Organizational Behavior

Human Behavior at Work

Organizational Behavior

Human Behavior at Work

ELEVENTH EDITION

JOHN W. NEWSTROM, PH.D.
University of Minnesota Duluth

KEITH DAVIS, PH.D.
Arizona State University

Boston   Burr Ridge, IL   Dubuque, IA   Madison, WI   New York   San Francisco   St. Louis
Bangkok   Bogotá   Caracas   Kuala Lumpur   Lisbon   London   Madrid   Mexico City
Milan   Montreal   New Delhi   Santiago   Seoul   Singapore   Sydney   Taipei   Toronto

McGraw-Hill Higher Education

A Division of The McGraw-Hill Companies

ORGANIZATIONAL BEHAVIOR: HUMAN BEHAVIOR AT WORK

Published by McGraw-Hill/Irwin, an imprint of The McGraw-Hill Companies, Inc. 1221 Avenue of the Americas, New York, NY 10020. Copyright © 2002, 1997, 1993, 1989, 1985, 1981, 1977, 1972, 1967, 1962, 1957, by The McGraw-Hill Companies, Inc. All rights reserved. No part of this publication may be reproduced or distributed in any form or by any means, or stored in a data base or retrieval system, without the prior written consent of The McGraw-Hill Companies, Inc., including, but not limited to, in any network or other electronic storage or transmission, or broadcast for distance learning.

Some ancillaries, including electronic and print components, may not be available to customers outside the United States.

This book is printed on acid-free paper.

domestic   4 5 6 7 8 9 0 DOW/DOW 0 9 8 7 6 5
international   3 4 5 6 7 8 9 0 DOW/DOW 0 9 8 7 6 5

ISBN 0-07-239675-X

Publisher: *John E. Biernat*
Senior editor: *John Weimeister*
Editorial assistant: *Trina Hauger*
Marketing manager: *Lisa Nicks*
Project manager: *Rebecca Nordbrock*
Senior production supervisor: *Michael R. McCormick*
Freelance design coordinator: *Pam Verros*
Interior design: *ZGraphics*
Cover design: *JoAnne Schopler*
Cover photograph: *© Photonica*
Supplement producer: *Nate Perry*
Producer, media technology: *Jenny R. Williams*
Compositor: *GTS Graphics, Inc.*
Typeface: *10/12 Times Roman*
Printer: *R. R. Donnelley & Sons Company*

Library of Congress Cataloging-in-Publication Data

Newstrom, John W.
    Organizational behavior: human behavior at work / John W. Newstrom, Keith Davis.
        p. cm.
    Includes bibliographical references and indexes.
    ISBN 0-07-239675-X (alk. paper)
    1. Organizational behavior. 2. Industrial sociology. I. Davis, Keith, 1918– II. Title.
    HD58.7 .D36 2002
    658.3—dc21   2001030197

INTERNATIONAL EDITION ISBN 0-07-118057-5
Copyright © 2002. Exclusive rights by The McGraw-Hill Companies, Inc. for manufacture and export. This book cannot be re-exported from the country to which it is sold by McGraw-Hill. The International Edition is not available in North America.

www.mhhe.com

To my mother Lillian,
wife Diane,
son Scott,
and daughter Heidi—
my sources of family support, and
my life's greatest treasures
JOHN W. NEWSTROM

To my mother Grace,
wife Sue,
son Charles,
daughter Jean,
and my delightful grandchildren
KEITH DAVIS

John W. Newstrom has taught at the University of Minnesota Duluth (UMD) for more than twenty-five years. He received his Ph.D. in management from the University of Minnesota, Minneapolis, and then taught at Arizona State University. He teaches courses in organizational behavior and management, interpersonal relations, and managing change to advanced undergraduates in the School of Business and Economics at UMD. He is a recipient of both the Chancellor's Outstanding Advisor award and the Horace T. Morse/University of Minnesota Alumni Association award for Outstanding Contributions to Undergraduate Education. He is a member of the University's Academy of Distinguished Teachers.

Newstrom is the coauthor of over thirty books for both academic and practitioner audiences. His products include *Supervision* (8th ed., 2001, with Lester Bittel), *Leaders and the Leadership Process* (2nd ed., 2000, with Jon L. Pierce), *The Manager's Bookshelf* (6th ed., 2002, with Jon L. Pierce), and ten popular books in support of human resource development professionals (the *Games Trainers Play* series, with Edward Scannell).

Newstrom has also published more than eighty-five journal articles and professional papers. His practitioner articles have appeared in *Business Horizons, Training, Training and Development, Workforce, The Personnel Administrator, Supervisory Management, Journal of Management Development, Supervision,* and *Personnel Journal.* He has published research-based and conceptual articles in the *Academy of Management Journal, Personnel Psychology, Journal of Occupational Behavior, Journal of Management, Compensation Review, Journal of Business Communication,* and *California Management Review.*

In the service domain, Newstrom has held elective leadership positions at the national level in the Academy of Management (chair of the Management Education and Development Division) and the American Society for Training and Development (board of directors). He has served as an editorial reviewer for the *Academy of Management Journal, Academy of Management Review, Academy of Management Executive, Journal of Management Development, Human Resource Development Quarterly, Personnel Administrator,* and *Advanced Management Journal.* He has been active in his local community, serving on various boards of directors and volunteering his time and resources to Habitat for Humanity, Arrowhead Regional Blood Center, "Four To Go" (a barbershop quartet), and serving as a mentor to his "best friend," Mickey Fry.

Keith Davis is Professor Emeritus of Management in the College of Business at Arizona State University. He is the author of prominent books on management and a past consulting editor for more than 130 books in the McGraw-Hill Series in Management. He is a Fellow in both the Academy of Management and the International Academy of Management.

Prior to entering the teaching field, Davis was a personnel specialist in industry and a personnel manager in government. He received his Ph.D. from Ohio State University and has taught at the University of Texas and at Indiana University. His fields of work are organizational behavior, personnel management, and social issues in management.

He has been visiting professor at a number of universities, including the University of Western Australia and Georgia Institute of Technology. In addition, he has served as consultant to a number of business and government institutions, including Mobil Oil Company, Texaco, the U.S. Internal Revenue Service, and the state of Hawaii.

Davis is a former president of the Academy of Management, and he received the National Human Relations Award from the Society for Advancement of Management. He also has been a National Beta Gamma Sigma Distinguished Scholar and is an Accredited Senior Professional in Human Resources. He received the Distinguished Educator Award from the Academy of Management in recognition of his influence on an entire generation of management practitioners and teachers through his writings and leadership in the field.

Another popular book prepared by Davis (with William B Werther, Jr.) is *Human Resources and Personnel Management* (5th ed., 1996), published by The McGraw-Hill Companies, Inc. Professor Davis was also a pioneer textbook author in the business, government, and society domain, producing the forerunner of the current *Business and Society: Corporate Strategy, Public Policy, Ethics* (8th ed., 1996) written by James E. Post, William C. Frederick, Anne T. Lawrence, and James Weber, published by The McGraw-Hill Companies, Inc. He also has contributed chapters to more than 100 other books and is the author of more than 150 articles in journals such as *Harvard Business Review, Academy of Management Journal, Management International,* and *California Management Review.* Four of his books have been translated into other languages.

Keith Davis was the creator of the predecessor to this book, which was then called *Human Relations at Work: Dynamics of Organizational Behavior.* For the first six editions, he was the sole author.

CONTENTS IN BRIEF

CONTENTS

PART TWO
Motivation and Reward Systems

xvi

PART EIGHT
Case Problems

PREFACE

Most students today have had at least part-time experiences in some form of work organization. You have quickly learned that not all behavior—whether your own, your manager's, or that of your workmates—is entirely rational. And you may have pondered a series of questions about what you saw and felt:

- Why do people behave as they do at work?
- How can individuals, groups, and whole organizations work together more effectively within the increasing pace of corporate change, dramatic restructurings and downsizings, and advancing global competition?
- What can managers do to motivate employees toward greater productivity?
- What responsibility do managers have for ensuring employee satisfaction?
- What can you learn from theory, research, and the experiences of other managers to help you become an effective future manager?

These and many other questions provide the background for this eleventh edition of *Organizational Behavior: Human Behavior at Work.*

Great progress has been made in the field of organizational behavior since this book was first published. The study and practice known as organizational behavior goes beyond the integration and application of behavioral science to work situations. It is an emerging field in which many questions and opportunities for improvement remain. This book provides rich insights into people at work in all kinds of situations and organizations.

We have tested earlier editions of this book on the firing line in university classrooms and in organizations for more than forty years. Many ideas offered by long-time users of previous editions and other insightful reviewers are incorporated in this new edition. Many topical ideas, figures, and applied examples have been provided by professors and managers from around the country. We actively solicit comments from both faculty and students to help us make the book even more useful in the future. We listen, *we care about your input,* and we strive to use it to produce a high-quality product. We invite you to contact the lead author by mail (at the University of Minnesota Duluth, Duluth, Minnesota 55812, by phone (218-726-8499), or via the Internet (jnewstro@d.umn.edu) with any comments, ideas, or questions you may have.

THE AUTHORS' ROLES

How do we create a book like this? We begin by continuously immersing ourselves in the thinking, research, and practice of organizational behavior to gain an in-depth understanding. We keep abreast of new developments by regularly reading dozens of journals and books, as well as interacting with managers in a variety of organizations. Then we develop a logical and engaging organizational framework and proceed to identify the most important elements for inclusion. Finally, we organize and present the information in ways that will help readers learn and retain the ideas.

Our final objective is to produce a book that is accurate, useful, up-to-date, and engaging. We emphasize content and substance, and we present the material in an organized and provocative fashion that will enable readers to integrate the various parts of this discipline into a whole philosophy of organizational behavior. The eleventh edition has been upgraded by thorough citations to recent research and practice, which indicate the basis for our conclusions.

Where appropriate, we include alternative viewpoints on a subject or express the weaknesses inherent in a particular model or concept. There are no simple answers to complex behavioral issues. We encourage readers to do their own thinking and to integrate a variety of perspectives. Consequently, we believe that this book will serve as a valuable foundation of behavioral knowledge. We hope it will stimulate readers to enrich their understanding through continued study of organizational behavior. Many prior students have chosen to retain their copy of *Organizational Behavior,* and they refer to it as a valuable reference manual when they encounter real-world problems and issues.

FEATURES OF THE BOOK

Many features of *Organizational Behavior: Human Behavior at Work* stand out in the eyes of its users. The most notable is its **careful blending of theory with practice,** so that its basic theories come to life in a realistic context. Readers learn that concepts and models do apply in the real world and help to build better organizations for a better society. The ideas and skills learned in organizational behavior can help readers cope better with every aspect of their lives.

Another popular feature is the hundreds of **examples of real organizational situations.** These real-life vignettes show how actual organizations operate and how people act (sometimes unexpectedly!) in specific situations. Most of the major concepts in this book are illustrated with one or more of these true examples.

A feature highly appreciated by both faculty and students is the book's **readability.** Following standard guidelines developed by Flesch and Gunning, we have maintained a moderate, but descriptive, vocabulary level, manageable sentence length, and a readable style to present a complex field in understandable language. Variety—provided by figures, practical illustrations, and research results—enhances the readability by presenting a refreshing change of pace from content discussions.

Other features of the book include:

- A detailed table of contents to locate major topics
- Provocative quotes at the beginning of each chapter to stimulate thought and in-class discussion, and margin notes to highlight key concepts
- Chapter-opening illustrations preceding every chapter to engage the reader in a real-life issue
- A widely accepted, and specially updated, presentation of five models of organizational behavior that provides an integrating framework throughout the book
- Strong, and early, coverage of employee communication, much of it based on the authors' own research
- A comprehensive chapter on motivational theories and another on their application to reward systems in organizations

- A chapter on empowerment and participation that is unique among organizational behavior books in capturing this highly contemporary approach
- Discussion of international issues in organizational behavior so students can later examine how selected concepts might require adaptation to other cultures
- A unique discussion of the limitations of organizational behavior to provide yet another balanced perspective
- At least one behavioral incident for analysis and one experiential exercise to involve students in their own learning, at the end of every chapter
- A comprehensive glossary of terms at the end of the book, providing a concise definition-at-a-glance for hundreds of key organizational behavior terms

Significant features in the eleventh edition include:

- A significantly streamlined sixteen-chapter structure that accents the issues of greatest importance in organizations today—motivation, leadership, interpersonal behavior, groups and teams, and the nature of change and its effects
- Substantial coverage of teams—their organizational context, factors that make them successful, and team-building processes that help members work together more effectively
- A unique feature, called "What Managers Are Reading," that provides concise summaries of recent best-selling books related to the chapter content
- Boxes within each chapter that focus on ethical questions, diversity issues, or international aspects of organizational behavior
- Special emphasis on practicality, as evidenced by the inclusion of "Advice to Future Managers" to guide managers toward improved practice of organizational behavior

LEARNING AIDS

Major features included in each chapter are chapter objectives, introductory quotations and incidents, a chapter summary, terms and concepts for review, and true case incidents for analysis in terms of chapter ideas. All chapters contain thorough and up-to-date references that provide a rich source of additional information for the interested reader. These come from a wide variety of sources, covering both academic and practitioner-related publications, to demonstrate that useful knowledge and illustrations can be found in many places. We encourage students to refer to these references regularly, as they not only indicate the source of information but often provide an interesting historical perspective on an issue or a countervailing viewpoint. There are also numerous discussion questions, many of which require thought, encourage insight, or invite readers to analyze their own experiences in terms of the ideas in the chapter. Other questions suggest appropriate group projects. Each chapter also contains an experiential exercise to involve students in the application of a chapter concept.

INSTRUCTIONAL AIDS

Since this book has been used in classrooms for ten previous editions, several classroom-proven instructional aids have been developed and refined over the years:

Instructor's Manual/Test Bank, prepared by Amit Shah (Frostburg State University)

The **Instructor's Manual** portion of this supplement is designed to save instructors time. It includes sample assignment sheets for quarter and semester schedules; chapter synopses; teaching suggestions; a detailed analysis for each of the end-of-chapter case incidents; and suggested answers to the end-of-chapter discussion questions and cases in the last part of the text. Blank lines are incorporated throughout the teaching material so that instructors can write notes about the subject matter. The **Test Bank** portion contains multiple-choice and true-false questions for each of the text's chapters and solutions for each.

Computerized Test Bank

A computerized version of the printed Test Bank is available on a CD-ROM that contains both Mac and Windows versions. This powerful system, which has online testing capabilities, allows tests to be prepared quickly and easily. Instructors can view questions as they are selected for a test; scramble questions; add, delete, and edit questions; select questions by type, objective, and difficulty level; and view and save tests.

Overhead Transparencies

A set of color transparencies is available to help instructors demonstrate key principles and concepts during their lectures. Transparencies consist of illustrations from other sources that will supplement text material, as well as selected text figures.

PowerPoint Presentations

The color **Overhead Transparencies** will also be available as slides for Microsoft PowerPoint 97.

McGraw-Hill Video Series in Organizational Behavior

Videos, selected from NBC News Archives, are available for instructors to enhance their lectures.

ACKNOWLEDGMENTS

Many scholars, managers, and students have contributed to this book, and we wish to express our appreciation for their aid. In a sense, it is their book, for we are only the agents who prepared it. We are especially grateful for thorough and competent reviews of the book by Paul Wilkens, Florida State University; Chan Hellman, Tulsa Community College; Edward Miller, Kean University/University of Bridgeport; Robert A. Figler, University of Akron; Marilee Smith, Kirkwood Community College; Bill Wickham, Heidelberg College; and Michele A. Govekar, Ohio Northern University. Their comments, questions, and suggestions have been carefully studied, found to be of substantial merit, and incorporated into the text wherever possible.

Many of our academic associates have directly or indirectly provided valuable insights, collegial support, and ongoing encouragement, and for that we wish to thank Jon Pierce, Steve Rubenfeld, and Dean Kjell Knudsen of the University of Minnesota Duluth. We also appreciate the help of the many McGraw-Hill employees—especially John Weimeister and Trina Hauger—who took a sincere and professional interest in improving the quality of the book.

John W. Newstrom
Keith Davis

Part One

Fundamentals of Organizational Behavior

Chapter 1

The Dynamics of People and Organizations

People tend to be very effective at managing relationships when they can understand and control their own emotions and can empathize with the feelings of others.

–Daniel Goleman[1]

All in all, a wealth of [organizational behavior] strategies are available to help practitioners improve their organization's operations.

–Karlene H. Roberts, et al.[2]

CHAPTER OBJECTIVES

TO UNDERSTAND

- The Meaning of Organizational Behavior
- The Key Goals and Forces with Which It Is Concerned
- Basic Concepts of Organizational Behavior
- Major Approaches Taken in This Book
- How Organizational Behavior Affects Organizational Performance
- Limitations of Organizational Behavior

Chris Hoffman graduated from college and was excited to begin her new job as a sales representative with IBM. The first few months at work were extremely hectic for her. She attended numerous formal training sessions, learned about the wide array of products she was to sell, and tried hard to understand the complex and fluid nature of her new employer.

Returning to her home late one night, she was too confused to fall asleep immediately. Many questions raced through her mind, based on her observations at work in recent weeks: "Why are some of my colleagues more successful than others? How can we act as a team when we are working out of our homes and interacting primarily through our laptop computers? How will I ever learn to handle the stress of meeting my sales quotas? Why doesn't my colleague Carrie cooperate with me when I ask her for assistance? Why does my manager ask me for suggestions, and then go ahead without using my input? How is the new 'IBM culture' different from the old one? And why is it constantly changing, anyway?"

Chris is already learning some key facts about life at work. *Organizations are complex systems.* If Chris wishes to be an effective employee and later a manager, she'll need to understand how such systems operate. Organizations like IBM effectively combine people and science—humanity and technology. With the rapid discoveries and improvements that science has provided in this century, mastering technology itself is difficult enough. When you add people to this situation, you get an immensely complex sociotechnical system that almost defies understanding. However, the progress of society in the twenty-first century depends heavily on understanding and managing effective organizations today.

Chris also sees that *human behavior in organizations is rather unpredictable.* The behavior of her colleagues, manager, and customers arises from their deep-seated needs, lifetime experiences, and personal value systems. However, *human behavior in an organization can be partially understood* in the frameworks of behavioral science, management, and other disciplines; exploring the various facets of such behavior is the objective of this book. *There are no perfect solutions to organizational problems,* as Chris will soon discover. However, employees can increase their understanding and skills so that work relationships can be upgraded. The task is challenging, but the results are worthwhile.

On occasion, Chris may become so frustrated that she will be tempted to withdraw from her job. The uncooperative colleague may limit Chris's effectiveness; the behavior of her manager may sometimes be difficult to understand. Whether she likes the behavior of these individuals or not, Chris does not have the luxury of *not* working with or relating to other people. Therefore, it is imperative that she learn about human behavior, explore how to improve her interpersonal skills, and begin to manage her relationships with others at work. These are areas where knowledge of organizational behavior can make a significant contribution to her effectiveness.

Organizational behavior is needed.

UNDERSTANDING ORGANIZATIONAL BEHAVIOR

In order to provide an understanding of what goes on at the workplace, we begin with the definition, goals, forces, and major characteristics of organizational behavior (OB). Later in the chapter we introduce the key concepts that OB deals with, lay out the four basic approaches taken in this book, and identify some factors that limit the success of OB.

Definition

Organizational behavior is the study and application of knowledge about how people—as individuals and as groups—act within organizations. It strives to identify ways in which people can act more effectively. Organizational behavior is a scientific discipline in which a large number of research studies and conceptual developments are constantly adding to its knowledge base. It is also an applied science, in that information about effective practices in one organization is being extended to many others.

Organizational behavior provides a useful set of tools at many levels of analysis. For example, it helps managers look at the behavior of *individuals* within an organization. It also aids their understanding of the complexities involved in *interpersonal* relations, when two people (two coworkers or a superior-subordinate pair) interact. At the next level, organizational behavior is valuable for examining the dynamics of relationships within small *groups,* both formal teams and informal groups. When two or more groups need to coordinate their efforts, such as engineering and sales, managers become interested in the *intergroup* relations that emerge. Finally, organizations can also be viewed, and managed, as *whole systems* that have interorganizational relationships (e.g., mergers and joint ventures).

Goals

Most sciences share four goals—to describe, understand, predict, and control some phenomena. These are also the **goals of organizational behavior.** The first objective is to *describe,* systematically, how people behave under a variety of conditions. Achieving this goal allows managers to communicate about human behavior at work using a common language. For example, one benefit from the study of this book is the acquisition of a new vocabulary about organizational behavior (see, for example, the Glossary at the end of this book).

A second goal is to *understand* why people behave as they do. Managers would be highly frustrated if they could only talk about behaviors of their employees, but not understand the reasons behind those actions. Therefore, inquisitive managers learn to probe for underlying explanations. *Predicting* future employee behavior is another goal of organizational behavior. Ideally, managers would have the capacity to predict which employees might be dedicated and productive or which ones might be absent, tardy, or disruptive on a certain day (so that managers could take preventive actions). The final goal of organizational behavior is to *control,* at least partially, and develop some human activity at work. Since managers are held responsible for performance outcomes, they are vitally interested in being able to make an impact on employee behavior, skill development, team effort, and productivity. Managers need to be able to improve results through the actions they and their employees take, and organizational behavior can aid them in their pursuit of this goal.

Some people may fear that the tools of organizational behavior will be used to limit their freedom and take away their rights. Although that scenario is possible, it is not likely, for the actions of most managers today are subject to intense scrutiny. Managers need to remember that organizational behavior is a human tool for human benefit. It applies broadly to the behavior of people in all types of organizations, such as businesses, government, schools, and service organizations. Wherever organizations are, there is a need to describe, understand, predict, and better manage human behavior.

Forces

A complex set of forces affects the nature of organizations today. A wide array of issues and trends in these forces can be classified into four areas—people, structure, technology, and the environment in which the organization operates (see Figure 1–1).

Applied science

Four goals of OB are to describe, understand, predict, and control.

Four key forces

4

FIGURE 1–1

Key forces affecting
organizational behavior   **5**

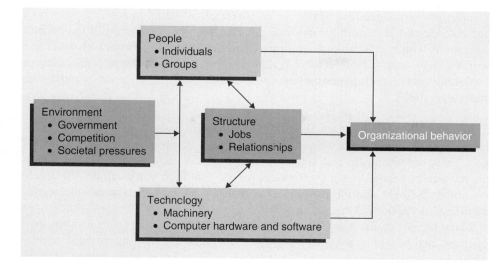

When people work together in an organization to accomplish an objective, some kind of structure of formal relationships is required. People also use technology to help get the job done, so there is an interaction of people, structure, and technology. In addition, these elements are influenced by the external environment, and they influence it. Each of the four forces affecting organizational behavior, and some illustrations of each, is considered briefly in the following sections.

People   People make up the internal social system of the organization. That system consists of individuals and groups, and large groups as well as small ones. There are unofficial, informal groups and more official, formal ones. Groups are dynamic. They form, change, and disband. People are the living, thinking, feeling beings who work in the organization to achieve their objectives. We must remember that organizations exist to serve people, rather than people existing to serve organizations.

The human organization of today is not the same as it was yesterday, or the day before. In particular, the workforce has become richly *diverse,* which means that employees bring a wide array of educational backgrounds, talents, and perspectives to their jobs. Occasionally, this diversity presents challenges for management to resolve, as when some employees express themselves through alternative dress or jewelry, while others present unique challenges through their unique lifestyles and recreational interests. Other employees have examined their values and are determined to put their personal goals ahead of total commitment to the organization. Managers need to be tuned in to these diverse patterns and trends, and be prepared to adapt to them.

> Some of the changes in the labor force are as follows: There has been a decline in the work ethic and a rise in emphasis on leisure, self-expression, fulfillment, and personal growth. The automatic acceptance of authority by employees has decreased, while desires for participation, autonomy, and control have increased. At the same time, several major factors are affecting the workforce. Skills become obsolete as a result of technological advances, and manual workers must either be retrained for knowledge-oriented jobs or be displaced. Security needs become foremost in the minds of millions of workers (and loyalty diminishes) because of the threat or the reality of downsizings. And even in eras of controlled inflation, the absence of meaningful salary growth for many employees has placed renewed emphasis on money as a motivator.

Indeed, there is a new labor force, and management's leadership practices must change to match the new conditions. These fast-moving developments have given new emphasis to leadership ability. Some companies are discovering that demonstrating a sense of caring, really listening to employees, and being concerned with both competence and relationships are among the keys to the motivation of the present workforce. Other companies are urging their managers to respond to a diverse workforce by building pride without devaluing others, empowering some without exploiting others, and demonstrating openness, confidence, authentic compassion, and vulnerability.[3]

Structure   Structure defines the formal relationship and use of people in organizations. Different jobs are required to accomplish all of an organization's activities. There are managers and employees, accountants and assemblers. These people have to be related in some structural way so that their work can be effectively coordinated. These relationships create complex problems of cooperation, negotiation, and decision making.

Many organizational structures have become flatter (containing fewer levels, a goal often attained by cutting middle-management positions). This downsizing and restructuring has occurred as a result of the pressure to lower costs while remaining competitive. Other structures have grown more complex as a result of mergers, acquisitions, and new ventures. Several organizations have experimented with hiring contingent workforces (temporary, part-time, or contract employees). Finally, many firms have moved from a traditional structure to a team-based one (a trend that is discussed in Chapter 13).

Technology   Technology provides the resources with which people work and affects the tasks that they perform. They cannot accomplish much with their bare hands, so they build buildings, design machines, create work processes, and assemble resources. The technology used has a significant influence on working relationships. An assembly line is not the same as a research laboratory, and a steel mill does not have the same working conditions as a hospital. The great benefit of technology is that it allows people to do more and better work, but it also restricts people in various ways. It has costs as well as benefits. Examples of the impact of technology include the increasing use of robots and automated control systems in assembly lines, the dramatic shift from a manufacturing to a service economy, the impressive advances in computer hardware and software capabilities, the rapid move toward widespread use of the information highway (Internet), and the need to respond to societal demands for improved quality of goods and services at acceptable prices. Each of these technological advancements, in its own way, places increased pressure on OB to maintain the delicate balance between technical and social systems.

Environment   All organizations operate within an internal and an external environment. A single organization does not exist alone. It is part of a larger system that contains many other elements, such as government, the family, and other organizations. Numerous changes in the environment create demands on organizations. Citizens expect organizations to be socially responsible; new products and competition for customers come from around the globe; the direct impact of unions (as measured by the proportion of the labor force that is unionized) diminishes; the dramatic pace of change in society quickens. All these factors—but especially the rapid globalization of the marketplace, whose impact on OB is discussed in Chapter 16—influence one another in a complex system that creates a dynamic (even chaotic) context for a group of people.

Individual organizations, such as a factory or a school, cannot escape being influenced by this external environment. It influences the attitudes of people, affects working conditions, and provides competition for resources and power. It must be considered in the study of human behavior in organizations.

Positive Characteristics of the Organizational Behavior Field

One major strength of organizational behavior is its *interdisciplinary* nature. It integrates the behavioral sciences (the systematic body of knowledge pertaining to why and how people behave as they do) with other social sciences that can contribute to the subject. It applies from these disciplines any ideas that will improve the relationships between people and organizations. Its interdisciplinary nature is similar to that of medicine, which applies knowledge from the physical, biological, and social sciences into a workable medical practice.

Interdisciplinary

Another strength of organizational behavior is its emerging base of *research knowledge and conceptual frameworks*. The field of organizational behavior has grown in depth and breadth, and it will continue to mature. The keys to its past and future success revolve around the related processes of theory development, research, and managerial practice. **Theories** offer explanations of how and why people think, feel, and act as they do. Theories identify important variables and link them to form tentative propositions that can be tested through research. Good theories are also practical—they address significant behavioral issues, they contribute to our understanding, and they provide guidelines for managerial thought and action. You will be introduced to several practical and interesting theories in this book, presented in a straightforward fashion.

Research is the process of gathering and interpreting relevant evidence that will either support a behavioral theory or help change it. Research hypotheses are testable statements connecting the variables in a theory, and they guide the process of data collection. Data are generated through various research methods, such as case studies, field and laboratory experiments, and surveys.[4] The results of these research studies, as reported in various journals, can affect both the theory being examined and future managerial practices.

Research is an ongoing process through which valuable behavioral knowledge is continually uncovered. Examining a stream of research is like exploring the Mississippi River from its gentle source in northern Minnesota to its powerful ending in the Gulf of Mexico. Just as a trip down the entire river allows us to better appreciate its growth and its impact, so does a review of research help us better understand how the major ideas in organizational behavior evolved over time. Consequently, the highlights of dozens of relevant research studies are briefly presented to you in appropriate places in this text.

Neither research nor theory can stand alone and be useful, however. Managers apply the theoretical models to structure their thinking; they use research results to provide relevant guides to their own situations. In these ways, there is a natural and healthy flow from theory and research to **practice**, which is the conscious application of conceptual models and research results in order to improve individual and organizational performance at work.

There is also a vital role for managers to play in the other direction—the development of theory and conduct of research. Feedback from practitioners can suggest whether theories and models are simple or complex, realistic or artificial, and useful or useless. Organizations serve as research sites and provide the subjects for various studies. As shown in Figure 1–2, there is a two-way interaction between each pair of processes, and all three processes are critical to the future of organizational behavior.

FIGURE 1–2

The interaction of
theory, research,
and practice in
organizational behavior,
and sample sources for
each

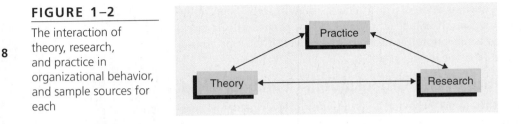

Sample Sources		
Theory Information	**Research Information**	**Practice Information**
Academy of Management Review	*Academy of Management Journal*	*Academy of Management Executive*
Human Relations	*Journal of Applied Psychology*	*Organizational Dynamics*
Administrative Science Quarterly	*Journal of Management*	*Harvard Business Review*
Psychological Bulletin	*Organizational Behavior and Human Decision Processes*	*Business Horizons*
Annual Review of Psychology	*Journal of Organizational Behavior*	*California Management Review*

Better models must be developed, theory-based research needs to be conducted, and managers need to be receptive to both sources and apply them to their work.

Fortunately, a third major strength of organizational behavior is the increasing *acceptance of theory and research* by practicing managers. This willingness of managers to explore new ideas explains why this eleventh edition of *Organizational Behavior* includes a broad sampling of theory and research results. Managers today are more receptive to new models, they support related research, and they hungrily experiment with new ideas. Examples of this increasing dialogue between the world of science and the world of practice abound, as seen in the experiments with self-managing teams, a practice which we describe later (Chapter 13). These illustrate the kinds of organizational practices which, when coupled with theory development and research, will continue to produce improved organizational performance. Researchers have identified key questions, designed appropriate studies, and reported the results and their conclusions. Others have examined related studies, and used them to construct models and theories that explain sets of findings and help guide future studies. As a result, organizational behavior has progressed substantially, and will continue to be vitally important in the twenty-first century. Sample sources of OB theory, research, and practice information are shown in Figure 1–2.

FUNDAMENTAL CONCEPTS

Every field of social science, or even physical science, has a philosophical foundation of basic concepts that guide its development. In accounting, for example, a fundamental concept is that "for every debit there will be a credit." The entire system of double-entry accounting was built on this equation when that system replaced single-entry bookkeeping many years ago. In physics, a basic belief is that elements of nature are uniform. The law of gravity operates uniformly in Tokyo and London, and an atom of hydrogen is identical in Moscow and Washington, D.C. Even though such uniformity cannot be applied to people, certain basic concepts regarding human behavior do exist.

As shown in Figure 1–3, organizational behavior starts with a set of fundamental concepts revolving around the nature of people and organizations. These concepts are the enduring principles that form a strong foundation for OB. A summary of these ideas follows, and they are woven into later chapters.

The Nature of People

With regard to people, there are six basic concepts: individual differences, perception, a whole person, motivated behavior, desire for involvement, and value of the person.

Individual Differences   People have much in common (they become excited by an achievement; they are grieved by the loss of a loved one), but each person in the world is also individually different (and we expect that all who follow will be different!). The idea of **individual differences** is supported by science. Each person is different from all others, probably in millions of ways, just as each person's DNA profile is different, as far as we know. And these differences are usually substantial rather than meaningless. Think, for example, of a person's billion brain cells and the billions of possible combinations of connections and bits of experience that are stored there. All people are different, and this diversity needs to be recognized and viewed as a valuable asset to organizations.

The idea of individual differences comes originally from psychology. From the day of birth, each person is unique (the impact of *nature*), and individual experiences after birth tend to make people even more different (the influence of *nurture*). Individual differences mean that management can motivate employees best by treating them differently. If it were not for individual differences, some standard, across-the-board way of dealing with employees could be adopted, and minimum judgment would be required thereafter. Individual differences require that a manager's approach to employees be individual, not statistical. This belief that each person is different from all others is typically called the **law of individual differences.**

Law of individual differences

Perception   People look at the world and see things differently. Even when presented with the same object, two people may view it in two different ways. Their view of their objective environment is filtered by **perception,** which is the unique way in

The nature of people	The nature of organizations
• Individual differences	• Social systems
• Perception	• Mutual interest
• A whole person	• Ethics
• Motivated behavior	
• Desire for involvement	
• Value of the person	

FIGURE 1–3

Fundamental concepts of organizational behavior

10

which each person sees, organizes, and interprets things. People use an organized framework that they have built out of a lifetime of experiences and accumulated values. Having unique views is another way in which people insist on acting like human beings rather than rational machines.

Employees see their work worlds differently for a variety of reasons. They may differ in their personalities, needs, demographic factors, and past experiences, or they may find themselves in different physical settings, time periods, or social surroundings. Whatever the reasons, *they tend to act on the basis of their perceptions.* Essentially, each person seems to be saying, "I react not to an objective world, but to a world judged in terms of my own beliefs, values, and expectations." This way of *Selective perception* reacting leads to the process of **selective perception,** in which people tend to pay attention to those features of their work environment that are consistent with or reinforce their own expectations. Selective perceptions can not only cause misinterpretations of single events at work but also lead to future rigidity in the search for new experiences. Managers must learn to expect perceptual differences among their employees, accept people as emotional beings, and manage them in individual ways.

A Whole Person   Although some organizations may wish they could employ only a person's skill or brain, they actually employ a whole person rather than certain characteristics. Different human traits may be studied separately, but in the final analysis they are all part of one system making up a whole person. Skill does not exist apart from background or knowledge. Home life is not totally separable from work life, and emotional conditions are not separate from physical conditions. People function as total human beings.

> For example, a supervisor wanted to hire a new telemarketer named Anika Wilkins. She was talented, experienced, and willing to work the second shift. However, when Anika was offered the job, she responded by saying that she would need to start a half hour late on Wednesdays because her child-care service was not available until then. Also, since she had a minor handicap, her workstation required a substantial adjustment in height. So her supervisor had to consider her needs as a whole person, not just as a worker.

Better person   When management practices organizational behavior, it is trying to develop a better employee, but it also wants to develop a better *person* in terms of growth and fulfillment. Jobs shape people somewhat as they perform them, so management needs to care about the job's effect on the whole person. Employees belong to many organizations other than their employer, and they play many roles inside and outside the firm. If the whole person can be improved, then benefits will extend beyond the firm into the larger society in which each employee lives.

Motivated Behavior   From psychology we learn that normal behavior has certain causes. These may relate to a person's needs or the consequences that result from acts. In the case of needs, people are motivated not by what *we* think they ought to have but by what *they* themselves want. To an outside observer, a person's needs may be unrealistic, but they are still controlling. This fact leaves management with two basic ways to motivate people. It can show them how certain actions will increase their need fulfillment, or it can threaten decreased need fulfillment if they follow an undesirable course of action. Clearly, a path toward increased need fulfillment is the better approach. Motivation is essential to the operation of organizations. No matter how much technology and equipment an organization has, these resources cannot be put to use until they are released and guided by people who have been motivated.

Think for a minute in terms of the Concorde—a supersonic passenger plane sitting at the end of a runway at a New York City airport. The plane has been refueled for its return to Europe, the baggage has been loaded, tickets have been sold, and the passengers are on board. A flight plan has been filed, and the plane has been cleared for takeoff. No matter how well this preliminary work has been done, the plane cannot move an inch down the runway until the pilot starts the ignition and provides fuel to the jet engines—that is, until motive power is supplied. Similarly, in an organization, motivation turns on the power to start and keep the organization running effectively.

Desire for Involvement   Many employees today are actively seeking opportunities at work to become involved in relevant decisions, thereby contributing their talents and ideas to the organization's success. They hunger for the chance to share what they know and to learn from the experience. Consequently, organizations need to provide opportunities for meaningful involvement. This can be achieved through employee empowerment—a practice that will result in mutual benefit for both parties.

Value of the Person   People deserve to be treated differently from other factors of production (land, capital, technology) because they are of a higher order in the universe. Because of this distinction, they want to be treated with caring, respect, and dignity; increasingly, they demand such treatment from their employers. They refuse to accept the old idea that they are simply economic tools. They want to be valued for their skills and abilities and to be provided with opportunities to develop themselves.

The Nature of Organizations

With regard to organizations, the three key concepts are that they are social systems, they are formed on the basis of mutual interest, and they must treat employees ethically.

Social Systems   From sociology we learn that organizations are social systems; consequently, activities therein are governed by social laws as well as psychological laws. Just as people have psychological needs, they also have social roles and status. Their behavior is influenced by their group as well as by their individual drives. In fact, two types of social systems exist side by side in organizations. One is the formal (official) social system, and the other is the informal social system.

The existence of a social system implies that the organizational environment is one of dynamic change rather than a static set of relations as pictured on an organization chart. All parts of the system are interdependent, and each part is subject to influence by any other part. Everything is related to everything else.

The effects of the broader social system can be seen in the experience of a supervisor, Glenda Ortiz. Ortiz disciplined an employee for a safety violation. The action was within the rules and considered routine by Ortiz. However, the local union already was upset because of what it considered to be unfair discipline for safety violations in another branch of the company. It wanted to show sympathy for its fellow members in the other branch, and it also wanted to show management that it would not accept similar treatment in this branch. In addition, the union president, Jimmie Swallen, was running for reelection, and he wanted to show members that he was protecting their interests.

The union encouraged the employee to file a grievance about Ortiz's action, and the simple disciplinary matter became a complex labor relations problem that consumed the time of many people.

12

The idea of a social system provides a framework for analyzing organizational behavior issues. It helps make organizational behavior problems understandable and manageable.

Mutual Interest   Organizations need people, and people need organizations. Organizations have a human purpose. They are formed and maintained on the basis of some **mutuality of interest** among their participants. Managers need employees to help them reach organizational objectives; people need organizations to help them reach individual objectives.[5] If mutuality is lacking, it makes no sense to try to assemble a group and develop cooperation, because there is no common base on which to build. As shown in Figure 1–4, mutual interest provides a superordinate goal—one that can be attained only through the integrated efforts of individuals and their employers.

Ethics   In order to attract and retain valuable employees in an era in which good workers are constantly recruited away, **ethical treatment** is necessary. To succeed, organizations must treat employees in an ethical fashion. More and more firms are recognizing this need and are responding with a variety of programs to ensure a higher standard of ethical performance by managers and employees alike. Companies have established codes of ethics, publicized statements of ethical values, provided ethics training, rewarded employees for notable ethical behavior, publicized positive role models, and set up internal procedures to handle misconduct. They have begun to recognize that since organizational behavior always involves people, ethical philosophy is involved in one way or another in each action they take. (See "What Managers Are Reading.") Because of the importance of ethics, this theme will be addressed periodically throughout the text.

Triple reward system   When the organization's goals and actions are ethical, mutuality creates a **triple reward system** in which individual, organizational, and social objectives are all met. People find more satisfaction in work when there is cooperation and teamwork. They are learning, growing, and contributing. The organization is also more successful, because it operates more effectively. Quality is better, service is improved, and costs are reduced. Perhaps the greatest beneficiary of the triple reward system is society itself, because it has better products and services, more capable citizens, and an overall climate of cooperation and progress. There is a three-party win-win-win result in which there need not be any losers.

Ethical treatment

FIGURE 1–4

Mutual interest provides a superordinate goal for employees, the organization, and society.

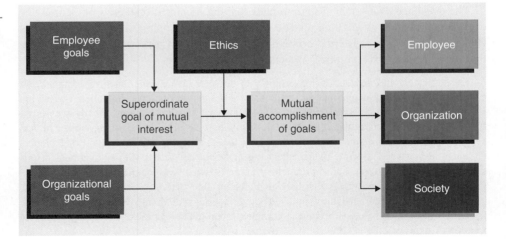

In his book *Choosing the Right Thing to Do,* David Shapiro contends that employees of all ages have a growing need for moral guidance at work—perhaps due to an absence of such ethical preparation in their upbringing. Organizations, he suggests, need some assurance that their workers will take ethical actions on a consistent basis even in the absence of direct supervision. Rather than distribute detailed lists of ethical guidelines, Shapiro urges managers to offer a set of "moral prisms" through which their employees can determine the right thing for themselves to do. These prisms, with the primary question to be asked under each, include:

- *Virtue ethic*—What would a highly virtuous person do in this situation?

- *Results ethic*—What actions would most effectively ensure the attainment of my goals, both short-term and long-term?
- *Universal ethic*—What would happen if everyone in the world engaged in a similar behavior as I am considering?
- *Public exposure ethic*—If everyone knew what I planned to do, how would I act then?
- *Caring ethic*—Which action would best contribute to, and sustain, a caring relationship with the people impacted by this action?

Source: David A. Shapiro, *Choosing the Right Thing to Do,* San Francisco: Berrett-Koehler Publishers, 1999.

BASIC APPROACHES OF THIS BOOK

Organizational behavior seeks to integrate the four elements of people, structure, technology, and environment. It rests on an interdisciplinary foundation of fundamental concepts about the nature of people and organizations. The four basic approaches—human resources, contingency, results-oriented, and systems—are interwoven throughout subsequent chapters (Figure 1–5).

A Human Resources (Supportive) Approach

The **human resources approach** is developmental. It is concerned with the growth and development of people toward higher levels of competency, creativity, and fulfillment, because people are the central resource in any organization and any society. The nature of the human resources approach can be understood by comparing it with the traditional management approach of the early 1900s. In the traditional approach, managers decided what should be done and then closely controlled employees to ensure task performance. Management was directive and controlling.

The human resources approach, on the other hand, is supportive. It helps employees become better, more responsible people, and then it tries to create a climate in which they may contribute to the limits of their improved abilities.[6] It assumes that expanded capabilities and opportunities for people will lead directly to improvements in operating effectiveness. Work satisfaction also will be a direct result when employees make fuller use of their abilities. Essentially, the human resources approach means that better people achieve better results. It is somewhat illustrated by the ancient proverb that follows:

> *Give a person a fish, and you feed that person for a day;*
> *Teach a person to fish, and you feed that person for life.*

Another name for the human resources approach is the **supportive approach,** because the manager's primary role changes from control of employees to active support of their growth and performance. The supportive model of organizational behavior is more fully discussed in Chapter 2.

Supportive approach

FIGURE 1–5

Basic approaches of the book

Human resources (supportive)	Employee growth and development are encouraged and supported.
Contingency	Different managerial behaviors are required by different environments for effectiveness.
Results-oriented	Outcomes of organizational behavior programs are assessed in terms of their efficiency.
Systems	All parts of an organization interact in a complex relationship.

A Contingency Approach

Traditional management relied on principles to provide "one best way" of managing. There was a correct way to organize, to delegate, and to divide work. The correct way applied regardless of the type of organization or situation involved. Management principles were considered to be universal. As the field of organizational behavior developed, many of its followers also supported the concept of universality. Behavioral ideas were supposed to apply in any type of situation. One example was the belief that employee-oriented leadership should consistently be better than task-oriented leadership, whatever the circumstances. An occasional exception might be admitted, but in general early ideas were applied in a universal manner.

The more accepted view in the twenty-first century is that there are few across-the-board concepts that apply in all instances. Situations are much more complex than first perceived, and the different variables may require different behavioral approaches. The result is the **contingency approach** to organizational behavior, which means that *different situations require different behavioral practices for effectiveness.*

The key question is *when* to use a specific approach, which is a point often overlooked in a discussion of contingency OB. Solid theory and careful use of research findings can help move managers beyond the glib statement of "it all depends." The whole point of becoming familiar with OB research findings and relevant OB models is to help managers find the answers to the "when" question. *Managers need to know under what conditions they should choose one behavioral approach over another,* and the contingency framework can help them do this.

No one best way

No longer is there one best way. Each situation must be analyzed carefully to determine the significant variables that exist in order to establish the kinds of practices that will be most effective. The strength of the contingency approach is that it encourages analysis of each situation prior to action while at the same time discouraging habitual practice based on universal assumptions about people. The contingency approach also is more interdisciplinary, more system-oriented, and more research-oriented than the traditional approach. Thus it helps managers use in the most appropriate manner all the current knowledge about people in organizations.

A Results-Oriented Approach

All organizations need to achieve some relevant outcomes, or results. A dominant goal for many is to be productive, so this **results orientation** is a common thread woven

Productivity

through organizational behavior. **Productivity,** at its simplest, is a ratio that compares units of output with units of input, often against a predetermined standard. If more outputs can be produced from the same amount of inputs, productivity is improved. Or if fewer inputs can be used to produce the same amount of outputs, productivity has increased. The idea of productivity does not imply that one should produce more output; rather, it is a measure of how efficiently one produces whatever output is desired. Consequently, better productivity is a valuable measure of how well resources are used in society. It means that less is consumed to produce each unit of output. There is less waste and better conservation of resources—a result increasingly valued by many in society.

Productivity often is measured in terms of economic inputs and outputs, but human and social inputs and outputs also are important. For example, if better organizational behavior can improve job satisfaction, a human output or result occurs. In the same manner, when employee development programs lead to a by-product of better citizens in a community, a valuable social result occurs. Organizational behavior decisions typically involve human, social, or economic issues, and so a number of results-oriented outcomes of effective organizational behavior are discussed throughout this book.

Multiple inputs and outputs

Many of these measures are intertwined in the popular practice of **total quality management (TQM).** TQM is an integrated attempt to improve the quality of a firm's products or services through a variety of techniques and training. It typically focuses on creating high customer satisfaction through listening carefully to customers, building partnerships with suppliers, searching for continuous improvements in operational methods, training employees in the understanding and use of statistical tools, and meaningfully involving employees in team-based systems.

A Formula   The role that organizational behavior plays in creating organizational results is illustrated by a set of factors and the relationships between the factors (Figure 1–6). Let us look first at a worker's ability. It is generally accepted that the product of knowledge and one's skill in applying it constitute the human trait called *ability* (see equation 1). Abilities can be improved through hiring better workers (e.g., those with high potential for learning, greater previous experience, and a desire to succeed) or providing existing employees with job-related training. *Motivation* results from a person's attitudes reacting in a specific situation (see equation 2). This book emphasizes employee attitudes (covered in depth in Chapter 9) and how they are affected by situational factors (such as leadership, discussed in Chapter 7) to determine motivation.

The interaction of motivation and ability determines a person's *potential performance* in any activity (see equation 3). Of course, organizational behavior also plays a part in motivating workers to acquire the other factor, ability. The potential for human performance has to be mixed with *resources,* and a worker must be

1. Knowledge × skill	=	ability
2. Attitude × situation	=	motivation
3. Ability × motivation	=	potential human performance
4. Potential performance × resources × opportunity	=	organizational results

FIGURE 1–6

Equations showing the role of organizational behavior in work systems

16

given the *opportunity* to perform to get *organizational results* (as indicated by equation 4).[7] Resources, such as tools, power, and supplies, relate primarily to economic, material, and technical factors in an organization. Organizational behavior plays a key role in providing the opportunity to perform, as we discuss in the need for empowerment in Chapter 8.

A Systems Approach

Treating an organization as a system is critically important to its success. The fundamental elements of the **systems approach** include:

1. There are many variables within a system.
2. The parts of a system are interdependent (one part affects many other parts and is affected by many in a complex way).
3. There are many subsystems contained within larger systems.
4. Systems generally require inputs, engage in some process, and produce outputs.
5. The input-process-output mechanism is cyclical and self-sustaining (it is ongoing, repetitive, and uses feedback to adjust itself).
6. Systems produce both positive and negative results.
7. Systems produce both intended and unintended consequences.
8. The consequences of systems may be short-term, long-term, or both.

Holistic OB

Thus, the systems approach compels managers to take a holistic view of the subject. **Holistic organizational behavior** interprets people–organization relationships in terms of the whole person, whole group, whole organization, and whole social system. It takes an across-the-board view of people in organizations in an effort to understand as many of the factors as possible that influence people's behavior. Issues are analyzed in terms of the total situation affecting them rather than in terms of an isolated event or problem.

A systems viewpoint should be the concern of every person in an organization. The clerk at a service counter, the machinist, and the manager all work with people and thereby influence the behavioral quality of life in an organization and the organization's outputs. Managers, however, tend to have a larger responsibility, because they are the ones who make more of the decisions affecting human issues, and most of their daily activities are people-related. The role of managers, then, is to use organizational behavior to help achieve individual, organizational, and societal goals. Managers help build an organizational culture in which talents are utilized and further developed, people are motivated, teams become productive, organizations achieve their goals, and society reaps the rewards.

Cost-benefit analysis

However, negative effects as well as positive effects sometimes result from the behavioral actions of managers. It is necessary to make a **cost-benefit analysis** to determine whether potential actions will have a net positive or net negative effect (see Figure 1–7). Managers need to ask themselves what they might gain from rigid adherence to a policy, from a new reward system, or from different methods of organizing work. At the same time, they need to recognize that there may be both direct and indirect costs of any actions they take. These costs can include work slowdowns, higher absenteeism rates, or other consequences of worker dissatisfaction. The process of creating a cost-benefit analysis also forces managers to look beyond the immediate implications of their actions. Making such an analysis would have been beneficial for the supervisor in this furniture factory:

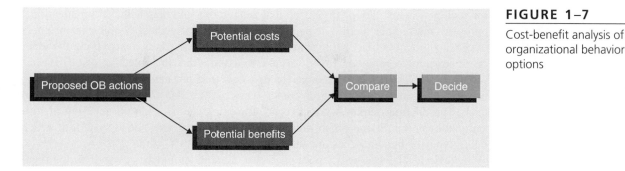

In the upholstery department of a furniture factory, a supervisor refused to allow an employee to take leave without pay to attend the funeral of a second cousin in a city 200 miles away. The employee claimed that special family relationships with this cousin required her attendance, and she took two days off without permission. When she returned, the supervisor disciplined her by giving her one day off without pay. Employees in other departments heard about the incident, and they felt that the discipline was unfair; so all plant employees walked off the job in a wildcat strike, threatening to remain off the job until the supervisor withdrew her penalty. The supervisor had failed to realize that actions in her department could have effects beyond that department in the larger factory system.

The systems approach applies especially to the social system and the idea of organizational culture discussed in Chapter 4.

LIMITATIONS OF ORGANIZATIONAL BEHAVIOR

This book is written from a specialized point of view that emphasizes primarily the human side of organizations and the kinds of benefits that attention to that side can bring. We continually report research results identifying payoffs in the areas of absenteeism, turnover, stress levels, and employee performance. Nevertheless, we also recognize the limitations of organizational behavior. It will not abolish conflict and frustration; it can only reduce them. It is a way to improve, not an absolute answer to problems. Furthermore, it is but part of the whole cloth of an organization. We can discuss organizational behavior as a separate subject, but to apply it, we must tie it to the whole of reality. Improved organizational behavior will not solve unemployment. It will not make up for our own deficiencies. It cannot substitute for poor planning, inept organizing, or inadequate controls. It is only one of many systems operating within a larger social system. This section is designed to alert you to three major limitations of OB (behavioral bias, diminishing returns, and unethical manipulation), as well as some other problems.

Problems exist in OB's nature and use.

Behavioral Bias

People who lack system understanding may develop a **behavioral bias,** which gives them a narrow viewpoint that emphasizes satisfying employee experiences while overlooking the broader system of the organization in relation to all its publics. This condition is a reflection of **tunnel vision,** in which people have narrow viewpoints, as if they were looking through a tunnel. They see only the tiny view at the other end of the tunnel while missing the broader landscape.

Tunnel vision restricts objectivity.

It should be evident that concern for employees can be so greatly overdone that the original purpose of bringing people together—productive organizational outputs

18

for society—is lost. Sound organizational behavior should help achieve organizational purposes, not replace them. The person who ignores the needs of people as consumers of organizational outputs while championing employee needs is misapplying the ideas of organizational behavior. It is a mistake to assume that the objective of OB is simply to create a satisfied workforce, for that goal will not automatically translate into new products and outstanding customer service. It is also true that the person who pushes production outputs without regard for employee needs is misapplying organizational behavior. Sound organizational behavior recognizes a social system in which many types of human needs are served in many ways.

Behavioral bias can be so misapplied that it harms employees as well as the organization. Some people, in spite of their good intentions, so overwhelm others with care that the recipients of such care are reduced to dependent—and unproductive—indignity. They become content, not fulfilled. They find excuses for failure rather than take responsibility for progress. They lack self-discipline and self-respect. As happened with scientific management years ago, concern for people can be misapplied by overeager partisans until it becomes harmful.

The Law of Diminishing Returns

A limiting factor

Overemphasis on an organizational behavior practice may produce negative results, as indicated by the **law of diminishing returns.**[8] It is a limiting factor in organizational behavior the same way that it is in economics. In economics the law of diminishing returns refers to a declining amount of extra outputs when more of a desirable input is added to an economic situation. After a certain point, the output from each unit of added input tends to become smaller. The added output eventually may reach zero and even continue to decline when more units of input are added.

> A farmer who has a laborer working on 20 acres of land can double the output by adding another laborer. Similar results can occur by doubling the workforce to four people, but soon a point will be reached where the increase in output from adding workers is smaller and smaller. Eventually, production will decline as the field becomes overcrowded with workers, coordination deteriorates, and crops are trampled by the crowd.

How does the law work in organizational behavior?

The law of diminishing returns in organizational behavior works in a similar way. It states that at some point, increases of a desirable practice produce declining returns, eventually zero returns, and then negative returns as more increases are added. The concept implies that *for any situation there is an optimum amount of a desirable practice,* such as recognition or participation. When that point is exceeded, there is a decline in returns. In other words, the fact that a practice is desirable does not mean that more of it is more desirable. *More of a good thing is not necessarily good.*

> The diminishing returns associated with various incentives for enlisting in the U.S. Navy were studied in interviews with 1,700 civilian males. Substantially different levels of incentives were offered: $1,000 versus $3,000 bonuses, two years versus four years of free college, and 10 versus 25 percent of base pay for exceptional performance. None of the three larger incentives produced more favorable dispositions to enlist. In fact, the respondents found the 10 percent bonus more attractive, leading the researchers to conclude that not only is more not necessarily better but it "can be worse."[9]

Diminishing returns may not apply to every human situation, but the idea applies so widely that it is of general use. Furthermore, the exact point at which an application becomes excessive will vary with the circumstances, but an excess can be reached with nearly any practice.

Why does the law of diminishing returns exist? Essentially, it is a system concept. It applies because of the complex system relationships of many variables in a situation. The facts state that when an excess of one variable develops, although that variable is desirable, it tends to restrict the operating benefits of other variables so substantially that net effectiveness declines. For example, too much security may lead to less employee initiative and growth. This relationship shows that *organizational effectiveness is achieved not by maximizing one human variable but by working all system variables together in a balanced way.*

Unethical Manipulation of People

A significant concern about organizational behavior is that *its knowledge and techniques can be used to manipulate people unethically as well as to help them develop their potential.* People who lack respect for the basic dignity of the human being could learn organizational behavior ideas and use them for selfish ends. They could use what they know about motivation or communication in the **manipulation of people** without regard for human welfare. People who lack ethical values could use people in unethical ways.

The *philosophy of organizational behavior is supportive* and oriented toward human resources. It seeks to improve the human environment and help people grow toward their potential. However, the *knowledge and techniques of this subject may be used for negative as well as positive consequences.* This possibility is true of knowledge in almost any field, so it is no special limitation of organizational behavior. Nevertheless, we must be cautious so that what is known about people is not used to manipulate them. The possibility of manipulation means that people in power in organizations must maintain high ethical and moral integrity and not misuse their power. Without ethical leadership, the new knowledge that is learned about people becomes a dangerous instrument for possible misuse. **Ethical leadership** will recognize such principles as the following:[10]

Ethical managers will not manipulate people.

- *Social responsibility*   Responsibility to others arises whenever people have power in an organization.
- *Open communication*   The organization shall operate as a two-way, open system, with open receipt of inputs from people and open disclosure of its operations to them.
- *Cost-benefit analysis*   In addition to economic costs and benefits, human and social costs and benefits of an activity shall be analyzed in determining whether to proceed with the activity.

As the general population learns more about organizational behavior, it will be more difficult to manipulate people, but the possibility is always there. That is why society needs ethical leaders.

CONTINUING CHALLENGES

Seeking Quick Fixes

One problem that has plagued organizational behavior has been the tendency for business firms to have short time horizons for the expected payoff from behavioral programs. This search for a **quick fix** sometimes leads managers to embrace the newest fad, to address the symptoms while neglecting underlying problems, or to fragment their efforts within the firm. The emergence of organizational development programs

Immediate expectations are not realistic.

1. Remember that your actions have implications at one or more levels of OB: individual, interpersonal, group, intergroup, and whole system. Therefore, try to increase your skills by predicting the results and monitoring the consequences of your decisions.

2. Discipline yourself to read, and search for applications of, at least one item from the literature in OB theory, research, and practice each month.

3. Create an inventory of the observed differences you see across your employees. Then state the implications of those differences (how will you treat them based on what you know about them?).

4. Identify the ethical issues you face. Share these with your employees so that they understand them, and tell them which moral prisms most likely affect your resolution of the issues.

5. Analyze the organizational results you are currently responsible for. Identify which of the major contributing factors (knowledge, skill, attitude, situation, or resources) is most under your control, and develop a plan for improving that one.

6. Examine a potential change you are considering making. Identify its costs and benefits, both direct and indirect, and use that information to help determine your decision.

---

that focus on systemwide change and the creation of long-term strategic plans for the management of human resources has helped bring about more realistic expectations concerning employees as a productive asset.

Some management consultants and writers have been labeled "witch doctors" because of their blind advocacy of a single approach as a way to solve an entire organization's problems. Some of the management concepts that have been blindly promoted by one or more authors are management by objectives, job enlargement, sensitivity training, flextime, quality circles, visioning, and strategic planning. Unfortunately, these quick fixes have often been promoted on the basis of only interesting stories and personal anecdotes. Managers are urged to be cautious consumers of these perspectives.[11]

Varying Environments

Can organizational behavior adapt to change?

Another challenge that confronts organizational behavior is to see whether the ideas that have been developed and tested during periods of organizational growth and economic plenty will endure with equal success under new conditions. Specifically, the environment in the future may be marked by shrinking demand, scarce resources, and more intense competition. When organizations stagnate, decline, or have their survival threatened, there is evidence that stress and conflict increase. Will the same motivational models be useful in these situations? Are different leadership styles called for? Will the trend toward participative processes be reversed? Since no easy answers to these and many other questions exist, it is clear that there is still tremendous room for further development of organizational behavior.

Lack of a Single Definition

Organizational behavior, as a relatively new discipline, has experienced some difficulty emerging as a clearly defined field of study and application. There is a lack of consensus regarding its *unit of analysis* (individual, group, or total organization), its greatest *need* (as a source of empirical data and integrating theory, or as a basis for applied information), its major *focus* (micro or macro issues), and its major *contributions* to date.[12] This lack of clear definition has been compounded by the multiple criteria that can be used to assess its effectiveness. Issues here include identification of the relevant stakeholders, short or long time frame to wait for results, and reliance on soft or hard data (perceptions or records). All these issues deserve attention and clarification.

SUMMARY

Organizational behavior is the study and application of knowledge about how people—as individuals and groups—act in organizations. Its goals are to make managers more effective at describing, understanding, predicting, and controlling human behavior. Key elements to consider are people, structure, technology, and the external environment. Organizational behavior has emerged as an interdisciplinary field of value to managers. It builds on an increasingly solid research foundation, and it draws upon useful ideas and conceptual models from many of the behavioral sciences to make managers more effective.

Fundamental concepts of organizational behavior relate to the nature of people (individual differences, perception, a whole person, motivated behavior, desire for involvement, and value of the person) and to the nature of organizations (social systems, mutual interest, and ethics). Managerial actions should be oriented holistically to attain superordinate goals of interest to employees, the organization, and society. Effective management can best be attained through the understanding and use of the human resources, contingency, results-oriented, and systems approaches.

A behavioral bias, the law of diminishing returns, and unethical use of behavioral tools can all limit the effectiveness of organizational behavior. Managers must guard against using OB as a quick fix, failing to recognize the impact of different environments, and assuming that OB is interpreted in the same way universally. If these factors are overcome, OB should produce a higher quality of life in which there is improved harmony within each person, among people, and among the organizations of the future.

Behavioral bias	Perception	**Terms and Concepts for Review**
Contingency approach	Practice	
Cost-benefit analysis	Productivity	
Ethical leadership	Quick fix	
Ethical treatment	Research	
Goals of organizational behavior	Results orientation	
Holistic organizational behavior	Selective perception	
Human resources approach	Supportive approach	
Individual differences	Systems approach	
Law of diminishing returns	Theories	
Law of individual differences	Total quality management (TQM)	
Manipulation of people	Triple reward system	
Mutuality of interest	Tunnel vision	
Organizational behavior		

1. Define organizational behavior in your own words. Ask a friend or work associate to do the same. Identify and explore the nature of any differences between the two definitions.
2. Assume that a friend states, "Organizational behavior is selfish and manipulative, because it serves only the interests of management." How would you respond?

Discussion Questions

22

3. As you begin to understand organizational behavior, why do you think it has become a popular field of interest?
4. Consider the statement "Organizations need people, and people need organizations." Is this assertion true for all types of organizations? Give examples of where it is and where it probably isn't true.
5. Review the fundamental concepts that form the basis of organizational behavior. Which concepts do you think are more important than the others? Explain.
6. Select one of your work associates or friends. Identify the qualities that make that person substantially different from you. In what ways are you basically similar? Which dominates, the differences or the similarities?
7. Discuss the major features of the social system in an organization where you have worked. In what ways did that social system affect you and your job performance, either positively or negatively?
8. Review the four approaches to organizational behavior. As you read this book, keep a list of the ways in which those themes are reflected in each major topic.
9. Examine the formulas leading to effective organizational productivity. Which factors do you think have the greatest potential for making a difference between organizations? What can be done to affect the other ones?
10. Are behavioral bias and diminishing returns from organizational behavior practices the same or different? Discuss.

Assess Your Own Skills

How well do you understand organizational behavior?

Read the following statements carefully. Circle the number on the response scale that most closely reflects the degree to which each statement accurately describes you. Add up your total points, and prepare a brief action plan for self-improvement. Be ready to report your score for tabulation across the entire group.

	Good description								Poor description	
1. I thoroughly understand the nature and definition of organizational behavior.	10	9	8	7	6	5	4	3	2	1
2. I can list and explain the four primary goals of organizational behavior.	10	9	8	7	6	5	4	3	2	1
3. I feel comfortable explaining the interaction between theory, research, and practice in organizational behavior.	10	9	8	7	6	5	4	3	2	1
4. I am fully aware of the ways in which people act on the basis of their perceived world.	10	9	8	7	6	5	4	3	2	1
5. I believe that most employees have a strong desire to be involved in decision making.	10	9	8	7	6	5	4	3	2	1
6. I feel comfortable explaining the role of ethics in organizational behavior.	10	9	8	7	6	5	4	3	2	1

7. I can easily summarize the basic nature of the contingency approach to organizational behavior.   10 9 8 7 6 5 4 3 2 1

8. I can list and explain each of the factors in the formula for producing organizational results.   10 9 8 7 6 5 4 3 2 1

9. I can explain why a systems approach to organizational behavior is appropriate.   10 9 8 7 6 5 4 3 2 1

10. I understand the relationship among the systems viewpoint, behavioral bias, and the law of diminishing returns in organizational behavior.   10 9 8 7 6 5 4 3 2 1

Scoring and Interpretation Add up your total points for the ten questions. Record that number here, and report it when it is requested. _____

- If you scored between 81–100 points, you appear to have a solid understanding of organizational behavior basics.
- If you scored between 61–80 points, you should take a close look at the items with lower self-assessment scores and review the related material again.
- If you scored less than 60 points, you should be aware that a weaker understanding of several items could be detrimental to your future success as a manager. We encourage you to review the entire chapter.

Now identify your three lowest scores, and write the question numbers here: _____, _____, _____. Write a brief paragraph, detailing to yourself an action plan for how you might sharpen each of these skills.

The Transferred Sales Representative   **Incident**

Harold Burns served as district sales representative for an appliance firm. His district covered the central part of a midwestern state, and it included about 100 retail outlets. He had been with the company for twenty years and in his present job and location for five years. During that time he met his district sales quota each year.

One day Burns learned through local friends that the wife of a sales representative in another district was in town to try to rent a house. She told the real estate agency that her family would be moving there in a few days because her husband was replacing Burns. When Burns heard this news, he refused to believe it.

Two days later, on January 28, he received an express mail letter, postmarked the previous day, from the regional sales manager. The letter read:

Dear Harold:
Because of personnel vacancies we are requesting that you move to the Gunning district, effective February 1. Mr. George Dowd from the Parsons district will replace you. Will you please see that your inventory and property are properly transferred to him? I know that you will like your new district. Congratulations!
Sincerely yours,
(Signature)

In the same mail he received his twenty-year service pin. The accompanying letter from the regional sales manager read:

> *Dear Harold:*
> *I am happy to enclose your twenty-year service pin. You have a long and excellent record with the company. We are honored to give you this recognition, and I hope you will wear it proudly.*
> *Our company is proud to have many long-service employees. We want you to know that we take a personal interest in your welfare because people like you are the backbone of our company.*
> *Sincerely yours,*
> *(Signature)*

Harold Burns checked his quarterly sales bulletin and found that sales for the Gunning district were running 10 percent below those in his present district.

Questions

1. Comment on the positive and negative events in this case as they relate to organizational behavior.
2. Was a human resources approach to Burns applied in this instance? Discuss.

Experiential Exercise

Ethics in Organizational Behavior

Examine the following statements. Assess each situation according to the degree to which you believe a potential ethical problem is inherent in it. After recording your answers, meet in small groups (three to five persons) and discuss any significant differences you find among answers given by members of your group.

	No ethical problem				Ethical problem
1. A manager, following the law of individual differences, allows her six employees to establish their own starting times for work each day.	0	1	2	3	4
2. A supervisor finds that members of a certain minority group are faster workers than whites, and thereafter hires only those minorities for particular jobs.	0	1	2	3	4
3. An organization, frustrated over continual complaints about its appraisal system and pay, decides that "equal pay for all employees" (despite differences in their performance) will work best.	0	1	2	3	4
4. An organization is faced with a possible union certification election. To find out what employees are thinking, top management installs					

electronic eavesdropping equipment
in the cafeteria.   0   1   2   3   4

5. A company hires a consulting firm to
    conduct an attitude survey of its
    employees. When the consultants
    suggest that they could code the
    questionnaires secretly so that
    responses could be traced back to
    individuals, the company agrees that
    it would be "interesting."   0   1   2   3   4

Chapter 2

Models of Organizational Behavior

It's been a remarkable journey, painfully slow, from the days in which companies succeeded—and for a time they succeeded stupendously—by denying employees' humanity.

—Geoffrey Colvin[1]

[Many popular] books have a common theme: the longing to create a workplace where everyone from the top down shares a unified vision and sense of purpose beyond making money.

—Pamela Leigh[2]

CHAPTER OBJECTIVES

TO UNDERSTAND

- The Elements of an Organizational Behavior System
- The Role of Management's Philosophy and Paradigms
- Alternative Models of Organizational Behavior and Their Effects
- Trends in the Use of These Models

One of the authors recently boarded a plane on a winter day in Duluth and flew to Phoenix to visit his coauthor. The differences between the weather conditions in the two geographical areas were easily apparent. One was cold, damp, and windy; the other was warm, dry, and calm. As a matter of fact, the temperature differential between the two cities was over 100 degrees!

The differences between organizations can sometimes be equally extreme. In addition, organizations have undergone tremendous changes during the past two centuries. Although employers in early days had no systematic program for managing their employees, their simple rules still exerted a powerful influence on the organization. Many of the old rules are now out of date, and increasing numbers of organizations today are experimenting with exciting new ways to attract and motivate their workers. A century from now, though, people may look back on these practices and consider them outdated, too. Clearly, work rules vary across organizations, time, and cultures.

A century ago, farmers' and industrialists' reference to employees as "hands" was a natural reflection of the prevailing model of organizational behavior at that time. Employers took the narrow economic view that they were purchasing the commodity of labor—that is, the skill of the *hands* of the employees. Continuing the major themes introduced in Chapter 1 (human resources, contingency, results-oriented, and systems/holistic approaches), this chapter presents five alternative models of organizational behavior. Some of these reflect more progressive approaches that are well adapted to contemporary issues and trends. We see that even the words used to refer to employees (such as "hands," as contrasted to the use in some organizations of terms like "associates" or "partners" to convey equality) tell a lot about the underlying model in use.

This chapter builds on the fundamental concepts presented in Chapter 1 by showing how all behavioral factors can be combined to develop an effective organization. We discuss the interrelated elements of an organizational behavior system and offer a road map for where these elements appear in this book. After a brief review of the historical highlights of OB, we present five alternative models of organizational behavior and propose several conclusions about the use of these models.

AN ORGANIZATIONAL BEHAVIOR SYSTEM

Organizations achieve their goals by creating, communicating, and operating an **organizational behavior system,** as shown in Figure 2–1. Major elements of a good organizational behavior system are introduced on the following pages and presented in detail throughout the book. These systems exist in every organization, but sometimes in varying forms. They have a greater chance of being successful, though, if they have been *consciously created* and *regularly examined and updated* to meet new and emerging conditions. Updating is done by drawing upon the constantly growing behavioral science base of knowledge mentioned in the previous chapter.

The primary purposes of organizational behavior systems are to identify and then help manipulate the major human and organizational variables that affect the results organizations are trying to achieve. For some of these variables, managers can only be aware of them and acknowledge their impact; for others, managers can exert some control over them. The outcomes, or end results, are typically measured in various forms of three basic criteria: *performance* (e.g., quantity and quality of products and services;

FIGURE 2–1

An organizational
behavior system

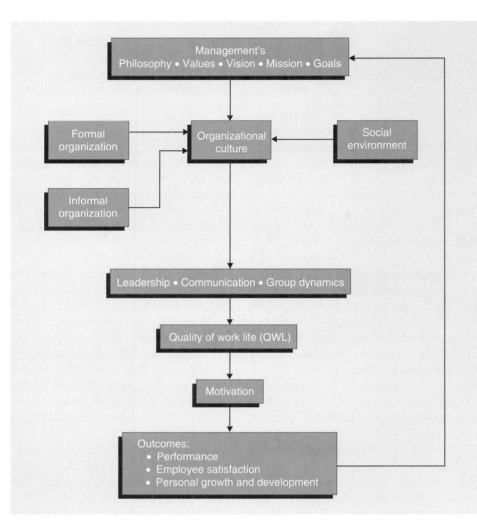

level of customer service), *employee satisfaction* (often exhibited through lower absenteeism, tardiness, or turnover), or *personal growth and development* (the acquisition of lifelong knowledge and skills leading to continued employability). The effect of organizational behavior practices on these outcomes is discussed throughout this book.

Elements of the System

The system's base rests on the fundamental beliefs and intentions of those who join to create it (such as owners) and of the managers who currently administer it. The **philosophy** (model) of organizational behavior held by management consists of an integrated set of assumptions and beliefs about the way things are, the purpose for these activities, and the way they should be. These philosophies are sometimes explicit, and occasionally implicit, in the minds of managers. Five major organizational behavior philosophies—autocratic, custodial, supportive, collegial, and system—and their implications are discussed later in this chapter.

The philosophy of organizational behavior held by a manager stems from two sources—fact premises and value premises. **Fact premises** represent our descriptive view of how the world behaves. They are drawn from both behavioral science research and our personal experiences (important things we have learned). For example, you would not throw an expensive video camera from a ten-story building, because you believe gravity would pull it downward uncontrollably and crush it against the ground, and you don't want this to happen. Fact premises, then, are acquired through direct and indirect lifelong learning and are very useful in guiding our behavior.

Fact and value premises

Value premises, on the other hand, represent our view of the desirability of certain goals and activities. If you had been very unhappy with the video camera's performance, then you might choose to throw it from the ten-story building. You still accept the fact premise of gravity, but now your value premises have changed (at least momentarily!). As this illustration shows, value premises are variable beliefs we hold and are therefore under our control. We can choose, modify, discard, or replace them (although they are often deeply entrenched). Many organizations have sought to identify and state the values they cherish, as shown in the following illustration:

> A group of 800 professional staff in the FMC Corporation were given the goal of creating "user satisfaction" with the services they provided to the firm's 28,000 employees. The key to achieving this goal, however, lay in a four-day meeting that produced a statement of philosophy (see Figure 2–2). This clarification of values, coupled with other organizational changes and skill-building sessions, resulted in dramatic improvements in employee satisfaction and quality of service to the staff's internal "clients." FMC reported a 50 percent reduction in turnover of key employees following this value-clarification process.[3]

Managers also have primary responsibility for instilling three other elements into the organizational behavior system—vision, mission, and goals. **Vision** represents a challenging portrait of what the organization and its members can be—a possible, and desirable, future. Leaders need to create exciting projections about where the organization should go and what major changes lie ahead. Once the vision is established, persistent and enthusiastic communication is required to sell it throughout the ranks of employees so they will embrace it with commitment.[4]

Vision

An organization also typically creates a **mission** statement, which identifies the business it is in, the market niches it tries to serve, the types of customers it is likely to have, and the reasons for its existence. Many mission statements even include a brief listing of the competitive advantages, or strengths, that the firm believes it has. In contrast to visions, mission statements are more descriptive and less future-oriented. They are still rather broad, and need to be converted to goals to become operational and useful.

Mission

- We are committed to quality, cost-effectiveness, and technical excellence.

- People should treat each other with consideration, trust, and respect.

- Each person is valuable, is unique, and makes a contribution.

- All employees should be unfailingly committed to excellent performance.

- Teamwork can, and should, produce far more than the sum of individual efforts. Team members must be reliable and committed to the team.

- Innovation is essential.

- Open communications are important for attaining success.

- Decisions should be reached participatively.

FIGURE 2–2

Selected elements of a philosophy statement
Source: Adapted from FMC Corporation's management information systems' "Mission, Values, and Policies," as reported in Edmund J. Metz, "Managing Change toward a Leading-Edge Information Culture," *Organizational Dynamics,* Autumn 1986, pp. 28–40.

Goals

Goals are relatively concrete formulations of achievements the organization is aiming for within set periods of time, such as one to five years. Goal setting is a complex process, for top management's goals need to be merged with those of employees, who bring their psychological, social, and economic needs with them to an organization. Further, goals may exist at the individual, group, and larger organization level, so substantial integration is required before a working social system can emerge. Elements of effective goals are discussed in Chapter 5.

Philosophy feeds into value premises, which help shape vision. Vision is a stretching version of mission, and goals provide a way to pinpoint targets for achieving that mission. Together, philosophy, values, vision, mission, and goals exist in a hierarchy of increasing specificity (philosophy is most general; goals are most specific). They all help create a recognizable organizational culture, which is discussed in Chapter 4. This culture is also a reflection of the formal organization with its formal policies, structures, and procedures, and the existing social and cultural (global) environment (Chapter 16). Managers also need to be aware of the informal organization (discussed in Chapter 12) and must work with its members to create positive norms. Together, the formal and informal organizations provide the glue that binds the varied elements of the institution into an effective working team.

Managers are then expected to use a leadership style (Chapter 7), communication skills (Chapter 3), and their knowledge of interpersonal and group dynamics (Chapters 11 and 12) to create an appropriate quality of work life for their employees (Chapter 10). When this task is done properly, employees will become motivated toward the achievement of organizational goals (Chapter 5). Their motivation, however, is also a product of their underlying attitudes and specific situational factors at a certain point in time. If any of the previous factors in the organizational system are changed, motivation will also be different. Because of this interaction, leaders must learn to manage employee motivation contingently. For example, if a procedure is arbitrarily changed but attitudes and the prevailing situation remain the same, motivation may change and produce different results. The social equilibrium has been upset, and the effects will inevitably show up. Numerous examples of this cause-and-effect relationship exist, as illustrated in the following report:

> Contrasting effects of organizational behavior systems were seen in some of the efforts to revitalize airline companies in the past decade. In the face of financial crises, employees in some firms willingly accepted the necessity of drastic cost-saving actions and responded with increased (and successful) efforts to save their companies and jobs. Employees in other firms, such as Eastern Airlines, fearful for their jobs and resentful of management's previous autocratic actions, strongly resisted attempts to modernize old work rules and pay systems. As a consequence of the failure to adopt new work practices, bankruptcy followed.

The result of an effective organizational behavior system is motivation which, when combined with employee skills and abilities, results in the achievement of performance goals (as we saw in the formulas in Chapter 1) as well as individual satisfaction. It builds two-way relationships that are mutually supportive, meaning that manager and employee are jointly influencing each other and jointly benefiting. Supportive OB systems are characterized by power *with* people rather than power *over* them, which is consistent with present human values regarding how people wish to be treated (with dignity). Alternatively, if goals are not being achieved, managers need to use this information to examine and revise their organizational behavior system.

MODELS OF ORGANIZATIONAL BEHAVIOR

Organizations differ in the nature of the systems they develop and maintain and in the results they achieve. Varying results predictably follow from different **models** of organizational behavior. These models constitute the belief system that dominates management's thought and affects management's actions in each organization. It is highly important that managers recognize the nature, significance, and effectiveness of their own models, as well as the models of others around them.

Douglas McGregor was one of the first writers to call attention to managerial models. In 1957, he presented a convincing argument that most management actions flow directly from whatever theory of human behavior the managers hold.[5] He suggested that management philosophy controls practice. Management's human resource policies, decision-making styles, operating practices, and even organizational designs flow from key *assumptions about human behavior.* The assumptions may be implicit rather than explicit, but they can be inferred from observing the kinds of actions that managers take.

Theory X is a traditional set of assumptions about people. As shown in Figure 2–3, it assumes that most people dislike work and will try to avoid it if they can. Workers are seen as being inclined to restrict work output, having little ambition, and avoiding responsibility if at all possible. They are believed to be relatively self-centered, indifferent to organizational needs, and resistant to change. Common rewards cannot overcome this natural dislike for work, so management is almost forced (under Theory X assumptions and subsequent logic) to coerce, control, and threaten employees to obtain satisfactory performance. Though managers may deny that they hold this view of people, many of their historical actions suggest that Theory X has been a typical management view of employees.

Theory X assumptions

Theory X	Theory Y
• The typical person dislikes work and will avoid it if possible.	• Work is as natural as play or rest.
• The typical person lacks responsibility, has little ambition, and seeks security above all.	• People are not inherently lazy. They have become that way as a result of experience.
• Most people must be coerced, controlled, and threatened with punishment to get them to work.	• People will exercise self-direction and self-control in the service of objectives to which they are committed.
	• People have potential. Under proper conditions they learn to accept and seek responsibility. They have imagination, ingenuity, and creativity that can be applied to work.
With these assumptions the managerial role is to coerce and control employees.	With these assumptions the managerial role is to develop the potential in employees and help them release that potential toward common objectives.

FIGURE 2–3

McGregor's Theory X and Theory Y, alternative assumptions about employees

Theory Y assumptions

Theory Y implies a more humanistic and supportive approach to managing people. It assumes that people are not inherently lazy. Any appearance they have of being that way is the result of their experiences with less-enlightened organizations, and if management will provide the proper environment to release their potential, work will become as natural to them as recreational play or rest and relaxation. Under Theory Y assumptions, management believes that employees are capable of exercising self-direction and self-control in the service of objectives to which they are committed. Management's role is to provide an environment in which the potential of people can be released at work.

McGregor's argument was that management had been ignoring the facts about people. It had been following an outmoded set of assumptions about people because it adhered to Theory X when the facts are that the Theory Y set of assumptions is more truly representative of most people. There will always be important differences among people, so a few individuals will fit the assumptions of the Theory X model. Nearly all employees, however, have some potential for growth in their capabilities and demonstrated performance. Therefore, McGregor argued, management needed to change to a whole new set of assumptions about people—one based on emerging behavioral science research. These new assumptions had a powerful impact on subsequent managerial actions.

When seen through the lenses of history, McGregor deserves credit for a number of contributions. First, he stimulated subsequent generations of managers to think consciously about their belief systems and management models. Second, he was an early advocate of the practical value of reading and using research findings to better understand human behavior. Third, he introduced and publicized one of the early theories of motivation—the hierarchy of needs model by A. H. Maslow (explained in Chapter 5). Finally, he became a spokesman for a trend that had been developing over a long period of time—the need to bring human values into balance with other values at work.

Impact of paradigms

Models such as Theory X and Theory Y are also called **paradigms,** or frameworks of possible explanations about how things work. Any model that a manager holds usually begins with certain assumptions about people and leads to certain interpretations, implications, and even predictions of events. Underlying paradigms, whether consciously or unconsciously developed, become powerful guides to managerial behavior. Managers tend to act as they think, because they are guided by their dominant thoughts.

Managerial paradigms, according to popular author Joel Barker, act in several important ways:

- They influence managerial perceptions of the world around them.
- They define one's boundaries and provide prescriptions for how to behave.
- They encourage resistance to change, since they have often worked in the past.
- They may either consciously or unconsciously affect one's behavior.
- When new paradigms appear, they provide alternative ways of viewing the world and solving problems.[6]

Examples of paradigm shifts abound in the commercial world. A decade ago, throngs of citizens mobbed shopping malls across the country in the weeks and days before a major holiday; today, millions of people do some or all of their shopping via the Internet while sitting at home. In the automotive realm, internal combustion engines were the sole source of energy for many decades; now, battery-powered cars have become a reality for some buyers. In communications, U.S. citizens relied almost exclusively on the Postal Service to deliver their letters throughout much of the twentieth century; today, millions of messages are almost instantaneously transmitted via e-mail systems. Paradigms are changing everywhere!

Top management's models are particularly important to identify, for the underlying model that exists within a firm's chief executive officer tends to extend throughout that firm. For this reason, models of organizational behavior are highly significant. Examples abound of the impact throughout the firm of a single executive, such as CEOs Carly Fiorina at Hewlett-Packard, Jeff Bezos at Amazon, Jerry Yang at Yahoo, Meg Whitman at eBay, or Steve Ballmer at Microsoft.

We highlight in this chapter the following five models (paradigms): autocratic, custodial, supportive, collegial, and system. These five models are summarized in Figure 2–4. In the order mentioned, they represent an approximate historical evolution in management practice during the last 100 years or more. Although one model tends to dominate at a particular time in history, each of the other models is practiced by some organizations.

Just as organizations differ among themselves, so practices may vary within the departments or branches of one organization. The production department may work within a custodial model while the supportive model is being tried in the research department. And, of course, the practices of individual managers may differ from their organization's prevailing model because of those managers' personal preferences or different conditions in their department. Thus no one model of organizational behavior is sufficient to describe all that happens in an organization, but identifying a model can help distinguish one way of organizational life from another.

The selection of a model by a manager is determined by a number of factors. As we discussed earlier, the prevailing philosophy, values, vision, mission, and goals of managers affect, and are affected by, their organizational behavior model. In addition,

FIGURE 2–4

Five models of organizational behavior

	Autocratic	Custodial	Supportive	Collegial	System
Basis of model	Power	Economic resources	Leadership	Partnership	Trust, community, meaning
Managerial orientation	Authority	Money	Support	Teamwork	Caring, compassion
Employee orientation	Obedience	Security and benefits	Job performance	Responsible behavior	Psychological ownership
Employee psychological result	Dependence on boss	Dependence on organization	Participation	Self-discipline	Self-motivation
Employee needs met	Subsistence	Security	Status and recognition	Self-actualization	Wide range
Performance result	Minimum	Passive cooperation	Awakened drives	Moderate enthusiasm	Passion and commitment to organizational goals

environmental conditions help determine which model will be most effective. The current turbulent conditions in some industries, for example, may drive firms toward the more collegial models, since rapid decision making and flexibility are needed. This suggests that the model should not be static and unchanging but adapted across time. Our discussion of five models, beginning with the autocratic, roughly follows their historical evolution.

The Autocratic Model

The autocratic model has its roots in history, and certainly, it became the prevailing model of the industrial revolution. As shown in Figure 2–4 the **autocratic model** depends on *power*. Those who are in command must have the power to demand "you do this—or else," meaning that an employee who does not follow orders will be penalized.

Power and authority are used.

In an autocratic environment the managerial orientation is formal, official *authority*. This authority is delegated by right of command over the people to whom it applies. Management believes that it knows what is best and that the employee's obligation is to follow orders. It assumes that employees have to be directed, persuaded, and pushed into performance, and such prompting is management's task. Management does the thinking; the employees obey the orders. This conventional view of management leads to tight control of employees at work. When combined with the often brutal and backbreaking physical tasks of that era and the intolerable conditions of disease, filth, danger, and scarcity of resources, the autocratic model was intensely disliked by many employees (and still is).

Under autocratic conditions the employee orientation is *obedience* to a boss, not respect for a manager. The psychological result for employees is *dependence* on their boss, whose power to hire, fire, and "perspire" them is almost absolute. The boss pays minimum wages because *minimum performance* is given by employees. They are willing to give minimum performance—though sometimes reluctantly—because they must satisfy *subsistence* needs for themselves and their families. Some employees give higher performance because of internal achievement drives, because they personally like their boss, because the boss is "a natural-born leader," or because of some other factor; but most of them give only minimum performance.

The autocratic model is a useful way to accomplish work. It is not a complete failure. The picture of the autocratic model just presented is an extreme one; actually, the model exists in all shades of gray, from rather dark to rather light. This view of work built great railroad systems, operated giant steel mills, and produced the dynamic industrial civilization that developed in the United States. It does get results, but usually only moderate results. *Its principal weakness is its high human costs.*

Autocratic model works.

The autocratic model was an acceptable approach to guide managerial behavior when there were no well-known alternatives, and it still can be useful under some conditions, such as organizational crises.[7] However, the combination of emerging knowledge about the needs of employees and changing societal values suggested that there were better ways to manage organizational systems. A second step in the ladder of progress was needed, and it was soon forthcoming.

The Custodial Model

As managers began to study their employees, they soon recognized that although autocratically managed employees did not talk back to their boss, they certainly "thought back." There were many things they wanted to say, and sometimes they did say them when they quit or lost their tempers. Employees were filled with insecurity, frustrations, and aggressions toward their boss. Since they could not vent these feelings directly, sometimes they went home and vented them on their families and neighbors; so the entire community might suffer from this relationship.

> An example of the effects of management-induced frustration on the behavior of employees occurred in a wood-processing plant. Managers treated workers crudely, sometimes even to the point of physical abuse. Since employees could not strike back directly for fear of losing their jobs, they found another way to do it. They *symbolically* fed their supervisor to a log-shredding machine! They did this by purposely destroying good sheets of veneer, which made the supervisor look bad when monthly efficiency reports were prepared.[8]

It seemed rather obvious to progressive employers that there ought to be some way to develop better employee satisfactions and security. If the insecurities, frustrations, and aggressions of employees could be dispelled, the employees might feel more like working. In any case, they would have a better quality of work life.

To satisfy the security needs of employees, a number of companies began welfare programs in the 1890s and 1900s. In their worst form these welfare programs later became known as *paternalism*. In the 1930s welfare programs evolved into a variety of fringe benefits to provide employee security. Employers—and unions and government—began caring for the security needs of workers. They were applying a **custodial model** of organizational behavior.

> Employee security remains a high priority for millions of workers in today's uncertain job market where lifetime employment is seldom promised to any employee. Many firms have historically gone out of their way to stabilize their workforce and preserve employee jobs. To avoid layoffs, they constantly retrain employees, reduce overtime, freeze hiring, encourage both job transfers and relocations, provide early retirement incentives, and reduce subcontracting to adjust to slowdowns in the computer industry.[9]

As shown in Figure 2–4, a successful custodial approach depends on *economic resources*. The resulting managerial orientation is toward *money* to pay wages and benefits. Since employees' physical needs are already reasonably met, the employer looks to *security* needs as a motivating force. If an organization does not have the wealth to provide pensions and pay other benefits, it cannot follow a custodial approach.

The custodial approach leads to employee *dependence on the organization*. Rather than being dependent on their boss for their weekly bread, employees now depend on organizations for their security and welfare. Perhaps more accurately stated, an organizational dependence is *added* to a reduced personal dependence on the boss. If employees have ten years of seniority under the union contract and a good pension program, they cannot afford to quit even if the grass looks greener somewhere else.

Employees become dependent.

> There are many programs consistent with a custodial environment at the workplace. The Calvert Group, a Maryland-based mutual funds company, provides support for physical fitness, massage therapy, wellness seminars, parental leave, dependent-care time, and child-care programs. Calvert reported that the turnover rate has fallen sharply from its preprogram level of 30 percent annually, the number of sick days taken is down, health care expenses are lower, and recruitment and training costs have been reduced.[10] Apparently, employees become dependent on these custodial practices and then are reluctant to change employers.

Employees working in a custodial environment become psychologically preoccupied with their economic rewards and benefits. As a result of their treatment, they are well maintained and contented. However, contentment does not necessarily produce

36

strong motivation; it may produce only *passive cooperation*. The result tends to be that employees do not perform much more effectively than under the old autocratic approach.

The custodial model is described in its extreme in order to show its emphasis on material rewards, security, and organizational dependence. In actual practice, this model also has various shades of gray, from dark to light. Its great benefit is that it brings security and satisfaction to workers, but it does have substantial flaws. The most evident flaw is that most employees are not producing anywhere near their capacities, nor are they motivated to grow to the greater capacities of which they are capable. Though employees are happy, most of them really do not feel fulfilled or motivated. In confirmation of this condition, a series of studies at the University of Michigan in the 1940s and 1950s reported that "the happy employee is not necessarily the most productive employee."[11] Consequently, managers and academic leaders started to ask again, "Is there a better way?"

The search for a better way is not a condemnation of the custodial model as a whole but rather a condemnation of the assumption that this is "the final answer"— the one best way to motivate employees. The error in reasoning occurs when people perceive the custodial model as so desirable that there is no need to build on it toward something better. Although the custodial model is desirable to provide employee security, it is best viewed as the foundation for growth to the next step.

The Supportive Model

The **supportive model** of organizational behavior had its origins in the "principle of supportive relationships" as stated by Rensis Likert, who said:

> The leadership and other processes of the organization must be such as to ensure a maximum probability that in all interactions and all relationships with the organization each member will, in the light of his [or her] background, values, and expectations, view the experience as supportive and one which builds and maintains his [or her] sense of personal worth and importance.[12]

Likert's principle is similar to the human resources approach mentioned in Chapter 1.

One key spark for the supportive approach was a series of research studies at the Hawthorne Plant of Western Electric in the 1920s and 1930s.[13] Led by Elton Mayo and F. J. Roethlisberger, the researchers gave academic stature to the study of human behavior at work by applying keen insight, straight thinking, and sociological backgrounds to industrial experiments. They concluded that an organization is a social system and the worker is indeed the most important element in it. Their experiments concluded that the worker is not a simple tool but a complex personality that often is difficult to understand. The studies also suggested that an understanding of group dynamics, coupled with the application of supportive supervision, was important.

Development of research

The Mayo-Roethlisberger research has been strongly criticized as being inadequately controlled and overinterpreted,[14] but its basic ideas, such as a social system within the work environment, have stood the test of time. The important point is that it was substantial research about human behavior at work, and its influence was widespread and enduring. The studies have truly been a landmark in the historical evolution of organizational behavior and awakened further interest in the supportive model.

The supportive model depends on *leadership* instead of power or money. Through leadership, management provides a climate to help employees grow and accomplish in the interests of the organization the things of which they are capable. The leader assumes that workers are not by nature passive and resistant to organizational needs, but that they are made so by an inadequately supportive climate at work. They will take responsibility, develop a drive to contribute, and improve themselves if management will give them a chance. Management's orientation, therefore, is to *support the employee's job performance* rather than to simply support employee benefit payments as in the custodial approach.

Since management supports employees in their work, the psychological result is a feeling of *participation and task involvement* in the organization. Employees may say "we" instead of "they" when referring to their organization. They are more strongly motivated than by earlier models because their *status and recognition* needs are better met. Thus they have *awakened drives* for work.

Supportive behavior is not the kind of behavior that requires money. Rather, it is a part of management's lifestyle at work, reflected in the way that it deals with other people. The manager's role is one of helping employees solve their problems and accomplish their work. Following is an example of a supportive approach:

Employees are helped to become productive.

> Juanita Salinas, a young divorcee with one child, had a record of frequent tardiness as an assembler in an electronics plant. Her supervisor, Helen Ferguson, scolded her several times about her tardiness, and each time Salinas improved for two or three weeks but then lapsed back into her normal pattern. At about this time Ferguson attended a company training program for supervisors, so she decided to try the supportive approach with Salinas.
>
> The next time Salinas was tardy, Ferguson approached her with concern about what might have caused her tardiness. Rather than scolding her, Ferguson showed a genuine interest in Salinas's problems, asking, "How can I help?" and "Is there anything we can do at the company?" When the discussion focused on delays in getting the child ready for school early in the morning, Ferguson arranged for Salinas to talk with other mothers in the department. When Salinas talked about the distance she had to walk to catch a bus, Ferguson worked with the personnel department to get her into a dependable car pool.
>
> Although the new car pool undoubtedly helped, an important point was that Salinas seemed to appreciate the recognition and concern that was expressed, so she was more motivated to come to work on time. She also was more cooperative and interested in her job. It was evident that the supportive approach influenced Salinas's behavior. An important by-product was that Ferguson's job became easier because of Salinas's better performance.

The supportive model works well with both employees and managers, and it has been widely accepted—at least philosophically—by many managers in the United States. Of course, their agreement with supportive ideas does not necessarily mean that all of them *practice* those approaches regularly or effectively. *The step from theory to practice is a difficult one.* Nevertheless, there are more and more reports of companies that reap the benefits of a supportive approach.

Are theory and practice consistent?

The supportive model of organizational behavior tends to be especially effective in affluent nations because it responds to employee drives toward a wide array of emerging needs. It has less immediate application in the developing nations, because their employees' current needs and social conditions are often quite different. However, as those needs for material rewards and security become satisfied, and as employees become aware of managerial practices in other parts of the world, we may also expect employees in those countries to demand a more supportive approach. Consequently, their progression through the models is frequently a more rapid one.

The Collegial Model

A useful extension of the supportive model is the **collegial model.** The term "collegial" relates to a body of people working together cooperatively. The collegial model, which embodies a team concept, first achieved widespread applications in research laboratories and similar work environments. More recently it has been applied in a wide range of other work situations as well.

The collegial model traditionally was used less on assembly lines, because the rigid work environment made it difficult to develop there. A contingency relationship exists in which the collegial model tends to be more useful with unprogrammed work, an intellectual environment, and considerable job freedom. In other environments management often believes that other models may be more successful.

As shown in Figure 2–4, the collegial model depends on management's building a feeling of *partnership* with employees. The result is that employees feel needed and useful. They feel that managers are contributing also, so it is easy to accept and respect their roles in the organization. Managers are seen as joint contributors rather than as bosses.

> The feeling of partnerships can be built in many ways. Some organizations have abolished the use of reserved parking spaces for executives, so every employee has an equal chance of finding a space close to the workplace. Some firms have tried to eliminate the use of terms like "bosses" and "subordinates," feeling that those terms simply create perceptions of psychological distance between managers and nonmanagers. Other employers have removed time clocks, set up "fun committees," sponsored company canoe trips, or required managers to spend a week or two annually working in field or factory locations. All these approaches are designed to build a spirit of mutuality, in which every person makes contributions and appreciates those of others.

Teamwork is required.   The managerial orientation is toward *teamwork.* Management is the coach that builds a better team. The employee response to this situation is *responsibility.* For example, employees produce quality work not because management tells them to do so or because the inspector will catch them if they do not, but because they feel inside themselves an obligation to provide others with high quality. They also feel an obligation to uphold quality standards that will bring credit to their jobs and company.

The psychological result of the collegial approach for the employee is *self-discipline.* Feeling responsible, employees discipline themselves for performance on the team in the same way that the members of a football team discipline themselves to training standards and the rules of the game. In this kind of environment employees normally feel some degree of fulfillment, worthwhile contribution, and *self-actualization,* even though the amount may be modest in some situations. This self-actualization will lead to *moderate enthusiasm* in performance.

> The collegial model tends to produce improved results in situations where it is appropriate. One study covered scientists in three large research laboratories. Laboratories A and B were operated in a relatively traditional hierarchical manner. Laboratory C was operated in a more open, participative, collegial manner. There were four measures of performance: esteem of fellow scientists, contribution to knowledge, sense of personal achievement, and contribution to management objectives. All four were higher in laboratory C, and the first three were significantly higher.[15]

The System Model

An emerging model of organizational behavior is the **system model.** It is the result of a strong search for higher *meaning* at work by many of today's employees; they want more than just a paycheck and job security from their jobs (see "What Managers Are Reading"). Since they are being asked to spend many hours of their day at work, they want a work context there that is ethical, infused with integrity and *trust,* and provides an opportunity to experience a growing sense of *community* among coworkers. To accomplish this, managers must increasingly demonstrate a sense of *caring and compassion,* being sensitive to the needs of a diverse workforce with rapidly changing needs and complex personal and family needs.

A new term is seeping slowly into the managerial lexicon—"spirituality." As espoused in a wide range of books, including *Soul of a Business, Leading with Soul, The Search for Meaning in the Workplace, Live the Life You Love,* and *Reawakening the Spirit at Work,* spirituality often focuses on an opportunity for employees to know their deepest selves better, to grow personally, to make a meaningful contribution to society, and to demonstrate integrity in every action taken. Spirituality incorporates the principle of self-awareness, encouraging people to "know thyselves" while honoring and respecting the diverse beliefs of others. As individuals search for and identify universal values—via reading, meditation, journal writing, or workshops—they are urged to live and act authentically, congruently, and joyfully. Perhaps as a consequence of this movement, one of Robert Levering's criteria for judging the "Best Companies to Work for in America" is the degree to which employees respond positively to the statement "My work has special meaning." And many companies, such as Tom's of Maine, Xerox, Aetna, and Medtronic, have actively incorporated elements of spirituality into their daily operations.

Under the system model, managers try to convey to each worker, "You are an important part of our whole system. We sincerely care about each of you. We want to join together to achieve a better product or service, local community, and society at large. We will make every effort to make products that are environmentally friendly." The role of a manager becomes one of *facilitating employee acomplishments* through a variety of actions (see Figure 2–5).

In response, many employees embrace the goal of organizational effectiveness, and recognize the mutuality of company-employee obligations in a system viewpoint. They experience a sense of *psychological ownership* for the organization and its products or services. They go beyond the self-discipline of the collegial approach until they reach a state of *self-motivation,* in which they take responsibility for their own goals and actions. As a result, the employee needs that are met are wide-ranging but often include the *highest-order needs* (e.g., social, status, esteem, autonomy, self-actualization). Because it provides employees an opportunity to meet these needs through their work as well as understand the organization's perspectives, this new model can engender employees' *passion* and *commitment* to organizational goals. They are inspired; they feel important; they believe in the usefulness and viability of their system for the common good. Their hopes and ideals are built around what the system accomplishes rather than solely what they as individuals can do.

> Starbucks Coffee Co. is an example of a firm that is strongly committed to creating a humanized workplace that exemplifies the ideals of the system model of OB. Its CEO, Howard Schultz, has written a book (*Pour Your Heart Into It*) that very publicly announces the firm's values—employee self-esteem, self-respect, and appreciation for them. Managers there recognize outstanding achievements of the employees, honor the passion they put into their work, promote an open environment, and award stock options to every level of the organization. Results show up in effective customer service, new product ideas, employee loyalty, and low turnover rates.[16]

Conclusions about the Models

Several conclusions can be made about the models of organizational behavior: They are, in practice, subject to evolutionary change; they are a function of prevailing employee needs; there is a trend toward the newer models; and any of the models can be successfully applied in some situations. In addition, the models can be modified and extended in a variety of ways.

Evolving Usage   Managerial and, on a broader scale, organizational, use of these models tends to evolve over time.[17] As our individual or collective understanding of human behavior increases or as new social conditions develop, we

FIGURE 2–5

Facilitator roles for managers in the system model of OB

- Support employee commitment to short- and long-term goals.

- Coach individuals and groups in appropriate skills and behaviors.

- Model and foster self-esteem.

- Show genuine concern and empathy for people.

- Offer timely and acceptable feedback.

- Influence people to learn continuously and share that learning with others.

- Help individuals identify and confront issues in ethical ways.

- Stimulate insights through interviews, questions, and suggestions.

- Encourage people to feel comfortable with change and uncertainty.

- Build cohesive, productive work teams.

move somewhat slowly to newer models. It is a mistake to assume that one particular model is a "best" model that will endure for the long run. This mistake was made by some managers about both the autocratic model and the custodial model, with the result that they became psychologically locked into those models and had difficulty altering their practices when conditions demanded it. Eventually, the supportive model may also fall to limited use. There is no one permanently "best" model, because what is best is contingent on what is known about human behavior in whatever environment exists at that time. In some conditions the collegial model may be inappropriate; in others the autocratic or custodial models should still be used.

Effectiveness of current models

The primary challenge for management is to *identify the model it is actually using and then assess its current effectiveness*. This self-examination can be a challenge for managers, who tend to profess publicly one model (e.g., the supportive, collegial, or system) yet practice another. (This may occur in multinational firms; see "Managing across National Boundaries.") In effect, a manager has two key tasks—to acquire a new set of values as models evolve and to learn and apply the behavioral skills that are consistent with those values. These tasks can be very difficult to accomplish.

Relation of Models to Human Needs   A second conclusion is that the five models discussed in this chapter are closely related to human needs. New models have been developed to serve the different needs that became important at the time. For example, the custodial model is directed toward the satisfaction of employees' security needs. It moves one step above the autocratic model, which reasonably serves subsistence needs but does not meet needs for security. Similarly, the supportive model is an effort to meet employees' other needs, such as affiliation and esteem, which the custodial model is unable to serve.

Effect of satisfied needs

A number of people have assumed that emphasis on one model of organizational behavior is an automatic rejection of other models, but comparison suggests that *each model is built upon the accomplishments of the other*. For example, adoption of a supportive approach does not mean abandonment of custodial practices that

Managing across National Boundaries

Several U.S. firms have chosen to lower their costs by setting up assembly plants in less-developed countries, such as Mexico, where the wage scale is lower. The firms ship parts to the assembly plant, use cheap labor to perform assembly operations, and then ship the finished product back to markets in the United States. While this practice helps the firms remain competitive from a price standpoint, it raises some interesting behavioral issues. For example, is it appropriate for firms to implement one model of organizational behavior (e.g., a supportive or collegial one) in their U.S. facilities and consciously choose another model (e.g., a custodial one) in Mexico? Another interesting dilemma arises when jobs in the United States are lost as a result of these foreign assembly plants—does a firm need to revert to a custodial model in the U.S. operations when it senses that employees there fear that their job security is becoming highly threatened?

serve necessary employee security needs. What it does mean is that custodial practices are given secondary emphasis, because employees have progressed to a condition in which newer needs dominate. In other words, the supportive model is the appropriate model to use at that point because subsistence and security needs are already reasonably met by a suitable structure and security system. If a misdirected modern manager should abandon these basic organizational needs, the system would move back quickly to seek structure and security in order to satisfy those needs for its people.

Increasing Use of Some Models   A third conclusion is that the trend toward the supportive, collegial, and system models will probably continue. Despite rapid advances in computers and management information systems, top managers of giant, complex organizations cannot be authoritarian in the traditional sense and also be effective. Because they cannot know all that is happening in their organization, they must learn to depend on other centers of power nearer to operating problems. They are often forced to literally redefine the old psychological contract and embrace a newer, more participative one.[18] In addition, many employees are not readily motivated toward creative and intellectual duties by the autocratic model. Only the newer models can offer the satisfaction of their needs for esteem, autonomy, and self-actualization.

Contingent Use of All Models   A fourth conclusion is that, though one model may be most used at any given time, some appropriate uses will remain for other models. Knowledge and skills vary among managers. Role expectations of employees differ, depending upon cultural history. Policies and ways of life vary among organizations. Perhaps more important, task conditions are different. Some jobs may require routine, low-skilled, highly programmed work that will be mostly determined by higher authority and will provide mostly material rewards and security (autocratic and custodial conditions). Other jobs will be unprogrammed and intellectual, requiring teamwork and self-motivation. Employees in such jobs generally respond best to supportive, collegial, and system approaches. Therefore, probably all five models will continue to be used, but the more advanced models will have growing use as progress is made.

Managerial Flexibility   The preceding discussion rests on a central conclusion: *Managers not only need to identify their current behavioral model but also must keep it flexible and current.* There is great danger in paradigm rigidity, when the changing nature of people and conditions demands new responses, but managers cling to old beliefs and practices. Managers need to read, to reflect, to interact with others, and to be receptive to challenges to their thinking from their colleagues and employees. The following analogy illustrates this process:

> Skydivers know that a parachute tightly packed for long periods of time might develop undesirable permanent folds in the fabric, which could keep it from opening properly when needed. To prevent this, all parachutes are periodically unpacked and hung in storage sheds to "get the kinks out." Then they are repacked for safe usage. Similarly, wise managers benefit from occasionally sharing their organizational behavior models with others, thus opening them up to public scrutiny. Then, after making appropriate revisions to their models, the managers "pack them up" and put the improved paradigms back to work again.

SUMMARY

Every firm has an organizational behavior system. It includes the organization's stated or unstated philosophy, values, vision, mission, and goals; the quality of leadership, communication, and group dynamics; the nature of both the formal and informal organizations; and the influence of the social environment. These items combine to create a culture in which the personal attitudes of employees and situational factors can produce motivation and goal achievement.

Five models of organizational behavior are the autocratic, custodial, supportive, collegial, and system. The supportive, collegial, and system models are more consistent with contemporary employee needs and, therefore, will predictably obtain more effective results in many situations. Managers need to examine the model they are using, determine whether it is the most appropriate one, and remain flexible in their use of alternative and emerging models.

Communication, a major tool for expressing managerial models, provides the focus for Chapter 3. Then the idea of organizational behavior models is extended in Chapter 4, as we discuss social systems, roles, and status. Specifically, we look at the creation and impact of organizational cultures, which help employees sense which organizational behavior model is in use.

Terms and Concepts for Review

Autocratic model	Paradigms
Collegial model	Philosophy
Custodial model	Supportive model
Fact premises	System model
Goals	Theory X
Mission	Theory Y
Models	Value premises
Organizational behavior system	Vision

1. Remind yourself to think about organizational behavior from a system perspective, envisioning how any one element of the system or action by yourself will likely impact other parts of the OB system.

2. List, examine, and reevaluate your fact premises about people periodically to see if they need updating. Then create a separate list of your value premises and share these with a colleague or friend to see if they withstand open scrutiny.

3. Show your employees the list of assumptions that underlie Theory X and Theory Y. Then ask them for illustrations that indicate you are using either of the two paradigms. Invite them to help you make your actions more consistent with Theory Y.

4. Examine the five models of OB every so often. Search for ways in which you could be using features from the more advanced models (supportive, collegial, system).

5. Report to a close friend the ways in which you have actively changed your underlying OB model in the past few years. Be ready to provide specific examples.

Discussion Questions

1. Interview some managers to identify their visions for their organizations. What are those visions? Where did they come from? How successfully have they been communicated to the employees, and how successfully have they been embraced by the employees?

2. Both philosophy and vision are somewhat hazy concepts. How can they be made clear to employees? Why are philosophy and vision included as early elements in the organizational behavior system? Give an example of an organizational vision that you have read about or heard of.

3. Distinguish between fact premises and value premises. What are their implications for managers?

4. Consider an organization where you now work (or where you have worked). What model (paradigm) of organizational behavior does (did) your supervisor follow? Is (Was) it the same as top management's model?

5. Discuss similarities and differences among the five models of organizational behavior.

6. What model of organizational behavior would be most appropriate in each of the following situations? (Assume that you must use the kinds of employees and supervisors currently available in your local labor market.)
   a. Long-distance telephone operators in a very large office
   b. Accountants with a small certified professional accounting firm
   c. Food servers in a local restaurant of a prominent fast-food chain
   d. Salesclerks in a large discount department store
   e. Circus laborers temporarily employed to work the week that the circus is in the city

7. Discuss why the supportive, collegial, and system models of organizational behavior are especially appropriate for use in the more affluent nations.

8. Interview a supervisor or manager to identify the model of organizational behavior that person believes in. Explain why you think that the supervisor's or manager's behavior would or would not reflect those beliefs.

9. Examine the trends in the models of organizational behavior as they have developed over a period of time. Why have the trends moved in this direction?

10. Assume that a friend of yours contends that "the system model is obviously 'best' to use with all employees, or it wouldn't have been placed on the right side of the figure." How would you respond?

Assess Your Own Skills

How well do you exhibit facilitator skills?

Read the following statements carefully. Circle the number on the response scale that most closely reflects the degree to which each statement accurately describes you. Add up your total points and prepare a brief action plan for self-improvement. Be ready to report your score for tabulation across the entire group.

	Good description						**Poor description**			
1. I know how to support employee commitment to short- and long-term goals.	10	9	8	7	6	5	4	3	2	1
2. I could coach individuals and groups in appropriate skills and behaviors.	10	9	8	7	6	5	4	3	2	1
3. I feel comfortable modeling and fostering self-esteem.	10	9	8	7	6	5	4	3	2	1
4. I am likely to show genuine concern and empathy for people.	10	9	8	7	6	5	4	3	2	1
5. I would feel comfortable offering timely and acceptable feedback to others.	10	9	8	7	6	5	4	3	2	1
6. I am dedicated to influencing people to learn continuously and to share that learning with others.	10	9	8	7	6	5	4	3	2	1
7. I would help individuals identify and confront issues in ethical ways.	10	9	8	7	6	5	4	3	2	1
8. I feel comfortable stimulating insights through interviews, questions, and suggestions.	10	9	8	7	6	5	4	3	2	1
9. I believe in encouraging people to feel comfortable with change and uncertainty.	10	9	8	7	6	5	4	3	2	1
10. I would work hard to build cohesive, productive work teams.	10	9	8	7	6	5	4	3	2	1

Scoring and Interpretation   Add up your total points for the ten questions. Record that number here, and report it when it is requested. _____

- If you scored between 81–100 points, you appear to have a solid capability for demonstrating facilitative skills.
- If you scored between 61–80 points, you should take a close look at the items with lower self-assessment scores and explore ways to improve those items.
- If you scored less than 60 points, you should be aware that a weaker skill level regarding several items could be detrimental to your future success as a manager. We encourage you to review the entire chapter and watch for relevant material in subsequent chapters and other sources.

Now identify your three lowest scores, and write the question numbers here: _____,

_____, _____. Write a brief paragraph, detailing to yourself an action plan for how you might sharpen each of these skills.

Incident

The New Plant Manager

Toby Butterfield worked his way upward in the Montclair Company until he became assistant plant manager in the Illinois plant. Finally, his opportunity for a promotion came. The Houston plant was having difficulty meeting its budget and production quotas, so he was promoted to plant manager and transferred to the Houston plant with instructions to "straighten it out."

Butterfield was ambitious and somewhat power-oriented. He believed that the best way to solve problems was to take control, make decisions, and use his authority to carry out his decisions. After preliminary study, he issued orders for each department to cut its budget 5 percent. A week later he instructed all departments to increase production 10 percent by the following month. He required several new reports and kept a close watch on operations. At the end of the second month he dismissed three supervisors who had failed to meet their production quotas. Five other supervisors resigned. Butterfield insisted that all rules and budgets should be followed, and he allowed no exceptions.

Butterfield's efforts produced remarkable results. Productivity quickly exceeded standard by 7 percent, and within five months the plant was within budget. His record was so outstanding that he was promoted to the New York home office near the end of his second year. Within a month after he left, productivity in the Houston plant collapsed to 15 percent below standard, and the budget again was in trouble.

Questions
1. Discuss the model of organizational behavior Butterfield used and the kind of organizational climate he created.
2. Discuss why productivity dropped when Butterfield left the Houston plant.
3. If you were Butterfield's New York manager, what would you tell him about his approach? How might he respond?

The Rapid Corporation

Experiential Exercise

The Rapid Corporation is a refrigeration service organization in a large city. It has about seventy employees, mostly refrigeration service representatives. For many years the company's policies have been dominated by its president and principal owner, Otto Blumberg, who takes pride in being a "self-made man."

Recently Otto and his office manager attended an organizational behavior seminar in which the value of a written corporate philosophy for employees was discussed. Both men agreed to draft one and compare their efforts.

1. Divide the class into three types of groups. One set of groups should draft statements for the Rapid Corporation based on the autocratic model; the second set should create comparable statements of philosophy using the supportive model as a basis; the third set should use the system model.
2. Ask representatives of each group (autocratic, supportive and system) to read their statements to the class. Discuss their major differences. Have the class debate the usefulness of philosophy statements for guiding the organizational behavior system in a firm of this type.

Chapter 3

Managing Communications

Listening can reduce stress, frustration, and conflict in the workplace.

—Jennifer J. Salopek[1]

E-mail and voice mail are efficient, but face-to-face contact is still essential to true communication.

—Edward M. Hallowell[2]

CHAPTER OBJECTIVES

TO UNDERSTAND

- The Two-Way Communication Process
- Barriers to Communication
- Factors Leading to Effective Communication
- Downward and Upward Communications Problems
- The Roles of Questioning and Listening
- The Impact of Electronic Communications
- Organizational Grapevines and Rumors

A Hollywood movie company was filming a movie near a small western town. The script involved some narrow-gauge-railway scenes, and a local resident, regularly a railroad engineer, had been selected as engineer of the narrow-gauge train. He was very proud of his assignment. One evening when both the Hollywood visitors and the engineer were in a local bar, the engineer walked over to the director of the movie company and asked, "John, how did I do with those train scenes today?"

The director, in a good mood, gave his most favorable Hollywood response, "Joe, you are doing one hell of a job."

Joe, not understanding the favorable meaning of this colloquialism,[3] took it as a criticism and was immediately ruffled, replying, "Oh, I don't know about that. You couldn't do any better."

The director, still trying to communicate (but in terms of his own frame of reference), said, "That's what I said, Joe. You are doing one hell of a job." At this point Joe became angry and an argument broke out, with Joe vowing that he wouldn't be talked to that way in front of friends. Eventually, it was necessary to separate the two men to prevent a fight.

Whether in a movie company, a manufacturing or service firm, or the federal government, communication is the ever-present activity by which people relate to one another and combine their efforts. Communication is necessary to perpetuate the health of the organization. Just as people may develop arteriosclerosis, a hardening of the arteries that restricts the flow of blood and the nutrients it carries, so may an organization develop similar problems with its information arteries. The result is the same—unnecessarily reduced efficiency due to key information's being blocked or restricted at various points throughout the organization. And just like the medical ailment, preventing the problem may be easier than trying to find a cure.

Today's employees have a powerful desire to know what is going on and how they fit into the larger picture. More than ever before, managers need to engage in systematic and extensive communications in upward, downward, and lateral directions. As you can see from the opening quote, listening skills remain highly important in the communication process. Further, as technology spreads ever wider, the human element of communication must not be forgotten. In this chapter the significance of communication in the workplace is explored in depth. Also discussed are its relation to organizational behavior and the impact of electronic technology.

COMMUNICATION FUNDAMENTALS

Communication is the transfer of information and understanding from one person to another person. It is a way of reaching others by transmitting ideas, facts, thoughts, feelings, and values. Its goal is to have the receiver understand the message as it was intended. When communication is effective, it provides a bridge of meaning between the two people so that they can each share what they feel and know. By using this bridge, both parties can safely cross the river of misunderstanding that sometimes separates people.

Communication always involves at least two people—a sender and a receiver. One person alone cannot communicate. Only one or more receivers can complete the communication act. This fact is obvious when you think of being lost on an island and calling for help when there is no one near enough to hear the call. The need for a receiver is not so obvious to managers who send out memos to employees. They tend

Two people are required.

47

to think that when their messages are sent, they have communicated; but transmission of the message is only a beginning. A manager may send a hundred messages, but there is no communication until each one is received, read, and understood. Communication is what the receiver understands, not what the sender says.

Understanding is critical for success.

The Importance of Communication

Organizations cannot exist without communication. If there is no communication, employees cannot know what their coworkers are doing, management cannot receive information inputs, and supervisors and team leaders cannot give instructions. Coordination of work is impossible, and the organization will collapse for lack of it. Cooperation also becomes impossible, because people cannot communicate their needs and feelings to others. We can say with confidence that *every act of communication influences the organization in some way,* just as the flapping of a butterfly's wings in California influences (however slightly) the subsequent wind velocity in Boston. Communication helps accomplish all the basic management functions—planning, organizing, leading, and controlling—so that organizations can achieve their goals and meet their challenges.

When communication is effective, it tends to encourage better performance and job satisfaction.[4] People understand their jobs better and feel more involved in them. In some instances they even will voluntarily give up some of their long-established privileges because they see that a sacrifice is necessary.

> Management in one firm persuaded production employees to bring their own coffee and have coffee breaks at their machines instead of taking a regular lost-time coffee break in the cafeteria. The company had dealt directly and frankly with them. It presented to employee group meetings a chart of electricity use for the plant, showing how power use was less than half of normal for fifteen minutes before and after coffee break, plus the normal production loss during the break. The company made a sound case for the fact that this long period of inactivity and partial activity prevented profitable operation. The power-use charts were convincing, and employees readily accepted the new coffee-break policy.

Open communication

The positive response of those employees supports one of the basic propositions of organizational behavior—that *open communication is generally better than restricted communication.* (See "What Managers Are Reading.") In effect, if employees know the problems an organization is facing and hear what managers are trying to do, they will usually respond favorably.

It would be easy to focus solely on communication with employees and ignore the needs of managers, but that approach would provide a limited view. Management's role is critical, for managers not only initiate communications but also pass them on to and interpret them for employees. Just as a photograph can be no clearer than the negative from which it is printed, managers cannot transmit a message more clearly than their own understanding of it.

> Kiki, a department supervisor, received a copy of a 110-page report. Instead of distributing it directly to her staff and expecting them to read the entire report, she prepared a two-page summary and gave it to each member. Although they appreciated the time saved, they realized that they were now dependent on her interpretation of the total report. Similarly, the quality of Kiki's summary depended on the readability of the original report as well as her own skills of interpretation.

Managers need timely, useful information to make sound decisions. Inadequate or poor data can affect a broad area of performance because the scope of managerial influence is quite wide. Very simply, managerial decisions affect many people and many activities.

John Case, in his series of books on open-book management, contends that organizations require willing, eager, talented employees who care about the success of their employer. To achieve this success, management must make sure that employees:

1. View the organization and its practices as open and transparent
2. See themselves as partners in the enterprise (have a stake in its success)
3. Are empowered on a daily basis to help run the workplace
4. Understand what the business is all about (know what its critical numbers are, what they mean, and how they can be influenced)

Open-book management systems provide employees with the company's financial and other operating numbers, which enables them to independently track and understand the organization's performance. Then employees must be expected and allowed to take appropriate actions to improve those numbers. Finally, employees must trust that they will receive some direct benefit from the organization's success.

Source: John Case, *The Open-Book Experience*, Reading, MA: Addison-Wesley, 1998.

The Two-Way Communication Process

The two-way communication process is the method by which a sender reaches a receiver with a message. The process always requires eight steps, whether the two parties talk, use hand signals, or employ some advanced-technology means of communication. The steps are shown in Figure 3–1.

Eight steps in the process

Develop an Idea   Step 1 is to *develop an idea* that the sender wishes to transmit. This is the key step, because unless there is a worthwhile message, all the other steps are somewhat useless. This step is represented by the sign, sometimes seen on office or factory walls, that reads, "Be sure brain is engaged before putting mouth in gear."

Encode   Step 2 is to *encode* (convert) the idea into suitable words, charts, or other symbols for transmission. At this point the sender determines the method of transmission so that the words and symbols may be organized in suitable fashion for the type of transmission. For example, back-and-forth conversation usually is not organized the same way as a written memorandum.

Transmit   When the message finally is developed, step 3 is to *transmit* it by the method chosen, such as by memo, phone call, or personal visit. The sender also chooses a certain channel, such as bypassing or not bypassing the superintendent, and communicates with careful timing. For example, the sender may decide that today

FIGURE 3–1

The communication process

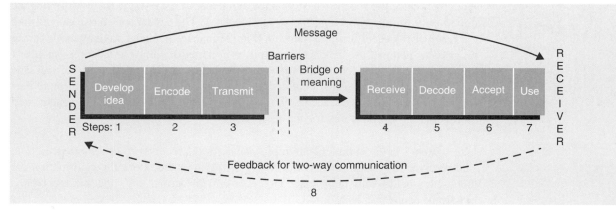

may not be the right day to talk to the manager about that pay raise. The sender also tries to keep the communication channel free of barriers, or interference, as shown in Figure 3–1, so that the message has a chance to reach the receiver and hold his or her attention. In employment interviewing or performance appraisals, for example, freedom from distraction is desirable.

Receiver controls steps 4 to 8.

Receive   Transmission allows another person to *receive* a message, which is step 4. In this step the initiative transfers to the receiver, who tunes in to receive the message. If it is oral, the receiver needs to be a good listener, a skill that is discussed shortly. If the receiver does not function, the message is lost.

> Andrea sent an urgent request to a professional colleague across the country for a copy of a diagram she needed for a presentation later that day. "I'll fax it to you," Derrick responded. Each time he tried, however, a message appeared telling him that the fax transmission did not go through. After he called Andrea to explain this perplexing problem, she checked her machine and found it had run out of paper. Only after fixing the problem did she receive the needed message.

Need for understanding

Decode   Step 5 is to *decode* the message so that it can be understood. The sender wants the receiver to understand the message exactly as it was sent. For example, if the sender transmits the equivalent of a square and the decoding step produces a circle, then a message has been sent, but not much understanding has taken place.

Understanding can occur only in a receiver's mind. A communicator may make others listen, but there is no way to make them understand. The receiver alone chooses whether to understand or not. Many employers overlook this fact when giving instructions or explanations. They think that telling someone is sufficient, but the communication cannot proceed until there is understanding. This process is known as "getting through" to a person.

> The encoding-decoding sequence is somewhat like the activity involved when modern log homes are first constructed near the timber source rather than at the final site. The completed home cannot be moved in one piece, so it has to be disassembled log by log, with each log marked as to its proper location. This process is similar to the action of a sender who has an idea and encodes (dismantles) it into a series of words, each marked by location and other means to guide the receiver. In order to move the idea (transmit it), the sender needs to take it apart by putting it into words. The reassembly of the home log by log at its final destination is similar to the action of a receiver who takes the words received and mentally reassembles them into whole ideas. If one log (or word) is misused, the entire structure (message) may be weakened.

Accept   Once the receiver has obtained and decoded a message, that person has the opportunity to *accept or reject* it, which is step 6. The sender, of course, would like the receiver to accept the communication in the manner intended so that activities can progress as planned. Acceptance, however, is a matter of choice and degree, such that the receiver has considerable control over whether or not to embrace all the message or just parts of it. Some factors affecting the acceptance decision revolve around perceptions of the message's accuracy, the authority and credibility of the sender, and the behavioral implications for the receiver.

Use   Step 7 in the communication process is for the receiver to *use the information*. The receiver may discard it, perform the task as directed, store the information for the future, or do something else. This is a critical action step, and the receiver is largely in control of what to do.

Provide Feedback When the receiver acknowledges the message and responds to the sender, *feedback* has occurred. Feedback completes the communication loop, because there is a message flow from the sender to the receiver and back to the sender, as shown by the feedback arrow (step 8) at the bottom of Figure 3–1.

> Engaging in two-way communication can be compared to playing the game of tennis. Consider the process that must go on in the mind of one of its promising young stars, Venus Williams. As Venus serves the ball, she cannot tell herself, "My next shot will be a cross-court forehand." Her next shot, to be effective, must depend on feedback from the receiver, that is, on where and how her opponent returns the serve. Venus undoubtedly has an overall strategy for the match, but each of her shots must be contingent on the way the ball is returned to her—its force, spin, and placement—and on the position of her opponent on the opposite side of the court. If Venus fails to match her shots to her opponent's game, she will find that her game is not as effective as it could have been that day. As is the case in communication, ignoring feedback limits the likelihood that the exchange will be successful.

Two-way communication, made possible by feedback, has a back-and-forth pattern. In two-way communication, the speaker sends a message and the receiver's response comes back to the speaker. The result is a developing play-by-play situation in which the speaker can, and should, adjust the next message to fit the previous response of the receiver. The sender needs feedback—the final step—because it tells whether the message was received, decoded properly, accepted, and used. If necessary, the sender should seek and request feedback from the receiver. When this two-way communication occurs, both parties experience greater satisfaction, frustration is prevented, and work accuracy is much improved.

Senders require feedback.

Potential Problems

Two-way communication is not exclusively beneficial. It also can cause difficulties. Two people may strongly disagree about some item but not realize it until they establish two-way communication. When they expose their different viewpoints, they may become even more **polarized,** taking even more extreme positions. When threatened with the potential embarrassment of losing an argument, people tend to abandon logic and rationality, and engage in **defensive reasoning.**[5] They blame others, selectively gather and use data, seek to remain in control, and suppress negative feelings. Defensive reasoning is designed to avoid risk and the appearance of incompetence, but it typically results in a drive toward control and winning. These objectives predictably detract from effective communications.

Another difficulty that may occur is **cognitive dissonance.** This is the internal conflict and anxiety that occurs when people receive information incompatible with their value systems, prior decisions, or other information they may have. Since people do not feel comfortable with dissonance, they try to remove or reduce it. Perhaps they will try to obtain new communication inputs, change their interpretation of the inputs, reverse their decision, or change their values. They may even refuse to believe the dissonant input, or they may rationalize it out of the way.

Possible problem of cognitive dissonance

Senders always need to communicate with care, because communication is a potent form of self-revelation to others as well as a source of possible evaluation. Not only are we disclosing something about ourselves (content) when we speak, but others are judging us at the same time. This aspect of communication creates pressure to engage in **face-saving**—an attempt to preserve our valued self-concept from attack. Our very self-esteem is threatened when people say something to us that we wish they had not. Sometimes they, too, regret having said something that challenges our **self-concept.** Although such regrettable messages are often unintended, they usually create hard

Face-saving

feelings in the recipient, place stress on the relationship, or even cause the relationship to deteriorate. Regrettable messages may include several types, such as outright verbal blunders, personal attacks, stereotyped slurs, sarcastic criticism, or harmful information. People often send regrettable messages during an emotional confrontation, as in this example:

> Damian (an accounting supervisor) and Janny (a marketing manager) had both interviewed a series of candidates for the position of auditor. Later, they got together with three other department heads to make the final selection. When Janny pointed out a weakness she saw in one candidate, Damian reacted sharply by questioning her capacity to assess auditing skills, due to the fact that she had spent her entire career in marketing. Janny, of course, was furious at having her integrity attacked. Although Damian later apologized to her and claimed he regretted the incident, Janny never forgot the remark.

Communication Barriers

Even when the receiver receives the message and makes a genuine effort to decode it, a number of interferences may limit the receiver's understanding. These obstacles act as **noise,** or barriers to communication, and may emerge in either the physical surroundings (such as a coworker's radio overshadowing your phone conversation) or within an individual's emotions (the distraction of the receiver's concern about a sick relative). Noise may entirely prevent a communication, filter out part of it, or give it incorrect meaning. Three types of barriers are personal, physical, and semantic.

Personal Barriers   **Personal barriers** are communication interferences that arise from human emotions, values, and poor listening habits. They may also stem from differences in education, race, sex, socioeconomic status, and other factors. Personal barriers are a common occurrence in work situations, with common examples including distracting verbal habits (e.g., needless repetition of "ah" or ending nearly every sentence with "you know"). We all have experienced how our personal feelings can limit our communication with other people, and these situations happen at work just as they do in private life.

Psychological distance   Personal barriers often involve a **psychological distance**—a feeling of being emotionally separated—between people that is similar to actual physical distance. For example, Marsha talks down to Janet, who resents this treatment, and Janet's resentment separates them.

Our emotions act as perceptual filters in nearly all our communications. We see and hear what we are emotionally tuned to see and hear, so communication is guided by our expectations. We also communicate our interpretation of reality instead of reality itself. Someone has said, "No matter what you say a thing is, it isn't," meaning that the sender is merely giving an emotionally filtered perception of it. Under these conditions, when the sender's and receiver's perceptions are reasonably close together, their communication will be more effective.

Physical Barriers   **Physical barriers** are communication interferences that occur in the environment in which the communication takes place. A typical physical barrier is a sudden distracting noise that temporarily drowns out a voice message. Other physical barriers include distances between people, walls, or static that interferes with radio messages. People frequently recognize when physical interference occurs and try to compensate for it.

Ecological control   For example, physical barriers can be converted into positive forces through **ecological control,** in which the surroundings are altered by the sender so as to influence the receiver's feelings and behavior. Moderate tidiness, open desk placement, a reasonable amount of status symbols, plants, and wall decorations may all affect a visitor's perceptions. Consider how ecological control operates in this situation:

> When visitors came to her office, Carmen Valencia used to sit rigidly behind her desk, leaving the other person somewhat distant on the other side of the desk. This arrangement created a psychological distance and clearly established her as the leader and superior in the interaction. Then she rearranged her office so that a visitor sat beside her on the same side of her desk. This arrangement suggested more receptiveness and equality of interaction with visitors. It also had the advantage of providing a work area on her desk for mutual examination of work documents. When she wished to establish a more informal relationship, particularly with her team members, she came around to the front of the desk and sat in a chair near the employee.

Carmen's behavior also illustrates the practice of maintaining proper physical distance between two parties as they communicate. The study of such spatial separation is called **proxemics;** it involves the exploration of different practices and feelings about interpersonal space within and across cultures. In the United States, general practice allows *intimate* communications between close friends to occur at very short range (e.g., 6 to 18 inches). Conversations with acquaintances are often held at a 3- or 4-foot *personal* distance. Work-related discussions between colleagues may occur at a *social* distance of 4 to 12 feet, with more impersonal and formal conversations in *public* occurring at even greater distances. Not only is it important to know and observe common practice with regard to the nature of the underlying relationships (intimate, friendly, work-related, or casual) between the two parties, it is also imperative that these practices be adapted for cultural differences. In some societies, sharply different practices prevail. For example, Latin American and Asian cultures generally favor closer distances for personal conversations, and workers in Arab countries often maintain extremely close contact. Therefore, the sender should be aware of cultural norms and the receiver's preferences, and make an effort to understand and adapt to them.

Proper distance

Semantic Barriers   **Semantics** is the science of meaning, as contrasted with *phonetics,* the science of sounds. Nearly all communication is symbolic; that is, it is achieved using symbols (words, pictures, and actions) that suggest certain meanings. These symbols are merely a map that describes a territory, but they are not the real territory itself; hence they must be decoded and interpreted by the receiver. Before we introduce the three types of symbols, however, an additional form of barrier, one that has its origin in semantics, deserves mention.

Semantic barriers arise from limitations in the symbols with which we communicate. Symbols usually have a variety of meanings, and we have to choose one meaning from many. Sometimes we choose the wrong meaning and misunderstanding occurs. An illustration is the case of the railroad engineer at the beginning of this chapter. He misunderstood what the slang phrase "hell of a job" meant, so he became emotional. In that instance a semantic barrier also led to an emotional barrier, and further communication was blocked.

Semantics presents a particularly difficult challenge when people from different cultures attempt to communicate with each other. Not only must both parties learn the literal meanings of words in the other language, they must also interpret the words within their context and the way in which they are used (tone, volume, and accompanying nonverbal gestures). Clearly, the emerging global economy demands that sensitive managers everywhere overcome the extra burden that semantic barriers place on their intercultural communications.

Fact versus inference

Whenever we interpret a symbol on the basis of our assumptions instead of the facts, we are making an **inference.** Inferences are an essential part of most communication. We cannot avoid them by waiting until all communication is factual before accepting it. However, since inferences can give a wrong signal, we need always to be aware of them and to appraise them carefully. When doubts arise, more information can be sought.

Communication Symbols

Words Words are the main communication symbol used on the job. Many employees spend more than 50 percent of their time in some form of verbal communication. A major difficulty occurs, however, since nearly every common word has several meanings. Multiple meanings are necessary because we are trying to talk about an infinitely complex world while using only a limited number of words. The complexities of a single language are compounded when people from diverse backgrounds—such as different educational levels, ethnic heritages, or cultures—attempt to communicate. No wonder we have trouble communicating with one another!

Context provides meaning.

If words really have no single meaning, how can managers make sense with them in communicating with employees? The answer lies in *context,* which is the environment surrounding the use of a word. For example, using the term "dummy" to describe another person in an argument at the office may be derogatory, but using it to refer to the person serving as dummy in a social game of bridge is acceptable. We need to surround key words with the context of other words and symbols until their meanings are narrowed to fairly certain limits and potential confusion is minimized. Consequently, effective communicators are idea-centered rather than just word-centered. They know that *words do not provide meaning, but people do.*

Social cues

Context provides meaning to words partially through the cues people receive from their social environment, such as friends and coworkers. **Social cues** are positive or negative bits of information that influence how people react to a communication. Examples of social cues are job titles, patterns of dress, and the historical use of words in a particular region of the country or ethnic group. Our susceptibility to being influenced by these cues varies, depending on the credibility of the source, our past exposure to the item, the ambiguity of the cue, and individual differences such as diverse cultural backgrounds. It is always important for us to be aware of social cues, because use of language with inadequate context creates a semantic smog. Like a real smog, it irritates our senses and interferes with the accuracy of our perceptions.

Readability

Since the meaning of words is difficult to impart even with the use of context, a reasonable assumption is that if these symbols can be simplified, the receiver will understand them more easily. Further, if symbols of the type that receivers prefer are used, the receivers will be more receptive. This assumption is behind the idea of **readability,** which is the process of making writing and speech more understandable. Readability was popularized by Rudolf Flesch and others, who developed formulas that can be applied to magazines, bulletins, speeches, policy manuals, and other communications in order to judge their level of readability.[6]

Figure 3–2 offers some guidelines for more readable writing according to the Flesch formula. Then it applies the guidelines to show how the complex writing in the original paragraph can be simplified in the second one. When you write your next report for a class, check it before submitting it to see if you have successfully practiced the ideas in Figure 3–2.

Much of the organizational literature sent to employees and customers is more dif-

FIGURE 3–2

Clear writing: Guidelines
and an example

Source: Adapted from
*Readingease: The Key to
Understanding,* Employee
Relations Staff. General
Motors Corporation, n.d.

55

Guidelines for Readable Writing

- Use *simple* and *familiar* words and phrases, such as "improve" instead of "ameliorate" and "like" instead of "in a manner similar to that of." These ease the reader's task, and make comprehension more likely.

- Use *personal pronouns* such as "you" and "them," if the style permits. These help the receiver relate to the message.

- Use *illustrations, examples, and charts.* Remember that "a picture is worth a thousand words."

- Use *short sentences and paragraphs.* You want to express your thoughts efficiently. Avoid excessive conjunctions and divide long paragraphs.

- Use *active verbs,* such as "The manager decided . . . " rather than "The manager came to the conclusion that . . . " Active words carry more impact.

- Use only *necessary* words. For example, in the sentence "Bad weather conditions served to prevent my trip," the word "conditions" is not needed and "served to prevent" can be shortened. Say, "Bad weather prevented my trip."

- Use a clear *structure.* Use headings and subheadings to demonstrate that you are following an outline. Apply techniques of emphasis (e.g., underlining or italics) to accent the ideas you believe are most important. Include helpful lists of key points, accented by numbers or bullets.

ficult than standard levels of readability. Employee handbooks, codes of conduct, annual reports to stockholders, product assembly manuals, strategic plans, and union contracts are consistently rated "difficult" and "very difficult." Such ratings indicate that the writing is beyond the level of standard reading even for typical adults.

Monitoring readability and simplifying documents is a critical communication task. For example, many members of the U.S. labor force have some language difficulties. *Millions of Americans are functionally illiterate.* This means that they do not always have the reading skills necessary to comprehend even basic job descriptions or work orders assigning them to tasks. In addition, as increasing proportions of the workforce are drawn from diverse cultural backgrounds, English is a second language for many. This means that English terms and phrases that are common to some workers may appear strange to others. Such language needs to be avoided, or at least clarified. Since the main purpose of communication is to make ourselves understood, there is a clear need to consider the needs of receivers and adapt our use of words to *their* level.

Pictures   A second type of symbol is the picture, which is used to clarify word communication. Organizations make extensive use of pictures, such as blueprints, progress charts, fishbone diagrams, causal maps, visual aids in training programs, scale models of products, and similar devices. Pictures can provide powerful visual images, as suggested by the proverb "A picture is worth a thousand words." To be most effective, however, pictures should be combined with well-chosen words and actions to tell a complete story.

56

One organization, Lake Superior Paper Industries, planned to build a state-of-the-art paper mill. Because of the complexity of the technology involved, the $400 million construction cost, and the serious impact of any delays in the mill's construction, the company decided to build a three-dimensional room-sized model of the entire building and its contents. Company officials claimed that this one "picture," created at a cost of over $1 million, saved them many times that amount by letting designers and construction personnel see precisely where layout problems would occur before costly conflicts actually arose.

Action (Nonverbal Communication)

Actions have meaning.

Action (Nonverbal Communication)   A third type of communication symbol is action, also known as **nonverbal communication.** Often people forget that what they do is a means of communication to the extent that such action is open to interpretation by others. For example, a handshake and a smile have meaning. A raise in pay or being late for an appointment also has meaning.

Two significant points about action are sometimes overlooked. One point is that failure to act is an important way of communicating. A manager who fails to praise an employee for a job well done or fails to provide promised resources is sending a message to that person. Since we send messages by both action and inaction, we communicate almost all the time at work, *regardless of our intentions.*

A second point is that actions speak louder than words, at least in the long run. Managers who say one thing but do another will soon find that their employees "listen" mostly to what they do. The manager's *behavior* is the stronger social cue. A typical example is an executive who verbally advocates ethical behavior but repeatedly violates the company's own code of conduct. Employees receive mixed signals and may find it convenient to mimic the executive's unethical actions.

Credibility gaps cause problems.

When there is a difference between what someone says and does, a **credibility gap** exists. Communication credibility is based on three factors: trustworthiness, expertise, and dynamism.[7] These three factors suggest that managers must act with integrity, speak from a strong base of knowledge, and deliver their messages with confidence and enthusiasm. Although a manager's credibility can take years to develop, only a few moments are required to destroy it. The following illustration shows how a large credibility gap can result in the loss of confidence in a leader:

> Willie Beacon, the zone manager of a sales office, emphasized the idea that he depended upon his employees to help him do a good job because, as he stated it, "You salespeople are the ones in direct contact with the customer, and you get much valuable information and many useful suggestions." In most of his sales meetings he said that he always welcomed employees' ideas and suggestions. But here is how he translated his words into action: In those same sales meetings the schedule was so tight that by the time he finished his pep talk, there was no time for anyone to present problems or ask questions, and he would hardly tolerate an interruption during his talk because he claimed that interruptions destroyed its punch.
>
> If a salesperson tried to present a suggestion in Willie's office, Willie usually began with, "Fine, I'm glad you brought in your suggestion." Before long, however, he would direct the conversation to some subject on his mind, or would have to keep an appointment, or would find some other reason for never quite getting to the suggestion. The few suggestions that did get through, he rebuffed with, "Yeah, I thought of that a long time ago, but it won't work." The eventual result was that he received no suggestions. His actions spoke louder than his words. His credibility gap was too large for employees to overcome.

Body language provides meaning.

An important part of nonverbal communication is **body language,** by which people communicate meaning to others with their bodies in interpersonal interaction. Body language is an important supplement to verbal communication in most parts of the world.

Facial expressions are especially important sources of body language in work situations. Examples are eye contact, eye movement, smiles and frowns, and a furrowed brow. In one instance a manager frowned when an employee brought a suggestion, and the employee interpreted the frown as a rejection when in fact it was a headache. In another instance a smile at an inappropriate time was interpreted as a derisive sneer, and an argument erupted. Nonverbal cues can be either inadvertent, as in the preceding examples, or intentional, thus adding complexity to the communication process. Other types of body language are physical touch, hand and hip movements, leaning forward or back, crossing one's arms or legs, and sighing or yawning. Despite the wealth of data available from nonverbal cues, their interpretation is highly subjective and loaded with the potential for error. Caution is in order.

The Impact of Barriers on the Communication Process

We have now reviewed a sampling of the barriers that impede the exchange of communication between two people. Next, it is valuable to examine which of those barriers exert their impact on the actions in the eight-step communication process outlined previously in Figure 3–1. This allows managers, as students of organizational behavior, to direct their attention toward minimizing the effects of specific barriers.

Examination of Figure 3–3 indicates that the personal barriers have a pervasive effect on communications. Emotions can affect the development of an idea for presentation, the method and form of its transmission, how it is decoded, and most certainly whether or not it is accepted. Listening skills (discussed on pages 63–64) have a powerful impact on the effectiveness of a message's receipt and interpretation (decoding). Feelings of psychological distance largely impact the receipt, acceptance, and usage of a message, in addition to the quality of feedback provided to the sender.

Physical barriers such as noise and geographical distance primarily affect the transmission and receipt of messages, whereas semantic issues and various communication

FIGURE 3–3

Primary impact of barriers on the steps in communication

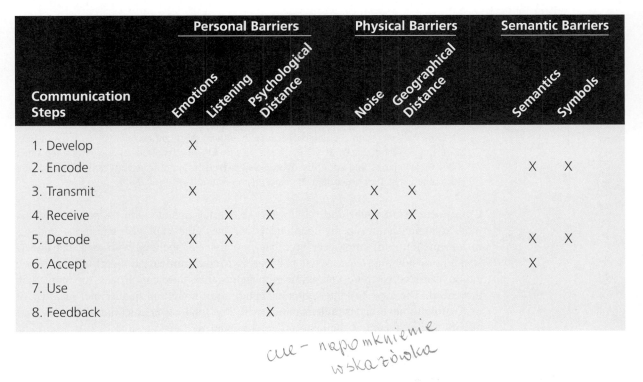

Communication Steps	Personal Barriers			Physical Barriers		Semantic Barriers	
	Emotions	Listening	Psychological Distance	Noise	Geographical Distance	Semantics	Symbols
1. Develop	X						
2. Encode						X	X
3. Transmit	X			X	X		
4. Receive		X	X	X	X		
5. Decode	X	X				X	X
6. Accept	X		X			X	
7. Use			X				
8. Feedback			X				

cue — napomknienie
wskazówka

symbols most often create problems in the encoding, decoding, and acceptance stages. The overall message for managers is that barriers can—and do—affect the effectiveness of communications at all eight stages. The active participants in a communication exchange—just like two acrobats on a trapeze—dare not let their guards down for even an instant, or the negative consequences can be long-lasting!

DOWNWARD COMMUNICATION

Downward communication in an organization is the flow of information from higher to lower levels of authority. Almost one-half of managerial communications are with subordinates, with the remainder divided among superiors, peers, and external recipients. To communicate downward, some executives rely on colorful booklets, flashy PowerPoint presentations, and elaborately planned employee meetings. These approaches, while attention-getting, often fail to achieve employee understanding—one of the goals of effective communication. The key to better communication lies not just in the use of color, action, and electronic aids but in the presentation of information by more sensitive managers who prepare carefully and convey their messages with candor and warmth. Managers who communicate successfully are sensitive to human needs and open to true dialogue with their employees.

Prerequisites and Problems

Four prerequisites

Part of management's failure has been that it has not prepared for effective communication. It has failed to lay a good foundation, so its communication house has been built upon sand. A solid foundation has four cornerstones that act as prerequisites for an effective approach. First, managers need to *develop a positive communication attitude.* They must convince themselves that communication is an important part of their jobs, as research on managerial responsibilities convincingly shows. Second, managers must continually work to *get informed.* They need to seek out relevant information of interest to employees, share it, and help employees feel informed. Third, managers need to consciously *plan for communication,* and they must do this at the beginning of a course of action. Finally, managers must *develop trust;* as mentioned earlier, trust between senders and receivers is important in all communication. If subordinates do not trust their superiors, they are not as likely to listen to or to believe management's messages.

> Consider the case of two employees from the same firm who were told by their manager not to discuss pay with each other, because the other one might be unhappy to learn of having a lower salary. Later, at a New Year's Eve party, they started talking with each other about their salaries and soon discovered that they were earning exactly the same amount. How much will they trust their manager in the future?

Communication Overload   Managers sometimes operate with the philosophy that more communication is better communication. They give employees enormous amounts of information until employees find that they are overwhelmed with data, but understanding is not improved. What happens is a **communication overload,** in which employees receive more communication inputs than they can process or more than they need. The keys to better communication are timing and quality, not quantity. It is possible to have better understanding with less total communication if it is of high quality and delivered at the appropriate moment.

Acceptance of a Communication   As pointed out earlier, acceptance of a message by the receiver is critical; without acceptance, communication breaks down. Several conditions encourage acceptance of a communication:

Quality is preferable to quantity.

- Acknowledged legitimacy of the sender to send a message
- Perceived competence of the sender relative to the issue
- Trust in the sender as a leader and as a person
- Perceived credibility of the message received
- Acceptance of the tasks and goals that the communication is trying to accomplish
- Power of the sender to enforce sanctions on the receiver either directly or indirectly

If overload can be prevented and the likelihood of acceptance ensured through the use of these six conditions, then managers can turn their attention toward the satisfaction of four important communication needs of employees.

Communication Needs

Employees at lower levels have a number of communication needs. Managers think that they understand employees' needs, but often their employees do not think so.[8] This fundamental difference in perception tends to exist at each level in organizations, thereby making communication more difficult. It causes downward communicators to be overconfident and probably not take enough care with their downward messages.

Job Instruction   One communication need of employees is proper instruction regarding their work. Managers secure better results if they state their instructions in terms of the objective requirements of the job as well as the opportunities and potential problem areas. The consequences of inadequate job instructions can be disastrous, as in this example:

> A manufacturer of small tools hired a new sales representative, gave him a tour of the plant and a copy of the product catalog, and assigned him to a territory. In a few weeks the representative jubilantly sent in an order for 100,000 units of a multipurpose tool. Only then did the company realize it had neglected to tell him that that product was never promoted to its customers because the tool was priced well below the company's cost of producing it (in order to match a competitor's price). The result was that the company lost over $10,000 on this one order!

The need for objective information is especially important for employees in a new job or organization. Because their high expectations often conflict with reality, they quickly become dissatisfied. To prevent such discontent, firms are using **realistic job previews,** in which job candidates are given a small sample of organizational reality. The realistic preview minimizes the employee's unmet expectations by providing both positive and negative information about the potential work environment. When this method is used, turnover of new employees is reduced.

Turnover is reduced by realistic job previews.

Managers also need to adjust their communications according to the task needs of their receivers. For example, as the uncertainty of a task increases, there is a predictable need for increased information flow in order to maintain a comparable level of performance. Thus an employee performing a standardized, repetitive machine task needs little communication input about the task. On the other hand, an engineer working on a new product may require substantial communication input in order to perform successfully. Such varying task needs are reflected in the emerging trend toward **just-in-time training,** whereby key information is available to employees in convenient small modules, to be accessed when needed.

60

Performance is improved by feedback.

Feedback-seeking behavior

Performance Feedback   Employees also need feedback about their performance. Feedback helps them know what to do and how well they are meeting their own goals. It shows that others are interested in what they are doing. Assuming that performance is satisfactory, feedback enhances employees' self-image and feelings of competence. Generally, **performance feedback** leads to both improved performance and improved attitudes.

Giving feedback is a challenging task for managers. The process is discussed in depth in Chapter 6. Some dedicated employees engage in **feedback-seeking behavior,** in which they search for information about their prior performance and possible areas of improvement. Feedback-seeking individuals can actively monitor cues regarding their own performance ("This report tells me I'm still 3 percent over my budget") and inquire about progress toward their goals ("How am I doing?"). Employees are more likely to engage in feedback-seeking behavior if they have a strong competence motive and a powerful drive to self-evaluate, if they currently lack feedback from others, and if the results are not expected to threaten their self-esteem.[9] Managers should encourage this behavior and attempt to satisfy employees' needs for performance-related information.

News   Downward messages should reach employees as fresh and timely news rather than as a stale confirmation of what already has been learned from other sources. Employees are impatient, and rightfully so, for they cannot act effectively on the basis of old information. Historically, employers distributed information via newsletters, postings on bulletin boards, or inserts in pay envelopes. More contemporary methods include closed-circuit television, daily recorded telephone messages that employees can receive by dialing a certain number (even from their homes), electronic mail systems, and websites.

> Aircraft manufacturer McDonnell Douglas has sharply expanded its news-dissemination program. Staff writers prepare daily, monthly, and quarterly newsletters on a wide range of operating topics (costs, scrap numbers, progress reports, stock price, and problems). These are transmitted electronically to everybody associated with the program—employees, customers, suppliers, and management. Everybody is kept informed, and promptly.[10]

Social Support   Another communication need that employees have at work is **social support,** which is the perception that they are cared for, esteemed, and valued. When interpersonal warmth and trust are displayed by managers, there may be positive impacts on psychological and physical health, as well as job satisfaction and performance. It is interesting to note, though, that whether a manager communicates about task assignments, career subjects, or personal matters; or provides performance feedback; or responds to questions raised, employees report feeling a greater level of social support.[11] Apparently, it is the *presence* (and caring delivery) of communication, not the topic, that is most important for satisfying this particular need.

UPWARD COMMUNICATION

If the two-way flow of information is broken by poor **upward communication,** management loses touch with employee needs and lacks sufficient information to make sound decisions. It is, therefore, unable to provide needed task and social support for employees. Management needs to tune in to employees in the same way a person with a radio tunes in. This process requires initiative, positive action, sensitivity to weak signals, and adaptability to different channels of employee information. It primarily requires an awareness and belief that upward messages are important, as the following illustration shows:

> The need for upward communication is demonstrated by the difficult experience of a manufacturing company that grew rapidly over two or three years. Despite work standards, supervisory pressure, and extensive downward communication, employee enthusiasm lagged and productivity declined.
>
> Finally, management brought in an interviewing team from the home office. Most complaints were petty ones, but there did seem to be a general feeling among older supervisors and employees that as the company grew, they had become more and more separated from higher management. They felt isolated and unable to discuss their problems with anyone. Gradually, they became alienated from management and tended to spread their alienation to the newer employees who were being hired as the company expanded.
>
> As soon as management discovered the basic problem, it was able to take corrective action. However, most of these difficulties could have been prevented if management had developed effective procedures early enough to encourage upward communication.

Difficulties

Several problems plague upward communication, especially in larger, more complex organizations. The first is *delay,* which is the unnecessarily slow movement of information up to higher levels. Indecisive managers hesitate to take a problem upward because doing so implies an admission of failure; therefore each level delays the communication while trying to decide how to solve the problem. The second, and closely intertwined, factor is *filtering*. This partial screening out of information occurs because of the natural tendency for an employee to tell a superior only what the employee thinks the superior wants to hear.

Delay

Filtering

However, there may be legitimate reasons for filtering. The total message may be technically overwhelming, or the information may be speculative and require additional confirmation. In some cases the supervisor may have previously requested the employee to pass along only the highlights of a situation. These explanations indicate that filtering is not necessarily a problem in communications.

Sometimes, in an effort to avoid filtering, people *short-circuit* around their superior, which means that they skip one or more steps in the communication hierarchy. On the positive side, **short-circuiting** reduces filtering and delays; on the negative side, since it upsets those who are bypassed, employers usually discourage it. Another problem revolves around an employee's legitimate *need for a response.* Since employees initiate upward communication, they are now the senders, and they have strong expectations that feedback will occur (and soon). If management provides a quick response, further upward messages will be encouraged. Conversely, lack of response suppresses future upward communications, as the following example indicates:

Short-circuiting

Need for response

> Managers of sales branches in one company received a memorandum that encouraged them to make suggestions to improve the firm's customer relations. Shortly after receiving the memo, Esther Helbring, a branch manager, asked the company to review a fine-print clause in one of its sales contracts because several customers had objected to it. Not long after sending her letter, she received a telephone call from a member of higher management requesting clarification. One year later, however, she had received no further feedback and the clause had not been amended. She commented to the interviewer, "A response of this kind doesn't encourage further upward communication."

Diversity in Communications

Do men and women use unique patterns of communication? Research on gender-based communication styles has begun to show some fascinating diversity between the two groups. Numerous studies have explored whether men and women use different (learned) communication styles.

In general, men and women display marked diversity in the way in which they communicate at work. Men emphasize power, while women stress rapport; men are more likely than women to claim credit for accomplishments; men tend to downplay their uncertainty rather than admit it; women ask questions to learn more, while men fear that asking questions will make them look ignorant; women make more ritualistic apologies, exchange compliments with each other, invite honest feedback, and soften their criticism with praise; men look for one-up chances, engage in ritualistic arguments, and seek recognition. Overall, men tend to speak more directly, while women often prefer an indirect approach.

Awareness of these gender-based linguistic styles leads to several useful conclusions for managers.

1. Recognize that everyone lives in a different communication "world"; men and women simply value different patterns.
2. Accept that the way you talk is only one of many possible ways.
3. Learn that people (male or female) will expect, value, and reward communication styles like their own.
4. Managers need to read key signals in their interactions with others and adjust their communication styles accordingly.
5. Managers should allow a person with something to contribute to be heard, regardless of their own style preferences.

Sources: Deborah Tannen, "The Power of Talk: Who Gets Heard and Why," *Harvard Business Review,* September–October 1995, pp. 138–48; Deborah Tannen, *You Just Don't Understand: Women and Men in Conversation* (William Morrow, 1990); and Deborah Tannen, *Talking from 9 to 5* (Avon Books, 1995).

Distortion

A final communication difficulty concerns *distortion.* This is the willful modification of a message so as to achieve one's personal objectives. For example, some employees may exaggerate their achievements, hoping for more recognition or larger salary increases. Others may cover up operating difficulties in their department, hoping to avoid a painful confrontation with their supervisor. Any message distortion robs a manager of accurate information and the capacity to make enlightened decisions. Worse yet, it represents unethical behavior that can destroy trust between two parties. Managers need to recognize the potential for all these upward communication problems and must actively seek to prevent them.

Upward Communication Practices

A starting point for building better upward communications is to establish a general policy stating what kinds of upward messages are desired. This could include areas where higher management is accountable, controversial topics, matters requiring managerial advice, or any corporate policy exceptions or changes being recommended. In addition to policy statements, various practices are needed to improve upward communications. Counseling sessions, grievance systems, participative management, suggestion systems, job satisfaction surveys, and other practices are discussed in later chapters. Additional practices discussed at this point are questioning, listening, employee meetings, open-door policies, and participation in social groups.

Questioning   Managers can encourage upward communications by asking good questions. This practice shows employees that management takes an interest in their opinions, desires additional information, and values their input. Questions can take several forms, but the most common types are open and closed. **Open questions** introduce a broad topic and give others an opportunity to respond in many ways. "How are things going?" is a classic open question, and the responses received can provide rich clues for the manager to follow up. By contrast, **closed questions** focus on a narrower topic and invite the receiver to provide a more specific response. An example is, "What are the cost implications of the proposed early retirement plan?" Both open and closed questions can be useful for initiating upward communications. No matter how well questions are asked, however, they are useless unless the questions are accompanied by skillful listening and the responses are probed for their meaning.

Listening   **Active listening** is more than hearing; it requires use of the ears and the mind. Effective listening works on two levels—it helps receivers understand both the factual idea and the emotional message the sender intended. Good listeners not only hear what the person is saying but also learn about the feelings and emotions of that person. Equally important, managers who listen effectively send a key signal that they care about the employee. Although many people are not skilled listeners, they can improve their ability through training courses—and focused practice. Participants in listening courses are often taught to avoid daydreaming, to focus on the speaker's objective, to weigh the evidence, to search for examples and clues to meaning, and to use idle time to review mentally what has already been said. Other suggestions for active listening are given in Figure 3–4.

Employee Meetings   One useful method of building upward communications is to meet with small groups of employees. In these "town hall" meetings employees are encouraged to talk about job problems, needs, and management practices that both help and interfere with job performance. The meetings attempt to probe in some depth the issues that are on the minds of employees. As a consequence (assuming follow-up action is taken), employee attitudes improve and turnover declines.

> One such employee meeting system is used in the Haworth company, in Holland, Michigan. Meetings called "sensing sessions" provide opportunities for employees to inform management what is on their minds. Some questions asked by management are open, used to discover what is going well and what is not and to seek suggestions for improvement. Others are more focused on a specific issue. Led by corporate executives as facilitators, the sensing sessions have been useful in obtaining ideas, as well as building partnerships and encouraging collaboration on improvements within the organization.[12]

An Open-Door Policy   An **open-door policy** is a statement that encourages employees to come to their supervisor or higher management with any matter that concerns them. Usually, employees are encouraged to see their supervisor first. If their problem is not resolved by the supervisor, then higher management may be approached. The goal is to remove blocks to upward communication. It is a worthy goal, but it is not easy to implement because there often are real or perceived barriers between managers and employees. Although the manager's door is physically open, psychological

FIGURE 3–4

Guidelines for effective listening

1. **Stop talking!**
   You cannot listen if you are talking.
   Polonius *(Hamlet):* "Give every man thine ear, but few thy voice."
2. **Put the talker at ease.**
   Welcome the person, and express your availability.
   Help a person feel free to talk by making him or her comfortable.
   Create a permissive atmosphere by establishing rapport.
3. **Show a talker that you want to listen.**
   Look interested. Establish eye contact and give nonverbal responses.
   Act interested. Do not read your mail while someone talks.
   Listen to understand rather than to oppose.
4. **Remove distractions.**
   Don't doodle, tap, or shuffle papers.
   Offer to shut the door.
5. **Empathize with a talker.**
   Try to see the other person's point of view.
   Connect with the person by sharing a similar experience.
6. **Be patient.**
   Allow plenty of time. Do not interrupt a talker. Wait out the short pauses.
   Don't start for the door or walk away.
7. **Hold your temper.**
   Pause before you speak or respond.
   An angry person takes the wrong meaning from words.
8. **Go easy on argument and criticism.**
   These approaches put a talker on the defensive, and she or he may clam up or become angry.
   Do not argue. Even if you win, you lose.
9. **Ask relevant questions.**
   Asking questions encourages a talker and shows that you are listening.
   It helps develop points further, and discloses relevant emotions.
10. **Stop talking!**
    This guideline is both first and last, because all others depend on it.
    You cannot be an effective listener while you are talking.

- Nature gave people two ears but only one tongue, which is a gentle hint that they should listen more than they talk.

- Listening requires two ears, one for meaning and one for feeling.

- Decision makers who do not listen have less information for making sound decisions.

and social barriers exist that make employees reluctant to enter. Some employees do not want to admit that they lack information or have a problem. Others are afraid they will incur their manager's disfavor if they raise disruptive issues.

Barriers may limit its use.

An even more effective "open door" is for managers to walk through their own doors and get out among their people. This approach reinforces the open-door policy with a powerful social cue. In this way managers will learn more than they ever would by simply sitting in their offices. This practice can be described as **management by walking around (MBWA),** in which the manager takes the initiative to systematically make contact with a large number of employees. By walking out through the door, the manager can not only discover key information from employees but also use the opportunity to project a supportive atmosphere. In this way, both parties gain.

Participation in Social Groups   Informal, casual recreational events furnish superb opportunities for unplanned upward communication. This spontaneous information sharing reveals true conditions better than most formal communications. There are departmental parties, sports events, bowling groups, hobby groups, picnics, and other employer-sponsored activities. Upward communication is not the primary purpose of these events, but it can be an important by-product of them.

OTHER FORMS OF COMMUNICATION

Not all communication takes place directly down or up the organizational hierarchy, not all is formally prescribed by the firm, and not all of it takes place either at work or through face-to-face interaction. This section provides an overview of lateral communication and the impact of some electronic forms of communication.

Lateral Communication

Managers engage in a large amount of **lateral communication,** or *cross-communication,* which is communication across chains of command. It is necessary for job coordination with people in other departments. It also is done because people prefer the informality of lateral communication rather than the up-and-down process of the official chain of command. Lateral communication often is the dominant pattern within management.

Cross-communication

Employees who play a major role in lateral communication are referred to as **boundary spanners.** Boundary-spanning employees have strong communication links within their department, with people in other units, and often with the external community. These connections with other units allow boundary spanners to gather large amounts of information, which they may filter or transfer to others. This gives them a source of status and potential power.

Boundary spanners

Networks   Whereas boundary spanners acquire their roles through formal task responsibilities, much other lateral communication takes place in less formal ways. A **network** is a group of people who develop and maintain contact to exchange information informally, usually about a shared interest. An employee who becomes active in such a group is said to be **networking.** Although networks can exist within as well as outside a company, usually they are built around external interests, such as recreation, social clubs, minority status, professional groups, career interests, and trade meetings.

Networking

> Deb Caldwin, an engineer, is in a network of research people who keep in touch at professional meetings and occasionally by telephone. She is also an excellent golfer and is part of a golf network at a local country club. Therefore, she knows personally the top executives of several local corporations, as well as other influential people in the area. Some of her networks are business-related; some, career-related; and others, purely social.

Networks help broaden the interests of employees, keep them more informed about new technical developments, and make them more visible to others. Networks help employees learn who knows what and even who knows those who know. As a result, an alert networker can gain access to influential people and centers of power by drawing upon common backgrounds, bonds of friendship, complementary organizational roles, or community ties. By obtaining job-related information and developing productive working relationships through effective networks, employees gain valuable skills and can perform their jobs better. Several practical suggestions for developing networks are provided in Figure 3–5.

Ombudsperson   Another device for aiding communication is the use of an **ombudsperson.** This position is created to receive and respond to inquiries, complaints, requests for policy clarifications, or allegations of wrongdoing from employees who do not feel comfortable going through normal channels. All contacts are typically confidential to encourage candor. The ombudsperson investigates the matter and intervenes where necessary to right a wrong and correct the system to prevent future errors. In this way, a streamlined alternative to the chain of command is created, and employees feel that their problem will receive a fair and impartial hearing.

Electronic Communication

Electronic networks

Electronic Mail   **Electronic mail** (e-mail) is a computer-based communication system that allows you to send a message to someone—or to a hundred people—almost instantaneously. It is stored within the computer system until the recipients turn on their networked personal computers and read the message at their convenience, at which time they can respond in the same manner. Some electronic mail systems can send messages in various modes (such as a letter to one correspondent who does not have a computer), and others can translate the message into a foreign language. The primary advantages of electronic mail systems are their dramatic speed and convenience; the major disadvantages include the loss of face-to-face contact, the temptation to send flaming (spontaneous, emotion-laden) messages, the risks of using acronyms and emoticons (keyboard versions of various psychological states) that will be misunderstood, and the associated difficulty of accurately conveying and interpreting emotions and subtleties in brief and somewhat sterile printed messages.

FIGURE 3–5

Suggestions for developing and using a personal network

1. Inventory your personal resources so that you know what you have to offer others.
2. Clarify your purpose for establishing or joining a network.
3. Join significant community organizations and contribute to them.
4. Initiate contacts with people whenever you can find (or create) a reason.
5. Share news, information, and ideas with others, thereby creating an obligation for them to reciprocate.
6. Seek out responsibilities that will bring you into contact with key people.
7. Demonstrate to other networkers that you can be trusted with confidential information.
8. Identify the key members of your network—those who have the most influence, connections, and willingness to help.
9. Don't hesitate to tap into members of your network for general advice, career contacts, and other useful information.
10. Find various ways to help your network colleagues satisfy their needs.

FIGURE 3–6

Sample guidelines for
e-mail netiquette

67

1. Provide your recipient with an informative subject for your message.
2. Indicate the degree of urgency with which you need a response.
3. Limit the use of acronyms and emoticons unless the receiver is thoroughly familiar with them and receptive to them.
4. Be cautious about forwarding messages and replying to them; ensure that the message is going only to the right persons.
5. Don't assume that everyone is equally comfortable with e-mail or checks their messages as frequently as you do.
6. Scan your inbox several times a day to assess which messages have the highest priority and respond to them first. Nevertheless, try to get back to all messages requiring your response within 24 hours.
7. Be brief.
8. Exercise as much care in spelling and punctuation as you would with a printed message; recipients often judge you on the basis of your care and attention to detail.

In response to these challenges, organizations have begun developing communication policies regarding which topics are appropriate for e-mail and which are not, who should be on distribution lists, what language is unacceptable, and even the frequency with which e-mail should be used (versus voice mail or face-to-face meetings). The whole field of e-mail courtesy ("netiquette") has sprung up, with a set of guidelines (see Figure 3–6) emerging to help managers decide how best to proceed via e-mail.[13]

Psychiatrist Edward Hallowell, who teaches at the Harvard Medical School, believes that the present era of technologically assisted communications has created a totally new challenge, one of combining high tech with high touch. Managers, he asserts, need to connect on an emotional level in order to have effective communication take place—and this cannot be done by either voice mail or e-mail. He advocates creating time for the *human moment*—an authentic encounter between two people. This requires physical presence in mutual space, tuning in to the other psychologically, and focusing on the other with high energy. The benefits? Less loneliness and isolation, a higher sense of meaningful relationships, and greater stimulation of mental activity.

Telecommuting   A member of a Chicago law firm maintains a permanent residence at a ski resort community in Colorado. An information processing operator works half of the time at home and the other half at a downtown bank. An author in a California beach house, working against a deadline, finishes a manuscript just before 8 A.M. and has a copy on the editor's desk hundreds of miles away just minutes later, about the time the author steps into the ocean for a swim. These people are all engaged in **telecommuting,** also called the *electronic cottage.* Telecommuters accomplish all or part of their work at home, or at a satellite location, through computer links to their offices.

Research suggests that the personal advantages of telecommuting include freedom from the distractions of the workplace, a reduction in the time and money spent on commuting, the opportunity to reduce expenditures for work-relevant clothing, and the opportunity to spend more time with family members or even to provide for their care at home. Corporate advantages include improved productivity (sometimes as much as 15 to 25 percent), reduced space requirements, the opportunity to hire key talent who will telecommute from a distant city, increased employee loyalty because the employer "went the extra mile" by setting up the system, and the capacity to accommodate disabled or chronically ill employees.[14] Society benefits, too—from a reduction in auto traffic and pollution and from the employment of people who are unable to work outside the home. Some employees are even inclined to contribute more time and effort in exchange for the comfort of working in their homes.

The number of Americans working at home by telecommuting has already passed 10 million and could eventually include up to 25 percent of the workforce, according to some optimistic estimates. The growth of telecommuting practices will depend largely on the ability of managers to overcome their fear of a loss of direct control over employees they cannot visually monitor. A number of other substantial problems can also arise for telecommuters. These include the possibility of being overlooked at promotion time through lesser daily visibility, the risk of getting burned out from the temptation to put in more hours daily, and especially, the social isolation that at-home employees may feel.[15]

As a consequence of this physical isolation, telecommuters may feel out of touch with their regular (social) networks, unable to experience intellectual stimulation from their peers, removed from informal channels of communication, and insulated from most sources of social support. The emotional costs may be unacceptably high unless the employer carefully screens participants, briefs them in advance so they know what to expect, and makes a strong attempt to maintain contact with them. Clearly, technological progress in communication is not easily gained without some human costs and organizational effort.

Virtual Offices   The impact of technological developments on communication offers both great promise and some problems as well. Some companies, such as Compaq, Hewlett-Packard, IBM, and AT&T, have implemented **virtual offices,** in which physical office space and individual desks are being replaced with an amazing array of portable communication tools—electronic mail, cellular phones, Thinkpads, voice mail systems, laptop computers, fax machines, modems, and videoconferencing systems. Employees armed with these tools can perform their work not just in their homes, as telecommuters do, but almost anywhere—in their cars, in restaurants, in customers' offices, or in airports. Electronic communication tools allow employers to greatly reduce the office space needed for each employee, sometimes enabling them to replace dozens of desks with a single "productivity center" that employees can use for holding meetings, responding to mail, and accomplishing other short-term tasks. One significant risk is the loss of an opportunity for social interaction; employees still need to gather informally, exchange ideas and experiences face-to-face, and develop a sense of teamwork.[16]

INFORMAL COMMUNICATION

The **grapevine** is an informal communication system. It coexists with management's formal communication system. The term "grapevine" arose during the Civil War. Intelligence telegraph lines were strung loosely from tree to tree in the manner of a grapevine, and wild grapevines grew over the lines in some areas. Since messages from the lines often were incorrect or confusing, any rumor was said to be from the grapevine. Today the term applies to all informal communication, including company information that is communicated informally between employees and people in the community.

Although grapevine information tends to be sent orally, it may be written. Handwritten or typed notes sometimes are used, but in the modern electronic office these messages typically are flashed on computer screens, creating the new era of the **electronic grapevine.** This system can speed the transmission of more units of information within a very short time. It will not replace the face-to-face grapevine, however, for two reasons: (1) not every employee has access to a network of personal computers at work, and (2) many workers enjoy the more personal social interaction gained through the traditional grapevine.

Since the grapevine arises from social interaction, it is as fickle, dynamic, and varied as people are. It is the expression of their natural motivation to communicate. It is the exercise of their freedom of speech and is a natural, normal activity. In fact, only employees who are totally disinterested in their work do not engage in shoptalk about it. Employee interest in associates is illustrated by this experience in one company:

> The wife of a plant supervisor had a baby at 11 P.M., and a plant survey the next day at 2 P.M. showed that 46 percent of the management personnel knew of the event through the grapevine.[17]

Features of the Grapevine

Several aspects distinguish the grapevine and help us to understand it better. The pattern that grapevine information usually follows is called a **cluster chain,** because each link in the chain tends to inform a cluster of other people instead of only one person. In addition, only a few people are active communicators on the grapevine for any specific unit of information. These people are called **liaison individuals.**

> In one company, when a quality-control problem occured, 68 percent of the executives knew about it but only 20 percent of them spread the information. In another case, when a manager planned to resign, 81 percent of the executives knew about it but only 11 percent passed the news on to others.

As this example illustrates, the grapevine is often more a product of the situation than it is of the person. This means that *given the proper situation and motivation, anyone would tend to become active on the grapevine.* Some of the factors that encourage people to be active are listed in Figure 3–7.

Typical examples of situations prompting grapevine activity include layoffs or takeovers, firings or promotions, or the introduction of new technology. Some jobs, such as secretaries, are central funneling points for information and thus lead the holders of those jobs into participation in the grapevine. Some employees simply have personalities that make them active (e.g., they like to talk with others about others). There does not seem to be any gender difference in grapevine activity, as both men and women are equally active on the grapevine.

- Excitement and insecurity
- Involvement of friends and associates
- Recent information
- Procedure that brings people into contact
- Work that allows conversation
- Job that provides information desired by others
- Personality of communicator

FIGURE 3–7

Factors that encourage grapevine activity

We also know that, contrary to common perceptions, well over three-fourths of grapevine information is accurate.[18] However, the grapevine may also be incomplete; it generally carries the truth but not the whole truth. In addition, the grapevine is fast, flexible, and personal. Its speed makes it difficult for management to stop undesirable rumors or to release significant news in time to prevent rumor formation. Much feedback about employees and their jobs is carried by the grapevine to a manager who is attentive to it, and it can also tell employees useful things about their manager ("Don't talk to Carrie; she's really busy today"). In conclusion, the evidence shows that *the grapevine is influential, both favorably and unfavorably.* The grapevine accomplishes so much positively and so much negatively that it is difficult to determine whether its net effects are positive or negative. Undoubtedly, its effects vary among work groups and organizations. Research with managers and white-collar employees reported that 53 percent of them viewed the grapevine as a negative factor in the organization. Only 27 percent viewed it as a positive factor, and 20 percent considered it neutral.[19]

Rumor

Definition of rumor

The major problem with the grapevine—and the one that gives the grapevine its poor reputation—is **rumor.** The word "rumor" sometimes is used as a synonym for "grapevine," but technically, there is an important difference between the two terms. Rumor is grapevine information that is communicated without secure standards of evidence being present. It is the unverified and untrue part of the grapevine. It could by chance be correct, but generally it is incorrect; thus it is presumed to be undesirable.

Interest and ambiguity lead to rumor.

Rumor is primarily a result of both interest and ambiguity in a situation. If a subject is unimportant or has no interest to a person, then that person has no cause to pass along a rumor about it. For example, the authors of this book have never rumored about the coconut output on the island of Martinique for the preceding year. Similarly, if there is no ambiguity in a situation, a person has no cause to spread rumor because the correct facts are known. Two factors—*interest and ambiguity—normally must be present* both to begin and to maintain a rumor. Following is an example of these two factors in action in the financial community:

> The rumor flew around the country that "the roof caved in on Bank X." The origin of the rumor, of course, was an ambiguous situation with different meanings. There were water leaks in the ceiling of the bank's building and this, coupled with the interest of both employees and financial analysts, was translated into a rumor of financial problems at the bank. Once the ambiguity was clarified, the rumor disappeared.

Details are lost.

Since rumor largely depends on ambiguity and the interest that each person has, it tends to change as it passes from person to person. Its general theme usually can be maintained, but not its details. It is subject to **filtering,** by which it is reduced to a few basic details that can be remembered and passed on to others. Generally, people choose details in the rumor to fit their own interest and view of the world.

People also add new details, often making the story worse, in order to include their own strong feelings and reasoning; this process is called **elaborating.**

> Marlo Green, a factory worker, heard a rumor that an employee in another department had been injured. When she passed the rumor to someone else, she elaborated by saying that the injury probably was caused by the supervisor's poor machine maintenance. Apparently, she made this elaboration because she did not like the supervisor, and she felt that if someone was injured, it must have been the supervisor's fault.

FIGURE 3–8

Guidelines for control
of rumor

71

- Remove its causes in order to prevent it.

- Apply efforts primarily to serious rumors.

- Refute rumor with facts.

- Deal with rumor as soon as possible.

- Emphasize face-to-face supply of facts, confirmed in writing if necessary.

- Provide facts from reliable sources.

- Refrain from repeating rumor while refuting it.

- Encourage assistance of informal and union leaders if they are cooperative.

- Listen to all rumors in order to understand what they may mean.

Types of Rumors The previous illustrations (the bank roof and the factory injury) suggest that *there are different kinds of rumors.* Some are historical and explanatory; they attempt to make meaning out of incomplete prior events. Others are more spontaneous and action-oriented; they arise without much forethought and represent attempts to change a current situation. Occasionally, rumors are negative, such as those which drive a wedge between people or groups, destroy loyalties, and perpetuate hostilities. They may also be positive, as when employees speculate about the beneficial effects of a new product just released. The existence of a variety of rumor types reminds managers that rumors should not be universally condemned even though they sometimes create problems.

Control of Rumor Since rumor generally is incorrect, a major outbreak of it can be a devastating epidemic that sweeps through an organization as fast as a summer tornado—and usually with as much damage. Rumor should be dealt with firmly and consistently, but how and what to attack must be known. It is a serious mistake to strike at the whole grapevine merely because it happens to be the agent that carried the rumor; that approach would be as unwise as throwing away a computer's keyboard because of a few misspelled words. Several ways to control rumor are summarized in Figure 3–8. The best approach is to prevent it by removing its causes. When rumors do circulate, however, a face-to-face supply of facts—if provided early—helps answer the ambiguities in each person's mind.

Use preventive approach.

SUMMARY

Communication is the transfer of information and understanding from one person to another person. Organizations need effective communication in downward, upward, and lateral directions. The two-way communication process consists of these eight steps: develop an idea, encode, transmit, receive, decode, accept, use, and provide feedback. To overcome personal, physical, and semantic barriers, managers must pay close attention to communication symbols, such as words, pictures, and nonverbal actions. Effective communication requires study and use of semantics—the science of meaning—to encourage understanding.

Managers play a key role in downward and upward communication, sometimes even delaying or filtering the flow of information. Many tools are available for their

Advice to Future Managers

1. Think of communication as much more than *sending* a message; you also need to anticipate the recipient's reaction and ensure that it matches your intentions.

2. Be alert to some of the many behavioral considerations in communication (e.g., polarized positions, defensiveness, face-saving) and work to avoid these in yourself and prevent these in others.

3. Sharpen your written presentation skills, whether it be in formal reports or informal e-mail messages. Challenge yourself to learn more about good writing by paying attention to good reading.

4. Think of ways in which you can practice social support for others, convincing them through every communication that they are valued individuals.

5. Whatever your gender is, work at minimizing your typical negative tendencies as you communicate and building upon your positive ones.

6. Obtain feedback from others on what it would take to make you into a world-class listener. Now follow their advice, capitalizing on every significant human moment that you can.

use, such as providing performance feedback and social support or establishing open-door policies and holding employee meetings. Listening, however, remains one of the most powerful tools. Networks have become popular ways for employees to find out what is going on around them, while the rapid development and use of computers and other tools have made possible electronic mail systems, telecommuting, and virtual offices for some employees.

Informal communication systems, called the grapevine, develop in the form of a cluster chain. Overall, the grapevine is accurate, fast, and influential, but sometimes details are omitted and rarely is the whole story communicated. Rumor is grapevine information communicated without secure standards of evidence. It occurs when there is ambiguity and interest in information. Managers can have some influence over the grapevine, and their basic objective is to integrate interests of the formal and informal communication systems so that the two systems can work together better.

Terms and Concepts for Review

Active listening
Body language
Boundary spanners
Closed questions
Cluster chain
Cognitive dissonance
Communication
Communication overload
Credibility gap
Defensive reasoning
Downward communication
Ecological control
Elaborating
Electronic grapevine
Electronic mail
Face-saving
Feedback-seeking behavior

Filtering
Grapevine
Inference
Just-in-time training
Lateral communication
Liaison individuals
Management by walking around (MBWA)
Network
Networking
Noise
Nonverbal communication
Ombudsperson
Open-book management
Open-door policy
Open questions
Performance feedback
Personal barriers

Physical barriers

Polarized

Proxemics

Psychological distance

Readability

Realistic job previews

Rumor

Self-concept

Semantic barriers

Semantics

Short-circuiting

Social cues

Social support

Telecommuting

Two-way communication process

Upward communication

Virtual offices

Discussion Questions

1. Think of a job that you have had and a situation in which the communication failed or was ineffective. Discuss how the communication process applied in that situation and where (during which of the eight steps) the breakdown occurred.
2. Discuss the barriers to communication that exist when you discuss a subject with your instructor in the classroom.
3. Select a situation in which you made a wrong inference. Analyze how the misinterpretation was made, and discuss how you might avoid similar misinterpretations in the future. How important is feedback as an aid to avoiding inference problems?
4. Observe your own behavior, and discuss what nonverbal communication habits you typically use. What do you intend as the message of each of them? Are there some behaviors you have that may mislead receivers?
5. Visit an instructor's office, and record your feelings of relative comfort there. What physical elements in the office contributed to your reaction? Discuss the instructor's apparent use of space (proxemics).
6. Examine the guidelines for effective listening in Figure 3–4. Which ones do you practice best? Which ones could you improve upon? Create a plan for improving your listening skills, and solicit feedback from a friend in three months to monitor your improvement.
7. Think of a part-time or full-time job that you have had.
   a. Discuss any communication overload you experienced.
   b. Discuss how well management handled downward communication to you.
   c. Explain any upward communication difficulties that you had and what you did to try to overcome them.
   d. Did you engage in feedback-seeking behavior? Describe what you did, or explain why you did not.
8. What networks do you belong to? Explain how you became a part of them and what they have done for you. What are your future networking plans?
9. Assess electronic mail in the context of this chapter. How does it fit with the eight steps of the communication process? What barriers are most likely to arise when it is used? How can they be overcome, or at least minimized?
10. Select a grapevine story that you heard, and discuss how it was communicated to you and how accurate it was.

How well do you exhibit good communication skills?

   Read the following statements carefully. Circle the number on the response scale that most closely reflects the degree to which each statement accurately describes you. Add up your total points and prepare a brief action plan for self-improvement. Be ready to report your score for tabulation across the entire group.

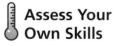 **Assess Your Own Skills**

	Good description									Poor description
1. I would be a strong practitioner of open communications and open-book management.	10	9	8	7	6	5	4	3	2	1
2. I am conscious of the need to pay attention to all eight steps in the communication process.	10	9	8	7	6	5	4	3	2	1
3. I am aware of my tendencies to engage in defensive reasoning and face-saving.	10	9	8	7	6	5	4	3	2	1
4. I understand which barriers affect each stage of the communication process.	10	9	8	7	6	5	4	3	2	1
5. I can recite several guidelines for creating more readable writing.	10	9	8	7	6	5	4	3	2	1
6. I consciously seek to manage the messages that are sent by my body language.	10	9	8	7	6	5	4	3	2	1
7. When it is important to achieve receiver acceptance of a message, I know which conditions to create for that purpose.	10	9	8	7	6	5	4	3	2	1
8. I can point out three substantial ways in which males and females differ in their communication patterns.	10	9	8	7	6	5	4	3	2	1
9. I regularly exhibit many of the classic guidelines for effective listening.	10	9	8	7	6	5	4	3	2	1
10. I maintain—and use—an active network of personal contacts for mutual benefit.	10	9	8	7	6	5	4	3	2	1

Scoring and Interpretation   Add up your total points for the ten questions. Record that number here, and report it when it is requested. _____

- If you scored between 81–100 points, you appear to have a solid capability for demonstrating good communication skills.

- If you scored between 61–80 points, you should take a close look at the items with lower self-assessment scores and explore ways to improve those items.

- If you scored less than 60 points, you should be aware that a weaker skill level regarding several items could be detrimental to your future success as a manager. We encourage you to review the entire chapter and watch for relevant material in subsequent chapters and other sources.

Now identify your three lowest scores, and write the question numbers here: _____, _____, _____. Write a brief paragraph, detailing to yourself an action plan for how you might sharpen each of these skills.

A Breakdown in Communications

Linda Barry, a single mother with three children, was hired as an order-entry clerk for a trucking firm. Her first two weeks on the job were spent in a special class from 8 A.M. to 4 P.M., where she learned how to sort, code, and enter the orders on the computer. An instructor worked with her constantly at first, and then less frequently as she gained skill and confidence. Linda was happy to have the job and enjoyed her work schedule. When the training was completed, she was told to report to the order-entry department the following Monday.

When she was first employed, either Linda failed to read and understand the printed information about her regular work schedule or perhaps the recruiter forgot to tell her that she was to fill a spot in a special shift that worked from 4 A.M. until noon. In any case, Linda failed to report to work on the early schedule on the first day of regular work. When she did arrive at 8 A.M., her supervisor criticized her for lack of responsibility. Barry responded by saying that she could not work the early shift because she had to prepare her children for school, and she threatened to resign if she could not work on the later shift. Because of a heavy workload and a difficult labor market, the supervisor needed Linda to do the job, yet had no room for her in the 8 A.M. to 4 P.M. shift.

Questions

1. Analyze the communication blockages in this case. Discuss ideas such as upward and downward communication, listening, realistic job previews, feedback, and inference.
2. Explain how you would handle the employment situation at the end of the case. What ideas from the chapter could be applied to help resolve this problem?

Communication Style

Read the following three paragraphs, and then rank them (1 = highest; 3 = lowest) according to the degree to which they describe your communication style. Be sure to use all three numbers (1, 2, and 3), where 1 is most descriptive and 3 is least descriptive.

_____ A. I like to *see* an idea in the form of charts, diagrams, maps, figures, and models; I prefer to receive written communications over oral; I like concrete examples and specific directions; I tend to give oral feedback ("I see what you're driving at").

_____ B. I like to *hear* ideas from others, and then I enjoy discussing and debating them; I may repeat others' ideas in order to cement them in my mind; I can be distracted by excess background noise; I tend to give oral clues to others ("I hear what you're saying").

_____ C. I like to *do* something; that is the way I learn best. I thrive on examples, and am generally quite active as a hands-on person; I tend to give oral clues in a physical way ("I need to get a handle on this before I can decide").

Now form into groups of three persons, and engage in a discussion of some stimulating issue of concern to the three of you. After 5–10 minutes, assess the other two persons in items of whether they are more likely to describe themselves as an A, a B, or a C above. Then compare notes with each other to see how accurate you are at perceiving the communication style of others.

Chapter 4

Social Systems and Organizational Culture

The greatest gift a mentor can give protégés is to demonstrate authenticity and realness.

–Chip Bell[1]

Day in and day out, we're champions of the culture, guaranteeing that consideration for people plays into business decisions.

–Sally Gore[2]

CHAPTER OBJECTIVES

TO UNDERSTAND

- The Operation of a Social System
- The Psychological Contract
- Social Cultures and Their Impact
- The Value of Cultural Diversity
- Role and Role Conflict in Organizations
- Status and Status Symbols
- Organizational Culture and Its Effects

Employees at Herman Miller, Inc., a large office furniture manufacturer, work very hard to create well-designed, top-quality products, such as desk consoles, cabinets, and chairs. Although the company's innovative products are well known throughout the industrial design world, Herman Miller, Inc., is even more widely recognized for its distinctive organizational culture.[3]

Prospective employees are closely examined for their overall character and their ability to get along with people. Employees are organized into work teams, where leaders and members evaluate each other twice each year. Employees can qualify to receive quarterly bonuses, based on cost-saving suggestions and other contributions. But the primary key to the company's culture resides in a "covenant" that is established between top management and all employees. In this covenant, the company asserts that it will attempt to "share values, ideals, goals, respect for each person, [and] the process of our work together." As a result, the Herman Miller company has achieved significant success, consistently ranking in the top 5 percent in evaluations of America's "most admired corporations."

Employees at companies like Herman Miller, Southwest Airlines, and Dell Computers work within complex social systems that have a significant influence on them. These organizational cultures reflect the beliefs and values of the companies' founders as well as those of the current staff. Moreover, social systems have a profound effect on the ways that employees work together. Cultures provide both direct and indirect cues telling workers how to succeed. Direct cues include orientation training, policy statements, and advice from supervisors and peers. Indirect cues are more subtle, including inferences made from promotions and apparent patterns of acceptable dress. This chapter introduces major ideas about social systems, such as social equilibrium, the effects of system changes, psychological contracts, cultural diversity, and the impact of role and status. We also examine the nature and effects of both societal culture (existing at a national level) and organizational culture (existing within a firm).

UNDERSTANDING A SOCIAL SYSTEM

A **social system** is a complex set of human relationships interacting in many ways. Possible interactions are as limitless as the stars in the universe. Each small group is a subsystem within larger groups that are subsystems of even larger groups, and so on, until all the world's population is included. Within a single organization, the social system includes all the people in it and their relationships to one another and to the outside world.

Two points stand out in the complex interactions among people in a social system. First, the behavior of any one member can have an impact, directly or indirectly, on the behavior of any other. Although these impacts may be large or small, *all parts of the system are mutually interdependent.* Simply stated, a change in one part of a system affects all other parts, even though its impact may be slight.

A second important point revolves around a system's boundaries. Any social system engages in exchanges with its environment, receiving input from it and providing output to it (which then becomes inputs for its adjacent systems). Social systems are, therefore, **open systems** that interact with their surroundings. Consequently, members of a system should be aware of the nature of their environments and their impact on other members both within and outside their own social system. This social system awareness is increasingly important in the twenty-first century, as global trade and

Open systems

international marketplaces for a firm's products and services vastly expand the need for organizations and their employees to anticipate and react to changes in their competitive environments.

Social Equilibrium

A system is said to be in **social equilibrium** when there is a dynamic working balance among its interdependent parts. Equilibrium is a dynamic concept, not a static one. Despite constant change and movement in every organization, the system's working balance can still be retained. The system is like a sea: There is continuous motion and even substantial disruption from storms, but over time the sea's basic character changes very little.

When minor changes occur in a social system, they are soon absorbed by adjustments within the system and equilibrium is regained. On the other hand, a single significant change (a shock, such as the resignation of a key executive) or a series of smaller but rapid changes may throw an organization out of balance, seriously reducing its forward progress until it can reach a new equilibrium. In a sense, when it is in disequilibrium, its parts are working against one another instead of in harmony. Here is an example:

> American automobile manufacturers have faced a significant challenge in responding to the design, quality, and cost advantages of international automakers such as Toyota, Nissan, Honda, and Mazda. In particular, the U.S. companies sometimes found that it took them much longer to bring a new car to market (total time from its conception to early production). Among many reasons offered is the internal struggle among seemingly competing units of an auto firm, such as product design, factory engineering, and sales and marketing. An unfortunate, and unproductive, disequilibrium sometimes exists.
>
> To combat this problem, Ford Motor Company creates cross-functional teams of line managers charged with the task of speeding product development. These teams are housed in the same work area, which makes communication much easier. They also share a common goal—reduction of product development costs by 20 percent. In this way, Ford maintains a more productive equilibrium within its system and keeps the functional subgroups working together.[4]

Functional and Dysfunctional Effects

Effects of changes

A change such as the introduction of cross-functional design teams has a **functional effect** when it is favorable for the system. When an action or a change creates unfavorable effects, such as a decline in productivity, for the system it has a **dysfunctional effect.** A major management task is to appraise both actual and proposed changes in the social system to determine their possible functional or dysfunctional effects, so that appropriate responses can be anticipated and made. Managers also need to predict both short-term and long-term effects, measure "hard" (e.g., productivity) and "soft" (e.g., satisfaction and commitment) criteria, and consider the probable effects on various stakeholder groups, such as employees, management, and stockholders. Assessing the overall functionality of a particular managerial action is clearly a complex process.

Employees can also have functional or dysfunctional effects on the organization. They can be creative, productive, and enthusiastic and actively seek to improve the quality of the organization's product or service. On the other hand, they can be tardy, absent frequently, unwilling to use their talents, and resistant to organizational changes. In order for employees to exhibit functional behaviors, they need to receive clear expectations and promises of reward. Furthermore, in exchange, the organization needs to receive a commitment from the employees.

Psychological and Economic Contracts

When employees join an organization, they make an unwritten **psychological contract** with it, although often they are not conscious of doing so. As shown in Figure 4–1, this contract is in addition to the economic contract where time, talent, and energy are exchanged for wages, hours, and reasonable working conditions. The psychological contract defines the conditions of each employee's psychological involvement—both contributions and expectations—with the social system. Employees agree to give a certain amount of loyalty, creativity, and extra effort, but in return they expect more than economic rewards from the system. They seek job security, fair treatment (human dignity), rewarding relationships with coworkers, and organizational support in fulfilling their development expectations.

If the organization honors only the economic contract and not the psychological contract, employees tend to have lower satisfaction because not all their expectations are being met. They may also withhold some of their work-related contributions. On the other hand, if both their psychological and economic expectations are met, they tend to experience satisfaction, stay with the organization, and perform well.

> The reciprocal obligations regarding the relationship between an employee and the organization can be violated either through an inability to fulfill them or by one party purposefully reneging on a promise. Research shows that when this happens, employees experience feelings of anger and betrayal. To prevent breakdowns of the psychological contract, employers are urged to help employees clarify their expectations and perceptions, initiate explicit discussions of mutual obligations, exercise caution when conveying promises, provide candid explanations for broken promises, and alert employees to the realistic prospects of reneging (e.g., when a business downturn forces an employer to withdraw previous commitments).[5]

As indicated in Figure 4–1, management responds in a similar way to the economic and psychological contracts that it sees. It expects responses such as high performance,

FIGURE 4–1

The results of the psychological contract and the economic contract

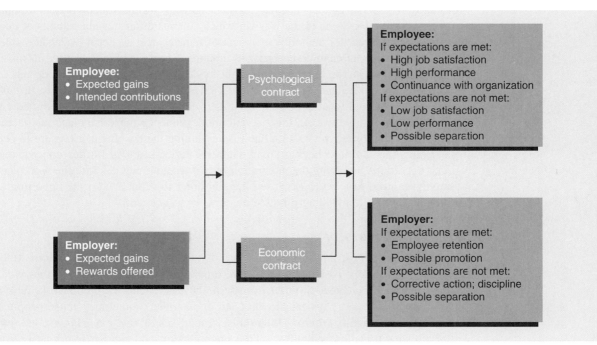

80

Exchange theory

continuous quality improvements, commitment to the organization, and friendly service to its customers. When these results occur, an employee is retained and may earn a promotion. However, if cooperation and performance do not meet expectations, corrective action and even termination may occur.

The psychological contract builds upon the concept of *exchange theory*. This theory simply suggests that whenever a continuing relationship exists between two parties, each person regularly examines the rewards and costs of that interaction. In order to remain positively attracted to the relationship, *both* parties must believe that a net positive ratio (rewards to costs) exists from their perspective. Consequently, the psychological contract is continually examined and often revised as new needs emerge and new rewards become available.

SOCIAL CULTURE

Whenever people act in accordance with the expectations of others, their behavior is social, as in the case of an employee named Maria. Like all other workers, Maria grows to be an adult in a **social culture,** which is her environment of human-created beliefs, customs, knowledge, and practices. Culture is the conventional behavior of her society, and it influences all her actions even though it seldom enters her conscious thoughts. Maria drives to work on the right or left side of the road, depending on the culture of her society, but she seldom consciously stops to think of this. Similarly, the car she drives, the drama she attends, the type of food she eats, and the organization that employs her are evidence of her social culture.

Social cultures are often portrayed as consistent within a nation, thereby producing a so-called national culture. At the simplest level, national cultures can be compared on the bases of how their members relate to each other, accomplish work, and respond to change.[6] However, there can be distinctive social cultures *within* a nation, as well, as seen in the tragic dispute between people of various ancestry within the former country of Yugoslavia. Social cultures can have dramatic effects on behavior at work, as we illustrate in Chapter 16. Some of the ways in which cultures differ include patterns of decision making, respect for authority, treatment of females, and accepted leadership styles. Knowledge of social cultures is especially important because managers need to understand and appreciate the backgrounds and beliefs of all members of their work unit.

People learn to depend on their culture. It gives them stability and security, because they can understand what is happening in their cultural community and know how to respond while in it. However, this one-culture dependency may also place intellectual blinders on employees, preventing them from gaining the benefits of exposure to people from other cultural backgrounds. Cultural dependency is further compounded under conditions involving the integration of two or more cultures into the workplace. Employees need to learn to adapt to others in order to capitalize on the opportunities they present, while avoiding possible negative consequences.

Cultural Diversity

Employees in almost any organization are divided into subgroups of various kinds. Formation of groups is determined by two broad sets of conditions. First, *job-related* (organizationally created) differences and similarities, such as type of work, rank in the organization, and physical proximity to one another, sometimes cause people to align themselves into groups. However, a second set of *non-job-related* conditions (those related to culture, ethnicity, socioeconomics, sex, and race) arise primarily from an individual's personal background; these conditions are highly important for legal, moral, and economic reasons. In particular, the U.S. workforce has rapidly become much more diverse, with females, African Americans, Hispanics, and Asian immigrants bringing their talents to employers in record numbers. This **cultural diversity,** or rich variety of differences among people at work, raises the issue of fair treatment for workers who are not in positions of authority.

EEO Laws   An early attempt to deal with cultural diversity at work and fair treatment for employees was through federal and state legislation. **Equal employment opportunity (EEO)** is the provision of equal opportunities to secure jobs and earn rewards in them, regardless of conditions unrelated to job performance. It was established by Title VII of the Civil Rights Act of 1964 (as amended) and has been extended and supported by a variety of subsequent federal and state legislation and executive orders. It requires employers, labor unions, and employment agencies to treat all people equally, without regard to race, color, religion, national origin, gender, handicap, sexual preference, or age, in all phases of employment.

EEO laws

EEO laws prohibit discrimination on factors other than job performance. In response, many organizations voluntarily developed **affirmative-action** plans, in which they adopted nondiscrimination policies, reviewed their personnel practices, and monitored their progress. Affirmative-action programs, designed to expand the opportunities for qualified people, have three major goals.

- To provide redress for past (societal) discrimination
- To correct current discrimination
- To pursue greater diversity as a valuable objective[7]

If EEO were completely successful, it would produce the benefits shown in Figure 4–2. Although considerable progress has been made, it has often been slow, and problems still remain while a societal debate over the merits of affirmative action

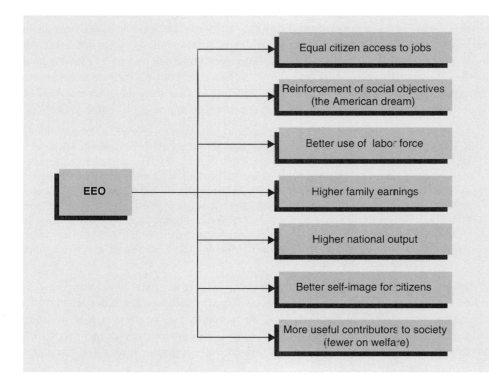

FIGURE 4–2

Potential social benefits of EEO

Discrimination and prejudice

has raged. Problems may persist because of a key difference in this context between **discrimination** and **prejudice.** *Discrimination is generally exhibited as an action, whereas prejudice is an attitude.* Either may exist without the other. The law focuses on an employer's actions, not feelings. If actions lead to what is legally determined to be discriminatory results, such actions are unlawful regardless of the employer's alleged good intentions.

A promising approach to overcoming discriminatory practices actually attempts to change the underlying attitudes. Programs aimed at managing and **valuing diversity** build from a key premise: Prejudicial stereotypes develop from unfounded assumptions about others and from their overlooked qualities. *Differences need to be recognized, acknowledged, appreciated, and used to collective advantage.* The workforce of the future (whether in the United States, the European Union, or elsewhere) will contain a rich blend of people representing diverse cultural and social conditions. *All* participants—males and females, members of differing racial groups, people of all ages, working parents, dual-career couples—will need to explore their differences, learn from others around them, and use that information to build a stronger organization.[8]

Changing one's own, or another employee's, attitude is seldom easy, yet there are constant political, economic, social, and technical pressures on people and organizations to change. More and more employees will encounter both subtle and substantial cultural differences among their work colleagues as the workforce becomes more diverse.[9] Recognition of these changes provides a powerful cultural force to which employers must adapt. If they actively manage diversity, there is a high likelihood that they will gain a competitive advantage—their workforce quality will be enriched, market sensitivity will increase, and both individual and group performance will improve.[10]

Social Culture Values

The Work Ethic For many years the culture of much of the western world has emphasized work as a desirable and fulfilling activity. This attitude is also strong in parts of Asia, such as Japan. The result of this cultural emphasis is a **work ethic** for many people, meaning that they view work as very important and as a desirable goal in life. They tend to like work and derive satisfaction from it. They usually have a stronger commitment to the organization and to its goals than do other employees. These characteristics of the work ethic make it highly appealing to employers.

> An illustration of the value placed upon the work ethic occurred when a taconite mining company, LTV Steel, decided to close down its iron ore operation in northern Minnesota. This dramatic action would put 1,600 steelworkers out of work. The governor of the state, Jesse Ventura, appeared on national television ("The Tonight Show") within a few weeks and announced to Jay Leno and a nationwide audience that he had a "gold mine" of competent workers looking for jobs there if any employer was interested in moving to the area. And what was the single major selling point? Governor Ventura touted the extraordinarily high work ethic reportedly possessed by those 1,600 workers. Within days, several interested employers—some from as far away as California—had contacted the governor's office to seek additional information.

Group differences

In spite of its prevalence, the work ethic is a subject of continuing controversy. Is it healthy? Is it declining? Is it a dead issue? The available research indicates that two conclusions can be safely reached. First, the proportion of employees with a strong work ethic varies sharply among sample groups. Differences depend on factors such as personal background, type of work performed, and geographical location. The range is quite broad, with the proportion of employees in different jobs who report that work is a central life interest extending from 15 to 85 percent.

A second conclusion is that the general level of the work ethic has declined grad-ually over many decades. The decline is most evident in the different attitudes between younger and older workers. Not only are younger employees not as supportive of the work ethic, but the level of support that young people once exhibited has dropped substantially. This decline carries serious implications for industrial productivity, espe-cially as international competition intensifies.

Gradual decline

Why has the work ethic declined? Dramatic social changes have brought about the work ethic's deterioration. Competing social values have emerged, such as a leisure ethic (a high priority placed on personal gratification), desire for intimacy (an emphasis on close personal relationships), and entitlement (a belief that peo-ple should receive benefits without having to work). In addition, changes in social policy and tax laws have reduced incentives to work and occasionally even penal-ized hard work and success (in the minds of some workers, at least). Finally, the "instant wealth" phenomenon has blossomed in recent times. This occurs when thousands of people—either as employees in high-tech start-up companies or as fortunate investors in the stock market—become millionaires after just a few years of work. The dramatic change they experience in their financial assets has led to a belief among some people that there are vast sums of money to be made by simply being in the right place at the right time, regardless of their belief in the work ethic. These factors all represent additional illustrations of complex social relationships in action, and they show how an employee's work ethic is contingent on factors in the larger social system. In the twenty-first century, managers will no longer be able to rely on the work ethic alone to drive employees to be productive.

Social Responsibility   Every action that organizations take involves costs as well as benefits. In recent years there has been a strong social drive to improve the cost-benefit relationship to make it possible for society to gain benefits from organizations and for the benefits to be fairly distributed. **Social responsibility** is the recognition that organizations have significant influence on the social system and that this influence must be properly considered and balanced in all organiza-tional actions.

An Ethics Question

Many entrepreneurs have a strongly developed work ethic. They also believe that their *employees* should demonstrate a strong commitment to work and should reflect this commitment in their customer service orientation, attendance and tardiness records, concern for quality, willingness to work beyond normal hours, and overall productivity. But some employees brush aside the argument that "work is a fulfilling activity" and ask instead, "What's in it for me?" The key issue boils down to the debatable right of an employer to impose the work ethic and its expectations on employees. Classic exam-ples include the Japanese concept of *karoshi,* where it is virtually a matter of pride to die from overwork, or the right of an auto manufacturer to demand that an employee work overtime. What do *you* think is the ethical thing for an employer to do regarding the work ethic?

One bit of evidence that organizations are increasingly concerned about social responsibility is provided by the criteria used to publicly judge their overall performance. *Fortune* magazine annually assesses "America's Most Admired Companies," and does so by evaluating over 300 organizations.[11] One of the criteria used is "social responsibility." Firms such as GE, Microsoft, Dell, Cisco, Wal-Mart, Home Depot, and Southwest Airlines have received high overall ratings.

The presence of strong social values such as social responsibility has a powerful impact on organizations and their actions. It leads them to use a *socioeconomic model of decision making,* in which both social costs and benefits are considered along with the traditional economic and technical values. Organizations take a broader view of their role within a social system, and accept their interdependence with it.

ROLE

Expected actions

A **role** is the pattern of actions expected of a person in activities involving others. Role reflects a person's position in the social system, with its accompanying rights and obligations, power and responsibility. In order to be able to interact with one another, people need some way of anticipating others' behavior. Role performs this function in the social system.

A person has roles both on the job and away from it, as shown in Figure 4–3. One person performs the occupational role of worker, the family role of parent, the social role of club president, and many others. In those various roles, a person is both buyer and seller, supervisor and subordinate, and giver and seeker of advice. Each role calls for different types of behavior. Within the work environment alone, a worker may have more than one role, such as a worker in group A, a subordinate to supervisor B, a machinist, a member of a union, and a representative on the safety committee.

FIGURE 4–3

Each employee performs many roles.

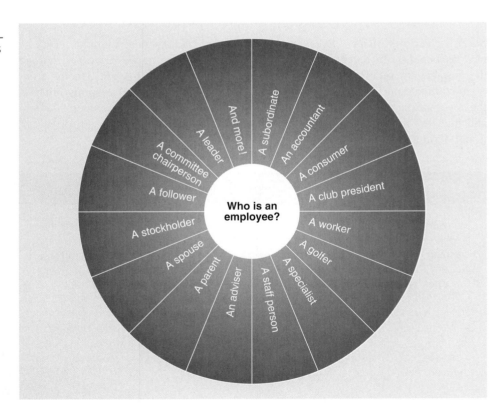

Role Perceptions

Activities of managers and workers alike are guided by their **role perceptions,** that is, how they think they are supposed to act in their own roles and how others should act in their roles. Since managers perform many different roles, they must be highly adaptive (exhibiting *role flexibility*) in order to change from one role to another quickly. Supervisors especially need to change roles rapidly as they work with subordinates and superiors and with technical and nontechnical activities.

When two people, such as a manager and an employee, interact, each one needs to understand at least three role perceptions, as shown in Figure 4–4. For a manager, the three roles are as follows: First there is the manager's role perception as required by the job being performed (A). Then there is the manager's perception of the role of the employee being contacted (B). Finally there is the manager's perception of his or her role as likely to be seen by the employee (C). Obviously, one cannot meet the needs of others unless one can perceive what they expect. Three related role perceptions (D, E, and F) exist from the employee's perspective, with dramatic differences (from the manager's perceptions) possible—especially in the direct comparisons such as A–D, B–E, and C–D. The key is for *both* parties to gain accurate role perceptions for their own roles and for the roles of the other. Reaching such an understanding requires studying the available job descriptions, as well as opening up lines of communication to discover the other's perceptions. Unless roles are clarified and agreed upon by both parties, conflicts will inevitably arise.

Mentors

Where can employees get information regarding their work-related roles so that they will have accurate role perceptions? In addition to traditional sources of information, such as job descriptions and orientation sessions, many organizations have formal or informal mentorship programs. A **mentor** is a **role model** who guides another employee (a **protégé**) by sharing valuable advice on roles to play and behaviors to avoid. Mentors teach, advise, coach, support, encourage, act as sounding boards, and sponsor their protégés so as to expedite their career progress. The advantages of successful mentoring programs include stronger employee loyalty, faster movement up the learning curve, better succession planning through development of replacements,

Role modeling by mentors

FIGURE 4–4

The complex web of manager-employee role perceptions

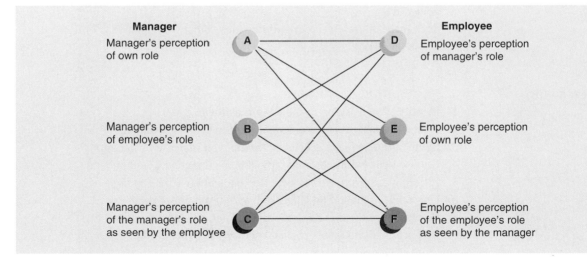

and increased level of goal accomplishments.[12] Some organizations actually assign protégés to various mentors, but this practice can create problems of resentment, abuse of power, and unwillingness to serve. As a result, other firms simply allow employees to seek out their own mentors. Tips for protégés working with mentors are provided in Figure 4–5(a); tips for mentors are shown in Figure 4–5(b).

Mentors are usually older, successful themselves, and respected by their peers (influential). They also must be willing to commit time and energy to help another person move up the corporate ladder, be able to communicate effectively and share ideas in a nonthreatening fashion, and enjoy one-on-one development of others. Mentors are often not the employee's direct supervisor; therefore they can provide additional support to aid an employee's career progress. Their detachment from a supervisory role also allows them to be more objective about the strengths and weaknesses observed with a protégé.

Several problems can arise in mentoring programs, however.[13] Some mentors are more effective role models than others, or simply more interested in being good mentors. Similarly, some protégés are more aggressive in seeking out the prime candidates for a mentor, leaving other protégés with less skilled mentors. In other cases, a mentor might provide advice or information to a protégé that actually hinders the

FIGURE 4–5(a)

Tips for protégés using mentors

1. Select more than one mentor. Draw your mentors from your peer group, higher management levels, or even professional colleagues outside the organization.
2. Consult them periodically. Discipline yourself to meet with them at regular intervals.
3. Brief them on your progress, current issues, and problems you are facing.
4. Seek feedback from them. Inquire how your work is regarded. Show them samples of your work, and ask for suggestions for improvement.
5. Share a summary of your own strengths and weaknesses, and your action plan for overcoming your limitations. Compare your view with their perceptions of your strengths, and probe them for improvement ideas for the areas where you need work.
6. Ask your mentors to watch for new opportunities opening up that might use your skills.
7. Seek their advice on career-building moves that will enhance your promotability.

FIGURE 4–5(b)

Tips for mentors

1. Identify protégé strengths, and build on them.
2. Foster self-discovery, by asking insight-generating questions.
3. Let the protégé make decisions, for that will increase ownership.
4. Choose your words carefully; avoid being directive or judgmental.
5. Listen; watch from a distance; intervene only when necessary.
6. Don't place yourself on a pedestal; avoid sounding like an expert.
7. Be real; be authentic; be supportive; eliminate signs of power.
8. Be open to alternative views and choices; help the protégé refine them.

employee's development. A special problem sometimes confronting women and minorities is the difficulty of finding successful role models from the same gender or ethnic group. When there are gender differences in the mentor-protégé relationship, difficult issues sometimes arise, such as when one party exploits the other's efforts and time, or when a legitimate but close emotional bond stimulates rumors of a sexual relationship. Finally, a protégé's career might be stifled abruptly if the mentor is transferred or leaves the organization. For these and other reasons, common practice is to have more than one mentor for each protégé, resulting in a constellation of relations from which the protégé can derive role perceptions. Despite well-meaning attempts, efforts to establish mentoring relationships sometimes fail, as in the following example:

> Kenneth Benton, a senior employee, offered to play the role of adviser and helper for a new and promising office employee, Ben Grossman. However, Grossman misinterpreted Benton's initiatives and felt that accepting help would imply an admission of weakness. Grossman also resented the idea of being bossed by someone who had no right to give him orders, so he abruptly rejected all offers of help.
>
> Rebuffed once as a mentor, Benton refused to share his insights on other topics with Grossman for years afterward, even when directly asked for assistance. Grossman later wound up committing several minor errors that slowed his career progress slightly. These mistakes might have been prevented had the mentor-protégé relationship between them been allowed to develop.

Role Conflict

When others have different perceptions or expectations of a person's role, that person tends to experience **role conflict.** Such conflict makes it difficult to meet one set of expectations without rejecting another. A company president faced role conflict, for example, when she learned that both the controller and the personnel director wanted her to allocate the new organizational planning function to their departments.

> Role conflict at work is fairly common. A national sample of wage and salary workers reported that 48 percent experienced role conflict from time to time and 15 percent said that role conflict was a frequent and serious problem.[14] Role conflict was most difficult for employees with many job contacts outside the organization, that is, with *boundary roles.* They found that their external roles placed demands on their jobs different from the demands of their internal roles, so role conflict resulted. When people were classified according to the number of their outside job contacts, those with few contacts had the least role conflict and those with frequent contacts had the most conflict.

Role Ambiguity

When roles are inadequately defined or are substantially unknown, **role ambiguity** exists, because people are not sure how they should act in situations of this type. When role conflict and role ambiguity exist, job satisfaction and organizational commitment will likely decline. On the other hand, employees tend to be more satisfied with their jobs when their roles are clearly defined by job descriptions and statements of performance expectations. A better understanding of roles helps people know what others expect of them and how they should act. If any role misunderstanding exists when people interact, then problems are likely to occur, as illustrated in this example:

> A factory employee, Bryce Bailey, was a union steward. He came to his supervisor, Shelly Parrish, for guidance on a work problem. Parrish thought Bailey was approaching in his role as union steward and trying to challenge her authority. Because of the misunderstood roles, the two people were not able to communicate, and the problem remained unsolved.

STATUS

Social rank

Status is the social rank of a person in a group. It is a mark of the amount of recognition, honor, and acceptance given to a person. Within groups, differences in status apparently have been recognized ever since civilization began. Wherever people gather into groups, status distinctions are likely to arise, because they enable people to affirm the different characteristics and abilities of group members.

Individuals are bound together in **status systems,** or status hierarchies, which define their rank relative to others in the group. If they become seriously upset over their status, they are said to feel **status anxiety.**

Loss of status—sometimes called "losing face" or **status deprivation**—is a serious event for most people; it is considered a much more devastating condition, however, in certain societies. People, therefore, become quite responsible in order to protect and develop their status. One of management's pioneers, Chester Barnard, stated, "The desire for improvement of status and especially the desire to protect status appears to be the basis of a sense of general responsibility."[15]

Since status is important to people, they will work hard to earn it. If it can be tied to actions that further the company's goals, then employees are strongly motivated to support their company.

> Bob Pike, president of Creative Training Techniques and an internationally renowned trainer, suggests that employees have their "emotional radio stations" tuned to two frequencies. In each, the employee is listening intently for the answer to a question or a demand. The first frequency is WIIFM, and the second is MMFIAM. WIIFM asks "What's In It For Me?" while MMFIAM pleads for a response to "Make Me Feel Important About Myself." Both of these show that employees are egocentric—they are hungry for information that either rewards them or reinforces their self-image and perceived status. Consequently, managers must act like radio disk jockeys who play the tunes that listeners request—feeding the status needs of their workers.

Status Relationships

Effects of status

High-status people within a group usually have more power and influence than those with low status. They also receive more privileges from their group and tend to participate more in group activities. They interact more with their peers than with those of lower rank. Basically, high status gives people an opportunity to play a more important role in an organization. As a result, lower-status members tend to feel isolated from the mainstream and to show more stress symptoms than higher-ranked members.

In a work organization, status provides a system by which people can relate to one another as they work. Without it, they would tend to be confused and spend much of their time trying to learn how to work together. Though status can be abused, normally it is beneficial because it helps people cooperate with one another.

Status Symbols

The status system reaches its ultimate end with **status symbols.** These are the visible, external things that attach to a person or workplace and serve as evidence of social rank. They exist in the office, shop, warehouse, refinery, or wherever work groups congregate. They are most in evidence among different levels of managers, because each successive level usually has the authority to provide itself with surroundings just a little different from those of people lower in the structure.

FIGURE 4–6

Typical symbols of status

89

- Furniture, such as a mahogany desk or a conference table

- Interior decorations, such as carpeting, draperies, and artwork

- Location of workplace, such as a corner office or an office having a window with a view

- Facilities at workplace, such as a computer terminal or fax machine

- Quality and newness of equipment used, such as a new vehicle or tools

- Type of clothes normally worn, such as a suit

- Privileges given, such as a club membership or company automobile

- Job title or organizational level, such as vice president

- Employees assigned, such as a private secretary

- Degree of financial discretion, such as authorizing up to $5,000 expenditures

- Organizational membership, such as a position on the executive committee

As shown in Figure 4–6, there are a variety of symbols of status, depending on what employees feel is important. For example, in one office the type of wastebasket is a mark of distinction. In another, significant symbols are type of desk and telephones. In the executive offices, such items of rank as rugs, bookcases, curtains, and pictures on the wall are important. Another classic symbol of much significance is a corner office, because those offices are often larger and have windows on two sides. There may even be distinctions between an office with windows and one with no windows. Outside the office, the truck driver who operates the newest or largest truck has a symbol of status.

All this concern for symbols of status may seem amusing, but status symbols are a serious matter. They may endanger job satisfaction because employees who do not have a certain symbol, and think they should, can become preoccupied with that need. When, for example, an employee gives unreasonable attention to status symbols, there is evidence of status anxiety, and this situation requires management attention.

Many organizations have a policy that persons of equal rank in the same department should receive approximately equal status symbols. There may be some variation between departments, such as production and sales, because the work is different and rank is not directly comparable. In any case, managers need to face the fact that status differences exist and must be managed successfully. Managers have the power to influence and control status relationships somewhat. The organization gives some status, and it can take some away.

Sources of Status

The sources of status are numerous, but in a typical work situation several sources are easily identified. As shown in Figure 4–7, education and job level are two important sources of higher status. A person's abilities, job skills, and type of work also are major sources of status.

Other sources of status are amount of pay, seniority, age, and stock options. Pay gives economic recognition and an opportunity to have more of the amenities of life, such as travel. Seniority and age often earn for their holder certain privileges, such

FIGURE 4–7

Major sources of status on the job

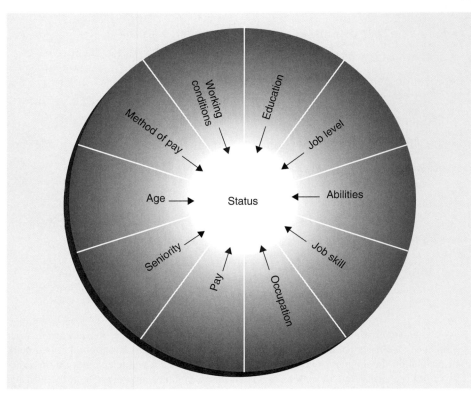

as first choice of vacation dates, or the respect of coworkers for their longevity at work. Method of pay (hourly versus salary) and working conditions also provide important status distinctions, such as distinguishing blue-collar and white-collar work. Stock options provide employees with the opportunity to share the financial success of the firm.

Significance of Status

Status is significant to organizational behavior in several ways. When employees are consumed by the desire for status, it often is the source of employee problems and conflicts that management needs to solve. It influences the kinds of transfers that employees will take, because they don't want a low-status location or job assignment. It helps determine who will be an informal leader of a group, and it definitely serves to motivate those seeking to advance in the organization. Some people are status seekers, wanting a job of high status regardless of other working conditions. These people can be encouraged to qualify themselves for high-status jobs so that they will feel rewarded.

Some organizations have consciously sought to use their knowledge of the impact of status symbols to reduce these indicators. National Bank of Georgia chose an open-office layout in its new headquarters so as to foster open communications and consensus. Top executives at Home Box Office avoided choosing the prestigious top (fifteenth) floor of their new building and instead selected the eighth floor for greater proximity to the marketing and programming departments. Executives at Lake Superior Paper Company choose to wear casual clothes (similar to those of the mill employees) so as to remove the potential status barrier between the two groups. More and more, organizations are removing reserved parking spots and placing everyone on an equal basis in the parking lot, too.

These illustrations provide some evidence that there has been a backlash in our society against too many status symbols. Some speakers argue that an overemphasis on status has created, or at least magnified, a gap between the haves and the have-nots. As a result, some contemporary employees *reject* traditional symbols of status even when those are available to them. They choose to wear clothes of their own choice to work; they don't always drive higher-priced cars; and they prefer to mingle with other employees despite having access to an executive dining room after receiving a promotion.

ORGANIZATIONAL CULTURE

Social (national) culture creates the wide-ranging context in which organizations operate. It provides the complex social system of laws, values, and customs in which organizational behavior occurs. Employee behavior (B), according to social psychologist Kurt Lewin, is a function of the interaction between personal characteristics (P) and the environment (E) around the person, or B = f (P, E). Part of that environment is the social culture in which the individual lives and works, which provides broad clues as to how a person with a given background will behave. The previous discussion indicated how employee actions are sharply affected by the roles assigned to them and the status level accorded to them.

Inside the organization lies another powerful force for determining individual and group behavior. **Organizational culture** is the set of assumptions, beliefs, values, and norms that are shared by an organization's members.[16] This culture may have been consciously created by its key members, or it may have simply evolved across time. It represents a key element of the work environment in which employees perform their jobs. This idea of organizational culture is somewhat intangible, for we cannot see it or touch it, but it is present and pervasive. Like the air in a room, it surrounds and affects everything that happens in an organization. Because it is a dynamic systems concept, culture is also affected by almost everything that occurs within an organization.

Shared norms help define culture.

Organizational cultures are important to a firm's success for several reasons. They give an organizational identity to employees—a defining vision of what the organization represents. They are also an important source of stability and continuity to the organization, which provides a sense of security to its members. At the same time, knowledge of the organizational culture helps newer employees interpret what goes on inside the organization, by providing an important context for events that would otherwise seem confusing. More than anything else, perhaps, cultures help stimulate employee enthusiasm for their tasks. Cultures attract attention, convey a vision, and typically honor high-producing and creative individuals as heroes. By recognizing and rewarding these people, organizational cultures are identifying them as role models to emulate.

Characteristics of Cultures

Organizations, like fingerprints and snowflakes, are unique. Each has its own history, patterns of communication, systems and procedures, mission statements and visions, stories and myths which, in their totality, constitute its *distinctive* culture. Cultures are relatively *stable* in nature, usually changing only slowly over time. Exceptions to this condition may occur when a major crisis threatens a firm or when two organizations merge with each other (requiring a careful blending of the two so as to avoid culture clash).

Cultures are distinctive, stable, implicit, and symbolic.

Jack Welch, former CEO of General Electric, led that company to an outstanding level of success for more than twenty years. He has been referred to as the "most successful chief executive ever" by many business magazines and corporate observers. He achieved his results by defining, emphasizing, and rewarding a corporate culture built around several valued principles:

- Removing boundaries that inhibit the flow of ideas
- Increasing speed and simplicity by "delayering" the organization
- Setting "stretch" goals for employees and rewarding their achievement

- Following a "six sigma" program for improving quality and performance
- Emphasizing the importance of customer satisfaction
- Creating a learning culture that stresses high morals, open exchanges of ideas, and high levels of contributions from each employee.

Source: Robert Slater, *Jack Welch and the GE Way*, New York: McGraw-Hill, 1998.

Most organizational cultures have historically been *implicit* rather than explicit. More recently, though, organizations have begun talking about their intended cultures, and many top leaders see one of their major roles as speaking out about the kind of environment they would like to create within their firms. (See "What Managers Are Reading.") A final defining characteristic of most cultures is that they are seen as *symbolic representations* of underlying beliefs and values. Seldom do we read a description of a firm's culture. More frequently, employees make inferences about it from hearing stories about the way things are done, from reading slogans that portray corporate ideals, from observing key artifacts, or from watching ceremonies in which certain types of employees are honored.

Examples of symbolic representations abound in General Mills, headquartered in Minneapolis, Minnesota.[17] Executives refer to the "company of champions" culture, and point with pride to a statement of company values that is reinforced by rewards, recognition programs, and employee development systems. A popular slogan proclaims that "Eagles dare to win," and this statement adorns many awards given to employees and their units for exceptional work. A training program, "The Championship Way," provides an opportunity for the corporation to communicate its corporate values and discover barriers to their achievement.

Over time, an organization's culture becomes perpetuated by its tendency to attract and retain people who fit its values and beliefs. Just as people may choose to move to a certain region because of geographic characteristics such as temperature, humidity, and rainfall, employees also will gravitate toward the organizational culture they prefer as a work environment. This results in a good fit of employer and employee.

Unfortunately, examples abound of corporate mergers whose partners experienced a clash of cultures. Novell's acquisition of WordPerfect, the marriage of Daimler-Benz with Chrysler, the blending of General Electric with Honeywell, and the merger of Wells Fargo with Norwest Bank all encountered difficulties that delayed expected payoffs. As a result, even major accounting firms are demanding that potential merger partners answer a series of due diligence questions before moving ahead. Most important among these questions is "Will there be a good fit between the two?"[18]

Several other dimensions of culture are important to note. For one, there is *no best culture* for all firms; culture clearly depends on the organization's goals, industry, nature of competition, and other factors in its environment. Cultures will be more easily recognized when their elements are generally *integrated* and consistent with each other; in other words, they fit together like pieces of a puzzle. Also, most members must at least *accept,* if not embrace, the assumptions and values of the culture.

Historically, employees seldom talked explicitly about the culture in which they worked; more recently, culture has become an increasingly acceptable conversation topic among employees. Most cultures evolve directly from *top management,* who can have a powerful influence on their employees by what they say. However, management's *actions* are even more important to watchful employees, who can quickly detect when managers give only lip service but not true support to certain ideals, such as customer service and quality products. A culture may exist across an entire organization, or it may be made up of various *subcultures*—the environment within a single division, branch, plant, or department. Finally, cultures have varying strengths—they can be characterized as relatively strong or weak, depending largely on the degree of their impact on employee behavior and how widely the underlying beliefs and values are held. The ten characteristics of cultures are summarized in Figure 4–8.

The effect of organizational culture on employee behavior is difficult to establish. Some research indicates that there must be, and is, a positive relationship between certain organizational cultures and performance. Agreement within an organization on a culture should result in a larger degree of cooperation, acceptance of decision making and control, communication, and commitment to the employer. Such a result is especially likely when a firm consciously seeks to create a performance-enhancing culture that removes barriers to success. Just as yeast is a critical ingredient in baking bread, a culture of productivity is an essential element in organizational success. However, if the wrong ingredient is accented, the results can be costly, as the following research shows.

A study of five international accounting firms examined their cultures, employee retention (turnover) rates for new hires, and the opportunity costs associated with employee departures. Two primary cultures were identified. One emphasized the work task values of detail and stability; the other emphasized the interpersonal relationship values of team orientation and respect for people. Newly hired professionals working in the culture accenting interpersonal relations stayed, on average, fourteen months longer than their counterparts in the other culture. The estimated cost (in lost profits) to a single firm of higher turnover (presumably due to the more task-oriented culture) was $6–9 million for the fourteen months.[19]

Measuring Organizational Culture

Systematic measurement and comparison of cultures is difficult at best. Most early attempts by researchers relied on examination of stories, symbols, rituals, and ceremonies to obtain clues and construct a composite portrait. Others have used interviews and open-ended questionnaires in an attempt to assess employee values and beliefs. In other cases, examination of corporate philosophy statements has provided insight into the espoused culture (the beliefs and values that the organization states publicly). Another approach is to survey employees directly and seek their percep-

• Distinctive	• Integrated
• Stable	• Accepted
• Implicit	• A reflection of top management
• Symbolic	• Subcultures
• No one type is best	• Of varying strength

FIGURE 4–8

Characteristics of organizational cultures

tions of the organization's culture. One of the more interesting methods is to become a member of the organization and engage in participant observation. This approach allows direct sensing from the perspective of a member who is experiencing the culture.

> Prudential Insurance Company of America used a standard pencil-and-paper instrument to identify part of its culture. Prudential measured current norms and found strong perceptions of conformity, caution, competition with other work groups, risk avoidance, and top-down decision making. Then the company assessed desired norms, and found major gaps. Employees wanted a culture that stressed teamwork, collaboration, customer service, initiative, training, and cooperation. This measurement process allowed Prudential to involve employees in changing to a new culture—one where managers are measured against their culture-change goals.[20]

Any attempt to measure organizational culture can be only an imperfect assessment. Such measurements capture only a snapshot of the culture at a single point in time. In reality, many organizational cultures are in the process of changing and need to be monitored regularly and by a variety of methods to gain a truer picture.

Communicating and Changing Culture

If organizations are to consciously create and manage their cultures, they must be able to communicate them to employees, especially the newly hired ones. People are generally more willing to adapt when they want to please others, gain approval, and learn about their new work environment. Similarly, organizations are anxious to have the new employees fit in, and therefore an intentional approach that helps make this happen is used by many firms. Examples of formal communication vehicles for transmitting organizational cultures include executive visions of the firm's future, corporate philosophy statements, and codes of ethical conduct. Informal means involve publicly recognizing heroes and heroines, retelling historical success stories, and even allowing myths to become exaggerated without popping the hot-air balloon. Of course, elements of the organization's culture are also unintentionally communicated to employees in a variety of ways, such as when news of a manager's error and an executive's forgiveness of it are accidentally leaked throughout the firm.

Socialization affects employees.

Collectively, these cultural communication acts may be lumped under the umbrella of **organizational socialization,** which is the continuous process of transmitting key elements of an organization's culture to its employees. It consists of both formal methods (such as military indoctrination at boot camp or corporate orientation training for new employees) and informal means (like the role modeling provided by mentors, discussed earlier in this chapter). All these approaches help shape the attitudes, thoughts, and behavior of employees. Viewed from the organization's perspective, organizational socialization is like placing an organization's fingerprints on people or stamping its own genetic code on them. From the employee's viewpoint, it is the essential process of learning the ropes to survive and prosper within the firm. The important point is that socialization can be functional for both workers and their employers.

Managers are encouraged to engage in **storytelling** as a way to forge a culture and build organizational identity. Good stories tap into the emotions of an audience and have proven to be powerful ways to create shared meaning and purpose. Stories convey a sense of tradition, explain how past problems have been solved, convey personal frailty through tales of mistakes made and learned from, and enhance cohesion around key values. The most memorable stories entertain as well as inform and uplift as well as teach. These stories highlight purposeful plots and patterns that the organization cherishes, they point out consequences of actions, and they provide valuable lessons that carry forward the wisdom gained through previous years.[21] Storytelling, then, is a key means for achieving socialization of employees.

A reciprocal process emerges when changes occur in the other direction. Employees can also have an active impact on the nature of the organization's culture and operations. **Individualization** occurs when employees successfully exert influence on the social system around them at work by challenging the culture or deviating from it. The interaction between socialization and individualization is portrayed in Figure 4–9, which shows the types of employees who accept or reject an organization's norms and values while exerting various degrees of influence. The two extremes—*rebellion* and total *conformity*—may prove dysfunctional for the organization and the individual's career in the long run. *Isolation,* of course, is seldom a productive course of action. If we assume that the culture of a certain organization invites its employees to challenge, question, and experiment while also not being too disruptive, then the *creative individualist* can infuse new life and ideas for the organization's benefit, as this example demonstrates:

Individualization affects the organization.

> Delbert Little is an engineer who works for a major American electronics firm. A highly creative, energetic, and talented worker, he prides himself on giving 110 percent effort to his job. Although he totally accepts his employer's values regarding the need to create new and improved products through technological breakthroughs, he also flaunts his rejection of some corporate norms regarding personal behavior (mode of dress and deference to authority). He communicates to his workers with great passion, regularly imploring them to exercise similar innovativeness. Whenever he thinks his employer is moving in the wrong product or market direction, he writes passionate memos to top executives detailing his reasoning and trying to persuade them to change their minds.
>
> Delbert can be described as exercising creative individualism (but bordering on rebellion). He accepts some norms and values but rejects others (and therefore is moderately socialized). He fights fiercely for what he thinks is right and attempts to change others' thinking, too. Consequently, he has a relatively high impact on his portion of the

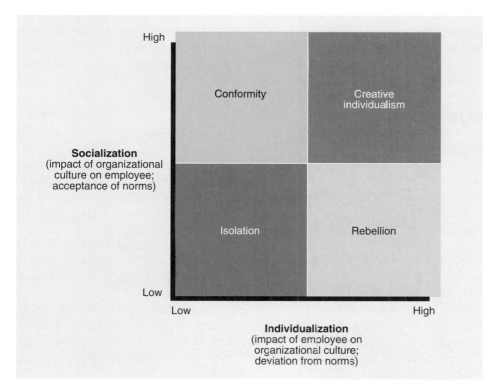

FIGURE 4–9

Four combinations of socialization and individualization

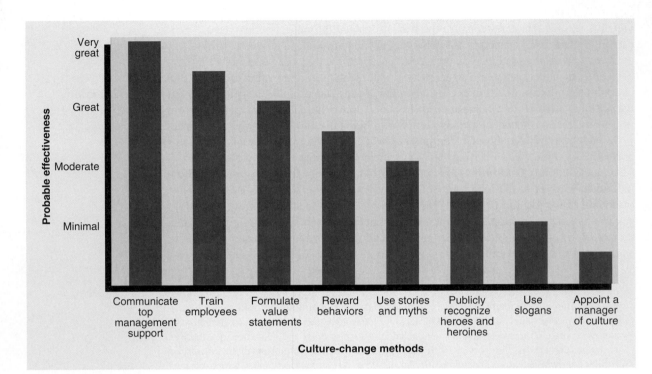

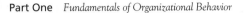

FIGURE 4–10

Effectiveness of methods
for changing
organizational culture

organization (individualism). "The company tolerates my behavior," he laughed one day, "only because I have produced over 100 patents while working here!"

Can culture be changed? A study of corporate cultures at nine large companies—Federal Express, Johnson & Johnson, 3M, AT&T, Corning, Du Pont, Ford, IBM, and Motorola—suggests that it can change. However, it requires a long-term effort, often spanning five to ten years to complete. Figure 4–10 indicates the relative effectiveness of a variety of methods for changing culture.[22] Clearly, an open display of top-management commitment and support for the new values and beliefs is critically important, as is the training of employees to enable them to change.

SUMMARY

When people join a work group, they become part of that organization's social system. It is the medium by which they relate to the world of work. The variables in an organizational system operate in a working balance called social equilibrium. Individuals make a psychological contract that defines their personal relationship with the system. When they contribute to the organization's success, we call their behavior functional.

The broad environment that people live in is their social culture. People need to accept and appreciate the value that a diversity of cultural backgrounds can contribute to the success of an organization. Other important cultural factors include the work ethic and corporate attitudes toward social responsibility.

Role is the pattern of action expected of a person in activities involving others. Related ideas are role perception, mentors, role conflict, and role ambiguity. Status is the social rank of a person in a group, and it leads to status systems and possibly status anxiety. Status symbols are sought as if they were magical herbs, because they often provide external evidence of status for their possessors.

1. Look at your organization as a social system, and ask yourself whether it is in balance or not. If it is not, is the disequilibrium functional for the organization?

2. Seek to understand, and actively manage, the psychological contract you have with each of your employees.

3. Inventory the positive ways in which each of your employees is different. Make sure that your workplace capitalizes on these aspects of diversity.

4. Find, and use, at least one active mentor for yourself. Also, offer yourself as a mentor to at least one person who does not report directly to you.

5. Analyze the status symbols that are apparent in your organization. Decide whether they are functional or dysfunctional for employee morale and performance.

6. Paint a comprehensive verbal portrait of the organizational culture at your workplace. Is the culture strong or weak? Describe what you could do to clarify it and strengthen it.

Organizational cultures reflect the assumptions and values that guide a firm. They are intangible but powerful influences on employee behavior. Participants learn about their organization's culture through the process of socialization and influence it through individualization. Organizational cultures can be changed, but the process is time-consuming.

Terms and Concepts for Review

Affirmative action

Cultural diversity

Discrimination

Dysfunctional effect

Equal employment opportunity (EEO)

Functional effect

Individualization

Mentor

Open systems

Organizational culture

Organizational socialization

Prejudice

Protégé

Psychological contract

Role

Role ambiguity

Role conflict

Role model

Role perceptions

Social culture

Social equilibrium

Social responsibility

Social system

Status

Status anxiety

Status deprivation

Status symbols

Status systems

Storytelling

Valuing diversity

Work ethic

Discussion Questions

1. What psychological contract do you feel is present in this course? Describe its key features.

2. Consider the continuing debate in the United States regarding the merits of affirmative action. Identify three arguments for and three against the concept.

3. Look around your classroom, dormitory, or student organization. In what ways does it reflect cultural diversity? Suggest ways by which the resources represented in that diversity could be used to greater advantage for the benefit of all participants.

4. A management specialist recently commented about the work ethic, saying, "You can discover if you personally have a work ethic if you think more about the

salary you make than about the quality of the product you make (or the service you provide)." Comment.

5. What does social responsibility mean to you? Does it apply to people as well as institutions? Describe three acts of social responsibility that you have seen, or performed, in the last month.

6. Describe a situation in which you have experienced role conflict or role ambiguity. What caused it? How are the two ideas related, and how are they different?

7. Interview a manager to discover what that person believes to be the five most important status symbols in the work situation. Identify whether the importance of status symbols is increasing or decreasing there.

8. Describe the organizational culture that seems to exist in your class. What are some of the implicit or explicit norms, values, and assumptions?

9. Reflect back on your first few days in college, or in a part-time or summer job. In what ways were you socialized? How did you feel about what was happening to you?

10. Now look at the reciprocal process of individualization. In what ways did you make an impact on the college, or on the job?

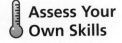

Assess Your Own Skills

How well do you exhibit good mentoring skills?

Read the following statements carefully. Circle the number on the response scale that most closely reflects the degree to which each statement accurately describes you when you have played a role to someone else as a mentor. Add up your total points and prepare a brief action plan for self-improvement. Be ready to report your score for tabulation across the entire group.

	Good description									Poor description
1. I make myself available for contact whenever my protégé needs me.	10	9	8	7	6	5	4	3	2	1
2. I give constructive feedback whenever it is appropriate.	10	9	8	7	6	5	4	3	2	1
3. I share tales of my own successes and failures when I think examples are needed.	10	9	8	7	6	5	4	3	2	1
4. I provide emotional support when I sense the timing is right.	10	9	8	7	6	5	4	3	2	1
5. I follow through on any commitments I make, to establish an image of integrity.	10	9	8	7	6	5	4	3	2	1
6. I view all information gained as personal and confidential, disclosing it to no one.	10	9	8	7	6	5	4	3	2	1
7. I work hard to remain open to the needs and objectives of my protégé.	10	9	8	7	6	5	4	3	2	1
8. I make sure that I listen attentively to both the words and feelings of my protégé.	10	9	8	7	6	5	4	3	2	1
9. I try to be available for immediate contact whenever my protégé needs me.	10	9	8	7	6	5	4	3	2	1
10. I recognize the need to provide support and encouragement to my protégé.	10	9	8	7	6	5	4	3	2	1

Scoring and Interpretation   Add up your total points for the ten questions. Record that number here, and report it when it is requested. ____

- If you scored between 81–100 points, you appear to have a solid capability for demonstrating good mentoring skills.
- If you scored between 61–80 points, you should take a close look at the items with lower self-assessment scores and explore ways to improve those items.
- If you scored less than 60 points, you should be aware that a weaker skill level regarding several items could be detrimental to your future success as a mentor. We encourage you to review relevant sections of the chapter and watch for related material in subsequent chapters and other sources.

Now identify your three lowest scores, and write the question numbers here: ____, ____, ____. Write a brief paragraph, detailing to yourself an action plan for how you might sharpen each of these skills.

Liberty Construction Company

Incident

Liberty Construction Company is a small company in Colorado. Over half its revenue is derived from the installation of underground water and power lines, so much of its work is seasonal and there is high turnover among its employees.

Michael Federico, a college student, had been employed by Liberty as a backhoe operator for the last three summers. On his return to work for the fourth summer, Federico was assigned the second newest of the company's five backhoes. The owner reasoned that Federico had nine months of work seniority, so according to strict seniority, he should have the second backhoe. This action required the present operator of the backhoe, Pedro Alvarez, a regular employee who had been with the company seven months, to be reassigned to an older machine. Alvarez was strongly dissatisfied with this; he felt that as a regular employee he should have retained the newer machine instead of having to give it to a temporary employee. The other employees soon fell into two camps, one supporting Alvarez and one supporting Federico. Job conflicts arose, and each group seemed to delight in causing work problems for the other group. In less than a month Alvarez left the company.

Question

Discuss this case in terms of the social system, equilibrium, the psychological contract, role, status, and status symbols.

Role Perceptions of Students and Instructors

Experiential Exercise

Consider yourself as the subordinate in this class, with the instructor as your manager.

1. (Work individually). In the student-instructor relationship in this class, identify:
   a. Your perception of your student roles
   b. Your perception of the instructor's roles
   c. Your perception of the instructor's perception of your roles as a student
   (At the same time, the instructor should be identifying his or her perception of the instructor's roles, the instructor's perception of the students' roles, and the instructor's perception of the students' perceptions of his or her roles.)
2. Meeting in small groups of students, combine your ideas into collective statements of perceptions.
3. Report your group's perceptions to the class on all three factors. Request that the instructor share his or her perceptions with the class.

Part Two

Motivation and Reward Systems

Chapter 5

Motivation

As simple as they may seem, praise and thanks still are the most neglected social gestures in the workplace.

–Brenda Paik Sunoo[1]

Expectancy theory is practical, is simple, is mainstream psychology, has been around a long time, is easy to apply, and—most important, it works.

–Thomas L. Quick[2]

CHAPTER OBJECTIVES

TO UNDERSTAND

- The Motivational Process
- Motivational Drives
- Need Category Systems
- Behavior Modification and Reinforcement
- Goal Setting and Its Effects
- The Expectancy Model of Motivation
- Equity Comparisons

Hyatt Hotels Corporation had a problem. It hired bright, energetic young people to help run its Hyatt Regency hotels. They worked for a few years as switchboard operators, as assistant housekeeping managers, or in other positions while learning hotel operations. Then they would desire faster promotions into management positions and, seeing the long road ahead, search for a new employer.

Part of the problem lay in the slow expansion of the company, which often slowed individual progression rates into management from the previous time span of three years to eight years or more. To prevent high turnover and capitalize on existing talent, Hyatt started giving its employees opportunities to create new ventures in related fields, such as party catering and rental shops. The motivational impact of the autonomy provided by these entrepreneurial ventures enabled Hyatt to retain over 60 percent of its managers, while increasing its revenues and providing valuable experience to its workforce.[3]

The Hyatt situation provides an opportunity for us to look both backward (at Part One) and forward (to this chapter and the next). Certainly the new program in the hotels created a different organizational culture there; the executives in charge showed how supportive they were by searching for ways to retain valuable human resources; and they began to listen carefully to what employees were telling them to discover how to respond. Motivation, then, takes place within a culture, reflects an organizational behavior model, and requires communication skills.

Motivation also requires discovering and understanding employee drives and needs, since it originates within an individual. Positive acts performed for the organization—such as creating customer satisfaction through personalized service—need to be reinforced. And employees will be more motivated when they have clear goals to achieve. Needs, reinforcement, goals, expectancies, and feelings of equity are the main thrusts of this chapter.

A MODEL OF MOTIVATION

Although a few human activities occur without motivation, nearly all conscious behavior is motivated, or caused. It requires no motivation to grow hair, but getting a haircut does. Eventually, anyone will fall asleep without motivation (although parents with young children may doubt this), but going to bed is a conscious act requiring motivation. A manager's job is to identify employees' drives and needs and to channel their behavior, to motivate them, toward task performance.

The role of motivation in performance is summarized in the model of motivation in Figure 5–1. Internal needs and drives create tensions that are affected by one's environment. For example, the need for food produces a tension of hunger. The hungry person then examines the surroundings to see which foods (external incentives) are available to satisfy that hunger. Since environment affects one's appetite for particular kinds of food, a South Seas native may want roast fish, whereas a Colorado rancher may prefer broiled steak. Both persons are ready to achieve their goals, but they will seek different foods to satisfy their needs. This is an example of both individual differences and cultural influences in action.

As we saw in the formulas in Chapter 1, potential performance (P) is a product of ability (A) and motivation (M). Results occur when motivated employees are provided with the opportunity (such as the proper training) to perform and the resources (such as the proper tools) to do so. The presence of goals and the awareness of

$P = A \times M$

FIGURE 5–1

A model of motivation

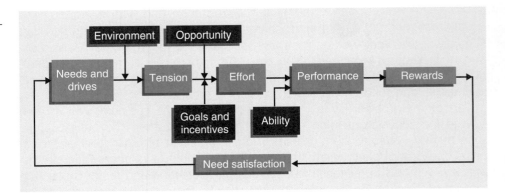

incentives to satisfy one's needs are also powerful motivational factors leading to the release of effort. When an employee is productive and the organization takes note of it, rewards will be distributed. If those rewards are appropriate in nature, timing, and distribution, the employee's original needs and drives are satisfied. At that time, new needs may emerge and the cycle will begin again.

It should be apparent, therefore, that an important starting point lies in *understanding employee needs*. Several traditional approaches to classifying drives and needs are presented first; these models attempt to help managers understand how employees' internal needs affect their subsequent behaviors. These historical approaches are logically followed by a discussion of a systematic way of modifying employee behavior through the use of rewards that satisfy those needs.

MOTIVATIONAL DRIVES

People tend to develop certain motivational **drives** as a product of the cultural environment in which they live, and these drives affect the way people view their jobs and approach their lives. Much of the interest in these patterns of motivation was generated by the research of David C. McClelland of Harvard University.[4] He developed a classification scheme highlighting three of the more dominant drives and pointed out their significance to motivation. His studies revealed that people's motivational drives reflect elements of the culture in which they grow up—their family, school, church, and books. In most nations, one or two of the motivational patterns tend to be strong among the workers because they have grown up with similar backgrounds. McClelland's research focused on the drives for achievement, affiliation, and power (see Figure 5–2).

Three drives

Achievement Motivation

Achievement motivation is a drive some people have to pursue and attain goals. An individual with this drive wishes to achieve objectives and advance up the ladder of success. Accomplishment is seen as important primarily for its own sake, not just for the rewards that accompany it.

Characteristics of achievers

A number of characteristics define achievement-oriented employees. They work harder when they perceive that they will receive personal credit for their efforts, when there is only moderate risk of failure, and when they receive specific feedback about their past performance. People with a high drive for achievement take responsibility for their actions and results, control their destiny, seek regular feedback, and enjoy being part of a winning achievement through individual or collective effort. As man-

FIGURE 5–2

Motivational drives

105

Achievement	A drive to accomplish objectives and get ahead
Affiliation	A drive to relate to people effectively
Power	A drive to influence people and situations

agers, they tend to expect that their employees will also be oriented toward achievement. These high expectations sometimes make it difficult for achievement-oriented managers to delegate effectively and for "average" employees to satisfy their manager's demands.

Affiliation Motivation

Affiliation motivation is a drive to relate to people on a social basis. Comparisons of achievement-motivated employees with affiliation-motivation employees illustrate how the two patterns influence behavior. Achievement-oriented people work harder when their supervisors provide detailed evaluations of their work behavior. But people with affiliation motives work better when they are complimented for their favorable attitudes and cooperation. Achievement-motivated people select assistants who are technically capable, with little regard for personal feelings about them; those who are affiliation-motivated tend to select friends to surround them. They receive inner satisfactions from being with friends, and they want the job freedom to develop those relationships.

Comparing achievement and affiliation drives

Managers with strong needs for affiliation may have difficulty being effective managers. Although a high concern for positive social relationships usually results in a cooperative work environment where employees genuinely enjoy working together, managerial overemphasis on the social dimension may interfere with the usual process of getting things done. Affiliation-oriented managers may have difficulty assigning challenging tasks, directing work activities, and monitoring work effectiveness.

Power Motivation

Power motivation is a drive to influence people and change situations. Power-motivated people wish to create an impact on their organizations and are willing to take risks to do so. Once this power is obtained, it may be used either constructively or destructively.

Power-motivated people make excellent managers if their drives are for institutional power instead of personal power. *Institutional power* is the need to influence others' behavior for the good of the whole organization. People with this need seek power through legitimate means, rise to leadership positions through successful performance, and therefore are accepted by others. However, if an employee's drives are toward personal power, that person tends to be an unsuccessful organizational leader.

Institutional versus personal power

Managerial Application of the Drives

Knowledge of the differences among the three motivational drives requires managers to understand the work attitudes of each employee. They can then deal with employees differently according to the strongest motivational drive that they identify in each employee. In this way, the supervisor communicates with each employee according to that particular person's needs. As one employee said, "My supervisor talks to me in my language." Although various tests can be used to identify the strength of employee drives, direct observation of employees' behavior is one of the best methods for determining what they will respond to.

HUMAN NEEDS

When a machine malfunctions, people recognize that it needs something. Managers try to find the causes of the breakdown in an analytical manner based on their knowledge of the operations and needs of the machine. Like the machine, an operator who malfunctions does so because of definite causes that may be related to needs. In order for improvement to occur, the operator requires skilled and professional care just as the machine does. If we treated (maintained) people as well as we do expensive machines, we would have more productive, and hence more satisfied, workers. First we must identify the needs that are important to them.

Types of Needs

Primary needs

There are various ways to classify needs. A simple one is (1) basic physical needs, called **primary needs,** and (2) social and psychological needs, called **secondary needs.** The physical needs include food, water, sex, sleep, air, and reasonably comfortable temperature. These needs arise from the basic requirements of life and are important for survival of the human race. They are, therefore, virtually universal, but they vary in intensity from one person to another. For example, a child needs much more sleep than an older person.

Needs also are conditioned by social practice. If it is customary to eat three meals a day, then a person tends to become hungry for three, even though two might be adequate. If a coffee hour is introduced in the morning, then that becomes a habit of appetite satisfaction as well as a social need.

Secondary needs

Secondary needs are more vague because they represent needs of the mind and spirit rather than of the physical body. Many of these needs are developed as people mature. Examples are needs that pertain to self-esteem, sense of duty, competitiveness, self-assertion, and to giving, belonging, and receiving affection. The secondary needs are the ones that complicate the motivational efforts of managers. Nearly any action that management takes will affect secondary needs; *therefore, managerial planning should consider the effect of any proposed action on the secondary needs of employees.*

Here are seven key conclusions about secondary needs. They:

- Are strongly conditioned by experience
- Vary in type and intensity among people
- Are subject to change across time within any individual
- Cannot usually be isolated, but rather, work in combination and influence one another
- Are often hidden from conscious recognition
- Are vague feelings as opposed to specific physical needs
- Influence behavior

Whereas the three motivational drives identified earlier were not grouped in any particular pattern, the three major theories of human needs presented in the following sections attempt to classify those needs. At least implicitly, the theories of Maslow,

Herzberg, and Alderfer each build on the distinction between primary and secondary needs. Also, there are some similarities as well as important differences among the three approaches. Despite their limitations, all three approaches to human needs help create an important basis for the more advanced motivational models to be discussed later.

Maslow's Hierarchy of Needs

According to A. H. Maslow, human needs are not of equal strength, and they emerge in a definite sequence. In particular, as the primary needs become reasonably well satisfied, a person places more emphasis on the secondary needs. Maslow's **hierarchy of needs** focuses attention on five levels, as shown in Figure 5–3.[5] This hierarchy is briefly presented and then interpreted in the following sections.

Lower-Order Needs   First-level needs involve basic survival and include physiological needs for food, air, water, and sleep. The second need level that tends to dominate is bodily safety (such as freedom from a dangerous work environment) and economic security (such as a no-layoff guarantee or a comfortable retirement plan). These two need levels together are typically called **lower-order needs,** and they are similar to the primary needs discussed earlier.

FIGURE 5–3

A comparison of Maslow's, Herzberg's, and Alderfer's models

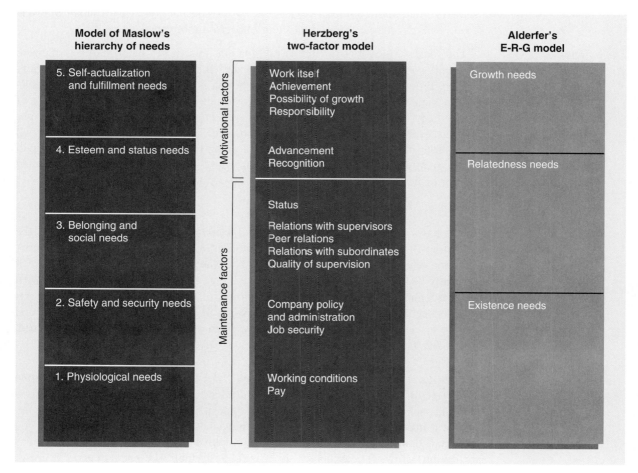

Higher-Order Needs   There are three levels of **higher-order needs.** The third level in the hierarchy concerns love, belonging, and social involvement at work (friendships and compatible associates). The needs at the fourth level include those for esteem and status, including one's feelings of self-worth and of competence. The feeling of competence, which derives from the assurance of others, provides status. The fifth-level need is **self-actualization,** which means becoming all that one is capable of becoming, using one's skills to the fullest, and stretching talents to the maximum.

Interpreting the Hierarchy of Needs   Maslow's need-hierarchy model essentially says that people have needs they wish to satisfy and that gratified needs are not as strongly motivating as unmet needs. *Employees are more enthusiastically motivated by what they are currently seeking than by receiving more of what they already have.* A fully satisfied need will not be a strong motivator.

Interpreted in this way, the Maslow hierarchy of needs has had a powerful impact on contemporary managers, offering some useful ideas for helping managers think about motivating their employees. As a result of widespread familiarity with the model, today's managers need to

- Identify and accept employee needs
- Recognize that needs may differ among employees
- Offer satisfaction for the particular needs currently unmet
- Realize that giving more of the same reward (especially one which satisfies lower-order needs) may have a diminishing impact on motivation

Limitations   The Maslow model also has many limitations, and it has been sharply criticized. As a philosophical framework, it has been difficult to study and has not been fully verified. From a practical perspective, it is not easy to provide opportunities for self-actualization to all employees. In addition, research has not supported the presence of all five need levels as unique, nor has the five-step progression from lowest to highest need levels been established. There is, however, some evidence that unless the two lower-order needs (physiological and security) are basically satisfied, employees will not be greatly concerned with higher-order needs.[6] The evidence for a more limited number of need levels is consistent with each of the two models discussed next.

Herzberg's Two-Factor Model

On the basis of research with engineers and accountants, Frederick Herzberg, in the 1950s, developed a **two-factor model of motivation.**[7] He asked his subjects to think of a time when they felt especially good about their jobs and a time when they felt especially bad about their jobs. He also asked them to describe the conditions that led to those feelings. Herzberg found that employees named different types of conditions that produced good and bad feelings. That is, if a feeling of achievement led to a good feeling, the lack of achievement was rarely given as cause for bad feelings. Instead, some other factor, such as company policy, was given as a cause of bad feelings.

Maintenance and Motivational Factors   Herzberg concluded that two separate sets of factors influenced motivation. Prior to that time, people assumed that motivation and lack of motivation were merely opposites of one factor on a continuum. Herzberg upset the traditional view by stating that certain job factors, such as job security and working conditions, dissatisfy employees primarily when the conditions are absent. However, as shown in Figure 5–4, their presence generally brings

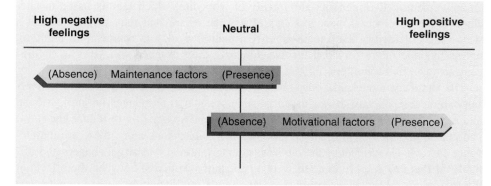

FIGURE 5–4

Effects of maintenance and motivational factors

109

employees only to a neutral state. The factors are not strongly motivating. These potent dissatisfiers are called **hygiene factors,** or *maintenance factors,* because they must not be ignored. They are necessary for building a foundation on which to maintain a reasonable level of motivation in employees.

Hygiene factors

Other job conditions operate primarily to build this motivation, but their absence rarely is strongly dissatisfying. These conditions are known as **motivational factors,** *motivators,* or *satisfiers.* For many years managers had been wondering why their custodial policies and wide array of fringe benefits were not increasing employee motivation. The idea of separate motivational and maintenance factors helped answer their question, because fringe benefits and personnel policies were primarily maintenance factors, according to Herzberg.

Motivational factors

Job Content and Context   Figure 5–3 shows the Herzberg factors. Motivational factors such as achievement and responsibility are related, for the most part, directly to the job itself, the employee's performance, and the personal recognition and growth that employees experience. Motivators mostly are job-centered; they relate to **job content.**

On the other hand, maintenance factors are mainly related to **job context,** because they are more related to the environment surrounding the job. This difference between job content and job context is a significant one. It shows that employees are motivated primarily by what they do for themselves. When they take responsibility or gain recognition through their own behavior, they are strongly motivated.

Intrinsic and Extrinsic Motivators   The difference between job content and job context is similar to the difference between intrinsic and extrinsic motivators in psychology. **Intrinsic motivators** are internal rewards that a person feels when performing a job, so there is a direct and often immediate connection between work and rewards. An employee in this situation is self-motivated. **Extrinsic motivators** are external rewards that occur apart from the nature of work, providing no direct satisfaction at the time the work is performed. Examples are retirement plans, health insurance, and vacations. Although employees value these items, they are not effective motivators.

Intrinsic and extrinsic motivators

Interpreting the Two-Factor Model   Herzberg's model provides a useful distinction between maintenance factors, which are necessary but not sufficient, and motivational factors, which have the potential for improving employee effort. The two-factor model broadened managers' perspectives by showing the potentially powerful role of intrinsic rewards that evolve from the work itself. (This conclusion ties in with a number of other important behavioral developments, such as job enrichment,

110

empowerment, self-leadership, and quality of work life, which are discussed in later chapters.) Nevertheless, managers should now be aware that they cannot neglect a wide range of factors that create at least a neutral work environment. In addition, unless hygiene factors are reasonably addressed, their absence will serve as significant distractions to workers.

The Herzberg model, like Maslow's, has been widely criticized.[8] It is not universally applicable, because it was based on and applies best to managerial, professional, and upper-level white-collar employees. The model also *appears* to reduce the motivational importance of pay, status, and relations with others, since these are maintenance factors. This aspect of the model is counterintuitive to many managers and difficult for them to accept. Since there is no absolute distinction between the effects of the two major factors (see Figure 5–4), the model outlines only general tendencies; maintenance factors may be motivators to some people, and motivators may be maintenance factors to others. Finally, the model also seems to be method-bound, meaning that only Herzberg's approach (asking for self-reports of favorable and unfavorable job experiences) produces the two-factor model. In short, there may be an appearance of two factors when in reality there is only one factor.

Alderfer's E-R-G Model

Building upon earlier need models (primarily Maslow's) and seeking to overcome some of their weaknesses, Clayton Alderfer proposed a modified need hierarchy—the E-R-G model—with just three levels (see Figure 5–3).[9] He suggested that employees are initially interested in satisfying their **existence needs,** which combine physiological and security factors. Pay, physical working conditions, job security, and fringe benefits can all address these needs. **Relatedness needs** are at the next level, and these involve being understood and accepted by people above, below, and around the employee at work and away from it. **Growth needs** are in the third category; these involve the desire for both self-esteem and self-actualization.

Existence

Relatedness

Growth

> The president of a chain of clothing stores thought things were going well. The company was about to add ten new stores to its ninety outlets as part of an ambitious corporate expansion program. One day the president's key marketing manager walked into the office and announced that he hated his job. "What could he possibly want?" the president thought, as she invited him to sit down and talk about his needs and aspirations. "It shouldn't be job security, or better working conditions. Perhaps he feels the need to learn new skills and develop executive capabilities."

The impending conversation between the president and the marketing manager could be structured around Alderfer's **E-R-G model.** The president may first wish to identify which level or levels seem to be satisfied. For example, a large disparity between their salaries could lead the marketing manager to be frustrated with his existence needs, despite a respectable salary-and-bonus package. Or his immersion in his work through long hours and heavy travel as the stores prepared to open could have left his relatedness needs unsatisfied. Finally, assuming he has mastered his present job assignments, he may be experiencing the need to develop his nonmarketing capabilities and grow into new areas.

In addition to condensing Maslow's five need levels into three that are more consistent with research, the E-R-G model differs in other ways. For example, the E-R-G model does not assume as rigorous a progression from level to level. Instead, it accepts the likelihood that all three levels might be active at any time— or even that just one of the higher levels might be active. It also suggests that a person frustrated at either of the two higher levels may return to concentrate on a lower level and then progress again. Finally, whereas the first two levels are somewhat limited in their requirements for satisfaction, the growth needs not only are unlimited but are actually further awakened each time some satisfaction is attained.

Comparison of the Maslow, Herzberg, and Alderfer Models

The similarities among the three models of human needs are quite apparent, as shown in Figure 5–3, but there are important contrasts, too. Maslow and Alderfer focus on the internal needs of the employee, whereas Herzberg also identifies and differentiates the conditions (job content or job context) that could be provided for need satisfaction. Popular interpretations of the Maslow and Herzberg models suggest that in modern societies many workers have already satisfied their lower-order needs, so they are now motivated mainly by higher-order needs and motivators. Alderfer suggests that the failure to satisfy relatedness or growth needs will cause renewed interest in existence needs. (The consequences of unsatisfied needs, whether they produce frustration or constructive coping, are discussed in Chapter 15.) Finally, all three models indicate that before a manager tries to administer a reward, he or she would find it useful to discover which need or needs dominate a particular employee at the time. In this way, all need models provide a foundation for the understanding and application of behavior modification.

BEHAVIOR MODIFICATION

The models of motivation that have been discussed up to this point are known as *content theories of motivation* because they focus on the content (nature) of items that may motivate a person. They relate to the person's inner self and how that person's internal state of needs determines behavior.   *Content theories*

   The major difficulty with content models of motivation is that the needs people have are not subject to observation by managers or to precise measurement for monitoring purposes. It is difficult, for example, to measure an employee's esteem needs or to assess how they change over time. Further, simply knowing about an employee's needs does not directly suggest to managers what they should do with that information. As a result, there has been considerable interest in motivational models that rely more heavily on intended results, careful measurement, and systematic application of incentives. **Organizational behavior modification,** or **OB Mod,** is the application in   *OB Mod* organizations of the principles of behavior modification, which evolved from the work of B. F. Skinner.[10] OB Mod and the next several models are *process theories* of moti-   *Process theories* vation, since they provide perspectives on the dynamics by which employees can be motivated.

Law of Effect

OB Mod is based on the idea that *behavior depends on its consequences;* therefore, it is possible for managers to control, or at least affect, a number of employee behaviors by manipulating their consequences. OB Mod relies heavily on the **law of effect,** which states that a person tends to repeat behavior that is accompanied by favorable consequences (reinforcement) and tends not to repeat behavior that is accompanied by unfavorable consequences. Two conditions are required for successful application of OB Mod—the manager must be able to *identify* some powerful consequences (as perceived by the employee) and then must be able to *administer* them in such a way that the employee will see the connection between the behavior to be affected and the consequences.

Some professional sports have developed reward systems that appear to build on these principles. For example, on the Ladies Professional Golf Association (LPGA) tour, only those players who complete all four rounds of a tournament and have the better total scores collect checks when they are done. Furthermore, the winner's check is nearly double what the second-place finisher receives. The LPGA has identified money as a favorable consequence and tied its distribution directly to the level of short-term performance by its members. This system presumably encourages the players to participate in numerous tournaments, play all four rounds, and excel.

Focus on consequences

The law of effect comes from learning theory, which suggests that we learn best under pleasant surroundings. Whereas content theories argue that *internal needs lead to behavior,* OB Mod states that *external consequences tend to determine behavior.* The advantage of OB Mod is that it places a greater degree of control, and responsibility, in the hands of the manager. Several firms, including Frito-Lay, Weyerhaeuser, and B. F. Goodrich, have used various forms of behavior modification successfully.

Alternative Consequences

OB Mod places great emphasis on the use of rewards (see the model of motivation in Figure 5–1) and alternative consequences to sustain behavior. Before using OB Mod, however, managers must decide whether they wish to increase the probability of a person's continued behavior or to decrease it. Once they have decided on their objective, they have two further choices to make which determine the type of consequence to be applied. First, should they use a positive or a negative consequence? Second, should they apply it or withhold it? The answers to those two questions result in four unique alternative consequences, as shown in Figure 5–5 and in the discussion that follows.

FIGURE 5–5

OB Mod uses four alternative consequences

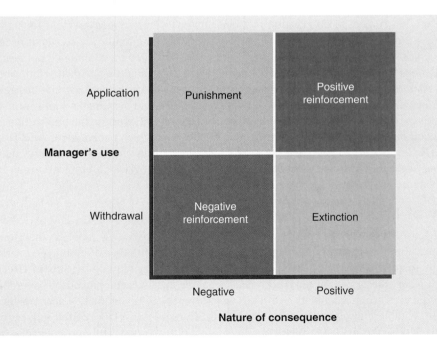

Behavior is encouraged primarily through positive reinforcement. **Positive reinforcement** provides a favorable consequence that encourages repetition of a behavior. An employee, for example, may find that when high-quality work is done, the supervisor gives a reward of recognition. Since the employee likes recognition, behavior is reinforced, and the employee tends to want to do high-quality work again. The reinforcement always should be contingent on the employee's correct behavior.

Positive reinforcement

The variety of rewards available to managers is almost limitless, not always expensive, and often touching to the recipients. Here are a few examples:

- Blandin Paper Company emphasizes recognition from supervisors plus rewards such as T-shirts, coffee mugs, and gift certificates to be used at local restaurants.
- Pfeiffer-Hamilton Publishers invites all employees to a "celebration of creativity" party each year and also gives each employee a free autographed copy of every book the company publishes.
- Grandma's Restaurant chain not only gives ten-year employees a gold watch but also creates placemats for its tables with the employee's picture and background information on them.
- Other companies advocate the use of personal notes praising an employee's performance, provide workers with a free lunch on their birthdays, or place the signatures of employees inside the products they produce. The key is to make the rewards as personal and spontaneous as possible.[11]

Shaping is a systematic and progressive application of positive reinforcement. It occurs when more frequent, or more powerful, reinforcements are successively given as the employee comes closer to the desired behavior. Even though the completely correct behavior does not yet occur, it is encouraged by giving reinforcement for behavior in the desired direction. Shaping is especially useful for teaching complex tasks.

Shaping

An illustration of shaping is the training procedure used by a supervisor in a retail store. The store was so small that it had no centralized training program for sales clerks, so all sales training was a responsibility of the supervisor. In the beginning, when a new salesclerk did not know how to deal with customers effectively, the supervisor explained the proper sales procedure. The supervisor observed the clerk's behavior, and from time to time when the clerk showed improved behavior in some part of the procedure, the supervisor expressed approval and encouraged the employee. Since this was favorable recognition for the employee, it helped shape behavior in the correct direction.

Negative reinforcement occurs when behavior is accompanied by *removal* of an unfavorable consequence; therefore, it is not the same as punishment, which normally *adds* something unfavorable. Consistent with the law of effect, behavior responsible for the removal of something unfavorable is repeated when that unfavorable state is again encountered. An example of negative reinforcement is the experience of a jet aircraft mechanic who learned that if she wore noise suppressors over her ears, she could prevent discomfort from the jet engine noise—the unfavorable consequence; this reinforcement encouraged her to wear the proper noise equipment.

Negative reinforcement

Punishment is the administration of an unfavorable consequence that discourages a certain behavior. Although punishment may be necessary occasionally to discourage an undesirable behavior, it needs to be used with caution because it has certain limitations. It does not directly encourage any kind of desirable behavior unless the person receiving it is clearly aware of the alternative path to follow; it may cause managers acting as punishers to become disliked for their disciplinary actions; and it could happen that people who are punished may be unclear about what specific part of their behavior is being punished.

Punishment

Extinction

Extinction is the withholding of significant positive consequences that were previously provided for a desirable behavior. Such desirable learned behavior needs to be reinforced to encourage the person to repeat the action in the future. If no reinforcement by the manager, the employee, or anyone else occurs, the behavior tends to diminish (become extinguished) through lack of reinforcement.

Schedules of Reinforcement

Baseline

Before various types of consequences can be applied, managers should monitor employee behavior to learn how often, or how well, employees are performing. The frequency of the behavior creates a *baseline,* or standard, against which improvements can be compared. Then the manager can select a reinforcement schedule, which is the frequency with which the chosen consequence accompanies a desired behavior.

Continuous reinforcement

Reinforcement may be either continuous or partial. **Continuous reinforcement** occurs when a reinforcer accompanies each correct behavior by an employee. In some instances, this level of reinforcement may be desirable to encourage quick learning, but in the typical work situation it usually is not possible to reward even one employee for every correct behavior—much less several employees. An example of continuous reinforcement is payment of employees for each acceptable item that they produce.

Partial reinforcement

Partial reinforcement occurs when only some of the correct behaviors are reinforced. Learning is slower with partial reinforcement than with continuous reinforcement. However, a unique feature of partial reinforcement is that learning tends to be retained longer when it is secured under conditions of partial reinforcement. There are four types of partial reinforcement schedules—fixed-interval, variable-interval, fixed-ratio, and variable-ratio schedules—which offer a variety of reinforcement approaches.

Reinforcement schedules

A **fixed-interval** schedule provides a reinforcement after a certain period of time. A typical example is a paycheck that arrives every two weeks. **Variable-interval** schedules give reinforcement after a variety of time periods. Usually the variations are grouped around some target, or average, period of reinforcement. **Fixed-ratio** schedules occur when there is reinforcement after a certain number of correct responses. An example is payment of sales bonuses after a certain number of large items (such as automobiles) is sold. **A variable-ratio** schedule is a reinforcement after a variable, but undisclosed, number of correct responses, such as reinforcement after nineteen, then fifteen, then twelve, then twenty-four, and then seventeen responses. This type of reinforcement schedule provokes much interest and is preferred by employees for some tasks. It tends to be the most powerful of all the reinforcement schedules.

Interpreting Behavior Modification

Contributions

The major benefit of behavior modification is that it makes managers become conscious motivators. It encourages managers to analyze employee behavior, explore why it occurs and how often, and identify specific consequences that will help change it when those consequences are applied systematically. Application of this process often encourages effective supervisors to devote more time to monitoring employee behaviors. Performance feedback and recognition are often parts of this strategy because they tend to be widely desired and therefore are strong reinforcements. General guidelines for a behavior modification strategy are shown in Figure 5–6. When

FIGURE 5–6

General guidelines for
applying behavior
modification

115

- Identify the exact behavior to be modified.

- Make sure the expected behavior is within the employee's capabilities.

- Determine not only the rewards that employees value but also the magnitude that would affect their behavior.

- Clarify the connection between desired behavior and rewards.

- Use positive reinforcement whenever possible.

- Use punishment only in unusual circumstances and for specific behaviors.

- Ignore minor undesirable behavior to allow its extinction.

- Use shaping procedures to develop correct complex behavior.

- Minimize the time between the correct response and reinforcement.

- Provide reinforcement frequently, and on some chosen schedule.

specific behaviors can be identified and desired reinforcements are properly applied, behavior modification can lead to substantial improvements in specific areas, such as absences, tardiness, and error rates.

> Collins Food International used behavior modification with clerical employees in its accounting department.[12] One of the items selected for modification was billing error rates. Management measured existing error rates and then met with employees to discuss and set goals for improvement. It also praised employees for reduction of errors, and it reported error results to them regularly. Employees in the accounts payable department responded by reducing error rates from more than 8 percent to less than 0.2 percent.

Behavior modification has been criticized on several grounds, including its philosophy, methods, and practicality (see "What Managers Are Reading"). Because of the strong power of desired consequences, behavior modification may effectively force people to change their behavior. In this way it manipulates people and is inconsistent with humanistic assumptions discussed earlier that people want to be autonomous and self-actualizing. Some critics also fear that behavior modification gives too much power to the managers, and they raise the question, Who will control the controllers?

Limitations

Other critics say that behavior modification insults people's intelligence. At the extreme, people could be treated like rats in a training box when in fact they are intelligent, thinking, self-controlled individuals who are capable of making their own choices and perhaps motivating themselves. Another problem is that behavior modification has limited applicability to complex jobs. For example, it is difficult to identify specific behaviors in the jobs of corporate lawyers, software developers, or chief executive officers and reinforce them. This challenge has become increasingly difficult as the U.S. economy becomes more and more service-based.

GOAL SETTING

Goals are targets and objectives for future performance. They help focus employees' attention on items of greater importance to the organization, encourage better planning for the allocation of critical resources (time, money, and energy), and stimulate

Alfie Kohn argues that corporate incentive plans not only fail to work as intended but also undermine the objectives they intended to achieve. This result is due, he suggests, to inadequate psychological assumptions on which reward systems are based. Explaining his position in *Punished by Rewards,* Kohn argues:

- Rewards punish people—their use confirms that someone else is in control of the employee; additionally, some people do not get the rewards they were hoping for.
- Rewards rupture relationships—they magnify the effects of power differences, and they create competition where teamwork and collaboration are desired.
- Rewards ignore reasons—they relieve managers from the urgent need to explore *why* an employee is effective or ineffective.

- Rewards discourage risk taking—employees tend to do exactly what is required to earn the reward, and not much more.
- Rewards undermine interest—they distract both manager and employee from consideration of intrinsic motivation.

Kohn is often asked, "But don't rewards work?" "Absolutely," he replies. "They motivate people to *get* rewards" but not to do anything more than the minimum.

Source: Alfie Kohn, *Punished by Rewards: The Trouble with Gold Stars, Incentive Plans, A's, Praise, and Other Bribes,* Boston: Houghton-Mifflin, 1993.

the preparation of action plans for goal attainment. Goals appear in our model of motivation (see Figure 5–1) *before* employee performance, which accents their role as a cue to acceptable behavior. Goals are also useful *after* the desired behavior, as managers compare employee results with their aims and explore reasons for any differences.

Goal setting works as a motivational process because it creates a discrepancy between current and expected performance. This results in a feeling of tension, which the employee can diminish through future goal attainment. Meeting goals also helps satisfy a person's achievement drive, contributes to feelings of competence and self-esteem, and further stimulates personal growth needs. Individuals who successfully achieve goals tend to set even higher goals in the future.

A major factor in the success of goal setting is **self-efficacy.** This is an internal belief regarding one's job-related capabilities and competencies. (Self-efficacy is different from self-esteem, which is a broader feeling of like or dislike for oneself.)[13] Self-efficacy can be judged either on a specific task or across a variety of performance duties. If employees have high self-efficacies, they will tend to set higher personal goals under the belief that they are attainable. The first key to successful goal setting is to build and reinforce employee self-efficacy (see the practical tips in Figure 5–7). Following this step, managers should try to incorporate the four essential elements of goal setting, which are discussed next.

Elements of Goal Setting

Goal setting, as a motivational tool, is most effective when all its major elements are present. These are goal acceptance, specificity, challenge, and performance monitoring and feedback. Each is discussed briefly in the following sections.

Goal Acceptance Effective goals need to be not only understood but also *accepted.* Simply assigning goals to employees may not result in their commitment to those goals, especially if the goal will be difficult to accomplish. Minimally, supervisors need to explain the purpose behind goals and the necessity for them. A more powerful method of obtaining acceptance is to allow the employees to participate in

FIGURE 5–7

Tips for building
employee self-efficacy

117

1. Don't imply that employees are incompetent.
2. Don't talk down to them about their jobs.
3. Don't find petty faults with their results.
4. Don't criticize their work in front of their peers.
5. Don't belittle the importance of their jobs or tasks.
6. Do praise them for their appropriate efforts.
7. Do ask for their input.
8. Do listen carefully to their ideas for improvements.
9. Do share positive feedback from their peers with them.
10. Do provide formal recognition for their achievements.

the goal-setting process. A public statement of performance intentions also contributes to the commitment of employees to their achievement.

Specificity   Goals need to be as specific, clear, and measurable as possible so that employees will know when a goal is reached. It is not very helpful to ask employees to improve, to work harder, or to do better, because that kind of goal does not give them a focused target to seek. Specific goals let them know what to reach for and allow them to measure their own progress.

Challenge   Perhaps surprisingly, most employees work harder when they have difficult goals to accomplish rather than easy ones. Hard goals present a challenge that appeals to the achievement drive within many employees. These goals must, however, still be achievable, given the experience of the individual and the resources available.

> The motivational value of a challenge was demonstrated by a motel owner in a small city. Richard Fann was concerned about the time required by housekeepers to change the beds when they cleaned a room. The average time used was about seven minutes, including numerous trips around the bed to strip the sheets and replace the covers. Suggestions made to the housekeepers to reduce their wasted motions were only marginally successful in speeding up the process. Finally, Richard decided to stage a contest and pit the housekeepers against one another. Not only did the strategy work, but the results overwhelmed him. The winning employee was able to change a bed in less than one minute and to do this by staying on one side! "Why hadn't they done this earlier?" Richard inquired. "Because you didn't challenge us," they responded.

Performance Monitoring and Feedback   Even after employees have participated in setting well-defined and challenging goals, two other closely related steps are important to complete the process. **Performance monitoring**—observing behavior, inspecting output, or studying documents of performance indicators—provides at least subtle cues to employees that their tasks are important, their effort is needed, and their contributions are valued. This monitoring heightens their awareness of the role they play in contributing to organizational effectiveness.

Simply monitoring results, however, may not be enough. Many employees are hungry for information about how well they are performing. Without **performance feedback**—the timely provision of data or judgment regarding task-related results—employees will be working in the dark and have no true idea how successful they are. A ball team needs to know the score of the game; a trapshooter needs to see the clay

118

pigeons break into pieces; and the woodchopper needs to see the chips fly and the pile of firewood grow. The same can be said for a team on the production line or a retail salesclerk. Performance feedback tends to encourage better job performance, and self-generated feedback is an especially powerful motivational tool.

> Researchers examined the financial performance of 437 companies to explore the effects of setting goals, giving feedback, reviewing results, and rewarding behavior. They discovered that firms with these performance management programs had greater profits, better cash flow, and stronger stock market performance than those that did not have them. Further, in a comparison of the before and after performances of the firms with performance management, the average shareholder return increased by 25 percent and productivity gains averaged 94 percent![14]

THE EXPECTANCY MODEL

V × E × I = M

A widely accepted approach to motivation is the **expectancy model,** also known as *expectancy theory,* that was developed by Victor H. Vroom and has been expanded and refined by Porter and Lawler and others.[15] Vroom explains that motivation is a product of three factors: how much one wants a reward (valence), one's estimate of the probability that effort will result in successful performance (expectancy), and one's estimate that performance will result in receiving the reward (instrumentality). This relationship is stated in the following formula:

$$\text{Valence} \times \text{Expectancy} \times \text{Instrumentality} = \text{Motivation}$$

The Three Factors

Reward preference

Valence **Valence** refers to the strength of a person's preference for receiving a reward. It is an expression of the amount of one's desire to reach a goal. For example, if an employee strongly wants a promotion, then promotion has high valence for that employee. Valence for a reward is unique to each employee and thus is a reflection of the concept of individual differences introduced in Chapter 1. An individual's valence for a reward is conditioned by experience, and it may vary substantially over a period of time as old needs become satisfied and new ones emerge.

It is important to understand the difference between the implications of need-based models of motivation and the idea of valence in the expectancy model. In the need-based models, broad generalizations are used to predict where a *group of employees* may have the strongest drives or the greatest unsatisfied needs. In the expectancy model, managers need to gather specific information about *an individual employee's* preferences among a set of rewards and then continue to monitor changes in those preferences.

Can valence be negative?

Since people may have positive or negative preferences for an outcome, valence may be negative as well as positive. When a person prefers *not* attaining an outcome, as compared with attaining it, valence is a negative figure. If a person is indifferent to an outcome, the valence is 0. The total range is from −1 to +1, as shown in Figure 5–8.

Some employees will find intrinsic valence in the work itself, particularly if they have a strong work ethic or competence motivation. They derive satisfaction directly from their work through a sense of completion, of doing a task right, or of creating something. In this instance, outcomes are largely within the employee's own control and less subject to management's reward system. These employees are self-motivated.

Expectancy **Expectancy** is the strength of belief that one's work-related effort will result in completion of a task. For example, a person selling magazine subscriptions door-to-door may know from experience that volume of sales is directly related to the number of sales calls made. Expectancies are stated as probabilities—the employee's estimate of the degree to which performance will be determined by the amount of effort expended. Since expectancy is the probability of a connection between effort and performance, its value may range from 0 to 1. If an employee sees no chance that effort will lead to the desired performance, the expectancy is 0. At the other extreme, if the employee is totally confident that the task will be completed, the expectancy has a value of 1. Normally, employee estimates of expectancy lie somewhere between the two extremes.

Effort → performance probability

One of the forces contributing to effort-performance expectancies is the individual's self-efficacy. Employees with high levels of self-efficacy are more likely to believe that exerting effort will result in satisfactory performance. High self-efficacy creates a high expectancy assessment.

In contrast to high self-efficacy, some employees suffer from the **imposter phenomenon.** Imposters believe that they are not really as capable as they appear to be and, consequently, fear that their incompetence will be revealed to others. They are filled with self-doubt, afraid to take risks, and seldom ask for help. Because they believe they lack the necessary competence, they are also likely to doubt that any amount of their own effort will result in high performance. Imposters, therefore, will predictably have low expectancy assessments for themselves. The self-efficacy and imposter concepts demonstrate the importance of understanding broad characteristics of individual employees as a predictor of their specific motivational drives.

Imposters

Instrumentality **Instrumentality** represents the employee's belief that a reward will be received once the task is accomplished. Here the employee makes another subjective judgment about the probability that the organization *values* the employee's performance and *will administer rewards on a contingent basis.* The value of instrumentality effectively ranges from 0 to 1.[16] For example, if an employee sees that promotions are usually based on performance data, instrumentality will be rated high.

Performance → reward probability

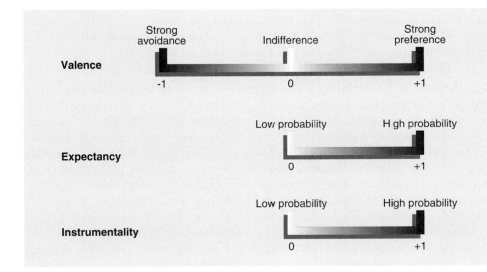

FIGURE 5–8

Range of valence, expectancy, and instrumentality

However, if the basis for such decisions is unclear or managerial favoritism is suspected, a low instrumentality estimate will be made.

120

How the Model Works

The product of valence, expectancy, and instrumentality is **motivation.** It is defined as the strength of the drive toward an action. Below is an example of the expectancy model in operation.

> Marty Fulmer, age thirty-one, works as a welder in a large factory. Fulmer has very strong desires (high valence) to be in white-collar work instead of his present job, which he no longer enjoys.
>
> Fulmer recognizes that good welding will result in high performance appraisals by his supervisor (high expectancy). However, all white-collar jobs in the plant require a college degree, and Fulmer has only a high school diploma. Because of this barrier, Fulmer's instrumentality estimate is low. Being a good welder will not result in promotion to the desired position. Despite his strong desire for something, he sees no viable way to achieve it and, therefore, is not motivated to perform his job better.

The three factors in the expectancy model may exist in an infinite number of combinations. The multiplicative combination that produces the strongest motivation is high positive valence, high expectancy, and high instrumentality. If desire for a reward is high, but either of the probability estimates is low, then motivation will likely be moderate, at best. If both expectancy and instrumentality are low, then motivation will be weak even if the reward has high valence.

A special case occurs when valence is negative. For example, some employees would prefer *not* to be promoted into management because of the stress, loss of overtime pay, or additional responsibilities they would bear. In particular, the widespread corporate downsizings of the past decade clearly targeted middle managers and produced insecurity in those who remained. In situations like these, where promotion has a negative valence, the employee will try to avoid earning the promotion. The strength of avoidance behavior depends not only on the negative valence but on the expectancy and instrumentality factors as well.

Through experience, people learn to place a different value on the rewards available to them and also on the varying levels of rewards offered. They also develop expectancy and instrumentality estimates through both their direct experiences and their observations of what happens to others. As a consequence, employees perform a type of cost-benefit analysis, often implicit, for their own behavior at work. If the estimated benefit is worth the cost, then employees are likely to apply more effort.

The Impact of Uncertainty   The expectancy model depends on the employee's perception of the relationship between effort, performance, and rewards. The connection between effort and ultimate reward is often uncertain. There are so many causes and effects in a situation that rarely can an employee be sure that a desired reward will follow a given action. In addition, there are both primary and secondary outcomes. The **primary outcomes** result directly from an action. Then the **secondary outcomes** follow from the primary ones. For example, an employee secures more training and eventually earns the primary outcome of a promotion and the pay that goes with it. Then secondary outcomes follow. The promotion brings more status and recognition from associates. The higher pay allows the employee and her or his family to purchase more products and services that they want. The result is a complex and variable series of outcomes from almost any major action.

Primary and secondary outcomes

Another cause of outcome uncertainty is that many outcomes are controlled by others and the employee cannot be sure how others will act. In the case of the employee who is seeking a promotion, both the promotion and the higher pay are given by management, and the higher status is given by the employee's associates. This second-party relationship often creates great uncertainty.

There are two major ways for managers to address this uncertainty as they apply the expectancy model. First, they can work to strengthen both the *actual* value of the rewards offered and the formal *connections* between effort and performance and between performance and rewards. (This approach incorporates the principles of organizational behavior modification, discussed earlier, in which the manager establishes strong relationships between desired behaviors and effective rewards.)

The second approach requires that managers recognize and accept the legitimacy of an employee's *perception* of the rewards. An employee may not perceive that rewards are worthwhile (valence) or that there is a strong probability of receiving one (the effort-performance and performance-reward connections). Consequently, a simple, straightforward incentive is often more motivating than a complex one. The complex one may involve so much uncertainty that the employee does not sufficiently connect the desired work behavior with a valued reward. The simple incentive, on the other hand, offers a practical course of action that the employee can picture and understand; therefore, it carries higher values for expectancy and instrumentality. In order to make the expectancy model work, the manager must *clarify employee perceptions*. This is just one area where a manager's communication skills (Chapter 3) can be invaluable.

Interpreting the Expectancy Model

Advantages The expectancy model is a valuable tool for helping managers think about the mental processes through which motivation occurs. In this model, employees do not act simply because of strong internal drives, unmet needs, or the application of rewards and punishments. Instead, they are *thinking individuals* whose beliefs, perceptions, and probability estimates powerfully influence their behavior. The model reflects Theory Y assumptions about people as capable individuals and in this way values human dignity.

The expectancy approach also encourages managers to design a motivational climate that will stimulate appropriate employee behavior. Managers need to communicate with employees, asking them three kinds of questions:

- Which of the rewards available do you value the most?
- Do you believe your effort will result in successful performance? (And if not, what can I do to reassure you?)
- How likely is it that you will receive your desired rewards if you perform well?

Then some difficult tasks may face managers, such as telling employees why some desired rewards are currently unavailable, or explaining to them why other factors may restrict employee performance despite their strong efforts. Even if employees cannot receive all that they desire, their expectations will be more realistic after effective communication has occurred.

Limitations Despite its general appeal, the expectancy model has some problems. It needs further testing to build a broad base of research evidence for support. Its

Temporary Workers: Another Form of Diversity

In their attempts to control costs and gain workforce flexibility, many firms have begun using increasing numbers of temporary, part-time, or contract workers to fill jobs—especially those of a seasonal or special-project nature. Several million workers now hold temporary jobs, and many of these people are seeking full-time positions while recognizing that their present jobs may last only a few weeks or months.

How do you motivate temporary workers? The answers seem to lie in logical adaptation of existing OB concepts and motivational models. For example, managers are urged to

- Screen temporary workers on criteria similar to those used for permanent employees (set a challenging hurdle for them to surpass)
- Integrate them carefully into the workforce (communicate comprehensively; provide a detailed orientation; spend time learning their career aspirations)
- Compensate them at market rates (help assure that they perceive equity)
- Discover their interest in challenging work and give them assignments on a par with their skills
- Provide autonomy, invite their participation, and demonstrate trust in them

Above all, employers are urged never to refer to a temporary worker as *the temp*, which sets that worker apart from the others.* Even a seemingly innocuous term like "temp" can make that worker feel isolated, insecure, and ostracized. As a consequence, the worker may withhold his or her creative inputs. This discussion about temporary workers shows how important it is for managers to discover the things that employees value (the first step in the expectancy model of motivation).

*Shari Caudron, "Are Your Temps Doing Their Best?" *Personnel Journal*, November 1995, pp. 33–38.

---

multiplicative combination of the three elements needs further substantiation. Both intrinsic and extrinsic rewards need to be considered. The predicted effects of multiple outcomes from the same effort must be built into the model.

In addition, reliable measures of valence, expectancy, and instrumentality need to be developed. There is a special need to develop measures that managers can use in actual work settings. When possible, managers need to learn both what employees perceive and *why* they hold those valence, expectancy, and instrumentality beliefs.

The model also needs to be made more complete while still remaining practical enough for managers to use. Recent indications are that some additional factors can be added to it to better explain employee behavior. For example, there are often several different rewards available to employees. The valence of each reward must be assessed and combined with the valences of other rewards to estimate the total motivational force for each employee. Another possible addition involves providing motivated employees with the *opportunity* to perform (refer to Figure 5–1).

The model raises some fundamental questions: Is it so complex that managers will tend to use only its highlights and not explore its details and implications? Will other managers ignore it altogether? Many managers in operating situations do not have the time or resources to use a complex motivational system on the job. However, as they begin to learn about it, perhaps they can use parts of it.

THE EQUITY MODEL

The previous discussions of motivational models have viewed the employee as an individual, virtually independent of other employees. As is pointed out in Chapter 1, however, employees work in a social system in which each is dependent to some degree on the others. Employees interact with one another on tasks and on social occasions. They observe one another, judge one another, and make comparisons. The next model to be discussed builds on this notion of comparison to add new dimensions to our overall understanding of employee motivation.

Most employees are concerned about more than just having their needs satisfied; they also want their reward system to be *fair*. This issue of fairness applies to all types of rewards—psychological, social, and economic—and it makes the managerial job of motivation much more complex. J. Stacy Adams's **equity theory** states that employees tend to judge fairness by comparing the outcomes they receive with their relevant inputs and also by comparing this *ratio* (not always the absolute level of rewards) with the ratios of other people (Figure 5–9), as this formula shows:[17]

$$\frac{\text{One's own outcomes}}{\text{One's own inputs}} \overset{?}{=} \frac{\text{Others' outcomes}}{\text{Others' inputs}}$$

Inputs include all the rich and diverse elements that employees believe they bring, or contribute, to the job—their education, seniority, prior work experiences, loyalty and commitment, time and effort, creativity, and job performance. **Outcomes** are the rewards they perceive they get from their jobs and employers; outcomes include direct pay and bonuses, fringe benefits, job security, social rewards, and psychological rewards.

Inputs and outcomes are compared.

Employees analyze the fairness of their own outcome/input "contract," and then compare their contract with contracts of other workers in similar jobs and even with those outside of their job. Fairness of rewards (equity) may even be judged in comparison with relatively arbitrary criteria like *age,* as the following example shows:

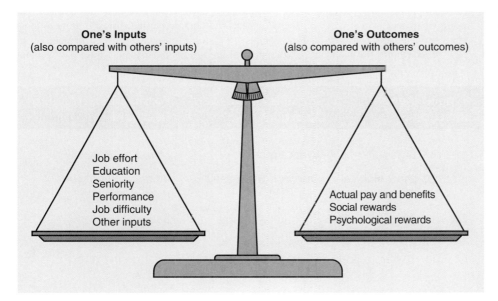

FIGURE 5–9

Key factors in equity assessment

124

Irene Nickerson is a supervisor in a large public utility. For several years her friends told her she could consider herself successful when her salary (in thousands of dollars) surpassed her age. One year, at age thirty-four, she received a substantial salary increase that placed her income at $33,865. She was frustrated, incensed, and demoralized for weeks afterwards, for she did not receive what she dearly wanted! For an extra $135, the company could have matched her equity expectations and continued to have a motivated employee.

Equity

Pay was a symbolic scorecard by which Nickerson compared her outcomes with her inputs (since she included age with her other inputs of education, experience, and effort). Her reaction is only one of the three combinations that can occur from social comparisons—equity, overreward, and underreward. If employees perceive *equity,* they will continue to contribute at about the same level. Otherwise, under conditions of inequity, they will experience tension that will create the motivation to reduce the inequity. The resulting actions can be either physical or psychological, and internal or external.

Overreward

If employees feel *overrewarded,* equity theory predicts that they will feel an imbalance in their relationship with their employer and seek to restore that balance. They might work harder (shown as an internal and physical response in Figure 5–10), they might discount the value of the rewards received (internal and psychological), they could try to convince other employees to ask for more rewards (external and physical), or they might simply choose someone else for comparison purposes (external and psychological).

Underreward

Workers who feel they have been *underrewarded* seek to reduce their feelings of inequity through the same types of strategies, but some of their specific actions are now reversed. They might lower the quantity or quality of their productivity, they could inflate the perceived value of the rewards received, or they could bargain for more actual rewards. Again, they could find someone else to compare themselves (more favorably) with, or they might simply quit. In any event, they are reacting to inequity by bringing their inputs into balance with their outcomes. Knowledge of outcome/input ratios allows managers to predict part of their employees' behavior through understanding when, and under what conditions, workers will experience inequity.

An example of employee reaction to underpayment occurred in a manufacturing plant that made small mechanical parts for the aerospace and automotive industries.[18] Some important contracts were canceled, and the company was forced to announce a 15 percent cut in pay for all employees. Compared with a control group in another plant whose pay was not

FIGURE 5–10

Possible reactions to perceived inequity

Type of Inequity Reaction	Possible Overreward Reactions	Possible Underreward Reactions
Internal, physical	Work harder	Lower productivity
Internal, psychological	Discount the reward	Inflate value of the reward
External, physical	Encourage the referent person to obtain more	Bargain for more; possibly quit
External, psychological	Change the referent person	Change the referent person

cut, the affected employees reacted by doubling their normal theft rate (tools and supplies stolen from the company). Turnover also jumped to 23 percent, compared with a normal rate of 5 percent. Apparently the employees experienced a change from relative equity to underpayment inequity. They reacted to their perceived mistreatment by making unofficial transfers of organizational resources to themselves. When the pay cut ended after ten weeks, the theft rate returned to normal levels.

Interpreting the Equity Model

An understanding of equity should remind managers that employees work within *several* social systems. Employees may actually select a number of reference groups both inside and outside the organization. Employees are also inclined to shift the basis for their comparisons to the standard that is most favorable to them. Educated people often inflate the value of their education, while employees with longer service emphasize seniority as the dominant criterion. Other employees choose somewhat higher (economic) groups as their reference. Many employees have strong egos and high opinions of themselves. Consequently, all these factors (multiple reference groups, shifting standards, upward orientation, and personal egos) make the task of predicting when inequity will occur somewhat complex.

Equity theory has generated extensive research, with many of the results being supportive. In particular, underreward seems to produce motivational tension with predictable (negative) consequences; less consistent results are found for the overreward condition. The different research results may be reconciled by the idea of **equity sensitivity,** which suggests that individuals have different preferences for equity. Some people seem to prefer overreward, some conform to the traditional equity model, and others prefer to be underrewarded.[19] Identifying which employees fall into each class would help managers predict who would experience inequity and how important it would be in affecting their behavior.

Equity sensitivity

Similar elements—effort (inputs) and rewards (outcomes)—can be seen when comparing the equity and expectancy models. In both approaches, perception plays a key role, again suggesting how valuable it is for a manager to gather information *from* employees instead of trying to impose perceptions onto them. The major challenges for a manager using the equity model lie in measuring employee assessments of their inputs and outcomes, identifying their choice of references, and evaluating employee perceptions of inputs and outcomes.

INTERPRETING MOTIVATIONAL MODELS

Several motivational models are presented in this chapter. All the models have strengths and weaknesses, advocates and critics. No model is perfect, but all of them add something to our understanding of the motivational process. Other models are being developed, and attempts are being made to integrate existing approaches.

The cognitive (process) models are likely to continue dominating organizational practice for some time. They are most consistent with our supportive and holistic view of people as thinking individuals who make somewhat conscious decisions about their behavior. However, behavior modification also has some usefulness, especially in stable situations with minimum complexity, where there appears to be a direct connection between behavior and its consequences. In more complex, dynamic situations, cognitive models will be used more often. In other words, the motivational model used must be adapted to the situation as well as blended with other models.

Contingent use of motivational models

Advice to Future Managers

1. Identify each employee's needs and drives and how they change over time.

2. Reduce the distracting influence of hygiene factors before turning your attention to providing motivators.

3. Establish strong connections between desired behaviors and rewards given; provide rewards that recognize high achievers more than other employees; administer rewards on a systematic basis (e.g., a variable-ratio reinforcement schedule).

4. Set performance-oriented goals that are specific, challenging, and acceptable.

5. Seek information regarding employee perceptions of valence, expectancy, and instrumentality; share key information with employees to improve their assessments.

6. Discover the referent people or groups and perceived outcome/input ratios for employees' equity computation; compare your assessments of likely equity with theirs.

SUMMARY

When people join an organization, they bring with them certain drives and needs that affect their on-the-job performance. Sometimes these are immediately apparent, but often they not only are difficult to determine and satisfy but also vary greatly from one person to another. It is useful, though, to understand how needs create tensions which stimulate effort to perform and how effective performance brings the satisfaction of rewards.

Several approaches to understanding internal drives and needs within employees are examined in the chapter. Each model makes a contribution to our understanding of motivation. All the models share some similiarities. In general, they encourage managers not only to consider lower-order, maintenance, and extrinsic factors but to use higher-order, motivational, and intrinsic factors as well.

Behavior modification focuses on the external environment by stating that a number of employee behaviors can be affected by manipulating their consequences. The alternative consequences include positive and negative reinforcement, punishment, and extinction. Reinforcement can be applied according to either continuous or partial schedules.

A blending of internal and external approaches is obtained through consideration of goal setting. Managers are encouraged to use cues—such as goals that are accepted, challenging, and specific—to stimulate desired employee behavior. In this way, goal setting, combined with the reinforcement of performance feedback, provides a balanced approach to motivation.

Additional approaches to motivation presented in this chapter are the expectancy and equity models. The expectancy model states that motivation is a product of how much one wants something and the probabilities that effort will lead to task accomplishment and reward. The formula is valence $\times$ expectancy $\times$ instrumentality = motivation. Valence is the strength of a person's preference for an outcome. Expectancy is the strength of belief that one's effort will be successful in accomplishing a task. Instrumentality is the strength of belief that successful performance will be followed by a reward.

The expectancy and equity motivational models relate specifically to the employee's intellectual processes. The equity model has a double comparison in it—a match between an employee's perceived inputs and outcomes, coupled with a comparison with some referent person's rewards for her or his input level.

Managers are encouraged to combine the perspectives of several models to create a complete motivational environment for their employees.

Terms and Concepts for Review

Discussion Questions

1. Think of someone who, in the past, did an excellent job of motivating you. Describe how this was done. Which of the following approaches did that person use (either explicitly or implicitly)?
   a. Lower-order or higher-order needs?
   b. Maintenance or motivational factors? If so, which one(s)?
   c. Existence, relatedness, or growth needs?
   d. Behavior modification?
   e. Goal setting?
2. In your role as a student, do you feel that you are motivated more by Maslow's lower-order or higher-order needs? Explain. Describe how you expect motivation to change once you graduate.
3. Which one factor in Herzberg's two-factor model is most motivating to you at the present time? Explain. Is this a maintenance or motivational factor?
4. It is relatively easy for a manager to manipulate *extrinsic* rewards. Describe some ways in which a manager could affect *intrinsic* satisfaction of an employee.
5. Discuss how behavior modification operates to motivate people. Why is it still important to understand people's needs when using this approach?

6. Explain the differences between negative reinforcement and punishment.
7. Divide the class into two groups (one in favor and one opposed) and debate this proposition: "Rewards motivate people."
8. How would you use the expectancy model in the following situations?
   a. You want two employees to switch their vacations from the summer to the spring so that job needs will be filled suitably during the summer.
   b. You believe that one of your employees has excellent potential for promotion and want to encourage her to prepare for it.
   c. You have a sprained ankle and want a friend to walk to a fast-food restaurant and get you a hamburger.
9. Apply the equity model to yourself as a student. How do you measure your inputs and outcomes? Whom have you chosen as referent individuals? Do you perceive equity? If not, how will you attain it?
10. The text suggests that an individual's equity perceptions can be distorted. If that is the case, how would you go about correcting or adjusting them?

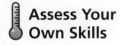
Assess Your Own Skills

How well do you exhibit good motivational skills?

Read the following statements carefully. Circle the number on the response scale that most closely reflects the degree to which each statement accurately describes you when you have tried to motivate someone else. Add up your total points and prepare a brief action plan for self-improvement. Be ready to report your score for tabulation across the entire group.

	Good description								Poor description
1. I consciously follow an integrated model of motivation such as Figure 5–1 when motivating people.	10 9 8 7 6 5 4 3 2 1								
2. I determine whether people are achievement, affliation, or power driven and respond accordingly.	10 9 8 7 6 5 4 3 2 1								
3. I try to determine which level of the need hierarchy is most powerful for each employee.	10 9 8 7 6 5 4 3 2 1								
4. I make sure that I eliminate dissatisfiers in the work context before I focus on providing motivational factors to my employees.	10 9 8 7 6 5 4 3 2 1								
5. I recognize that employees might be interested in the satisfaction of their growth needs, as indicated by the Maslow, Herzberg, and Alderfer models.	10 9 8 7 6 5 4 3 2 1								
6. I am conscious of the need to provide systematic consequences, both positive and negative, to employees to utilize the law of effect.	10 9 8 7 6 5 4 3 2 1								

7. I recognize that negative reinforcement and punishment are very different strategies.   10 9 8 7 6 5 4 3 2 1

8. Whenever possible, I use the variable-ratio schedule for administering rewards.   10 9 8 7 6 5 4 3 2 1

9. I seek to provide the conditions that will allow employees to improve their level of self-efficacy.   10 9 8 7 6 5 4 3 2 1

10. I carefully monitor each employee's level of performance and provide constructive feedback as needed.   10 9 8 7 6 5 4 3 2 1

Scoring and Interpretation   Add up your total points for the ten questions. Record that number here, and report it when it is requested. _____

- If you scored between 81–100 points, you appear to have a solid capability for demonstrating good motivational skills.
- If you scored between 61–80 points, you should take a close look at the items with lower self-assessment scores and explore ways to improve those items.
- If you scored less than 60 points, you should be aware that a weaker skill level regarding several items could be detrimental to your future success as a motivator. We encourage you to review relevant sections of the chapter and watch for related material in subsequent chapters and other sources.

Now identify your three lowest scores, and write the question numbers here: _____, _____, _____. Write a brief paragraph, detailing to yourself an action plan for how you might sharpen each of these skills.

The Downsized Firm

Role-Play

Instructions   Divide into groups of four persons, with one person taking the role of Phil, Sue, John, and Linda. Each person should read only their role. When everyone is ready, Phil should meet with each person and attempt to create a motivational atmosphere that will encourage each person to remain with the firm and be productive.

Phil   You are the supervisor of the circulation department for a scientific publisher. Your department has recently been downsized, and you lost two customer service representatives. They were terminated for business reasons that had nothing to do with their job performance. You have three remaining representatives—Sue, John, and Linda—and are about to meet with each of them to try to convince them to remain motivated and productive (doing the work of five person previously) and stay with the firm.

Sue   Your department has recently been downsized, and two of the five customer service representatives were laid off. They were allegedly terminated for business reasons that had nothing to do with their job performance. You are one of the three remaining representatives (the others are John and Linda). You are a single mother and have to take extra days off when your children are sick. Sometimes you work a

130

flexible schedule of hours to accommodate the children's schedules. You are beginning to wonder if these allowances will make you more vulnerable in any future round of layoffs. You are about to meet with Phil now.

John   Your department has recently been downsized, and two of the five customer service representatives were laid off. They were allegedly terminated for business reasons that had nothing to do with their job performance. You are one of the three remaining representatives (the others are Sue and Linda). You have been on the job for two years. You attend college at night and see the job as a stepping-stone into a management position. However, after seeing your two colleagues (and friends) terminated, you are beginning to wonder if this company is one that you want to stay with. You are about to meet with Phil now.

Linda   Your department has recently been downsized, and two of the five customer service representatives were laid off. They were allegedly terminated for business reasons that had nothing to do with their job performance. You are one of the three remaining representatives (the others are Sue and Linda). You have worked in customer service for fifteen years and have always felt like you made a lifetime commitment to work. Now even you are beginning to wonder how secure your job is. After all, if it happened to two of your colleagues, it might happen to you, too. You are about to meet with Phil now.

Discussion
1. What major motivational model(s) did Phil use with Sue, John, and Linda?
2. What other approaches might have worked better?
3. What are the major lessons you can derive from this exercise?

Incident

The Piano Builder[20]

Waverly Bird builds pianos from scratch. He is a consultant to a piano manufacturer. He is on call and works about one week a month, including some travel, to solve problems of customers. He also rebuilds about a dozen grand pianos every year for special customers; but, according to Bird, the most satisfying part of his life is his hobby of building pianos from the beginning. "It's the part that keeps a man alive," he says. The challenge of the work is what lures Bird onward. He derives satisfaction from precision and quality, and he comments, "Details make the difference. When you cut a little corner here and a little corner there, you've cut a big hole. A piano is like the human body; all the parts are important."

Bird has a substantial challenge in making a whole piano. His work combines skills in cabinetmaking, metalworking, and engineering, with knowledge of acoustics and a keen ear for music. It requires great precision, because a tiny misalignment would ruin a piano's tune. It also requires versatility: A keyboard must be balanced to respond to the touch of a finger; the pinblock, on the other hand, must withstand up to 20 tons of pressure. In addition, Bird had to make many of his own piano construction tools.

Bird has built forty pianos in his thirty-four-year career. Though construction takes nearly a year, he sells his pianos at the modest price of a commercial piano. He is seeking not money but challenge and satisfaction. He says, "The whole business is a series of closed doors. You learn one thing, and there's another closed door waiting to be opened." Bird says his big dream is to build a grand piano: "It is the one thing I haven't done yet and want to do."

Questions

1. Discuss the nature of Bird's motivation in building pianos. What are his drives and needs? Would a behavior modification program affect his motivation? Why or why not? What would be the effect of setting a goal of two pianos per year for him?
2. How could a manufacturer of pianos build the motivation Bird has now into its employees?

Are Grades Motivators?

1. Assess the valence of receiving an A in this course. Assign that A a valence somewhere between −1 and +1, using gradations of one-tenth (e.g., 0.8, 0.9, 1.0).
2. Now assess the probability (between 0.0 and 1.0) that the level of effort you expect to commit to this course will result in high enough performance to merit an A letter grade. This constitutes your expectancy score.
3. Then assess the probability (between 0.0 and 1.0) that your stellar performance in this course (an A) will substantially improve your overall grade-point average. This represents your instrumentality score.
4. Now multiply your V, E, and I scores to produce an overall measure of your likely motivation (on this one task and for this reward). This overall score should fall between −1.0 and +1.0. Enter your name and data on line 1 below.
5. Share your four scores with classmates in a format like that shown here. Note the range of responses within the class for each item.

Student's Name	Valence	Expectancy	Instrumentality	Motivation
1.				
2.				
3.				
4.				
5.				
etc.				

Chapter 6

Appraising and Rewarding Performance

But sometimes—and we would venture to say often—an employee's poor performance can be blamed largely on his [or her] boss.
—Jean-Francois Manzoni and Jean-Louis Barsoux[1]

Most people want feedback, as long, of course, as it mirrors their self perception. When it does, they tend to like it. When it doesn't, they don't.
—Larry Cipolla[2]

CHAPTER OBJECTIVES

TO UNDERSTAND

- Total Reward Systems
- Money as an Economic and Social Medium of Exchange
- The Role of Money in Motivational Models
- Behavioral Considerations in Performance Appraisal
- The Characteristics of Good Feedback Programs
- The Process of Attribution
- How and Why to Link Pay with Performance
- Uses of Profit-Sharing, Gain-Sharing, and Skill-Based Pay Programs

For twenty-four years Mark McCann worked as a bank teller in a small town. He was the senior person among three tellers, and on rare occasions when both bank officers were away, he was left in charge of the bank. In his community he was a respected citizen. He belonged to a downtown business club and was an elder in his church. Recently he confided to a trusted friend, "I'm looking for another job—just anything to get away from that bank." Further questioning revealed that he had been quite satisfied with his job and was still satisfied except for one event. Because of a local labor shortage, one teller's position went unfilled for three months. Finally, in desperation, the bank recruited a young, untrained college man from another city. In order to get him, the bank paid him a monthly salary $25 higher than Mark's. Mark suddenly felt bypassed and forgotten. His whole world had come tumbling down the day he learned of the new teller's rate. He felt that his community social standing had collapsed and that his self-image was destroyed. The employee he was training was earning $25 more each month!

This case illustrates how economic rewards are important to employees and how pay relationships carry immense social value. Management has not always recognized their social importance to workers. In the nineteenth and early twentieth centuries employees were presumed to want primarily money; therefore, money was believed to produce direct motivation—the more money offered, the more motivation. Roethlisberger and his followers successfully buried this idea by showing that economic rewards operated through the attitudes of workers in the social system to produce an *indirect* incentive.

In this chapter we discuss the complex relationship between economic reward systems and organizational behavior. More details about these systems will be found in books about compensation and human resource management; only their significant behavioral aspects are examined here. The chapter focuses first on how **incentives** are combined with other parts of wage administration to build a complete reward system that encourages motivation. Then we discuss money as a means of rewarding employees, motivational models applied to pay, cost-reward comparisons, and behavioral considerations in performance appraisal. Finally, we discuss incentive pay, an approach in which each worker's pay varies in relation to employee or organizational performance.

A COMPLETE PROGRAM

Many types of pay are required for a complete economic reward system.[3] Job analysis and wage surveys rate *jobs*, comparing one job with another to determine base pay (according to levels of responsibility and market pressure). Performance appraisal and incentives rate *employees* on their performance and reward their contributions. Profit sharing rates the *organization* in terms of its general economic performance and rewards employees as partners in it. Together these three systems—base pay, performance rewards, and profit sharing—are the incentive foundation of a complete pay program, as diagrammed in the reward pyramid in Figure 6–1. Each can contribute something to the employee's economic satisfaction.

The three systems are complementary because each reflects a different set of factors in the total situation. Base pay and skill-based pay motivate employees to progress to jobs of higher skills and responsibility. Performance pay is an incentive to improve performance on the job. Profit sharing motivates workers toward teamwork to improve an organization's performance.

Relating pay to objectives

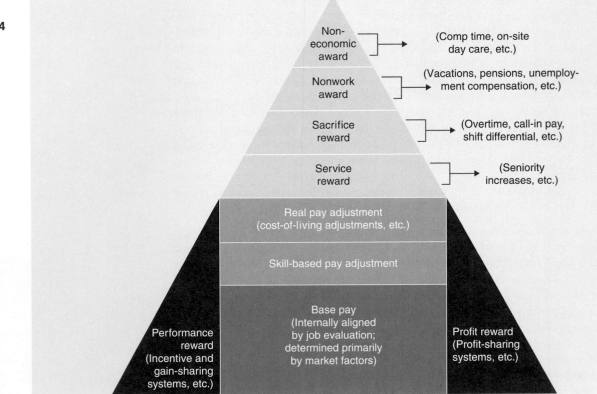

FIGURE 6–1

The reward pyramid: The makeup of a complete pay program *(read from bottom)*

Other payments, primarily nonincentive in nature, are added to the incentive foundation. Seniority pay adjustments are made to reward workers for extended service and to encourage them to remain with their employer. If an employer asks workers to sacrifice by working overtime, working on their day off, or working undesirable hours, the workers may be paid extra for the inconvenience. Other payments are given for periods when an employee does not work, such as vacations, holidays, jury service, and layoffs subject to guaranteed pay.

The additions to the incentive foundation of the reward pyramid have little direct incentive value because they do not increase according to improved job performance. Some of these additions may result in indirect incentive through better attitudes. Other additions, such as seniority pay, actually may decrease worker incentive. It is clear that not one factor but many factors enter into computation of a worker's paycheck. Some of these factors are related less to incentive than they are to such broad objectives as security, equity, and social justice. An effective program of economic rewards is a balance of most of these factors, as shown in this example:

Lincoln Electric Company provides a classic and unique combination of compensation programs to its employees to create a complete reward program, in conjunction with other distinctive management policies.[4] It offers piecework pay, shared profits, suggestion systems, year-end bonuses, and stock-ownership opportunities. It couples these with no paid holidays or sick days, mandatory overtime, no seniority system, and no definite lines of promotion. It does, however, boast a 50-year record of no layoffs, which provides a huge measure of job security in this era of downsizing. The results are clear: Its sales level per employee is 2 to 3 times the manufacturing standard; its products are noted for their reliability; and the post-probationary turnover rate is less than 3 percent per year—including deaths and retirements.

A wide range of noneconomic programs also exists to supplement an organization's complete pay program. Some firms reward their employees with contingent time off for exemplary performance; others allow employees to earn "comp time" (compensatory time) for hours worked but not paid for. Many firms provide a wide array of other benefits for their employees, such as on-site day care facilities and wellness programs. The number of options and their costs to employers have risen dramatically and are often as much as 35 to 40 percent of total compensation.

MONEY AS A MEANS OF REWARDING EMPLOYEES

It is evident from Figure 6–1 that money is important to employees for a number of reasons. Certainly, money is valuable because of the goods and services that it will purchase. This aspect is its economic value as a medium of exchange for allocation of economic resources; however, money also is a *social medium of exchange.* All of us have seen its importance as a status symbol for those who have it and can thus save it, spend it conspicuously, or give it away generously. Money has status value when it is being received and when it is being spent. It represents to employees what their employer thinks of them. It is also an indication of one employee's status relative to that of other employees. It has about as many values as it has possessors. Here is an example of how people respond differently to it:

Money has social value.

> A manager gave two field sales representatives the same increase in pay because each had done a good job. One sales representative was highly pleased with this recognition. She felt she was respected and rewarded because the raise placed her in a higher income bracket. The other sales representative was angered because he knew the raise amounted to the minimum standard available; so he considered it an insult rather than an adequate reward for the outstanding job he felt he was doing. He felt that he was not properly recognized, and he saw this small raise as a serious blow to his own esteem and self-respect. This same raise also affected the security of the two employees in a different manner. The first employee now felt she had obtained more security, but the second employee felt that his security was in jeopardy.

Application of the Motivational Models

A useful way to think about money as a reward is to apply it to some of the motivational models presented in Chapter 5.

Drives   Achievement-oriented employees maintain a symbolic scorecard in their minds by monitoring their total pay and comparing it with that of others. Their pay is a measure of their accomplishments. Money also relates to other drives, since people can use it to buy their way into expensive clubs (affiliation) and give them the capacity (power) to influence others, such as through political contributions.

Money satisfies many drives and needs.

Needs   In the Herzberg model, pay is viewed primarily as a hygiene factor, although it may have at least short-term motivational value as well. In the other need-based models, pay is most easily seen in its capacity to satisfy the lower-order needs (such as Maslow's physiological and security needs or Alderfer's existence needs).

However, we can easily see how it relates to other levels as well, like Mark McCann's esteem needs in the opening example for this chapter.

Expectancy   As you will recall, expectancy theory states that

$$\text{Valence} \times \text{Expectancy} \times \text{Instrumentality} = \text{Motivation}$$

This means that if money is to act as a strong motivator, an employee must want more of it (valence), must believe that effort will be successful in producing desired performance (expectancy), and must trust that the monetary reward will follow better performance (instrumentality).

Money often has high valence.

Valence of money is not easily influenced by management. It is contingent upon an employee's personal values, experiences, and needs as well as the macromotivational environment. For example, if an employee has an independent income, a small increase in pay may have little valence. The same conclusion applies to an employee who cherishes other values and desires only a subsistence income. Similarly, the direct value of money to people in an affluent society tends to decline, since money tends to satisfy lower-order needs more directly than higher-order needs. However, since money has many social meanings to people, employees may seek it for its social value (a measure of status and esteem) even when its economic value has low valence. This dual role means that *most employees do respond to money as a reward* (it has valence for them).

With regard to instrumentality, many employees are not sure that additional performance will lead to additional pay (the performance-reward connection). They see some employees deliver minimum performance, yet receive almost the same pay increases as high performers. They often believe that promotions are based more on seniority or personal relationships than on performance. Instrumentality is an area where management has much opportunity for building trust and taking positive action, because it can change substantially the connection between increased performance and reward.

High instrumentality is desired.

Behavior Modification   The two desired conditions for applying contingent rewards under behavior modification principles are shown in Figure 6–2 as situations 1 and 4. In each case employees can see that there is a direct connection between performance and reward (instrumentality is high). The undesirable states are situations 2 and 3, where rewards are withheld from high performers or given to low performers (instrumentality is low). When these conditions are allowed to occur, many employees will at least be confused about how to perform and may even be highly dissatisfied with the reward system.

> Consider the cases of four employees, each of whom was treated differently by the employer, and the possible thoughts running through their minds. Shannon received a substantial pay increase for her outstanding performance ("I think I'll try even harder in the future, since good work is obviously noticed"). Chet's productivity record mirrored Shannon's, but he received only a token salary increase ("If that's all my effort is worth to them, I'm going to really cut back next year"). Travis did not have a good performance record, but because the organization enjoyed a successful year, he was still given a healthy raise ("This is a great place to work; I can slide by and still do all right"). Pam had an equally poor record, so her supervisor withheld any increase from her ("I guess if I want to get ahead, I need to perform better in the future"). In each case the reward received (when compared with performance) sent a strong signal—but not always the intended one—to the employee about the likelihood of future rewards based on performance.

FIGURE 6–2

Desirable and
undesirable
instrumentality
conditions

Situation	Level of Performance	Level of Economic Reward	Instrumentality Condition
1	High	High	Desirable
2	High	Low	Undesirable
3	Low	High	Undesirable
4	Low	Low	Desirable

Equity There is no simple answer for employers in their attempts to create workable systems of economic rewards for increased productivity, but they must at least attempt to understand the employee's perspective. The employee's approach to this complex problem is to make a rough type of **cost-reward comparison,** similar to the break-even analysis that is used in financial assessments. The employee identifies and compares personal costs and rewards to determine the point at which they are approximately equal, as shown in Figure 6–3. Employees consider all the costs of higher performance, such as effort, time, acquisition of knowledge and new skills, and the mental energy that must be devoted to innovation and problem solving. Then they compare those costs with all the possible rewards, both economic (such as pay, benefits, and holidays) and noneconomic (such as status, esteem, and autonomy, although the value of these may be more difficult to assess). This input-outcome comparison process is similar to part of the equity model of motivation discussed in Chapter 5, except that in this analysis we assume that the employees do not yet compare themselves with others. Both costs (inputs) and rewards (outcomes) are always valued.

*Cost-reward
comparison*

The break-even point is the point at which costs and rewards are equal for a certain level of expected performance, as shown by point *B* on the chart. Employee performance tends to be near the break-even point, but generally below it, for two reasons. First, the employee typically cannot be so precise as to pinpoint the exact break-even point. Second, the employee tries to maintain a personally satisfactory

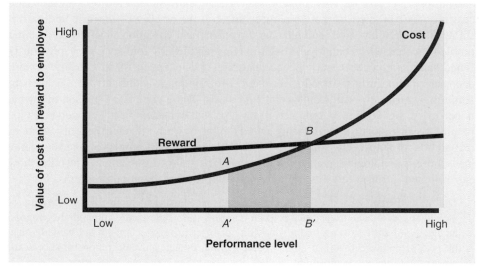

FIGURE 6–3

Cost of performance in
relation to reward for an
employee. Employee
performance level will
tend to be between *A'*
and *B'*.

relationship in which rewards are relatively favorable in relation to costs.[5] Performance tends to be somewhere in the range of line $A'B'$.

Several reservations must be expressed about this analysis, however. In Figure 6–3 employee costs are shown rising more steeply near the highest level of performance expectation to represent the additional effort and concentration required. Further, the shape of each employee's lines (and the location of each one's break-even point) will be unique, representing the personal value placed on both costs and rewards (an illustration of individual differences in action). Also, the reward line is shown as a straight line, such as that provided by a piece-rate system, but in most instances it rises only in steps after a certain amount of performance improvement occurs. If management can make the perceived reward line rise more steeply by means of offering or emphasizing larger or different rewards, then the break-even point will be at a higher level of performance. Alternatively, if management can convince employees that their cost line is not really that steep, then the break-even point will also appear at a higher level of performance.

> Many salespeople work on some form of commission plan that provides them with periodic bonuses. In many cases, the bonuses become larger as the salesperson reaches higher levels of performance, under the assumption that this will stretch the employee to excel. However, this principle is sometimes ignored, as it was by a distributor interviewed by one of the authors. He actually *reduced* the level of bonuses provided as his salespeople reached new plateaus of sales during the month. His explanation? "I don't want my employees getting rich off of me," he said.

Additional Considerations in the Use of Money

Extrinsic and Intrinsic Rewards   Money is essentially an extrinsic reward rather than an intrinsic one, so it is easily administered in behavior modification programs. However, it also has all the limitations of extrinsic benefits. No matter how closely management attaches pay to performance, pay is still something that originates outside the job and is useful only away from the job. Therefore, it tends to be less immediately satisfying than intrinsic job rewards. For example, the personal satisfaction of a job well done is a powerful motivator for many people. Economic rewards, by contrast, cannot provide all the needed rewards for a psychologically healthy person.

Difficult to integrate   An important task for management is integrating extrinsic and intrinsic rewards successfully. One problem is that employees differ in the amount of intrinsic and extrinsic rewards that they want, and jobs and organizational conditions also differ. Another problem occurs when employers begin paying employees for work they previously found satisfying, since some evidence indicates that payment of an extrinsic reward decreases the intrinsic satisfaction received.[6] In addition, it is difficult for managers to administer intrinsic rewards on a systematic basis. These conditions suggest that what is needed is a contingency approach to rewards that considers needs of workers, type of job, organizational environment, and different rewards. Special benefits, such as recognition or status, are sometimes especially valuable to employees because they have more psychological and social meaning. The following example illustrates how extrinsic and intrinsic rewards are often intertwined in recognition programs:

> The Wells Fargo Bank developed a program to recognize and reinforce the behavior of individuals who made exceptional contributions to customer service.[7] Although the program included both cash rewards and a wide array of other prize selections of substantial value, its peak experience revolved around a recognition dinner and celebration for the award winners with the top company executives at a classy San Francisco restaurant.

Compliance with the Law   In addition to the complexities involved in applying various motivational models and building on both extrinsic and intrinsic factors, compensation management is also complicated by the need to comply with a wide range of federal and state laws. The most significant one is the federal **Equal Pay Act of 1963,** which affects employers who are engaged in interstate commerce and most employees of federal, state, and local governments. Also legislated by many states, the law demands that reward systems be designed and administered so that people doing the same work receive equal pay regardless of the sex of the person holding the job. This law is designed to prevent one form of sexual discrimination, eliminating historical discrepancies in which females were sometimes paid less than males.

Another program, called **comparable worth,** also seeks to guarantee equal pay for equal work. This approach demands that reward systems be designed so that people in comparable jobs—those of equal *value* to the employer—receive similar levels of pay. For example, a hospital might determine that a laboratory technician position requires comparable education, decision-making ability, and stress management skills as that of an internal auditor and therefore might set comparable levels of compensation for each. This program also has the intent of ending historical patterns of discrimination against those people who hold sex-stereotyped jobs (such as females working as registered nurses).

Comparable worth

Other Factors   Many other elements confound the compensation process. In contrast to legal and psychological pressures for equity (matching inputs and outcomes in comparison with those of others), some individuals advocate *equality.* They would prefer that all employees receive the same rewards, regardless of their unique skills or level of performance. Clearly, equity and equality are totally different bases for comparing compensation. *Secrecy* in pay programs is sometimes subject to debate. Some organizations guard all information about compensation from employees; others freely share it in the belief that openness is preferable. *Control* can also be an issue. Should reward systems be designed by staff experts, or should employees be allowed to participate in their creation and governance? The level of *flexibility* has been subject to debate. Even though some clothing products claim "one size fits all," it may not be reasonable to expect that all dimensions of compensation will meet the needs of all employees. Clearly, the administration of organizational reward systems involves many issues, and unique answers will be provided by different firms.

ORGANIZATIONAL BEHAVIOR AND PERFORMANCE APPRAISAL

Organizations require consistent levels of high performance from their employees in order to survive in a highly competitive environment (see "What Managers Are Reading"). Many firms use some form of results-oriented planning and control systems. **Management by objectives (MBO)** is a cyclical process that often consists of four steps as a way to attain desired performance:

1. *Objective setting*—joint determination by manager and employee of appropriate levels of future performance for the employee, within the context of overall unit goals and resources. These objectives are often set for the next calendar year.
2. *Action planning*—participative or even independent planning by the employee as to *how* to reach those objectives. Providing some autonomy to employees is

invaluable; they are more likely to use their ingenuity, as well as feel more committed to the plan's success.

3. *Periodic reviews*—joint assessment of progress toward objectives by manager and employee, performed informally and sometimes spontaneously.

4. *Annual evaluation*—more formal assessment of success in achieving the employee's annual objectives, coupled with a renewal of the planning cycle. Some MBO systems also use performance appraisal to tie rewards for employees to the level of results attained.

Reasons for employee appraisal

Performance appraisal plays a key role in reward systems. It is the process of evaluating the performance of employees, sharing that information with them, and searching for ways to improve their performance. Appraisal is necessary in order to (1) allocate resources in a dynamic environment, (2) motivate and reward employees, (3) give employees feedback about their work, (4) maintain fair relationships within groups, (5) coach and develop employees, and (6) comply with regulations. It is also a formal opportunity to do what should be done much more frequently in organizations—express appreciation for employee contributions.[8] Appraisal systems, therefore, are necessary for proper management and for employee development.

The social environment surrounding organizations has changed considerably in recent years. Federal and state laws have added to the complexity and difficulty of appraisal plans. For example, as shown in Figure 6–4, criteria for compliance with equal employment opportunity laws are stringent. Management needs to design and operate its appraisal systems carefully in order to comply with these laws.

Appraisal Philosophy

Performance emphasis and goals

A generation ago, appraisal programs tended to emphasize employee traits, deficiencies, and abilities, but modern appraisal philosophy emphasizes present performance and future goals. Modern philosophy also stresses employee participation in mutually setting goals with the supervisor and knowledge of results. Thus the hallmarks of modern appraisal philosophy are as follows:

1. *Performance orientation*—it is not enough for employees to put forth *effort;* that effort must result in the attainment of desired *outcomes* (products or services).

2. *Focus on goals or objectives*—as the discussion of MBO shows, employees need to have a clear idea of what they are supposed to be doing and the priorities

The performance appraisal system

- Is an organizational necessity

- Is based on well-defined, objective criteria

- Is based on careful job analysis

- Uses only job-related criteria

- Is supported by adequate studies

- Is applied by trained, qualified raters

- Is applied objectively throughout the organization

- Can be shown to be nondiscriminatory as defined by law

among their tasks; as the saying goes, "If you know where you want to go, you are more likely to get there."

3. *Mutual goal setting between supervisor and employee*—this is the belief that people will work harder for goals or objectives that they have participated in setting. Among their desires are to perform a worthwhile task, share in a group effort, share in setting their objectives, share in the rewards of their efforts, and continue personal growth. The (Theory Y) assumption is that people want to satisfy some of their needs through work and that they will do so if management will provide them with a supportive environment.

4. *Clarification of behavioral expectations*—this is often done via a *behaviorally anchored rating scale* (BARS), which provides the employee and manager with concrete examples of various levels of behaviors. Brief descriptions of outstanding, very good, acceptable, below average, and unacceptable behaviors are specified for each major dimension of a job, thus cueing the employee in advance regarding the organization's expectations. BARS help reduce a manager's tendency to focus on attitudes, personality, and quirks of an employee and shift the emphasis toward productive behaviors.

5. *Extensive feedback systems*—employees can fine-tune their performance better if they know how they are doing in the eyes of the organization.

Mutual goal setting and feedback

The Appraisal Interview

Most organizational appraisal systems require supervisors to assess employees on various aspects of their productivity (results), behavior, or personal traits. Examples of these three dimensions include quality of work and quantity of output, attendance and initiative, and general attitude. Many appraisal systems also point toward both historical performance and the individual's potential for growth and advancement. The actual forms and procedures used for assessing this information vary widely. Some organizations ask supervisors to write essays describing the employee's performance; others recommend that they accumulate a record of critical incidents (both positive and negative); many firms use various types of graphic rating scales that grade employees on A-B-C-D-E or 1-2-3-4-5 systems.

Regardless of the system used, the assessment is then communicated to the employee in an **appraisal interview.** This is a session in which the supervisor

142

provides feedback to the employee on past performance, discusses any problems that have arisen, and invites a response. Then the two parties set objectives for the next time period, and the employee is informed about her or his future salary. The appraisal interview also provides a rich opportunity to motivate the employee. Using the Herzberg model, for example, might encourage a manager to explore which maintenance factors currently create dissatisfaction for an employee. If those can be resolved, then the discussion can turn toward ways to build into the job more opportunities for achievement, responsibility, and challenge.

Suggested Approaches   Extensive research has been done on the appraisal process and the characteristics of the most effective ones. Appraisal interviews are most likely to be successful when the appraiser

- Is knowledgeable about the employee's job
- Has previously set measurable performance standards
- Has gathered specific evidence frequently about performance
- Seeks and uses inputs from other observers in the organization
- Sharply limits the amount of criticism to a few major items (so the employees can *focus* their improvement efforts)
- Provides support, acceptance, and praise for tasks well done
- Listens actively to the employee's input and reactions
- Shares responsibility for outcomes and offers future assistance
- Allows participation in the discussion

Self-appraisal

The last point has been extended even further in recent approaches to the performance appraisal interview. Some organizations in both the private and public sectors include, as a formal part of the process, **self-appraisal.** This is an opportunity for the employee to be introspective and to offer a personal assessment of his or her accomplishments, strengths, and weaknesses. Questions directed to the employee might include "What has gone extremely well for you during this period?" "What kinds of problems have you had?" "What ideas do you have for improving your contributions?" Employee responses to these questions are then compared with the supervisor's evaluation of the employee. This approach allows differences of opinion to be discussed openly and resolved.

Problems can arise in self-appraisals, however.[9] Some poor performers tend to diminish their level of difficulties and attribute their problems to situational factors around them, and a few will rate themselves too leniently. These limitations, however, are offset by the fact that most employees are quite candid when asked to identify their strengths and weaknesses, and are able to compare their performance with previous expectations. In addition, self-assessments are much less threatening to one's self-esteem than are those received from others. Therefore, self-appraisals provide a more fertile soil for growth and change.

360-Degree Feedback Programs

All appraisal systems build on the assumption that employees need feedback about their performance (a basic element of the communication model described in Chapter 3). Feedback helps them know what to do and how well they are meeting their goals. It shows that others are interested in what they are doing. Assuming that performance is satisfactory, feedback enhances an employee's self-image and feeling of competence. Generally, **performance feedback** leads to both improved performance and improved attitudes—if handled properly by the manager.

Giving feedback is a challenging task for managers, however. Feedback is more likely to be accepted and cause some improvement when it is properly presented (see the guidelines for effective feedback in Figure 6–5). In general, it should focus on specific job behaviors, rely on objective data rather than subjective opinions and inferences, be well-timed by being given soon after a critical event, and be checked for understanding by the receiver. Overall, it has the greatest chance for inducing a behavioral change if it is genuinely desired by the employee and is connected to job tasks and if the receiver is allowed to choose a new behavior from alternative recommendations offered.

In spite of the importance of performance feedback, many managers fail to provide enough of it on an ongoing basis. They may feel too busy, they may assume that employees are already aware of their performance level, or they may be reluctant to share bad news because of the negative reaction they expect it to generate.

Another possible reason—not having enough valid information to create a substantive conclusion—can be overcome by the fast-growing practice of **360-degree feedback** (also known as multirater feedback or full-circle feedback). This is the process of systematically gathering data on a person's skills, abilities, and behaviors from a variety of sources—the manager, peers, subordinates, and even customers or clients.[10] These perspectives are examined to see where problems exist in the eyes of one or more groups. The results can also be compared across time to see if improvements have been made or compared with organizational norms to see if a person is better or worse than others. The 360-degree feedback system works best if individuals match the data gathered with their own self-assessments, for this approach encourages candid confrontation of one's need for change. The product of this multidirectional appraisal approach is rich feedback (both positive and negative) that, if used properly, can aid in performance improvements. It requires the cooperation of others to provide honest feedback, assurances that the data will remain confidential, and skilled facilitators to help recipients understand the complex information and develop

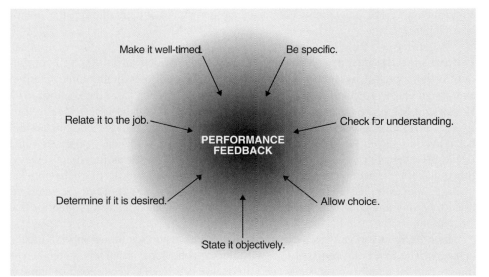

FIGURE 6–5

Guidelines for effective performance feedback

144

useful action plans for improvement. However, 360-degree feedback programs can be time-consuming, intimidating to the recipients, and expensive (development and administration of rating forms and training in how to use them).

> The role of a skilled facilitator is vital to the success of 360-degree feedback at AT&T, where a trained staff person from human resources often fills that role.[11] The facilitators there consolidate the inputs, identify the points of consensus, help the appraisee convert the natural focus on negative feedback into a discussion of using strengths to overcome flaws, and aid in developing concrete action plans for creating necessary changes. The presence of a facilitator also acts as a buffer, preventing the manager from attacking those who provided honest inputs.

Appraisal Problems   The need to perform the multiple functions in the appraisal process makes the appraisal interview difficult and even threatening for many managers. In addition, there are several behavioral problems inherent in the process.[12] It can be *confrontational,* because each party is trying to convince the other that her or his view is more accurate. (These views are distorted by attributional tendencies, as we discuss later in this chapter.) It is typically *emotional,* since the manager's role calls for a critical perspective, while the employee's desire to save face easily leads to defensiveness. It is *judgmental,* because the manager must evaluate the employee's behavior and results, and this aspect places the employee in a clearly subordinate position. Further, performance appraisals are *complex* tasks for managers, requiring job understanding, careful observation of performance, and sensitivity to the needs of employees. Managers are also called upon to handle the issues that arise spontaneously within the discussion itself.

Managers sometimes fail to conduct effective appraisal interviews because they lack vital skills. Perhaps they failed to gather data systematically. Maybe they weren't specific on the expected performance improvements in the previous appraisal. They could be reluctant to address difficult topics, or they could fail to involve the employee in the assessment process and discussion. Some managers may have grown cynical about the probability that attitudinal or behavioral changes will occur. A few may see appraisals as a meaningless game and even intentionally distort the ratings and feedback given. All these factors can place powerful limits on the usefulness of the appraisal interview, unless it is conducted properly or modified through the use of other inputs.

Attributions are causal explanations.

Nature of Attributions   Attribution theory has provided an intriguing contribution to the appraisal literature. **Attribution** is the process by which people interpret and assign causes for their own and others' behavior. It stems from the work of Fritz Heider and has been expanded and refined by Harold Kelley and others.[13]

The attribution process closely parallels the four basic goals of organizational behavior outlined in Chapter 1. As shown in Figure 6–6, a manager *observes* some employee's behavior or its consequences and often *describes* it as functional or dysfunctional for the work unit. Seeking to *understand* and diagnose the behavior, the manager makes a causal attribution (tentative explanation) for it. Then the manager tries to *predict* and *control* (influence) future employee behaviors as a product of that attribution.

Three basic factors are assessed as attributions are made regarding an individual's behavior. The first is its *consistency*—whether the behavior is relatively stable across time (a similar pattern) or unstable (an infrequent occurrence). The second dimension is its *distinctiveness*—whether the person's performance is different on this task than

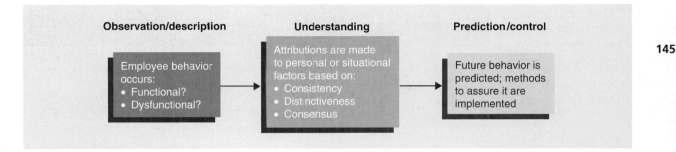

Observation/description	Understanding	Prediction/control
Employee behavior occurs: • Functional? • Dysfunctional?	Attributions are made to personal or situational factors based on: • Consistency • Distinctiveness • Consensus	Future behavior is predicted; methods to assure it are implemented

FIGURE 6–6

The process of making and using attributions

on most other tasks in the person's job. The third element is its *consensus*—the degree to which the person's peers behave in a similar fashion.

The combination of these three assessments results in several potential explanations for an employee's performance on a task. It could be attributed to high or low ability, to greater or lesser effort, to a difficult or an easy task, or to good or poor luck. Ability and effort are *personal* attributions; they tend to be given as explanations when there is a judgment of high consistency and low distinctiveness and low consensus. Task difficulty and luck are *situational* attributions; they tend to be used as explanations when the behavior stands out as distinctive and different from that of peers, while also being inconsistent. Following is an example of how the attribution process can be used:

Personal versus situational attributions

> After each professional football game, the head coach sits down with the assistant coaches and grades each player's performance. Did the athlete play better or worse than normal? Did the player perform better or worse than teammates? Did the player excel at some tasks and not at others? After appraising the athlete's conduct, the coach must also determine whether the strong or weak performance was the result of superior or inferior ability, greater or lesser effort, an experienced or inexperienced opponent, or good or bad luck (attributions). Then the coach will likely give some praise and constructive feedback to the players.

Since attributions are subjective assessments, we are interested in what affects the choice of explanations. One important factor is whether we are evaluating our own behavior or interpreting another's. In general, people tend to exhibit a **self-serving bias,** claiming undue credit for success and minimizing their own responsibility for problems. This tendency is seen when they overestimate the influence of internal factors (personal traits) when assessing their own successes and assign external (situational) causes for their own less successful outcomes (Figure 6–7).

Self-serving bias

The opposite pattern—a **fundamental attribution bias**—is often exhibited when judging others. People tend to attribute others' achievements to good luck or easy tasks, and they assume that others failed to try hard enough or simply lacked the appropriate personal characteristics or overall ability if they failed. The interpersonal comparison process is at work, with each party trying to improve his or her own relative self-image by manipulating assessments and attributions. Attributional tendencies accent the existing role differences between managers and employees, and these biases emerge clearly during managerial appraisals of employees.

Fundamental attribution bias

Related Ideas   Attributions illustrate the effects of **perceptual set;** that is, people tend to perceive what they expect to perceive. (Remember how an optimist sees the glass as half full, whereas the pessimist sees the same glass as half empty?) Perceptual sets sometimes cause us to misread a situation and see only what we expect to see. In this way, perceptual sets are much like the paradigms discussed in Chapter 2. Managers, therefore, need to be aware of their own perceptual sets and the effects of

Perceptual set

FIGURE 6–7

Different attributions for
an employee's behavior

Level of Employee Performance	Perceived by	Probable Attribution
Success →	Employee →	Personal characteristics (high ability or strong effort)
	Manager →	Situational factors (easy task or good luck)
Failure →	Employee →	Situational factors (hard task or bad luck)
	Manager →	Personal characteristics (low ability or poor effort)

those sets on their appraisals of others. Similarly, they need to be aware of their employees' perceptual sets in order to understand their workers better.

Self-fulfilling prophecy

The relatively passive idea of perceptual set extends into the behavior of individuals when we witness the power of the **self-fulfilling prophecy,** or the Pygmalion effect. The self-fulfilling prophecy suggests that a manager's expectations for an employee will cause the manager to treat the employee differently and that the employee will respond in a way that confirms the initial expectations.[14] For example, if a supervisor is told that a new employee is competent, the supervisor is more likely not only to perceive that competence but also to provide opportunities for the employee to demonstrate competence on the job. The supervisor then attributes the task performance to the employee's ability. This example shows how important perceptual set and the self-fulfilling prophecy can be in reversing the natural attributional tendencies discussed earlier.

> One supervisor's experience shows the roles that perceptual sets and self-fulfilling expectations can play. One of his machinists strongly wanted three days of vacation in order to go deer hunting. Since the department was so rushed that it was even working overtime every Saturday, the supervisor would not give him time off.
>
> The machinist also had a record of tardiness. One morning he arrived thirty minutes late. The harassed supervisor, without giving much thought to his words, threatened the employee with three days off without pay if he was tardy again that month.
>
> Guess who was tardy the next morning? You are correct. The machinist perceived the threat as an opportunity to go on his desired deer hunt. The supervisor saw no other choice than to give the machinist a disciplinary penalty of three days off without pay. In this way, the management policies were applied and the machinist reached his goal of going deer hunting, but the needed work was not done on schedule.

Applications of Attribution   The attributional model can be easily integrated with our earlier discussion (see Chapter 5) of other motivational approaches. For example, achievement-oriented people may claim that their accomplishments are the direct result of their high level of effort. Although goals are most motivational when they are challenging, employees will examine them closely to determine if they are too difficult to attain.

In conjunction with the expectancy model, an employee who fails on a task may feel that the environment prevents success and, therefore, may reduce the level of future effort. Users of behavior modification are cautioned to consider carefully their

An Ethics Question

Managers are often caught in a bind between conflicting pressures, with no apparent "perfect" solution. For example, consider a behaviorally aware manager who accepts the need to provide performance feedback to employees. While practicing the guidelines for effective feedback, however, the manager discovers that employees often experience a profound face-saving issue—they hear that their actual performance is not as good as they had perceived it to be. Upon hearing this, some become stoic and quiet, others cry, and a few become overtly angry, hostile, and verbally abusive.

After reflecting on this situation, the manager poses a general question: "Is it ethical for managers to share their honest perceptions of employee performance, at the risk of hurting them?" What do *you* think?

response to an employee's successful performance. A manager may assume it was due to luck or an easy task and withhold appropriate recognition. The employee, who believes that success was the result of ability or effort, may experience a decline in motivation for the lack of a reward.

Managers might benefit from greater awareness of their own attributional processes and how those processes affect their behavior toward employees. They could also seek to reinforce among subordinates the belief that success is due to the workers' own efforts (effort-performance expectancies) and abilities, while discouraging the employee attribution that failure is due to task difficulty or bad luck. Simple attributions should be avoided, since employee behavior is also partly determined by the task, social context, and environment, as outlined in Chapter 1.

Managerial Effects   Conducting performance appraisals also has substantial impact on the appraiser. On the positive side, a formal appraisal system encourages managers to do more analytical and constructive thinking about their employees. The requirement of a face-to-face interview encourages managers to be more specific about identifying each employee's abilities, interests, and motivation. Managers often begin to perceive that each employee is truly different and must be treated that way. For example, greater participation may be more appropriate when an employee is knowledgeable, has a strong independence need, and has demonstrated acceptable performance in the past.

Realistically, however, managers sometimes avoid giving appraisals because they do not want to disrupt an existing smooth relationship with an employee by providing negative feedback. It is particularly difficult to deal with low-performing employees, who may require more frequent monitoring and reviews. In other cases, managers simply do not see any organizational rewards coming to them from the appraisal process. Where there is no extrinsic or intrinsic incentive to perform the task, managers may neglect it entirely, as in this example:

Gordy, an employee in a utility, reported that for many years his supervisor would simply hand him a folded slip of paper with his next year's salary written on it. This was the sum total of his "performance appraisal"! Only recently did the utility become concerned about effective organizational behavior practices and begin training and rewarding its managers for appraising employees. Now Gordy enjoys the benefits of open discussion of his performance and mutual goal setting.

148

Even when appraisal interviews are capably conducted by managers, it is doubtful whether they will produce long-term performance changes by themselves. The appraisal acts only as a source of feedback and a psychic reward, and economic incentives are still needed to obtain employee motivation. Various economic incentive approaches are described next, along with assessments of their advantages and disadvantages.

ECONOMIC INCENTIVE SYSTEMS

Purposes and Types

An **economic incentive system** of some type can be applied to almost any job. The basic idea of such systems is to induce a high level of individual, group, or organizational performance by making an employee's pay contingent on one or more of those dimensions. Additional objectives include making it easier to recruit and retain good employees, stimulating desirable role behaviors such as creativity, encouraging the development of valued skills, and satisfying key employee needs. The criteria for these incentives could include employee output, company profit, cost savings, units shipped, level of customer service, or the ratio of labor cost to total sales. Evaluation of performance may be individual or collective, and the payment may be immediate or delayed, as in a profit-sharing plan.

Our discussion of economic incentives focuses on their overall nature, purpose, and behavior implications. We do not attempt to discuss all types of incentives or all details about them. The ones selected for presentation are wage incentives, which are a widely used individual incentive, and profit sharing and gain sharing, which are popular group incentives. Skill-based pay systems are increasing in popularity, especially in new industrial operations. Readers are urged to review Figure 6–1 to see how incentives are combined with other parts of wage administration to make a **complete pay program.**

Although most of our discussion is on long-run incentive programs, temporary incentives also have a role to play in compensation. Sometimes they provide just the right amount of added motivation to cause a desired increase in performance. Here is an example:

> A manufacturer of specialized business equipment experienced a substantial decline in sales for one of its models. The decline was so severe that it had scheduled a one-month closing of this model's production line during the Christmas season. At the sales manager's suggestion, the company offered to give its salespeople a new $10 bill for each item of this model sold during the month of December. The offer was made in the context of an extra Christmas bonus opportunity. The response was so great that the production line was kept operating, and some salespeople earned over $4,000 in bonus money paid in $10 bills. A $4,000 bonus amounted to 10 to 20 percent of a typical salesperson's annual income.

Incentives Linking Pay with Performance

There are several broad types of incentives that link pay with performance. Major ones are shown in Figure 6–8. Perhaps the most popular measure is for the amount of output

Piece rate

to determine pay, as illustrated by a sales commission or a **piece rate.** It provides a simple, direct connection between performance and reward. Those workers who produce more are rewarded more. Often pay is determined by a combination quantity-quality measure in order to ensure that a high quality of product or service is maintained. For example, a piece rate usually is paid for only those pieces that meet quality standards.

In other instances an incentive bonus is given only to those employees who

FIGURE 6–8

Major incentive
measures to link pay
with performance

149

Incentive Measure	Example
Amount of output	Piece rate; sales commission
Quality of output	Piece rate only for pieces meeting the standard; commission only for sales that are without bad debts
Success in reaching goals	Bonus for selling an established number of items during a predetermined time span
Amount of profit	Profit sharing
Cost efficiency	Gain sharing
Employee skills	Skill-based pay

reach established goals. For example, a bonus might be given for selling fifteen automobiles during a month, but there would be no bonus for selling only fourteen. Rewards also may be given on the basis of profit success, as in a profit-sharing plan. Another measure is to link pay with cost efficiency. An example is gain sharing, discussed later in this chapter. Skill-based pay systems reward individuals for their capabilities. Regardless of the type of incentive that is used, its objective is to link a portion of a worker's pay to some measure of employee or organizational performance.

Advantages   Incentives provide several potential employee advantages. A major advantage is that *they increase employee beliefs (instrumentality) that reward will follow high performance.* If we assume that money has valence to an employee, then motivation should increase.

Incentives also appear favorable from the point of view of equity theory. Those who perform better are rewarded more. This kind of input-outcome balance is perceived by many people to be equitable. Further, if more pay is a valued reward, then incentive systems are favorable from the point of view of behavior modification. They provide a desirable consequence (pay) that should reinforce behavior. Rewards, such as sales commissions, often are rather immediate and frequent, which is consistent with the philosophy of behavior modification.

Improved motivation

Another advantage from the employee's point of view is that incentives are comparatively objective. They can be computed from the number of pieces, dollars, or similar objective criteria. Compared with a supervisor's subjective performance ratings, the objective approach tends to have higher acceptance by employees.

Difficulties   With so many favorable conditions supporting incentives, it seems that workers would welcome almost any incentive because of the rewards it could bring. However, there are difficulties that tend to offset some of the advantages. Potential equity is offset by other developments that are perceived as inequities. In behavior modification terms, certain unfavorable consequences exist alongside the favorable consequences of more pay, so they tend to reduce the potential advantages of incentive pay. When workers make their cost-reward analyses, they find that costs have risen along with rewards. The result may be that the break-even point has changed very

150

Evaluate pros and cons.

little, if at all. The extra problems caused by the incentive may offset much of the economic gain expected. For example, new employees may have difficulty learning the system; other employees with declining energy may experience a decrease in total pay; and some unions may resist the incentive idea.

The organization, too, can experience problems. It is difficult to establish a fair basis for incentive pay—one that motivates higher performance across a broad range of employees without producing undesirable side effects. Some incentive systems are also costly to monitor, requiring extensive record-keeping procedures. The key thought is that *incentive systems produce both positive and negative employee consequences,* as shown in Figure 6–9. Both must be evaluated in determining the desirability of an incentive system. Economic consequences are likely to be positive, but the direction of psychological and social consequences is less certain.

Wage Incentives

More Pay for More Production   Basically, **wage incentives** provide more pay for more production. The main reason for use of wage incentives is clear: They nearly always increase productivity while decreasing unit labor costs. Workers under normal conditions without wage incentives have the capacity to produce more, and wage incentives are one way to release that potential. The increased productivity often is substantial.

> One example is Nucor, a builder and operator of steel-producing minimills. It pays weekly bonuses, based on a measure of acceptable production. Groups typically receive a bonus more than 100 percent above base pay. Turnover rates, after the start-up period, are so small that the company does not even bother measuring them.[15]

Criteria for incentive systems

In order to be successful, a wage incentive needs to be simple enough for employees to have a strong belief that reward will follow performance. If the plan is so complex that workers have difficulty relating performance to reward, then higher motivation is less likely to develop. The objectives, eligibility requirements, performance criteria, and payment system all need to be established and understood by the participants.

When incentive systems operate successfully, they are evaluated favorably by participants, probably because they provide psychological as well as economic rewards. Employees receive satisfaction from a job well done, which fulfills their achievement drive. Their self-image may improve because of greater feelings of competence. They

FIGURE 6–9

Advantages and disadvantages of incentives linking pay with performance

Advantages	Disadvantages
• Strengthen instrumentality beliefs	• Cost (to both employer and employee)
• Create perceptions of equity	• System complexity
• Reinforce desirable behaviors	• Declining or variable pay
• Provide objective basis for rewards	• Union resistance
	• Delay in receipt
	• Rigidity of system
	• Narrowness of performance

may even feel they are making a contribution to society by helping in the attempt to regain a productivity leadership position among nations. Some incentives may encourage cooperation between workers because of the need for employees to work together to earn incentive awards.

> One of the authors visited a small assembly plant in rural Illinois. After other workers performed a variety of preliminary tasks, two-person crews on an incentive system installed a variety of hardware—hinges, braces, locks, decorative trim, and handles—on large pieces of furniture. The work speed of the crew that was observed was almost unbelievable, as the workers seemed to be flying around their workstation. Their productive interaction was almost like a ballet—it was perfectly choreographed and wordlessly performed. They always seemed to know not only their individual assignment but what their partner would be doing, with only an occasional nod of the head needed as a signal between them. They had been given a fair piece rate, they had the necessary skills and tools, and they both wanted to earn higher pay. As a result they worked furiously for a couple of hours at a time, took breaks whenever they needed them, and still earned more incentive pay than any other team in the factory.

Difficulties   Production wage incentives furnish an example of the kinds of difficulties that may develop with many incentive plans, despite their potential benefits. Management's job is to try to prevent or reduce the problems while increasing benefits, so that the incentive plan works more effectively.

The basic human difficulty with wage incentives of this type is that *disruptions in the social system may lead to feelings of inequity and dissatisfaction.* At times these disruptions are severe enough to make incentive workers less satisfied with their pay than workers who are paid an hourly wage, even though the incentive workers are earning more. *Disruption of social systems*

For any wage incentive plan to be successful, it needs to be coordinated carefully with the whole operating system. If there are long periods when employees must wait for work to arrive at their workplace, then the incentive loses its punch. If the incentive is likely to replace workers, then management needs to plan for their use elsewhere so that employee security is not threatened. If work methods are erratic, then they must be standardized so that a fair rate of reward can be established. This is a complex process leading to many difficulties.

1. Wage incentives normally require establishment of performance standards. **Rate setting** is the process of determining the standard output for each job, which becomes the fair day's work for the operator. Rate setters are often resented not only because subjective judgment is involved but also because they are believed to be a cause of change and more difficult standards. *Rate setting*

2. Wage incentives may make the supervisor's job more complex. Supervisors must be familiar with the system, so that they can explain it to employees. Paperwork increases, resulting in greater chance of error and more employee dissatisfaction. Relationships are compounded, and supervisors are required to resolve different expectations from higher management, rate setters, workers, and unions.

3. A thorny problem with production wage incentives involves **loose rates.** A rate is "loose" when employees are able to reach standard output with less than normal effort. When management adjusts the rate to a higher standard, employees predictably experience a feeling of inequity. *Loose rates*

4. Wage incentives may cause disharmony between incentive workers and hourly workers. When the two groups perform work in a sequence, hourly workers may feel discriminated against because they earn less. If the incentive workers increase output, hourly workers farther along the process must work faster to prevent a

152

bottleneck. The incentive workers earn more for their increased output, but the hourly workers do not.

Hourly workers who precede incentive workers in the production process can on occasion take it easy and produce less with no cut in pay. But the incentive worker's income is cut when less work is available. The same problem occurs if an hourly worker is absent and reduces the flow of material to incentive workers. Conflicts of this type are so difficult to resolve that it is best for management not to mix the two groups in any closely integrated production sequence.

Output restrictions

5. Another difficulty with wage incentives is that they may result in **output restriction,** by which workers limit their production and thus defeat the purpose of the incentive. This phenomenon is caused by several factors—group insecurities that the production standard will be raised, resistance to change by the informal social organization, and the fact that people are not comfortable always working at full capacity.

Profit Sharing

Nature and Merits   **Profit sharing** is a system that distributes to employees some portion of the profits of business, either immediately (in the form of cash bonuses) or deferred until a later date (held in trust in the form of employee-owned shares). The growth of profit sharing has been encouraged by federal tax laws that allow employee income taxes to be deferred on funds placed in profit-sharing pension plans.

Mutual interest is emphasized.

Basic pay rates, performance pay increases, and most other incentive systems recognize individual differences, whereas profit sharing recognizes *mutual* interests. Employees become interested in the economic success of their employer when they see that their own rewards are affected by it. Greater institutional teamwork tends to develop.

Smaller organizations in competitive industries that demand high commitment from employees in order to make technological breakthroughs or bring new products to market faster are prime candidates for profit-sharing programs. If the firms are successful, the rewards are great. This possibility builds strong motivation among employees to see the big picture and allows the organization to forge ahead of its competitors.

> The Andersen Corporation is a billion-dollar company that makes various types of windows for the housing industry. The company began a profit-sharing plan in 1914, and it has grown with the success of the company ever since then. In a recent year, the company distributed over $100 million to its full-time employees through its profit-sharing plan. This bonus amounted to approximately forty-three weeks of extra compensation for each employee.[16]

In general, profit sharing tends to work better for fast-growing, profitable organizations in which there are opportunities for substantial employee rewards. It also works better, of course, when general economic conditions are favorable. It is less likely to be useful in stable and declining organizations with low profit margins and intense competition. Profit sharing generally is well received and understood by managers and high-level professional people, because their decisions and actions are more likely to have a significant effect on their firm's profits. Since operating workers, especially in large firms, have more difficulty connecting their individual actions with the firm's profitability, profit sharing may have less initial appeal to them. In situations where it has worked effectively, managers have openly shared financial reports with all levels of workers, actively trained employees to understand financial statements, and provided on-site computer terminals for immediate access to relevant information whenever employees want it. (You may wish to review the discussion of open-book management in "What Managers Are Reading" in Chapter 3.)

153

Difficulties   Even in those situations where profit sharing seems appropriate, some general disadvantages exist:

1. Profits are not directly related to an employee's effort on the job. Poor market conditions may nullify an employee's hard work.

   Indirect relationship

2. Employees must wait for their reward, and this lengthy delay diminishes its impact.

   Delay

3. Since profits are somewhat unpredictable, total worker income may vary from year to year. Some workers may prefer the security of a more stable wage or salary.

   Lack of predictability

4. Some union leaders have historically been suspicious of profit sharing. They fear that it would undermine union loyalty, result in varied total earnings from company to company, and weaken their organizing campaigns. More progressive unions have, however, welcomed the opportunity for their members to share in corporate profits.

   Union skepticism

The social aspects of profit sharing are just as significant as its economic and tax aspects, if not more so. For profit sharing to develop a genuine community of interest, workers need to understand how it works and feel a sense of fairness in its provisions. If they do not, they may resent it, as in the following situation:

> Marvin Schmidt, an idealistic owner of a small retail store, employed twenty-five people. He had worked hard to build his meager investment into a prosperous store in the short period of seven years. Much of his success resulted from loyal, cooperative employees who had worked for him several years. He recognized their contributions and wanted to give them extra rewards, but he always had been short of capital.
>
> Finally, he had a very prosperous year, so he decided to begin a cash profit-sharing plan to be given as a bonus at Christmas. The generous bonus amounted to 30 percent of each person's pay for the year. It was announced and given as a surprise with the weekly paycheck immediately preceding Christmas. Not one employee thanked him, and most of his employees were cool and uncooperative thereafter. He eventually learned that they felt if he could give that large a bonus, he must have been unjustly exploiting them for years, even though they admitted they had been receiving more than the prevailing wage.

Gain Sharing

Another useful group incentive is **gain sharing,** or production sharing. A **gain-sharing plan** is a program that establishes a historical base period of organizational performance, measures improvements, and shares the gains with employees on some formula basis. Examples of the performance factors measured include inventory levels, labor hours per unit of product, usage of materials and supplies, and quality of finished goods.[17] The idea is to pinpoint areas that are controllable by employees and then give them an incentive for identifying and implementing ideas that will result in cost savings, as the following example shows:

> An example of gain-sharing plans is the one used at Turner Brothers Trucking—a company that tears down and reassembles drilling rigs, services pipe, and operates large cranes.[18] To reduce its huge liability and workers' compensation premiums, the company offered a group of employees $50 each for every month in which total losses from injuries, cargo damage, and driving accidents were less than $300. The results were dramatic; the ratio of the gain-sharing amount paid to employees compared with expected safety costs was 1:4 for the first

154

few years after the program was introduced, and it dropped even further thereafter. This win-win program demonstrated that employees could not only control their safety record but would do so for a fairly modest cost to the organization.

Behavioral Basis   Gain-sharing plans use several fundamental ideas from organizational behavior and are much more than pay systems. They encourage employee suggestions, provide an incentive for coordination and teamwork, and promote improved communication. Union-management relations often improve, since the union gains status because it takes responsibility for the benefits gained. Attitudes toward technological change improve because workers are aware that greater efficiency leads to larger bonuses. Gain sharing broadens the understanding of employees as they see a larger picture of the system through their participation rather than confining their outlook to the narrow specialty of their job.

Contingency Factors   The success of gain sharing is contingent upon a number of key factors, such as moderately small size of the unit, sufficient operating history to allow creation of standards, existence of controllable cost areas, and relative stability of the business. In addition, management must be receptive to employee participation, the organization must be willing to share the benefits of production increases with employees, and the union should be favorable to such a cooperative effort. Managers need to be receptive to ideas and tolerant of criticism from employees.

> A gain-sharing program replaced a piece-rate system at Tech Form Industries (TFI), a small (400-employee) producer of tubular exhaust systems for cars.[19] The company was experiencing severe external problems with rejected products and customer dissatisfaction, and internally the state of labor-management relations was severely strained. After careful design and implementation of the new program, a two-year follow-up study revealed a decrease of 83 percent in defective products returned, a 50 percent decline in direct labor hours spent on repairs, and a grievance rate that diminished by 41 percent. TFI, its customers, and its employees were delighted with the results.

At-risk pay

Some gain-sharing programs have broadened the basic idea to include the notion that employees must share in both gains and losses. Du Pont's fibers department designates a portion of the employee's base salary (for example, 6 percent of it) as **at-risk pay**.[20] If the work unit does not achieve its growth objectives, employees may receive as little as 94 percent of their target pay rate; if objectives are met, workers may receive up to a 12 percent bonus. In this way, employees can truly experience both the positive and negative effects of their efforts.

Skill-Based Pay

In contrast to salaries (which pay someone to hold a job) and wage incentives (which pay for the level of performance), **skill-based pay** (also called *knowledge-based pay* or *multiskill pay*) rewards individuals for what they know how to do. Employees are paid for the range, depth, and types of skills in which they demonstrate capabilities.[21] They start working at a flat hourly rate and receive increases for either developing skills within their primary job or learning how to perform other jobs within their work unit. Some companies provide increases for each new job learned; most others require employees to acquire blocks of related new skills, which may take several years to learn. Substantial amounts of training must be made available for the system to work, and methods for fairly pricing jobs and certifying employee skill levels need to be established. Some skill-based pay systems have supervisors evaluate the knowledge and skill of their employees; others allow work teams to assess the progress of each trainee.

1. Seek to establish accurate measures of performance, and make the connection between performance and rewards clear to all.
2. Provide rewards that people value; if you don't know what they value, ask them.
3. Make it clear to employees how the organization's monetary rewards relate to their various needs and drives.
4. Make sure that employees believe their goals are attainable if they perform well.
5. If you are trying to promote teamwork, provide team-based, not individual, rewards.
6. Be aware of the unintended consequences that are associated with any reward system, and try to minimize these.
7. Utilize the advantages of 360-degree feedback systems for providing employees with a broad and rich source of performance feedback.
8. Monitor your own behavior, and that of your employees, for signs of inappropriate attributions of behavior during performance appraisals.

Advantages   Although skill-based pay systems are quite new, they have several potential strengths. They provide strong motivation for employees to develop their work-related skills, they reinforce an employee's sense of self-esteem, and they provide the organization with a highly flexible workforce that can fill in when someone is absent. Since workers rotate among jobs to learn them, boredom should be reduced, at least temporarily. Pay satisfaction should be relatively high, for two reasons. First, the employee's hourly rate received (for having multiple skills) is often higher than the rate that would be paid for the task being performed, since only in a perfect system would all employees be constantly using their highest skills. As a result, some employees may even feel temporarily overpaid. Second, workers should perceive the system as equitable both in the sense of their costs and rewards being matched and in the knowledge that all employees with the same skills earn the same pay.

Disadvantages   There are several disadvantages to skill-based pay, and some firms have backed away from early experiments with it. First, since most employees will voluntarily learn higher-level jobs, the average hourly pay rate will be greater than normal. (This increased cost should be more than offset by productivity increases, however.) Second, a substantial investment in employee training must be made, especially in the time spent coaching by supervisors and peers. Third, not all employees like skill-based pay because it places pressure on them to move up the skill ladder. The subsequent dissatisfaction may lead to a variety of consequences, including employee turnover. Fourth, some employees will qualify themselves for skill areas that they will be unlikely to use, causing the organization to pay them higher rates than they deserve from a performance standpoint.

Skill-based pay, like other incentive programs, works best when the organizational culture of the firm is generally supportive and trusting. The system should be understood by employees, they must have realistic expectations about their prospects for higher pay levels, it must be possible for them to learn new skills and to have these skills promptly evaluated, and there must be some limits on which skills they can qualify for. Under these conditions, the program is consistent with the other incentives discussed in this chapter, since it links employee pay with the potential for increased performance.

SUMMARY

Economic rewards provide social as well as economic value. They play a key role within several motivational models, blending with expectancy, equity, behavior modification, and need-based approaches. Employees perform a rough cost-reward comparison and work somewhat near but below the break-even point.

Performance appraisal provides a systematic basis for assessment of employee contributions, coaching for improved performance, and distribution of economic rewards. Modern appraisal philosophy focuses on performance, objectives, mutual goal setting, and feedback. Newer appraisal approaches, such as self-appraisal and 360-degree feedback systems, provide additional perspectives on employee performance and suggestions for improvement. Nevertheless, the appraisal interview can be difficult for both manager and employee.

One significant confounding factor in appraisals is the likelihood that one or both parties will engage in inappropriate attributions. These are the perceptual assignment of alternative causes to one's behavior based on preconceptions and faulty reasoning; they serve to cause difficulties between the manager and the appraisee unless they are resolved through careful analysis.

Incentive systems provide different amounts of pay in relation to some measure of performance. They tend to increase employee expectations that rewards will follow performance, although the delay may range from a week to a year. Incentives often stimulate greater productivity but also tend to produce some offsetting negative consequences. Wage incentives reward greater output by individuals or groups, whereas profit sharing emphasizes mutual interest with the employer to build a successful organization. Gain sharing emphasizes improvement in various indexes of organizational performance, whereas skill-based pay rewards employees for acquiring greater levels or types of skills. Since employees have different needs to be served, many types of pay programs are required for a complete economic reward system.

Terms and Concepts for Review

Appraisal interview	Output restriction
At-risk pay	Perceptual set
Attribution	Performance appraisal
Comparable worth	Performance feedback
Complete pay program	Piece rate
Cost-reward comparison	Profit sharing
Economic incentive system	Rate setting
Equal Pay Act of 1963	Self-appraisal
Fundamental attribution bias	Self-fulfilling prophecy
Gain sharing	Self-serving bias
Gain-sharing plan	Skill-based pay
Incentives	360-degree feedback
Loose rates	Wage incentives
Management by objectives (MBO)	

Discussion Questions

1. Explain how money can be both an economic and a social medium of exchange. As a student, how do *you* use money as a social medium of exchange?
2. Think of a job that you formerly had or now have.
   a. Discuss specifically how the expectancy model applied (applies) to your pay.
   b. Discuss how you felt (feel) about the equity of your pay and why you felt (feel) that way.
   c. Develop and explain a cost-reward comparison chart for your pay and effort.

3. Think of a time when you assessed, either formally or informally, someone else's level of performance and found it deficient by your standards. To what did you attribute the reasons for the inadequate performance? Were you engaging in any attributional tendencies? How could you avoid doing so?

4. Assume that, in the first six months of your first job, your manager asks you to participate in filling out a feedback form describing his or her strengths and weaknesses. How comfortable will you feel in doing this? Now assume that your manager asks you to engage in the same process, seeking feedback from your peers, manager, and customers. Now what is your reaction? Explain.

5. What are the major measures used to link pay with production? Which ones, if any, were used in the last job you had? Discuss the effectiveness of the measure or measures used.

6. Would you use profit sharing, gain sharing, skill-based pay, or wage incentives in any of the following jobs? Discuss your choice in each instance.
   a. Employee in a small, fast-growing computer company
   b. Teacher in a public school
   c. Clerk processing insurance claims in an insurance office
   d. Automobile repair mechanic in a small repair shop
   e. Farm worker picking peaches
   f. Production worker in a shoe factory making men's shoes

7. Divide into small groups, each led by a member who has worked for a sales commission. Discuss how the commission related to both equity theory and expectancy theory, and report highlights of your discussion to your entire classroom group.

8. Have you ever participated in restriction of output in a job or in an academic course? If so, discuss why you did it and what its consequences were.

9. "Skill-based pay is a waste of company money, because we are paying for *potential* performance instead of *actual* performance." Discuss this statement.

10. During your first ten years after leaving college, what fraction of your salary would you be willing to put at risk—both for possible gain and for possible loss? During the last ten years before you retire, how much would you be willing to put at risk? Explain.

How well do you exhibit good reward and performance appraisal skills?

Read the following statements carefully. Circle the number on the response scale that most closely reflects the degree to which each statement accurately describes you when you reward employees and conduct a performance appraisal. Add up your total points, and prepare a brief action plan for self-improvement. Be ready to report your score for tabulation across the entire group.

Assess Your Own Skills

	Good description									Poor description
1. I recognize and understand the roles that money plays in each of the motivational models.	10	9	8	7	6	5	4	3	2	1
2. I plan to administer monetary rewards on a contingent basis, providing high rewards for good performance and much lesser rewards for weaker performance.	10	9	8	7	6	5	4	3	2	1

158

3. I recognize the importance of helping employees understand the need for balance between their rewards and their contributions.   10   9   8   7   6   5   4   3   2   1

4. I understand the necessity of providing employees with opportunities for both extrinsic and intrinsic rewards.   10   9   8   7   6   5   4   3   2   1

5. I am comfortable with the five hallmarks of modern appraisal philosophy and would use those in my own appraisals of employees.   10   9   8   7   6   5   4   3   2   1

6. I envision the performance appraisal interview as an opportunity for much more than simply giving feedback to employees.   10   9   8   7   6   5   4   3   2   1

7. I would be comfortable receiving feedback from all participants in a 360-degree appraisal process.   10   9   8   7   6   5   4   3   2   1

8. I could readily follow the guidelines for giving performance feedback to employees.   10   9   8   7   6   5   4   3   2   1

9. I can easily see how an employee's self-serving bias could distort that person's self-appraisal.   10   9   8   7   6   5   4   3   2   1

10. I understand the fundamental attribution bias and believe that I could successfully avoid it.   10   9   8   7   6   5   4   3   2   1

Scoring and Interpretation   Add up your total points for the ten questions. Record that number here, and report it when it is requested.____

- If you scored between 81–100 points, you appear to have a solid capability for demonstrating good reward and performance appraisal skills.
- If you scored between 61–80 points, you should take a close look at the items with lower self-assessment scores and explore ways to improve those items.
- If you scored less than 60 points, you should be aware that a weaker skill level regarding several items could be detrimental to your future success as a manager. We encourage you to review relevant sections of the chapter and watch for related material in subsequent chapters and other sources.

Now identify your three lowest scores, and write the question numbers here: ____, ____, ____. Write a brief paragraph, detailing to yourself an action plan for how you might sharpen each of these skills.

Incident

Plaza Grocery

Brad Holden was the executive vice president for Plaza Grocery, a family-owned chain of six grocery stores in a medium-sized metropolitan area. The current problem he was facing dealt with the stock clerks/carryout workers in the stores. Despite paying them the usual wage rate (the minimum federal hourly wage), he had trouble obtaining enough applicants for the job. Worse still, many of them seemed to lack motivation once he hired them. This situation created problems of empty shelves and slow service at the checkout lanes.

In an attempt to solve the problem, Brad met with small groups of the workers to get their ideas. He also consulted with a local expert on compensation issues. Some workers said they wanted a higher hourly wage rate; others said they wanted some incentive to work faster; some had no comment whatsoever. The consultant recommended that Brad consider using some of the more contemporary compensation systems.

Questions

1. Which of the major economic incentive systems discussed in this chapter has the best chance of working for Brad?
2. Can two or more incentive systems be combined, with an even greater likelihood of success? What might be gained through a combination, and what would be the costs (for both Plaza Grocery and the employees)?
3. In your recommendation, which motivational theories are you most specifically using?

Performance Appraisal/Reward Philosophy

Experiential Exercise

1. Read the following set of statements about people and indicate your degree of agreement or disagreement on the rating scales.

	Strongly agree				Strongly disagree
a. Most people don't want equity; they want to earn more than their peers.	1	2	3	4	5
b. Skill-based pay won't work well because employees will learn the minimum necessary to earn a higher rate and then forget what they learned.	1	2	3	4	5
c. Most employees are too comfortable with the status quo to want to devote effort to learning new skills.	1	2	3	4	5
d. Most employees neither understand what profits are nor appreciate their importance; therefore profit-sharing systems are doomed to fail.	1	2	3	4	5
e. If asked to participate in a 360-degree feedback program appraising their own manager, most employees would distort their assessments in some way rather than be honest.	1	2	3	4	5
f. The division between management and labor is so great that both gain-sharing and profit-sharing systems are likely to fail.	1	2	3	4	5

    g. Since people do not want to hear about
their weaknesses and failures, performance
appraisal interviews will not change
employee behavior.   1   2   3   4   5

    h. The idea that employees assess the costs
and rewards associated with any major
behavior is ridiculous; they simply decide
whether or not they feel like doing
something and then do it or don't do it.   1   2   3   4   5

2. Meeting in small discussion groups, tabulate the responses to each question (frequency distribution and mean) and explore reasons for any significant disagreements within your group's ratings.

3. In your group, develop alternative statements for any items you do not support (ratings of 3, 4, or 5) at present. Explain how your new statements reflect your knowledge of human behavior gained through reading the early chapters of this book.

Part Three

Leadership
and
Empowerment

Chapter 7

Leadership

It is important that people in an organization have something to be proud of.
–Percy Barnevik[1]

Clearly, the most critical attribute future managers must have is flexibility.
–Brent B. Allred, Charles C. Snow, and Raymond E. Miles[2]

CHAPTER OBJECTIVES

TO UNDERSTAND

- The Nature of Leadership and Followership

- The Difference between Traits and Behaviors

- Different Leadership Styles

- Early Approaches to Leadership

- Contingency Approaches to Leadership

- Substitutes for Leadership

- Self-Leadership and Superleadership

- Coaching as a Leadership Role

Al Dunlap was the CEO of Scott Paper Company for two years. Soon after being selected to lead the company, he acquired the nickname "Chainsaw Al" for the dramatic way in which he chopped up the organization and scaled back its operations. All in all, he cut 11,000 employees, slashed R&D by 50 percent, forbid community involvement by managers, and eliminated all corporate gifts to charities. His toughness and tenacity were focused on maximizing shareholder value. The result was an increase in stock price for Scott Paper of approximately 225 percent, and a successful merger with Kimberly-Clark.[3] Dunlap's later attempt to duplicate his feat at Sunbeam was disastrous, however.

THE NATURE OF LEADERSHIP

Leadership is the process of influencing and supporting others to work enthusiastically toward achieving objectives. It is the critical factor that helps an individual or a group identify its goals and then motivates and assists in achieving the stated goals. The three important elements in the definition are influence/support, voluntary effort, and goal achievement. Without leadership, an organization would be only a confusion of people and machines, just as an orchestra without a conductor would be only musicians and instruments. The orchestra and all other organizations require leadership to develop their precious assets to the fullest.

The leadership process is similar in effect to that of the secret chemical that turns a caterpillar into a butterfly with all the beauty that was the caterpillar's potential. *Leadership, then, is the catalyst that transforms potential into reality.* This role is often seen dramatically in giant organizations, as when CEO Jack Welch led the transformation of General Electric from a sleeping giant in 1980 into a sleek machine in the twenty-first century. It is equally important in smaller organizations like Microsoft Corporation, which Bill Gates started and guided to national prominence as a developer of microcomputer software and operating systems. The opening illustration about the successes and failures of Al Dunlap accents the catalyst role that leaders play while demonstrating the fact that many leadership styles have a "dark side" to them (e.g., the hardship to laid-off employees and the dangers of a narrow focus on a single goal). In all cases, leadership is the ultimate act that identifies, develops, channels, and enriches the potential that is already in an organization and its people.

A catalyst

In this chapter we discuss the nature of leadership—the behaviors, roles, and skills that combine to form different leadership styles. Behavioral approaches are *descriptive,* offering a variety of ways in which the *actions* of leaders often differ (e.g., leaders can be positive or negative, autocratic or participative, employee-oriented or task-oriented). Contingency approaches are more *analytical,* encouraging managers to examine their situation and select a style which best *fits* it. We conclude with a look at some of the newer ideas, such as substitutes for leadership, superleadership, and coaching.

Management and Leadership

Leadership is an important part of management, but it is not the whole story. *The primary role of a leader is to influence others to voluntarily seek defined objectives* (preferably with enthusiasm). Managers also plan activities, organize appropriate structures, and control resources. Managers hold formal positions, whereas anyone can use his or her informal influence while acting as a leader. Managers achieve results by directing the activities of others, whereas leaders create a vision and inspire others to achieve this vision and to stretch themselves beyond their normal capabilities. Because there is a difference between management and leadership, strong leaders may be weak managers if poor planning causes their group to move in the wrong directions. Though they can get their group going, they just cannot get it going in directions that best serve organizational objectives.

164

Other combinations also are possible. A person can be a weak leader and still be an effective manager, especially if she or he happens to be managing people who have a clear understanding of their jobs and a strong drive to work. This set of circumstances is less likely, and therefore we expect excellent managers to have reasonably high leadership ability among their other skills. Fortunately, leadership ability can be acquired through observation of effective role models, participation in management training, and learning from work experiences.[4]

Traits of Effective Leaders

People have been concerned about the nature of leadership since the beginning of history. Early research tried to identify the **traits**—physical, intellectual, or personality characteristics—that differed between leaders and nonleaders or between successful and unsuccessful leaders. Many cognitive and psychological factors, such as intelligence, ambition, and aggressiveness, were studied. Other researchers examined physical characteristics, such as height, body size and shape, and personal attractiveness. Many corporations today still use the controversial Myers-Briggs Type Indicator personality test, based on the work of psychologist Carl Jung, to label managers on four dimensions—as extroverts or introverts, thinkers or feelers, sensers or intuitors, and judges or perceivers. Clearly, interest and speculation persist about what characteristics make a good leader.

Myers-Briggs typology

The current research on leadership traits suggests that some factors do help differentiate leaders from nonleaders (see Figure 7–1).[5] The most important traits are a high level of personal drive, the desire to lead, personal integrity, and self-confidence. Cognitive (analytical) ability, business knowledge, charisma, creativity, flexibility, and personal warmth are also frequently desired.

Key traits

One important conclusion about these leadership traits is that they do not necessarily *guarantee* successful leadership. They are best viewed as personal competencies or resources that may or may not be developed and used. Many people have the capabilities to be effective leaders, but some choose not to demonstrate the traits they have. Others may have the necessary traits and the desire to use them, but the opportunity to do so never arises. A final issue is whether or not leadership traits can be acquired or embellished over time if someone aspires to leadership. While some traits may be difficult to accumulate in the short run, others (such as self-confidence and knowledge of the business) can likely be acquired by dedicated students.

Leadership Behavior

Much research has focused on identifying leadership *behaviors*. In this view, successful leadership depends more on appropriate behavior, skills, and actions, and less on personal traits. The difference is similar to that between latent energy and kinetic energy in physics: One type (the traits) provides the latent potential, and the other (the behaviors, skills, and actions) is the successful release and expression of those traits, much like kinetic energy. The distinction is a significant one, since behaviors and skills can be learned and changed, while many traits are relatively fixed in the short term. The three broad types of skills leaders use are technical, human, and conceptual. Although these skills are interrelated in practice, they can be considered separately.

Technical Skill   **Technical skill** refers to a person's knowledge of and ability in any type of process or technique. Examples are the skills learned by accountants, engi-

FIGURE 7–1

Leadership traits

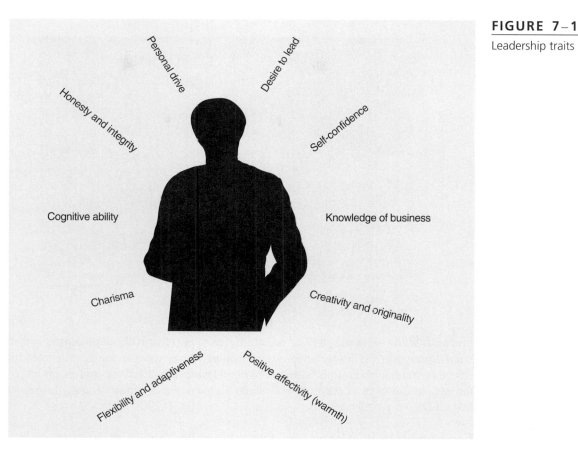

neers, word processing operators, and toolmakers. Technical skill is the distinguishing feature of job performance at the operating and professional levels, but as employees are promoted to leadership responsibilities, their technical skills become proportionately less important, as shown in Figure 7–2. As managers, they increasingly depend on the technical skills of their subordinates; in many cases they have never practiced some of the technical skills that they supervise.

An Ethics Question

Leaders are needed, and good leaders are valued by their organizations. They energize workforces with compelling visions of the future, guide their firms through difficult crises, create supportive corporate cultures, and increase shareholder value. When performance is positive, leaders are revered. But how much are they worth?

Many CEOs today are richly rewarded, earning several million dollars per year in salary, bonuses, and stock options. This is distressing to some observers, who feel that these corporate leaders are getting rich at the expense of other employees. The ratio of top CEO pay to that of the average worker has risen sharply in the past few decades, from about 20:1 to its current level of approximately 300:1. During a period when average worker compensation has been relatively steady, is it ethical to use corporate resources to pay CEOs increasingly huge sums while the gap between them and their employees widens? What do you think?

FIGURE 7–2

Variations in the use of leadership skills at different organizational levels

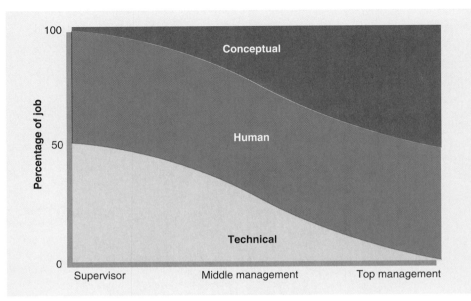

Human Skill   **Human skill** is the ability to work effectively with people and to build teamwork. No leader at any organizational level escapes the requirement for effective human skill. It is a major part of leadership behavior and is discussed throughout this book. Lack of human skills has been the downfall of many managers and CEOS.

Conceptual Skill   **Conceptual skill** is the ability to think in terms of models, frameworks, and broad relationships, such as long-range plans. It becomes increasingly important in higher managerial jobs. Conceptual skill deals with ideas, whereas human skill concerns people and technical skill involves things.

Analysis of leadership skills helps explain why outstanding department heads sometimes make poor vice presidents. They may not be using the proper mixture of skills required for the higher-level job, particularly additional conceptual skill.

Situational Aspects

Three elements to consider

Successful leadership requires behavior that unites and stimulates followers toward defined objectives in specific situations. All three elements—leader, followers, and situation—are variables that affect one another in determining appropriate leadership behavior.

It is evident that leadership is situational. In one situation, action A may be the best cluster of leadership acts, but in the next situation, action B will be best. To try to have all an organization's leaders fit a standard pattern will suppress creative differences and result in inefficiency as well, because many square pegs will be trying to fit into round holes. Leadership is part of a complex system, so there is no simple way to answer the question, What makes a leader?

Sometimes leaders must resist the temptation to be visible in a situation. Even though good leadership involves a set of behaviors, it should not be confused with mere activity when activity is not needed. Aggressiveness and constant interaction with others will not guarantee good leadership. At times the appropriate leadership action is to stay in the background keeping pressures off the group, to keep quiet so that others may talk, to be calm in times of uproar, to hesitate purposefully, and to delay decisions. At other times a leader must be more decisive, directive, and controlling. The key task for a leader is to *recognize different situations and adapt to them on a conscious basis.*

Followership

With few exceptions, leaders in organizations are also followers. They nearly always report to someone else. Even the president of a public firm or nonprofit organization reports to a board of directors. Leaders must be able to wear both hats, relating effectively both upward and downward. And just as leaders *give something to* their superiors and employees, they *need validation from* higher authority as much as they need support from followers.

In formal organizations of several levels, ability to follow (dynamic subordinancy) is one of the first requirements for good leadership. Being an effective follower is a testing ground for future leaders, a place where employees are closely observed to see if they exhibit potential for leadership. Skillful performance in current roles unlocks the door to future leadership opportunities. By contrast, many people fail in their jobs not as a result of any skill deficiencies, but because they lack followership skills. These skills help employees support their current leader and be effective subordinates.

Followership behaviors include

Followership behaviors

- Not competing with the leader to be in the limelight
- Being loyal and supportive, a team player
- Not being a "yes person" who automatically agrees
- Acting as a devil's advocate by raising penetrating questions
- Constructively confronting the leader's ideas, values, and actions
- Anticipating potential problems and preventing them

Good followers, then, need to succeed at their own jobs while helping their managers succeed at theirs. At the same time, effective subordinates can also prepare themselves for promotion by developing their conceptual and leadership skills. Similarly, good leaders should never forget what it is like in the trenches. Many effective leaders remind themselves of the importance of followership roles by periodically spending time visiting their stores, working a shift in a plant, and doing other things to remain in contact with first-level employees.

BEHAVIORAL APPROACHES TO LEADERSHIP STYLE

The total pattern of explicit and implicit leaders' actions as seen by employees is called **leadership style.** It represents a consistent combination of philosophy, skills, traits, and attitudes that are exhibited in a person's behavior. Each style also reflects, implicitly or explicitly, a manager's beliefs about a subordinate's capabilities (Theory X or Theory Y, discussed in Chapter 2). As emphasized throughout this book, employee *perceptions* of leadership style are all that really matters to them. Employees do not respond solely to what leaders think and do and say but to what they *perceive* leaders are. Leadership is truly in the eyes of the beholders.

This section discusses a variety of styles that differ on the basis of motivation, power, or orientation toward tasks and people. Many different classifications of leadership styles have been proposed and found to be useful. The simplest of these are based on a single dimension; others focus on two or more ways to distinguish among styles. Although each style is typically used in combination with others or even applied differently to various employees, the style classifications are discussed separately to highlight the contrasts among them. In general, the early classification schemes all took a universalist approach as they sought to identify the one best leadership style. However, this objective has subsequently proved to be impossible to attain.

Positive and Negative Leaders

Rewards or penalties?

There are differences in the ways leaders approach people to motivate them. If the approach emphasizes rewards—economic or otherwise—the leader uses *positive leadership.* Better employee education, greater demands for independence, and other factors have made satisfactory employee motivation more dependent on positive leadership.

If emphasis is placed on penalties, the leader is applying *negative leadership.* This approach can get acceptable performance in many situations, but it has high human costs. Negative leaders act domineering and superior with people. To get work done, they hold over their personnel such penalties as loss of job, reprimand in the presence of others, and a few days off without pay. They display authority in the false belief that it frightens everyone into productivity. They are bosses more than leaders.

A continuum of leadership styles exists, ranging from strongly positive to strongly negative.[6] Almost any manager uses a mix of positive and negative styles somewhere on the continuum every day, but the dominant style sets a tone within the group. Style is related to one's model of organizational behavior. The autocratic model tends to produce a negative style; the custodial model is somewhat positive; and the supportive, collegial, and system models are clearly positive. *Positive leadership generally results in higher job satisfaction and performance.*

Autocratic, Consultative, and Participative Leaders

Styles and the use of power

The way in which a leader uses power also establishes a type of style. Each style—autocratic, consultative, and participative—has its benefits and limitations. A leader often uses all three styles over a period of time, but one style tends to be the dominant one. An illustration is a factory supervisor who is normally autocratic, but she is participative in determining vacation schedules, and she is consultative in selecting a department representative for the safety committee.

Autocratic leaders centralize power and decision making in themselves. They structure the complete work situation for their employees, who are expected to do what they are told and not think for themselves. The leaders take full authority and assume full responsibility. Autocratic leadership typically is negative, based on threats and punishment, but it can appear to be positive, as demonstrated by the *benevolent autocrat* who chooses to give some rewards to employees.

Some advantages of autocratic leadership are that it is often satisfying for the leader, permits quick decisions, allows the use of less competent subordinates, and provides security and structure for employees. The main disadvantage is that most employees dislike it, especially if it is extreme enough to create fear and frustration. Further, it seldom generates the strong organizational commitment among employees that leads to low turnover and absenteeism rates. The leadership style of Al Dunlap, described in the opening for this chapter, is clearly an autocratic one.

Consultative leaders approach one or more employees and ask them for inputs prior to making a decision. These leaders may then choose to use or ignore the information and advice received, however. If the inputs are seen as used, employees are likely to feel as though they had a positive impact; if the inputs are consistently rejected, employees are likely to feel that their time has been wasted.

Participative leaders clearly decentralize authority. Participative decisions are not unilateral, as with the autocrat, because they *use* inputs from followers and participation by them. The leader and group are acting as a social unit. Employees are informed about conditions affecting their jobs and encouraged to express their ideas, make suggestions, *and take action*. The general trend is toward wider use of participative practices because they are consistent with the supportive and collegial models of organizational behavior. Because of its importance and increasingly widespread usage, participative management is discussed thoroughly in the next chapter.

Leader Use of Consideration and Structure

Two different leadership styles used with employees are **consideration** and **structure,** also known as *employee orientation* and *task orientation*. There is consistent evidence that leaders secure somewhat higher job satisfaction from employees if high consideration is their dominant leadership style. Considerate leaders are concerned about the human needs of their employees. They try to build teamwork, provide psychological support, and help employees with their problems. Structured, task-oriented leaders, on the other hand, believe that they get results by keeping people constantly busy, ignoring personal issues and emotions, and urging them to produce.

Employee and task orientations

> The difference between the two orientations is dramatically illustrated by the reply of Paul Blumberg, a mine superintendent in a western mining town. A clerk brought him the following news about one of his truck drivers: "John Jones just ran the truck off the road into Mile Deep Canyon." The superintendent's task-oriented reply was, "Get another truck out there right away and get that ore to the mill." (We wonder what happened to Jones.)

Consideration and structure appear to be somewhat independent of each other, so they should not necessarily be viewed as opposite ends of a continuum. A manager who becomes more considerate does not necessarily become less structured. A manager may have both orientations in varying degrees. If consideration exists alone, production may be bypassed for superficial popularity and contentment; so it appears that *the most successful managers are those who combine relatively high consideration and structure, giving somewhat more emphasis to consideration.*[7]

Early research on consideration and structure was done at the University of Michigan and at Ohio State University. In several types of environments, such as truck manufacturing, railroad construction, and insurance offices, the strongly considerate leader was shown to have achieved somewhat higher job satisfaction and productivity. Subsequent studies confirm this general tendency and report desirable side effects, such as lower grievance rates, lower turnover, and reduced stress within the group.[8] Conversely, turnover, stress, and other problems seemed likely to occur if a manager was unable to demonstrate consideration.

Blake and Mouton's Managerial Grid

Robert R. Blake and Jane S. Mouton developed the **managerial grid,** which is quite popular among managers as a tool for identifying their style.[9] The grid is based on the leadership style dimensions of concern for people and concern for production, which essentially mirrors the dimensions of consideration and structure discussed above. The grid clarifies, on two 9-point scales, how the two dimensions are related (see Figure 7–3). It also establishes a uniform language and framework for communication about appropriate leadership styles. The 1,9 leaders are high in concern for people but so low

170

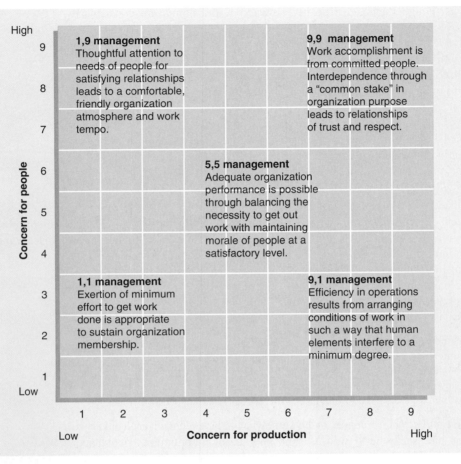

High

9 **1,9 management**
Thoughtful attention to
needs of people for
satisfying relationships
leads to a comfortable,
friendly organization
atmosphere and work
tempo.

9,9 management
Work accomplishment is
from committed people.
Interdependence through
a "common stake" in
organization purpose
leads to relationships
of trust and respect.

5,5 management
Adequate organization
performance is possible
through balancing the
necessity to get out
work with maintaining
morale of people at a
satisfactory level.

1,1 management
Exertion of minimum
effort to get work
done is appropriate
to sustain organization
membership.

9,1 management
Efficiency in operations
results from arranging
conditions of work in
such a way that human
elements interfere to a
minimum degree.

Concern for people

Low

1   2   3   4   5   6   7   8   9

Low   **Concern for production**   High

FIGURE 7–3

The managerial grid
Source: Robert R. Blake
and Jane S. Mouton,
"Managerial Facades,"
*Advanced Management
Journal,* July 1966, p. 31,
copyright. Used with
permission.

*A 9,9 style is
preferred.*

in concern for production that output is typically low. They are "country-club leaders."
In sharp contrast, the 9,1 leaders are overly concerned with production to the exclu-
sion of their employees' needs. The 9,1 leaders tend to be authoritarian bosses.

A 1,1 leader does not place adequate emphasis on either dimension and would predictably fail. A more desirable balance of the two dimensions is from 5,5 to 9,9—
with the latter assumed by Blake and Mouton to be the most effective style. The grid
can help individuals identify not only their primary leadership style but also their
backup style. The backup style is the one managers tend to use when their normal
style does not get results. In general, managers tend to be more autocratic and concerned with production when their primary style is unsuccessful.

Sally, a manager with a staff of seven supervisors reporting to her, saw herself as a 9,9
leader. When interviewed, she said that she tried hard to demonstrate support for her staff,
by including them in key decisions and communicating with them about current events in
the organization. She also expressed strong concerns about the need to meet their goals and
stay within their budgets. However, Sally's employees saw her differently. They reported
that whenever they would question or disagree with her, she would immediately switch to
her backup style, which they characterized as about an 8,2. She would become physically
rigid and emotionally unreceptive to their inputs and challenge them to "quit thinking about
themselves so much, and worry more about the bottom line." What is Sally's real leadership style—9,9 or 8,2?

Models like the managerial grid have been useful for highlighting multiple dimensions of leadership, getting managers to think and talk about their styles, and stimulating debate and further studies about leadership. Together, the early approaches to leadership styles served as a useful springboard to newer models, which are discussed in the next section.

CONTINGENCY APPROACHES TO LEADERSHIP STYLE

The positive, participative, considerate leadership style is not always the best style to use. At times there are exceptions, and the prime need for leaders is to identify when to use a different style. A number of models have been developed that explain these exceptions, and they are called *contingency approaches*. These models state that the most appropriate style of leadership depends on an analysis of the nature of the situation facing the leader. Key factors in the situation need to be identified first. When combined with research evidence, these factors will indicate which style should be more effective. Four contingency models of this nature are briefly examined.

Fiedler's Contingency Model

An early, but often controversial, **contingency model** of leadership was developed by Fred Fiedler and his associates.[10] This model builds upon the previous distinction between task and employee orientation and suggests that the most appropriate leadership style depends on whether the overall situation is favorable, unfavorable, or in an intermediate stage of favorability to the leader. As the situation varies, leadership requirements also vary.

Fiedler shows that a leader's effectiveness is determined by the interaction of employee orientation with three additional variables that relate to the followers, the task, and the organization. They are leader–member relations, task structure, and leader position power. **Leader–member relations** are determined by the manner in which the leader is accepted by the group. If, for example, there is group friction with the leader, rejection of the leader, and reluctant compliance with orders, then leader–member relations are low. **Task structure** reflects the degree to which one specific way is required to do the job. **Leader position power** describes the organizational power that goes with the position the leader occupies. Examples are power to hire and fire, status symbols, and power to give pay raises and promotions.

Three situational variables

The relationship among these variables is shown in Figure 7–4. High and low employee orientations are shown on the vertical scale. Various combinations of the other three variables are shown on the horizontal scale, arranged from leader-favorable conditions to leader-unfavorable conditions. Each dot on the chart represents the data from a specific research project. The chart clearly shows that the considerate, employee-oriented manager is most successful in situations that have intermediate favorableness to the leader (the middle of the chart). At the chart's extremes, which represent conditions either quite favorable or quite unfavorable to the leader, the structured, task-oriented leader seems to be more effective. For example, the members of an automobile assembly-line crew have a structured task and a supervisor with strong position power. If leader–member relations are positive, the situation is favorable for task-oriented leaders who can use their strengths. Similarly, a structured leader is more effective in a position of weak power, low task structure, and poor leader–member

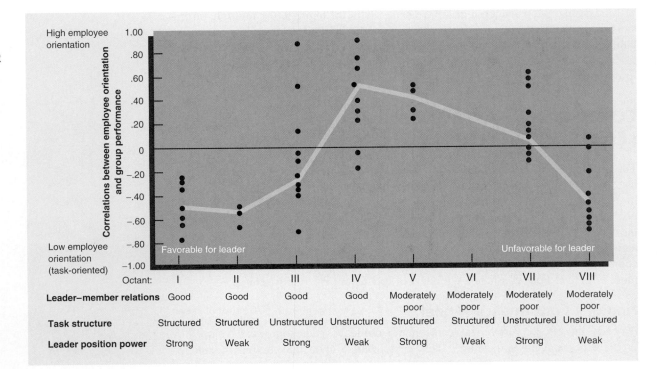

FIGURE 7–4

Research results as applied to Fiedler's contingency model of leadership

Source: Adapted from *A Theory of Leadership Effectiveness,* by Fred E. Fiedler, p. 146. Copyright © 1967 by McGraw-Hill Book Company. Used with permission of McGraw-Hill Book Company.

relations. However, in intermediate conditions of favorableness, the considerate leader is often the most effective; and these situations are the most common ones in work groups.

The conclusions of the Fiedler model may be explained in the following manner. In highly unstructured situations the leader's structure and control are seen as removing undesirable ambiguity and the anxiety that results from it, so a structured approach may be preferred by employees. In situations where the task is highly routine and the leader has good relations with the employees, they may perceive a task orientation as supportive to their job performance (clearing the path). The remaining broad middle ground requires better leader–member relations to be established, so a more considerate, employee-oriented leader is effective.

Despite criticism, Fiedler's contingency model has played a major role in stimulating discussions on leadership style and in generating useful guidelines. For example, managers are encouraged to

- Examine their situation—the people, task, and organization
- Be flexible in the use of various skills within an overall style
- Consider modifying elements of their jobs to obtain a better match with their preferred style

Hersey and Blanchard's Situational Leadership Model

Another contingency approach, the **situational leadership** (or life-cycle) **model** developed by Paul Hersey and Kenneth Blanchard, suggests that the most important factor affecting the selection of a leader's style is the development (maturity) level of a subordinate.[11] **Development level** is the task-specific combination of an employee's task competence and motivation to perform (commitment). Managers assess development level by examining an employee's level of job knowledge, skill, and ability, as well as willingness to take responsibility and capacity to act independently. Employees typically (according to Theory Y assumptions) become better developed on a task as they receive appropriate guidance, gain job experience, and see the rewards for cooperative behavior. Both the *competence* to perform a given task and the *commitment* to do so can vary among employees; therefore development levels demand different responses from leaders.

Competence and commitment after development level

Hersey and Blanchard use a combination of guidance and supportive (also called task and relationship) orientations to create four major styles—telling, selling (coaching), participating (supporting), and delegating. These are matched with the progressive development levels of the employees (see Figure 7–5), suggesting that a manager's leadership style should vary with the situation. The model is simple and intuitively appealing and accents an important contingency factor (the *individual* employee's capabilities on a specific task) that is sometimes overlooked. However, it ignores several other critical elements that determine leadership style, and it does not have a widely accepted research base.[12] Despite these limitations, it has achieved considerable popularity and also awakened many managers to the idea of contingency approaches to leadership style. Here is an example of the situational leadership model in use:

Four styles match four levels.

> Two employees named Cindi and Mary were hired by the same firm to perform similar jobs. Although they had comparable educational backgrounds, Cindi had several more years of relevant work experience than Mary did. Applying the situational leadership model, their supervisor identified Mary as being moderately low in development ("willing, but not yet fully able to perform"), while Cindi was assessed as having a moderately high development level ("fully able, but lacking some confidence to perform"). Following this analysis, the supervisor decided to treat them differently during their first months on the job, by "selling" with Mary and "participating" with Cindi. Approximately two years later, the supervisor was able to use different styles with each, now "participating" with Mary and "delegating" with Cindi, since each had gained skills and self-confidence.

Path-Goal Model of Leadership

Robert House and others have further developed a path-goal view of leadership initially presented by Martin G. Evans, which is derived from the expectancy model of motivation (see Chapter 5).[13] **Path-goal leadership** states that the leader's job is to use structure, support, and rewards to create a work environment that helps employees reach the organization's goals. The two major roles involved are to create a goal orientation and to improve the path toward the goals so that they will be attained.

Figure 7–6 shows the path-goal process. Leaders identify employee needs, provide appropriate goals, and then connect goal accomplishment to rewards by clarifying

Employee's Development Level	Leader's Recommended Style
1. Low ability; low willingness	Telling (directive; low support)
2. Low ability; high willingness	Selling/coaching (directive; supportive)
3. High ability; low willingness	Participating/supporting (supportive; low direction)
4. High ability; high willingness	Delegating (low direction; low support)

FIGURE 7–5

Situational leadership recommendations for leadership style to be used with each development level

FIGURE 7-6

174

The path-goal
leadership process

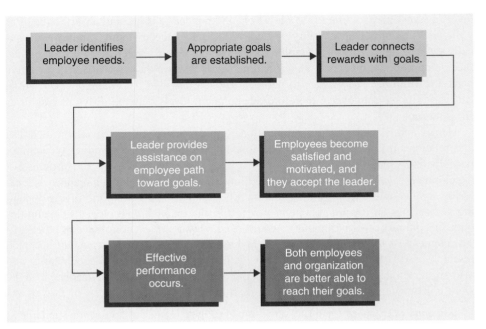

expectancy and instrumentality relationships. Barriers to performance are removed, and guidance is provided to the employee. The expected results of the process include job satisfaction, acceptance of the leader, and greater motivation. These should pay off further in effective performance and goal attainment.

Goal Setting   Goals play a central role in the path-goal process. Goal setting is the establishment of targets and objectives for successful performance, both long-run and short-run. It provides a measure of how well individuals and groups are meeting performance standards.

The basic premise underlying goal setting is that *human behavior is goal-directed,* as we discuss in Chapter 5. Group members need to feel that they have a worthwhile goal that can be reached with the resources and leadership available. Without goals, different members may go in different directions. This difficulty will continue as long as there is no common understanding of the goals involved.

Path Improvement   The steps surrounding goal setting represent only half of the path-goal leadership process. Leaders also need to consider some contingency factors and the range of leadership options open to them before deciding how to go about smoothing the path toward a goal. In particular, the need for two kinds of support must be weighed.

Leaders provide a balance of both task and psychological support for their employees, as logic would suggest. They provide **task support** when they help assemble the resources, budgets, power, and other elements that are essential to get the job done. Equally important, they can remove environmental constraints that sometimes inhibit the performance of the employee, exhibit upward influence, and provide recognition contingent upon effective effort and performance. But **psychological support** is also needed. Leaders must stimulate people to want to do the job. The combination of task and psychological support in a leader is described by a telephone company employee as follows:[14]

There is a supervisor here in the western area who is the epitome of a leader. The reason? He cares. He cares about people (psychological support) and about getting the job done right (task support). His enthusiasm is real, not forced, and it's quite contagious. His employees want to work for him and learn from him.

It all stems from two basic reasons: He knows what he's talking about and he treats subordinates as though they are rational human beings with the ability to do the job. And he expects them to do it. He gives them the recognition that their work is important. Therefore, people get the feeling that they are working with him to get the entire job done.

Leadership Styles According to path-goal theory, the leader's roles are to help employees understand what needs to be done (the goal) and how to do it (the path). Further, leaders need to help employees see how achieving the goals will be beneficial to them and the organization. This leadership action should result in perceptions of high expectancy (effort leading to goal achievement and hence to valued rewards). Leaders, however, have to decide which style to use with each employee; the path-goal model identifies four alternatives:

- *Directive leadership*—the leader focuses on clear task assignments, standards of successful performance, and work schedules.
- *Supportive leadership*—the leader demonstrates concern for employees' well-being and needs, while trying to create a pleasant work environment.
- *Achievement-oriented leadership*—the leader sets high expectations for employees, communicates confidence in their ability to achieve challenging goals, and enthusiastically models the desired behavior.
- *Participative leadership*—the leader invites employees to provide input to decisions, and seriously seeks to use their suggestions as final decisions are made.

Contingency Factors Two major factors must be analyzed—the general work environment and the specific characteristics of the employee. In the work environment, a leader must identify whether the employee's *task* is already structured or not, whether the *formal authority system* is most compatible with a directive or participative approach, and whether the existing *work group* already provides for satisfaction of employee social and esteem needs.

Similarly, the leader must assess three significant variables in each employee. **Locus of control** refers to alternative beliefs about whether an employee's achievements are the product of his or her own effort (an *internal locus,* which is more compatible with a participative style) or the result of outside forces (an *external locus,* which is more receptive to a directive approach). A second factor is the employee's **willingness to accept the influence of others.** If this variable is high, a directive approach will be more successful; if it is low, a participative style is more appropriate. The third individual characteristic is **self-perceived task ability.** Employees who have high confidence in their potential will react most favorably to a supportive leader. Alternatively, employees lacking a perception of their own task ability will more likely embrace an achievement-oriented leader.

Employee characteristics need to be assessed.

The path-goal model has made a contribution by identifying additional contingency variables, as well as broadening the range of leader behaviors to choose from. It is also somewhat unique in that it explicitly relates leadership style to an underlying motivational model. On the other hand, the entire model is still being tested through research studies, and it is somewhat speculative. Existing research indicates that use of the model does correlate with employee *satisfaction* with leadership, but its impact on performance is not yet fully documented.

Vroom's Decision-Making Model

A useful **decision-making model** for selecting among various degrees of leadership style (autocratic to participative) was developed by V. H. Vroom and others.[15] They recognized that problem-solving situations differ, so they developed a structured approach for managers to examine the nature of those differences and to respond appropriately.

Problem Attributes   In this model, managers assess a current decision situation according to its *problem attributes* (see the eight questions in Figure 7–7)— especially the perceived importance of technical quality and employee acceptance. *Decision-quality* dimensions include cost considerations and the availability of information and whether or not the problem is structured. *Employee-acceptance* dimensions include the need for their commitment, their prior approval, the congruence of their goals with the organization's, and the likelihood of conflict among the employees. By carefully following this analysis in a structured decision-tree format, managers can identify and classify several unique kinds of problems.

Leadership Options   After the type of problem being faced is determined, guidelines are then offered to help managers select one of five approaches to use. For example, items to consider are the time constraints, the geographical dispersion of subordinates, the leader's motivation to conserve time, and the leader's motivation to develop subordinates. These considerations all have an impact on the choice of whether to use a more autocratic or a more consultive approach from among the five described here:

- *Autocratic I*—leader individually solves the problem using the information already available.
- *Autocratic II*—leader obtains data from subordinates and then decides.
- *Consultative I*—leader explains problem to individual subordinates and obtains ideas from each before deciding.
- *Consultative II*—leader meets with group of subordinates to share the problem and obtain inputs, and then decides.
- *Group II*—leader shares problem with group and facilitates a discussion of alternatives and a reaching of group agreement on a solution.

The usefulness of Vroom's model rests on at least three key assumptions. First, it assumes that managers can accurately classify problems according to the criteria

FIGURE 7–7

Guiding questions in the Vroom decision-making model

1. How important is technical quality with regard to the decision being made?
2. How important is subordinate commitment to the decision (employee acceptance)?
3. Do you already have sufficient information to make a high-quality decision?
4. Is the problem well structured?
5. If you made the decision, would the subordinates be likely to accept it?
6. Do subordinates share the goals to be attained in solving the problem?
7. Is there likely to be conflict among subordinates over alternative solutions?
8. Do subordinates have sufficient information to allow them to reach a high-quality solution?

offered. Second, it assumes that managers are able and willing to adapt their leadership style to fit the contingency conditions they face for each major decision. Third, it assumes that employees will accept the legitimacy of different styles being used for different problems, as well as the validity of the leader's classification of the situation at hand. If all these assumptions are valid, the model holds considerable promise for helping managers choose the appropriate leadership style.

EMERGING APPROACHES TO LEADERSHIP

In the preceding sections of this chapter we traced the development of different views on leadership—those focusing on traits, behaviors, and contingency factors. Each model touches on something different, producing a different conclusion. In this way, they are similar to the ancient parable of the blind men encountering an elephant, with each describing it very differently, depending on whether he had touched an ear, a tail, a trunk, or a leg. Despite the seemingly substantial differences among the leadership models, they are remarkably consistent in some ways. Figure 7–8 identifies their common emphasis on two types of factors—"soft" and "hard."

Several additional perspectives—substitutes and enhancers for leadership, self- and superleadership, coaching, and two other approaches—are presented briefly in the following sections. These perspectives provide useful new ways of looking at leadership. Chapter 8 explores participative approaches in depth.

Substitutes and Enhancers for Leadership

A totally different approach to leadership that still has a modest contingency flavor has been proposed by Steven Kerr and others.[16] Previous leadership models have suggested that a formal leader is necessary to provide task direction, structure, and rewards, plus the consideration and social support that employees require. Unfortunately, these leadership roles may create an *unhealthy dependency* on the leaders that stifles the growth and autonomy of subordinates. A leader may also

Model	Soft Emphasis	Hard Emphasis
University of Michigan and Ohio State University studies	Consideration	Structure
Blake and Mouton's managerial grid	People	Production
Fiedler's contingency model	Employee orientation	Task orientation
Hersey and Blanchard's situational model	Relationships	Task guidance
Path-goal model	Psychological support	Task support
Vroom's decision-making model	Employee acceptance	Decision quality

FIGURE 7–8

Similarities across leadership models

177

lack the necessary traits, knowledge, and skills to fulfill those roles effectively or may not be able to be present at all times. Further, some **neutralizers** may intervene. These are attributes of subordinates, tasks, and organizations that actually interfere with or diminish the leader's attempts to influence the employees. Neutralizers include physical distance, rigid reward systems, and a practice of bypassing the managers by either subordinates or superiors.

If the situation or leader cannot be readily changed, there may be substitutes or enhancers for leadership. **Substitutes for leadership** are factors that make leadership roles unnecessary through replacing them with other sources. Examples of such factors are shown in Figure 7–9; they are found in the contingency factors of the task, organization, and employees. Presence of such substitutes as strong subordinate experience, clear rules, or a cohesive work group helps decrease the need for a leader's traditional task orientation. Other factors, such as intrinsically satisfying tasks, professional orientations by employees, or an employee's high need for independence, may diminish the need for a leader's consideration-oriented behavior.

Alternatively, a leader's existing characteristics and abilities may become clarified and aided through other factors. **Enhancers for leadership** are elements that amplify a leader's impact on the employees (see Figure 7–9).[17] A directive orientation may be improved by an increase in the leader's status or reward power or when that leadership style is used in jobs with frequent crises. A supportive leadership style may be enhanced by encouraging more team-based work activities or by increasing employee participation in decision making. The important contribution of the neutralizers/substitutes/enhancers approach is that organizations have an alternative remedy in those cases where it is not feasible to replace or train the

FIGURE 7–9

Potential neutralizers, substitutes, and enhancers for leadership

Neutralizers	Substitutes	Enhancers
Physical distance between leader and employee	Peer appraisal/feedback	Superordinate goals
Employee indifference toward rewards	Gain-sharing reward systems	Increased group status
Intrinsically satisfying tasks	Staff available for problems	Increased leader's status and reward power
Inflexible work rules	Jobs redesigned for more feedback	Leader as the central source of information supply
Rigid reward systems	Methods for resolving interpersonal conflict	
Cohesive work groups	Team building to help solve work-related problems	Increased subordinates' view of leader's expertise, influence, and image
Employees with high ability, experience, or knowledge	Intrinsic satisfaction from the work itself	Use of crises to demonstrate leader's capabilities
Practice of bypassing the manager (by subordinates or superiors)	Cohesive work groups	
	Employee needs for independence	

leader or to find a better match between leader and job. However, the leader's emotions are also at stake here; someone who previously thought she or he was critically important and now finds her- or himself partially replaceable can suffer a demoralizing loss of self-esteem.

Self-Leadership and Superleadership

The substitutes for leadership provide partial compensation for a leader's weakness and the enhancers build on a leader's strengths. In another emerging approach to leadership, a dramatic substitute for leadership is the idea of **self-leadership,** which has been advocated by Charles Manz and Henry Sims.[18] This process has two thrusts: leading oneself to perform naturally motivating tasks and managing oneself to do work that is required but not naturally rewarding. Self-leadership requires employees to apply the *behavioral skills* of self-observation, self-set goals, management of cues, self-reward, rehearsal of activities prior to performance, and self-criticism. It also involves the *mental activities* of building natural rewards into tasks, focusing thinking on natural rewards, and establishing effective thought patterns such as mental imagery and self-talk. The net result is employees who influence themselves to use their self-motivation and self-direction to perform well.

> Denise is the manager of safety and training at Lakehead Pipeline Company, which pumps crude oil from northern Canada to areas in the northern and eastern United States. Many of the company's 300 field employees work in geographically isolated locations in very small groups. Some are totally independent, with no supervisor available within a hundred miles. To prepare these field employees for possible oil-spill crises, Denise's training programs encourage the workers to be *self-leaders* (while working within the limits of standard operating policies). Thus, workers must set their own daily goals, observe their own behavior, and mentally rehearse safety procedures before tackling dangerous tasks. Then, with no supervisor present, they must critique their own safety practices and praise themselves where appropriate.

How can employees learn to become self-leaders? The answer lies in the support of *superleaders,* or people who actively work to unleash the abilities of their subordinates.[19] **Superleadership** begins with a set of positive beliefs about workers, such as those in Theory Y. It requires practicing self-leadership oneself and modeling it for others to see. Superleaders also communicate positive self-expectations to employees, reward their progress toward self-leadership, and make self-leadership an essential part of the unit's desired culture. Just as with other substitutes for leadership, superleadership can be challenging for managers to work toward, because they must give up some of the direct control that they have learned to exercise and that they find comfortable.

Coaching

A rapidly emerging metaphor for the leader is that of a **coach.** Borrowed and adapted from the sports domain (see "What Managers Are Reading"), coaching means that the leader prepares, guides, and directs a "player" but *does not play the game.* These leaders recognize that they are on the sidelines, not on the playing field. Their role is to select the right players, to teach and develop subordinates, to be available for problem-oriented consultation, to review resource needs, to ask questions, and to listen to inputs from employees. Some managers report that they spend 50 to 60 percent of their time coaching.[20] They cajole, prod, enable, inspire, exhibit warmth and support, and hold informal conversations. Coaches see themselves as cheerleaders and facilitators while also recognizing the occasional need to be tough and demanding.

Don Shula—the highly successful former coach of the Miami Dolphins—and management author Ken Blanchard teamed up to explore their mutual thoughts on leadership. They concluded that all leaders need to COACH their team members. What does coaching mean to them? They suggest that good managerial coaches have five characteristics:

- **C**onviction-driven—they have a clear vision of where they want the organization to go and sell that vision with passion to their employees.
- **O**verlearning—they devote extensive time and energy to preparing their employees for performance of their tasks at a high level of skill.
- **A**udible-ready—they recognize the need for momentary adaptations to changing circumstances and allow their key employees the autonomy to deviate from the original plan.

- **C**onsistency—they recognize employee hunger for clarity and predictability in managerial behaviors from day to day and strive to demonstrate consistent actions across both time and situations.
- **H**onesty—they identify and articulate their personal values and serve as role models to employees in their ethical behaviors.

Shula and Blanchard believe that coaching is not limited to the sports arena but is universally applicable to all manager-employee relationships as a way to help others develop to their full potential.

Source: Don Shula and Kenneth Blanchard, *Everyone's a Coach,* New York: HarperBusiness, 1995.

Coaching can be a powerful leadership tool, if handled correctly. It has been described as a secret weapon of some outstanding organizations that allows them to build an arsenal of well-prepared managers. Good coaching focuses mostly on enhanced performance as supported by high expectations and timely feedback while building on the tools of trust, mutual respect, integrity, openness, and common purpose. The specific areas that most managers admit needing coaching in are:

- Improving their interaction style
- Dealing more effectively with change
- Developing their listening and speaking skills[21]

To facilitate change through coaching, skillful leaders initiate periodic dialogues that maintain a healthy balance between building the employee's self-esteem and introducing creative tension for change. Prerequisites to successful coaching include the employee's willingness to change, capability of changing, and the opportunity to practice new behaviors.

Other Approaches

Two other perspectives on leadership deserve mention. Visionary leaders—those who can paint a portrait of what the organization needs to become and then use their communication skills to motivate others to achieve the vision—play especially important roles during times of transition. Transformational leadership and the trait of charisma are discussed in Chapter 14. A second approach looks at the reciprocal nature of influence between managers and their employees and studies the exchanges that take place between them. Since this approach serves as the basis for participative management, in which both parties give and gain something, it is introduced in the next chapter.

SUMMARY

Leadership is the process of influencing and supporting others to work enthusiastically toward achieving objectives. It is determined partially by traits, which provide the potential for leadership, and also by role behavior. Leaders' roles combine technical, human, and conceptual skills, which leaders apply in different degrees at various organizational levels. Their behavior as followers is also important to the organization.

1. Build upon and use your positive leadership traits; turn your weaknesses into strengths over time.
2. Recognize that there are many leadership models and many different dimensions as a foundation for them; accept their lessons while seeking ways to integrate them.
3. Embrace the contingency nature of leadership, recognizing that strong analytical skills are a prerequisite to effective application of most leadership models.
4. Remain appropriately wary of simplistic leadership models, especially those for which there is little available research support.
5. Recognize the need to flexibly vary your leadership style according to situational demands while also demonstrating some degree of consistency from day to day.
6. Accept the importance of your role as a coach, whose greatest assets include experience, empathy, objectivity, questioning skills, and listening capabilities.
7. Strive to become a superleader, whose major goal is to develop self-leadership capabilities in others.
8. Recognize when leadership is *not* necessary (due to substitutes) or not likely to be effective, and conserve your efforts.

Leaders apply different leadership styles, ranging from consultative to autocratic. Although a positive, participative, considerate leader tends to be more effective in many situations, the contingency approaches suggest that a variety of styles can be successful. Leaders must first analyze the situation and discover key factors in the task, employees, or organization that suggest which style might be best for that combination. Leaders should also recognize the possibility that they are not always directly needed because of available substitutes or enhancers. Also, it may be desirable to develop employees into self-leaders through effective coaching and the exercise of superleadership behaviors.

Terms and Concepts for Review

Autocratic leaders
Coach
Conceptual skill
Consideration
Consultative leaders
Contingency model
Decision-making model
Development level
Enhancers for leadership
Followership
Human skill
Leader–member relations
Leader position power
Leadership
Leadership style
Locus of control
Managerial grid
Neutralizers
Participative leaders
Path-goal leadership
Psychological support
Self-leadership
Self-perceived task ability
Situational leadership model
Structure
Substitutes for leadership
Superleadership
Task structure
Task support
Technical skill
Traits
Willingness to accept the influence of others

Discussion Questions

1. Explain the difference between management and leadership. Discuss why conceptual leadership skills become more important, and technical skills less important, at higher organizational levels.
2. A manager once told a subordinate, "To be a good leader, you must first become a good follower." Discuss what it means to be a good follower, whether you agree with the statement, and why or why not.

3. Think of the best leader you have ever worked with on a job, in sports, or in any other activity. Then think of the worst leader. Discuss the contrasting styles and skills used by the two. How did you respond to each? What could they have done differently?

4. Explain how Theory X and Theory Y relate to leadership styles, especially the contingency approaches and superleadership. Comment on the statement "management philosophy controls practice."

5. Think of situations in which you were a leader. What leadership style did you use? Using hindsight and the material in this chapter, what would you have done differently?

6. The contingency models are all more complex than the earlier trait or "one best style" approaches. Discuss the likelihood that practicing managers will understand, accept, and use each of the contingency models.

7. Consider the various substitutes for leadership and enhancers. Identify the three that you think have the greatest potential for positive impact, and explain why.

8. Vroom's decision-making model assumes that managers have the flexibility to shift from one style to another. Debate the feasibility of this model.

9. Why would a typical manager attempt to create self-leading employees? Would this competition between manager and employees eventually result in the loss of the manager's job if the attempt were fully successful? Why or why not?

10. Review the idea of the leader as a coach. Which of the leadership models relates more closely with coaching? Explain.

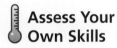

Assess Your Own Skills

How well do you exhibit good leadership traits?

Read the following statements carefully. Circle the number on the response scale that most closely reflects the degree to which each statement accurately describes you as a leader. Add up your total points and prepare a brief action plan for self-improvement. Be ready to report your score for tabulation across the entire group.

	Good description								Poor description	
1. I exhibit a healthy degree of charisma.	10	9	8	7	6	5	4	3	2	1
2. I have a high degree of cognitive ability.	10	9	8	7	6	5	4	3	2	1
3. I possess substantial creativity/originality.	10	9	8	7	6	5	4	3	2	1
4. I have a strong desire to be a leader.	10	9	8	7	6	5	4	3	2	1
5. I exhibit a powerful degree of drive.	10	9	8	7	6	5	4	3	2	1
6. I demonstrate high energy and enthusiasm.	10	9	8	7	6	5	4	3	2	1
7. I am generally flexible and adaptable.	10	9	8	7	6	5	4	3	2	1
8. I am known for my honesty and integrity.	10	9	8	7	6	5	4	3	2	1
9. I have a healthy degree of self-confidence.	10	9	8	7	6	5	4	3	2	1
10. I exhibit a high degree of warmth toward others.	10	9	8	7	6	5	4	3	2	1

Scoring and Interpretation   Add up your total points for the ten questions. Record that number here, and report it when it is requested. _____

• If you scored between 81–100 points, you appear to have a solid capability for demonstrating appropriate leadership traits.

• If you scored between 61–80 points, you should take a close look at the items with lower self-assessment scores and explore ways to improve those items.

• If you scored less than 60 points, you should be aware that a weaker level regarding several items could be detrimental to your future success as a leader. We encourage you to review relevant sections of the chapter and watch for related material in subsequent chapters and other sources.

Now identify your three lowest scores, and write the question numbers here:
_____, _____, _____. Write a brief paragraph, detailing to yourself an action plan for how you might sharpen each of these traits.

The Work Assignment

Incident

Effie Pardini supervised eleven accounting clerks in the budget and planning department of a large computer manufacturer. None of the clerks had accounting degrees, but all were skilled in handling records and figures. They primarily prepared budgetary plans and analyses for operating departments. Data inputs were secured from the departments and from company records. Pardini assigned projects to the clerks on the basis of their interests and skills. Some projects were more desirable than others because of prestige, challenge, the contacts required, or other factors; thus there were occasional conflicts over which clerk was to receive a desirable project. One clerk who seemed especially sensitive and regularly complained about this issue was Sonia Prosser.

On one occasion Pardini received a desirable project and assigned it to a clerk by the name of Joe Madden. Prosser was particularly distressed because she felt she should have had the assignment. She was so distressed that she retaliated by gathering up her present assignment and putting it away in her desk. Then she took a book from her desk and started reading it. Since all the clerks were together in the same office, most of them observed her actions. She announced to one in a voice loud enough to be heard by others, "Nobody around here ever gives me a good assignment."

Pardini overheard Prosser's comment and looked up from her desk, noting what was happening. Pardini was angered, but she sat at her desk for five minutes wondering what to do. Meanwhile Prosser continued reading her book.

Questions
1. What leadership issues are raised by this incident?
2. Discuss what action Pardini should take. Consider the path-goal model of leadership and the contingency approaches to leadership before making your decision.

Application of Leadership Models

Experiential Exercise

1. Divide into small groups of five to seven persons.
2. Select, as a focus of discussion, a visible leader with whom all members are reasonably familiar (e.g., your college's president, a local mayor, the state governor, or a major corporation's CEO).
3. Each group member should choose a different leadership model and relate it to that leader. Spend a few minutes explaining to the other group members how:
   a. Your model applies to that leader
   b. Your model fails to apply neatly to that leader and why
4. Hold a brief discussion to explore ways in which the models are similar, different, and potentially complementary to each other.
5. Derive a set of action implications for yourselves as future leaders, based on this discussion.

Chapter 8

Empowerment and Participation

Empowerment is a false promise, nothing more.

–Chris Argyris[1]

Great gains can be expected from the implementation of empowerment, but not without significant costs.

–Jay Klagge[2]

CHAPTER OBJECTIVES

TO UNDERSTAND

- The Nature of Empowerment
- The Idea of Participation
- The Participative Process
- Prerequisites for Participation
- Benefits of Participation
- Types of Participative Programs
- Limitations of Participation

● A large aircraft manufacturer employed from 5,000 to 20,000 shop workers during a ten-year period. It used a safety committee system in which each department was represented on the committee by one of its workers. During those ten years a surprising phenomenon emerged. When people became safety committee members, they ceased having disabling injuries. This record occurred despite the fact that there were hundreds of members during the decade, and sometimes accident-prone workers were appointed committee members in order to make them safety-conscious. The facts in this case show a significant difference between committee members and nonmembers with regard to disabling injuries.

The safety committee members in the aircraft firm probably changed their own behavior for many reasons. They became more *aware* of safety problems, they were *involved* in the process of improving safety practices, they were given some *resources*, and they felt as though they had not only responsibility but also some *power* to affect the outcomes. The idea of empowering employees serves as the foundation for participation.

As discussed in the preceding chapter, an employee orientation and a consultative or a participative style are often important for effective leadership. Participation has excellent potential for developing employees and building teamwork, but it is a difficult practice and can fail if poorly applied. When it is used effectively, two of the best results are acceptance of change and a strong commitment to goals that encourage better performance.

THE NATURE OF EMPOWERMENT AND PARTICIPATION

What Is Empowerment?

Almost every society has within it some minority groups that feel incapable of controlling their own destiny. Similarly, most work organizations have a number of employees who believe that they are dependent on others and that their own efforts will have little impact on performance. This powerlessness contributes to the frustrating experience of *low self-efficacy*—the conviction among people that they cannot successfully perform their jobs or make meaningful contributions. Problems with self-efficacy are often caused by major organizational changes that are beyond the employees' control (such as mergers). Problems may also stem from having to work under an authoritarian leader, within a reward system that fails to reinforce competence or innovation, or in a job that lacks variety, discretion, or role clarity.

Powerlessness causes low self-esteem.

Fortunately, individual perceptions of low levels of self-efficacy can be raised by empowering employees. **Empowerment** is *any process that provides greater autonomy to employees through the sharing of relevant information and the provision of control over factors affecting job performance.* Empowerment helps remove the conditions that cause powerlessness while enhancing employee feelings of self-efficacy.[3] Empowerment authorizes employees to cope with situations and enables them to take control of problems as they arise. Five broad approaches to empowerment have been suggested:

Empowerment

1. Helping employees achieve *job mastery* (giving proper training, coaching, and guided experience that will result in initial successes)
2. Allowing more *control* (giving them discretion over job performance and then holding them *accountable* for outcomes)[4]

Blanchard and his colleagues weave a fanciful, and engaging, tale of a manager's odyssey to the Land of Empowerment. Along the way, the authors draw upon their research and consulting experiences to point out that empowerment is not a gimmick, not easily accomplished, and not achieved without the support of top management. They build their approach on three fundamental principles:

1. Information needs to be widely shared with employees.
2. Empowered employees need autonomy, but they also need to know the boundaries around that autonomy.
3. Empowerment is constrained by hierarchies, which should be replaced by self-managed teams.

Consequently, the role of managers is to teach their employees to become less dependent on their superiors. Employees need to learn to accept their new independence and use the newly shared information to weave themselves into self-directed teams. With this new-found freedom to act, however, comes a new requirement—accountability. The journey to empowerment is long, scary, and difficult, but it is filled with powerful potential rewards.

Source: Ken Blanchard, John P. Carlos, and Alan Randolph, *Empowerment Takes More than a Minute*, New York: Fine Publications, 2000.

3. Providing successful *role models* (allowing them to observe peers who already perform successfully on the job)
4. Using *social reinforcement and persuasion* (giving praise, encouragement, and verbal feedback designed to raise self-confidence)
5. Giving *emotional support* (providing reduction of stress and anxiety through better role definition, task assistance, and honest caring)

When managers use these approaches, employees begin believing that they are competent and valued, that their jobs have meaning and impact, and that they have opportunities to use their talents. In effect, when they have been legitimately empowered, it is more likely that their efforts will pay off in both personal satisfaction and the kind of results that the organization values. This chain of events is illustrated in Figure 8–1.

A major review of the theoretical literature on empowerment concluded that it is the result of four cognitions by employees—meaning and purpose to one's work role, competence in the skills and abilities required, autonomy and control over how one does the work assigned, and a sense of personal impact over relevant organizational outcomes. A study conducted

FIGURE 8–1

The process of empowerment

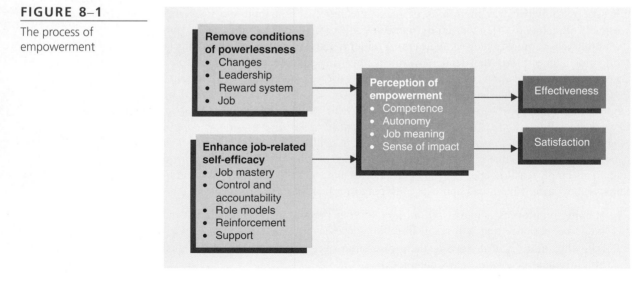

in a manufacturing firm and a service organization showed that all four of those dimensions were necessary to produce a positive impact on organizational effectiveness and individual satisfaction.[5]

Managers have many behavioral tools available to them to attack the powerlessness problem. Some of these tools, such as mutual goal setting, job feedback, modeling, and contingent reward systems, have already been discussed in previous chapters. A major approach, however, lies in the use of various programs for participative management. Such programs provide employees with varying degrees of perceived ownership, input into various steps in the decision-making process, and the key feeling of choice in their work environment.

What Is Participation?

Participative managers consult with their employees, bringing them in on problems and decisions so that they work together as a team. The managers are not autocrats, but neither are they managers who abandon their management responsibilities. Participative managers still retain ultimate responsibility for the operation of their units, but they have learned to share operating responsibility with those who perform the work. The result is that employees feel a sense of involvement in group goals. (You may wish to refer to Figure 2–4, which shows that the employee psychological result of supportive management is participation.) It follows that **participation** is *the mental and emotional involvement of people in group situations that encourages them to contribute to group goals and share responsibility for them.* There are three important ideas in this definition—involvement, contribution, and responsibility.

Elements in participation

Involvement   First, and probably foremost, participation means meaningful involvement rather than mere muscular activity. A person who participates is *ego-involved* instead of merely task-involved. Some managers mistake task involvement for true participation. They go through the motions of participation, but nothing more. They hold meetings, ask opinions, and so on, but all the time it is perfectly clear to employees that their manager is an autocratic boss who wants no ideas. These empty managerial actions constitute *pseudoparticipation,* with the result that employees fail to become ego-involved.

Ego involvement

Motivation to Contribute   A second concept in participation is that it motivates people to contribute. They are empowered to release their own resources of initiative and creativity toward the objectives of the organization, just as Theory Y predicts. In this way participation differs from consent. The practice of consent uses only the creativity of the manager, who brings ideas to the group for the members' consent. The consenters do not contribute; they merely approve. Participation is more than getting consent for something that has already been decided. Its great value is that it taps the creativity of all employees.

Employees use their creativity.

Participation especially improves motivation by helping employees understand and clarify their paths toward goals. According to the path-goal model of leadership, the improved understanding of path-goal relationships produces a heightened sense of responsibility for goal attainment. The result is improved motivation.

One of Xerox Corporation's manufacturing plants in New York was losing money.[6] Top management concluded that the only alternative was to subcontract the production of some components. In an attempt to save 180 employees from being laid off, an employee team was formed to gather proposals for cost savings. After six months of intense effort and analysis, the team proposed a wide-ranging series of changes that projected an annual savings of $3.7 million. The recommendations were accepted by management and the union, avoiding the layoffs and making the plant profitable again. The team members, with the help of many other interested employees, had a strong motivation to contribute, and they succeeded.

Acceptance of Responsibility   Finally, participation encourages people to accept responsibility in their group's activities. It is a social process by which people become self-involved in an organization and want to see it work successfully. When they talk about their organization, they begin to say "we," not "they." When they see a job problem, it is "ours," not "theirs." Participation helps them become good organizational citizens rather than nonresponsible, machinelike performers.

Responsibility builds teamwork.

As individuals begin to accept responsibility for group activities, they see in it a way to do what they want to do, that is, to get a job done for which they feel responsible. This idea of getting the group to want teamwork is a key step in developing it into a successful work unit. When people want to do something, they will find a way. Under these conditions employees see managers as supportive contributors to the team. Employees are ready to work actively with managers rather than reactively against them.

Why Is Participation Popular?

Managers have for years recognized various benefits of participation, but these benefits were first demonstrated experimentally in classic studies in industry by Roethlisberger, Coch and French, and others.[7] Conducted by skillful social scientists under controlled conditions, these experiments were useful in drawing attention to the potential value of participation. Their collective results suggested the general proposition that, *especially in the introduction of changes, participation tends to improve performance and job satisfaction.* Later research in organizations has repeatedly supported this proposition, as suggested by the authors of a comprehensive review: "Participation can have statistically significant effects on performance and satisfaction" (although the size of the effects is not always large).[8]

Research conclusions

There are good reasons for the enhanced interest in participation. U.S. businesses are struggling to compete in the global marketplace. Consequently, they are showing a keen interest in any managerial practice that offers to increase productivity or to speed the introduction of products to market.[9] Participative practices expedite these goals by placing more responsibility at lower levels of the organization and by speeding up the approval process. Participative practices may also provide power opportunities earlier to minority workers in an increasingly diverse workforce, since such workers need not wait until reaching higher organizational levels before being allowed to contribute meaningfully.

Spirit at work

Participation also seems to help satisfy the awakening employee need for meaning and fulfillment at work. This search for *spirit,* or harmony among all facets of life as guided by a higher (religious) power, has challenged organizations such as Tom's of Maine, Boeing, Lotus Development, and Medtronic to search for ways to restore a "soul" to their workplaces.[10] The organizations have found that employees are searching for a sense of significance, the opportunity to use their minds, and a chance to devote their efforts to a higher purpose in their work. Meaningful participation can help satisfy those needs.

Other reasons for the popular use of participative practices are noteworthy. The educational level of the workforce often provides workers with unique capacities that can be applied creatively to work problems. These employees have also acquired both a greater *desire* for influencing work-related decisions and an *expectation* that they will be allowed to participate in these decisions. An equally strong argument can be made that participation is an **ethical imperative** for managers. This view rests on the conclusion that highly nonparticipative jobs cause both psychological and physical harm to employees in the long run. As a result of these driving forces (see Figure 8–2), managers need to create participative conditions that will allow interested employees to experience feelings of empowerment in their work.

Benefits of Participation

In various types of organizations under many different operating conditions, participation has contributed to a variety of benefits. Some of these are direct; others are less tangible. Participation typically brings higher output and a better quality of output. In certain types of operations the quality improvement alone is worth the time invested in participation. Employees often make suggestions for both quality and quantity improvements. Although not all the ideas are useful, there are enough valuable ones to produce genuine long-run improvements.

Kelly is a supervisor of a crew in a U.S. steel mill. When she began her duties, she discovered that the annual cost for replacing work gloves (heavily insulated to withstand molten steel) was a phenomenal $144,000. Soon, she brought this problem to the attention of the work crew and asked for their involvement in reducing the cost. Based on their ideas and

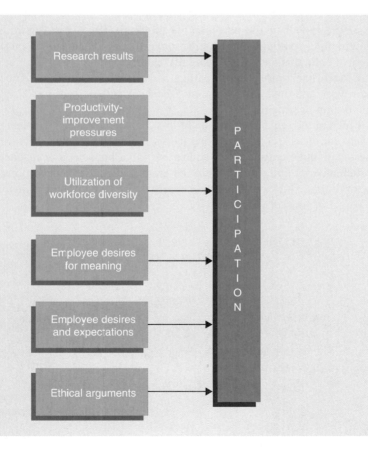

FIGURE 8–2

Forces affecting the greater use of participation

190

buy-in to their own solution, the cost of replacing the gloves soon plummeted to less than $1,000/month and stabilized at less than $9,000/year thereafter. Her participative approach had reduced this cost item to 6 percent of its previous level.

Participation tends to improve motivation because employees feel more accepted and involved in the situation. Their self-esteem, job satisfaction, and cooperation with management also may improve. The results often are reduced conflict and stress, more commitment to goals, and better acceptance of change.[11] Turnover and absences may be reduced because employees feel that they have a better place to work and that they are being more successful in their jobs. Finally, the act of participation in itself establishes better communication as people mutually discuss work problems. Management tends to provide workers with increased information about the organization's finances and operations, and this sharing of information allows employees to make better-quality suggestions.

Benefits may emerge slowly.

The results clearly show that participation has broad systems effects that favorably influence a variety of organizational outputs. The benefits may not appear immediately, however. When one company adopted participative management, it predicted it would take *ten years* to achieve the full effect. Once the organizational culture is changed (a slow process), then the system as a whole becomes more effective.

HOW PARTICIPATION WORKS

The Participative Process

A simple model of the participative process is shown in Figure 8–3. It indicates that in many situations participative programs result in mental and emotional involvement that produces generally favorable outcomes for both the employees and the organization. Participating employees are generally more satisfied with their work and their supervisor, and their self-efficacy rises as a result of their new-found empowerment.[12]

Much of the remaining portion of this chapter identifies important participative programs and discusses their relative merits. Before we review the range of practices in use today, three questions are addressed: What happens to a manager's power under participative programs? What are the prerequisites for successful participation? What factors in the situation affect the success of participative programs?

FIGURE 8–3

The participative process

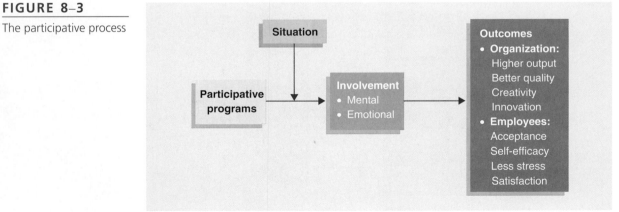

The Impact on Managerial Power

Leader–Member Exchange   Participation is a sharing process between managers and employees. It is built upon the **leader–member exchange model** of leadership.[13] This model suggests that leaders and their followers develop a somewhat unique reciprocal relationship, with the leader selectively delegating, informing, consulting, mentoring, praising, or rewarding each employee. In exchange, each subordinate contributes various degrees of task performance, loyalty, and respect to the manager. The quality of the relationships varies, depending on the balance of exchanges made, with some employees attaining favored status (the in-group) and others perceiving some unfairness in their treatment (the out-group). Managerial perceptions are important, too. If a manager believes that an employee has high ability and that a high-quality exchange relationship exists, the manager is more likely to allow a greater degree of influence in decisions.

Reciprocal relationships develop.

When managers first consider the need to empower employees through participation, they often ask, "If I share authority with my employees, don't I lose some of it?" This is a natural fear that stems from a view of managers as controllers, but it is not a justifiable one because participative managers often still retain final authority. All they do is share the use of authority so that employees will experience a greater sense of involvement in the organization. Managers engage in a two-way social exchange with workers, in contrast to imposing ideas from above. They demonstrate their trust in employee potential by giving employees some power, and they receive employee creativity and commitment in return.

Two Views of Power   Strange as it may seem, participation actually may increase the power of both managers and their employees. It is evident that employees gain more power with participation, but what about managers? The autocratic view of management is that power is a fixed quantity, so someone must lose what another gains.

However, as shown in Figure 8–4, the participative view is that power in a social system can be increased without taking it from someone else.[14] The process works like this: Managerial power depends partly on employee trust in management, a feeling of teamwork, and a sense of responsibility. Participation improves these conditions. Since employees feel more cooperative and responsible, they are likely to be more responsive to managerial attempts to influence them. In a sense, managers make social transactions with their work groups that build assets such

Participation expands influence.

Autocratic View	Participative View
Power	**Power**
• Is a fixed amount	• Is a variable amount
• Comes from the authority structure	• Comes from people through both official and unofficial channels
• Is applied by management	• Is applied by shared ideas and activities in a group
• Flows downward	• Flows in all directions

FIGURE 8–4

Two views of power and influence

192

as improved goodwill and responsibility. These assets are similar to a savings deposit that managers can draw upon later, perhaps with interest, when they need to apply their power. Here is an example that shows how a manager may increase power by sharing it:

> The manager of a computer operation having over fifty employees felt that some changes were needed. In the beginning she tried the usual autocratic approach, aided by a consultant. Desired changes were proposed, but the employees would not accept them. Finally, the effort was abandoned.
>
> The manager continued to think that changes were necessary, so a year later she decided to try again, using more participatory approaches. She discussed the need with her supervisors and several key employees. Then she set up committees to work on designated parts of a self-examination study. The groups worked hard, and in a few months they submitted a capable report that recommended a number of important changes. In this instance the members felt a sense of pride and ownership in the report. It was theirs. They had created it. The result was that they made a genuine effort to implement it. With the full support of the whole group, they made substantial changes. Participation had increased the manager's power and influence.

Prerequisites for Participation

The success of participation is directly related to how well certain prerequisite conditions are met, as shown in Figure 8–5. Some of these conditions occur in the participants; some exist in their environment. They show that participation works better in some situations than in others—and in certain situations it works not at all. Major prerequisites are as follows:

1. There must be *time to participate* before action is required. Participation is hardly appropriate in emergency situations.
2. The potential *benefits of participation should be greater than the costs.* For example, employees cannot spend so much time participating that they ignore their work.
3. The subject of participation must be *relevant and interesting* to the employees; otherwise employees will look upon it merely as busywork.
4. The participants should have the *ability,* such as intelligence and technical knowledge, *to participate.* It is hardly advisable, for example, to ask custodians in a pharmaceutical laboratory to participate in deciding which of five chemical formulas deserve research priority; but they might participate in helping resolve other problems related to their work.
5. The participants must be *mutually able to communicate*—to talk each other's language—in order to be able to exchange ideas.
6. *Neither party should feel that its position is threatened* by participation. If workers think their status will be adversely affected, they will not participate. If

FIGURE 8–5

Prerequisites for participation

1. Adequate time to participate
2. Potential benefits greater than costs
3. Relevance to employee interests
4. Adequate employee abilities to deal with the subject
5. Mutual ability to communicate
6. No feeling of threat to either party
7. Restriction to the area of job freedom

managers feel that their authority is threatened, they will refuse participation or will be defensive. If employees feel their job security is at risk, they are less likely to participate fully.

7. Participation for deciding a course of action in an organization can take place only *within the group's area of job freedom.* Some degree of restriction is required with regard to the parts of an organization in order to maintain unity for the whole. Each separate subunit cannot make decisions that violate policy, collective-bargaining agreements, legal requirements, and similar restraints. Likewise, there are restraints due to the physical environment (a flood that results in the closing of a plant is an extreme example) and due to personal limitations (such as an employee's not understanding electronics). The **area of job freedom** for any department is its area of discretion after all restraints have been applied. In no organization is there complete freedom, even for the top executive.

Area of job freedom

Within the area of job freedom, participation exists along a continuum, as shown in Figure 8–6. Over a period of time a manager will practice participation at various points along the continuum. That is, a manager may seek the group's ideas before deciding vacation schedules, but that same manager may decide overtime schedules independently. Similarly, a manager may find it necessary to limit the

FIGURE 8–6

Participation exists along a continuum.

Source: Adapted from Robert Tannenbaum and Warren H. Schmidt, "How to Choose a Leadership Pattern," *Harvard Business Review,* March–April 1958, p. 96.

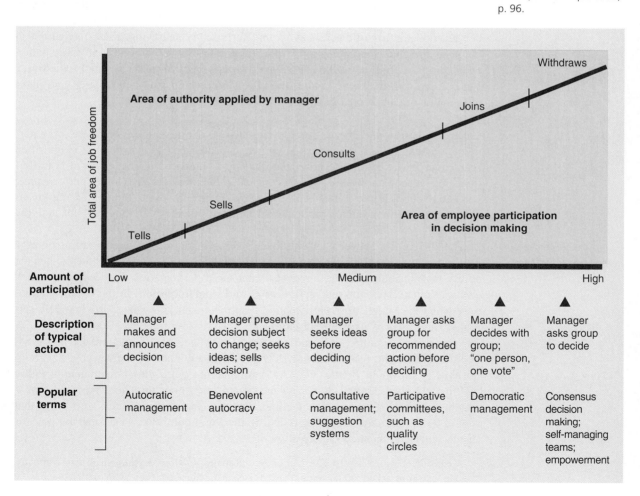

participation used with one employee while consulting freely with another (this practice is consistent with the Hersey-Blanchard model discussed in Chapter 7). Since a consistent approach provides employees with a predictable environment, each manager gradually becomes identified with some general style of participation as a usual practice. The popular terms designated for amounts of participation along the continuum are representative of a broad area on the continuum instead of a certain point. Several of the terms are defined later in this chapter.

Contingency Factors

As with the use of many behavioral ideas, several contingency factors influence the success of participative programs. These may be found in the environment, the organization, its leadership, the nature of tasks performed, or the employees. For example, national cultures and political systems vary sharply across the world, resulting in a restrictive environment for participation in a dictatorship and a more supportive one in a democracy. Organizational practices also need to be adapted to the pace of change in their environments, which can range from stable to turbulent.

In Chapter 7 we discussed the impact of Theory X or Theory Y beliefs on a manager's selection of a leadership style. There is also evidence that top executives' beliefs and values, as reflected in the organization's culture, have a strong impact on the use of participation by lower managers. Task characteristics need to be examined before choosing a participative program; intrinsically satisfying tasks may diminish the need for greater participation, while routine tasks may suggest that participation could produce fruitful results. There are also a variety of tasks in which employees can be involved, including goal setting, decision making, problem solving, and planning major organizational changes.

Differing Employee Needs for Participation   Some employees desire more participation than others. As indicated earlier, educated and higher-level workers often seek more participation, because they feel more prepared to make useful contributions. When they are not allowed to contribute, they tend to have lower performance, less satisfaction, lower self-esteem, and more stress. However, some other employees desire only a minimum of participation and are not upset if they are not actively involved.

Compare desired and actual participation.

The difference between an employee's desired and actual participation gives a measure of the potential effectiveness of participation, assuming the employee has the ability to contribute. When employees want more participation than they have, they are "participatively deprived" and there is **underparticipation.** In the opposite situation, when they have more participation than they want, they are "participatively saturated" and there is **overparticipation.**

Where there is either underparticipation or overparticipation, people are less satisfied than those who participate in a degree that closely matches their needs. This relationship is shown in Figure 8–7. As participation comes closer to matching either high or low needs, satisfaction with the organization goes up. Conversely, as a mismatch increases, these positive feelings decline. Participation is not something that should be applied equally to everyone. Rather, it should match each person's needs (if the other contingency factors allow it).

A consultant was asked to assess employee attitudes within a department in one company. One question asked of the employees focused on the frequency with which they were

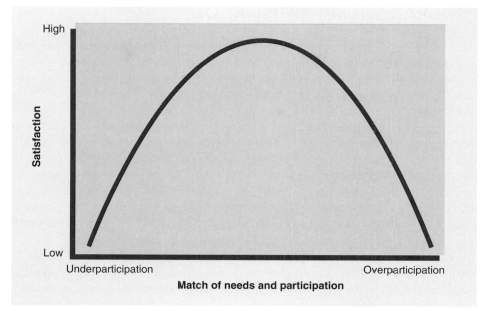

FIGURE 8–7

The relation of
satisfaction to the match
of needs and actual
participation

allowed to participate in decision making. The contrast in responses was striking. For example, one employee replied, "All the time—about three or four times a week." Another responded by saying, "Almost never—only three or four times a week."

It is apparent from this example that employee *perceptions* of the situation are highly important. The evidence suggests that participation will be more successful where employees feel they have a valid contribution to make, it will be valued by the organization, and they will be rewarded for it. It is also imperative that they believe that management is truly interested in their ideas and will use them, so that their time and energy will not be wasted.

Responsibilities of Employees and Manager   A critical contingency element in the success of any participative program is the degree to which all employees recognize that the opportunities provided are accompanied by a set of responsibilities. Ideally, all employees would agree to

- Be fully responsible for their actions and their consequences
- Operate within the relevant organizational policies
- Be contributing team members
- Respect and seek to use the perspectives of others
- Be dependable and ethical in their empowered actions
- Demonstrate responsible self-leadership

Expectations for employees

These responsibilities of employees provide a balance to those of the manager:

- Identifying the issues to be addressed
- Specifying the level of involvement desired
- Providing relevant information and training
- Allocating fair rewards

Expectations for managers

PROGRAMS FOR PARTICIPATION

We can further understand how participation works if we examine selected programs to develop it. An array of programs, ranging roughly from modest to more substantial in their degree of participation, is presented in Figure 8–8. These programs usually are clusters of similar practices that focus on specific approaches to participation. One or more can be used within a single company. Some organizations give their managers some discretion to choose which program to use in their own areas, whereas other organizations mandate a particular approach throughout the company. In addition to differing considerably in nature, they also vary in their formality, degree of direct or indirect involvement, opportunity to exert influence, and time length of the involvement. When a company uses either a very significant approach with widespread application or a sufficient number of programs to develop a substantial sense of empowerment among its employees, it is said to practice **participative management.**

Suggestion Programs

Suggestion programs are formal plans to invite individual employees to recommend work improvements. In most companies the employee whose suggestion results in a cost savings may receive a monetary award in proportion to the first year's savings. Thus, the award can range from as low as $25 to as high as $50,000 in outstanding cases. The suggestions are screened for applicability and cost-benefit ratio, resulting in an acceptance rate of about 25 percent in most organizations.[15]

Problem areas

Although many suggestion programs provide useful ideas, they are a limited form of participation that accents individual initiative instead of group problem solving and teamwork. Only a small fraction of employees regularly make suggestions, and the rest may not feel any significant level of involvement in the program. In addition, delays in processing suggestions and rejections of seemingly good ideas can cause a backlash among contributors. Perhaps most significantly, some supervisors find it hard to look constructively upon the suggestions and instead view them as criticisms of their own ability and practices.

Quality Emphasis

For many years, both union and nonunion firms have organized groups of workers and their managers into committees to consider and solve job problems. These groups may be called work committees, labor-management committees, work-

FIGURE 8–8

Selected types of
participative programs

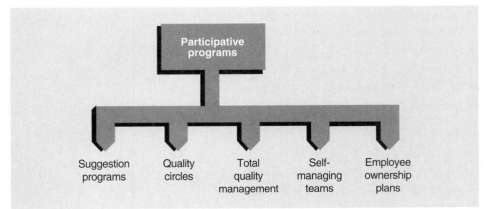

improvement task forces, or involvement teams. They have broad usefulness for improving productivity and communications because most of the employees can be involved. Popular approaches for this purpose are quality circles and total quality management.

Quality Circles   Voluntary groups that receive training in statistical techniques and problem-solving skills and then meet to produce ideas for improving productivity and working conditions are known as **quality circles.** They meet regularly—often on company time—and generate solutions for management to evaluate and implement. Quality circles expanded rapidly as an involvement technique in the United States and Europe after achieving widespread success and popularity in Japan.

> One research study in a manufacturing firm compared the attitudes and performance of six quality circles with a matched group of noninvolved workers.[16] Quality-circle participation favorably influenced employee attitudes toward decision making, group communication, and a feeling of having accomplished something worthwhile. Productivity rose by 23 percent, versus a 2 percent increase in the control group. Absenteeism declined steadily in the quality-circle group to a level 27 percent below where it began, while it showed erratic movement in the comparison group.

Effects of quality circles

The quality-circle approach helps employees feel that they have some influence on their organization even if not all their recommendations are accepted by higher management. Quality circles provide opportunities for personal growth, achievement, and recognition. Further, employees are committed to the solutions they generate, because they "own" them.

To be successful, quality circles should be used according to these guidelines:

- Use them for measurable, short-term problems.
- Obtain continuous support from top management.
- Apply the group's skills to problems within the circle's work area.
- Train supervisors in facilitation skills.
- View quality circles as one starting point for other more participative approaches to be used in the future.

Guidelines

Total Quality Management   Not all quality circles have been successful, and some firms using quality circles experienced a number of problems with them. Not all employees participated, and when they did, they often addressed rather trivial issues at first. Some quality-circle groups felt isolated in their efforts, and they could not see their impact on the larger organization.

In response to this checkered experience, continued competitive pressures, and the opportunity to compete for national recognition (for example, the Malcolm Baldrige National Quality Award), several firms have initiated a **total quality management (TQM)** program.[17] The TQM approach gets every employee involved in the process of searching for continuous improvements in their operations. Quality of product and service becomes a rallying cry for employees to focus on, and every step in the firm's processes is subjected to intense and regular scrutiny for ways to improve it. Employees are provided with extensive training in problem solving, group decision making, and statistical methods. The total quality management approach constitutes a formal program with direct participation of all employees. Almost any issue is subject to exploration, and the process is a continuing one of long duration. Consequently, TQM holds promise as a substantial program in participative management.

Wide involvement; high training

International Forms of Participation

Participative management is not unique to the United States, although its form may be different around the world. **Industrial democracy** is a program of government-mandated worker participation at various levels of the organization with regard to decisions that affect workers. Occasionally, the term also is applied to voluntary programs rather than mandated ones. At lower levels it is applied through *works councils;* at the top level it is called **codetermination.** Several European nations have laws requiring codetermination, which provides for legislated worker representation on the board of directors, and sometimes other committees, of major companies.

The idea of industrial democracy is to institutionalize what many see as a good thing—increased worker participation in higher managerial levels, giving the employees some voice in major policy and operating decisions. Although the problems addressed are highly significant, it is a *representative* form of participation with only a small fraction of workers directly involved. It also places restrictions on multinational organizations that are not familiar with the practice in their home countries.

Self-Managing Teams

Some firms have moved beyond limited forms of participation, allowing a number of major decisions to be made by employee groups (see extreme right side of Figure 8–6). These progressive approaches incorporate extensive use of group discussion, which makes full use of group ideas and group influence. These groups often seek to achieve consensus support for their actions, and this reflects many of the ideas adapted from successful Japanese firms.

A more formal version of the group-decision approach is the self-managing team. Sometimes called *semi-autonomous work groups* or *sociotechnical teams,* **self-managing teams** are natural work groups that are given a large degree of decision-making autonomy; they are expected to control their own behavior and results. A key feature is the diminished (or dramatically changed) role of the manager as the team members learn to acquire new skills. Because of their widespread use and importance, teams are discussed more extensively in Chapter 13.

Employee Ownership Plans

Employees have often been urged to "buy the product you make"; today, that slogan has occasionally been replaced with "buy the company you work for." **Employee ownership** of a firm emerges when employees provide the capital to purchase control of an existing operation. The stimulus often comes from threatened closings of marginally profitable plants, where workers see little hope of other employment in a devastated local economy. Employee ownership has been tried in diverse industries, such as plywood, meat packing, steel, and furniture manufacturing. On the surface, these plans appear to offer the highest degree of participative decision making, as employees take control. Better management, heightened morale, and improved productivity have all been predicted to follow.

The National Center for Employee Ownership surveyed 3,000 participants in 37 employee-owned companies.[18] Stock ownership generally increased employee interest in the company's financial success and encouraged workers to remain with the company longer. However, it did not increase their perception of influence in decision making, they did not feel like they were treated more equally by their managers, and they did not report working harder on the job. It appears that the potential financial rewards, coupled with a greater understanding of organizational problems and practices, are the biggest benefits from employee ownership.

The use of employee ownership plans continues to expand, with as many as 10 million employees covered in the United States alone. Although some large firms, such as Hallmark and W. L. Gore, have some form of employee ownership or stock trusts, the financial benefits may be more apparent to employees in smaller firms. Job security also has been gained for thousands of workers who were in danger of losing their jobs, but there still is no guaranteed employment if business declines. However, employee ownership plans do not necessarily result in greater day-to-day control or direct involvement by employees in key decisions.[19] Some firms have even found that the compensation gaps between workers and management have widened and labor-management relations have sometimes deteriorated from previous levels. Clearly, employee ownership has costs as well as benefits as a participative tool.

Does ownership imply involvement?

IMPORTANT CONSIDERATIONS IN PARTICIPATION

Labor Union Attitudes toward Participation

Some union leaders traditionally felt that if they participated in helping management decide courses of action, the union's ability to challenge those actions would be weakened. These union leaders preferred to remain aloof, having the freedom to express disagreement with management and to challenge it at any time. The opposite point of view, held by more progressive leaders, is that participation gives them an opportunity to get on the inside and to express their viewpoints *before* action is taken, which is superior to disagreement and protest *after* a decision is made. In practice most union viewpoints are somewhere between the two extremes: some types of participation are considered acceptable, but others are not.

> A preliminary danger signal regarding union responses to some forms of participation was raised when the National Labor Relations Board (NLRB) issued rulings in the Electromation and du Pont cases.[20] In effect, the NLRB upheld the decisions of the administrative law judge by ruling that the employers had created and structured action committees constituting labor organizations, had dominated and assisted them, and were allowing them to address conditions of employment (a violation of the National Labor Relations Act).

Companies are well advised to avoid the appearance of domination, set clear goals and boundaries, allow employees to select some members, and provide the committees with decision-making autonomy.

Limitations of Participation

In the early part of this chapter we identified the major forces pushing toward an increase in the practice of participation. As strong as those forces are, they are partially offset by other factors pushing in the opposite direction, such as those shown in Figure 8–9. Following is one example of such *limitations of participation:*

> One insurance company found that employee decision making became *too* independent after a participative approach was implemented. Sometimes two employees were calling on the same customer. Other employees were seeking only easy accounts, leaving the hard ones for someone else. Eventually, the company had to restore some controls.

FIGURE 8–9

Forces affecting the
lesser use of
participation

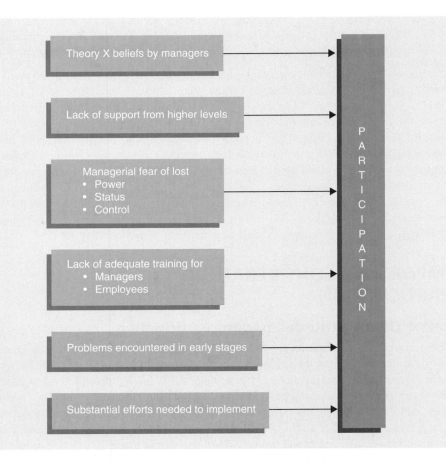

Even though failures of this type may be the result of improper planning and implementation, they often receive undue publicity, which encourages other managers to avoid participation.

Managerial Concerns about Participation

Some managers have difficulty adjusting to their new roles in a high-involvement system. They may still cling to Theory X beliefs and assumptions, they may fear losing their former status as key decision makers, or they may be concerned that they will have less power and control than previously. To a large degree, these are perceptual sources of resistance but still very real factors.

Impediments to success   Even more powerful forces acting against the success of participative programs are an organization's failure to properly prepare either their managers or employees for new roles in an empowered environment. A substantial investment in training is often required, and key issues need to be addressed, such as the philosophy underlying participation and the specific tools that help make it work effectively. Carefully designed pilot programs often help pave the way to later success, or else problems encountered in early stages may sabotage the larger effort. One of the greatest impediments to success is the lack of support for, or even resistance to, participative programs by top management. One set of observers put it bluntly when they said, "It is nearly impossible for unempowered people to empower others."[21] Just as it is important for the lead dog and all others on a sled dog team to be pulling in the

1. Let workers progress from involvement on simple issues to more complex ones.

2. Provide employees with relevant training so that they understand broader organizational issues and financial statements.

3. Communicate in advance their areas of decisional freedom and the associated boundaries.

4. Don't force workers to participate if they do not wish to do so.

5. Provide counseling for supervisors so that they will know how to handle power sharing.

6. Set realistic goals for the early stages of any participative process.

7. Keep the guiding philosophy behind participation firmly in mind at all times.

8. Never attempt to manipulate a decision under the guise of participation.

9. Maintain a delicate balance between overparticipation and underparticipation.

10. Monitor employee perceptions of the level of empowerment experienced.

same direction, it is critical that participation receive both verbal and behavioral support from the CEO's office on down throughout the organization.

Managers need to start relinquishing their roles of judge and critic and begin viewing themselves as *partners* with employees. They still need to communicate a direction for their unit, help set challenging goals, and monitor resources. But their new role invites them to view themselves as stewards of a broad range of human and technical resources. This stewardship paradigm shifts their emphasis from direction and control to that of *servant leadership,* where their challenge is to help others attain relevant goals while developing their skills and abilities.[22]

Concluding Thoughts

In spite of its numerous limitations, participation generally has achieved substantial success. It is not the answer to all organization problems, but experience does show its general usefulness. The demand of employees to gain more power and use their talents is neither a passing fancy nor a competitive advantage to be ignored. It appears to be rooted deeply in the culture of free people around the world, and it is probably a basic drive in human beings. Employees want some control over things that affect them and some meaning in their work. Organizational leaders need to devote long-range efforts and continuing discussion to promote participation as a means of building some of the human values needed at work. Participation has been so successful in practice that it has become widely accepted in more advanced nations, and will become an important tool in the progress of developing nations.

SUMMARY

Many employees want to become more empowered. If they are allowed to play a meaningful role in the organization, their feelings of self-esteem will increase and they will contribute their abilities and efforts to help the organization succeed.

Participation is an important vehicle for empowering employees. Participation is the mental and emotional involvement of people in group situations that encourages them to contribute to group goals and share responsibility for them. For employees, it is the psychological result of supportive management.

Participation is a sharing process that may increase the power of both employees and the manager, because power is an expandable resource. When the prerequisites of participation are met, it can provide a variety of benefits for both employees and employers. Some employees desire more participation than others, so a participative approach is most effective when it reasonably matches individual needs. Where there is underparticipation or overparticipation, both satisfaction and performance may decline.

A number of participative programs can be effective, and they vary in the degree to which they meet the criteria for full involvement. All have their benefits as well as their limitations. A program that is desirable for some employees is not necessarily good for all of them. Managers need to redefine themselves as stewards of resources and seek to fulfill a servant leadership role that helps others grow and develop.

Terms and Concepts for Review

Area of job freedom	Participation
Codetermination	Participative management
Employee ownership	Quality circles
Empowerment	Self-managing teams
Ethical imperative	Suggestion programs
Industrial democracy	Total quality management (TQM)
Leader–member exchange model	Underparticipation
Overparticipation	

Discussion Questions

1. Explain what empowerment means to you. Give an illustration of a time when you truly felt empowered.
2. Ask several persons outside of class what "participation" means. If their answers differ, explain why you think they do.
3. How is it possible for participation to increase the power and influence of both manager and employee?
4. Discuss the prerequisites for effective participation. Which of these are more difficult to fulfill? Do the more-difficult prerequisites help explain why some managers are still relatively autocratic?
5. Many employees desire a higher level of participation than they are currently allowed. Why is it that managers do not provide more opportunities for participation now?
6. List the several benefits that can flow from participation. Compare the various programs on the basis of the degree to which they are likely to provide those benefits.
7. Apply the leader–member exchange model to the professor–student relationship. What does each party have to give to the other?
8. What was the area of freedom in your last job? Was it adequate for your needs? What groups or institutions restricted this freedom? In what ways was it too large an area?
9. Consider the use of self-managing teams. What possible negative consequences can you predict once they are begun?
10. Consider your instructor's use of the stewardship role. In what ways does she or he demonstrate partnership building, service, and empowerment?

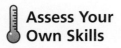 Assess Your Own Skills

How well do you exhibit good reward and empowerment skills?

Read the following statements carefully. Circle the number on the response scale that most closely reflects the degree to which each statement accurately describes you when you empower employees. Add up your total points and prepare a brief action plan for self-improvement. Be ready to report your score for tabulation across the entire group.

	Good description									Poor description
1. I fully believe in the value of providing greater autonomy to employees.	10	9	8	7	6	5	4	3	2	1
2. I fully believe in the value of widely sharing relevant information with employees.	10	9	8	7	6	5	4	3	2	1
3. I believe that some employees currently feel a sense of powerlessness in their jobs.	10	9	8	7	6	5	4	3	2	1
4. I believe that most employees want to feel a sense of competence in their jobs.	10	9	8	7	6	5	4	3	2	1
5. I believe that a participative approach can result in both performance and satisfaction improvements.	10	9	8	7	6	5	4	3	2	1
6. I believe in creating individualized relationships with each of my employees.	10	9	8	7	6	5	4	3	2	1
7. I place a high priority on developing the task-related sense of self-efficacy in each employee.	10	9	8	7	6	5	4	3	2	1
8. I accept the fact that power for both employee and manager can increase under participative systems.	10	9	8	7	6	5	4	3	2	1
9. I recognize that an effective way of providing employees with autonomy is to clarify their area of job freedom (boundaries).	10	9	8	7	6	5	4	3	2	1
10. I accept the fact that there may be a wide degree of variation in the amount of participation desired by each employee.	10	9	8	7	6	5	4	3	2	1

Scoring and Interpretation   Add up your total points for the ten questions. Record that number here, and report it when it is requested. _____

- If you scored between 81–100 points, you appear to have a solid capability for demonstrating good empowerment skills.
- If you scored between 61–80 points, you should take a close look at the items with lower self-assessment scores and explore ways to improve those items.
- If you scored less than 60 points, you should be aware that a weaker skill level regarding several items could be detrimental to your future success as a manager. We encourage you to review relevant sections of the chapter and watch for related material in subsequent chapters and other sources.

Now identify your three lowest scores, and write the question numbers here: _____, _____, _____. Write a brief paragraph, detailing to yourself an action plan for how you might sharpen each of these skills.

Incident

Joe Adams

Joe Adams is supervisor in the final-assembly department of an automobile body plant. Work in this department is not dependable, with temporary layoffs or short weeks occurring three or four times a year. The work is physically difficult, and since the skill required is minimal, most employees are high school graduates only. Some do not even have a high school education. About one-third of the workforce comes from ethnic and racial minority groups. The work procedure and pace of work are tightly controlled by industrial engineers and other staff groups.

Adams attended a one-day conference of his supervisors' association recently and learned the many potential benefits of participation. In his own words, "This conference sold me on participation," and now he wishes to establish it in his assembly department.

Management feels that conditions on an assembly line are not suitable for participation. Further, it believes that the majority of workers employed have an autocratic role expectation of supervision. In addition, management has said that the production schedule will not allow time off for participation during the workday. This means that if Adams wants to hold any meetings about participation, he will have to do so after work and on the workers' own time. Adams feels sure that his employees will not wish to remain after work on their own time; in fact, he is not even sure that they would do so if he paid them overtime.

Questions

1. Recommend a course of action for Adams.
2. Would any ideas from the following be helpful in this case: McGregor, Herzberg, McClelland, Fiedler, models of organizational behavior, prerequisites for participation, area of job freedom, and programs for participation?

Experiential Exercise

Empowerment through Participation

Empowerment fully occurs when employees feel competent and valued, when they have opportunities to use their talents, and when their jobs have meaning and impact. Working in groups of three or four persons, rate (1 = low, 10 = high) the degree to which the group feels that each participative program would produce these feelings of empowerment. Share your ratings with other groups and discuss the implications of your assessments.

Programs	*Feeling of Empowerment*			
	Competence	Value	Talent Use	Meaningful Job
1. Suggestion programs				
2. Quality circles				
3. Total quality management				
4. Self-managing teams				
5. Employee ownership				

Part Four

Individual and Interpersonal Behavior

Chapter 9

Employee Attitudes and Their Effects

Employee satisfaction is not a frill; it is a foundation of growth.
—George M. C. Fisher[1]

With loyalty no longer guaranteed and competition for skilled workers at its highest level ever, companies are doing all they can to keep employees happy, productive, stress free, and committed to their jobs.
—Diane E. Lewis[2]

CHAPTER OBJECTIVES

TO UNDERSTAND

- The Nature of Attitudes and Job Satisfaction
- The Relationship between Performance and Satisfaction
- Job Involvement and Organizational Commitment
- Some Positive and Negative Effects of Employee Attitudes
- Organizational Citizenship Behaviors
- Benefits of Studying Employee Attitudes
- Design and Use of Job Satisfaction Surveys

Hugh Aaron ran a small plastics materials company that had suffered through three painful recessions—painful because each time Hugh had to lay off highly trained and motivated employees.[3] Not only was it emotionally tough to release them, but every time business improved, some former workers had already found other jobs. The loss of those workers required him to hire inexperienced workers, who delayed the company's return to former efficiency levels. Even those who were rehired had lost some of their skills and often had bitter attitudes remaining about the layoff. Seeking to protect themselves as a future recession approached, they would slow the pace of their work in an attempt to delay their next layoff. This practice, however, only sped up the pace of layoffs, contributing to the vicious circle.

After studying some revolutionary behavioral practices of Japanese companies, Hugh introduced certain major changes. In exchange for a simple promise to eliminate future layoffs, the employees agreed to work any necessary overtime and they were cross-trained to perform a wider variety of jobs. Any additional help needed was drawn from retirees and college students.

The results were beyond expectations. Pride was evident; turnover was negligible; morale shot up; unemployment insurance and health benefit costs were reduced by having a smaller and more stable workforce. Attitudes also improved, as illustrated by employees' willingness to exert extra effort and by a sense of cohesiveness within the "family" team. Best of all, no layoffs were required during the next eight years, despite two more recessions.

Employee attitudes are clearly important to organizations, as seen in the preceding story. When attitudes are negative, they are both a *symptom* of underlying problems and a contributing *cause* of forthcoming difficulties in an organization. Declining attitudes may result in wildcat strikes, work slowdowns, absences, and employee turnover. They may also be a part of grievances, low performance, poor product quality and shabby customer service, employee theft, and disciplinary problems. The organizational costs associated with poor employee attitudes may severely reduce an organization's competitiveness.

Favorable attitudes, on the other hand, are desired by management because they tend to be connected with some of the positive outcomes that managers want. Employee satisfaction, along with high productivity, is a hallmark of well-managed organizations. However, many people hold a classic misconception about the satisfaction-productivity relationship—one that is discussed later in this chapter.

A key challenge for managers is dealing with employees who increasingly *expect* to have concern shown for their attitudes and feelings as well as to receive rewards. They have an attitude of *entitlement*—believing they deserve things because society owes it to them. However, these expectations can be unrealistic. Effective behavioral management that continuously works to build a supportive human climate in an organization can help produce favorable attitudes. This chapter focuses on the attitudes of employees toward their jobs, ways to obtain information about those attitudes, and ways to use this information effectively to monitor and improve employee satisfaction.

THE NATURE OF EMPLOYEE ATTITUDES

Attitudes are the feelings and beliefs that largely determine how employees will perceive their environment, commit themselves to intended actions, and ultimately behave. Attitudes form a mental set that affects how we view something else, much

Attitudes affect perceptions.

as a window provides a framework for our view into or out of a building. The window allows us to see some things, but the size and shape of the frame prevent us from observing other elements. In addition, the color of the glass may affect the accuracy of our perception, just as the "color" of our attitudes has an impact on how we view and judge our surroundings at work. Managers of organizational behavior are vitally interested in the nature of the attitudes of their employees toward their jobs, toward their careers, and toward the organization itself.

Although many of the factors contributing to job satisfaction are under the control of managers, it is also true that people do differ in their personal dispositions as they enter organizations.[4] Some people are optimistic, upbeat, cheerful, and courteous; they are said to have **positive affectivity.** Others are generally pessimistic, downbeat, irritable, and even abrasive; they are said to have **negative affectivity**. It appears that people are predisposed to be satisfied or dissatisfied, and managers can only partially affect the responses of employees. Nevertheless, it is important to explore the nature and effects of job satisfaction.

Job Satisfaction

Feelings, thoughts, and intentions

Elements   **Job satisfaction** is a set of favorable or unfavorable feelings and emotions with which employees view their work. Job satisfaction is an affective attitude— a *feeling* of relative like or dislike toward something (for example, a satisfied employee may comment that "I enjoy having a variety of tasks to do"). There is an important difference between these job-related feelings of satisfaction and two other elements of employee attitudes. The same employee may have an intellectual response to her work, stating the *objective thought* (belief) that "my work is quite complex." On another occasion, the employee may voice her *behavioral intentions* to a coworker ("I plan to quit this job in three months"). Attitudes, then, consist of feelings, thoughts, and intentions to act.

Morale is group satisfaction.

Individual Focus   Job satisfaction typically refers to the attitudes of a single employee. For example, an administrator might conclude, "Antonio Ortega seems very pleased with his recent promotion." When assessments of individual satisfaction are averaged across all members of a work unit, the general term used to describe overall group satisfaction is **morale.** Group morale is especially important to monitor since individuals often take their social cues from their work associates and adapt their own attitudes to conform to those of the group.

Elements of job satisfaction

Overall or Multidimensional?   Job satisfaction can be viewed as an overall attitude, or it can apply to the various parts of an individual's job. If it is viewed only as an overall attitude, however, managers may miss seeing some key hidden exceptions as they assess an employee's overall satisfaction. For example, although Antonio Ortega's general job satisfaction may be high, it is important to discover both that he likes his promotion and that he is dissatisfied with his vacation schedule this year. Job satisfaction studies, therefore, often focus on the various parts that are believed to be important, since these *job-related attitudes predispose an employee to behave in certain ways.* Important aspects of job satisfaction include pay, one's supervisor, the nature of tasks performed, an employee's coworkers or team, and the immediate working conditions.

Since job satisfaction is best viewed as being multidimensional, managers are cautioned not to allow an employee's high satisfaction on one element to offset high dissatisfaction on another by arithmetically blending both feelings into an average rating. The studies may, however, usefully divide their attention between those elements which are directly related to *job content* (the nature of the job) and those which are part of the *job context* (the supervisor, coworkers, and organization).

Stability of Job Satisfaction   Attitudes are generally acquired over a long period of time. Similarly, job satisfaction or dissatisfaction emerges as an employee gains more and more information about the workplace. Nevertheless, *job satisfaction is dynamic,* for it can decline even more quickly than it develops. Managers cannot establish the conditions leading to high satisfaction now and later neglect it, for employee needs may fluctuate suddenly. Managers need to pay attention to employee attitudes week after week, month after month, year after year.

Satisfaction levels vary.

Environmental Impact   Job satisfaction is one part of life satisfaction. The nature of a worker's environment off the job indirectly influences his or her feelings on the job. Similarly, since a job is an important part of life for many workers, job satisfaction influences general life satisfaction. The result is that there is a **spillover effect** that occurs in *both* directions between job and life satisfaction. Consequently, managers need to monitor not only the job and immediate work environment but also their employees' attitudes toward other parts of life, as shown in Figure 9–1 and illustrated in this incident:

Spillover effect

> The behavior of Nancy Rickson, a secretary in a small office, was difficult for her supervisor to understand. She had recently received a promotion and a raise but soon became increasingly unhappy, distracted, and careless in her work habits. Numerous conversations that probed her job-related attitudes provided no direct clues as to the source of her dissatisfaction.
>
> One day the supervisor happened to ask about one of Nancy's children, whose pictures were on her desk. Almost immediately, Nancy poured out a series of heart-wrenching tales including her two divorces, the delinquency of her children, the lack of support from her parents, and her failure to master an attempted recreational pursuit (tennis). These problems,

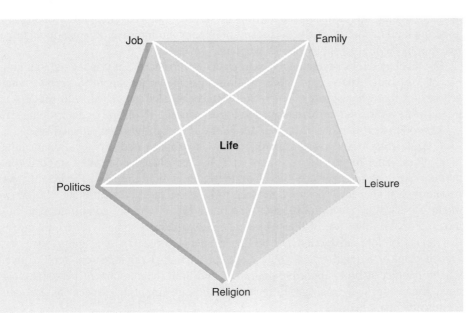

FIGURE 9–1

Some related elements of life satisfaction

and having no one to share them with, were obviously affecting her job attitudes and performance. As the complete picture emerged, the supervisor began to be aware of the intimate connection between Nancy's life satisfaction and job satisfaction.

Importance   Nancy Rickson's situation provides one piece of evidence that supervisors need to be alert to subtle clues about employee satisfaction levels. Should managers also systematically study the job satisfaction of their employees and seek to improve it where appropriate? One affirmative answer to this question lies in the idea of promoting human dignity, as advocated in this book; we believe it is important to apply knowledge of organizational behavior to build better organizations. Then both individuals and society can benefit. Additional perspectives on the issue revolve around several critical questions addressed later in this chapter:

- Is there room for improvement? (Is there currently a gap or deficiency, and can it be lessened at reasonable cost?)
- Which employees are currently the most dissatisfied?
- What other attitudes besides job satisfaction should be studied?
- What are the effects of negative employee attitudes?
- How can information about attitudes be gained?
- How can knowledge of employee attitudes be used constructively?

Level of Job Satisfaction   Long-term nationwide studies indicate that general job satisfaction has been relatively high and stable in the United States. Although worker expectations have both increased and changed in their focus over time, the quality of management practices also has improved. As a result, more than 80 percent of those in the workforce usually report that they are reasonably satisfied with their jobs.[5] Managers should not be complacent, however, for this statistic also suggests that millions of workers (the other 20 percent) are unhappy, and many other millions are probably dissatisfied with some specific aspect of their jobs. In addition, many of the "satisfied" workers may have simply resigned themselves to their work situations, with the result that they are neither satisfied nor dissatisfied. Moreover, many workers live under a cloud of job insecurity as a result of attempts to improve organizational effectiveness by laying off thousands of workers.

The level of job satisfaction across groups is not constant, but it is related to a number of variables. Analysis of these relationships allows managers to predict which groups are more likely to exhibit the problem behaviors associated with dissatisfaction. The key variables revolve around age, occupational level, and organizational size.

As workers grow older, they initially tend to be slightly more satisfied with their jobs. Apparently, they lower their expectations to more realistic levels and adjust themselves better to their work situations. Later, their satisfaction may suffer as promotions are less frequent and they face the realities of retirement. Predictably, too, people with higher-level occupations tend to be more satisfied with their jobs. As we might expect, they are usually better paid, have better working conditions, and hold jobs that make fuller use of their abilities. Finally, there is some evidence to suggest that levels of job satisfaction are higher in smaller organizational units, such as a branch plant or a small Silicon Valley enterprise. Larger organizations tend to overwhelm people, disrupt supportive processes, and limit the amounts of personal closeness, friendship, and small-group teamwork that are important aspects of job satisfaction for many people.

Most workers are satisfied.

Who is satisfied?

210

Authors Catlette and Hadden contrasted six organizations that are notorious as great places to work (e.g., Hewlett-Packard and Lincoln Electric) with six other competitive firms. The employees with the higher reputations collectively assume that employees desire meaningful work, want to be employed by firms with high standards and a clear sense of purpose, seek freedom and autonomy, want to experience a sense of caring and justice, and desire to be and feel competent. In response, these successful firms work hard to:

- Find and keep people who will be committed to the organization's core purpose

- Send messages of all types to their employees that they are valued, important, and cared about
- Enable their employees to perform (via provision of resources and training)

These practices, the authors contend, result in more satisfied employees who then provide better, not necessarily more, products and services; hence the book's title of *Contented Cows Give Better Milk*.

Source: Bill Catlette and Richard Hadden, *Contented Cows Give Better Milk*, Williford Communications, 2000.

Job Involvement

In addition to job satisfaction, three other distinct, but related, employee attitudes are important to many employers. **Job involvement** is the degree to which employees immerse themselves in their jobs, invest time and energy in them, and view work as a central part of their overall lives. Holding meaningful jobs and performing them well are important inputs to their own self-images, which helps explain the traumatic effects of job loss on their esteem needs. Job-involved employees are likely to believe in the work ethic, to exhibit high growth needs, and to enjoy participation in decision making. As a result, they seldom will be tardy or absent, they are willing to work long hours, and they will attempt to be high performers.

Organizational Commitment

Organizational commitment, or employee *loyalty,* is the degree to which an employee identifies with the organization and wants to continue actively participating in it. Like a strong magnetic force attracting one metallic object to another, it is a measure of the employee's willingness to remain with a firm in the future. It often reflects the employee's belief in the mission and goals of the firm, willingness to expend effort in their accomplishment, and intentions to continue working there. Commitment is usually stronger among longer-term employees, those who have experienced personal success in the organization, and those working within a committed employee group. Organizationally committed employees will usually have good attendance records, demonstrate a willing adherence to company policies, and have lower turnover rates. In particular, their broader base of job knowledge often translates into loyal customers who buy more from them, make referrals resulting in new customers, and even pay a premium price.[6]

Work Moods

Employees also have feelings about their jobs that are highly dynamic; they can change within a day, hour, or minute. These variable attitudes toward their jobs are called **work moods.** An employee's work mood can be described as ranging from negative ("I hate this task") to positive ("I'm excited by this new challenge") and from weak to strong and intense. When workers experience strongly positive work moods, it is often visible in terms of their energy, activity, and enthusiasm. These types of work moods are important to a manager, because they will predictably result in closer attention to customer service, lower absenteeism, greater creativity, and

An Ethics Question

"The squeaky wheel gets the grease." This saying may describe the situation in certain organizations. Dissatisfied employees—especially those who voice their dissatisfaction to their managers—often get undue attention. They may receive more communications, they may get preferential task assignments, they may get a lighter workload, or they may receive newer equipment sooner. But note the ultimate irony here—while managers strive valiantly to diminish the dissatisfaction of some employees, they may be simultaneously increasing the dissatisfaction of many others who feel that such special treatment is unfair. It appears that managers are on the horns of a dilemma. If they try to reduce dissatisfaction for some, they risk raising it for others. But if they ignore it in the few, it may become more intense and spread to others anyway. What would *you* recommend?

interpersonal cooperation.[7] Work moods are directly affected by managerial actions such as sharing praise, creating an atmosphere filled with occasional fun, humor, and levity, providing a workplace filled with pleasant surroundings, and engaging in and encouraging a reasonable amount of social interaction.

Because job satisfaction has received much attention from both researchers and managers, we take a careful look at some of the effects of job satisfaction and dissatisfaction. However, a comprehensive approach to organizational behavior suggests that a manager should consider ways in which the work environment can help produce all four key employee attitudes—job satisfaction, job involvement, organizational commitment, and positive work mood.

EFFECTS OF EMPLOYEE ATTITUDES

Attitudes are reasonably good predictors of behaviors. They provide clues to an employee's behavioral intentions or inclinations to act in a certain way. Positive job attitudes help predict constructive behaviors; negative job attitudes help predict undesirable behaviors. When employees are dissatisfied with their jobs, lack job involvement, are low in their commitment to the organization, and have strongly negative moods, a wide variety of consequences may follow. This result is especially likely if the feelings are both strong and persistent. Dissatisfied employees may engage in **psychological withdrawal** (e.g., daydreaming on the job), **physical withdrawal** (e.g., unauthorized absences, early departures, extended breaks, or work slowdowns), or even overt acts of **aggression** and retaliation for presumed wrongs. On the other hand, satisfied employees may provide acts of customer service beyond the call of duty, have sparkling work records, and actively pursue excellence in all areas of their jobs.[8] A large number of studies have addressed the outcomes of satisfaction and dissatisfaction, and the basic nature of the results is reported here in the areas of performance, turnover, absences and tardiness, theft, violence, and other behaviors. These are all important outcomes that organizations are vitally concerned about controlling.

Employee Performance

Some managers cling to an old myth—that high satisfaction always leads to high employee performance—but this assumption is *not* correct. Satisfied workers actually may be high, average, or even low producers, and they will tend to continue the level of performance that previously brought them satisfaction (according to the behavior modification model). The satisfaction-performance relationship is more complex than the simple path of "satisfaction leads to performance."

A complex relationship

> Professional athletes often experience the effects of becoming overly satisfied with their performances. Past successes periodically lead them to become complacent and to play carelessly, with the result that their team suffers a subsequent defeat. Some of the roles of a coach are to keep the players *dissatisfied* with their own contributions, to instill a renewed desire to win, and to motivate the players to perform even better. In this case, *dissatisfaction* may lead to better performance!

A more accurate statement of the relationship is that *high performance contributes to high job satisfaction.*[9] The sequence, shown in Figure 9–2, is that better performance typically leads to higher economic, sociological, and psychological rewards. If these rewards are seen as fair and equitable, then improved satisfaction develops because employees feel that they are receiving rewards in proportion to their performance. On the other hand, if rewards are seen as inadequate for the level of performance, dissatisfaction tends to arise. In either case, the level of satisfaction leads to either greater or lesser commitment, which then affects effort and eventually affects performance again. The result is a continuously operating **performance-satisfaction-effort loop.** The implication for management is to *devote its efforts to aiding employee performance,* which will likely produce satisfaction as a by-product.

Importance of equitable rewards

Alternatively, a different scenario emerges if performance is low. Employees might not receive the rewards they were hoping for, and dissatisfaction can result. Under these circumstances, the employee might exhibit one or more negative behaviors, such as turnover, absenteeism, tardiness, theft, violence, or poor organizational citizenship. Each of these undesirable by-products of dissatisfaction (seen in the lower portion of Figure 9–2) will now be explored.

Turnover

As might be expected, higher job satisfaction is associated with lower employee **turnover,** which is the proportion of employees leaving an organization during a given time period (usually one year). The more-satisfied employees are less likely to go through a progressive process in which they think about quitting or announce their intention to quit. Thus they are more likely to stay with their employer longer. Similarly, as shown in Figure 9–3, those employees who have lower satisfaction usually have higher rates of turnover. They may lack self-fulfillment, receive little recognition on the job, or experience continual conflicts with a supervisor or peer, or they may have reached a personal plateau in their career. As a result they are more likely

Who tends to leave?

FIGURE 9–2

The performance-satisfaction-effort loop

FIGURE 9–3

Relationship of job satisfaction to turnover and absences

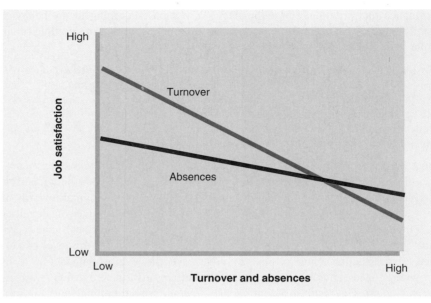

to seek greener pastures elsewhere and leave their employers, while their more satisfied associates remain.

Research studies by Mobley and others suggest that voluntary turnover is usually not a simple decisional process ("Should I stay or should I leave?").[10] While some dissatisfied workers never become turnover statistics (unless released by their employers), many of them engage in a conscious process that follows several steps to greater or lesser degrees. After experiencing job dissatisfaction for a while, an employee may begin to think about what it would be like to quit. This is followed by weighing the probable gains and losses from quitting. If the balance leans toward a net gain, the employee likely makes a decision to start searching for job alternatives, and then does so. Assuming that more than one alternative emerges, the possibilities are analyzed against each other and against the existing job held. At some point the employee must reach a decision (vividly described as "I had to decide whether to fish or cut bait" by one procrastinator) regarding intention to stay or depart and then follow through with the appropriate action. For managers, the value of knowing that this is a multistage process allows them to pay attention to available cues from employees and intervene before it is too late (for the valuable employee whom they wish to encourage to stay).

Employee turnover can have several negative consequences, especially if the turnover rate is high. Often it is difficult to replace the departed employees, and the direct and indirect costs to the organization of replacing workers are expensive. The remaining employees may be demoralized from the loss of valued coworkers, and both work and social patterns may be disrupted until replacements are found. Also, the organization's reputation in the community may suffer. However, some benefits may arise from turnover, such as more opportunities for internal promotion and the infusion of expertise from newly hired employees. In other words, *turnover may have functional effects.*

Figure 9–4 illustrates the relationship between employee attitudes toward the organization and the organization's attitudes toward the employee. Desirable turnover is represented by cells *b* and *d;* the undesirable turnover of cell *c* should be minimized. Situations contributing to cell *a* should be encouraged; in this cell are valued employees who wish to remain with the organization. The message for managers is to look beyond overall turnover rates and *examine instead the functionality of each departure.*

Some turnover is functional.

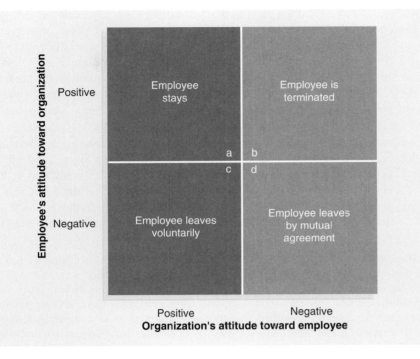

FIGURE 9–4

Four products of employee-organization attitudes

215

Managers need to ask themselves these questions—"Are the *right* people staying, and are the *right* people departing?" This is an extremely critical analytical issue during downsizing. However, the best approach is a preventive one, as this example shows:

> A study of 43,000 job applicants determined that a simple preemployment questionnaire could predict the likelihood of an individual's later being fired or quitting within 30 days of being hired.[11] The results identified a "turnover personality" that consisted of these traits: bitterness, cynicism, outspokenness, lack of involvement, hedonism, and avoidance of involvement and challenge. Identification of these factors in applicants could potentially reduce unplanned or uncontrolled turnover.

Many organizations have become more savvy in recent years regarding employee retention in the face of intense competition for talent and the extraordinary costs of recruiting and training new employees. Valero Energy works to foster a sense of family and community among its employees; General Electric identifies its best people and then invests heavily in training and mentoring them to start them on successful careers; Home Depot allows all employees extensive decision-making authority; Goldman Sachs tries to create a culture of exclusivity and a reputation as a market leader; and SAS Institute gives employees the opportunity to balance the demands between work and family. And a Gallup poll found that the employers with lower turnover clarify job expectations, provide opportunities for employees to excel and use their talents, offer recognition and praise regularly, and make sure that each employee feels that someone cares about him or her as a person.[12]

Absences and Tardiness

Figure 9–3 also shows that those employees who have low job satisfaction tend to be absent more often. The connection is not always sharp, for a couple of reasons. First, some **absences** are caused by legitimate medical reasons; therefore a satisfied   *Absenteeism reasons* employee may have a valid absence. Second, dissatisfied employees do not necessarily plan to be absent, but they seem to find it easier to respond to the opportunities to do so. These voluntary (attitudinal) absences often occur with high frequency among a certain cluster of employees and usually occur on Mondays or Fridays. Whereas involuntary (medically related) absenteeism can sometimes be predicted (e.g., for surgery) and often be reduced through the use of more thorough preemployment physical exams and work-history record checks, different approaches are needed for absences caused by poor attitudes.

Some employers place all of an employee's accrued time off into a *paid leave bank* of usable days (also known as paid time off). Vacation time, sick leave, holidays, and personal days all enter the bank, and the employee can use them for any reason. This approach gives the employee greater *control* over when to take days off, and the employer gains greater *predictability* of those occasions. Other employers have successfully used incentives to control absenteeism, as the following example shows:

> Statistically, Drakenfeld Colors Corporation did not have an overall absenteeism problem (0.89 percent).[13] As a matter of fact, almost half (44 percent) of its 250 employees had perfect records. However, a small handful of employees missed several days per year, and they were perceived to be taking advantage of the company and their working colleagues. Drakenfeld attacked this problem by offering small cash bonuses for those with perfect attendance every six months, a sweepstakes opportunity featuring an all-expenses-paid trip for two to a resort for the perfect-record winner of a drawing, and a progressive disciplinary procedure for abusers of the attendance policy. The results? Absenteeism fell to 0.35 percent, the number of significant abusers fell by 90 percent, and the proportion of employees with perfect attendance increased to 62 percent. This case demonstrates that absenteeism *can* be controlled.

Tardiness

Another way in which employees may exhibit their dissatisfaction with job conditions is through **tardiness.** A tardy employee is one who comes to work but arrives beyond the designated starting time. Tardiness is a type of short-period absenteeism ranging from a few minutes to several hours for each event, and it is another way in which employees physically withdraw from active involvement in the organization. It may impede the timely completion of work and disrupt productive relationships with coworkers. Although there may be legitimate reasons for an occasional tardy arrival (like a sudden traffic jam), a pattern of tardiness is often a symptom of negative attitudes requiring managerial attention.

Theft

> One of the authors once toured a pizza-production plant. Toward the completion of the tour, the guide was asked what the major human problems were. Without hesitation, she replied, "Theft." "You mean the employees steal the pizzas?" she was asked. "Oh no," she replied, "they aren't worth that much. But we do lose hundreds of pepperoni sticks each year." Then she showed us a cart of the sticks. They were each about 40 inches long and 3 inches in diameter, and each weighed perhaps 20 pounds. "We don't know how the employees get them out the door," she said, "but we assume they steal them as indirect compensation for the relatively low wages they receive [minimum wage] and the monotonous [assembly-line] jobs they perform." Looking back at Figure 9–2, we can see that a perception of inequity produced dissatisfaction, which apparently caused some employees to rationalize stealing from the firm.

Some employees steal products, like the pepperoni sticks described above. Others use company services without authorization, such as when they make personal long-distance calls at work (thereby "stealing" both the cost of the call and their productive time). Others forge checks or commit other types of fraud. All these acts represent **theft,** or the unauthorized removal of company resources.[14] Although there are many causes of employee theft, some employees may steal because they feel exploited, overworked, or frustrated by the impersonal treatment that they receive from their organization. In their own minds, employees may justify this unethical behavior as a way of reestablishing a perception of lost equity, or even gaining revenge for what they consider ill treatment at the hands of a supervisor. In contrast to the situation with absenteeism and tardiness, tighter organizational controls or incentive systems do not always solve theft problems, since they are directed at the symptoms and not at the underlying causes such as severe dissatisfaction.

Violence

One of the most extreme consequences of employee dissatisfaction is exhibited through **violence,** or various forms of verbal or physical aggression at work. Although the source of violence can include customers and strangers, the effect is the same— millions of workers are now the victims of workplace violence annually, and many more live under the direct or perceived threat of harm. The cost to U.S. businesses is astronomical—estimated to be $36 billion a year.[15] Ironically, work stress can be both a cause of violence and the aftermath of it. Managers must increasingly be on the lookout for signs that employee dissatisfaction might turn into verbal or physical harm at work, and they must take appropriate preventive actions.

Other Effects

Low productivity, turnover, absenteeism, tardiness, theft, and violence are all typically negative behaviors, for they harm the organization and sometimes its members. Many employees, however, hold positive attitudes toward their work and organization, and these pay off in both obvious and more subtle ways. In particular, employees sometimes demonstrate **organizational citizenship behaviors,** which are discretionary actions that promote the organization's success.[15] Organizational citizenship is often marked by its spontaneity, its voluntary nature, its constructive impact on results, its unexpected helpfulness to others, and the fact that it is optional. For example, Mary Jo may exhibit unusual conscientiousness in carrying out normal job responsibilities; Willy may exercise a high level of innovation and creativity on a troublesome problem. Even volunteering for extra assignments or sharing equipment with another worker is a demonstration of organizational citizenship. Like the thousands of grains of dry yeast that make the other ingredients in bread dough rise, thousands of tiny bits of extra effort (helping, donating, cooperating) help organizations rise past their competitors.

Organizational citizenship

Acts of good organizational citizenship include the use of courtesy in touching bases with others before taking action, sportsmanlike tolerance of daily nuisances on the job, unusual conscientiousness, helping behaviors, and a variety of civic behaviors, such as attending meetings even though reluctant to do so. Research suggests that these "good soldiers" engage in these actions for any of three reasons:

- Their personality disposes them to do so.
- They hope that by doing so they will receive special recognition or rewards.
- They are attempting to engage in image-enhancement through managing the impressions that others form of them.[17]

Regardless of their motivation, organizational citizenship behaviors are usually appreciated by the organization and coworkers alike.

STUDYING JOB SATISFACTION

Management needs information on employee job satisfaction in order to make sound decisions, both in preventing and solving employee problems. This section discusses the types of benefits that management can gain and the conditions under which a study of job satisfaction will be most likely to succeed. Some of the more popular survey methods are explained, and guidelines for the use of surveys are given.

Job satisfaction surveys

A typical method used is a job satisfaction survey, also known as a morale, opinion, attitude, or quality-of-work-life survey. A **job satisfaction survey** is a procedure by which employees report their feelings toward their jobs and work environment. Individual responses are then combined and analyzed.

Benefits of Job Satisfaction Studies

If job satisfaction studies are properly planned and administered, they will usually produce a number of important benefits, both general and specific.

Monitoring Attitudes   One benefit of attitude studies is that they give management an indication of general levels of satisfaction in a company. Surveys also indicate the specific areas of satisfaction or dissatisfaction (such as employee services) and the particular groups of employees (such as the marketing department or those employees who are approaching retirement). In other words, a survey tells how employees feel about their jobs, what parts of their jobs these feelings are focused on, which departments are particularly affected, and whose feelings are involved (e.g., supervisors, employees, or staff specialists). The survey is a powerful diagnostic instrument for assessing broad employee problems.

Additional Benefits   Surveys have many other benefits as well. The *flow of communication* in all directions is improved as people plan the survey, take it, and discuss its results. Surveys can serve as a *safety valve,* or emotional release, for people to get things off their chests and later feel better about them. *Training needs* can be identified, since employees can report how well they feel their supervisor performs certain parts of the job, such as delegating work and giving adequate instructions. Surveys can also help managers *plan and monitor new programs,* by getting feedback on proposed changes in advance and then conducting a follow-up survey to evaluate the actual response. The following example illustrates the multiple payoffs from attitude surveys:

> Aaron Goldberg had strong feelings about how management could improve its ways of working with people. He felt that some changes were needed. For more than a year he had been waiting for the right opportunity to express his viewpoints, but the opportunity never seemed to develop. His ideas were bottled up within him, and he was beginning to feel agitated. At about this time management distributed a job satisfaction survey that included generous space for employee comments. Aaron filled out the comments pages and then felt much better because finally he had a chance to give management his ideas. The firm gained both useful ideas and a more satisfied employee.

Ideal Survey Conditions

Desired prerequisites

Surveys are most likely to produce some of the benefits reviewed above when the following conditions are met:

- Top management actively supports the survey.
- Employees are fully involved in planning the survey.

- A clear objective exists for conducting the survey.
- The study is designed and administered in a manner consistent with standards for sound research.
- Management is capable of taking, and willing to take, follow-up action.
- Both the results and action plans are communicated to employees.

Use of Existing Job Satisfaction Information

Before they conduct formal job satisfaction surveys, managers might examine two other methods for learning about current employee feelings—daily contacts and existing data. These approaches recognize that formal job satisfaction surveys are similar to an annual accounting audit in the sense that both are merely periodic activities; yet there is a day-to-day need to monitor job satisfaction just as there is a regular need to keep up with the financial accounts.

Daily contacts

Management stays in touch with the level of employee satisfaction primarily through face-to-face contact and communication. This is a practical and timely method of determining the job satisfaction level of individuals, but there are also a number of other satisfaction indicators already available in an organization. As shown in Figure 9–5, examples include absences, grievances, and exit interviews. This information is usually collected separately for other purposes, but it can readily be assembled into a monthly report that gives management insights into the general level of satisfaction among employees.

Existing data

Some of the items in Figure 9–5 are behavioral indicators of job satisfaction, such as turnover, absenteeism, and tardiness, while others, such as medical and training

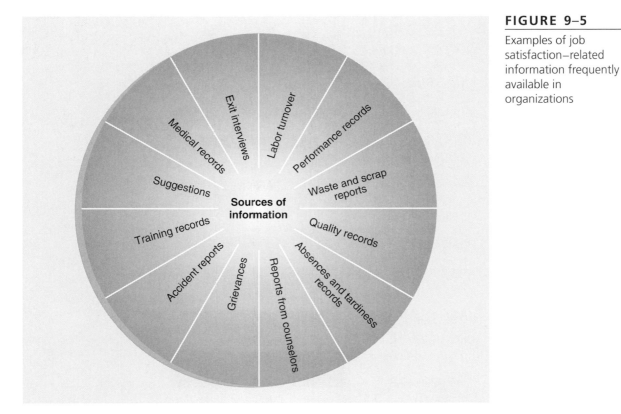

FIGURE 9–5

Examples of job satisfaction–related information frequently available in organizations

219

220

records, provide only indirect clues that something may be wrong. Carefully interpreted, the data can provide a rich portrait of the satisfaction of workers in an organization. The chief advantages of employee records are that in most cases they are already available, many of them provide quantifiable data, and they are a good measure of trends over a period of time.

SURVEY DESIGN AND FOLLOW-UP

Steps in the process

A systematic approach to conducting surveys is shown in Figure 9–6. In general, managers need to identify a purpose for the attitude assessment, obtain top management and union support, and then develop the measurement instrument. Intermediate steps consist of administering the survey, followed by tabulating and analyzing the results. Conclusions should be fed back to the participants *soon* afterward, and action plans need to be developed by groups of employees and managers working together, and then activated. Because the reasons for monitoring employee attitudes have already been suggested, this section focuses on the types of survey instruments that can be designed. It concludes with an examination of related factors for their successful use.

Types of Survey Questions

Providing structured responses

Studies of job satisfaction typically gather data either by survey questionnaires or by interviews. Whichever method is used, careful attention should be paid to the form of question asked and the nature of the response allowed. **Closed-end questions** present a choice of answers in such a way that employees simply select and mark the

FIGURE 9–6

Major steps in a systematic approach to conducting surveys

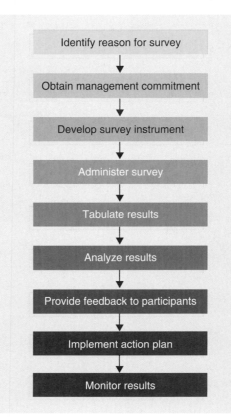

Identify reason for survey

Obtain management commitment

Develop survey instrument

Administer survey

Tabulate results

Analyze results

Provide feedback to participants

Implement action plan

Monitor results

answers that best represent their own feelings. **Open-end questions** present a variety of topics but let employees answer in their own words. The typical survey form uses both approaches.

Closed-End Questions   There are various kinds of closed-end questions, but a hallmark of each is the high degree of structure in the response categories.[18] One popular type, the *Index of Organizational Reactions,* uses multiple-choice questions. Here respondents read all the answers to each question and then mark the response that comes closest to their own feelings. Other surveys use questions with "true or false" or "agree or disagree" answers. The frequently used *Job Descriptive Index* provides respondents with a set of statements (e.g., "My work is routine") and asks them to indicate whether the term describes their work situation by checking either "Yes," "No," or "?" ("I can't decide") responses. Somewhat more flexible are the surveys that present statements and request employees to respond by checking a numerical scale to indicate their degree of agreement or disagreement, as shown here:

My feeling of security in my job (circle one number):
  How much is there now?   (min.) 1   2   3   4   5 (max.)

In addition, many surveys attempt to capture employee sentiment about the deficiency of a certain item (such as job security) by comparing the "now" responses with perceptions of desired states. They might ask,

How much should there be?   (min.) 1   2   3   4   5 (max.)
How important is this factor to you?   (min.) 1   2   3   4   5 (max.)

Another approach is to ask respondents for their "hindsight" ratings; employees are asked to assess the degree to which the item was present at some past point in time (e.g., three months or one year) as well as the present.[19] This allows an organization to estimate the degree of change in employee satisfaction as a result of introducing new programs, in spite of not having measured it before the change. An example is,

How satisfied were you with the level of communications before the newsletter was introduced?   (min.) 1   2   3   4   5 (max.)

Because of concern over the meaning that employees may attach to only numbers in a response scale, instruments like the *Minnesota Satisfaction Questionnaire* provide brief descriptions for each number on the scale—for example, 1 = not satisfied, 2 = slightly satisfied, 3 = satisfied, 4 = very satisfied, and 5 = extremely satisfied. These descriptions aid employees in selecting their responses and help management interpret the data.

The chief advantage of surveys with closed-end questions is that they are easy to administer and to analyze statistically. Much of the tabulation and analysis can be performed by computers, which minimizes clerical time, costs, and errors when large numbers of employees are surveyed.

The Chief Learning Officer for Sears Roebuck reports that they have found causal linkages between several key variables.[20] They regularly monitor employee satisfaction, and if they can increase it by five units in one quarter, then customer satisfaction scores go up in the next quarter. And when customer satisfaction scores increase, two other key indicators improve—customer retention and customer recommendations of the store to other shoppers. The combination of returning shoppers and new shoppers translates directly to improved financial performance. Employee satisfaction counts on the bottom line, according to Sears.

222

The chief defect of closed-end questions is that management or a survey consultant writes all the structured responses available to employees. None of these responses may be viewed as an accurate expression of employees' real feelings. In other words, this approach really does not give employees a full opportunity to express themselves.

Seeking personal feelings

Open-End Questions   In contrast to closed-end questions, open-end questions seek responses from employees in their own words. This unstructured approach permits employees to express their feelings, thoughts, and intentions fully. These more personal comments usually make a strong impression on management, especially if large numbers of employees mention a particular problem area and state their feelings in powerful language. For example, managers may not be too impressed if they discover that thirty-nine employees think the sick-leave plan is poor, but how would they react to thirty-nine comments similar to the following: "Our sick-leave plan stinks! You don't let us carry over unused leave more than two years, so I have no protection for serious illness that causes me to be absent more than a month." Now management may be more inclined to listen, and respond.

There are two types of open-end questions. *Directed* questions focus employee attention on specific parts of the job and ask questions about those aspects. This approach permits in-depth analysis of satisfaction with a specific job condition. On the other hand, *undirected* questions ask for general comments about the job. In this way management learns about the topics that currently are troubling employees and seem important to them.

Critical Issues

Reliability

Job satisfaction survey procedures are more complicated than they appear to be at first glance. It seems simple enough to go to employees, get their responses, and then interpret them, but experience shows that careless errors in survey design can seriously limit the usefulness of a survey. Reliability and validity are two elements that serve as the backbone of any effective study. **Reliability** is the capacity of a survey instrument to produce consistent results, regardless of who administers it. If an instrument is reliable, we can be confident that any difference found between two groups is real, and not the product of employee mood changes or widely varying administrative procedures.

Validity

In addition to reliability, studies of job satisfaction need **validity,** or the capacity to measure what they claim to measure. The difference between reliability and validity becomes clear when we attempt to use a wooden yardstick to measure metric distances. In this case, the yardstick is consistently accurate at what it does (it is reliable), but it is invalid since it measures the wrong thing. Obviously, we need to be sure of *both* the reliability and validity of our measures of job satisfaction. This task is easier with closed-end questions; it is much more difficult with the qualitative nature of open-end questions.

Social desirability bias

Many critical issues arise in the process of question construction and survey administration.[21] As shown in Figure 9–7, particular attention needs to be given to sample selection, maintenance of anonymity of employees, the use of norms in interpreting data, the voluntary participation of employees, and other factors. Response rates can be raised by requiring that surveys be returned in a short period of time, by sending periodic reminders, or by offering a small incentive. The tendency of employees to have a **social desirability bias** (e.g., overestimating the importance of challenge in their job because they think that is what society values) can be controlled. To do this, benchmarked norms from comparable organizations can be obtained and used to interpret response patterns.

- Should participation be voluntary or mandated?

- Should a sample or the total population be used?

- Should responses be signed or anonymous?

- Should norms be used for comparison?

- Should the forms be returned to the supervisor or to an independent consulting firm?

- Should the survey be designed and conducted by internal staff or by external consultants?

- Should a deadline be stated for return of the surveys, or should no date be set?

- Should a standardized instrument be used, or should one be created for this situation?

- How should feedback be given to employees?

FIGURE 9–7

Some issues in survey design and administration

223

Using Survey Information

Once job satisfaction information has been collected and tabulated, the big question remaining is: What does all this mean in terms of the organization and its employees? Although gathering this information is chiefly a matter of technique, analysis and use of the resulting data require skilled management judgment. It is the final important step in a job satisfaction survey. When appropriate action is taken, results can be excellent.

Communicating the Results   The first step in using job satisfaction information is to communicate it to all managers so that they can understand it and prepare to use it. This document is known as a *survey report*. Managers will be the ones to make any changes suggested by the data, and they will want to see the evidence in order to make their own judgments. The recommendations of job satisfaction specialists are helpful, but managers must make the final decisions.

Managers require evidence.

Comparative Data   In larger organizations, *comparisons among departments* are an effective way to encourage managers to sit up and take note of satisfaction data. Just as a lagging baseball team makes every effort to pass other teams in its league, managers whose departments do not show high job satisfaction will be spurred to improve their employees' attitudes by the time the next study is made. Comparisons of this type must be handled with skill so that the lower performers will not feel intimidated.

Survey data spur competition.

If earlier surveys have been made, *trends over time* can be plotted. More elaborate statistical comparisons and correlations can be made if the evidence looks promising. For example, do those who say their supervisor is a good manager say also that they take more pride in their organization as a place in which to work? Ultimately, all the questions and job satisfaction categories can be compared with one another in a search for meaningful relationships.

The managers' interests in job satisfaction statistics are heightened by asking them to *predict their subordinates' attitudes* toward various items and then to compare their predictions with actual survey results. Wherever their prediction misses its mark, they are forced to ask themselves why they misjudged this condition. Even if a prediction is accurate, it may still encourage soul searching. Consider the case of a department head who predicted his employees would report dissatisfaction with grievance handling. They did report dissatisfaction, which forced him to ask: "If I knew about this condition before the survey—and apparently I did—why didn't I do something about it?"

Employee Comments   As mentioned earlier, employee comments are very useful. This information often makes a greater impression on management than scores, statistics, and charts do. In terms of communication, the comments get through to management because they are more personal.

Some comments are about very minor conditions, but these conditions do annoy someone and are therefore worthy of management's sincere attention. It is a mistake to correct only the big problems shown in a survey while ignoring many minor conditions that will add up to big problems.

> In a marketing department survey, the comments of several field sales representatives showed negative attitudes toward the sales paperwork required of them. Although the subject appeared to be minor, management redesigned the paperwork so that it was reduced by about 30 percent. The results were more sales calls each week and 8 percent higher unit sales with the same sales force. This change helped the salespeople earn more commissions and helped management reduce its costs, so both parties benefited.

Committee Work Follow-Up   One way to get managers to introduce change in their departments following a survey is to set up working committees (task forces) whose responsibility is to review the survey data and develop plans for corrective action.

> In one company the president appointed a special executive committee to follow up a survey and recommend changes. Then the general manager appointed supervisory committees in each department to discuss how the survey applied to local departmental problems. The supervisory committees worked out their own solutions on departmental matters, but if their proposed action affected other departments, it had to be forwarded to the executive committee for approval.
>
> *Committees recommend action.*   The human resource director chaired each committee, which usually met monthly. At each meeting a separate part of the survey was discussed in some depth. Meetings continued for more than a year, ensuring an extended follow-up of the information uncovered by the survey. This long-run approach kept executives thinking about the survey and allowed time for the information to sink in.

The long-run approach to using job satisfaction information is important. Too many employers make the mistake of giving a survey immense publicity and interest for a few weeks and then forgetting about it until another survey is run. They shoot the works, giving their surveys all the fanfare of a Mardi Gras celebration—but when Mardi Gras has passed, they return to their old way of living.

Feedback to Employees   When corrective action is taken as the result of a survey, details of what was learned and what was done should be shared with employees as soon as possible. Only in this way will the people who participated feel that management listened to them and took action on the basis of their ideas. Providing feedback also assures employees that their ideas really were wanted—and are

FIGURE 9–8

Guidelines for changing
employee attitudes

- Make the reward system closely tied to individual or team performance.

- Set challenging goals with employees so that those with achievement drives can experience the opportunity for satisfaction through their accomplishment.

- Define clear role expectations so that employees struggling with ambiguity can overcome that concern.

- Refrain from attacking the employee's attitude. Use active listening skills instead, because an undefended attitude is more receptive to change.

- Provide frequent feedback to satisfy the need for information about performance levels.

- Exhibit a caring, considerate orientation by showing concern for employee feelings.

- Provide opportunities for employees to participate in decision making.

- Show appreciation for appropriate effort and citizenship behaviors.

wanted still. In fact, good publicity to managers and employees is essential from start to finish in a job satisfaction study in order to explain what the study intends to accomplish, to report the information gathered, and to announce what corrective action has been taken. This type of publicity is the essence of effective feedback.

Feedback and action are required.

One thing is sure: If a job satisfaction survey is made, *management should be prepared to take action on the results.* Employees feel that if they cooperate in stating their feelings, management should try to make some of the improvements they suggest or at least explain why the changes are not feasible. A sure way to close off future expressions of employee opinion is to fail to take action on opinions already given. Since management asked employees for their ideas, employees are justified in believing that action will be taken on at least some of them.

CHANGING EMPLOYEE ATTITUDES

Inducing attitude shifts is not always easy, but the potential gains can make it worthwhile to try. If management desires to change employee attitudes in a more favorable direction, there are many routes to pursue, as shown by the guidelines in Figure 9–8.

Many other ideas exist that provide clues on changing attitudes. Sometimes misinformation exists, and simply providing new data (e.g., telling insecure individuals about the organization's projected economic future) is useful. It can also be revealing to have an employee's coworkers share their attitudes; this tactic can create implicit peer pressure to fall into line. Even a simple series of open meetings for group discussion can be useful as a forum for allowing employees to vent their emotions and then begin exploring ways to change a situation. Finally, it would be naive to assume that attitudes only influence behavior, for there is a reciprocal relationship between them such that *behavior also influences attitudes.* Sometimes, then, it is advisable to get employees to change their behavior first, and let the desired attitude shift follow later, as this illustration demonstrates:

Attitudes affect behavior; behavior affects attitudes.

1. Pay attention to employee attitudes; where possible, hire new staff who exhibit positive affectivity.

2. Remember the work-life satisfaction spillover effect; take time to explore and monitor employees' nonwork environment.

3. Consider your role as a manager of performance, and recognize how dramatically the administration of rewards affects employee attitudes.

4. View employee attitudes as multidimensional; differentiate among satisfaction, involvement, commitment, and work mood when discussing them.

5. Recognize that it may take different programs and actions to impact turnover, absenteeism, tardiness, theft, and citizenship behaviors.

6. Commit yourself to a regular and systematic process of measuring employee satisfaction; promptly follow through to make changes based on the results.

7. Involve employees in the purpose, design, administration, and interpretation of survey results.

8. Recognize that attitudes can be changed, including your own. It may take substantial time, effort, and persistence to do so.

Many workers initially feared and resisted the implementation of personal computers at work. Marilyn was one supervisor who, it seemed, was hoping that she could delay the use of computers in her office until after she retired. Since retirement was about five years away, her manager decided neither to wait until then nor to waste further effort in trying to change her attitude directly. The manager simply purchased the computers, installed them, and offered nonthreatening training courses on how to use them. Within a few weeks Marilyn was the department's most enthusiastic supporter for the computers. "I don't know why we waited so long to get them," she confided to a colleague. "We've needed these for a long time!"

SUMMARY

Employee attitudes are important to monitor, understand, and manage. They develop as the consequences of the feelings of equity or inequity in the reward system (discussed in Chapter 6), as well as from supervisory treatment (addressed in Chapter 8). Managers are particularly concerned with four types of attitudes—job satisfaction, job involvement, organizational commitment, and work mood.

Job dissatisfaction may lead to increased absenteeism, turnover, and other undesirable behaviors, so employers want to develop satisfaction among their employees. The vast majority of workers in the United States report that they are satisfied with their jobs, although they may be dissatisfied with specific aspects of them.

Higher job involvement leads to higher levels of dedication and productivity in workers. High performance and equitable rewards encourage high satisfaction through a performance-satisfaction-effort loop. Higher job satisfaction usually is associated with lower turnover and fewer absences. Committed employees are also more likely to embrace company values and beliefs (its culture).

We can obtain useful attitudinal information by using questionnaires and interviews, as well as by examining existing human resource data. Information is communicated to managers through survey feedback that uses summary data, makes relevant comparisons, and supports the conclusions with actual employee comments. Follow-up is accomplished by committees to assure employees that appropriate action is taken after a survey. Ultimately, information on employee attitudes is useful only if it influences managers to improve their own behavior and reward systems.

Absences

Attitudes

Behavioral intentions

Closed-end questions

Job involvement

Job satisfaction

Job satisfaction survey

Morale

Negative affectivity

Open-end questions

Organizational citizenship behaviors

Organizational commitment

Performance-satisfaction-effort loop

Physical withdrawal

Positive affectivity

Psychological withdrawal

Reliability

Social desirability bias

Spillover effect

Tardiness

Theft

Turnover

Validity

Violence

Work moods

Discussion Questions

1. Explain, in your own words, why you feel that employee attitudes are important. Do you think that today's managers overemphasize or underemphasize attitudes? Why?
2. Assume that a survey of the twenty employees in your department found that 90 percent of them were basically satisfied with their jobs. What are the implications for you as a manager?
3. "A happy employee is a productive employee." Discuss this statement.
4. Think of a job you have held. List the areas of your job in which you were most satisfied and those which satisfied you least. Note in each case the degree to which management had some control over the item mentioned. What could the managers have done to improve your satisfaction?
5. Assume that job satisfaction, job involvement, organizational commitment, and work mood are independent of one another—any one may be present without the others. Describe a situation in which an employee might be committed but not satisfied or involved. Tell what you would do with such an employee.
6. Prepare a series of directed and undirected questions, and interview three friends to determine their areas of satisfaction and dissatisfaction. Discuss the results.
7. Select an industry (e.g., financial institutions or hospitals), and contact three organizations within that industry to learn of their absenteeism and turnover rates. What have they done to reduce them?
8. Construct a short questionnaire using objective questions, and survey the members of a small work team about their job satisfaction. Tabulate and analyze your results; include a list of recommendations for change.
9. Prepare a plan for using the data from a job satisfaction survey in an insurance office to provide feedback to managers and employees.
10. Contact a local fast-food restaurant, and ask the manager to estimate the proportion of turnover that can be attributed to effective employees leaving of their own choice. What suggestions could you make to reduce this problem?

How well do you exhibit good employee attitude-management skills?

Read the following statements carefully. Circle the number on the response scale that most closely reflects the degree to which each statement accurately describes you when you empower employees. Add up your total points and prepare a brief action

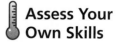

Assess Your Own Skills

plan for self-improvement. Be ready to report your score for tabulation across the entire group.

	Good description									Poor description
1. I pay as much attention to employee attitudes as I do to employee performance.	10	9	8	7	6	5	4	3	2	1
2. I am aware that my attitude may easily be reflected in the attitudes of my employees.	10	9	8	7	6	5	4	3	2	1
3. I listen carefully to differentiate among the feeling, thought, and behavioral intention components of employee attitudes.	10	9	8	7	6	5	4	3	2	1
4. I recognize that employee satisfaction is dynamic; I continually monitor and manage it.	10	9	8	7	6	5	4	3	2	1
5. I recognize the high costs and high likelihood of employee turnover, and therefore actively work to increase employee commitment/loyalty.	10	9	8	7	6	5	4	3	2	1
6. I could easily describe to my boss the research-based set of relationships among performance, rewards, satisfaction, and various products of satisfaction.	10	9	8	7	6	5	4	3	2	1
7. I observe the workplace for evidence of organizational citizenship behaviors and provide appropriate recognition for people who display them.	10	9	8	7	6	5	4	3	2	1
8. I conduct periodic surveys of employee satisfaction and introduce changes based on the results.	10	9	8	7	6	5	4	3	2	1
9. I regularly monitor existing indicators of employee satisfaction and search for explanations where these data differ from survey results.	10	9	8	7	6	5	4	3	2	1
10. I understand the need for reliability and validity of survey processes and take measures to assure those exist.	10	9	8	7	6	5	4	3	2	1

Scoring and Interpretation Add up your total points for the ten questions. Record that number here, and report it when it is requested. _____

- If you scored between 81–100 points, you appear to have a solid capability for demonstrating good employee attitude-management skills.
- If you scored between 61–80 points, you should take a close look at the items with lower self-assessment scores and explore ways to improve those items.

- If you scored less than 60 points, you should be aware that a weaker skill level regarding several items could be detrimental to your future success as a manager. We encourage you to review relevant sections of the chapter and watch for related material in subsequent chapters and other sources.

Now identify your three lowest scores, and write the question numbers here: _____, _____, _____. Write a brief paragraph, detailing to yourself an action plan for how you might sharpen each of these skills.

Barry Niland   **Incident**

Barry Niland, supervisor of a small sales department, noticed that one of his industrial sales representatives, Henry Hunter, had a problem. Among other signs, Hunter's sales had declined in the last six months, although most other sales representatives regularly were exceeding their quotas. Niland decided to try to boost his sales representative's performance by reminding him of the many opportunities for satisfaction in a sales job.

Niland explained his actions as follows:

> *I pointed out that in his customer's eyes he alone is the company. He has the opportunity to help his customer. He has the opportunity to show his ability and knowledge to many types of people. He has the opportunity through his own efforts to help many types of people. He has the opportunity to support the people who make our products, to reward the stockholders, and to control his financial return through his own know-how. He has the opportunity of testing his creative ideas, with immediate feedback about their value. He has the opportunity to meet constantly changing conditions, so there is no boredom in his job. There is no quicker way to achieve personal satisfaction than sales work.*

Questions
1. Comment on Niland's approach in dealing with his sales representative.
2. Suggest approaches for increasing Hunter's
   a. Job satisfaction
   b. Job performance
   c. Job involvement
   d. Organizational commitment

Attitudes in the Classroom   **Experiential**
                                                                 Exercise
The discussion of attitudes that is presented in this chapter can also be related to the college classroom.

1. Working individually, class members should rate, on a scale from 1 to 10 (1 = low, 10 = high) their
   a. Overall satisfaction with the course
   b. Feeling of involvement in the educational process
   c. Commitment to the college
2. The instructor should predict the average ratings of the class on each of the three items.
3. Share the ratings obtained in step 1, and compute averages for each.

4. Working in groups of four or five persons, discuss the reasons for the overall level of satisfaction, involvement, and commitment in the class. Is there a possible social desirability bias? Assess the accuracy of the instructor's predictions. Develop a realistic action plan for improving the level of each of the three dimensions.

5. Discuss the probable reliability and validity of the data gathered in steps 1 and 2. Suggest ways in which you could gather evidence of the data's reliability and validity.

6. What is the impact of using single-item response scales? Working in small groups, develop at least three response items for each of the three scales. Share these with other class members for their reactions.

Chapter 10

Issues between Organizations and Individuals

Companies are developing badges with electronic sensors that let a boss know where a worker is at any given minute of the workday.

—Samuel Greengard[1]

In fact, there may be negative consequences of whistle-blowing to managers, their organizations, and, in some instances, to society.

—Janet P. Near and Marcia P. Miceli[2]

CHAPTER OBJECTIVES

TO UNDERSTAND

- A Model of Legitimacy of Organizational Influence
- How Rights to Privacy Are Interpreted
- Bases for Discrimination at Work
- Using Discipline to Change Behaviors
- Quality of Work Life (QWL)
- Job Enrichment: Pros and Cons
- Mutual Individual-Organization Responsibilities
- Whistle-Blowing as a Prosocial Behavior

One of the most infamous cases of conformity to organizational authority occurred just hours before the U.S. space shuttle *Challenger* tragically exploded early in its flight. Morton Thiokol engineers had advised company executives not to recommend proceeding with the NASA flight in view of the cold weather. Overruled, the engineers remained silent. Liftoff occurred as scheduled, and the entire crew perished moments later in an explosion caused by parts not designed to operate effectively in lower temperatures. Why didn't the engineers speak out (publicly) in time? Why don't other employees "blow the whistle" when they spot employer practices that are potentially harmful?

The answer to these questions is complex. Certainly, it is true that people and organizations can live in a substantial degree of mutual interest and harmony. Individuals use organizations as instruments to achieve their goals just as much as organizations use people to reach objectives. There is a *mutual social transaction* in which each contributes to, and benefits from, the other. But *what is the nature of each group's rights and responsibilities toward the other,* such that disasters like the *Challenger* incident don't happen again?

This chapter is the second in a section that focuses on *micro*organizational behavior issues and processes. Whereas Chapter 9 identifies how employee attitudes can affect several dependent variables of concern to organizations (e.g., absenteeism and turnover). Chapters 10 and 11 examine important behavioral factors at the individual and interpersonal levels that can make the system more effective. In Chapter 10 we discuss some of the ways in which organizational policies and practices influence individuals, placing both demands and constraints on them and providing opportunities to them. Rights of privacy, policies regarding substance abuse, discriminatory practices, and discipline are discussed. Then we introduce job enrichment as a major organizational strategy for improving quality of work life for employees. Finally, we discuss some responsibilities of individuals to their organizations. In Chapter 11 we examine how people seek personal power over others, interact with them, and engage in and resolve conflict.

AREAS OF LEGITIMATE ORGANIZATIONAL INFLUENCE

Every organization develops certain policies and requirements for performance. If the organization and an individual define the boundaries of legitimate influence differently, then organizational conflict is likely to develop. It can be sufficient to interfere with effectiveness. For example, if employees believe that it is legitimate for management to control the personal telephone calls they make at work, they may dislike management's interference with their freedom on this matter, but they are unlikely to develop serious conflict with management about it. However, if employees believe that personal calls are their own private right, then this issue may become a focus of conflict with management.

This same type of reasoning applies to other issues. As long as there is agreement among the parties on the legitimacy of influence, each party should be satisfied with the power balance in the relationship. Research shows that there is reasonable agreement within the general population concerning legitimate areas of organizational influence on employees.[3] Studies covering labor leaders, business managers, Air Force officers, university students, and men compared with women showed that there is *substantial agreement among all groups.*

Agreement avoids conflict.

Following are sample areas of general approval of organizational influence:

- *Job conduct*—such as the tidiness of one's office and one's working hours (high legitimacy of influence)
- *Personal activities off the job*—such as the church one attends, where charge accounts are maintained, and where one goes on vacation (low legitimacy of influence)

Areas of agreement and disagreement

On the other hand, there is some disagreement between managers and others in a few areas, primarily those concerned with off-the-job conduct that could affect company reputation. Examples are degree of participation in various community affairs, personal use of company products, and even some areas of off-job unsafe habits or substance abuse. Obviously, if you work at a plant that assembles automobiles and you drive a competitor's automobile to work, your employer will be concerned about your lack of support of company products and the effect of your actions on product image.

A Model of Legitimacy of Organizational Influence

The model's variables

The model of **legitimacy of organizational influence** that has been developed from research is shown in Figure 10–1. The two key variables in the model are conduct on the job or off of it and conduct that is job-related or not job-related. As shown in the model, there is agreement on high legitimacy when conduct is on the job and job-related. Legitimacy tends to become less accepted as an act's connection with the job becomes more hazy. If the act is on the job but not job-related, such as playing cards during lunch hours, questions arise about legitimacy. Generally, only moderate legitimacy is supported, depending on the situation.

Management might accept a situation in which employees were playing cards but not gambling in a dining area in the manufacturing department during lunch. On the other hand, assume the card players are bank tellers playing poker with money at their desks in the public areas of a bank during lunch. Surely in this case both managers and others will agree that management has high legitimacy to forbid this conduct because of its possible effects on customers, even though the game is not being played on company time.

FIGURE 10–1

Model of legitimacy of organizational influence on employees

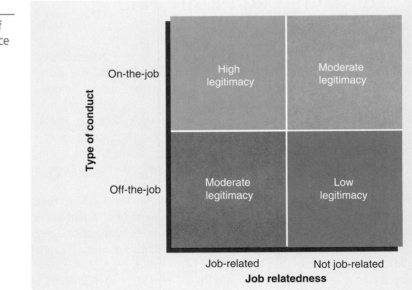

A challenging issue of balancing the individual's rights and the organization's temptation to interfere occurs in the area of romantic relationships between coworkers. Romance between coworkers in the work environment is not a new phenomenon. It does, however, expose one of the parties, and the employer, to the danger of sexual harassment if the relationship should sour. As a result, over three-quarters of CEOs surveyed frown upon such relationships and are inclined to forbid or at least discourage them. The vast majority of firms do permit office romances, however, and nine out of ten firms have not implemented formal policies regulating dating among coworkers.

Dennis Powers encourages firms to apply these strategies:

1. Maintain a neutral perspective toward interemployee dating.

2. Make timely and discreet responses to any problems that may arise.

3. Communicate the firm's policies, if any, on office romance, and intervene (mediate) where broken romance interferes with work performance.

4. Treat all parties with respect and fairness.

5. Recognize that about half of such romances will become long-term relationships, and support the parties with family-friendly work-life programs (e.g., day care).

Source: Dennis M. Powers, *The Office Romance: Playing with Fire without Getting Burned*, New York: AMACom, 1998.

Off-the-Job Conduct

The power of business to regulate employee conduct off the job is very limited. Certainly, when the conduct is not job-related, there is little reason for the employer to become involved. On the other hand, some activities off the job may affect the employer, so questions of organizational influence arise. The basic relationship is as follows: *The more job-related one's conduct is when off the job, the more support there is for organizational influence on the employee.*

Job-related conduct

Interpretations become difficult in some borderline situations. For example, what kinds of controls should be applied to off-job conduct of an employee living on company property at an oil pumping site and on twenty-four-hour call? Even when an employee has departed company property and is not on call, the boundaries of employer interest are still not fixed. Consider the angry employee who waited until the supervisor stepped outside the company gate and then struck the supervisor several times in the presence of other employees. In cases of this type, arbitrators consistently uphold company disciplinary action because the action is job-related. In the United States at least, the organization's jurisdictional line is clearly functional, related to the total job system and not the property line.

A number of issues potentially involving job-related behaviors currently receive extensive attention. These issues include surveillance, substance abuse, genetic screening of prospective employees for health risks, office romances (see "What Managers Are Reading"), and assessments of the ethical values of job applicants. Controversy arises out of concern for the accuracy of the measures used, as well as from conflicting views over the legitimacy of assessing such factors. These disagreements have served to focus attention on employee rights of privacy, which are discussed next.

RIGHTS OF PRIVACY

Rights of privacy primarily are related to organizational invasion of a person's private life and unauthorized release of confidential information about a person in a way that would cause emotional harm or suffering. Business activities that may involve

FIGURE 10–2

Business activities that may involve employee rights of privacy

- Lie detectors
- Personality tests
- Encounter groups
- Medical examinations
- Treatment of alcoholism
- Monitoring of employee lifestyles

- Treatment of drug abuse
- Surveillance devices
- Computer data banks
- Confidential records
- Genetic screening
- Inquiry into personal relationships

rights of privacy are listed in Figure 10–2, and several of these are discussed in the following paragraphs. As businesses intrude more deeply into domains of employee privacy, the potential for conflicts rises (see, for example, the first opening quote for this chapter).

Employees, customers, and others believe that their religious, political, and social beliefs are personal and should not be subject to snooping or analysis, although there are exceptions—such as when someone is employed by a church or a political party. The same view applies to personal acts, conversations, and locations, such as company rest rooms and private homes. Exceptions are permitted grudgingly only when job involvement is clearly proved, and still the burden of proof is on the employer. For example, it may be appropriate to know that a bank teller is deeply in debt as a result of betting on horse races or that an applicant for a national credit card twice has been convicted for stealing and using credit cards.

Conditions defining invasion of privacy

One research study surveyed over 2,000 employees to determine when they perceived that their privacy had been invaded.[4] Four conditions led to perception of invasion: personality (versus performance) information was used, no permission was obtained before disclosure, there were unfavorable consequences, and the disclosure was external (rather than inside the company). Clearly, these situations should be minimized to avoid employee reactions.

Policy Guidelines Relating to Privacy

Because of the importance of employee privacy, most large employers have developed policy guidelines to protect it. These guidelines also help establish uniform practices and make it easier to handle any unusual situations that may develop. Following are some of the policy guidelines on privacy that organizations are using:[5]

- *Relevance*—Only necessary, useful information should be recorded and retained.
- *Recency*—Obsolete information should be removed periodically.
- *Notice*—There should be no personal data system that is unknown to an employee.
- *Fiduciary duty*—The keeper of the information is responsible for its security.
- *Confidentiality*—Information should be released only to those who have a need to know, and release outside the organization normally should occur only with the employee's permission.
- *Due process*—The employee should be able to examine records and challenge them if they appear incorrect.
- *Protection of the psyche*—The employee's inner self should not be invaded or exposed except with prior consent and for compelling reasons.

Surveillance Devices

Protection of the psyche implies that, except for compelling reasons, there should be no surveillance of private places such as locker rooms or secret surveillance unknown to the employee, as with secret listening devices. Surveillance that is known to employees and has a compelling job reason usually is not considered to be an undue infringement on privacy. Banks and convenience stores, for example, have hidden cameras that take photographs during robberies. These photographs include employees, but this hardly infringes on their privacy provided that use of the photographs is confined to the original purpose.

Some surveillance is acceptable.

> An example of regular surveillance is provided by a fast-food chain that installed video cameras in a number of its stores. The camera photographed the cash register whenever it was open. Employees knew that it was there to control theft, although it also could photograph robberies. The camera worked effectively, providing an unexpected increase of about 10 percent in receipts.

Two other forms of **surveillance devices** have emerged through advances in computer technology. *Electronic sensor badges* are microcomputers in clip-on ID cards, which emit infrared signals. Employees wearing these badges can have their location monitored by sensors scattered throughout a building. Data are sent to a computer, which collects the information and distributes it to others in the organization. **Electronic monitoring** takes many forms, including automatic counting of keystrokes made by data entry clerks, remote observations of the screens of desktop computer operators, surreptitious reading of an employee's electronic mail, and voice-recording systems to assess the effectiveness of stockbrokers, travel agents, or other customer service personnel.

The availability of the Internet at work has resulted in a phenomenon known as *cybersurfing*. This is an activity done by employees who use work time and work computers to surf the Web, looking for a wide range of information of personal interest. Cybersurfers may use their terminal to check the stock market, get an update on a golf tournament, place a bid on a newly released video, or read a serialized version of the latest best-selling book. As a result of this unproductive time, employers have often turned to electronic monitoring to identify the most serious abusers of their Internet privileges.

Cybersurfing at work

The impact on employees of secret organizational monitoring can be detrimental, however. One study of telephone operators showed that those monitored reported higher levels of physiological and emotional distress, such as headaches, back pain, severe fatigue, shoulder soreness, sore wrists, and extreme anxiety.[6] The keys to employee acceptance of electronic surveillance lie in advance notification and explanation, use of information as an aid to performance improvement, and involvement of employees in setting up a fair system.

Honesty Testing

Employee theft is a major problem in U.S. businesses. It is estimated to cost employers over $40 billion per year, with up to three-fourths of employees participating at least once. Using a research methodology involving anonymous confessions, 62 percent of restaurant employees admitted to stealing, and 43 percent of grocery store employees acknowledged they had stolen cash or property.[7]

The Polygraph   Science has determined that conscience usually causes physiological changes when a person tells a significant lie. The **polygraph** (lie detector) is an instrument that was developed to record those changes and provide evidence of lying. It achieved significant popularity in business as a tool in honesty testing of employees.

However, the Employee Polygraph Protection Act was passed by Congress in 1988; this law largely prohibits or controls the use of polygraphs as a preemployment screening tool by many employers.[8]

The law was passed in response to two issues regarding the polygraph—its validity and its invasion of privacy. Because the validity of the polygraph is questionable, it runs the risk of falsely identifying innocent individuals (and failing to spot guilty ones). In regard to the second issue, some people believe that the use of the polygraph tends to invade their privacy. However, since the examinee has a choice of refusing the test, this argument is weakened somewhat. Employees have also resisted being routinely tested to prove themselves innocent, and this practice is now illegal for most organizations.

Psychological Stress Evaluator   A different kind of lie detector, the **psychological stress evaluator,** analyzes changes in voice patterns to determine whether a lie is being told. It requires no hookup to a machine, so it is not as visibly and physically invasive as the lie detector. As with the polygraph, the test taker's own conscience provides the evidence by showing vocal stress when a significant lie is told. Until this process has been fully validated, it is too risky to use by itself for honesty testing.

Paper-and-Pencil Tests   These **honesty tests,** also known as *integrity tests,* attempt to get the respondent to disclose information about their own previous or prospective honesty. They appear in two forms. *Overt tests* inquire about attitudes toward theft (e.g., "How common is it for employees to steal items at work?"), whereas *personality-based tests* more indirectly identify dishonest individuals by relating scores on selected personality-test items to a theft criterion. The validity of these tests is also controversial, and employers run some risks of legal action if they reject an applicant solely on the basis of integrity test scores. However, scores on one test (the honesty subscale of the Personnel Selection Inventory) have been found to predict accurately subsequent employee theft.[9]

Treatment of Alcoholism

Since alcoholism presents major medical and job problems, employers need to develop responsible policies and programs to deal with it without endangering rights of privacy. It is estimated that between 5 and 10 percent of employees are alcoholics and that they cost employers more than $10 billion annually in absenteeism, poor work, lost productivity, and related costs. Absence rates for alcoholic employees are two to four times those of other employees.

Alcoholics are found in all types of industries, occupations, and job levels. Sometimes the job environment may contribute to an employee's alcoholism, but the employee's personal habits and problems are also major contributors. In some instances employees are well on the road to alcoholism before they are hired.

Reasons for Company Programs   Regardless of the causes of alcoholism, an increasing number of firms are recognizing that they have a role to play in helping alcoholics control or break their habit. One reason is that the firm and employee already have a working relationship on which they can build. A second is that any success with the employee will save both a valuable person for the company and a valuable citizen for society. A third reason is that the job appears to be the best environment for supporting recovery because a job helps an alcoholic retain a self-image as a useful person in society.

Successful Programs   Successful employer programs treat alcoholism as an illness, focus on the job behavior caused by alcoholism, and provide both medical help and psychological support for alcoholics. As shown in Figure 10–3, the company demonstrates to alcoholics that it wants to help them and is willing to work with them over an extended period of time. A nonthreatening atmosphere is provided; however, there is always the implied threat that alcohol-induced behavior cannot be tolerated indefinitely. For example, if an employee refuses treatment and unsatisfactory behavior continues, the employer has little choice other than dismissal. Following is the way that one company operates:

> A supervisor named Mary Cortez notices that an employee named Bill Revson has a record of tardiness and absenteeism, poor work, an exhausted appearance, and related symptoms that may indicate alcoholism or another serious problem. She discusses only Revson's job behavior with him, giving him a chance to correct himself. When Revson's behavior continues unchanged, Cortez asks Revson to meet with her in the presence of a counselor. The supervisor presents her evidence of poor job behavior and then leaves the room so that the employee and counselor can discuss the situation privately. If the counselor concludes that a problem exists, treatment may be recommended for Bill. If the treatment is accepted and proves successful, the problem is solved.

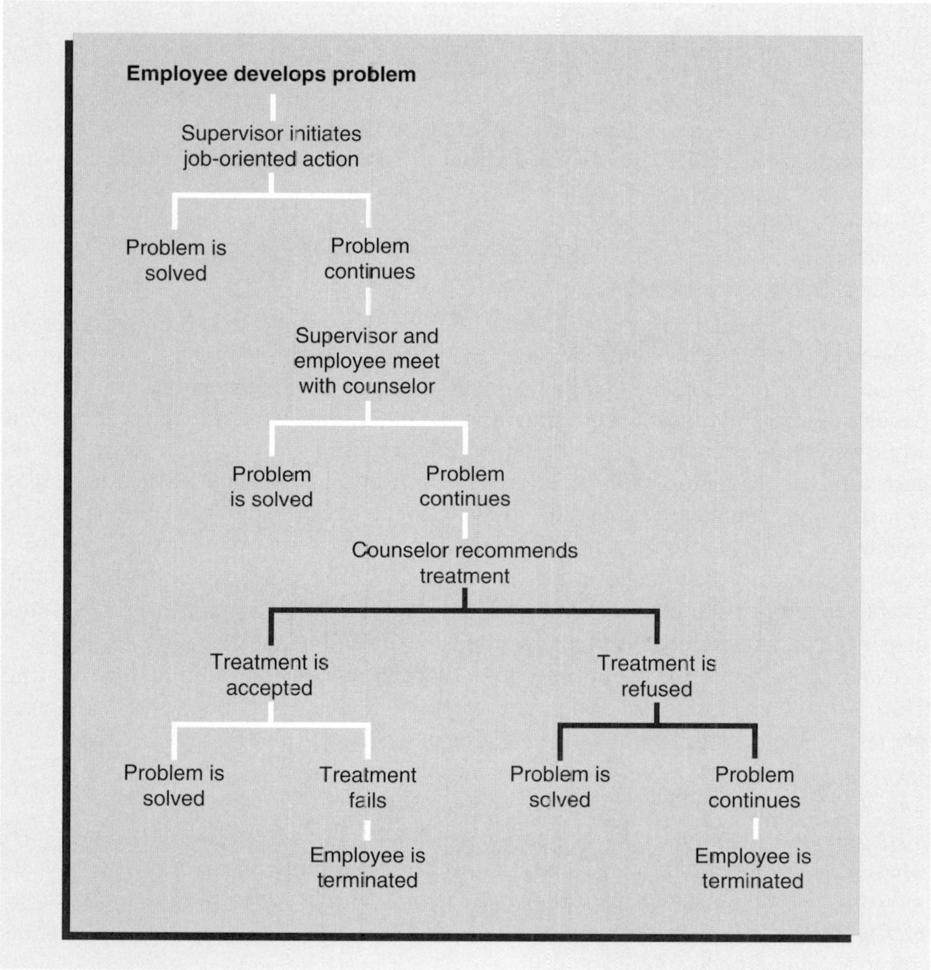

How should companies treat alcoholics?

239

FIGURE 10–3

Program for treatment of employees who are abusers of alcohol and other drugs

Drug Abuse

Abuse of drugs other than alcohol, particularly if used at work, may cause severe problems for the individual, the employer, and other employees. These drugs may include heroin, cocaine, crack, and marijuana, or the abuse may stem from the improper use of stimulants, barbiturates, and tranquilizers. In some job situations, such as those of a pilot, surgeon, railroad engineer, or crane operator, the direct effects of drug abuse can be disastrous.

Drug Testing   To employers, the direct consequences of employee drug abuse are enormous. Employee theft to support drug habits costs industry billions each year. Absentee rates for workers with drug problems may be as much as sixteen times higher than for nonusers, with accident rates four times as high. The lost productivity and additional health costs have been estimated to total as high as $70 billion annually. In addition, drug abuse takes a tragic toll on society.

To help combat this problem, the Drug-Free Workplace Act became law in the United States in 1988.[10] The law requires some employers (those with federal contracts over $25,000 and others obtaining financial assistance grants) to create and distribute to their employees policies prohibiting drug abuse at work. Other employers are encouraged to do the same. Many companies have adopted a policy of drug testing of both new and current employees. Some test job applicants as well. The tests may be done on a periodic schedule, administered randomly, or given only when there is reason to suspect an employee.

> Atlas Powder Company, a manufacturer of explosives, developed a drug policy for its Joplin, Missouri, plant.[11] All 425 employees receive annual physical examinations, which include mandatory drug testing for a wide range of controlled substances. During the first two years, seven people tested positive and received suspensions. In addition, 20 percent of Atlas's job applicants who were initially referred for hiring had positive drug screens for marijuana and were rejected.

Testing policies like those at Atlas can be highly controversial. One reason is that some tests are not satisfactorily accurate. Tests may fail to identify 5 percent of the users, while other employees may be incorrectly identified as users because the food they ate or the prescription drugs they took produced a falsely positive reaction. Usually, further investigation and repeated testing will support their innocence, but the harm to their reputation and self-esteem may already have occurred. Another objection to drug testing is the fear that it will reveal other medical conditions that an employee may prefer to keep private. In addition, some employees find it intrusive to be watched while providing samples for testing. A final privacy issue revolves around the presumed right to consume any substance one desires; however, the Constitution does not guarantee the right to possess and use illegal drugs.

A possible solution to the problems with drug testing lies in **impairment testing.** This method usually consists of a brief motor-skills test performed on a computer; the test is much like playing a video game.

> At the R. F. White Company, eye-hand coordination is assessed by comparing test results with a baseline measure for each employee.[12] Over a one-year period, this wholesale petroleum distribution company experienced reductions of accidents by 67 percent, errors and incidents by 92 percent, and worker's compensation claims costs by 64 percent. In addition to these benefits, the firm believed the process was cheaper, more timely, and more accurate than drug testing. It also shifts the focus from moralistic judgments of *why* an employee can't perform, to the capacity to perform itself.

Hiring Practices: Are They Driven by Ethics or Convenience?

The robust U.S. economy that marked the beginning of the twenty-first century brought about a low unemployment rate and very strong competition for skilled workers. As a result, some employers began making greater accommodations to their hiring practices so as to attract applicants. In particular, some firms threw out their drug-testing policies, while others no longer inquired about felony conviction records, as long as they believed that there was no threat to personal safety of their workforce. These firms found it timely to reverse their earlier policies in the face of a difficult labor market. Will they change their practices again when the economy softens?

Genetic Testing

The controversy over employee privacy rights has also emerged in the area of **genetic testing.** New developments in the field of genetics allow physicians to use medical tests to accurately predict whether an employee may be genetically susceptible to one or more types of illness or harmful substances. This is a more aggressive tool than **genetic monitoring,** which identifies harmful substances in the workplace, examines their effects on the genetic makeup of employees, and provides the basis for corrective action. Positive uses of genetic testing information include transferring the susceptible employees to other work areas where they will not be exposed to the substances, providing health warnings, and developing protective measures to shield the employees from danger. The negative side of genetic testing comes into play when a firm screens present employees or job applicants on the basis of genetic predispositions and uses the information to discriminate against them in an attempt to minimize the firm's future health costs. Similarly, a great challenge to individual privacy and opportunity occurs when a firm identifies those employees who smoke, drink socially, overeat, or engage in risky recreational activities and then attempts to affect their lifestyles.

Testing differs from monitoring.

Discrimination

As noted in Chapter 4, EEO laws generally prohibit job discrimination on the basis of race, color, national origin, sex, religion, handicapped status, and other factors. Two key EEO issues stand out as contemporary problems related to privacy. The first concerns sexual harassment on the job, in which the right to a nonoffensive work environment is violated. The second issue relates to a particular type of disease some employees may have and their right to maintain medical privacy, continue working, and receive medical care. Both of these topics will be discussed briefly.

Sexual Harassment   When supervisors make employment or promotion decisions contingent on sexual favors or when an employee's colleagues engage in any verbal or physical conduct that creates an offensive working environment, **sexual harassment** exists (see Figure 10–4). Although harassment is a *perceived* action by others, it is very real to the recipient. Since it is somewhat individually defined, there is some disagreement over what constitutes sexual harassment. Females responding to one survey generally included in their definition sexual propositions, unwanted physical

FIGURE 10–4

EEOC definition of sexual harassment

Source: Equal Employment Opportunity Commission's Guidelines on Discrimination Because of Sex, 1604.11 *(Sexual Harassment),* Nov. 10, 1980.

Unwelcome sexual advances, requests for sexual favors, and other verbal or physical conduct of a sexual nature constitute sexual harassment when:

1. Submission to such conduct is made either explicitly or implicitly a term or condition of an individual's employment.
2. Submission to or rejection of such conduct by an individual is used as the basis for employment decisions affecting such individual.
3. Such conduct has the purpose or effect of unreasonably interfering with an individual's work performance or creating an intimidating, hostile, or offensive working environment.

touching, sexual remarks and jokes, and suggestive gestures. Estimates of the extent of harassment indicate the problem is pervasive, with as many as 40 to 50 percent of females having experienced some form of it.[13] Such harassment can occur anywhere in a company, from executive offices to assembly lines. From a human point of view, it is distasteful and demeaning to its victims, and it is discriminatory according to EEO laws and federal and state guidelines. Sexual harassment is a violation of a person's personal rights and an offense to human dignity.

Preventive practices

In order to protect potential victims and prevent harassment, many employers have developed policies to prevent it. They also have conducted training programs to educate employees about the relevant law, identified actions that could constitute harassment, and communicated both the possible liabilities involved and the negative effects of harassment on its victims. In the absence of preventive programs, employers may be responsible for the harassment actions of their supervisors and employees. When it occurs, employers may be liable for reinstatement of the victims if they were unfairly discharged, and may have to pay back wages, punitive damages, and awards for psychological suffering and pain. Most victims of sexual harassment are women, but there have been instances in which men were victims.

AIDS   **Acquired immune deficiency syndrome (AIDS)** is a deadly viral disease of the human immune system. It is contagious through certain types of contact, incurable at this time, always fatal, and spreading rapidly in some areas of the world. Widespread public concern and lack of understanding, coupled with unclear legal status of employees with AIDS, have raised several key behavioral issues, such as the following:

AIDS-related issues at work

- Can the medical privacy of AIDS employees be protected?
- What can be done to help coworkers understand more about AIDS and about the way it affects its victims? In particular, how can the firm encourage employees to calmly accept a coworker with AIDS into the work group?
- How might the presence of AIDS employees affect teamwork and other participation in a group?
- How can managers prevent AIDS employees from becoming harassed or socially isolated through the possible loss of normal communications with their coworkers?
- Should employees be tested for the presence of the AIDS-related virus? If they test positive, should they be transferred to other jobs? (Note that the presence of the AIDS-related virus does *not* imply that a person now has the AIDS disease itself.)

Although these are difficult issues, employers need to consider them and develop their policies before the first case arises in their organization. In particular, they need to be aware of the relevant laws that appear to include persons with AIDS under the definition and protection of "handicapped" or "disabled." These include the Vocational Rehabilitation Act of 1973 and the Americans with Disabilities Act of 1990.[14]

DISCIPLINE

The area of discipline can have a strong impact on the individual in the organization. **Discipline** is management action to enforce organizational standards. There are two types, preventive and corrective.

Two types of discipline

Preventive discipline is action taken to encourage employees to follow standards and rules so that infractions do not occur. Prevention is best done by making company standards known and understood in advance. The basic objective, however, is to encourage employee self-discipline. In this way the employees maintain their own discipline rather than have management impose it. Employees are more likely to support standards that they have helped create. They also will give more support to standards that are stated positively instead of negatively, and when they have been told the reasons behind a standard so that it will make sense to them.

Corrective discipline is action that follows infraction of a rule; it seeks to discourage further infractions so that future acts will be in compliance with standards. Typically, the corrective action is a penalty of some type and is called a *disciplinary action.* Examples are a warning or suspension with or without pay.

The objectives of disciplinary action are positive, educational, and corrective, as follows:

Objectives of disciplinary action

- To reform the offender
- To deter others from similar actions
- To maintain consistent, effective group standards

Most employers apply a policy of **progressive discipline,** which means that there are stronger penalties for repeated offenses. The purpose is to give an employee an opportunity for self-correction before more serious penalties are applied. Progressive discipline also gives management time to work with an employee on a counseling basis to help correct infractions, such as unauthorized absences. A typical system of progressive discipline is shown in Figure 10–5.

Increasingly stronger penalties

FIGURE 10–5

A progressive discipline system

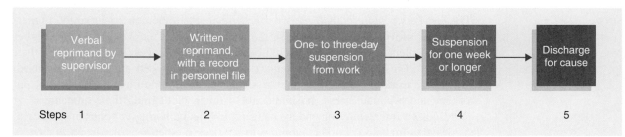

| Verbal reprimand by supervisor | Written reprimand, with a record in personnel file | One- to three-day suspension from work | Suspension for one week or longer | Discharge for cause |

Steps   1   2   3   4   5

QUALITY OF WORK LIFE

QWL programs

What is **quality of work life (QWL)**? The term refers to the favorableness or unfavorableness of a total job environment for people. QWL programs are another way in which *organizations recognize their responsibility to develop jobs and working conditions that are excellent for people as well as for the economic health of the organization.* The elements in a typical QWL program include many items discussed earlier in this book under the general area of supportive organizational behavior— open communications, equitable reward systems, a concern for employee job security and satisfying careers, a caring supervisor, and participation in decision making. Many early QWL efforts focused on job enrichment, which is a major topic in this section. In addition to improving the work system, QWL programs usually emphasize development of employee skills, the reduction of occupational stress, and the development of more cooperative labor-management relations.

A Rationale

Job specialization and simplification were popular in the early twentieth century. Employees were assigned narrow jobs and supported by a rigid hierarchy in the expectation that efficiency would improve. The idea was to lower costs by using unskilled workers who could be trained easily to do a small, repetitive part of each job.

Many difficulties developed from that classical job design, however. There was excessive division of labor. Workers became socially isolated from their coworkers because their highly specialized jobs weakened their community of interest in the whole product. De-skilled workers lost pride in their work and became bored with their jobs. Higher-order (social and growth) needs were left unsatisfied. The result was higher turnover and absenteeism, declines in quality, and alienated workers. Conflict often arose as workers sought to improve their conditions and organizations failed to respond appropriately. The real cause was that in many instances the job itself simply was not satisfying.

Forces for change

A factor contributing to the problem was that the workers themselves were changing. They became more educated, more affluent (partly because of the effectiveness of classical job design), and more independent. They began reaching for higher-order needs, something more than merely earning their bread. Employers now had two reasons for redesigning jobs and organizations for a better QWL:

- Classical design originally gave inadequate attention to human needs.
- The needs and aspirations of workers themselves were changing.

Humanized work through QWL

One option that emerged was to redesign jobs to have the attributes desired by people, and redesign organizations to have the environment desired by people. This approach seeks to improve QWL. There is a need to give workers more of a challenge, more of a whole task, more opportunity to use their ideas. *Close attention to QWL provides a more humanized work environment.* It attempts to serve the higher-order needs of workers as well as their more basic needs. It seeks to employ the higher skills of workers and to provide an environment that encourages them to improve their skills. The idea is that human resources should be developed and not simply used. Further, the work should not have excessively negative conditions. It should not put workers under undue stress. It should not damage or degrade their humanness. It should not be threatening or unduly dangerous. Finally, it should contribute to, or at least leave unimpaired, workers' abilities to perform in other life roles, such as citizen, spouse, and parent. That is, *work should contribute to general social advancement.*

Job Enlargement versus Job Enrichment

The modern interest in quality of work life was stimulated through efforts to change the scope of people's jobs in attempting to motivate them. **Job scope** has two dimensions—breadth and depth. **Job breadth** is the number of different tasks an individual is directly responsible for. It ranges from very narrow (one task performed repetitively) to wide (several tasks). Employees with narrow job breadth were sometimes given a wider variety of duties in order to reduce their monotony; this process is called **job enlargement.** In order to perform these additional duties, employees spend less time on each duty. Another approach to changing job breadth is called **job rotation,** which involves periodic assignment of an employee to completely different sets of job activities. Job rotation is an effective way to develop multiple skills in employees, which benefits the organization while creating greater job interest and career options for the employee.[15]

Enlargement provides breadth.

Job enrichment takes a different approach by adding additional motivators to a job to make it more rewarding. It was developed by Frederick Herzberg on the basis of his studies indicating that the most effective way to motivate workers was by focusing on higher-order needs. Job enrichment seeks to add **depth** to a job by giving workers more control, responsibility, and discretion over how their job is performed. The difference between enlargement and enrichment is illustrated in Figure 10–6. Here we see that job enrichment focuses on satisfying higher-order needs, whereas job enlargement concentrates on adding additional tasks to the worker's job for greater variety. The two approaches can even be blended, by both expanding the number of tasks and adding more motivators, for a two-pronged attempt to improve QWL.

Enrichment provides depth.

Job enrichment brings many benefits, as shown in Figure 10–7. Its general result is a role enrichment that encourages growth and self-actualization. The job is built in such a way that intrinsic motivation is encouraged. Because motivation is increased, performance should improve, thus providing both a more humanized and

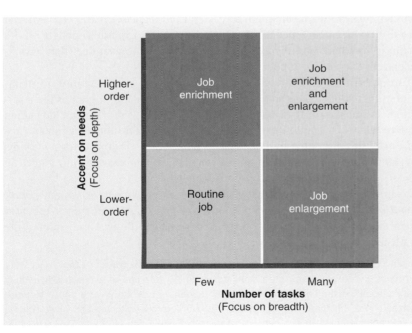

FIGURE 10–6

Difference between job enrichment and job enlargement

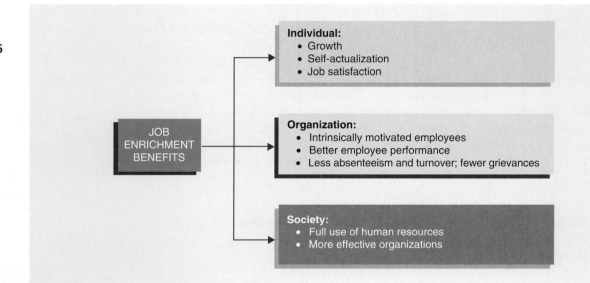

FIGURE 10–7

Benefits of job
enrichment emerge in
three areas.

a more productive job. Negative effects also tend to be reduced, such as turnover, absences, grievances, and idle time. In this manner both the worker and society benefit. The worker performs better, experiences greater job satisfaction, and becomes more self-actualized, thus being able to participate in all life roles more effectively. Society benefits from the more effectively functioning person as well as from better job performance.

Applying Job Enrichment

Viewed in terms of Herzberg's motivational factors, job enrichment occurs when the work itself is more challenging, when achievement is encouraged, when there is opportunity for growth, and when responsibility, feedback, and recognition are provided. However, *employees are the final judges of what enriches their jobs.* All that management can do is gather information about what tends to enrich jobs, try those changes in the job system, and then determine whether employees feel that enrichment has occurred.

In trying to build motivational factors, management also gives attention to maintenance factors. It attempts to keep maintenance factors constant or higher as the motivational factors are increased. If maintenance factors are allowed to decline during an enrichment program, then employees may be less responsive to the enrichment program because they are distracted by inadequate maintenance. The need for a systems approach to job enrichment is satisfied by the practice of gain sharing (introduced in Chapter 6).

*Gain sharing satisfies
maintenance needs.*

Since job enrichment must occur from each employee's personal viewpoint, *not all employees will choose enriched jobs if they have an option.* A contingency relationship exists in terms of different job needs, and some employees may prefer the simplicity and security of more routine jobs.

In one instance a manufacturer set up production in two different ways.[16] Employees were allowed to choose between work on a standard assembly line and at a bench where they individually assembled the entire product. In the beginning few employees chose to work at the enriched jobs, but gradually about half the workers chose them. The more routine assembly operation seemed to fit the needs of the other half.

Core Dimensions: A Job Characteristics Approach

How can jobs be enriched? And how does job enrichment produce its desired outcomes? J. Richard Hackman and Greg Oldham developed a job characteristics approach to job enrichment that identifies five **core dimensions**—skill variety, task identity, task significance, autonomy, and feedback.[17] Ideally, a job must have all five dimensions to be fully enriched. If one dimension is perceived to be missing, workers are psychologically deprived and motivation may be reduced.

Five dimensions

The core dimensions affect an employee's psychological state, which tends to improve performance, satisfaction, and quality of work, and to reduce turnover and absenteeism. Their effect on quantity of work is less dependable. Many managerial and white-collar jobs, as well as blue-collar jobs, often are deficient in some core dimensions. Although there are large individual differences in how employees react to core dimensions, the typical employee finds them to be basic for internal motivation. The dimensions and their effects are shown in Figure 10–8 and discussed briefly here.

Skill Variety   One core dimension is variety of skills used in the job. **Skill variety** allows employees to perform different operations that often require different skills. It differs from the job breadth element presented earlier, since an enlarged job may still use the same skills on different tasks or products. The need for some variety is illustrated by the following anecdote:

> A tourist in Mexico stopped at a woodcarver's shop to inquire about the price of a chair that was hand-carved. The woodcarver replied, "50 pesos." The tourist said that she liked the chair and wanted three more exactly like it. Hoping to receive a quantity discount, she asked, "How much for four chairs?" The woodcarver replied, "250 pesos for four chairs." Shocked that the price per unit for four chairs was more than for one chair, the tourist asked why. The woodcarver replied, "But, señorita, it is very boring to carve four chairs that are exactly alike."

FIGURE 10–8

How core job characteristics affect work outcomes through three psychological states

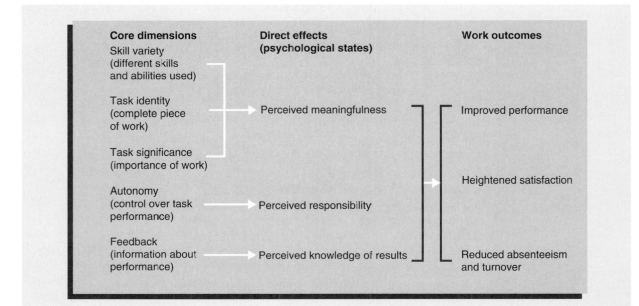

Jobs that are high in variety are seen by employees as more challenging because of the range of skills involved. These jobs also relieve monotony that develops from any repetitive activity. If the work is physical, different muscles are used, so that one muscle area is not so overworked and tired at the end of the day. Variety gives employees a greater sense of competence, because they can perform different kinds of work in different ways.

Task Identity   A second core job dimension is **task identity,** which allows employees to perform a complete piece of the work. In the past, individual employees worked on such a small part of the whole that they were unable to identify any product with their efforts. They could not feel any sense of completion or responsibility for the whole product. When tasks are broadened to produce a whole product or an identifiable part of it, then task identity has been established.

Task Significance   A third core dimension is **task significance.** It refers to the amount of impact, as perceived by the worker, that the work has on other people. The impact can be on others in the organization, as when the worker performs a key step in the work process, or it may be on those outside the firm, as when the worker helps make a lifesaving medical instrument. The key point is that workers should believe they are doing something important in their organization or society, or both.

> Even routine factory work can have task significance. St. Regis Paper Company had customer complaints about seams tearing and bottoms dropping out of about 6 percent of grocery bags made in three plants.[18] Management attempted to solve the problem by adding more inspectors and making production changes, but these efforts were not successful.
>
> Finally, management decided to work with the bag-machine operators to show them the significance of their work. One step was to circulate customer complaint letters so that the operators could see how serious the problem was. Management also arranged to have the signature of each operator imprinted on the bottom of the bags as follows: "Another quality product by St. Regis. Personally inspected by [employee's name]."
>
> Employees responded by reducing defective bags from 6 to ½ percent. They were proud of their work and its direct significance to customers. Employees even started taking their nameplates with them during rest breaks because they wanted to be responsible personally for bags that had their signature.

Autonomy   A fourth core dimension is **autonomy.** It is the job characteristic that gives employees some discretion and control over job-related decisions, and it appears to be fundamental in building a sense of responsibility in workers. Although they are *Empowerment practices*   willing to work within the broad constraints of an organization, workers also insist on a degree of freedom. Autonomy has become important to many people. The practice of management by objectives (MBO) is one way of establishing more autonomy because it provides a greater role for workers in setting their own goals and pursuing plans to achieve them.

Feedback   A fifth core dimension is **feedback.** Feedback refers to information that tells workers how well they are performing. It can come directly from the job itself (task feedback), or it can be given verbally by management and other employees. It can be positive or negative but is best when it is appropriately balanced. It should also be early and continuous rather than delayed and sporadic. The idea of feedback is a simple one, but it is of much significance to people at work. Since they are investing a substantial part of their lives in their work, they want to know how well they are doing. Further, they need to know rather often because they recognize that performance does vary, and the only way they can make adjustments is to know how they are performing now.

The Motivating Potential of Jobs

An instrument used to determine the relative presence of the five core dimensions in jobs is the **Job Diagnostic Survey.**[19] Before job enrichment is begun, an employer studies jobs to assess how high they are on skill variety, task identity, task significance, autonomy, and feedback. Scales are created for each dimension, and then each job is rated according to where it fits on each scale. For example, on a scale of 1 through 10, variety may be given a rating of 6 and autonomy a lower rating of 4. Employees need to be involved in this assessment process, since it is their perceptions that are most important.

Job Diagnostic Survey

After the data are collected, an overall index that measures the **motivating potential score (MPS)** of a job may be computed. The MPS indicates the degree to which the job is perceived to be meaningful (M, or average of skill variety, task identity, and task significance), foster responsibility (R, or autonomy), and provide knowledge of results (KR, or feedback). The formula is

Motivating potential score

$$MPS = M \times R \times KR$$

Jobs that have been enriched to create a high MPS increase the probability of high motivation, provided that employees

- Have adequate job knowledge and skills
- Desire to learn, grow, and develop
- Are satisfied with their work environment (are not distracted by negative hygiene factors)

Conditions for job enrichment

Most job enrichment attempts have been conducted in manufacturing operations, but many have also been attempted in banks, insurance companies, and other service organizations.

> Salespersons in a large department store were the subjects for a field experiment in job redesign for enrichment purposes.[20] After providing their perceptions of their current jobs as measured by a set of scales that produce a motivating potential score, they implemented a series of job changes designed to increase the skill variety, task identity, task significance, autonomy, and feedback gained from their jobs.
>
> The salespersons' MPS scores increased significantly (from 25.6 to 41.5) following the experiment, indicating that they believed their jobs had become enriched. Dysfunctional behaviors such as misuse of idle time and absence from the workstation decreased, whereas functional behaviors (selling and stocking) increased moderately. Several measures of employee satisfaction also improved.

Social Cues Affect Perceptions

Not all attempts to enrich jobs have been as successful as the experiment that was just described. In some cases employees do not report significant changes in their perceptions of the core characteristics after job enrichment despite objective evidence that the job actually was changed. This has produced considerable frustration for both job design specialists and managers.

One explanation for the lack of predicted changes from enrichment lies in the presence of social cues, which are often rather subtle bits of information workers receive

250

from their social surroundings. These social cues may come from coworkers, leaders, other organizational members, customers, and family members. Social cues may serve either to support or to counteract the direction of objective task characteristics, as shown in Figure 10–9.

The key to job enrichment lies in how employees use the social cues provided by their peers and others to arrive at their own perception of their jobs.[21] This activity, called **social information processing,** covers three elements. First, peers may suggest *which* of the job characteristics really count to them (as when a worker named Kaitlin asserts that "around here, the only thing I care about is how much control I'm allowed!"). Second, they may offer their personal model regarding the relative *weighting* of each core dimension (as when Lynn suggests to Dan that "I value skill variety and feedback the most, with the other three factors worth only a small amount"). Third, peers may provide direct or indirect clues about their own *judgments* of the dimensions (as when Alan confides that "despite what management claims, I still don't think my job is very important").

An integrated approach to job design suggests that managers must focus on managing the social context of job changes, as well as the objective job enrichment process itself. They must discover which groups are important sources of social cues, perhaps using group discussions to reinforce an employee's initial tendencies to assess job changes positively. Managers can also create expectations (in the minds of employees and coworkers) that the enriched jobs will have more of certain dimensions and therefore be more satisfying.

Contingency Factors Affecting Enrichment

Job enrichment does not apply to all types of situations. It appears to apply more easily to higher-level jobs, which are less likely to be dictated by the technological process. If the technology is stable and highly automated, the costs of job enrichment may be too great in relation to the rewards. Some workers do not want increased responsibility, and other workers do not adapt to the group interaction that is sometimes required.

FIGURE 10–9

Social cues affect
employee reactions to
tasks.

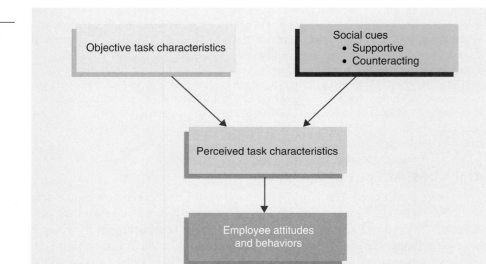

Job enrichment also may upset pay relationships. In particular, employees may expect more than intrinsic satisfaction for the additional duties and responsibilities they assume. There are many other costs and limitations in addition to pay, some of which are summarized in Figure 10–10. Equipment and floor space may have to be redesigned, with more space and tools needed so that teams can work independently. Inventories may need to be increased, training costs may go up, and turnover may initially increase. Unions may resist enrichment attempts if existing job classifications are upset.

Those planning job enrichment programs need to ask such questions as the following about employee needs and attitudes:

- Can the employee tolerate (and welcome) responsibility?
- How strong are the employee's growth and achievement needs?
- What is the employee's attitude and experience regarding group work?
- Can the employee intellectually and emotionally handle more complexity?
- How strong are the employee's drives for security and stability?
- Will the employees view the job changes as significant enough to justify the costs?
- Can a job be overenriched?

Key questions

There are many contingency elements to consider when exploring the possibility of job enrichment as a QWL approach. Both employee attitudes and the capabilities of employees to handle enriched tasks are crucial. Although it is tempting to consider job enrichment as good, it is more consistent with human values to recognize and respect individual differences that exist among employees.

- Some workers may not want enriched jobs.
  —If they are unable to tolerate increased responsibility
  —If they dislike more complex duties
  —If they are uncomfortable with group work
  —If they dislike relearning
  —If they prefer security and stability
  —If they are comfortable with supervisory authority
  —If their skills are not adaptable
  —If they prefer to quit their jobs

- Expensive equipment may not be adaptable.

- The program may unbalance the production system.

- Supervisory or staff roles may be reduced.

- Enriched jobs may increase pay dissatisfaction.

- Costs may increase.
  —Start-up costs (for example, for training)
  —Long-term costs (for example, for more equipment)

- Unions may oppose some enrichment efforts.

FIGURE 10–10

Some limitations of job enrichment and QWL programs

THE INDIVIDUAL'S RESPONSIBILITIES TO THE ORGANIZATION

A discussion of the individual in the organization is incomplete if it covers only the organization's impositions on, and obligations to, the individual. The employment relationship is two-way. Without question, *the organization has responsibilities to the individual,* but also—and again without question—*the individual has responsibilities to the organization.* Employment is a mutual transaction. Each employee makes certain membership investments in the organization and expects profitable rewards in return. The organization also invests in the individual, and it, too, expects profitable rewards.

A relationship is profitable for either party when benefits (outputs) are larger than costs (inputs) measured in a total value system. In the usual employment situation both parties benefit, just as they do in the usual social relationship. Both parties benefit because the social transaction between them produces new values that exceed the investment each makes.

The profitable relationship deteriorates if either party fails to act responsibly toward the needs of the other. The employees can fail to act responsibly, just as the organization can. If they do, they can expect the organization to respond by using tight controls to try to maintain a successful operating system.

Theft as an example

Consider the matter of theft, which was mentioned in connection with the polygraph. Overlook for the moment the legal-ethical-moral views of theft. From the point of view of the organizational system only, theft interferes with work operations. It upsets schedules and budgets. It causes reorders. It calls for more controls. In sum, it reduces both the reliability and the productivity of the organizational system. There is less output for the individual as well as for the organization. In this situation the organization must act to protect other employees as well as itself.

There are many ways, beyond acting productively and creatively, in which employees can demonstrate their larger responsibilities toward the organization. These include organizational citizenship and whistle-blowing.

Organizational Citizenship

Applying the social exchange idea makes it evident that employees are expected to go beyond their job descriptions and be good **organizational citizens.** This reciprocal relationship at the individual level parallels the way the organization is expected to behave in the broader society in which it operates. As we note in Chapter 9, employees who are organizational citizens engage in positive social acts designed to help others, such as volunteering their efforts on special projects, sharing their time and resources, and proactively cooperating with others. They also are expected to use their talents and energies fully to help the organization achieve its goals of efficiency and effectiveness.

Blowing the Whistle on Unethical Behavior

Despite the best ethical codes and individual voices, unethical organizational behavior may still arise. Being a good organizational citizen does not extend to blind conformity—supporting illegal activities of the organization, bending to organizational pressures (as in the *Challenger* example), or engaging in any other activities which seriously violate social standards. For example, when management disregards internal opposition to wrongful acts or fails to disclose information about defective products, an employee may choose a response from a wide array of alternatives (see Figure 10–11).[22] Several of these responses demonstrate a form of **whistle-blowing,** which is disclosing alleged misconduct to an internal or external source.

Some employees are more likely than others to be whistle-blowers in organizations.[23] They are workers who have strong evidence of having observed wrongdoing, who believe it to be a serious problem, and who feel that it directly affects them. In general, such conscientious people are likely to be professionals with long service, people previously recognized as good performers, and those who work in organizations perceived by others to be responsive to complaints. Their motivations may vary widely. Some employees blow the whistle because they feel obligated to protect the public; others do so in retaliation for the treatment they have received from their employer.

Who are the likely whistle-blowers?

> One employee of a military contractor made the headlines when he blew the whistle on his employer.[24] Christopher Urda claimed that his employer had systematically overbilled the Pentagon on its contracts. A federal judge fined the contractor over $55 million and awarded Mr. Urda $7.5 million under the provisions of the 1986 False Claims Act.

By going public, whistle-blowers hope to bring pressure on the organization to correct the problem. Although the legal system generally protects them, some employees have been the subject of employer retaliation, such as harassment, transfer, or **discharge.** The need for whistle-blowing can be diminished by creating a variety of ways for employees to voice their concerns inside the organization—and encouraging this behavior. Previously discussed devices for this purpose include suggestion systems, survey feedback, and employee-management meetings.

Mutual Trust

When whistle-blowing occurs, it usually signifies that a previous level of mutual trust has deteriorated or even been broken. **Mutual trust** is joint faith in the responsibility and actions of the parties involved; when it is present, each person has a strongly positive expectation that the other person will do the right thing. Development of mutual trust occurs over a period of time through the emergence of mutual understanding, the development of emotional bonds, and the demonstration of trustworthy behaviors. It can, however, be broken in an instant through inappropriate word or action by either party. Further, loss of trust results in a breakdown of the psychological contract (see Chapter 4). When managers lose the trust of their employees, it requires concerted and extended efforts to repair and re-earn it. Corporate leaders, and

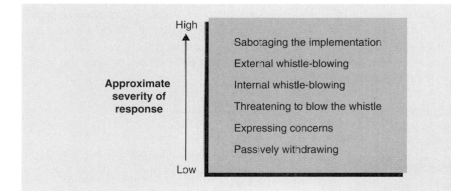

Approximate severity of response

High
- Sabotaging the implementation
- External whistle-blowing
- Internal whistle-blowing
- Threatening to blow the whistle
- Expressing concerns
- Passively withdrawing

Low

FIGURE 10–11

Alternative employee responses to wrongful acts

1. Before taking any significant actions that might influence employee behaviors, carefully weigh the degree to which those actions have a high degree of legitimacy.
2. Familiarize yourself with the organization's policies on employee rights to privacy and the reasons for those policies.
3. When unacceptable employee behaviors are likely to occur, focus first on preventive discipline and then, only if necessary, invoke corrective discipline.
4. Assess, through the eyes of employees, the level of quality of work life that they perceive to exist. Make appropriate changes and follow up to determine the impact.
5. Involve employees in efforts to redesign their jobs to incorporate higher degrees of skill variety, task identity, task significance, autonomy, or feedback, where appropriate.
6. Engage employees in regular discussions about their side of the psychological contract—their responsibility to act ethically, sustain trust, demonstrate good citizenship at work, and their obligation to blow the whistle if all else fails.

all managers, have a very visible role to play in shaping a strong organizational culture that clarifies the organization's values and expectations. When this is done, the level of trust is likely to be high.

SUMMARY

Some areas of potential individual-organization conflict are legitimacy of organizational influence, rights of privacy, and discipline. The main concern is to ensure that the employee's activities and choices are guided—but not unduly controlled to the detriment of the employee—by the organization. In order to protect both the organization and the worker, companies usually develop policies to guide their decisions about privacy, alcohol- and drug-abuse programs, genetic testing, sexual harassment, and other activities. To accomplish their goals, management uses both preventive and corrective discipline to ensure appropriate behavior.

One social obligation that many organizations have adopted is to improve the quality of work life (QWL) for its employees. QWL refers to the favorableness or unfavorableness of the job environment for people. This is never an easy nor a final task, since QWL exists in the perceptions of employees and is constantly changing.

Jobs vary in their breadth and depth. Job enrichment applies to any efforts to humanize jobs by the addition of more motivators. Core dimensions of jobs that especially provide enrichment are skill variety, task identity, task significance, autonomy, and feedback. In spite of job enrichment's objective desirability, its cues must be perceived by employees and valued by them to have substantial impact.

The social transaction of employment is a two-way street, with mutual responsibilities for the individual and the organization. The employee should be a good organizational citizen, exercise ethical leadership, or resort to whistle-blowing if necessary. Benefits will accrue to individuals, the organization, and society when this social exchange is fulfilled and mutual trust is evident.

Terms and Concepts for Review	Acquired immune deficiency syndrome (AIDS)	Discharge
	Autonomy	Discipline
	Core dimensions	Electronic monitoring
	Corrective discipline	Feedback
		Genetic monitoring

Genetic testing

Honesty tests

Impairment testing

Job breadth

Job depth

Job Diagnostic Survey

Job enlargement

Job enrichment

Job rotation

Job scope

Legitimacy of organizational
influence

Motivating potential score (MPS)

Mutual trust

Organizational citizens

Polygraph

Preventive discipline

Progressive discipline

Psychological stress evaluator

Quality of work life (QWL)

Rights of privacy

Sexual harassment

Skill variety

Social information processing

Surveillance devices

Task identity

Task significance

Whistle-blowing

1. Explain the basic model of legitimacy of organizational influence. Does it seem to be a reasonable one within which you could work? Provide personal examples for each of the four cells.
2. Think of a job you have had or now have. Did you feel that the employer invaded your right to privacy in any way? Discuss. Did the employer have a policy, explicit or implicit, with regard to right of privacy?
3. Assume that you are going to interview for a job as a teller with a bank and heard in advance that one of the forms of honesty tests discussed in the chapter would be used to explore your history and probability of honesty. Describe how you would feel about each type of test, and explain why you would feel that way.
4. Form small groups and visit a company to discuss its program for the treatment of alcoholism and hard-drug abuse. What other behaviors is the company concerned about from a health standpoint? Report the highlights of the program to your class, and give your appraisal of its probable effectiveness.
5. Assume that one of your employees has recently tested positive for the AIDS virus. Although he is still fully capable of performing his job duties, another employee has come to you and objected to working closely with him. How would you respond?
6. Form discussion groups of four to five people, and develop a list of the top six QWL items that your group wants in a job. Present your group report, along with your reasons, to other class members. Then discuss similarities and differences among group responses.
7. Think of the job you now have or a job that you formerly had. Discuss both the favorable and unfavorable QWL characteristics contained in it.
8. Debate this issue in class: "Job breadth is more important than job depth in motivating workers."
9. Think of a job you have had or now have. Were there any ways in which you did not act responsibly toward the organization or took unfair advantage of it? Discuss.
10. Consider your own role as a possible whistle-blower. Under what conditions would you publicly criticize your employer or another employee?

Discussion Questions

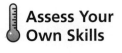

Assess Your Own Skills

How well do you exhibit good organizational-influence skills?

Read the following statements carefully. Circle the number on the response scale that most closely reflects the degree to which each statement accurately describes you as a leader. Add up your total points and prepare a brief action plan for self-improvement. Be ready to report your score for tabulation across the entire group.

	Good description									**Poor description**
1. I carefully differentiate between employee activities that occur on the job and those that occur off the job.	10	9	8	7	6	5	4	3	2	1
2. I am careful to respect an employee's rights to privacy when addressing topics surrounding religious, political, and social beliefs.	10	9	8	7	6	5	4	3	2	1
3. I carefully monitor my employees' use of their computers to ensure that they are not abusing their privileges.	10	9	8	7	6	5	4	3	2	1
4. I am observant for signs of alcohol or drug abuse among employees.	10	9	8	7	6	5	4	3	2	1
5. I take immediate and positive actions to ensure that employees do not engage in sexual harassment.	10	9	8	7	6	5	4	3	2	1
6. I place the bulk of my disciplinary emphasis on prevention of problems rather than corrective treatment of them.	10	9	8	7	6	5	4	3	2	1
7. I accept with enthusiasm my role in creating a quality of work life that is excellent for both employees and the organization.	10	9	8	7	6	5	4	3	2	1
8. I am fully aware of which employees would value enriched jobs and which would not.	10	9	8	7	6	5	4	3	2	1
9. I have clear ideas for how I could increase the levels of the five core dimensions in my employees' jobs.	10	9	8	7	6	5	4	3	2	1
10. I regularly spend time emphasizing to my employees their obligations to their employer (to balance the employer's responsibilities to them).	10	9	8	7	6	5	4	3	2	1

Scoring and Interpretation   Add up your total points for the ten questions. Record that number here, and report it when it is requested. _____

- If you scored between 81–100 points, you appear to have a solid capability for demonstrating appropriate organizational influence.
- If you scored between 61–80 points, you should take a close look at the items with lower self-assessment scores and explore ways to improve those items.

- If you scored less than 60 points, you should be aware that a weaker level regarding several items could be detrimental to your future success as a leader. We encourage you to review relevant sections of the chapter and watch for related material in subsequent chapters and other sources.

Now identify your three lowest scores, and write the question numbers here: _____, _____, _____. Write a brief paragraph, detailing to yourself an action plan for how you might sharpen each of these traits.

Two Accounting Clerks

Rosemary Janis and Mary Lopez were the only two clerks handling payments from customers in the office of Atlantic Plumbing Supply Company. They reported to the owner of the business. Janis had been employed for eighteen months and Lopez for fourteen months. Both were community college graduates, about twenty-three years old, and unmarried.

By manipulating the accounts in a rather ingenious way that would not normally be detected, Janis was stealing from account payments as they were received. During her third month of employment, Lopez learned of Janis's thefts, but she decided not to tell management, rationalizing that Janis's personal conduct was none of her business. Lopez did not benefit from Janis's thefts, and the two women were not close friends. Their duties allowed them to work rather independently of each other, each handling a different alphabetical portion of the accounts.

By the time the owner learned of Janis's thefts through the recent installation of hidden surveillance cameras, she had stolen approximately $5,700. During investigation of the thefts the owner learned that Lopez had known about them for several months, because it was evident that the thefts could not have occurred for an extended period without Lopez's knowledge. At the time of employment, both women had been instructed by the owner that they would be handling money and that strict honesty would be required of them.

Questions
1. What issues are raised by these events? Discuss.
2. What disciplinary action, either preventive or corrective, do you recommend for each of the two women? Why?
3. Is Lopez's failure to blow the whistle an issue?

The Enriched Student

1. Consider your academic "job" as a student. Rate it on each of the five core dimensions according to how much of each is presently in it (1 = low amount; 10 = high amount). Compute a motivating potential score for yourself by using the MPS formula given in the text. What does this information tell you?

Job Dimension	Your Rating	Group Average
Skill variety	_____	_____
Task identity	_____	_____
Task significance	_____	_____

Autonomy	_____	_____
Feedback	_____	_____
MPS score	_____	_____

2. Form groups of four to six persons, share your scores, and compute an average group score for each dimension. Then compute a motivating potential score for your group by using the MPS formula given in the text. What do the scores tell you?

3. Discuss five important steps that university administrators and professors could take to enrich your "job" if they had the data you generated.

Chapter 11

Interpersonal Behavior

The better [that employees] can understand their bosses' management styles, the better they'll be at interacting with them and getting things done.

—Jennifer Laabs[1]

All bad bosses fall into three groups: the boss with no brains; the boss with no courage; and the boss with no heart.

—Len Schlesinger[2]

CHAPTER OBJECTIVES

TO UNDERSTAND

- The Nature and Types of Conflict
- Conflict Outcomes and Resolution Strategies
- Different Personality Types
- Assertive Behavior
- Interpersonal Orientations and Stroking
- Types of Power
- Organizational Politics and Influence

Joyce and Joan were involved in a discussion which, had they allowed it to progress, might have driven them apart. "I think that we can best survive by growing larger," said Joyce, "and the best way to do this is by acquiring our two closest competitors." Joan responded by suggesting that "your approach will potentially bankrupt us; we could drown in a sea of debt payments."

"So what do *you* propose doing?" queried Joyce with a hint of sarcasm.

"I suggest that we focus on strengthening our current market position," responded Joan. "We should spend more on new product development, aggressively market our existing line, and trim our staff by 6 percent."

Before the debate could proceed further, Joan and Joyce agreed to examine the issue objectively and not let their emotions escalate. They decided to focus on jointly solving the problem, while understanding and respecting each other's point of view. In doing this, they successfully avoided some of the destructive pitfalls of typical conflicts.

Organizations, by definition, require people to work together and communicate with one another—often in pairs as in the interaction between Joyce and Joan. Ideally, these interpersonal relationships should be productive, cooperative, and satisfying. In reality, managers find that they are not always that way.

Almost every working relationship will produce some degree of conflict across time. Whether the conflicts will be destructive or constructive depends on the attitudes and skills of the participants (as well as time pressures and resource shortages). This chapter explores some approaches to conflict and examines the possible outcomes. It also suggests that employees may need to develop their assertiveness skills in order to be heard and respected by their peers. Guidelines are offered for understanding oneself and others and for communicating more effectively.

Interpersonal behavior in complex organizations inevitably produces power differences. Five sources of power are reviewed as a basis for seeing which are most constructive. We conclude the chapter with a discussion of organizational politics—the use of various strategies to gain greater interpersonal influence over decisions and people.

CONFLICT IN ORGANIZATIONS

The Nature of Conflict

Conflict is any situation in which two or more parties feel themselves in opposition. Conflict is an interpersonal process that arises from disagreements over the goals to attain or the methods to be used to accomplish those goals. In the potential argument reported above, Joyce and Joan differ over both the goal and the method of achieving it. Consequently, the conflict may be even more difficult to resolve, but they must find a way.

What is conflict?

In addition to conflicts over goals or methods, conflicts also arise due to task interdependence, ambiguity of roles, policies, and rules, personality differences, ineffective communications, the competition over scarce resources, and underlying differences in attitudes, beliefs, and experiences. In organizations everywhere, conflict among different interests is inevitable, and sometimes the amount of conflict is substantial. One survey reported that managers spend an estimated 20 percent of their time dealing with conflict.[3] They may be either direct participants or mediators trying to resolve conflict between two or more of their employees. In either case, knowledge and understanding of conflict and the methods for resolving it are important.

Several research studies over time have consistently indicated the important role of interpersonal behavior in the success or failure of managers.[4] One of the prime reasons for derailment of previously successful executives is insensitivity to others. Some female managers, lauded as exceptionally intelligent and sporting strong track records, later failed because of inability to adapt to a boss. And a composite portrait of failed European managers indicated that they were insensitive, manipulative, abusive, demeaning, overly critical, and incapable of building trusting relationships. Under these conditions, conflict—with peers and employees—inevitably emerges.

Levels of Conflict

Conflict can occur within an employee, between individuals or groups, and across organizations as they compete. Chapter 4 examines role conflict (different role expectations) and role ambiguity (lack of clarity over how to act).

Intrapersonal Conflict   Although most role conflict occurs when an employee's supervisor or peers send conflicting expectations to him or her, it is possible for intrapersonal role conflict to emerge from within an individual, as a result of competing roles taken. For example, Sabrina may see herself as both the manager of a team responsible for protecting and enlarging its resources and as a member of the executive staff charged with the task of reducing operating costs.

Interpersonal Conflict   Interpersonal conflicts are a serious problem to many people because they deeply affect a person's emotions. There is a need to protect one's self-image and self-esteem from damage by others. When self-concept is threatened, serious upset occurs and relationships deteriorate. Sometimes the temperaments of two persons are incompatible and their personalities clash. In other instances, conflicts develop from failures of communication or differences in perception.

> An office employee was upset by a conflict with another employee in a different department. It seemed to the first employee that there was no way to resolve the conflict. However, when a counselor explained the different organizational roles of the two employees as seen from the whole organization's point of view, the first employee's perceptions changed and the conflict vanished.

Intergroup Conflict   Intergroup conflicts, for example, between different departments, also cause problems. On a major scale such conflicts are something like the wars between juvenile gangs. Each group sets out to undermine the other, gain power, and improve its image. Conflicts arise from such causes as different viewpoints, group loyalties, and competition for resources. Resources are limited in any organization—and are increasingly tight as organizations struggle to be competitive. Since most groups feel that they need more than they can secure, the seeds of intergroup conflict exist wherever there are limited resources. For example, the production department may want new and more efficient machinery while, at the same time, the sales department wants to expand its sales force, but there are only enough resources to supply the needs of one group.

We noted earlier that *some conflict can be constructive,* and this is certainly true at the intergroup level. Here, conflict may provide a clue that a critical problem between two departments needs to be resolved rather than allowed to smolder. Unless issues are brought into the open, they cannot be fully understood or explored. Once intergroup conflict emerges, it creates a motivating force encouraging the two groups to resolve the conflict so as to move the relationship to a new equilibrium. Viewed this way, intergroup conflict is sometimes *escalated*—intentionally stimulated in organizations because of its constructive consequences. On other occasions it may be desirable to *de-escalate* it—intentionally decrease it because of its potentially destructive consequences. The managerial challenge is to *keep conflict at a moderate level* (where it is most likely to stimulate creative thought but not interfere with performance). Conflict should not become so intense that individual parties either hide it or escalate it to destructive levels.

Sources of Conflict

Interpersonal conflict arises from a variety of sources (see Figure 11–1):

- *Organizational change*—People hold differing views over the direction to go, the routes to take and their likely success, the resources to be used, and the probable outcomes. With the pace of technological, political, and social change increasing and the marketplace hurtling toward a global economy, organizational changes will be ever-present.

- *Different sets of values*—People also hold different beliefs and adhere to different value systems. Their philosophies may diverge, or their ethical values may lead them in different directions. The resulting disputes can be difficult to resolve, since they are less objective than disagreements over alternative products, inventory levels, or promotional campaigns.

- *Threats to status*—Chapter 4 suggests that status, or the social rank of a person in a group, is very important to many individuals. When one's status is threatened, face-saving becomes a powerful driving force as a person struggles to maintain a desired image. Conflict may arise between the defensive person and whoever created a threat to status. *Face-saving is important.*

- *Contrasting perceptions*—People perceive things differently as a result of their prior experiences and expectations. Since their perceptions are very real to them, and they feel that these perceptions must be equally apparent to others, they sometimes fail to realize that others may hold contrasting perceptions of the same object or event. Conflict may arise unless employees learn to see things as others see them and help others do the same.

- *Lack of trust*—Every continuing relationship requires some degree of **trust**—the capacity to depend on each other's word and actions. Trust opens up boundaries, provides opportunities in which to act, and enriches the entire social fabric of an organization. It takes time to build, but it can be destroyed in an instant. When someone has a real or perceived reason not to trust another, the potential for conflict rises.

- *Personality clashes*—We point out in Chapter 1 that the concept of individual differences is fundamental to organizational behavior. Not everyone thinks, feels, looks, or acts alike. Some people simply rub us the wrong way, and we cannot necessarily explain why. Although personality differences can cause conflict, they are also a rich resource for creative problem solving. Employees need to accept, respect, and learn how to use these differences when they arise.

Personality Differences   Henri is different from Maria, and Mathew is different from Adam. Even identical twins, for all their similarities, are different from each other. A manager's job is to identify the key differences across personalities, be sensitive to their effects, and adapt to them. If successful in this attempt, some conflicts can be prevented or at least softened.

How do personalities differ? Many traits have been identified, but they seem to

FIGURE 11–1

A model of the conflict resolution process

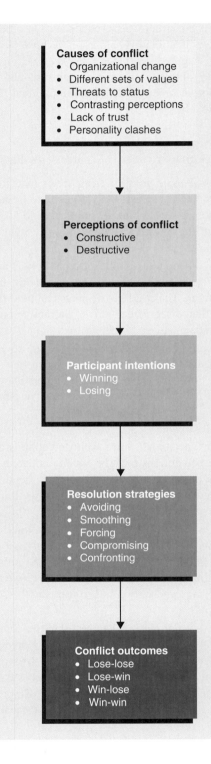

Causes of conflict
- Organizational change
- Different sets of values
- Threats to status
- Contrasting perceptions
- Lack of trust
- Personality clashes

Perceptions of conflict
- Constructive
- Destructive

Participant intentions
- Winning
- Losing

Resolution strategies
- Avoiding
- Smoothing
- Forcing
- Compromising
- Confronting

Conflict outcomes
- Lose-lose
- Lose-win
- Win-lose
- Win-win

cluster around five major factors: agreeableness, conscientiousness, openness to experience, emotional stability, and extroversion (the polar extremes of each are shown in Figure 11–2).[5] Conscientious employees have lower absenteeism rates, are careful regarding the quality of their work, set challenging performance goals for themselves,

FIGURE 11–2

Five major personality traits

265

One Extreme	Trait	Opposite Extreme
Caring, sensitive, empathetic	Agreeableness	Uncooperative, irritable
Dependable, self-disciplined	Conscientiousness	Disorganized, careless
Curious, flexible, receptive	Openness to experience	Closed, fixed, resistant
Calm, relaxed, comfortable	Emotional stability	Anxious, uptight, indecisive
Assertive, outgoing, talkative	Extroversion	Quiet, reserved, cautious

and demonstrate more frequent organizational citizenship behaviors. Emotionally stable individuals seem to handle stress better than others. Employees high on the openness to experience trait are less resistant in the face of rapid organizational change. Extroverted individuals are outgoing and often interact well with customers. Agreeable people tend to be patient, cooperative, and empathetic. Several of the traits (e.g., emotional stability, agreeableness, and conscientiousness) imply a lower likelihood of interpersonal conflict, since these types of individuals are more courteous, self-disciplined, and sensitive to the feelings and positions of others.

Sixteen different types

A highly popular personality test used in a wide array of organizations is the Myers-Briggs Type Indicator (MBTI).[6] The MBTI draws upon the work of Carl Jung, a psychiatrist, and differentiates people into sixteen major categories based on their preferences for *thinking* (using rational logic) versus *feeling* (considering the impact on others), *judging* (rapidly solving ordered problems) versus *perceiving* (preferring spontaneity), *extroversion* (asserting themselves confidently) versus *introversion* (preferring to work alone), and *sensing* (organizing details in a structured fashion) versus *intuition* (relying on subjective evidence and gut feelings). The MBTI has proven most useful in helping employees become more aware of their own idiosyncrasies while also sensitizing them to the unique characteristics of their coworkers. No one type is necessarily better than another nor more successful in the business world.

Effects of Conflict

Conflict is often seen by participants as destructive, but this is a limited view. In fact, if all conflict with coworkers is avoided, each party is likely deprived of useful information about the other's preferences and views. *Conflict is not all bad;* rather, it may result in either productive or nonproductive outcomes. A more positive view, then, is to see that conflict is nearly inevitable and to search for ways in which it can result in constructive outcomes.

Advantages

One of the benefits produced by conflict is that people are stimulated to search for improved approaches that lead to better results. It energizes them to be more creative and to experiment with new ideas. Another benefit is that once-hidden problems are brought to the surface, where they may be confronted and solved. Just as fermentation is necessary in the production of fine wines, a certain amount of ferment can create a deeper understanding among the parties involved in a conflict. And once the conflict is resolved, the individuals may be more committed to the outcome through their involvement in solving it.

Disadvantages

There are also possible disadvantages, especially if the conflict lasts a long period of time, becomes too intense, or is allowed to focus on personal issues. At the interpersonal level, cooperation and teamwork may deteriorate. Distrust may grow among people who need to coordinate their efforts. At the individual level some people may feel defeated, while the self-image of others will decline and personal stress levels (discussed in Chapter 15) will rise. Predictably, the motivation level of some employees will be reduced. It is important, then, for managers to be aware of the potential for interpersonal and intergroup conflicts, to anticipate their likely outcomes, and to use appropriate conflict resolution strategies.

A Model of Conflict

Conflict arises from many sources and directions. It also varies in the speed of its emergence and in the degree of its predictability. Sometimes it smolders for a long time like a hot ember and then springs to life like a flame when the hot coal is fanned. Other times it simply seems to explode without warning, like the sudden eruption of a dangerous volcano. And just like the flame that can warm us in need or sear us with its heat, conflict can be constructive or destructive. Managers, therefore, must know when to stimulate conflict and when to resolve it.

Part of the answer to this dilemma is shown in Figure 11–1, which portrays the conflict resolution process. The various sources discussed earlier give rise to constructive or destructive conflict. If conflict will be harmful, managers need to apply a conflict resolution strategy to prevent, diminish, or remove it. Then the outcomes of conflict (winning or losing) must be evaluated from the perspectives of both parties.

Four outcomes

Conflict Outcomes   Conflict may produce four distinct outcomes, depending on the approaches taken by the people involved. Figure 11–3 illustrates these outcomes. The first quadrant, termed "lose-lose," depicts a situation in which a conflict deteriorates to the point that both parties are worse off than they were before. An extreme example is the case of an executive who fires the only person who knows the secret formula for the organization's most successful product. The second quadrant is "lose-win," a situation in which one person (individual A) is defeated while the other one

FIGURE 11–3

Four possible outcomes of conflict; four possible intentions of the participants

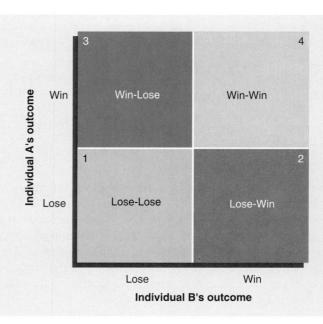

(individual B) is victorious. In quadrant three ("win-lose") the situation is reversed, with B losing to A. The fourth quadrant is the **win-win outcome of conflict,** in which both parties perceive that they are in a better position than they were before the conflict began. This is the preferred outcome to try to achieve in ongoing relationships, such as with suppliers, customers, and employees. Although it may be an unrealistic ideal in some situations, it is a fundamental organizational behavior perspective toward which all parties should aim.

Participant Intentions   Conflict outcomes are a product of the participants' *intentions,* as well as their *strategies.* For example, Jason may actually seek a lose-win outcome in a conflict with Becky because of the perceived benefits of being defeated on a particular issue. He may fear the consequences of retribution from too many earlier victories over Becky, or he may try to lose in the hope that Becky will reciprocate on another issue in the future. At the other extreme, Marcia may hope for a win-lose outcome in her conflict with Jessica. This intended effect is often caused by a "fixed-pie" (or zero-sum) viewpoint, in which Marcia believes that she can succeed only at the expense of Jessica.

Intentions affect strategies.

Resolution Strategies   Intentions help participants select their strategies. Once they have been chosen, the strategies implemented will have a substantial impact on the outcomes reached (*actual* winning or losing). The simplest strategies focus on the contrasting approaches of either cooperation or competition, but a widely used typology suggests that there are at least four clearly different strategies (and a combination one, called compromising). Each of these represents different degrees of concern for one's own outcomes and for another's results, and has a predictable outcome:[7]

Five strategies

- *Avoiding*—physical or mental withdrawal from the conflict. This approach reflects a low concern for either party's outcomes and often results in a lose-lose situation.
- *Smoothing*—accommodating the other party's interests. This approach places greatest emphasis on concern for others, usually to one's own detriment, resulting in a lose-win outcome.
- *Forcing*—using power tactics to achieve a win. This strategy relies on aggressiveness and dominance to achieve personal goals at the expense of the concern for the other party. The likely result is a win-lose situation.
- *Compromising*—searching for middle ground or being willing to give up something in exchange for gaining something else. This strategy reflects a moderate degree of concern for self and others, with no clear-cut outcome.
- *Confronting*—facing the conflict directly and working it through to a mutually satisfactory resolution. Also known as *problem solving* or *integrating,* this tactic seeks to maximize the achievement of both party's goals, resulting in a win-win outcome.

Any one of the strategies may be effective for its intended purpose of winning or losing. However, the avoiding and smoothing approaches are basically useful for *managing* the conflict process. This means that in some way these approaches control the degree of conflict and reduce its harmful side effects while it is under way, but the source of conflict still exists. The same is true when two parties compromise their positions just for the sake of reaching a solution. The idea of compromise is seductive if the objective is to escape from the conflict at minimal cost, but it often stifles creativity. The use of a forcing approach may achieve a short-term goal but often irreparably harms the relationship between the parties.

267

A Diversity of Preferences

Is there a single conflict resolution approach that all parties tend to use? Or might we find distinctive preferences and patterns among different groups, and even among different cultures? Although research evidence is not overwhelming, it suggests that these differences may exist:

- Males tend to use the forcing approach as their dominant style; females use forcing less and often rely on a range of other tactics.
- Managers tend to use the forcing approach; their employees prefer avoiding, smoothing, or compromising.
- American managers tend to be competitive; Japanese managers prefer to use a cooperative approach.

Other significant tendencies emerge, too. Each party in a conflict tends to mimic the style of the other (e.g., forcing induces forcing; accommodating induces accommodating). People tend to choose different resolution styles for different issues (e.g., confrontation is often used in performance appraisals; compromise is more likely used on issues involving personal habits and mannerisms). Once again, it is apparent that a variety of contingency factors (including group-diversity characteristics such as gender) affect the choice of a behavioral strategy.

Sources: James A. Wall, Jr., and Ronda Roberts Callister, "Conflict and Its Management," *Journal of Management,* Vol. 21, no. 3, 1995, pp. 515–58; Richard Hodgetts and Fred Luthans, *International Management,* 3d ed., New York: McGraw-Hill, 1997.

Only the **confronting** strategy can truly be viewed as a *resolution* approach, since this method addresses the basic differences involved and eventually removes them through creative problem solving. The confronting approach (see Figure 11–4 for a set of operating guidelines) has many behavioral benefits. Both parties will more likely see the recent conflict as productive, since both received gains. Also important is their perception that the process was a mutually supportive one in which problem solving and collaboration helped integrate the positions of both parties. As a result, participants find the confronting approach to be the most satisfying, as they maintain their self-respect and gain new respect for the other party. Many labor-management groups have been formed with the objective of seeking new ways to confront each other constructively in order to attain win-win relationships.

A wide variety of other tools and ideas have been successfully used to resolve conflicts. Sometimes the simple application of a relevant rule or policy can solve a dispute. Other times the parties can be separated by reassigning work spaces, removing one person from a committee, or placing workers on different shifts. Another alternative is to insert a third party into the interaction—a consultant, mediator, or other neutral person who can ignore personal issues and facilitate resolution. A constructive approach is to challenge the parties to work together toward a unifying goal, such as higher revenues or better customer satisfaction.

Negotiating Tactics   Much research has addressed the question, What kinds of behaviors help resolve conflicts in a win-win fashion? Time and again, some basic patterns show through: select a neutral site, arrange the seating in a comfortable fashion (preferably oriented toward a projection screen or writing surface), don't permit

1. Agree on the common goal: *to solve the problem.*
2. Commit yourself to fluid, not fixed, positions.
3. Clarify the strengths and weaknesses of both party's positions.
4. Recognize the other person's, and your own, possible need for face-saving.
5. Be candid and up-front; don't hold back key information.
6. Avoid arguing or using "yes-but" responses; maintain control over your emotions.
7. Strive to understand the other person's viewpoint, needs, and bottom line.
8. Ask questions to elicit needed information; probe for deeper meanings and support.
9. Make sure that both parties have a vested interest in making the outcome succeed.
10. Give the other party substantial credit when the conflict is over.

observers to be present (and implicitly place performance pressure on the negotiators), and set deadlines to force a resolution. Individual negotiators are advised to set minimum and optimum goals for themselves in advance, engage in a thorough data gathering process, listen carefully to what the other party says and how it is said, focus on issues and not personalities, and search for the areas where they can obtain concessions on important topics while making matching concessions in areas of lesser interest. If done well, these tactics should help result in an outcome that is fair for both parties, removes the underlying cause of the conflict, and is accomplished with a minimal investment of time and energy.[8]

ASSERTIVE BEHAVIOR

Confronting conflict is not easy for some people. When faced with the need to negotiate with others, some managers may feel inferior, lack necessary skills, or be in awe of the other person's power. Under these conditions they are likely to suppress their feelings (part of the avoidance strategy) or to strike out in unintended anger. Neither response is truly productive.

A constructive alternative is to practice assertive behaviors. **Assertiveness** is the process of expressing feelings, asking for legitimate changes, and giving and receiving honest feedback. An assertive individual is not afraid to request that another person change an offensive behavior and is not uncomfortable refusing unreasonable requests from someone else. Assertiveness training involves teaching people to develop effective ways of dealing with a variety of anxiety-producing situations.   *Assertiveness*

Assertive people are direct, honest, and expressive. They feel confident, gain self-respect, and make others feel valued. By contrast, aggressive people may humiliate others, and unassertive people elicit either pity or scorn from others. Both alternatives to assertiveness typically are less effective for achieving a desired goal.

Being assertive in a situation involves five stages, as shown in Figure 11–5. When confronted with an intolerable situation, assertive people describe it objectively, express their emotional reactions and feelings, and empathize with the other's position. Then they offer problem-solving alternatives and indicate the consequences (positive or negative) that will follow. Not all five steps may be necessary in all situations. As a minimum, it   *Stages in assertiveness*

FIGURE 11–5

Stages in assertive behavior

Stage	Example
1. Describe the behavior.	"When you do this . . ."
2. Express your feelings.	"I feel . . ."
3. Empathize.	"I understand why you . . ."
4. Offer problem-solving alternatives.	"I want you to consider changing to either . . ."
5. Indicate consequences.	"If you do (don't), I will . . ."

is important to describe the present situation and make recommendations for change. Use of the other steps would depend on the significance of the problem and the relationship between the people involved.

> Karla, the supervisor of a small office staff, had a problem. Her secretary, Maureen, had become increasingly careless about her morning arrival time. Not only did Maureen almost never arrive before 8 A.M., but her tardiness varied from a few minutes to nearly a half hour. Although Karla was reluctant to confront Maureen, she knew she must do so or the rest of the staff would be unhappy.
>
> Karla called Maureen into her office soon after Maureen arrived the next morning and drew upon her assertiveness training. "You have been arriving late almost every day for the past two weeks," she began. "This is unacceptable in an office that prides itself on prompt customer service beginning at 8 A.M. I recognize that there may be legitimate reasons for tardiness on occasion, but I want you to get to work on time most days in the future. If you don't, I will insert a letter into your personnel file and also note your behavior on your six-month performance appraisal. Will you agree to change?"

Assertive behavior generally is most effective when it integrates a number of verbal and nonverbal components. Eye contact is a means of expressing sincerity and self-confidence in many cultures, and an erect body posture and direct body positioning may increase the impact of a message. Appropriate gestures may be used, congruent facial expressions are essential, and a strong but modulated voice tone and volume will be convincing. Perhaps most important is the spontaneous and forceful expression of an honest reaction, such as "Tony, I get angry when you always turn in your report a day late!"

Interpersonal Orientations

Each person tends to exhibit one of four **interpersonal orientations**—a dominant way of relating to people.[9] That philosophy tends to remain with the person for a lifetime unless major experiences occur to change it. Although one orientation tends to dominate a person's transactions, other orientations may be exhibited from time to time in specific transactions. That is, one orientation dominates, but it is not the only position ever taken.

Viewing yourself and others

Interpersonal orientations stem from a combination of two viewpoints, as shown in Figure 11–6. First, how do people view themselves? Second, how do they view other people in general? The combination of either a positive response (OK) or a negative response (not OK) to each question results in four possible interpersonal orientations:

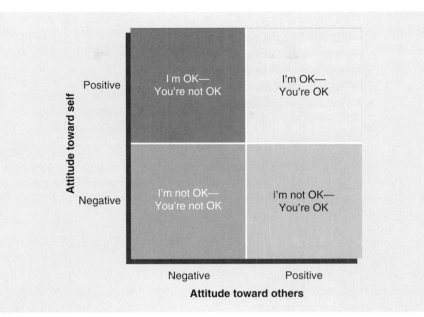

FIGURE 11–6

Four interpersonal orientations

271

- I'm not OK—You're OK.
- I'm not OK—You're not OK.
- I'm OK—You're not OK.
- I'm OK—You're OK.

The desirable perspective and the one that involves the greatest likelihood of healthy interactions is "I'm OK—You're OK." It shows healthy acceptance of self and respect for others. It is most likely to lead to constructive communications, productive conflict, and mutually satisfying confrontations. The other three orientations are less psychologically mature and less effective. The important point is that, regardless of one's present interpersonal orientation, the "I'm OK—You're OK" perspective can be learned. Therein lies society's hope for improved interpersonal transactions.

Stroking

People seek stroking in their interactions with others. **Stroking** is defined as any act of recognition for another. It applies to all types of recognition, such as physical, verbal, and nonverbal contact between people. In most jobs the primary method of stroking is verbal, such as "Pedro, you had an excellent sales record last month." Examples of physical strokes are a pat on the back and a firm handshake.

Strokes may be either positive, negative, or mixed. **Positive strokes** feel good when they are received, and they contribute to the recipient's sense of being OK. **Negative strokes** hurt physically or emotionally and make the recipient feel less OK about herself or himself. An example of a **mixed stroke** is this supervisor's comment: "Oscar, that's a good advertising layout, considering the small amount of experience you have in this field."

There also is a difference between conditional and unconditional strokes. **Conditional strokes** are offered to employees if they perform correctly or avoid problems. A

Types of strokes

Conditional and unconditional strokes

272

sales manager may promise an employee that "I will give you a raise if you sell three more insurance policies." **Unconditional strokes** are presented without any connection to behavior. Although they may make a person feel good (e.g., "You're a fine employee"), they may be confusing to employees because they do not indicate how more strokes may be earned. Supervisors will get better results if they give more strokes in a behavior modification framework, where the reward is contingent upon the desired activity. *Employee hunger for strokes,* and the occasional reluctance of supervisors to use them, is demonstrated in this conversation:

> Melissa, a stockbroker, had just made a presentation to a group of prospective customers. Later, she excitedly asked her manager how she had done. "You did a nice job," he began (and Melissa's eyes lit up in pleasure), "not a great job, but a nice job." Although she didn't show her disappointment, we can guess that her spirits were considerably dampened by his qualified remark.

Applications to Conflict Resolution   There are several natural connections between assertiveness, interpersonal orientation, and the approaches to resolving conflict discussed earlier in this chapter. The "I'm OK—You're OK" person is more likely to seek a win-win outcome, applying assertiveness and a confrontational strategy. Other probable connections are shown in Figure 11–7. Once more, the relationship among a number of behavioral ideas and actions is apparent.

Assertiveness training and stroking in combination can be powerful tools for increasing one's interpersonal effectiveness. They both share the goal of helping employees feel OK about themselves and others. The result is that they help improve communication and interpersonal cooperation. Although they can be practiced by individuals, these tools will be most effective when they are widely used throughout the organization and supported by top management.[10] Together, they form an important foundation for the more complex challenges that confront people who work in small groups and committees.

POWER AND POLITICS

All leaders deal with power and politics. **Power** is the ability to influence other people and events. It is the leader's stock-in-trade, the way that leaders extend their influence to others. It is somewhat different from authority, because authority is delegated by higher management. Power, on the other hand, is earned and gained by leaders on the basis of their personalities, activities, and the situations in which they operate.

FIGURE 11–7

Probable relationships of interpersonal orientations with conflict resolution strategies and behavior

Interpersonal Orientation	Conflict Resolution Strategy	Probable Behavior
I'm not OK—You're not OK	Avoidance	Nonassertiveness
I'm not OK—You're OK	Smoothing	Nonassertiveness
I'm OK—You're not OK	Forcing	Aggressiveness
I'm OK—You're OK	Confronting	Assertiveness

Types of Power

Power develops in a number of ways. There are five **bases of power,** and each has a unique source.[11]

Personal Power   **Personal power,** also called referent power, charismatic power, and power of personality, comes from each leader individually. It is the ability of leaders to develop followers from the strength of their own personalities. They have a personal magnetism, an air of confidence, and a passionate belief in objectives that attract and hold followers. People follow because they want to do so; their emotions tell them to do so. The leader senses the needs of people and promises success in reaching them. Well-known historical examples are Joan of Arc in France, Mahatma Gandhi in India, Winston Churchill in England, and John F. Kennedy and Martin Luther King in the United States.

Legitimate Power   **Legitimate power,** also known as position power and official power, comes from higher authority. It arises from the culture of society by which power is delegated legitimately from higher established authorities to others. It gives leaders the power to control resources and to reward and punish others. People accept this power because they believe it is desirable and necessary to maintain order and discourage anarchy in a society. There is social pressure from peers and friends who accept it and then expect others to accept it.

Expert Power   **Expert power,** also known as the authority of knowledge, comes from specialized learning. It is power that arises from a person's knowledge of and information about a complex situation. It depends on education, training, and experience, so it is an important type of power in our modern technological society. For example, if your spouse were having an asthma attack in a hospital emergency room, you would be likely to give your attention to the physician who comes in to provide treatment rather than to the helper who is delivering fresh laundry supplies. The reason is that you expect the physician to be a capable expert in the situation.

Reward Power   **Reward power** is the capacity to control and administer items that are valued by another. It arises from an individual's ability to give pay raises, recommend someone for promotion or transfer, or even make favorable work assignments. Many rewards may be under a manager's control, and these are not limited to material items. Reward power can also stem from the capacity to provide organizational recognition, to include an employee in a social group, or simply to give positive feedback for a job well done. Reward power serves as the basis for behavior modification programs, as discussed in Chapter 5.

Coercive Power   **Coercive power** is the capacity to punish another, or at least to create a perceived threat to do so. Managers with coercive power can threaten an employee's job security, make punitive changes in someone's work schedule, or, at the extreme, administer physical force. Coercive power uses fear as a motivator, which can be a powerful force in inducing short-term action. However, it is likely to have an overall negative impact on the receiver.

Effects of Power Bases

The five types of power are developed from different sources, but they are interrelated in practice. Reward, coercive, and legitimate power are essentially derived from one's position in the organization. Expert and personal power reside within the person.

When even one power base is removed from a supervisor, employees may perceive that other bases of influence will decline as well. The use of a power base must fit its organizational context in order to be effective.

Managers also need to be concerned about the effects of various power bases on employee motivation. Employees can respond in one of three ways, as shown in Figure 11–8. They may *resist* the leader's initiative, especially if coercive power is used consistently, without apparent cause, or in an arrogant manner.[12] They may *comply* with the leader's wishes by meeting minimal expectations while withholding extra effort. Legitimate power will likely result in compliance, as will reward power unless the rewards are substantial and directly related to employee needs. The most desirable outcome from wielding power is *commitment,* which is the enthusiastic release of energy and talent to satisfy the leader's requests. Referent and expert power are most likely to produce commitment, but legitimate and reward power can also work well under certain conditions.

Organizational Politics

Self-interest is the key.

While the five bases of power are essentially acquired and used to achieve formal organizational goals, many managers and employees resort to another (supplemental) set of behaviors to accomplish personal goals at work. **Organizational politics** refers to intentional behaviors that are designed to enhance or protect a person's influence and self-interest.[13] Used professionally, these behaviors may help attain a well-earned promotion, sell higher management on the merits of a proposal that will expand one's responsibilities and resources, or gain personal visibility. Other employees, however, choose either to avoid politics at all costs or to use politics in a self-serving, manipulative, and deceitful fashion. The risk is that unscrupulous employees involved in organizational politics might put their self-interest above that of their employer in their attempts to gain political power for short-term or long-term benefits.[14]

One survey of more than 400 managers provided insight into their views toward organizational politics.[15] To a large extent, the managers agreed that

- Politics is common in most organizations.
- Managers must be good at politics to succeed.
- Politics becomes more important at higher levels.
- Politics can detract from organizational efficiency.

Influence and Political Power

Managers, and all employees, in contemporary organizations must learn to produce results, elicit cooperation, and make things happen without reliance on traditional forms of power. As difficult as this goal sounds, it is still possible if managers begin with the premise that everyone is motivated primarily by her or his own self-interest. Knowing this, a person can influence others by making mutually beneficial exchanges

FIGURE 11–8

Possible responses to the use of power

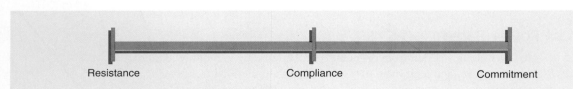

| Resistance | Compliance | Commitment |

with them to gain their cooperation. Here are seven steps to follow for increasing your influence:

1. Treat the other party as a potential ally.
2. Specify your objectives.
3. Learn about the other party's needs, interests, and goals.
4. Inventory your own resources to identify something of value you can offer.
5. Assess your current relationship with the other person.
6. Decide what to ask for and what to offer.
7. Make the actual exchange that produces a gain for both parties.[16]

There are also a number of tactics that leaders can use to gain political power. Several examples are given in Figure 11–9, and "What Managers Are Reading" on the following page provides a detailed set of guidelines. (*Networking*—developing and maintaining contacts among a group of people with shared interests—is another source of influence and is presented in Chapter 3.) Two of the most popular tactics are social exchanges and alliances of various types. *Social exchange* implies that "if you'll do something for me, I'll do something for you." It relies on the powerful **norm of reciprocity** in society, where two people in a continuing relationship feel a strong obligation to repay their social "debts" to each other. When these trade-offs are successfully arranged, both parties get something they want. Continuing exchanges over a period of time usually lead to an *alliance* in which two or more persons join in a longer-term power group to get benefits that they mutually desire.

Norm of reciprocity

Tactic Used	Example
Social exchange	In a trade-off the chief engineer helps the factory manager get a new machine approved if the manager will support an engineering project.
Alliances	The information system manager and the financial vice president work together on a proposal for a new computer system.
Identification with higher authority	The president's personal assistant makes minor decisions for her.
Control of information	The research and development manager controls new product information needed by the marketing manager.
Selective service	The purchasing manager selectively gives faster service to more cooperative associates.
Power and status symbols	The new controller arranges to double the size of the office, decorate lavishly, and employ a personal assistant.
Power plays	Manager A arranges with the vice president to transfer part of manager B's department to A.
Networks	A young manager joins a racquetball club.

FIGURE 11–9

Examples of tactics used to gain political power

Authors Bolman and Deal begin their book with the premise that *some* people, in *some* organizations, suffer from a "debilitating modern affliction"—cluelessness at work. Characteristics of such organizations are their immense size, chaotic and unpredictable internal work environments, powerless employees, dysfunctional policies, mysterious traditions, failed change efforts, pervasive cynicism and frustration, and general confusion. To combat the reality that organizations are political in nature, they offer several prescriptions:

- Identify the key political players and assess their clout on issues.
- Plot ways to gain allies and sway neutral persons to your side.
- Inventory your assets of personal, positional, and resource power.

- Clarify what you really want; settle for what you can likely get.
- Befriend your opponents.
- Invent win-win options that result in mutual gain.

Bolman and Deal predict that, as a consequence of combining a high level of organizational commitment and a high degree of political astuteness through tactics such as these, managers can develop reputations for being both reasonable and credible negotiators.

Source: Lee G. Bolman and Terrence E. Deal, *Escape from Cluelessness: A Guide for the Organizationally Challenged,* New York: AMACOM, 2000.

Another popular path toward political power is to *become identified with a higher authority* or a powerful figure in an organization. Then, as the saying goes, some of the power rubs off on you. Often this identification gains you special privileges, and in many cases you become recognized as a representative or spokesperson for the more powerful figure. Others may share problems with you, hoping that you will help them gain access to the higher figure. An example of identification is the president's personal assistant who represents the president in many contacts with others.

> In one company the president's personal assistant, Howard Janus, became widely accepted as the president's representative throughout the company. He issued instructions to other managers in the name of the president, and other managers accepted them as orders. He represented the president on special assignments. He controlled access to the president, and he partly controlled the flow of information both to and from the president. He handled power effectively and gradually became a major influence in the corporation. When the president retired, the assistant became a major executive and was accepted by other managers.

Another popular way to acquire political power is to *give service selectively* to your supporters. For example, a purchasing manager gives faster service and bends the rules to help friends who support the purchasing function. Another tactic is to *acquire power and status symbols* that imply that you are an important person in the firm, although this tactic can backfire if you do not have power equal to your symbols.

Some managers use the more aggressive tactic of applying power plays to *grab power from others.* This approach is risky because others may retaliate in ways that weaken the power-grabbing manager's power.

A common tactic for increasing power is to *join or form interest groups* that have a common objective. These networks operate on the basis of friendships and personal contacts, and may provide a meeting place for influential people. A young manager who joins the chamber of commerce or a racquetball club is opening the door to new contacts that may be useful.

As illustrated by the following example, power and politics are a basic part of leadership success in an organization:

1. Try to view interpersonal conflict as an opportunity for learning and growth and exploration.

2. Search for the underlying cause(s) of conflict so as to predict and understand it.

3. Be alert to clues regarding different personality traits among people; avoid judging them while using the patterns seen to react more positively to them.

4. Seek to view, and if possible to convert, potential conflict situations into win-win opportunities for both parties.

5. Refine your skills at being a constructively confrontational person; be candid, problem-oriented, questioning, and flexible.

6. Learn to express your feelings and positions in an assertive, honest, expressive fashion so as to get your own needs met.

7. Accept the enormous needs for recognition that most employees have; find legitimate opportunities for stroking them.

8. Assess the nature and strength of your sources of influence and power; learn to draw upon them to increase your chances of success in organizational politics.

9. After developing and demonstrating your technical skills, engage in impression management to polish your images in the eyes of others.

Management in a state office was considering whether to move a certain activity from one department to another. Finally, the director of the entire operation decided to hold a staff meeting of all senior managers to decide where the disputed activity should be located. Prior to the meeting the manager of the department that wanted the activity prepared an elaborate and convincing report that fully supported moving the activity to her department. Meanwhile the manager of the department that might lose the activity was visiting all committee members to mend fences, make trades, and support her department's point of view.

When the committee met two weeks later, most of its members already had decided in favor of the manager who used the political approach. The convincing logic of the written report was ignored, and the committee voted to retain the activity in its present location. Political skills won the dispute.

Managers soon realize that their political power comes from the support of key individuals or the group around them. It arises from a leader's ability to work with people and social systems to gain their allegiance and support. The effort to gain and use personal power for self-interest involves being alert to others' needs to save face, engaging in horse trading, making trade-offs, mending fences, developing ingenious compromises, and engaging in a variety of other activities.

High and low self-monitors

Research suggests that some people are more effective at using organizational politics than others.[17] In particular, *high self-monitors* are more adept at regulating themselves and adapting to situational and interpersonal cues. They are sensitive to shifting role expectations, concerned about their impression on others, and responsive to signals they receive. By meeting the expectations of others, they accomplish tasks and are seen as potential leaders. *Low self-monitors* are more insulated from social cues, behave as they wish, and show less concern for making positive impressions on others. This attitude negatively affects their relationships with others and diminishes their prospects for promotions.

Because many employees are vitally interested in their own career success, modern organizations are fertile places for politics to thrive. Observers say that leaders who are otherwise capable but who lack self-monitoring capacity and basic political skills will have trouble rising to the top in modern organizations. What they need (assuming high performance) is some emphasis on **impression management**—the ability to protect their self-image while intentionally affecting another's assessment of them. Some impression management strategies include sending positive nonverbal cues (e.g., smiles or eye contact), using flattery, and doing favors for others.[18] Clearly, a broad range of interpersonal skills is essential for leaders, both for their personal success and for smoothing the path to employee performance.

SUMMARY

Interpersonal and intergroup conflicts often arise when there is disagreement regarding goals or the methods of attaining them. These conflicts can be either constructive or destructive for the people involved. Several methods exist for resolving conflict (avoiding, smoothing, forcing, compromising, and confronting), and they vary in their potential effectiveness. A key issue revolves around intended outcomes for oneself and others: Does an individual want to win or to lose, and what is desired for the other party? Generally, a confronting approach has significant merit.

Assertive behavior is a useful response in many situations where a person's legitimate needs have been disregarded. Stroking is sought in social transactions, because it contributes to the satisfaction of recognition needs and reinforces an "I'm OK— You're OK" interpersonal orientation.

Power is needed to run an organization. The five bases of power are personal, legitimate, expert, reward, and coercive. Each of these has a different impact on employees, ranging from resistance to compliance to commitment. Organizational politics is the use of various behaviors that enhance or protect a person's influence and self-interest. In general, political behaviors in organizations are common, necessary for success, and increasingly important at higher levels.

Terms and Concepts for Review

Assertiveness	Negative strokes
Bases of power	Norm of reciprocity
Coercive power	Organizational politics
Conditional strokes	Personal power
Conflict	Positive strokes
Confronting	Power
Expert power	Reward power
Impression management	Stroking
Interpersonal orientation	Trust
Legitimate power	Unconditional strokes
Mixed stroke	Win-win outcome of conflict

Discussion Questions

1. Discuss the relationship between Theory X and Theory Y, conflict resolution strategies, and interpersonal orientations.
2. Pair up with another student and explore the concept of trust as a foundation for productive human relationships. Develop several strategies for increasing mutual trust.
3. How assertive are you (rate yourself from 1 = low to 10 = high)? Should you be more or less assertive? Under what conditions?
4. "Resolved: That all employees should be trained to become more assertive." Prepare to present the pros and cons in a class debate.
5. Identify which interpersonal orientation (combinations of "OK-ness" about yourself and others) fit you most closely. Develop an action plan for changing or maintaining your interpersonal orientation, according to your personal wishes.

6. Many people do not receive as many strokes as they feel they deserve on a regular basis. Why do they feel this way? What could their managers do about it? What could they do themselves?

7. Think of an organization you are familiar with. What types of power are used there? How do people react to those bases? What changes would you recommend?

8. Review and explain the idea of a norm of reciprocity as a basis for influencing others. Explain how you have seen it used in interpersonal relationships. How could you make use of it in the future?

9. Review the definition of organizational politics. Can an organization be totally free of political behavior? What would it be like? How could you make it happen?

10. Think about the idea of impression management. In what ways do students use it effectively in the classroom? What additional strategies could they adopt?

How well do you exhibit good interpersonal skills?

Read the following statements carefully. Circle the number on the response scale that most closely reflects the degree to which each statement accurately describes you when you have tried to work constructively with someone else. Add up your total points and prepare a brief action plan for self-improvement. Be ready to report your score for tabulation across the entire group.

Assess Your Own Skills

	Good description								**Poor description**	
1. I recognize the multiple sources of conflict and search for the likely cause before I go any further.	10	9	8	7	6	5	4	3	2	1
2. I am careful not to attack another person's self-esteem, nor do I let my self-esteem be threatened by what others say.	10	9	8	7	6	5	4	3	2	1
3. I know when to escalate a conflict and when it makes sense to de-escalate it.	10	9	8	7	6	5	4	3	2	1
4. I can recognize the strengths and weaknesses of each of the five major personality factors.	10	9	8	7	6	5	4	3	2	1
5. I actively attempt to assess the intended outcome of conflict that others seem to project; where necessary, I convert the goal to win-win.	10	9	8	7	6	5	4	3	2	1
6. I can flexibly shift my behavior among the five major conflict resolution strategies, although I generally prefer the confrontational one.	10	9	8	7	6	5	4	3	2	1
7. I know what it takes to be assertive, and I am comfortable expressing myself in this way.	10	9	8	7	6	5	4	3	2	1

8. I try to project an "I'm OK—
You're OK" orientation to others
around me and believe that I am
successful in conveying this.   10   9   8   7   6   5   4   3   2   1

9. I regularly assess, and attempt to
further develop, my various bases
of power.   10   9   8   7   6   5   4   3   2   1

10. I recognize the reality of organizational politics and consciously use
the norm of reciprocity to help
accomplish my goals.   10   9   8   7   6   5   4   3   2   1

Scoring and Interpretation   Add up your total points for the ten questions. Record that number here, and report it when it is requested. _____

- If you scored between 81–100 points, you appear to have a solid capability for demonstrating good interpersonal skills.
- If you scored between 61–80 points, you should take a close look at the items with lower self-assessment scores and explore ways to improve those items.
- If you scored less than 60 points, you should be aware that a weaker skill level regarding several items could be detrimental to your future success as a motivator. We encourage you to review relevant sections of the chapter and watch for related material in subsequent chapters and other sources.

Now identify your three lowest scores, and write the question numbers here: _____, _____, _____. Write a brief paragraph, detailing to yourself an action plan for how you might sharpen each of these skills.

Incident

The Angry Airline Passenger

Margie James was night supervisor for an airline in Denver. Her office was immediately behind the ticket counter, and occasionally she was called upon to deal with passengers who had unusual problems that employees could not solve. One evening about 11 P.M. she was asked to deal with an angry passenger who approached her with the comment, "Your incompetent employees have lost my bag again, and your !X?#*!! baggage attendant isn't helping me at all. I want some service. Is everybody incompetent around here? I have an important speech in that bag that I have to deliver at 9 o'clock in the morning, and if I don't get it, I'll sue this airline for sure."

Question
How should James respond to the passenger? Would stroking help her? Would assertiveness training help?

Experiential Exercise

Assessing Political Strategies

Working individually, rank-order the following political (influence) strategies according to your willingness to use them (1 = greatest; 8 = least) to advance your own self-interest at work. When you are through, form groups of about five persons and develop a group assessment (consensus) of the proportion of managers (0–100 percent) who might use each strategy. Then examine the key, and discuss any differences.

Self-Ranking		Group Assessment of Use by Managers
_____	A. Praising influential people to make them feel good	_____
_____	B. Lining up prior support for a decision to be made	_____
_____	C. Blaming others for problems (scapegoating)	_____
_____	D. Creating social debts by doing favors for others	_____
_____	E. Dressing to meet the organization's standards for successful grooming	_____
_____	F. Building a support network of influential people	_____
_____	G. Withholding or distorting information that sheds an unfavorable light on your performance	_____
_____	H. Forming coalitions with powerful individuals who can support you later	_____

Key: A = 25%, B = 37%, C = 54%, D = 13%, E = 53%, F = 24%, G = 54%, H = 25%.*

*Frequency data obtained from Robert W. Allen, Dan L. Madison, Lyman W. Porter, Patricia A. Renwick, and Bronston T. Mayes, "Organizational Politics: Tactics and Characteristics of Its Actors," *California Management Review,* Fall 1979, pp. 77–83.

Part Five

Group Behavior

Chapter 12

Informal and Formal Groups

Meetings are the most universal—and universally despised—part of business life.

—Eric Matson[1]

The more people in a meeting, the less that gets done. That may not be a cardinal rule of business, but it's close.

—Bob Filipczak[2]

CHAPTER OBJECTIVES

TO UNDERSTAND

- Group Dynamics
- The Nature and Effects of Informal Groups
- Informal Leaders
- Differences between Task and Social Leadership Roles
- Brainstorming, Nominal, Delphi, and Dialectic Techniques
- Weaknesses of Group Meetings

When Bill Smith graduated from engineering school and joined the laboratory of a large manufacturing company, he was assigned the task of supervising four laboratory technicians who checked production samples. In some ways he did supervise them. In other ways he was restricted by the group itself, which was quite frustrating to Bill. He soon found that each technician protected the others so that it was difficult to fix responsibility for sloppy work. The group appeared to restrict its work in such a way that about the same number of tests were made every day regardless of his urging to speed up the work. Although Bill was the designated supervisor, he observed that many times his technicians, instead of coming to him, took problems to an older technician across the aisle in another section.

Bill also observed that three of his technicians often had lunch together in the cafeteria, but the fourth technician usually ate with friends in an adjoining laboratory. Bill usually ate with other laboratory supervisors, and he learned much about company events during these lunches. He soon began to realize that these situations were evidence of an informal organization and that he had to work with it as well as with the formal organization.

GROUP DYNAMICS

This chapter and the next one turn our focus from interpersonal relations to group activities. Small groups have functioned since the time of the first human family. In recent years researchers have studied scientifically the processes by which small groups evolve and work. Some of the questions they have addressed are: What is the informal organization and how does it operate? What is the role of a leader in a small group? Does the role vary with different objectives? What structured approaches are most useful for accomplishing group objectives? In what ways and under what conditions are group decisions better or worse than individual ones? Answers to these questions have begun to emerge, producing useful information on the dynamics of behavior in small groups for supervisors such as Bill Smith.

The social process by which people interact face-to-face in small groups is called **group dynamics.** The word "dynamics" comes from the Greek word meaning "force"; hence group dynamics refers to the study of forces operating within a group. Two important historical landmarks in our understanding of small groups are the research of Elton Mayo and his associates in the 1920s and 1930s and the experiments in the 1930s of Kurt Lewin, the founder of the group dynamics movement. Mayo showed that workers tend to establish informal groups that affect job satisfaction and effectiveness. Lewin showed that different kinds of leadership produced different responses in groups.

What is group dynamics?

Groups have properties of their own that are different from the properties of the individuals who make up the group. This is similar to the physical situation in which a molecule of salt (sodium chloride) has different properties from the sodium and chlorine elements that form a "group" to make it. The special properties of groups are illustrated by a simple lesson in mathematics. Suppose we say "one plus one equals three." In the world of mathematics that is a logical error, and a rather elementary one at that. But in the world of group dynamics it is entirely rational to say "one plus one equals three." In a group there is no such thing as only two people, for no two people can be considered without including their relationship, and that relationship is the third element in the equation.

Types of Groups

Formal and informal

286

There are many ways of classifying groups. A key difference exists between **formal groups,** which are established by the organization and have a public identity and goal to achieve, and **informal groups,** which emerge on the basis of common interests, proximity, and friendships. This chapter discusses both types.

Another fundamental distinction is between two types of formal groups. Some have a relatively temporary life; they are created to accomplish a short-term task and then disband. An example of a temporary group is a committee or task force. The event at which group members discuss ideas or solve problems is generally called a *meeting.* The other type of formal group is a more natural and enduring work group. This type of group is formed when people perform tasks together as part of their job assignments and is called a *team.* Because of the immense importance of teams in today's organizations, we discuss teams in a separate chapter, Chapter 13.

Temporary and permanent

Beneath the cloak of formal relationships in every organization there is a more complex system of social relationships consisting of many small, informal groups. Although there are many varieties of informal groups, we refer to them collectively as the informal organization. These informal groups are a powerful influence on productivity and job satisfaction, as Bill Smith discovered in the opening illustration. This chapter begins with an overview of informal organizations at work.

THE NATURE OF INFORMAL ORGANIZATIONS

Comparison of Informal and Formal Organizations

Definition of informal organization

Informal power

Widespread interest in the informal organization developed as a result of the Western Electric studies in the 1930s, which concluded that it was an important part of the total work situation. These studies showed that the **informal organization** is a network of personal and social relations not established or required by the formal organization but arising spontaneously as people associate with one another. The emphasis within the informal organization is on people and their relationships, whereas the formal organization emphasizes official positions in terms of authority and responsibility. Informal power, therefore, attaches to a *person,* whereas formal authority attaches to a *position* and a person has it only when occupying that position. *Informal power is personal,* but formal authority is institutional. These differences are summarized in Figure 12–1.

FIGURE 12–1

Differences between informal and formal organizations

Basic of Comparison	Informal Organization	Formal Organization
General nature	Unofficial	Official
Major concepts	Power and politics	Authority and responsibility
Primary focus	Person	Position
Source of leader power	Given by group	Delegated by management
Guidelines for behavior	Norms	Rules
Sources of control	Sanctions	Rewards and penalties

Power in an informal organization is given by group members rather than delegated by managers; therefore, it does not follow the official chain of command. It is more likely to come from peers than from superiors in the formal hierarchy; and it may cut across organizational lines into other departments. It is usually more unstable than formal authority, since it is subject to the sentiments of people. Because of its subjective nature, the informal organization cannot be controlled by management in the way that the formal organization can.

A manager typically holds some informal (personal) power along with formal (positional) power, but usually a manager does not have more informal power than anyone else in the group. This means that *the manager and the informal leader usually are two different persons in work groups.*

As a result of differences between formal and informal sources of power, formal organizations may grow to immense size, but informal organizations (at least the closely knit ones) tend to remain small in order to keep within the limits of personal relationships. The result is that a large organization tends to have hundreds of informal organizations operating throughout it. Some of them are wholly within the institution; others are partially external to it. Because of their naturally small size and instability, informal organizations are not a suitable substitute for the large formal aggregates of people and resources that are needed for modern institutions. Instead, informal organizations complement the formal one.

How Does the Informal Organization Emerge?

The organization's structure is designed by management to be consistent with its environment, technology, and strategy. This structure, with its rules, procedures, and job descriptions, creates a set of prescriptions for employees to follow. Individuals and groups are expected to behave in certain ways. If they perform their tasks as prescribed, the organization is efficient. This ideal may not happen as much as managers would like, however, for several reasons.

The informal organization emerges from within the formal structure as predictably as flowers grow in the spring. The result of this combination is different from what managers may have expected in at least three ways.[3] First, *employees act differently* than required. They may work faster or slower than predicted, or they may gradually modify a work procedure on the basis of their experience and insight. Second, *employees often interact with different people,* or with different frequencies, than their jobs require. Georgia may seek advice from Melissa instead of Todd, and Candy may spend more time helping José than Steve. Third, *workers may embrace a set of attitudes, beliefs, and sentiments* different from those the organization expects of them. Instead of being loyal, committed, and enthusiastic about their work, some employees may become disenchanted; others are openly alienated. The lesson for managers is painfully obvious—they must be aware of the informal activities, interactions, and sentiments of employees in addition to the required ones. The *combination* of required and emergent behaviors sometimes makes it difficult to predict levels of employee performance and satisfaction, as shown in Figure 12–2.

Effects of the informal organization

Member Status and Informal Leaders

Among the members of the marketing department in one firm there were remarkable, but somewhat typical, differences. Their ages ranged from thirty to seventy-two; their seniority in the organization varied from newly hired to thirty-nine years; and the highest-paid member earned about 80 percent more than the lowest-paid member. Some of the group had

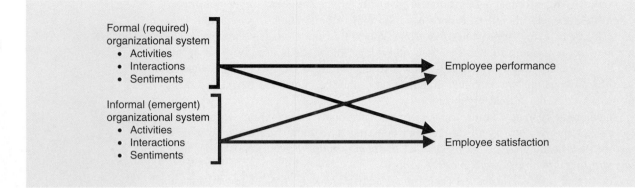

FIGURE 12–2

Formal and informal organizations and their effects

grown up in the local area, while others had moved across the United States to accept their jobs. Also, their offices differed in many dimensions, such as size, availability of natural lighting, and proximity to noise.

Members of work groups like that described above have identifiable characteristics that distinguish them from one another and give rise to status differences. As seen in the example, they differ in age, seniority, earnings, birthplace, and nature of their workplace. Other factors, such as technical competence, freedom to move around the work area, and personality, are also recognizable. Each of these elements can provide status to its holder, largely based on what the group members value. The causes of informal status are nearly numberless.

The employee with the largest amount of status in the informal organization usually becomes its **informal leader.** This person emerges from within the group, often acquiring considerable informal power. Informal leaders may help socialize new members into the organization, and they may be called upon by the group to perform the more complex tasks. A young neurosurgeon, for example, related how the group's senior partner would often stop by the operating room during a particularly delicate operation to assist briefly in the removal of a brain tumor, and then quietly move on when help was no longer needed.

Key roles of informal leaders

The informal leader plays several useful roles for a work unit. For example, the informal leader is expected to model and explain the key **norms** (informal standards of behavior) of the informal group for new members. And if someone fails to comply with the group's norms, the informal leader will likely play a dominant role in applying **sanctions**—various forms and degrees of punishment—to the individual to induce the desired behavior in the future. In addition, the informal leader often engages in a range of behaviors to help build and sustain the informal group's level of cohesiveness. For example, the leader may assume responsibility for recognizing the daily achievements of workers, for organizing after-hours social events, or for initiating a modest level of teasing and bantering among employees.

In return for their services, informal leaders usually enjoy certain rewards and privileges. Perhaps the informal leader is permitted by coworkers to choose a vacation time first, or the leader might be spared from a messy cleanup chore. A predictable reward is the high esteem in which the informal leader is held, and this is significant enough to balance the responsibilities the person shoulders.

Multiple informal leaders

Informal groups overlap to the extent that one person may be a member of several different groups, which means that there is not just one leader but several of varying importance. The group may look to one employee on matters pertaining to wages and to another to lead recreational plans. In this way several people in a department may be informal leaders of some type. There might be an experienced person who is looked upon as the expert on job problems, a listener who serves as counselor, and a communicator who is depended upon to convey key problems to the managers.

Identifying and Rewarding Informal Leaders   Sometimes the informal leadership of a group is unclear, at least to outside observers or managers. However, informal leaders often exhibit distinct behaviors that allow them to be identified. For example, Ellen may serve as the unofficial representative to management when workers have a question or complaint. Or managers may notice that other employees gather around Willie's workstation to swap stories whenever there is a coffee break. Sarah may voluntarily train new employees when they ask for technical help. These examples suggest that acting as a spokesperson, being the center of social attention, and offering well-received wisdom and guidance all provide useful clues regarding informal leadership.

Why are some employees, such as Ellen, Willie, and Sarah, willing to be informal leaders? To some workers informal leadership is a form of job enrichment, providing them with variety in their workday and a feeling of greater significance. Others find that it helps satisfy their social needs by dramatically increasing their interpersonal contacts during the day. Many find it a source of recognition for their esteem needs— a way of being acknowledged for their skills and experience while avoiding the responsibilities of formal supervision. By recognizing these rewards for informal leadership, managers can better understand the behavior of some individuals.

Although several persons in a group may be informal leaders of various types, there is usually one primary leader who has more influence than others. Each manager needs to learn who the key informal leader is in any group and to work with that leader to encourage behavior that furthers rather than hinders organizational objectives. When an informal leader is working against an employer, the leader's widespread influence can undermine motivation and job satisfaction.

One primary leader

Some Cautions   The informal organization is a desirable source of potential formal leaders, but it should be remembered that an informal leader does not always make the best formal manager. History is filled with examples of successful informal leaders who became arrogant bosses once they received formal authority. Some informal leaders fail as formal ones because they fear official responsibility—something they do not have as informal leaders. They often criticize management for lacking initiative or for not daring to be different, but when they take a managerial job, they become even more conservative because they are afraid to make a mistake. Other informal leaders fail because their area of official managerial authority is broader and more complex than the tiny area in which they had informal power. The fact that Joe is the leader in departmental social activities does not mean that he will be successful as the departmental manager.

> The difficult transition from informal to formal leader may be partially explained by the results of a research study of emergent leaders in small groups.[4] By using members' ratings of one another on the degree to which they were goal-directed and gave directions, summarized, and appeared self-assured after their first task, the researcher was able to predict eight out of nine emergent leaders. However, it was also discovered that the informal leaders typically rated quite highly as "quarrelsome," but not as "sensible." It appears that candidates for informal leadership require many of the same skills as formal leaders, but their other characteristics may later impair their effectiveness as formal leaders.

Benefits of Informal Organizations

Better total system

Although informal systems may lead to several problems, they also bring a number of benefits to both employers and employees, as shown in Figure 12–3. Most important is that they *blend with formal systems* to make an effective total system. Formal plans and policies cannot meet every problem in a dynamic situation because they are preestablished and partly inflexible. Some requirements can be met better by informal relations, which can be flexible and spontaneous.

Lighter workload for management

Another benefit of the informal organization is to *lighten the workload on management.* When managers know that the informal organization is working with them, they feel less compelled to check on the workers to be sure everything is shipshape. Managers are encouraged to delegate and decentralize because they are confident that employees will be cooperative. In general, informal group support of a manager probably leads to better cooperation and productivity. It helps get the work done.

The informal organization also may act to *fill in gaps in a manager's abilities.* If a manager is weak in planning, an employee may informally help with planning. In this way, planning is accomplished in spite of the manager's weakness.

Work group satisfaction

A significant benefit of the informal organization is that it *gives satisfaction and stability to work groups.* It is the means by which workers feel a sense of belonging and security, so satisfaction is increased and turnover reduced.

In a large office an employee named Rose McVail may feel like a mere payroll number, but her informal group gives her personal attachment and status. With the members of her group she is somebody, even though in the formal structure she is only one of a thousand employees. She may not look forward to monitoring 750 accounts daily, but the informal group gives more meaning to her day. When she thinks of meeting her friends, sharing their interests, and eating with them, her day takes on a new dimension that makes easier any difficulty or tedious routine in her work. Of course, these conditions can apply in reverse: The group may not accept her, thereby making her work more disagreeable and driving her to a transfer, to absenteeism, or to a resignation.

FIGURE 12–3

Potential benefits and problems associated with the informal organization

Benefits	Problems
• Makes a more effective total system	• Develops undesirable rumor
• Lightens workload on management	• Encourages negative attitudes
• Helps get the work done	• Resists change
• Tends to encourage cooperation	• Leads to interpersonal and intergroup conflicts
• Fills in gaps in a manager's abilities	• Rejects and harasses some employees
• Gives satisfaction and stability to work groups	• Weakens motivation and satisfaction
• Improves communication	• Operates outside of management's control
• Provides a safety valve for employee emotions	• Supports conformity
• Encourages managers to plan and act more carefully	• Develops role conflicts
• Contributes to higher cohesiveness	

An additional benefit is that the informal organization can be a *useful channel of employee communication.* It provides the means for people to keep in touch, to learn more about their work, and to understand what is happening in their environment.

Another benefit, often overlooked, is that the informal organization is a *safety valve for employee frustrations* and other emotional problems. Employees may relieve emotional pressures by discussing them with someone else in an open and friendly way, and one's associates in the informal group provide this type of environment.

A safety valve for emotions

> Consider the case of Max Schultz, who became frustrated with his supervisor, Frieda Schneider. He was so angry that he wanted to tell her what he thought of her, using uncomplimentary words, but he might have been disciplined for that. His next alternative was to have lunch with a close friend and to share with his friend exactly how he felt. Having vented his feelings, he was able to return to work and interact with Schneider in a more relaxed and acceptable manner.

A benefit of the informal organization that is seldom recognized is that its presence encourages managers to *plan and act more carefully* than they would otherwise. Managers who understand its power know that the informal organization provides a check on their unlimited use of authority. They introduce changes into their groups only after careful planning because they know that informal groups can undermine even a worthwhile project. They want their projects to succeed because they will have to answer to formal authority if they fail.

The benefits of the informal organization are more likely to appear if the group is cohesive and its members have favorable attitudes toward the firm.[5] **Cohesiveness** is indicated by how strongly the employees stick together, rely on each other, and desire to remain members of the group. *Productivity among members of cohesive groups is often quite uniform, and turnover is low.* Whether productivity will be high or low, however, is directly related to the cohesive group's internal work attitudes. If they are favorable toward the organization, performance will likely be higher; if they are negative, performance will likely be diminished.

Cohesiveness

Problems Associated with Informal Organizations

Many of the benefits of informal systems can be reversed to show potential problems. In other words, informal systems can help and harm an activity at the same time. For example, while useful information is being spread by one part of the system, another part may be communicating a malicious rumor. An informal system also can change its mood in a positive or negative way. A work group, for example, may accept, welcome, and nurture new employees and thus facilitate their feelings of comfort and performance levels. By contrast, the same group may confront, harass, and reject other employees, causing dissatisfaction and resignations.[6] Both positive and negative effects exist side by side in most informal systems.

One major problem with informal organizations is resistance to change. There is a tendency for a group to become overly protective of its way of life and to stand like a rock in the face of change. *What has been good is believed to be good enough for the future.* If, for example, job A has always had more status than job B, it must continue to have more status and more pay, even though conditions have changed to make job A less difficult. If restriction of productivity was necessary in the past with an autocratic management, the group might believe it to be necessary now, even though management is participative. Although informal organizations are bound by no chart on the wall, they are bound by convention, custom, and culture.

Resistance to change

Conformity

A related problem is that the informal organization can be a significant cause of employee conformity. The informal side of organizations is so much a part of the everyday life of workers that they hardly realize it is there, so they usually are unaware of the powerful pressures it applies to persuade them to conform to its way of life. The closer they are attached to it, the stronger its influence is.

Norms

Conformity is encouraged by **norms,** which are informal group requirements for the behavior of members.[7] These norms may be strong or weak (depending on the importance of the behavior to the group) and positive or negative (depending on their impact on the organization). Groups rigidly expect their members to follow strong norms; individuals may choose to accept or reject weak ones. Research studies show that groups have norms for both their task responsibilities and their personal relationships at work.[8] They also generate norms for their superior and subordinates, as well as their peers.

The group whose norms a person accepts is a **reference group.** Employees may have more than one reference group, such as the engineering manager who identifies with the engineering profession and its standards, plus one or more management groups. A reference group often uses rewards and penalties (sanctions) to persuade its members to conform to its norms. The combination of informal norms with their related sanctions consistently guides opinion and applies power to reduce any behavior that tends to vary from group norms. Nonconformers may be pressured and harassed until they capitulate or leave.

Treatment of nonconformers

> Examples of harassment are interference with work (such as hiding one of the offender's tools), ridicule, interference outside the workplace (such as letting the air out of the offender's automobile tires), and isolation from the group. In Britain it is said that a person isolated from the group is being "sent to Coventry."[9] In these instances the group refuses to talk with the offender for days or even weeks, and group members may even refuse to use any tool or machine the offender has used. Actions of this type can even drive a worker from a job.

Role conflict

Another problem that may develop is role conflict (see previous discussion in Chapter 4). Workers may want to meet the requirements of both their group and their employer, but frequently those requirements are somewhat in conflict. What is good for the employees is not always good for the organization. Coffee breaks may be desirable, but if employees spend an extra fifteen minutes socializing in the morning and afternoon, productivity may be reduced to the disadvantage of both the employer and consumers. Much of this role conflict can be avoided by carefully cultivating mutual interests with informal groups. The more the interests of formal and informal groups can be integrated, the more productivity and satisfaction can be expected. However, there always will be some differences between formal and informal organizations. This is not an area where perfect harmony exists.

A major difficulty with any informal organization is that it is not subject to management's direct control. The authority that it depends on is the social system rather than management. All that management can do is influence it here and there.

Personal and group conflicts

Informal organizations also develop interpersonal and intergroup conflicts that can be damaging to their organization. When employees give more of their thoughts and energies to opposing one another, they are likely to give less to their employer. Conflicts and self-interests can become so strong in informal organizations that they reduce both motivation and satisfaction. The result is less productivity, which harms both the employer and employees. No one gains.

Monitoring Informal Organizations

One way to gain a better understanding of an informal system is to prepare a visual portrait of it. These diagrams are called **network charts,** or *informal organization charts.*[10] They usually focus on either interpersonal *feelings expressed* (e.g., attraction, repulsion, or indifference) among individuals or actual *behaviors exhibited.* Identifying the feelings within a group can be useful for determining who trusts whom, or for selecting an individual to negotiate a satisfactory compromise on a sticky issue. Determining patterns of behaviors can be done either through direct observation of interactions, through collecting data on communication patterns, or by directly asking individuals involved (e.g., "From whom do you seek advice most frequently?"). Network charts like the simple one shown in Figure 12–4 can reveal central individuals ("stars," such as Tania or Jackie), isolated persons (Carolina) who are likely to feel overlooked, and dramatic differences between what outsiders think is happening versus what is actually occurring.

Influencing Informal Organizations

Management did not establish informal organizations, and it cannot abolish them. Nor would it want to do so. But management can learn to live with them and have some measure of influence on them. Management guidelines for action include the following:

1. Accept and understand informal organizations.
2. Identify various levels of attitudes and behaviors within them.
3. Consider possible effects on informal systems when taking any kind of action.

Guidelines for action

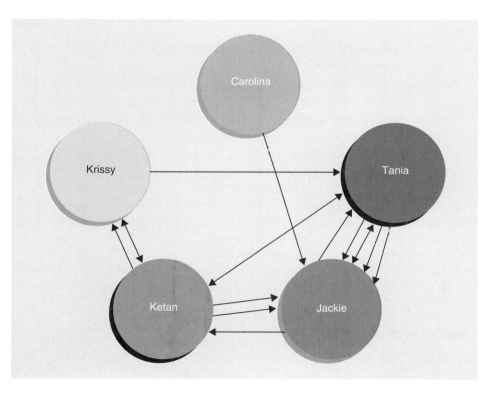

FIGURE 12–4

A sample network chart of task interactions at work

4. Integrate as far as possible the interests of informal groups with those of the formal organization.

5. Keep formal activities from unnecessarily threatening informal organizations.

Formal and informal combinations

The most desirable combination of formal and informal organizations appears to be a predominant formal system to maintain unity toward objectives, along with a well-developed informal system to maintain group cohesiveness and teamwork. In other words, the informal organization needs to be strong enough to be supportive, but not strong enough to dominate.

FORMAL GROUPS

"Oh no! Not another committee meeting," the executive groaned as she looked at her calendar for the morning. "It's only Wednesday morning, and I've been to five meetings already this week. When am I going to get my real work done?"

The executive's last remark reflects how many managers feel about meetings. One survey showed that managers felt time spent in group meetings was their most significant time waster. Whether called meetings, conferences, task forces, or committees, the time spent in formal groups has variously been described as a total waste of time, a source of confusion and misinformation, and an excuse for indecision on the part of an individual decision maker.

Here are some factors that contribute to the often-pervasive negative attitudes about time spent in committee meetings:

- A lack of trust causes participants to withhold their true feelings.
- A negative mind-set exists that "meetings aren't real work" and hence people don't take them seriously (e.g., they come late or leave early, they miss them completely, or they are distracted while there).
- Missing or incomplete information prevents participants from making important decisions when appropriate.
- Meetings are poorly run (the person in charge fails to have an agenda, a plan to follow, a finite length for the session, or the discipline to keep the discussion moving).
- Meetings are viewed as the end result, not the means to an end (the group fails to focus on creating a product or outcome).

In spite of such widespread condemnation, committees and other group activities have continued to flourish. Instead of becoming extinct because of widespread dislike, they continue to be an important part of daily organizational behavior.

Meetings are necessary, but they do introduce more complexity and more chances for problems to arise when improperly used. Some committees are used not to reach decisions but to put them off, not to obtain employee input but to sell a previously reached conclusion, and not to develop subordinates but to hide incompetence. On occasion, emotional issues overshadow the factual aspects of the decision to be made, and the sensitive interpersonal relations that emerge require understanding and delicate handling.

Committees

Formal groups are created for many purposes. Group members may be asked to generate ideas, make decisions, debate issues and negotiate resources, or provide status reports and receive constructive feedback.[11] A **committee** is a specific type of group meeting in which members in their group role have been delegated the authority to handle the problem at hand. The group's authority usually is expressed in terms of one vote for each member. This means that if a supervisor and a worker serve as members of the same committee, both usually have equal committee roles. The worker may even have greater actual influence on the committee's outcome as a result of differences in expertise, interest, or experience. Committees often create special human problems because people are unable to make adjustments from their normal work roles and relationships.

Systems Factors to Consider

A useful way to approach the management of committees is to apply the systems idea discussed in Chapter 1. As shown in Figure 12–5, effective committees require careful consideration of their inputs (size, composition, and agendas), the group process (leadership roles and alternative group structures), and outcomes (quality of the decision and the group's support for it). These factors are discussed next, followed by a review of the major problems and issues inherent in problem-solving groups.

Size   The size of a group tends to affect the way it works. If membership rises above seven, communication tends to be focused within a few members, with others feeling like they do not have adequate opportunity to communicate directly with one another. If it is necessary to have a larger committee to represent all relevant points of view, special effort and extra time are required to ensure good communication. A group of five people seems to be preferred for typical situations. A smaller group sometimes has difficulty functioning because conflicts of power develop.

Composition   Leaders of committees, problem-solving groups, and task forces often have the opportunity to select the members. When doing so, the leaders need to consider

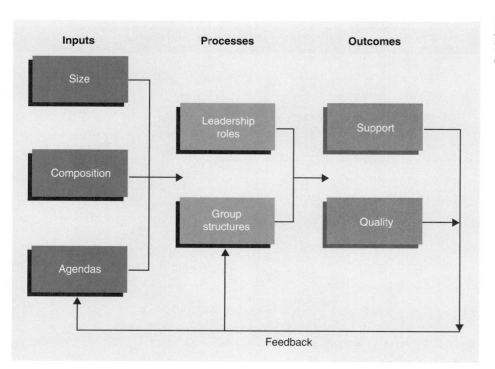

FIGURE 12–5

Systems view of effective committees

various factors, such as the committee's objective, the members' interest level and time available to serve, and the past history of working relationships among the potential members.

> One study examined the personal characteristics sought in appointees to seven types of committees.[12] In general, the top-level administrators preferred people who had a high stake (interest) in the outcome and were respected by their peers. Desire for people who were knowledgeable, who were cooperative, and who either advocated or opposed the official's position varied considerably, depending upon the type of committee to be created.

Surface and hidden agendas

Agendas Meetings work simultaneously at two different levels. One level is the official task of the group, known as the **surface agenda.**[13] The other level involves members' private emotions and motives, which they have brought with them but keep hidden. These are the **hidden agendas** of the meeting. Frequently, when a group reaches a crisis in its surface agenda, these hidden agendas come to life to complicate the situation. Conversely, sometimes a group seems to be making no progress and then suddenly everything is settled. What may have happened is that a hidden agenda finally was resolved, even though members did not know they were working on it, making it easy to settle the surface agenda. An example is that of the staff specialist who is searching for a way to retaliate against a supervisor, and the specialist is blind to everything else until the hidden agenda can be resolved satisfactorily.

Task roles

Leadership Roles Groups tend to require not one but two types of leadership roles: that of the **task leader** and that of the **social leader.**[14] Figure 12–6 provides illustrations of the nature of each role. The task leader's job in a meeting is to help the group accomplish its objectives and stay on target. The idea is to provide necessary structure by stating the problem, giving and seeking relevant facts, periodically summarizing the progress, and checking for agreement.

Difficulties sometimes arise because the task leader may irritate people and injure

FIGURE 12–6

Task and social leadership roles

Task Roles	Social Roles
• Define a problem or goal for the group.	• Support the contributions of others; encourage them by recognition.
• Request facts, ideas, or opinions from members.	• Sense the mood of the group and help members become aware of it.
• Provide facts, ideas, or opinions.	
• Clarify a confused situation; give examples; provide structure.	• Reduce the tension and reconcile disagreements.
• Summarize the discussion.	• Modify your position; admit an error.
• Determine whether agreement has been reached.	• Facilitate participation of all members.
	• Evaluate the group's effectiveness.

the unity of the group. It is the social leader's role to restore and maintain group relationships by recognizing contributions, reconciling disagreements, and playing a supportive role to help the group develop. An especially challenging job is to blend the
ideas of a deviant member with the thoughts of other participants. Although one person can fill both the task and social roles, often they are separate. When they are separate, it is important for the task leader to recognize the social leader and try to form
a coalition so that the two leaders are working together for improved effectiveness of
the group.

Social roles

An example of moderate group activity in a committee meeting is depicted in Figure 12–7.
In this committee all members except Fleming communicated with the leader. Seven of the
ten members communicated with members other than the leader, but they tended to talk
only to members near them, probably because of the committee's large size and layout.
Johnson, Smith, and Fleming participated the least; all the other members participated
actively. The chart shows clearly that the leader's principal means of creating discussion
was to ask questions.

In addition to relying on both task and social roles, effective meetings are also
facilitated by the application of a number of common-sense practices.[15] These include

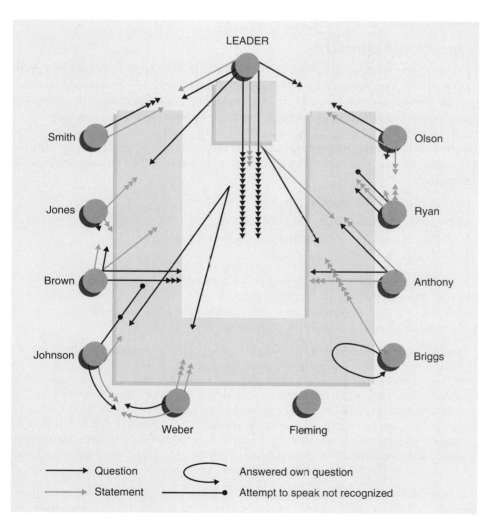

FIGURE 12–7

Participation diagram of
a meeting

*Source: Conference
Leadership,* U.S. Depart-
ment of the Air Force, n.d.,
pp. 9–11.

- Carefully considering *who* should be present, and for what parts of the meeting, and who does *not* need to be there
- Selecting a good *site* for the meeting (appropriate for the group's size, comfortable, and free of distractions)
- Using *technology* (e.g, computers hooked to printers and oversized monitors) to help capture ideas, allow for anonymous inputs, organize and expand upon them, record insights and criticisms, and create and edit documents before the participants leave
- Giving appropriate *credit* to those who participated, and drawing out those who didn't (such as Fleming in Figure 12–7)
- Using open questions to stimulate thought and directed questions to encourage a focus on a particular topic
- Balancing the serious discussions with time for a bit of lighthearted *fun*
- Summarizing progress, identifying issues yet unresolved, and making necessary *assignments* for the future (as captured in the cryptic phrase "Who does what by when?")

If followed regularly, these suggestions can greatly improve the productivity of committee meetings.

Structured Approaches

The committee meetings discussed above generally involve open discussion of a problem or issue. Other methods have been developed that work for specific objectives or provide greater control over the process. Four important alternative structures are brainstorming, nominal groups, Delphi decision making, and dialectic inquiry.

Brainstorming   **Brainstorming** is a popular method for encouraging creative thinking in groups of about eight people.[16] It is built around four basic guidelines for participants:

1. Generate as many ideas as possible.
2. Be creative, freewheeling, and imaginative.
3. Build upon (piggyback), extend, or combine earlier ideas.
4. Withhold criticism of others' ideas.

The success of brainstorming depends on each member's capacity and willingness to listen to others' thoughts, to use these thoughts as a stimulus to spark new ideas of their own, and then to feel free to express them. When this sequence takes place, a large number of new and different ideas can emerge.

> One company, Bachman Consulting, suggests modifying the basic brainstorming process for even greater success.[17] Their five-step process structures the flow to make sure that each set of ideas contributes value to the next step in the series. The first step looks backward to identify the causes of the problem to be solved. The second describes the criteria that the solutions must meet. The third step involves looking for all possible sources of models for solutions. In the fourth step participants are asked to relate the models and resources to the original objective to see how they might help. Finally, in the fifth step, the solutions identified are communicated to relevant stakeholders in the organization who might benefit from the product of the five-stage brainstorming effort.

Underlying principles   There are two main principles that underlie brainstorming. One is **deferred judgment,** by which all ideas—even unusual and impractical ones—are encouraged without criticism or evaluation. Ideas are recorded by a group member as fast as they are suggested; they are evaluated for usefulness at a later time. The purpose of deferred judgment is to separate idea creation from idea censorship. This principle encourages people to propose bold, unique ideas without worrying about what others think of them. The second principle is that *quantity breeds quality*. As more ideas come forth, eventually higher-quality ones will be developed. When these principles are followed, brainstorming typically produces more ideas than the conventional approach of combined thinking and judging. Brainstorming sessions last from ten minutes to one hour and require very little preparation.

Brainstorming has many advantages over other approaches. In brainstorming sessions group members are enthusiastic, participation is broader than normal, and the group maintains a strong task orientation. Ideas are built upon and extended, and members typically feel that the final product is a team solution. Its major difficulties include the residual fear among some members that their creative thoughts will be looked down upon, the fact that independent thought and later criticism of one's ideas do not contribute to group cohesion, and the very real fact that only one person can speak at a time (so as to be recorded clearly).

Pros and cons

The marriage of computer technology and groupware programs has allowed the development of a modified version of the method, known as **electronic brainstorming.** In this process, group members sit at personal computer terminals—sometimes in scattered locations—and receive a question, an issue, or a request for establishing priorities. In response, they type in their own ideas as they arise. As multiple inputs are received, a set of the group's ideas appears on their screens, available for response, editing, or even input of judgment or votes. Research shows that this process results in a higher number of ideas generated (because of the simultaneous generation and recording of ideas by participants) than through the traditional brainstorming process.[18] In addition, members feel they have more opportunity for participation and more flexibility, since they do not necessarily need to "meet" at the same time.

Nominal Group Technique

A **nominal group** exists in name only, with members having minimal interaction prior to producing a decision. Here are the steps that nominal groups often follow:

1. Individuals are brought together and presented with a problem.
2. They develop solutions independently, often writing them on cards.
3. Their ideas are shared with others in a structured format (e.g., a roundrobin process that ensures all members get the opportunity to present their ideas).
4. Brief time is allotted so that questions can be asked—but only for clarification.
5. Group members individually designate their preferences for the best alternatives by secret ballot.
6. The group decision is announced.

Work independently; combine ideas.

Advantages of the nominal group technique include the opportunity for equal participation by all members, the nondominance of discussion by any one member, and the tight control of time that the process allows. Disadvantages reported are that group members are frustrated by the rigidity of the procedure, gain no feelings of cohesiveness, and do not have the opportunity to benefit from cross-fertilization of ideas.

One research study explored the quality of solutions that were offered to a marketing strategy problem in a nominal group procedure.[19] Ideas generated at various stages of the process were scored on the basis of quality and creativity. Although the ideas with the greatest quality

Obtaining innovation and creativity in groups is not necessarily mysterious or an unreachable goal. On the contrary, argue the authors of *When Sparks Fly,* creativity can be managed—but it works best if the group is composed of a diverse range of opinions so that "creative abrasion" will appear. Further, creativity requires a supportive atmosphere, an appropriate infrastructure to support it, and the resources to encourage it.

Managers are urged to follow five basic steps:

1. *Preparation*—creating a knowledge base that can be tapped for new ideas.

2. *Innovation opportunity*—presenting the need for new ideas to be generated.

3. *Divergence*—generating a wide range of new ideas.

4. *Incubation*—allowing time for the members to ponder and review the options.

5. *Convergence*—helping the group select the best option(s).

Source: Dorothy Leonard and Walter Swap, *When Sparks Fly: Igniting Creativity in Groups,* Boston: Harvard Business School Press, 1999.

(practicality, pervasiveness, and long-range impact) generally appeared early in the nominal group discussion, the most creative ideas (which also had moderate quality) were generated late in the session. Two possible explanations were offered. The process may place pressure on participants to contribute their fair share as they see others continuing to provide suggestions. In addition, members may be encouraged to take greater risks to share nonconforming ideas as they see the structured process protect other members.

Survey the experts.

Delphi Decision Making

In **Delphi decision groups,** a panel of relevant people is chosen to address an issue. Members are selected because they are experts or have relevant information to share and the time available to do so. A series of questionnaires are sequentially distributed to the respondents, who do not need to meet face-to-face. All responses typically are in writing. Panelists may be asked to identify future problems, project market trends, or predict a future state of affairs (e.g., corporate sales in ten years). Explanations of their conclusions also can be shared. Replies are gathered from all participants, summarized, and fed back to the members for their review. Then participants are asked to make another decision, on the basis of new information. The process may be repeated several times until the responses converge satisfactorily and a final report is prepared.[20]

Delphi advantages

Success of the Delphi decision process depends on adequate time, participant expertise, communication skill, and the motivation of members to immerse themselves in the task. The major merits of the process include

- Elimination of interpersonal problems among panelists
- Efficient use of experts' time
- Adequate time for reflection and analysis by respondents
- Diversity and quantity of ideas generated
- Accuracy of predictions and forecasts made

Just as with electronic brainstorming, the increasingly wide availability of computers and the electronic transmission of responses have affected the Delphi process. Through their use, the interactive process of collecting input and feeding back group data can be greatly abbreviated. This use of advances in technology has helped overcome a previous limitation of the Delphi process.

Dialectic Decision Methods

Some face-to-face decision-making groups converge too quickly on one alternative while overlooking others. Their incomplete evaluation of options may reflect either the participants' dislike of meetings or their lack of willingness to raise and confront tough issues. The **dialectic decision method**

(DDM), which traces its roots to Plato and Aristotle. offers a way of overcoming these problems.[21] The steps of DDM are portrayed in Figure 12–8.

The dialectic process begins with a clear statement of a problem to be solved. Then two or more competing proposals are generated. A key step follows in which participants *identify the explicit or implicit assumptions* that underlie each proposal. The group then breaks into advocacy subgroups, which examine and argue the relative merits of their positions. Then the entire group makes a decision based on the competing presentations. This decision may mean embracing one of the alternatives, forging a compromise from several ideas, or generating a new proposal.

The merits of DDM include better understanding of the proposals, their underlying premises, and their pros and cons by the participants. Members are also likely to feel more confident about the choice they made. Disadvantages include the propensity to forge a compromise in order to avoid choosing sides and the tendency to focus more on who were the better debaters than what the best decision should be. Nevertheless, the dialectic method holds promise for future decision-making groups.

Potential Outcomes of Formal Group Processes

Support for Decisions   Probably the most important by-product of face-to-face group meetings is that *people who participate in making a decision feel more strongly motivated to accept it and carry it out.* In many instances this result is more than a

Acceptance

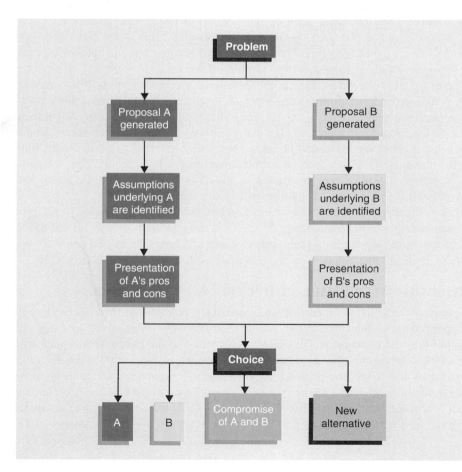

FIGURE 12–8

Steps in dialectic decision making

by-product—it is the primary purpose of the meeting. Meetings undoubtedly are one of the best means available of committing people to carry out a course of action. A person who has helped make a decision is more interested in seeing it work. Furthermore, if several group members are involved in carrying out a decision, group discussion helps each understand the part others will play, so that they can coordinate their efforts.

Group decisions also carry more weight with those who are not group members. Associates, subordinates, and even superiors are more likely to *accept* group decisions. They feel that decisions of this type are more free from individual prejudice because they are based on a combination of many viewpoints. Further, the combined social pressure of the entire group stands behind the decision.

Problem solving improves.

Quality of Decisions   In addition to supporting decisions, groups often are effective problem-solving tools. In comparison with an individual, groups typically have greater information available to them, a variety of experiences to draw upon, and the capacity to examine suggestions and reject the incorrect ones. As a result, groups can frequently produce more and better-quality solutions to some problems than individuals can.

Individual Development   When working in decision-making groups, some individuals are naturally more passive than others and may withhold their ideas. However, the group will benefit most if there is widespread and fairly even participation by all members. Participation also increases the likelihood of each member's developing new interactive skills that can be used later in other groups. How, then, does satisfactory individual participation occur? In addition to specific invitations ("Kristina, what ideas do you have?") and encouragement by other group members and the leader ("Great idea, Mario."), one explanation lies in **social facilitation.** This is the fact that group members often try harder to contribute on a task just because other people are around. *The presence of others stimulates them to perform better.*

There appear to be three reasons for this social facilitation effect. First, having other people around simply increases a person's general level of arousal and awareness, stimulating their cognitive activity. They simply think more carefully about their performance-related behavior. Second, the presence of others makes some people apprehensive about the likelihood of being appraised, formally or informally, by others, and thus they raise their level of performance so as to look good. Third, the presence of others may raise one's awareness of the discrepancy between the actual and ideal self and thereby stimulate the person to close that gap.

Increased participation may also be a product of implied group pressure to perform or a natural response to seeing others do so. Social facilitation is closely related to the idea of *role modeling,* where a group member sees and hears others perform well and wants to duplicate that behavior because of the social rewards it elicits from them.

Consensus: A Key Issue in Decision-Making Groups

Is unanimous agreement, or **consensus,** a necessary prerequisite for effective group decisions? Without total agreement, group members may be expected to carry out decisions they did not support. Divided votes also may set up disagreements that carry beyond the meeting. On the other hand, a *requirement,* or even implicit expectation, of unanimity has its disadvantages. It may become the paramount goal, causing people to suppress their opposition or to tell the group they agree when honestly they do not. It is frustrating to the majority of members to have to keep discussing a subject long after their minds are made up, simply because they are hoping to convince a few honest dissenters. This situation is a waste of time and an embarrassment to the dissenters. It can delay worthwhile projects unnecessarily.

Unless the decision is of utmost personal importance to the dissenter, agreement of most of the members should be sufficient for action. Though an isolated minority needs to be heard and respected, so does the majority. Organizations must get on with their work rather than stop to engage in endless debates in an effort to reach total agreement. Most employers, therefore, do not expect or require unanimity for committee decisions. In practice, consensus is often interpreted to mean that the group engaged in widespread input gathering, which resulted in a *shared level of understanding*. From a behavioral perspective, the key is for all members to feel they have had an honest opportunity to state their views and be heard.[22] At that time, most reasonable people will believe they can support the decision reached despite their reservations.

Specific ideas for facilitating consensus include the following:

1. Conduct a straw poll to identify where people stand.
2. Suggest a supermajority vote (e.g., requiring 90 percent approval for passage).
3. Ask members to withdraw controversial proposals, withdraw their concerns, or stand aside to allow the group to proceed without them.
4. Create a subgroup and empower it to make a decision.
5. Distill the concerns into major groups to pinpoint patterns of problems.
6. Expedite closing of discussion through use of a "go-round" (each member is given a time-limited chance to speak) or a "fishbowl" (representatives of major positions speak for all others on the issue).[23]

Weaknesses of Committees

> A distinguished executive was sitting at home one evening in 1927 as his wife was reading the newspaper account of Lindbergh's historic solo flight from New York to Paris. "Isn't it wonderful," she exclaimed, "and he did it all alone." Her husband's classic reply after a hard day at the office was, "Well, it would have been even more wonderful if he had done it with a committee!"

Because committees have weaknesses as well as strengths, some people have developed the attitude "you go to the meeting and I'll tend the store," meaning that meetings are unproductive labor and someone has to keep production humming. *Some* meetings are unproductive, but a single case does not prove the generality. Meetings are an essential and productive part of work organizations. Part of our trouble is that we expect too much of them, and when they do not meet our expectations, we criticize. But we will get nowhere criticizing a tennis court because it is a poor football field.

Properly conducted meetings can contribute to organizational progress by providing participation, integrating interests, improving decision making, committing and motivating members to carry out a course of action, encouraging creative thinking, broadening perspectives, and changing attitudes. The fundamental decision that must be made with groups, therefore, is not whether to have them but *how to make the best use of them*. To use them, one must know their weaknesses, which fall into five major categories: slowness and expensiveness, groupthink, polarization, escalating commitment, and divided responsibility.

Slowness and Expensiveness   As one manager observed, "Committees keep minutes and waste hours!" Meetings of all types are sometimes a slow and costly way to get things done. On occasion, delay is desirable. There is more time for thinking, for objective review of an idea, and for the suggestion of alternatives. But when quick, decisive action is necessary, an individual approach is more effective. A manager, for example, does not call a committee meeting to respond to a customer's urgent request for assistance.

> Some organizations have taken direct action to ensure that meetings move rapidly and end on time. Examples of successful techniques used include holding "stand up" meetings (where all the chairs are removed from the meeting room), requiring all presenters and dis-cussants to adhere to a rigid time schedule (e.g., 12 minutes for a major strategic proposal, including answering key criticisms of it), and providing a visible chart showing the accu-mulating cost of the meeting (computed as minutes elapsed $\times$ average salary of participants $\times$ number of participants present). These approaches demonstrate that the cost of meetings *can* be controlled.

Groupthink   One of the most convincing criticisms of meetings is that they often lead to conformity and compromise. This tendency of a tightly knit group to bring individual thinking in line with the group's thinking is called **groupthink,** or the lev-eling effect.[24] It occurs when a group values solidarity so much that it fails to criti-cally evaluate its own decisions and assumptions. Pressures are brought to bear on individuals to adapt to the desires of other members. The ideas of dominant mem-bers—those who have authority, speak with confidence, or are more vocal in their arguments—are more likely to be accepted whether or not they have value. This ten-dency weakens the group product.

Groupthink can be detected by watching for some of its classic symptoms, which include

- Self-censorship of critical thoughts
- Rationalization that what they are doing is acceptable to others
- Illusion of invulnerability
- Reliance on self-appointed mind-guards
- Illusion of unanimity within the group without testing for it
- Stereotyping others outside the group
- Illusion of morality
- Pressure on dissidents to give in and conform to the group

Groupthink is probably present when a group acts as though it is above the law and could not err, and when it assumes it has total support for its actions. The con-

The Need for Diversity in Groups

Nowhere is the need for diversity more apparent than in the composition of decision-making groups and task forces. Member *backgrounds* (e.g., age, gender, ethnicity) are becoming vitally important to consider so that product and service decisions can reflect market needs. In addition, member capacities to think differently and share alternative mind-sets can be vitally important for the prevention of deadly diseases like groupthink. As a consequence, wise managers consciously recruit individuals who have previously demonstrated the capacity to look at problems from a variety of angles. In the short term, this approach can create conflict, tension, and even chaos; in the long term, creating and using diversity is a healthy and constructive approach in group decision making.

sequences of groupthink include a deterioration in a group's judgment, failure to engage in reality testing, and lowered quality of its decision making.

One effective method of reducing or preventing groupthink is to designate a **devil's advocate** for each meeting. This person is expected to question the ideas of others, probe for supporting facts, and challenge their logic. Devil's advocates are guardians of clear and moral thinking and can help the group immeasurably by providing it with a stream of constructive criticism. Other methods used by organizations to prevent groupthink include rotating in new group members, inviting attendance by outsiders, and announcing a temporary delay before final decision making to give members one last chance to identify and voice their reservations.

Polarization   In contrast to groupthink, an alternative behavior that sometimes appears is group **polarization.** Here, individuals bring to the group their strong predispositions, either positive or negative, toward the topic. As ideas are explored and logic is challenged, some members become defensive. Their attitudes become rigid and even more extreme if they are aggressively confronted. Although group members' attitudes can become polarized in either direction (risky or conservative), research suggests that *some groups tend to make a* **risky shift** *in their thinking.* This tendency means that they are more willing to take chances with organizational resources as a group than they would if they were acting individually. Although risky decisions can have high payoffs, they also have the built-in potential for more disastrous consequences, as illustrated in this scenario:

> Picture a group of managers about to make a decision on expanding plant capacity despite the high cost of capital, intense competition, and an uncertain market. Two members who were mildly in favor of expansion before the meeting are surprised to hear a third argue persuasively for the decision. Another manager somewhat casually suggests that "five years from now the stockholders won't remember who made the decision, even if we're wrong." The fifth manager does not want to be known as a roadblock to progress and joins forces with the others to make it unanimous.

This meeting illustrates how the risky shift can quickly occur. While only one of the five members may really believe the decision is correct, the others allow themselves to be talked into it for a variety of reasons. Sometimes highly self-confident members can express themselves so persuasively that the rest accept their arguments without much debate. Other members feel that since they are not individually responsible for the decision, they can afford to take greater risks. The group must guard against these pitfalls.

Escalating Commitment   Closely related to the problem of groupthink is the idea that group members may persevere in advocating a course of action despite rational evidence that it will result in failure. In fact, they may even allocate additional resources to the project, thereby **escalating commitment** despite overwhelming evidence that it will fail. Examples abound of automakers continuing to make certain types of cars despite powerful consumer trends away from those types, pharmaceutical companies investing millions in the development of drugs that are not likely to receive federal approval, and communities spending heavily on tourist attractions in the face of evidence that they can never recoup their investments.

There are many reasons decision makers escalate their commitment. Sometimes they may unconsciously fall prey to selective perception and thus bias the choice of information used to support their arguments. The competence motive also affects their decisions, since their desire to protect their self-esteem prevents them from admitting failure until

306

the evidence is overwhelming. Having previously argued for an alternative in public makes it more difficult to demonstrate flexibility and reverse oneself (for fear of losing face). In many cultures there is strong admiration for leaders who are risk takers and persist in the face of adversity. All these forces suggest that members of groups need to be especially alert to the escalation phenomenon in themselves and others, and be willing to admit and accept their losses in some situations.

Divided Responsibility   Management literature has always recognized that divided responsibility is a problem whenever group decisions are made. It often is said that actions that are several bodies' responsibility are nobody's responsibility. Group decisions undoubtedly do dilute and thin out responsibility. They also give individual members a chance to shirk responsibility, using justifications such as "Why should I bother with this problem? I didn't support it in the meeting."

Overcoming the Weaknesses   Many of the disadvantages of group meetings can be overcome readily. The preceding discussions suggest that the proper group structures must be selected, that group size is an important factor, and that various leadership roles must be played. The "Advice to Future Managers" presents a set of additional guidelines for ensuring effective group meetings.

Emerging Directions

Variations in the use of groups

Three themes hold major promise for further advancing our knowledge about groups in organizations. One is the emergence of a broad array of *alternative group structuring techniques,* which occurred partially through the emphasis of TQM programs on group work.[25] Some of the methods try to stimulate creative thought; others equalize status differences, control discussion time, or vary the amount of anonymity for members. Supportive aids may include slips of paper, color-coded index cards, or flip charts hung on walls.

Contingency models

A second theme is the preliminary development of *contingency models.* A number of models are emerging that are designed to help managers know when to take different actions. Some of these approaches prescribe the amount of freedom to allow the group for decision-making purposes. Other models assess some of the desired outputs discussed earlier (such as acceptance and quality) and use that analysis to indicate whether nominal, Delphi, or group processes are most appropriate. When further refined, these models will help managers choose the method most effective for each situation.

Support systems

Another promising development is the **group decision support system.**[26] These support systems use computers, decision models, and technological advances to remove communication barriers, structure the decision process, and generally direct the group's discussion. An example is the electronic boardroom, featuring instant display of members' ideas on a large screen, computerized vote solicitation and display of results, and electronic transfer of messages among individual participants. The potential gains in quality of decisions are substantial from the integration of communication, computer, and decision technologies. What is not yet known are the effects on members' satisfaction, the participants' sense of involvement, or the balance of task and social roles that will be needed. Nevertheless, group decision support systems are an exciting development that holds substantial promise for the future.

1. Create and distribute the agenda and background materials for a meeting in advance. Clarify the objective (intended outcome or product) to all participants.

2. Compose the group appropriately according to both size and representativeness criteria; allow persons to come and go as they are needed in the meeting.

3. Encourage the expression and consideration of minority viewpoints; search for the underlying assumptions held and make these explicit.

4. Separate the idea-generation stage of a meeting from the idea-evaluation stage; control time spent on chitchat, tangents, and other topics.

5. Carefully test for the degree of support for a tentative decision about to be made.

6. End the meeting on a positive note regarding its success; commend individual contributors; and assign specific responsibilities for follow-up.

7. Engage the group in an evaluation of their own success during the meeting (what went well and what needs improvement in their own process); use these suggestions for improvement in the next meeting you conduct.

SUMMARY

Group dynamics is the process by which people interact face-to-face in small groups. Such groups may be informal or formal, and formal groups may be temporary or permanent.

The complex system of social relationships in an organization consists of many small, informal groups. These groups, which arise naturally from the interaction of people, are referred to collectively as the informal organization. Informal organizations have major benefits, but they also lead to problems that management cannot easily ignore. Informal organizations are characterized by a status system that produces informal leaders. Informal group norms are powerful influences on member behavior.

Formal groups, which are established by the organization, include committees, task forces, and other decision-making groups. Formal group meetings are a widely used form of group activity; they can create quality decisions that are supported by the participants.

Four structured approaches commonly used in group problem solving are brainstorming, nominal groups, the Delphi technique, and dialectic inquiry. Weaknesses of groups fall into five categories: slowness and expensiveness, groupthink, polarization, escalating commitment, and divided responsibility. Promising developments are occurring in the areas of alternative group structuring techniques, contingency models, and group decision support systems.

		Terms and Concepts for Review
Brainstorming	Group dynamics	
Cohesiveness	Groupthink	
Committee	Hidden agendas	
Consensus	Informal groups	
Deferred judgment	Informal leader	
Delphi decision groups	Informal organization	
Devil's advocate	Network charts	
Dialectic decision method (DDM)	Nominal group	
Electronic brainstorming	Norms	
Escalating commitment	Polarization	
Formal groups	Reference group	
Group decision support system	Risky shift	

Sanctions   Surface agenda

Social facilitation   Task leader

308   Social leader

Discussion Questions

1. Think of a part-time or full-time job that you now hold or formerly held. Identify the informal organization that is (was) affecting your job or work group, and its effects. Discuss how the informal leaders probably rose to their positions and how they operate.

2. Have you ever been in a situation where informal group norms put you in role conflict with formal organization standards? Discuss.

3. Discuss some of the benefits and problems that informal organizations may bring to both a work group and an employer.

4. Think of a small work group that you belonged to recently. Assess the level of its cohesiveness. What factors contributed to, or prevented, its cohesiveness?

5. Thinking of that small group, explain in what ways the members' actions, interactions, and sentiments were different in practice from what they were supposed to be when the group was formed.

6. Identify five specific things you will do to create an effective committee the next time you are a leader or member of one.

7. Divide a sheet of notebook paper into five columns. In the first column, under the heading "Strengths," list all the strengths that any of the types of group structures might have (e.g., "generates many solutions"). Write the four types of structured approaches as headings for the remaining columns. Indicate, by placing a check in the appropriate column(s), which approaches might have each of the strengths you listed. (Notice that, in essence, you are preparing your own contingency model.)

8. What does consensus mean to you, from your experience? Has your understanding of it changed since reading this chapter? What other interpretations do you think the term has for other people?

9. The chapter mentions five major weaknesses of decision-making groups. Prepare a counterargument that powerfully describes some of the benefits of using groups.

10. A manager complained recently that "meetings are not as much fun anymore since we started using structured approaches to group problem solving." Explain why this might be so. In addition to "fun," what criteria should the manager be using to judge group success?

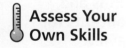 **Assess Your Own Skills**

How well do you exhibit good group leadership skills?

Read the following statements carefully. Circle the number on the response scale that most closely reflects the degree to which each statement accurately describes you when you have tried to lead a group or committee. Add up your total points and prepare a brief action plan for self-improvement. Be ready to report your score for tabulation across the entire group.

	Good description									Poor description
1. I am fully aware of the existence of the informal organization.	10	9	8	7	6	5	4	3	2	1
2. I actively seek to identify and utilize informal leaders to help accomplish my objectives.	10	9	8	7	6	5	4	3	2	1

3. I can readily list a half-dozen
   benefits of and problems with
   the informal organization.   10 9 8 7 6 5 4 3 2 1
4. I have used network charts to
   diagram an actual informal
   organization.   10 9 8 7 6 5 4 3 2 1
5. I understand why many people
   have negative attitudes toward
   committee meetings.   10 9 8 7 6 5 4 3 2 1
6. I can comfortably play both task
   and social leadership roles within
   a group.   10 9 8 7 6 5 4 3 2 1
7. I carefully monitor the interaction
   patterns within a committee
   meeting and take action to
   encourage a balance.   10 9 8 7 6 5 4 3 2 1
8. I have successfully used one of
   the structured approaches to
   group decision making.   10 9 8 7 6 5 4 3 2 1
9. I have a clear idea of what
   "consensus" means, and I
   communicate that to any group
   meeting I run.   10 9 8 7 6 5 4 3 2 1
10. I feel comfortable playing the role
    of devil's advocate in a group
    meeting.   10 9 8 7 6 5 4 3 2 1

Scoring and Interpretation   Add up your total points for the ten questions. Record that number here, and report it when it is requested. _____

- If you scored between 81–100 points, you appear to have a solid capability for demonstrating good group leadership skills.
- If you scored between 61–80 points, you should take a close look at the items with lower self-assessment scores and explore ways to improve those items.
- If you scored less than 60 points, you should be aware that a weaker skill level regarding several items could be detrimental to your future success as a motivator. We encourage you to review relevant sections of the chapter and watch for related material in subsequent chapters and other sources.

Now identify your three lowest scores, and write the question numbers here: _____, _____, _____. Write a brief paragraph, detailing to yourself an action plan for how you might sharpen each of these skills.

Excelsior Department Store   Incident

The Excelsior Department Store had a large department that employed six salesclerks. Most of these clerks were loyal and faithful employees who had worked in the department store more than ten years. They formed a closely knit social group.

The store embarked on an expansion program requiring four new clerks to be hired in the department within six months. These newcomers soon learned that the old-timers took the desirable times for coffee breaks, leaving the most undesirable periods for

310

newcomers. The old-time clerks also received priority from the old-time cashier, which required the newcomers to wait in line at the cash register until the old-timers had their sales recorded. A number of customers complained to store management about this practice.

In addition, the old-timers frequently instructed newcomers to straighten merchandise in the stockroom and to clean displays on the sales floor, although this work was just as much a responsibility of the old-timers. The result was that old-timers had more time to make sales and newcomers had less time. Since commissions were paid on sales, the newcomers complained to the department manager about this practice.

Questions

1. How is the informal organization involved in this case? Discuss.
2. As a manager of the department, what would you do about each of the practices? Discuss.

Choosing Your Leader

Experiential Exercise

1. Divide the class into groups of five to seven people. For the first ten minutes, have members introduce themselves by sharing not only their names but also other significant information (e.g., major accomplishments or future aspirations).
2. Now ask each group member to take out a piece of paper and write the name of the person who the member thinks would make the best leader of the small group. Then ask the members to collectively brainstorm, while recording the items on a sheet of paper, all the factors they used to select a leader (i.e., what characteristics were important to them?). Have them give all the slips to one person, who should tabulate the votes for leader. Have the new leader facilitate a discussion of the characteristics used to select him or her. Ask the groups to briefly discuss the validity of the selection process.
3. Now direct the groups to reflect on the discussion experience. Have them identify who the task and social leaders were, what the hidden agendas were, and who played the most assertive roles. How would they change their behavior if they were to do the exercise again?

Chapter 13

Teams and Team Building

Teamwork can be a great way for organizations to gain productivity, operate a redesigned operation, increase flexibility, reduce waste, and improve quality and customer satisfaction.

–Thomas R. Keen and Cherie N. Keen[1]

Like many management fads through the decades, teams haven't been exempt from overenthusiasm and mismanagement.

–David X. Swenson[2]

CHAPTER OBJECTIVES

TO UNDERSTAND

- Organizational Context for Teams
- The Nature of Teams
- Life Cycle of a Team
- Teamwork and the Characteristics of Mature Teams
- Process Consultation and Team-Building Skills
- Self-Managing Teams

Organizations are the grand strategies created to bring order out of chaos when people work together. Organizations provide the skeletal structure that helps create predictable relationships among people, technology, jobs, and resources. Wherever people join in a common effort, organization must be used to get productive results.

The necessity for organization—and the havoc of disorganization—are illustrated by disorganizing a short sentence: "riiggnagesnotztlsuse." In this form it is nonsense. Now let us reorganize it substantially: "organizinggetsresults." In this condition it is workable, but difficult. By the slight change of converting to a capital "O" and adding two spaces, it reads: "Organizing gets results." Yes, the organizing of people and things is essential for coordinated work.

In this chapter we introduce the key elements of classical and emerging organization design as they relate to organizational behavior. In particular, we show why many organizations have turned to various emphases on teams to overcome previous problems, provide employee need-satisfaction, and release the performance potential within groups. The need for careful development of teams is stressed, and a unique structure—self-managing teams—is explored.

ORGANIZATIONAL CONTEXT FOR TEAMS

Classical Concepts

Classical organization theory is the process of starting with the total amount of work to be done and dividing it into divisions, departments, work clusters, jobs, and assignments of responsibilities to people. Efficiency and integration of efforts are achieved by means of **division of work**—creating levels of authority and functional units—and **delegation**—assigning duties, authority, and responsibility to others. The result is an operating hierarchy, which is visually portrayed in an organization chart. Figure 13–1, for example, shows a simple organization consisting of four levels of authority, with nine operating units at the lowest level.

FIGURE 13–1

Likert's linking pin concept

Source: Adapted from *New Patterns of Management* by Rensis Likert, p. 13. Copyright © 1961 by McGraw-Hill Book Company.

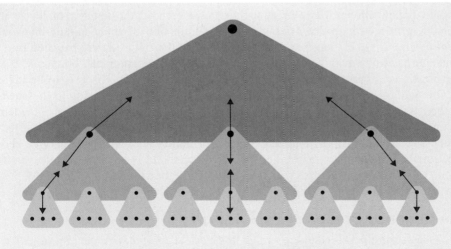

(The arrows illustrate the linking pin function.)

314

Each organization structures itself and uses delegation somewhat differently.[3] Some managers, for example, delegate more often than others do. One study of claims adjusters and their supervisors in an insurance company indicated that several factors apparently contributed to a higher degree of delegation. Among them were the supervisor's perceptions of subordinates as capable and trustworthy and the presence of a heavy workload on the supervisor. Delegation of authority is also more likely when supervisors believe that employees hold the necessary background information to make a wise decision and when the outcome of an employee's decision would create only minimal risk for the organization.

Classical organization design has its strengths as well as its weaknesses. For example, organizational structure can support people as well as suppress them. Classical structure provides much task support, such as specialized assistance, appropriate resources to perform the job, security, and fairly dependable conditions of work. On the other hand, although classical structure is strong in task support, *it is weak in psychological support.* What is needed is an organizational system that provides both task support and psychological support.

Managers as Linking Pins

Managers are links between groups.

When division of work and delegation are performed correctly, the result is an intricate web of relationships that links people into a smoothly working organization. Each level has functional teams that are linked to the next level above and below them. This is known as the linking pin concept, which is shown in Figure 13–1. Each manager serves as a **linking pin** connecting that manager's group with the remainder of the organization. If all linking pin connections are effective, then the organization can operate as an integrated whole. On the other hand, if there is a weakness anywhere in the chain of linking pins, the organization tends to be less effective.

When managers see themselves as linking pins uniting—and serving—the *whole* organization, they function more effectively. Maintaining such an organization-wide perspective can be difficult, especially when managers are held responsible for their *own* unit's results and are compensated on the basis of its performance. Nevertheless, when employees understand a manager's role as a linking pin for the whole organization, they can relate better to both their team and the organization as a whole and become more effective.

Decline in use of structure

New viewpoints are leading to a decline in the use of structure and authority in modern organizations. Many organizations have reduced the number of levels in their hierarchy through downsizing and the elimination of some middle-management positions. Others have attempted to eliminate the rigid barriers between functional units (known as "silos") by focusing on the creation of "boundaryless" organizations without artificial internal walls. The modern approach is to be more flexible with organizational systems, changing them rapidly according to the needs of their environment. One reason is changing social values, but it also is evident that horizontal relations between chains of command are more important for effectiveness than was formerly realized. Supervisory influence with peers, service people, suppliers, customers, and other chains of command is becoming more significant. The pace and complexity of work today make horizontal communication and flexible structures more necessary.

Contingency Organizational Design

As discussed in the preceding paragraph, *the trend is toward more contingency organizational design,* which recognizes that different organizational structures and processes are required for effectiveness in varying situations. Some major forces affecting the choice of structure are the organization's strategy, its technology, its size, and even the preferences of its top managers. Environments differ also, and what is an appropriate organizational design in one environment may not be appropriate in another. Since environments change over time, sometimes rapidly, *there is a special need for organizational designs to be flexible* so that they can be changed to best fit the changing environment.

The contingency point of view requires a fundamental change in philosophy from the traditional view that there are preferred ways of organizing that could remain relatively fixed over time. The next sections highlight these differences by contrasting two extreme organizational patterns and their likely use of teams. Then a flexible approach to organizing that creates a multitude of temporary project teams—the matrix structure—is reviewed.

Mechanistic and Organic Forms   Some of the earliest research on contingency design was by Tom Burns and George Stalker in Britain.[4] They distinguished between mechanistic and organic organizations. **Mechanistic organizations** fit the traditional hierarchical way of organizing. People are specialized into many activities that are directed by layers of supervision. Each higher level has more power and influence until the top is reached, where central direction of the whole organization takes place. Work is carefully scheduled, tasks are certain, roles are defined strictly, and most formal communication flows along the lines of hierarchy. The whole structure is organized like a well-designed machine and incorporates many of the characteristics of a bureaucracy.

Mechanistic characteristics

Organic organizations are more flexible and open. Tasks and roles are less rigidly defined, allowing people to adjust them to situational requirements. Communication is more multidirectional. It consists more of information and advice and joint problem solving rather than instructions and decisions. Authority and influence flow more directly from the person who has the ability to handle the problem at hand. Decision making is more decentralized, being shared by several levels and different functions. The organization also is more open to its environment.

Organic characteristics

Burns and Stalker showed that mechanistic forms are more effective than organic forms in certain situations. If tasks are stable and well defined, changing very little from month to month and year to year, a mechanistic form tends to be superior. If changes in the technology, market, and other parts of the environment are minimal, then a mechanistic structure seems to be more effective. Worker attitudes also are a contingency factor. If workers prefer more routine tasks and direction from others, then a mechanistic form better meets their needs. If they are threatened by ambiguity and insecurity, then a mechanistic approach is better.

Organic forms are more effective in other situations, and these situations tend to be more typical in the twenty-first century. Organic forms work better if the environment is dynamic, requiring frequent changes within the organization. They also work better when the tasks are not defined well enough to become routine. If employees seek autonomy, openness, variety, change, and opportunities to try new approaches, then an organic form is better. If they do not, a mechanistic form may still be preferred. *Teams are more likely to be used within an organic form of organization,* because they provide the flexibility that modern organizations require.

A contingency approach to organizing may be applied within an organization, with the result that various departments may be organized differently to meet their particular needs. The research department may have an organic structure, and the production department may require a mechanistic structure.

Matrix Organization

One development to meet changing organizational needs is **matrix organization.** It is an overlay of one type of organization on another so that there are two chains of command directing individual employees. It is used especially for large, specialized projects that temporarily require large numbers of technical people with different skills to work in project teams. A simple example of matrix organization is an annual United Way fund drive for contributions to community charities. It could be handled through the traditional hierarchy, but often it is assigned to a temporary hierarchy of employees as a part-time duty. They carry the assignment to completion and then the team is disbanded.

The effect of matrix structure is to separate some of the organization's activities into projects that then compete for allocations of people and resources. The traditional hierarchy provides the regular work group for an employee, but project groups are established temporarily for up to several years, as in Boeing's development of the 777 aircraft. Employees are assigned to a project for its limited life or as long as their specialty is needed on the project. As one assignment is completed, employees move back to permanent assignments in traditional departments, or they are assigned to other projects. In fact, an employee can be assigned part-time to two or more projects at the same time.

> Figure 13–2 portrays relationships of employees in Project Roger, a project in an electronics firm. It shows how ranks, peer relations, and supervisor-subordinate relationships vary between the permanent organizational structure and the matrix structure. With regard to rank, Diego's regular job places him in the fourth level of the permanent structure, but he has a key second-level rank in the matrix structure. With regard to peer relations, Georgia and Hart work in separate departments in the permanent organization, but they work together in the matrix organization. Concerning supervisor-subordinate relationships, Georgia works for Anne in the regular structure, but in the matrix structure she works for Carl, who is her peer in the regular structure.
>
> Together, Barb, Carl, Diego, Evan, Frank, and Izzy form a primary *project team* in the matrix system. In addition, Carl will be assisted by Georgia and Hart, while Jan and Kerry are temporarily reporting directly to Diego. In essence, matrix structure overlays one or more temporary project (team) structures simultaneously on the permanent organization.

Boundary roles

The Project Manager   In matrix organization a project manager (such as Diego) is established to direct all work toward completion of a major project, such as development of a new computer system. The project manager especially needs to have role adaptability to interact with people both within and without the structure. Project managers occupy **boundary roles** that require an ability to interact with a variety of groups in order to keep their project successful. They keep communication channels open and active by constantly sharing information with other units in, and out of, the organization. Each group has its own special language, values, and style of relationships, so project managers need to be sensitive and flexible in order to secure project needs from other groups. Since project managers often have relatively weak authority, their mission is best accomplished through communication, negotiation, development of challenging assignments, and powerful teamwork.

Effects of Matrix Organization   Matrix organization represents a dramatic change from simple organization structures, and its impact can vary from highly positive to negative. When first implemented, matrix structure can be confusing to its members. It requires multiple roles for people, and sometimes they get frustrated in

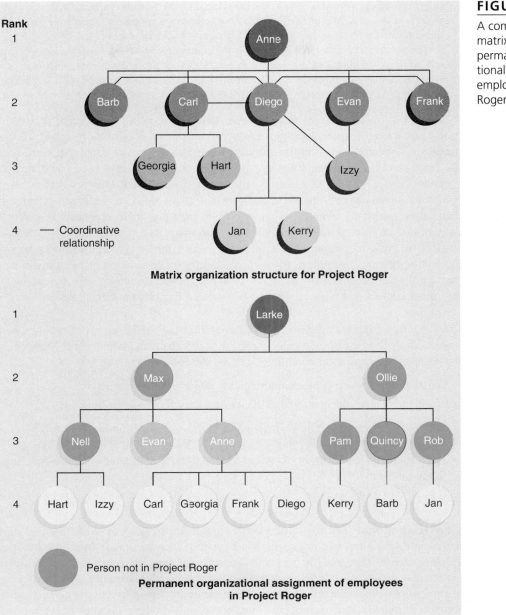

these ambiguous roles. Insecurities may arise over what will happen to them when the project is completed and the team is dissolved. The authority of the functional (line) manager who "loses" some staff temporarily may be diminished, while the problems of maintaining coordination and control increase. In addition, a condition called "projectitis" may arise, in which the commitment to the project team is so strong that unhealthy competition and rivalries appear. Some problems of the matrix form can be seen in the following illustration:

> The engineering division of an aircraft manufacturing firm was organized functionally, with separate groups for design, drafting, and testing.[5] A reorganization created a matrix struc-

ture, with project managers responsible for integrating the work on each of the development projects in progress. Measures of attitudes and behaviors were administered at various times and compared with those of a control group of employees in another location.

The most substantial effects occurred in the drafting group, where the physical relocation and work group restructuring were greatest. Although the quantity of communications increased, the quality declined. Role ambiguity increased, and both coordination and job satisfaction decreased. Surprisingly, employees did not report significant levels of role conflict.

In spite of its complexity, matrix organization is used for a number of reasons. It focuses on a single project, permitting better planning and control to meet budgets and deadlines. Especially on repetitive projects, the members gain valuable experience and the team develops a strong identity. Since the structure is more open and flexible (organic) than a traditional hierarchy, it can better handle the changes that occur in complex projects. Its distribution of authority and status also is more in agreement with democratic norms of technical employees. For example, more emphasis is given to authority of knowledge that a specialist can contribute to a project and less emphasis is given to rank in the permanent hierarchy. The matrix organization may improve motivation because people can focus more directly on completion of one project than they can in the traditional organization. It also improves communication by encouraging direct contact and reducing the inhibitions that result from formal rank.

Contingency Factors   Although matrix organization has limited application, where it does apply it is psychologically more advanced than traditional work hierarchies. Its use is contingent upon conditions such as the following:

- Existence of special projects, particularly major ones
- Need for diverse occupational skills, particularly higher-level ones
- Conditions of change during project operation
- Complex issues of coordination, problem solving, and scheduling
- High needs for authority of knowledge and expertise compared with existing functional authority
- Capacity of employees to understand teamwork and work within teams

Cross-Functional Teams   The matrix organizational process, when applied on a large scale across internal organizational boundaries, creates **cross-functional teams.** These are teams that draw their members from more than one specialty area and often several. By their very nature they contain a high element of diversity, at least in terms of professional backgrounds and work specializations. Cross-functional groups, while sometimes quickly constructed, pose special problems in the process of becoming true teams. Therefore, we will devote the remainder of this chapter to reviewing some key information regarding team formation, team building, and team operation.

TEAMWORK

Individual employees perform operating tasks, but the vast majority of them work in regular small groups where their efforts must fit together like the pieces of a picture puzzle. Where their work is interdependent, they act as a task team and seek to develop a cooperative state called teamwork. A **task team** is a cooperative small group in regular contact that is engaged in coordinated action. The frequency of team members' interaction and the team's ongoing existence make a task team clearly different from either a short-term decision-making group (committee) or a project team in a matrix structure.

When the members of a task team know their objectives, contribute responsibly and enthusiastically to the task, and support one another, they are exhibiting **teamwork.** At least four ingredients contribute to the development of teamwork: a supportive environment, skills matched to role requirements, superordinate goals, and team rewards. New teams typically progress through a series of developmental stages, which are described in the following section.

Contributors to teamwork

Life Cycle of a Team

When a number of individuals begin to work at interdependent jobs, they often pass through several stages as they learn to work together as a team (see Figure 13–3).[6] These **stages of team development** are not rigidly followed, but they do represent a broad pattern that may be observed and predicted in many settings across the team's time together. The stages are the result of a variety of questions and issues that the team predictably faces, such as those shown in Figure 13–3. In addition, members

FIGURE 13–3

Life cycle of a team and associated questions and issues faced at each stage

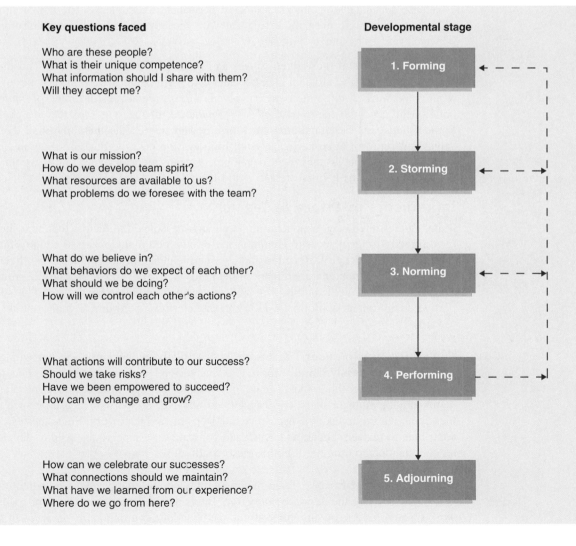

Key questions faced

Developmental stage

Who are these people?
What is their unique competence?
What information should I share with them?
Will they accept me?

1. Forming

What is our mission?
How do we develop team spirit?
What resources are available to us?
What problems do we foresee with the team?

2. Storming

What do we believe in?
What behaviors do we expect of each other?
What should we be doing?
How will we control each other's actions?

3. Norming

What actions will contribute to our success?
Should we take risks?
Have we been empowered to succeed?
How can we change and grow?

4. Performing

How can we celebrate our successes?
What connections should we maintain?
What have we learned from our experience?
Where do we go from here?

5. Adjourning

want to know which rules to follow and what each person should contribute. The typical stages in a team's evolution can be described as follows:

- *Forming*—Members share personal information, start to get to know and accept one another, and begin turning their attention toward the group's tasks. An aura of courtesy prevails, and interactions are often cautious.
- *Storming*—Members compete for status, jockey for positions of relative control, and argue about appropriate directions for the group. External pressures interfere with the group, and tensions rise between individuals as they assert themselves.
- *Norming*—The group begins moving together in a cooperative fashion, and a tentative balance among competing forces is struck. Group norms emerge to guide individual behavior, and cooperative feelings are increasingly evident.
- *Performing*—The group matures and learns to handle complex challenges. Functional roles are performed and fluidly exchanged as needed, and tasks are efficiently accomplished.
- *Adjourning*—Even the most successful groups, committees, and project teams disband sooner or later. Their breakup is called adjournment, which requires dissolving intense social relations and returning to permanent assignments. The adjournment stage is becoming even more frequent with the advent of flexible organizations, which feature temporary groups.

Advising teams of these likely stages can be helpful to group members and their leaders. Awareness by all team members can help them better understand what is happening and work through the issues involved. Groups are always different, of course; consequently, not all teams will clearly experience all the stages of the life cycle. Some groups may be temporarily stuck in a certain stage, and others may find themselves reverting to an earlier stage from time to time (see the dotted arrows in Figure 13–3). To expedite their own development, team members may find it useful to know what elements help create successful teams.

Ingredients of Effective Teams

Many studies have been conducted in an attempt to isolate the factors that contribute most directly to team success. Common items identified include careful composition, information sharing, clear direction and measurable goals for accountability, sufficient resources, integration and coordination, flexibility and innovativeness, and the stimulation of openness to learning.[7] We will focus on four major factors here—a supportive environment, appropriate skills and role clarity, superordinate goals, and team rewards.

Supportive Environment   Teamwork is most likely to develop when management builds a supportive environment for it. Creating such an environment involves encouraging members to think like a team, providing adequate time for meetings, and demonstrating faith in members' capacity to achieve. Supportive measures such as these help the group take the necessary first steps toward teamwork. Since these steps contribute to further cooperation, trust, and compatibility, supervisors need to develop an organizational culture that builds these conditions.

Skills and Role Clarity   Team members must be reasonably *qualified* to perform their jobs and have the *desire to cooperate*. Beyond these requirements, members can work together as a team only after all the members of the group *know the roles of all the others* with whom they will be interacting. When this understanding exists, members can act immediately as a team on the basis of the requirements of that situation, without waiting for someone to give an order. In other words, team members respond voluntarily to the demands of the job and take appropriate actions to accomplish team goals.

> An example is a hospital surgical team whose members all respond to a crisis during an operation. Their mutual recognition of the emergency alerts them to the need for simultaneous action and coordinated response. Each knows what the others can do, and trusts them to perform capably. The result is a highly efficient level of cooperation characteristic of a team.

If one member of a surgical team fails to perform in the right way at the right time, a person's life may be endangered. In more ordinary work situations, a life may not be in danger, but product quality or customer service may suffer by the failure of just one member. All the members are needed for effective teamwork. This interdependence is illustrated in Figure 13–4.

All members must contribute.

Superordinate Goals   A major responsibility of managers is to try to keep the team members oriented toward their overall task. Sometimes, unfortunately, an organization's policies, record-keeping requirements, and reward systems may fragment individual efforts and discourage teamwork. A district supervisor for a petroleum company tells the following story of the effect on sales representatives of below-quota reports:

> As in many businesses, each month we are expected to make our sales quota. Sales representatives are expected to make quotas in their individual territories in the same way that the Eastern district as a whole is expected to make its quota. Many times in the past the district has failed to make its quota in certain products—for instance, motor oil. It is a known practice for some of the sales representatives in the field to delay a delivery in their territories until the next month if they already have their quotas made.
>
>   The focus of the sales representatives is on their own quotas, not on the district quota. Any sales representative who is below quota in a product for a month must report the reason for the reduction. A sales representative who makes a large sale of several hundred gallons of motor oil to a customer knows that the next month or two that customer may not buy any oil, causing the representative to be below quota that month and to have to file a report.

The supervisor in the case just described might consider the creation of a **superordinate goal,** which is a higher goal that integrates the efforts of two or more persons. Superordinate goals can be attained only if all parties carry their weight. Such goals

FIGURE 13–4

Teamwork depends on the performance of every member.

What Is Needed fxr Teamwxrk?

My supervisxr txld me that teamwxrk depends xn the perfxrmance xf every single persxn xn the team. I ignxred that idea until my supervisxr shxwed me hxw my cxmputer keybxard perfxrms when just xne single key is xut xf xrder. All the xther keys xn my keybxard wxrk just fine except xne, but that xne destrxys the effectiveness xf the whxle keybxard. Nxw I knxw that even thxugh I am xnly xne persxn, I am needed if the team is tx wxrk as a successful team shxuld.

serve to focus attention, unify efforts, and stimulate more cohesive teams. For example, in a hospital meeting the leader said, "We are here to help the patient. Can we think of today's problem in those terms?" When the superordinate goal was recognized, several minor internal conflicts were resolved.

Team Rewards   Another element that can stimulate teamwork is the presence of team rewards. These may be financial, or they may be in the form of recognition. Rewards are most powerful if they are *valued* by the team members, perceived as *possible* to earn, and administered *contingent on the group's task performance.* In addition, organizations need to achieve a careful balance between encouraging and rewarding individual initiative and growth and stimulating full contributions to team success.[8] Innovative (nonfinancial) team rewards for responsible behavior may include the authority to select new members of the group, make recommendations regarding a new supervisor, or propose discipline for team members.

Potential Team Problems

Effective teams in action are a pleasure to observe. Members are committed to the firm's success, they share common values regarding product quality, safety, and customer satisfaction, and they share the responsibility for completing a project on schedule.

Changing Composition   Being complex and dynamic, teamwork is sensitive to all aspects of organizational environment. Like the mighty oak, teamwork grows slowly, but on occasion it declines quickly, like that same oak crashing to the forest floor. For example, too many changes and personnel transfers interfere with group relationships and prevent the growth of teamwork.

> An international company built a new plant in a community of about 1/2 million people where it already had three operating plants doing related work. The new plant was staffed for the most part by new hires, and within a short time excellent teamwork and productivity developed.
>
> In about three years there was a moderate layoff affecting all four plants. Since layoff was according to seniority among the four plants and since employees in the new plant had least seniority, people from the other plants forced new-plant employees into layoff. As a result, most teams in the newest plant received three to five transferees from other plants (about 25 to 50 percent of the team). Though these transfers-in were more experienced and had good records, teamwork was disrupted and deteriorated quickly. Visits for first aid tripled, accidents increased slightly, and production declined 30 to 50 percent. Nearly one year of effort and emotional strain was required to get the plant back on its feet. (We wonder if management considered these potential costs when it decided on the layoffs.)

It is rare that a team's composition remains constant from beginning to end of its task life. Members may be drafted onto higher-priority projects, they may experience a personal crisis and take a family medical leave, or they may be lured away to another company by better working conditions and rewards. And some teams—most notably those in the collegiate sports domain—automatically experience personnel changes as players depart for the professional arena or find other priorities in their lives. As a consequence, *most teams must learn to manage their internal turnover.*

How do they do this? The first key is to anticipate and accept that turnover within the team will happen and come to grips with that likelihood. The second is to develop a plan for managing team turnover right from the start. How much notice do they expect to receive? What steps must they engage in to obtain authorization to find new members? How will they recruit new additions? The third, and possibly most critical, step is to think through how best to integrate new members. How can they be made

Information technology has had powerful effects on individual behavior in organizations, and its effects are equally strong on social networks at the team level. Technology has allowed the emergence of **virtual teams**—groups that meet without all of their members being present in the same location. To overcome the inherent problems of coordination in virtual teams, Leigh Thompson suggests using one or more devices to substitute for daily face-to-face interaction. They include:

- A short, initial, face-to-face encounter to humanize fellow team members, which draws upon the practice of "schmoozing" (superficial social contacts)
- Temporary on-location projects among the virtual team members

- One-day videoconferences to introduce members, develop trust, and establish initial relationships
- Drop-in opportunities for isolated workers to touch bases with actual team members (advised for telecommuters, too, to overcome a feeling of loneliness)

Virtual teams, once thought to be unrealistic, are becoming commonplace on both a temporary and a permanent basis as organizations increasingly have global worksites.

Source: Leigh Thompson, *Making the Team: A Guide for Managers,* Saddle River, NJ: Prentice Hall, 2000.

---

to feel welcome? What background materials and training do they need to receive?[9] How long will it take them to get up to speed? How can they be helped to see the big picture as well as how each member fits into it? How will they be exposed to the team's values, norms, and objectives? In essence, a highly functioning team (functioning at the fourth stage as shown in Figure 13–3) needs to recognize a new member as an opportunity for its improvement (not a threat to its cohesiveness) and return at least briefly to earlier stages of the team development process.

Social Loafing   Other potential problems also exist. The departure from classical lines of authority may be difficult for some employees to handle responsibly. The extensive participation in decision making consumes large amounts of time. Experimentation with team activities may lead to charges of partiality from other employees. Also, the combination of individual efforts may not result in improved overall performance. For example, when employees think their contributions to a group cannot be measured, they may lessen their output and engage in **social loafing** (the free-rider effect). Causes of social loafing include a perception of unfair division of labor, a belief that coworkers are lazy, or a feeling of being able to hide in a crowd and therefore not be able to be singled out for blame. Social loafing may also arise if a member believes that others intend to withhold their efforts and thus he or she would be foolish not to do the same—the **sucker effect.**[10]

Social loafing

Since an improperly managed team can result in numerous problems, an effective manager needs to apply a contingency framework to determine whether to use a team approach. It is wise to analyze the nature of the task, the qualifications and desires of the participants, and the time and cost constraints. Many managers have found managing teams to be a whole new set of challenges after years of one-on-one supervision. (For example, see "What Managers Are Reading.)

TEAM BUILDING

Team members must work together to be effective; likewise, cooperation is needed among all the teams that make up the whole organization. Higher-level managers need to integrate all these groups into one collaborative group. To do this, managers often rely heavily on team building for both individual teams and large groups.[11] **Team building** encourages team members to examine how they work together, identify their weaknesses, and develop more effective ways of cooperating. The goal is to make the team more effective. High-performance teams accomplish their tasks, learn how to solve problems, and enjoy satisfying interpersonal relationships.[12]

Clues to Its Need

Not every team needs to engage in team building, nor does even a poor team need to devote constant attention to it. Many teams, however, could benefit from at least occasionally reexamining how they operate. Fortunately, a variety of clues can be detected that provide evidence when it is more appropriate to devote attention to the team-building process. These signals include:

- Interpersonal conflicts among team members, or between the team and its leader
- Low degree of team morale or low team cohesiveness
- Confusion or disagreement about roles within the team
- Large influx of new members
- Disagreement over the team's purpose and tasks
- Negative climate within the team, evidenced by criticism and bickering
- Stagnation within the team, with members resisting change and new ideas

In cases like these, it is likely that team building is called for and will have a positive effect on the team's functioning.

The Process

Teams work on task and process.

The team-building process follows the pattern shown in Figure 13–5. A highly participative process is used, with team members providing data and then using that data for self-examination. Often a skilled facilitator may assist the members in diagnosing and addressing a problem. Data are collected from individual group members and then fed back to the team for analysis. While the group works on development of action plans (their problem-solving *task* of the moment), members are also encouraged to direct equal attention toward the group's interaction *process*. By monitoring, examining, and adjusting its own actions, the group learns to evaluate and improve its own effectiveness. The result of this continuing process can be a high-performance team with high levels of morale and cooperation.

Specific Team-Building Issues

Team building usually focuses on one or more specific types of problems identified in the first stage of the developmental process portrayed in Figure 13–5. If team members seem to be unaware of, or in disagreement about, the *purpose* of the team, then the focus might best be placed on clarifying the goals and priorities of the team. When the team is confused about its *fit* within the larger organizational system, the focus might be on the nature of the organization's culture, its workplace facilities, its strategic directions, or the reward system. When there is confusion about *work relationships* between people and tasks, job functions may need definition, authority relationships might be revisited, and patterns of work flows might require clarification. When *interpersonal conflicts* seem to dominate the workplace, issues of respect and trust might be explored, listening skills might be reviewed, or various models for understanding interpersonal styles might be introduced. In effect, the best team-building approach is

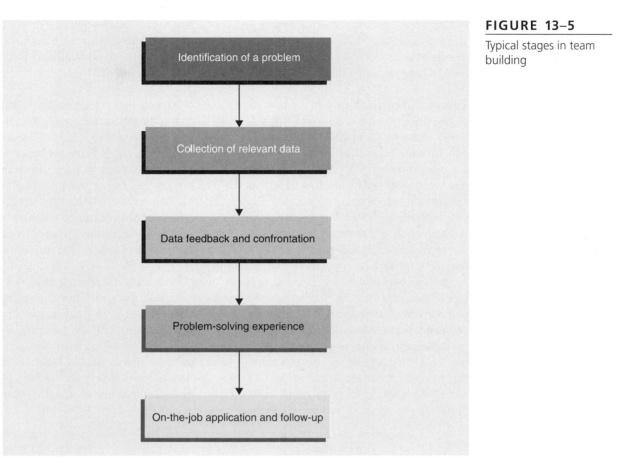

FIGURE 13–5

Typical stages in team building

325

one that is carefully built upon a database uncovered during the second stage and tailored to fit the specific team and team problem. The following illustration provides an example of a team-building approach that forces a team to confront issues of trust.[13]

Team building outdoors

A unique form of team building involves one of several varieties of "wilderness experiences."[14] In these courses, managers participate in week-long adventures such as mountain climbing, white-water rafting and kayaking, or outdoor obstacle courses. The physical challenge to survive is substantial, and many participants believe the experience prepares them for psychological survival in the corporate world.

Some programs have participants cross over raging rivers on wire cables, scale 13-foot-high walls, sleep on narrow mountain ledges, and cross imaginary snake pits on narrow boards and cinder blocks. Creativity and risk taking are encouraged, as are communication skills. Trust is essential, and groups recognize the importance of problem-solving skills. Team members learn to balance one another's strengths and weaknesses, and strong bonds of caring often emerge among members. A range of organizations from small (Fel-Pro, Inc.) to large (Martin Marietta and Xerox) have used wilderness experience laboratories with satisfactory results.

Skills Useful in Team Building

The facilitators who assist the development of effective teams need to apply a broad range of skills, including consultation skills (diagnosing, contracting, designing change), interpersonal skills (trust building, coaching, and listening, which is discussed in Chapter 3), research skills (planning and conducting a study and evaluating results), and presentational skills (public speaking and report preparation). Two additional and closely related skills stand out as critical to success—process consultation and feedback. These are skills that both team leaders and team members need.

Process Consultation   In contrast to the roles of experts (who share sophisticated technical information) and problem solvers (who define problems and suggest solutions), team building calls for yet another role—that of process consultant. **Process consultation** is a set of activities that help others focus on what is currently happening around them. In effect, the process consultant holds up a mirror to team members and helps them see themselves in action. The intent of process consultation is straightforward: to help team members perceive, understand, and react constructively to current behavioral events. Process consultants or team **facilitators** encourage employees to examine their intended versus their actual roles within the team, the ways in which the team discusses and solves problems, the use and abuse of power and authority, and the explicit and implicit communication patterns.

Process consultants observe, question, and confront.

Process consultants are helpers, drawing upon several key facilitating behaviors (see Figure 13–6).[15] They observe team meetings, recording conversational patterns and nonverbal behaviors. They ask probing questions designed to help others identify problems. They resist "owning" the team's problems, taking them off the hook, or giving expert advice. If necessary, they *confront* individuals by asking them to examine their behavior and its consequences or to explore new alternatives. All the while, the process consultant is attempting to *help other people learn to help themselves.* In other words, the goal is to create independence in team members so that they can more effectively think and act for themselves.

> Meg, a manager and successful team leader, was invited to attend a staff meeting of a community service organization she belonged to. She listened intently for the first half hour, often biting her tongue to remind herself not to engage in discussing the subject before the group. Soon the conversation strayed to several unrelated topics. Sarah turned to Meg and asked, "Should we stay more closely focused on the main topic?" Without answering yes or no, Meg used Sarah's question as an opportunity to highlight a group member's sensitivity to a process issue. In this way she hoped to encourage Sarah and others to be even more attentive to the group's processes in the future. Meg was acting as a process consultant at that moment.

FIGURE 13–6

Process consultants use facilitating behaviors to help teams function more effectively.

Facilitating Behaviors	Desired Effects on Team Members
• Encouraging open communication	• Examine intended versus actual roles
• Observing team meetings	• Identify problems
• Probing and questioning	• Examine consequences of behavior
• Confronting individuals	• React constructively to current behavioral events
• Stimulating problem solving	
• Attending to nonverbal cues	• Explore new alternatives
• Encouraging learning	• Think and act independently

Feedback   Team members need feedback so that they have useful data on which to base decisions. Feedback encourages them to understand how they are seen by others within their team and to take self-correcting action. Following is an example of a feedback exercise in one team-building program:

> Participants are separated into two groups representing two different viewpoints that exist in the team. Both groups are asked to develop answers to the following questions:
>
> • What characteristics best describe our group?
> • What characteristics best describe the other group?
> • How will the other group describe us?
>
> After the separate groups have prepared their answers, they assemble and present their answers to the other group. They give concrete feedback about impressions each group has of the other, and major misunderstandings are often uncovered. In this presentation no arguments are allowed. Questions are accepted only to *clarify* what the other group is saying.
>
> The groups again are separated to discuss two other questions:
>
> • How did these misunderstandings occur?
> • What can we do to correct them?
>
> With this new feedback, the groups meet to develop specific plans of action for solving their misunderstandings. In each instance feedback about themselves is the basis for their next activities.

Any team can use process consultation and feedback for its self-development. The need for continuous improvement is a cornerstone of total quality management programs, and a focus on teams is a critical structural element of many organizations as they operate in the twenty-first century.

Characteristics of Mature Teams

When teams regularly find themselves achieving and even surpassing their goals, they have attained the fourth stage of the team development model (see Figure 13–3). Is this realistic to expect? Yes. Many teams have become highly effective, although it seldom happens overnight. Even the United States Dream Team (men's Olympic basketball squad) struggles a bit every four years as team members learn their roles, assist each other, and adapt to a new coach and new rules.

What do most successful teams look like? They typically exhibit several characteristics that organizations value. Members take pride in their achievements and the contributions of their colleagues; they feel comfortable asking questions when they don't understand something; no one dominates the team, nor is anyone a wallflower or noncontributor; members know how to criticize others constructively and accept feedback from others; there is an atmosphere of respect and trust; the group is not threatened by instability or change; the atmosphere is relatively informal and tension-free; and members encourage and assist each other. "They are," as one team member put it, "a joy to behold, and to be a part of." Most of all, of course, the team consistently achieves its goals and sets progressively higher standards for itself.

Individual Territories versus Team Spaces

The use of teams at work increased at an astounding pace during the past decade. As a consequence, one interesting office design issue that arose was the use of physical space for employees. Specifically, managers needed to decide whether to provide enclosed work cubicles for each employee or to create a more open, landscaped work area with lower, or no, partitions between work spaces. A basic issue revolves around

Ethical Dilemmas within Teams

Team members often find themselves facing various dilemmas, problems for which no easy solutions are apparent. What would *you* do in each of these situations?

- *Team member appraisals*—Do you tell a teammate what is bugging you and risk offending the person, or do you withhold your feelings and let the group suffer?
- *Member assistance*—Several teammates stop by to ask if you need any help. You don't, but if you continue rejecting their offers, will they feel you are not a team player?
- *Team selection*—Your teammates want to hire new members who are similar to themselves. This approach is tempting for compatibility reasons, but how will you ever achieve greater diversity in the team?
- *Team perfection*—Enormous time and effort is spent on becoming the ideal team. However, you wonder if the team is losing its focus on the customer through its dominant focus on process.
- *Team rewards*—The team is rewarded on the basis of achieving its own performance goals. Yet, you wonder if such rewards prevent the team from seeing the larger organizational picture.

Territorial needs

the desire of some employees for privacy and personal space while they work. Many workers feel a need to establish their own **employee territories**—spaces they can call their own, within which they can control what happens. Cubicles provide an opportunity for them to have their own territory, design and modify their work layout, and even decorate to their own satisfaction.

Alternatively, a team-based organization may want a layout that encourages easy interaction, an exchange of ideas among employees engaged in related tasks, and a stronger feeling of team identity. Some firms have accomplished this goal by creating offices designed as activity settings, which include both home-base areas for privacy and bullpen areas for group interaction. These settings have proved especially effective for providing employees with a way to escape from their computer termi-

Social neighborhoods

nals for short periods of time. Other organizations have created **neighborhoods of offices,** which are centers of related individual offices to encourage the formation of social groups. This layout builds on the idea that proximity, or closeness, creates greater opportunities for interaction. The social groups that form contribute substantially toward satisfying employee needs for belonging.

Self-Managing Teams

One of the empowerment tools introduced in Chapter 8—**self-managing teams**—is also known as *self-reliant* or *self-directed teams.* They are natural work groups that are given substantial autonomy and in return are asked to control their own behavior and produce significant results. The *combination of empowerment and training* to plan, direct, monitor, and control their own activities distinguishes these teams from many others. They have wide-ranging autonomy and freedom, coupled with the capability to act like managers.

What is a self-managing team like? Typically, team members learn a wide range of relevant skills; this practice is called **multi-skilling.** As a result, members can flexibly float from area to area and task to task, depending on where they are needed most. They make joint decisions about work schedules, resource requirements, and assignment of tasks. Considerable time is spent in team meetings as members progressively take over many tasks that were formerly their manager's. Self-managing teams may begin by assuming responsibility for simple matters such as housekeeping issues and safety training. Later, they may begin to manage their own absenteeism, set overtime and vacation schedules, select and appraise team members, train coworkers, and engage in direct contact with key customers.[16] As they gain additional experience, these teams may even move beyond operational topics to refine their organization's mission statement, carve out a new compensation system, or provide input into expansion plans. Here is one example of self-managing teams in operation:

> Twenty firms were studied that each allowed work teams to hire, orient, and train new employees.[17] The firms reported that they were very satisfied with the quality of the employees selected, while risks of legal problems or simply bad decisions were minimized through careful training in using job-based criteria. The increased cost of having multiple sets of hiring teams was offset by low turnover of the individuals hired. The organizations in the survey especially valued the smooth acceptance of the new member by the team, which occurred as a result of the team's commitment to helping the new individual succeed (thus proving the wisdom of the team's selection decision).

Organizations using self-managing teams report several advantages:

- Improved flexibility of staff
- More efficient operations through the reduced number of job classifications
- Lower absenteeism and turnover rates
- Higher levels of organizational commitment and job satisfaction

By contrast, the disadvantages of this approach include

- The extended time to implement them (often covering several years)
- The high training investment
- Early inefficiencies due to job rotation
- The inability of some employees to adapt to a team structure

Self-managing teams are a powerful example of the application of OB knowledge about teamwork and successful participative methods. As a result, they are likely to increase in organizational use for several reasons. As a formal practice they are not likely to lose organizational support; they often directly involve 100 percent of the workforce; they wield substantial authority in many cases; and they are ongoing structures (not devoted to a single issue). However, firms have found that it may take

Traditional Structure	Self-Managing Team Structure
Authority figure	Coach and counselor
Expert	Champion and cheerleader
Teacher	Resource allocator
Problem solver	Liaison and boundary manager
Coordinator	Facilitator

FIGURE 13–7

Contrasting supervisory roles

1. Assess whether your employer exhibits more of the mechanistic or the organic characteristics of organizations. Then determine what drives this choice—inertia or rational assessment of the firm's competitive environment.

2. Resolve now to make yourself flexible enough to feel comfortable working in a matrix organization, in which you might have to report to multiple project managers.

3. Become an astute observer/analyst of teams, and try to assess whether they are in stage 1, 2, 3, or 4 of the team life cycle (refer to Figure 13–3).

4. Be on the alert for signs that the team you are in or managing is succumbing to some classic pitfalls. Take positive action to overcome these before they become magnified.

5. Read, study, observe others, and develop your own skills so that you can become effective at team building, process consultation, and providing feedback.

6. Prepare yourself for the possibility that you might be asked to create a self-managing team from a traditional one, with the associated role changes that switch would bring about for you.

several years for the teams to achieve their full potential. Cultural values emphasizing individualism can get in the way; rigid job classifications protected by labor contracts can be impediments; and managers can feel threatened by the loss of control and personal job security. Figure 13–7 portrays the sharp contrast between traditional supervisory roles and those required under a self-managing team structure.[18]

SUMMARY

Classical organization structures did not rely heavily on teams, despite the division of work into functional units and multiple levels. Managers played key roles as linking pins between units. More recently, organizations find that their structure needs to exist in a contingency relationship with their environments. Generally, mechanistic organization is more appropriate for stable environments, whereas organic organization is more appropriate in dynamic environments. Both the organic form and the matrix structure provide useful ways to adapt to turbulent environments, especially where large technical tasks are involved. Frequently, project teams are formed, which provide both a social relationship for workers and a valuable device for combining the talents of diverse workers.

Teams are cooperative groups that maintain regular contact and engage in coordinated action. They strive to achieve a high degree of teamwork, which is aided by a supportive environment, proper skills, superordinate goals, and team rewards. Newly formed teams often move through a series of developmental stages. Team building is an important and continuing process, which can be aided by managerial attention to process consultation (facilitation) and feedback skills.

Self-managing teams are empowered groups that are provided with the training, resources, and authority to assume responsibility for many management-level functions. They represent a creative and challenging way to formally tap the power of teams to help accomplish organizational goals. Employees gain, too, through greater autonomy and skill development.

Terms and Concepts for Review

Boundary roles	Employee territories
Cross-functional teams	Facilitators
Delegation	Linking pin
Division of work	Matrix organization

330

Mechanistic organizations	Stages of team development
Multi-skilling	Sucker effect
Neighborhoods of offices	Superordinate goal
Organic organizations	Task team
Process consultation	Team building
Self-managing teams	Teamwork
Social loafing	Virtual teams

Discussion Questions

1. Discuss how the linking pin concept can be a way to build a unified team within a whole organization.
2. Discuss the differences between mechanistic and organic organizations. What is the likely role of teams within each one?
3. Explain how matrix organization works. What are its strengths and weaknesses? What situations are more appropriate for its use?
4. Explain the relationship between a matrix organization and the use of cross-functional teams.
5. How do temporary groups and committees (discussed in Chapter 12) compare with teams? What are their similarities and differences?
6. Review the typical stages in a team's life cycle. Think of a time when you were a member of a work team. Were all those stages represented? Did they appear in a different order? Did some of them emerge more than once? Explain.
7. Assume that you are to be placed in charge of a student group in this class. Outline the key action steps you will take to make sure that the group develops into a real team.
8. Think of a time when you observed, or exhibited, social loafing. What contributed to it? How could it have been prevented or minimized?
9. Think about self-managing teams. Would you like to work in one? Why or why not?
10. The authors assert that "it may take several years for [self-managing] teams to achieve their full potential." Why might this be so? How could the process be shortened?

Assess Your Own Skills

How well do you exhibit good team management skills?

Read the following statements carefully. Circle the number on the response scale that most closely reflects the degree to which each statement accurately describes you when you have tried to participate in, or lead, a team. Add up your total points and prepare a brief action plan for self-improvement. Be ready to report your score for tabulation across the entire group.

	Good description									Poor description
1. I know the key differences between a group and a task team.	10	9	8	7	6	5	4	3	2	1
2. I can identify the developmental stage of a team by assessing which questions the members are currently addressing.	10	9	8	7	6	5	4	3	2	1
3. I could explain to a prospective team the key ingredients that will make them successful.	10	9	8	7	6	5	4	3	2	1

4. I could effectively help my team integrate a new member into its operations.	10	9	8	7	6	5	4	3	2	1
5. I know the major symptoms that ineffective teams exhibit.	10	9	8	7	6	5	4	3	2	1
6. I could choose the appropriate team-building focus, based upon the underlying problems that exist within the team.	10	9	8	7	6	5	4	3	2	1
7. I can comfortably apply many of the skills that are needed in process consultation.	10	9	8	7	6	5	4	3	2	1
8. I could list a half-dozen of the characteristics of successful mature teams.	10	9	8	7	6	5	4	3	2	1
9. I could explain the pros and cons of different uses of physical space to team members.	10	9	8	7	6	5	4	3	2	1
10. I am capable of moving from the traditional roles of a supervisor to those required by self-managing teams.	10	9	8	7	6	5	4	3	2	1

Scoring and Interpretation   Add up your total points for the ten questions. Record that number here, and report it when it is requested. _____

- If you scored between 81–100 points, you appear to have a solid capability for demonstrating good team management skills.
- If you scored between 61–80 points, you should take a close look at the items with lower self-assessment scores and explore ways to improve those items.
- If you scored less than 60 points, you should be aware that a weaker skill level regarding several items could be detrimental to your future success as a team leader. We encourage you to review relevant sections of the chapter and watch for relevant material in subsequent chapters and other sources.

Now identify your three lowest scores, and write the question numbers here: _____, _____, _____. Write a brief paragraph, detailing to yourself an action plan for how you might sharpen each of these skills.

Incident

Conflict in the Division

The engineering division of a firm consists of four departments, with the supervisor of each reporting to the division general manager (GM). The four departments range in size from two employees in the smallest (industrial engineering) to fourteen in the largest (sales engineering). The other two departments (design engineering and process engineering) each have eight employees.

Intense interdepartmental rivalry frequently arises over the allocation of resources. This problem is compounded by the favoritism that the GM allegedly shows toward the industrial and design engineering units and his reliance on majority-rule decision making (among his four supervisors and himself) at staff meetings. This practice, complain the supervisors of the sales and process engineering departments, often results in the leaders of the industrial and design engineering departments forming a coalition with the GM to make a decision, even though they represent only ten of the thirty-two employees. In response, the industrial and design engineering supervisors charge the supervisors of the sales and process engineering units with empire building, power plays, and a narrow view of the mission of the division.

Question
You are a friend of the GM, called in from another division to help resolve the problem. Outline the approach you would recommend that the GM take.

Readiness for Self-Managing Teams

Assume that you are the new owner of a fast-food restaurant employing approximately seventy-five employees across two shifts. Most of the employees are relatively young and inexperienced, but willing to learn. You are trying to decide to what degree to involve them in various decisions, in addition to their specific job assignments. In the list below indicate, with a check in the first column, those roles and responsibilities for which you are inclined to allow them to take control. Then discuss the issue with three or four other students. Combine your perspectives and indicate the group's response in the second column. Finally, review the pattern of items selected, and determine the apparent rationale used by the group for its choices.

	Col. 1 (Individual)	Col. 2 (Group)
1. Training new coworkers	_____	_____
2. Ordering food supplies	_____	_____
3. Conducting safety meetings	_____	_____
4. Disciplining tardy employees	_____	_____
5. Making minor equipment repairs	_____	_____
6. Selecting new coworkers	_____	_____
7. Recording hours worked	_____	_____
8. Making job assignments	_____	_____
9. Conducting problem-solving meetings	_____	_____
10. Dismissing unproductive workers	_____	_____

Team Building

Divide into groups of about five persons. In just a few minutes for each of the following tasks, develop a collective response and be prepared to share it with the class.

1. Select a unique *name* for your team.
2. Select a unique *cheer* for your team.
3. Select a unique *motto* (slogan) for your team.
4. Select a unique *color* (or set of colors) for your team.
5. Identify three things that each member *has in common* with all the others.
6. Identify one key *strength* that each member brings to the team.

7. Working together, and without any aids, answer these questions:
   a. How many centimeters long is a dollar bill?
   b. At what temperature are Fahrenheit and Centigrade equal?
   c. Who is the Chief Justice of the Supreme Court?
   d. What letter do the greatest number of words in the dictionary begin with?
   e. How many U.S. presidents are still alive, and who are they?

Share your answers to questions 1–7 with the class, and then discuss how those rather trivial exercises helped you to feel like a functioning team. What else could you do to continue your development as a team?

Part Six

Change and Its Effects

Chapter 14

Managing Change

Competent people resist change. Why? Because change threatens to make them less competent. And competent people like being competent.
                                                              —Seth Godin[1]

On the road to the future, there are drivers, there are passengers, and there is road kill.
                                    —Thomas S. Bateman and J. Michael Crant[2]

CHAPTER OBJECTIVES

TO UNDERSTAND

- The Nature of Change

- Costs and Benefits of Change

- Resistance to Change

- Basic Frameworks for Interpreting Change

- Role of Transformational Leadership in Change

- Practices to Build Support for Change

- Meaning and Characteristics of OD

- Benefits and Limitations of OD

"Life used to be so simple," lamented an independent logger in northern Minnesota. "My father cut the trees, hauled them to a sawmill, and got paid. The demand for wood was quite stable, the supply of trees was plentiful, and his logging equipment consisted of a chain saw, an axe, and a truck. Life was good in those days."

"So what is different now?" the logger was asked.

"Absolutely everything," he replied. "Current logging rigs cost hundreds of thousands of dollars. I need governmental permits for everything I do. Environmental groups protest against logging. Demand for my logs fluctuates wildly. And cutthroat competition makes it tough for me to make a buck anymore. I'm not sure I can keep my head above water."

The Minnesota logger is experiencing firsthand three facts of life about change: It is everywhere, it is constant, and its pace is accelerating. It is all around people—in the seasons, in their social environment, and in their own biological processes. Beginning with the shockingly new surroundings after birth, a person learns to meet change by being adaptive. A person's very first breath depends on the ability to adapt from one environment to another that is dramatically different. Throughout the rest of their lives, each hour of the day offers people new experiences and challenges.

Organizations are also encountering a wide variety of dramatic changes. Some face greater federal regulation, while others experience deregulation; some are more splintered, while others consolidate; some find their markets shrinking, while others find themselves thrown headlong into a global marketplace. Many organizations have experienced mergers or hostile takeovers, while others have implemented devastating downsizing programs producing wrenching psychological and economic effects on their employees. To survive, organizations need to decide not *whether* to change, but *when* and *how* to make it occur most successfully.

Human beings are certainly familiar with change and often prove themselves quite adaptive to it. Why, then, do they often resist change in their work environment? This question has troubled managers since the beginning of the industrial revolution. The faster pace of change required by the electronic age, of the shift to a service economy, and of the growth of global competition has made the solution to this question even more important. Even when managers use their most logical arguments and persuasive skills to support a change, they frequently discover that employees remain unconvinced of the need for it. This chapter examines the nature of change, reasons for resistance to it, and ways to introduce it more successfully, including organization development.

CHANGE AT WORK

The Nature of Change

Change is any alteration occurring in the work environment that affects the ways in which employees must act. These changes may be planned or unplanned, catastrophic or evolutionary, positive or negative, strong or weak, slow or rapid, and stimulated either internally or externally.[3] Regardless of their source, nature, origin, pace, or strength, changes can have profound effects on their recipients.

The effects of change can be illustrated by comparing an organization to an air-filled balloon. When a finger (which represents external change in this case) is pressed against a point on the balloon (which represents the organization), the contour of the balloon visibly changes (it becomes indented) at the point of contact. Here an obvious

338

Effects are widespread.

pressure, representing change, has produced an obvious deviation at the point of pressure. What is not so obvious, however, is that the entire balloon (the rest of the organization) has also been affected and has stretched slightly. In addition, the tension against the inner surface of the balloon has increased (not, it is hoped, to the breaking point). As shown by this illustration, a safe generalization is that *the whole organization tends to be affected by change in any part of it.*

The molecules of air in the balloon represent a firm's employees. It is apparent that those at the spot of pressure must make drastic adjustments. Though the change did not make direct contact with the employees (molecules), it has affected them indirectly. Though none is fired (i.e., leaves the balloon), the employees are displaced and must adjust to a new location in the balloon. This comparison illustrates an additional generalization: *Change is a human as well as a technical problem.*

Human and technical problem

The comparison using a balloon may be carried further. Repeated pressure at a certain point may weaken the balloon until it breaks. So it is with an organization. Changes may lead to pressures and conflicts that eventually cause a breakdown somewhere in the organization. An example is an employee who becomes dissatisfied and resigns.

Admittedly, the foregoing comparison is rough. An employing institution is not a balloon; a person is not a molecule; and people are not as free and flexible as air molecules in a balloon. What has been illustrated is a condition of molecular equilibrium. Organizations, too, tend to achieve an *equilibrium* in their social structure—a state of relative balance between opposing forces. This equilibrium is established when people develop a relatively stable set of relations with their environment. They learn how to deal with one another, how to perform their jobs, and what to expect next. Equilibrium exists; employees are adjusted. When change comes along, it requires them to make new adjustments as the organization seeks a new equilibrium. When employees are unable to make adequate adjustments, the organization is in a state of unbalance, or disequilibrium.

This disequilibrium highlights a dilemma for managers. On the one hand, the manager's role is to *introduce* continual organizational changes so as to bring about a better fit between the firm and its environment. Here, the manager's role is to be **proactive**—anticipating events, initiating change, and taking control of the organization's destiny. On the other hand, part of the manager's role is to *restore and maintain the group equilibrium* and personal adjustment that change upsets. In this role the manager is more **reactive**—responding to events, adapting to change, and tempering the consequences of change.

Proactive and reactive roles

Fortunately, many of the organizational changes that occur on a daily basis are somewhat minor. They may affect only a few people, and they may be incremental in nature and relatively predictable. For example, as new procedures evolve or as new members are added to a work group, existing employees generally do not need to change all dimensions of their jobs or acquire totally new behaviors. In such situations a new equilibrium may be reached readily.

A wide variety of forces, however, may bring about more dramatic changes that touch the entire core of an organization. Many of these have become much more common as the economy, competition, and pace of technological change have become more volatile. Examples include hostile takeovers of firms, leveraged buyouts and subsequent organizational restructuring, reengineering of organizations, acts of public terrorism, and natural disasters like oil spills and gas leaks. Crises like these, whether positive or negative, demand that managers help guide employees through the emotional shock that accompanies them, thereby bringing the organization to a new equilibrium.

Responses to Change

Work change is further complicated by the fact that it does not produce a direct adjust- **339**
ment, unlike the adjustment of air molecules in the balloon. Instead, *it operates through
each employee's attitudes* to produce a response that is conditioned by feelings toward
the change. This relationship was illustrated in a series of classical experiments—the
Hawthorne studies, conducted by F. J. Roethlisberger and his associates. In one instance
lighting was improved regularly according to the simplistic theory that better lighting *Experiments relating*
would lead to greater productivity. As was expected, productivity did increase. Then *lighting to productivity*
lighting was decreased to illustrate the reverse effect—reduced productivity. Instead,
productivity increased further. Lighting was again decreased. The result was still
greater productivity. Finally, lighting was decreased to 0.06 foot-candle, which is
approximately equivalent to moonlight. According to Roethlisberger, "Not until this
point was reached was there any appreciable decline in the output rate."[4]

How Individual Attitudes Affect Response to Change   Obviously, better lighting was not by itself causing greater output. There was no direct connection between
the change and the response. Some other intervening variable, later diagnosed as
employee attitudes, had crept in to upset the expected pattern. Roethlisberger later
explained the new pattern in the following way: Each change is interpreted by individuals according to their attitudes. *The way that people feel about a change is one
factor that determines how they will respond to it.* These feelings are not the result
of chance; they are caused. One cause is *personal history,* which refers to people's
biological processes, their backgrounds (e.g., family, job, education), and all their
social experiences away from work (see Figure 14–1). This history is what they bring
to the workplace. A second cause is the *work environment* itself. It reflects the fact
that workers are members of a group and their attitudes are influenced by its codes,
patterns, and norms.

   Feelings are not a matter of logic. They are neither logical nor illogical, but entirely *Feelings are nonlogical.*
apart from logic. They are *nonlogical.* Feelings and logic belong in two separate cat-
egories, just as inches and pounds do. For that reason, *logic alone is an ineffective
means of trying to modify feelings* because it does not get at them directly. Feelings
are not much better refuted by logic than this book's length in inches or centimeters
is refuted by its weight in pounds or kilograms.

The Hawthorne Effect   One cause of favorable feelings in the groups studied by
Roethlisberger was the interest shown by the researchers in employee problems. This
phenomenon later was called the **Hawthorne effect,** named after the factory where

Effects of a Diverse Workforce on Change

The workforce in the United States will become increasingly diverse (from a gender and
ethnic perspective) as we move into the twenty-first century. New jobs will be filled by
higher proportions of females, African-Americans, Hispanics, and Asians than ever
before. In addition, the typical education level of workers in this country has gradually
increased. What predictions can you make about the impact of these changes on the
employer's *likelihood* to change? On the employer's *capacity* to change? On the worker's
receptivity to change?

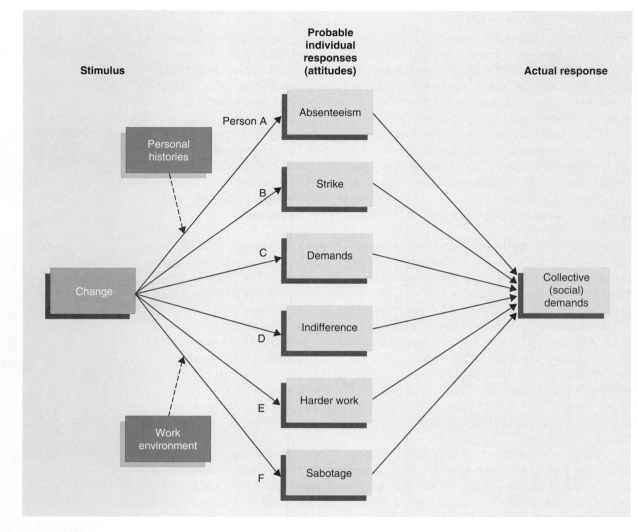

FIGURE 14–1

Unified social response to change

Observation affects behavior.

the research took place. The Hawthorne effect means that the mere observation of a group—or more precisely, the *perception* of being observed and one's *interpretation* of its significance—tends to change the group. *When people are observed, or believe that someone cares about them, they act differently.* These changes usually are unintended and not recognized. They contaminate the research design, but normally they cannot be prevented.

Group Response to Change   People interpret change individually and have their own probable response to it. However, they often show their attachment to the group by joining with other group members in some uniform response to the change, as shown in the "actual response" in Figure 14–1. This uniformity makes possible such seemingly illogical actions as walkouts when obviously only a few people actually want to walk out. Other employees who are unhappy seize upon the walkout as a chance to show their dissatisfaction and to confirm their affiliation with the group by joining with it in social action. Basically, the group responds with the feeling, "We're all in this together. Whatever happens to one of us affects all of us." John Donne, the seventeenth-century English poet, beautifully stated the philosophy of this relationship, as follows:

No man is an Iland, *intire of it selfe;*
every man is a peece of the Continent,
a part of the maine; if a Clod *be washed away*
by the Sea, Europe is the lesse, as well as if a
Promontorie *were, as well as if a* Mannor *of thy friends*
or of thine owne *were; any man's death diminishes me,*
because I am involved in Mankinde:
And therefore never send to know for whom the bell tolls;
It tolls for thee.[5]

Homeostasis   In trying to maintain equilibrium, a group is often inclined to engage in **backsliding**—to return to its perceived best way of life whenever any change occurs. Each pressure, therefore, elicits a counterpressure within the group. The net result is a self-correcting mechanism by which energies are called up to restore balance whenever change threatens. This self-correcting characteristic of organizations is called **homeostasis;** that is, people act to establish a steady state of need fulfillment and to protect themselves from disturbance of that balance. They want to maintain their previous sense of competence.

Costs and Benefits

All changes are likely to have some costs. For example, a new work procedure may require the inconvenience of learning new skills. It temporarily may disrupt work and reduce satisfaction. There also may be the cost of new equipment or relocation of old equipment. These costs are not merely economic; they also are psychological and social. They usually must be paid in order to gain the benefits of proposed changes.

Because of the costs associated with change, proposals for change are not always desirable. They require careful analysis to determine usefulness. Each change requires a detailed cost-benefit analysis. Unless changes can provide benefits above costs, there is no reason for the changes. It is illogical to emphasize benefits while ignoring costs. The organizational goal always is *benefits greater than costs.*

In a determination of benefits and costs, all types must be considered.[6] It is useless to examine only economic benefits and costs, because even if there is a net economic benefit, the social or psychological costs may be too large. Although it is not very practical to reduce psychological and social costs to numbers, they must nevertheless be included in the decision-making process. Almost any change, for example, involves some psychological loss because of the strain that it imposes on people as they try to adjust. Psychological costs also are called **psychic costs** because they affect   *Psychic costs*
a person's inner self, the psyche.

Knowledge of individual differences helps us predict that *people will react in different and widely varying ways to change.* Some will perceive only the benefits, while others see only what it costs them. Others will react fearfully at first, even though all the effects are actually positive for them. Others will appear initially to embrace the change but then gradually let their real feelings emerge.

Some people who have observed common reactions to traditional change efforts contend that the 20-50-30 rule applies.[7] According to this distribution of responses, about 20 percent of employees affected by a change will be receptive and possibly strongly supportive; about 50 percent will be rather neutral toward the change and possibly even open-minded and receptive; and about 30 percent will be close-minded, resist the change, and possibly attempt to sabotage it. The challenge for managers of a change process is to transform the 80 percent (neutrals and resisters) into supporters of the change for it to succeed.

342

In some cases the psychic costs of change can be so severe that they affect the psychological and even the physical health of employees. The tolerance level for change within a group of employees can range from relatively high for one person to relatively low for another. Whenever that level is exceeded, stressful responses develop that can undermine health. In some instances there is a sustained series of changes over a period of time, producing cumulative effects that finally overload a person's system. In other instances there is a single major change of such significance that it overloads a person's ability to cope with the situation. Examples include a move to a new location, bringing with it the need for a new house, new schools for children, a job search for the spouse, and loss of friendships, or a promotion involving new roles, status, work group, and job pressures. The effects of change in the form of job stress are discussed further in Chapter 15.

The reality of change is that frequently there is no clear-cut 100 percent benefit for all parties. Rather, there is a series of separate costs and benefits that must be considered on an individual basis. The supportive, collegial, and system models of organizational behavior imply that management should consider each substantial change, try to help each person understand it, and seek to have each person experience a net gain from it. Despite management's best efforts, however, change is not always welcomed. The next section explores the nature and effects of resistance to change.

RESISTANCE TO CHANGE

Why resistance occurs

Resistance to change consists of any employee behaviors designed to discredit, delay, or prevent the implementation of a work change. Employees resist change because it threatens their needs for security, social interaction, status, competence, or self-esteem.

Nature and Effects

The perceived threat stemming from a change may be real or imagined, intended or unintended, direct or indirect, large or small. Regardless of the nature of the change, some employees will try to protect themselves from its effects. Their actions may range from complaints, foot-dragging, and passive resistance to absenteeism, sabotage, and work slowdowns.

All types of employees tend to resist change because of the psychic costs that accompany it. Managers as well as workers resist it. Change can be resisted just as stubbornly by a white-collar worker as by a blue-collar worker. It does not respect either type of dress or job.

Although people tend to resist change, this tendency is offset by their desire for new experiences and for the rewards that come with change. Certainly, not all changes are resisted; some are actively sought by employees. Other changes are so trivial and routine that resistance, if any, is too weak to be evident. One lesson for management is that a change is likely to be either a success or a problem, *depending on how skillfully it is managed to minimize resistance.*

Chain-reaction effect

Insecurity and change are conditions that illustrate how a **chain-reaction effect** may develop in organizational behavior. A chain-reaction effect is a situation in which a change, or other condition, that directly affects only one person or a few persons may lead to a direct or indirect reaction from many people, even hundreds or thousands, because of their mutual interest in it. This is quite similar to multicar rear-end collisions on a foggy freeway, where each collision is followed by another one.

In one firm an assistant general manager for sales was promoted to assistant general manager for administration. The promotion of this high-ranking manager set off a cascading series of events that led to the promotion of ten other people at lower levels. The subsequent moves affected numerous divisions, territories, and offices. This example illustrates the wide impact of a single major change, and the chain-reaction effects of a single precipitating event.

Reasons for Resistance

Employees may resist changes for three broad reasons. First, they may not feel comfortable with the *nature of the change itself*. It may violate their moral belief system, they may believe the decision is technically incorrect, or they may simply be reluctant to exchange the comfort of certainty and familiarity for uncertainty. People may resist change because of their fear of the unknown, threats to their job security, or the lack of a demonstrated problem. A second reason for resistance stems from the *method* by which change is introduced.[8] People may resent having been ill-informed, or they may reject an insensitive and authoritarian approach that did not involve them in the change process. The method of introducing change may also revolve around a perception of poor timing. A third reason for resistance is the inequity experienced when people perceive themselves being changed while *someone else appears to gain the benefits* of the change. Their resistance will be even more intense if all three reasons exist: People disagree with the nature of the change, dislike the method used, and do not see a personal gain for themselves.

Resistance stems from nature of change, method used, and perceptions of inequity.

> Elisabeth Kübler-Ross, in her book *Death and Dying,* studied the reactions of individuals when told that they had an incurable (life-threatening) illness and faced death. She concluded that these people typically went through a series of five stages: denial, anger, depression, search for alternatives, and eventual acceptance of the prognosis. Many change managers also believe that employees go through a comparable experience, although certainly on a lesser scale, when faced with organizational change; they first fight the change, then strike out in anger and maintain their rigid resistance, then express their sadness and withdraw, then begin to explore and acknowledge the possible value of the change, and ultimately embrace the change as a new way of life.

From resistance to acceptance

Types of Resistance

There are three different types of resistance to change, as shown in Figure 14–2. These types work in combination to produce each employee's total attitude toward a change. The three types may be expressed by three different uses of the word "logical."

Logical Resistance　This is based on disagreement with the facts, rational reasoning, logic, and science. Logical resistance arises from the actual time and effort required to adjust to change, including new job duties that must be learned. These are true costs borne by the employees. Even though a change may be favorable for employees in the long run, these short-run costs must first be paid.

Rational resistance

Psychological Resistance　This is typically based on emotions, sentiments, and attitudes. Psychological resistance is internally logical from the perspective of the employees' attitudes and feelings about change. Employees may fear the unknown, mistrust management's leadership, or feel that their security and self-esteem are threatened. Even though management may believe there is no justification for these feelings, they are very real to employees, and managers *must* deal with them.

Emotional resistance

FIGURE 14–2

Types of resistance to change among employees

Logical, rational objections

- Time required to adjust

- Extra effort to relearn

- Possibility of less desirable conditions, such as skill downgrading

- Economic costs of change

- Questioned technical feasibility of change

Psychological, emotional attitudes

- Fear of the unknown

- Low tolerance of change

- Dislike of management or other change agent

- Lack of trust in others

- Need for security; desire for status quo

Sociological factors; group interests

- Political coalitions

- Opposing group values

- Parochial, narrow outlook

- Vested interests

- Desire to retain existing friendships

Social resistance

Sociological Resistance   Sociological resistance also is logical, when it is seen as a product of a challenge to group interests, norms, and values. Since social values are powerful forces in the environment, they must be carefully considered. There are political coalitions, labor union values, and even different community values. On a small-group level there are work friendships and status relationships that may be disrupted by changes. Employees will ask such questions as, "Is the change consistent with group values?" "Does it maintain teamwork?" Since employees have these kinds of questions on their minds, managers must try to make these conditions as favorable as possible if they intend to deal successfully with sociological resistance.

Implications of Resistance   Clearly, all three types of resistance must be anticipated and treated effectively if employees are to accept change cooperatively. If administrators work with only the technical, logical dimension of change, they have failed in their human responsibilities. It can be seen that psychological resistance and sociological resistance are not illogical or irrational; rather, they are logical according to different sets of values. Recognizing the impact of psychological and social factors is critically important to the success of proposed change.

In a typical operating situation, full support cannot be gained for every change that is made. Some moderate support, weak support, and even opposition can be expected. People are different and will not give identical support to each change. What management seeks is a climate in which people trust managers, have a positive feeling toward most changes, and feel secure enough to tolerate other changes. If management cannot win support, it may need to use authority. However, it must recognize that authority can be used only sparingly. If authority is overused, it eventually will become worthless.

Possible Benefits of Resistance

Resistance is not *all* bad. It can bring some benefits. Resistance may encourage management to reexamine its change proposals, thus making sure they are appropriate. In this way employees operate as part of a system of checks and balances that ensures that management properly plans and implements change. If reasonable employee resistance causes management to screen its proposed changes more carefully, then employees have discouraged careless management decisions.

Resistance also can help identify specific problem areas where a change is likely to cause difficulties, so that management can take corrective action before serious problems develop. At the same time, management may be encouraged to do a better job of communicating the change, an approach that in the long run should lead to better acceptance. Resistance also gives management information about the intensity of employee emotions on an issue, provides emotional release for pent-up employee feelings, and may encourage employees to think and talk more about a change so that they understand it better.

IMPLEMENTING CHANGE SUCCESSFULLY

Some changes originate within the organization, but many come from the external environment. Government passes laws, and the organization must comply. New developments in technology arise, and products must incorporate the changes. Competitors introduce new services, and the firm must respond. Then there are pressures from customers, labor unions, communities, and others who initiate changes. Although stable environments mean less change, *dynamic environments are now the norm,* and they require more change. On occasion they can cause difficulties for employees, as in this incident:

> Mary Manusco worked in an office in one of many buildings at a corporate complex that spread over 40 acres. She cheerfully returned from a two-week vacation to find that the whole office of fifty people had disappeared, leaving a bare room. Mary was startled and bewildered; she felt excluded and momentarily was concerned about her job security.
>
> She later learned that some quick changes had become necessary to prepare her building for new activities. Her office group had been suddenly moved to another building during her absence. Nevertheless, the way the move was handled raised legitimate questions for Mary. She asked, "Why didn't they tell me? They knew where I was, so they could have telephoned me. At least they could have written to me so that I would have a letter at home when I returned. Why didn't a friend call me at home the night before, or why didn't my supervisor try to contact me? *Does anybody care?* Is this the way future changes will be handled, too?"

Transformational Leadership and Change

Management has a key role in initiating and implementing change successfully, as illustrated by its failure to contact Mary Manusco. Not only do managers sometimes overlook simple but important details, but they may fail to develop a master strategy for planned change. An overall plan should address behavioral issues, such as employees' difficulty in letting go of old methods, the uncertainties inherent in change that cause workers to be fearful, and the general need to create an organization that *welcomes* change.

Transformational leaders are instrumental in this process.[9] They are managers who initiate bold strategic changes to position the organization for its future. They articulate a vision and promote it vigorously. They help employees rise above their narrow focus on their individual jobs or departments to see a broader picture. Transformational leaders stimulate employees to action and charismatically model the desired behaviors. They attempt to create learning individuals and learning organizations that will be better prepared for the unknown challenges that lie ahead. These important elements of transformational leadership—creating vision, exhibiting charisma, and stimulating learning—are explored in the following sections. Then a three-stage model of the change process is presented.

Learning organizations are needed.

Creating Vision   Transformational leaders create and communicate a vision for the organization. A **vision** is a crystallized long-range image or idea of what can and should be accomplished (you may wish to review the organizational behavior system model in Chapter 2).[10] It typically stretches people beyond their current capabilities and thinking, and it excites them to new levels of commitment and enthusiasm. A vision may also integrate the shared beliefs and values that serve as a basis for changing an organization's culture.

> The value, and the complexity, of instilling a vision is illustrated by the experience of a new university president. He was chosen to lead the institution when the interview team was impressed with his master plan for transforming the university from a position of mediocrity to one of focused excellence. However, he incorrectly assumed that the positive reaction to his general vision would automatically translate into acceptance of his specific proposals. Here he met opposition from legislators, regents, faculty, students, and alumni. He soon learned that having a dramatic vision was only the first step in the transformational leadership process.

Communicating Charisma   Even if employees are intellectually convinced that the vision is desirable, leaders still have two tasks: to persuade employees that the vision is urgent and to motivate their employees to achieve it. **Charisma** is a leadership characteristic that can help influence employees to take early and sustained action. Charismatic leaders are dynamic risk takers who show their depth of expertise and well-deserved self-confidence, express high performance expectations, and use provocative symbols and language to inspire others.[11] They can also be warm mentors who treat employees individually and guide them to take action. In response, employees respect and trust charismatic leaders as they introduce change, and tend to be more emotionally committed to the vision of such leaders. Charismatic leaders also need to recognize the "emotional vulnerability" that employees experience during change and to allay employees' fears while stimulating their energy for change.

Stimulating Learning   Transformational leaders recognize that the legacy they leave behind is not simply the change itself but an organization that will *continue* to change. Their critical task is to develop people's capacity to learn from the experience of change. This process is called **double-loop learning.** Its name is derived from the fact that the way a change is handled should not only reflect current information gathered (the first loop) but also prepare the participants to manage future changes even more effectively (the second loop).[12] Double-loop learners develop the ability

Double-loop learners challenge their own thinking.

to anticipate problems, prevent many situations from arising, and, in particular, challenge their own limiting assumptions and paradigms. This process is in sharp contrast to **single-loop learning,** in which employees simply solve current problems and blindly adapt to changes which have been imposed on them. The double-loop process not only makes the current change more successful but also increases the chances that employees will be more ready for the next change to be introduced, or better yet, will make it themselves.

> Johnsonville Foods, a sausage-maker in Sheboygan, Wisconsin, has worked to change itself into a double-loop learning organization.[13] A young supervisor there (we'll call him "Mac") was a brilliant technician and coach. When employees brought a problem to him, he told them precisely what to do, and then they would fix it. Mac felt good about this role; he was *needed.* This single-loop process might have continued indefinitely, except that Mac got tired of being awakened by third-shift crew members in the middle of the night. The next time they called, he asked them some key questions about the problem and encouraged them to suggest a solution. He not only endorsed their answer but also suggested that they had the ability to solve similar problems without his help. As a consequence, all of Mac's crews learned to become problem-solving individuals and teams. They were double-loop learners.

Three Stages in Change

Behavioral awareness in managing change is aided by viewing change as a three-step process:[14]

- Unfreezing
- Changing
- Refreezing

Unfreezing means that old ideas and practices need to be cast aside so that new ones can be learned. Often this step of getting rid of old practices is just as difficult as learning the new ones. It is an easy step to overlook while concentrating on the proposed change itself, but failure to cast aside old ideas is what often leads to resistance to change. Just as a farmer must clear a field before planting new seeds, so must a manager help employees clear their minds of old roles and old purposes. Only then will they be able to embrace new ideas.

Changing is the step in which the new ideas and practices are learned. This process involves helping an employee think, reason, and perform in new ways. It can be a time of confusion, disorientation, overload, and despair. Fortunately, the changing step usually is also mixed with hope, discovery, and excitement.

Refreezing means that what has been learned is integrated into actual practice. In addition to being intellectually accepted, the new practices become emotionally embraced and incorporated into the employee's routine behavior. Merely knowing a new procedure is not enough to ensure its use. As a farmer once said when confronted by an agricultural extension agent with suggestions for crop improvement, "I'm not farming half as good as I already know how." Successful on-the-job practice, then, must be the ultimate goal of the refreezing step.

> An extreme example of the three-stage change process comes from rehabilitation programs for victims of strokes who have one side of their body partially paralyzed. Their tendency is to use their "good-side" arm for self-feeding, for example, which inhibits their full recovery. Therapists have found it to be extremely beneficial to bind the patient's good-side arm against their body and encourage the patient to use their weak-side arm for 8–10 hours per day. Incredible stories of regained usefulness have been reported using this method. The binding process illustrates a physical method of unfreezing (forced discard of the old way);

the daily practice with the weak arm is the change introduced; and the dramatic gains experienced by the patient serve to reward the patient and refreeze the new behavior. Similarly, managers may need to find ways to unfreeze old habits of employees by physically preventing them from using old equipment or software before they will turn their attention to accepting new methods.

Manipulating the Forces

Social psychologist Kurt Lewin, who identified the three stages of change, also suggested that any organization (as a social system) is a dynamic balance of forces supporting and restraining any existing practice; there is an **equilibrium,** as shown in Figure 14–3.

In a factory operation there are pressures both for and against higher output. Management typically wants the higher output. Industrial engineers conduct studies to try to improve it. Supervisors push for it. Some workers, on the other hand, may feel that they are already working hard enough. More effort would cause feelings of inequity, and they do not want additional strain and tension. They do not want to feel more tired when they go home. They enjoy their rest breaks. The result is that they act as a restraining force, and the current amount of output will tend to continue until some type of change is introduced.

Change is introduced within a group by a variety of methods, as follows:[15]

Supporting and restraining forces

- Adding new supporting forces
- Removing restraining forces
- Increasing the strength of a supporting force
- Decreasing the strength of a restraining force
- Converting a restraining force into a supporting force

At least one of these approaches must be used to change the equilibrium, with greater success likely when more than one is adopted. The idea is to help change be accepted and integrated into new practices. For example, making people responsible for the quality of the product they produce has been used as a supporting force for higher-quality work. Another supporting force involves implementing programs to increase the employees' pride in their work. In the other direction, restraining forces on quality can be reduced by providing better maintenance of machines, so that better work can be done on them.

FIGURE 14–3

A model of the equilibrium state and change process

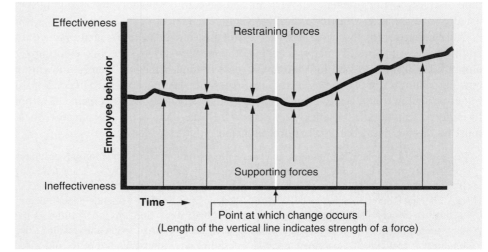

Building Support for Change

If we assume that management is following the model of the change process in Figure 14–3, then forces of support need to be built before, during, and after a change. A wide variety of positive activities to build support are described below. Others, such as manipulation and coercion, typically antagonize employees and sabotage the long-term success of the change program.

Use of Group Forces   Effective change focuses not only on the individuals but also on the group itself. The group is an instrument for bringing strong pressure on its members to change. Since behavior is firmly grounded in the groups to which a person belongs, any changes in group forces will encourage changes in the individual behavior. The idea is to help the group join with management to encourage desired change.

The power of a group to stimulate change in its members depends partly on the strength of their attachment to it. The more attractive the group is to each member, the greater its influence on a group member can be. Influence is further increased if members with high status in the group support a change.

Change should not disrupt the group's social system more than is necessary. Any change that threatens the group will tend to meet with resistance.

Providing a Rationale for Change   Capable leadership reinforces a climate of psychological support for change. The effective leader presents change on the basis of the impersonal requirements of the situation, rather than on personal grounds. It is generally better to provide objective (performance-related) reasons for the change. If they are compelling and substantial, they should be given. If not, maybe the intended change needs to be abandoned. Ordinary requests for change should also be in accord with the objectives and vision of the organization. Only a strong personal leader can use personal reasons for change without arousing resistance.

Change is more likely to be successful if the leaders introducing it have high expectations of success. In other words, managerial and employee *expectations of change* may be as important as the technology of change. This concept was suggested earlier in Figure 14–1, which showed the importance of attitudes toward change. Creating positive expectations of change is a demonstration of the powerful self-fulfilling prophecy (introduced in Chapter 5), which is illustrated in this example:

Expectations are important.

> A manufacturer of clothing patterns had four almost identical plants. When a job enrichment and rotation program was introduced, managers in two of the plants were given inputs predicting that the program would increase productivity. Managers of the other two plants were told that the program would improve employee relations but not productivity.
>
> During the next twelve months, productivity did increase significantly in the two plants where the managers were expecting it. In the two plants where the managers were not expecting it, it did not increase. The result showed that high leader expectations were the key factor in making the change successful.[16]

Expectations alone are not powerful enough to induce or discourage significant change. How, then, does the process really work? The expectations tend to get translated into specific managerial behaviors that increase or decrease the likelihood of change. *By believing that the change will work, the manager acts so as to fulfill that belief* (e.g., by providing more resources or by reinforcing new employee behaviors). This belief is transferred to employees, who buy into the probability of success and change their behaviors accordingly. This process creates an integrated system of expectations of success and of appropriate behaviors leading up to it.

Participation   A fundamental way to build support for change is through participation, which is discussed in Chapter 8. It encourages employees to discuss, to communicate, to make suggestions, and to become interested in change. Participation
encourages commitment rather than mere compliance with change. Commitment implies
motivation to support a change and to work to ensure that the change is effective.

As shown in Figure 14–4, it is generally true that *as participation increases, resistance to change tends to decrease.* Resistance declines because employees have less
cause to resist. Since their needs are being considered, they feel secure in a changing
situation.

Employees need to participate in a change *before* it occurs, not after. When they
can be involved from the beginning, they feel protected from surprises and feel that
their ideas are wanted. On the other hand, employees are likely to feel that involvement after a change is nothing more than a selling device and manipulation by
management.

Shared Rewards   Another way to build employee support for change is to be sure
that there are enough rewards for employees in the change situation. It is only natural for employees to ask, "What's in this for me?" If they see that a change brings
them losses and no gains, they can hardly be enthusiastic about it.

Rewards say to employees, "We care. We want you as well as us to benefit from
this change." Rewards also give employees a sense that progress accompanies a
change. Both economic and psychic rewards are useful. Employees appreciate a pay
increase or promotion, but they also appreciate emotional support, training in new
skills, and recognition from management.

*Economic and psychic
rewards*

It is desirable for a change to pay off as directly and as soon as possible. From an
employee's point of view, what's good in general is not necessarily good for the
employee, and what's good for the long run may not be good for the short run.

An example of successful change through employee participation and shared rewards
occurred at Delphi Corporation's Oak Creek plant in Wisconsin.[17] Through a major redesign
of its assembly operations for catalytic converters into a modularized system, employees
found ways to save 500,000 square feet of floor space, simplify processes, improve adaptability, increase productivity 25 percent, and raise participation in the suggestion system to
99 percent. Many employees also take advantage of the stock ownership program and thus
feel and act like owners.

FIGURE 14–4

A model of participation
and resistance to change

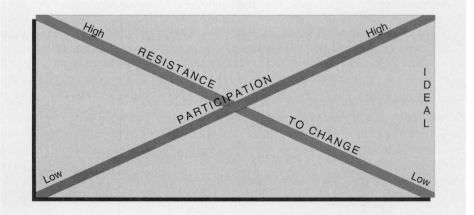

Employee Security   Along with shared rewards, existing employee benefits need to be protected. Security during a change is essential. Many employers guarantee workers protection from reduced earnings when new technology and methods are introduced. Others offer retraining and delay installation of labor-saving equipment until normal labor turnover can absorb displaced workers. Seniority rights, opportunities for advancement, and other benefits are safeguarded when a change is made. Grievance systems give employees a feeling of security that benefits will be protected and differences about them fairly resolved. All these practices help employees feel secure in the presence of change.

Communication and Education   Communication is essential in gaining support for change. Even though a change will affect only one or two in a work group of ten persons, all of them need to be informed about the change in order to feel secure and to maintain group cooperation. Management often does not realize that activities that help get change accepted, such as communication and education, usually are disrupted by change. In other words, since the flow of information may be weakest at the time it is needed most, special effort is required to maintain it in times of change.

Stimulating Employee Readiness   Closely related to communication is the idea of helping employees become aware of the need for a change. This approach builds on the premise that *change is more likely to be accepted if the people affected by it recognize a need for it before it occurs*. This awareness may happen naturally, as when a crisis occurs, or it can be induced by management through sharing operating information with employees, as is done in open-book management programs. One of the more powerful ways, however, occurs when workers discover for themselves that a situation requires improvement. Then they will truly be ready, as this incident shows:

Dissatisfaction stimulates change.

> The human resources director of a major bank aided the self-discovery process by hiring a consultant to conduct an assessment of the department's innovativeness. The provocative conclusions shocked the staff into awareness that changes were needed. According to the director, the results of the report "seemed to crystallize new perspectives about the potential of the department." Task forces were created, and their recommendations were implemented. Desired new behaviors emerged—risk taking, self-reliance, and decentralized decision making. All this activity occurred because the employees suddenly became aware that a problem existed, and they personally experienced the need for some changes.

Working with the Total System   Resistance to change can be reduced by a broader understanding of employee attitudes and natural reactions to change. Management's role is to help employees recognize the need for each change and to invite them to participate in it and gain from it.[18] It is also essential for managers to take a broader, systems-oriented perspective on change to identify the complex relationships involved. Organization development can be a useful method for achieving this objective.

UNDERSTANDING ORGANIZATION DEVELOPMENT

Organization development (OD) is the systematic application of behavioral science knowledge at various levels (group, intergroup, and total organization) to bring about planned change.[19] Its objectives include a higher quality of work life, productivity, adaptability, and effectiveness. It seeks to use behavioral knowledge to change beliefs, attitudes, values, strategies, structures, and practices so that the organization can better adapt to competitive actions, technological advances, and the fast pace of other changes in the environment.

OD helps managers recognize that organizations are systems with dynamic interpersonal relationships holding them together. The reasonable next step was to try to change groups, units, and entire organizations so that they would support, not necessarily replace, change efforts. In short, the general objective of OD is to change all parts of the organization in order to make it more humanly responsive, more effective, and more capable of organizational learning and self-renewal. OD relies on a systems orientation, causal models, and a set of key assumptions to guide it.

Foundations of OD

Systems Orientation   Change is so abundant in modern society that organizations need all their parts working together in order to solve the problems—and capitalize on the opportunities—that are brought about by change.[20] Some organizations have grown so large that it is difficult to maintain coordinated effort among their parts. Organization development is a comprehensive program that is concerned with the interactions of various parts of the organization as they affect one another. OD is concerned with the interplay of structure, technology, and people. It is concerned with the behavior of employees in different groups, departments, and locations. It focuses on answering the question, How effective are all these parts as they combine to work together? Emphasis is on the manner in which the parts relate, not just on the parts themselves.

Understanding Causality   One contribution of the systems orientation is to help managers view their organizational processes in terms of a model with three types of variables.[21] They are causal, intervening, and end-result variables, as shown in Figure 14–5. The *causal variables* are the significant ones, because they affect both intervening and end-result variables. Causal variables are the ones that management can change most directly; they include organizational structure, controls, policies, training, a broad range of leadership behaviors, and OD efforts. The *intervening variables* are those which are immediately affected by the causal variables. They include employee attitudes, perceptions, motivation, and skilled behaviors, as well as teamwork and even intergroup relationships. Finally, the *end-result variables* represent the objectives sought by management. They usually include improved productivity, increased sales, lower costs, more loyal customers, and higher earnings. They represent the reason that the OD program was initiated.

Causal, intervening, and end-result variables

Assumptions Underlying Organization Development   OD practitioners make a set of assumptions that guide their actions. Sometimes these assumptions are implicit

FIGURE 14–5

Variables in the organization development approach

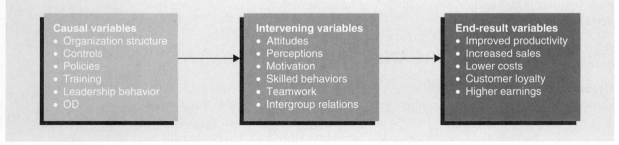

and need to be examined to enable double-loop learning. It is important for managers to identify those assumptions so that they will be aware of their impact (just as we argue in Chapter 2 that managers need to be aware of, and update, their paradigms). OD assumptions need to be shared with managers and employees so that those groups will clearly understand the basis for the OD program.

A wide range of assumptions can be made, but certain ones are relatively common at the individual, group, and organizational level. A sample of them is described here and is summarized in Figure 14–6. OD advocates typically hold a highly positive viewpoint regarding the capabilities, unused potential, and interests of all individuals. This stems from the humanistic values that are implicit in OD theory. Groups and teams are seen as vital building blocks of an organization, but since they are powerful and complex they are not always easy to change. Traditional organizations are viewed as rigid bureaucracies that have sometimes stifled employee development and growth, but possibilities are seen for positive conflict and goal compatibility.

Individual

Group

Organization

Characteristics of Organization Development

A number of characteristics, such as its systems orientation, are implied in the definition of OD. Many of these are consistent with the dominant themes of organizational behavior presented earlier in this book. The characteristics are discussed in the following paragraphs. Although some of the characteristics of organization development differ substantially from traditional change efforts, OD has begun to have an impact on the way organizational change programs are designed and presented.

Humanistic Values OD programs typically are based on **humanistic values,** which are positive beliefs about the potential and desire for growth among employees. To be effective and self-renewing, an organization needs employees who want to expand their skills and increase their contributions. The best climate for such growth

What does OD value?

Individuals

- People want to grow and mature.

- Employees have much to offer (e.g., energy and creativity) that is not now being used at work.

- Most employees desire the opportunity to contribute (they desire, seek, and appreciate empowerment).

Groups

- Groups and teams are critical to organizational success.

- Groups have powerful influences on individual behavior.

- The complex roles to be played in groups require skill development.

Organization

- Excessive controls, policies, and rules are detrimental.

- Conflict can be functional if properly channeled.

- Individual and organizational goals can be compatible.

FIGURE 14–6

Common organization development assumptions

is one that stresses collaboration, open communications, interpersonal trust, shared power, and constructive confrontation. These factors all provide a value base for OD efforts and help ensure that the new organization will be responsive to human needs.

Use of a Change Agent   OD programs generally use one or more **change agents,** whose role is to stimulate, facilitate, and coordinate change. The change agent usually acts as a catalyst, sparking change within the system while remaining somewhat independent of it. Although change agents may be either external or internal, they are usually consultants from outside the company. Advantages of using external change agents are that they are more objective and have diverse experiences. They are also able to operate independently without ties to the hierarchy and politics of the firm.

To offset their limited familiarity with the organization, external change agents usually are paired with an internal coordinator from the human resources department. These two then work with line management. The result is a three-way relationship that draws on the strengths of each component for balance, much like a team approach to modern health care requires the cooperation of a physician, medical support staff, and the patient. Sometimes, especially in large firms, the organization has its own in-house OD specialist. This person replaces the external consultant and works directly with the firm's managers to facilitate improvement efforts.

Problem Solving   OD emphasizes the process of problem solving. It trains participants to identify and solve problems that are important to them. These are the actual problems that the participants are currently facing at work, so the issues are stimulating and their resolution challenging. The approach commonly used to improve problem-solving skills is to have employees identify system problems, gather data about them, take corrective action, assess progress, and make ongoing adjustments. This cyclical process of using research to guide action, which generates new data as the basis for new actions, is known as **action research,** or *action science*. By studying their own problem-solving process through action research, employees learn how to learn from their experiences, so that they can solve new problems in the future on their own. This process is another example of double-loop learning, discussed earlier in this chapter.

Experiential Learning   When participants learn by experiencing in the training environment the kinds of human problems they face on the job, the process is called **experiential learning.** Participants can discuss and analyze their own immediate experiences and learn from them. This approach tends to produce more changed behavior than the traditional lecture and discussion alone, in which people only hear and talk about abstract theories and concepts. The theory provided by those traditional approaches is necessary and desirable, but participants need to learn how it applies in a real situation. OD helps provide some of the applied answers. Participant experiences help solidify, or refreeze, new learning.

Interventions at Many Levels   The general goal of organization development is to build more effective organizations—ones that will continue to learn, adapt, and improve. OD accomplishes this goal by recognizing that problems may occur at the individual, interpersonal, group, intergroup, or total organization level. An overall OD strategy is then developed with one or more **interventions,** which are structured activities designed to help individuals or groups improve their work effectiveness. These interventions are often classified by their emphasis on individuals (such as career planning) or groups

Merrill Anderson contends that three key trends have forced OD to accelerate its pace of change as well as to become more concerned with adding value for its clients: the speed with which competitive changes take place, the increasing need for organizations to be viewed as complex and dynamic systems, and the increasing emphasis of OD on strategic issues. As a consequence, OD practitioners are expected to have three new sets of competencies:

- Fluency in the language of business (e.g., finance)
- Sound grasp of strategic formulation tools and conceptual models

- Explorational and investigative tools to identify market challenges, industry trends, leader backgrounds and motivations, and company histories

From this base, OD experts are expected to draw upon their toolkit of search conferences, organizational redesign, kaizen, team building, fast-cycle learning, and coaching to help organizations achieve outstanding business results in these times of tumultuous change.

Source: Merrill Anderson & Associates, *Fast Cycle Organization Development*, Cincinnati: South-Western, 2000.

(such as team building). Another way to view interventions is to look at whether they focus on *what* people are doing (such as clarifying and changing their job tasks) or on *how* they are doing it (improving the interpersonal process that occurs).

OD interventions can be classified.

Contingency Orientation / Organization development is usually described as contingency-oriented. Although some OD practitioners rely on just one or a few approaches, most OD people are flexible and pragmatic, selecting and adapting actions to fit assessed needs. Diagnosis plays a key role in determining how to proceed, and usually there is open discussion of several useful alternatives rather than the imposition of a single best way to proceed.

Summary and Application The OD process applies behavioral science knowledge and strategies to improve an organization. It is a long-range, continuing effort that tries to build cooperative work relationships through the use of a change agent. It seeks to integrate into an effective unit the four elements that affect organizational behavior—people, structure, technology, and environment—which are discussed in Chapter 1.

> An OD intervention in a public-sector organization occurred at the Utah Department of Public Safety.[22] Using an action research approach, 750 employees completed a diagnostic survey focused on nineteen areas of organizational and managerial effectiveness. Then they received feedback on the results and helped develop action plans where deficiencies were noted.
>
> In a follow-up study two years later, most of the supervisors reported that communications had improved, teams were more cohesive, and participative management was used more frequently. Employees were receiving more feedback on their performance and had a greater sense of ownership and responsibility for work outcomes. In units where the OD approach was less successful, the barriers were related to a lack of managerial support, resource constraints, and low support from peers.

The Organization Development Process

OD is a complex process. It may take a year or more to design and implement, and the process may continue indefinitely. OD tries to move the organization from where it is now (requiring diagnosis) to where it should be (by action interventions). Even then the process continues, as it is desirable to evaluate the outcomes and maintain the momentum. Although there are many different approaches to OD, a typical complete program includes most of the following steps (as shown in Figure 14–7):

FIGURE 14–7

356

Typical stages in
organization
development

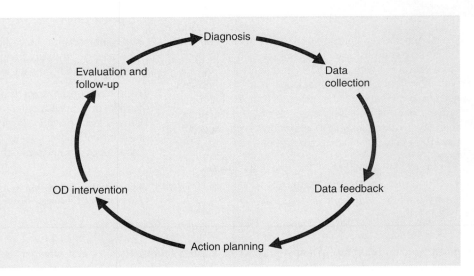

Steps in OD

1. *Initial diagnosis*—The consultant meets with top management to determine the nature of the firm's problems, to develop the OD approaches most likely to be successful, and to ensure the full support of top management. During this step the consultant may seek inputs by means of interviews with various people in the organization.

2. *Data collection*—Surveys may be made to determine organizational climate and behavioral problems. The consultant usually meets with groups away from work to develop information from questions such as these:

   a. What kinds of conditions contribute most to your job effectiveness?

   b. What kinds of conditions interfere with your job effectiveness?

   c. What would you most like to change in the way this organization operates?

   The by-products of data collection include the identification of **performance gaps**—deficiencies in the way the organization operates—and **baseline information**—a portrait of the organization's current level of operations for later comparison with the effects of OD efforts.

3. *Data feedback and confrontation*—Work groups are assigned to review the data collected, to mediate areas of disagreement, and to establish priorities for change.

4. *Action planning and problem solving*—Groups use the data to develop specific recommendations for change. Discussion focuses on actual problems in the organization. Plans are specific, including who is responsible and when the action should be completed.

5. *Use of interventions*—Once the action planning is completed, the consultant helps the participants select and use appropriate OD interventions. Depending on the nature of the key problems, the intervention may focus on individuals, teams, interdepartmental relations, or the total organization.

6. *Evaluation and follow-up*—The consultant helps the organization evaluate the results of its OD efforts and develop additional programs in areas where additional results are needed.

In one organization the consultant asked managers to provide tapes of committee meetings that they chaired after the program's start. The consultant analyzed these tapes and used them to discuss with managers how well each was applying what was learned in the OD program.

Since the steps in OD are part of a whole process, all of them need to be applied if a firm expects to gain the full benefits of OD. A firm that applies only two or three steps, such as diagnosis and team building, is likely to be disappointed with the results; however, the whole process can produce quite favorable results.

Mobil Oil has implemented numerous OD programs, and it reports these results:

- Improved supervisor-employee communications
- Streamlined paperwork requirements
- More systematic problem analysis and problem solving
- Better interdepartmental relationships

The company concluded that the most critical step in OD is the first one—obtaining permission, active support, and total involvement from top management.[23]

Benefits and Limitations of OD

Organization development is a useful organizational intervention. Its chief advantage is that it tries to deal with changes in a whole organization or a major unit of it. In this manner it accomplishes more widely dispersed improvement. Other benefits include improved motivation, productivity, quality of work, job satisfaction, teamwork, and resolution of conflict. There also are reduced negative factors such as absences and turnover.[24] The benefits and limitations are summarized in Figure 14–8 and illustrated in the following research summary:

Benefits of OD	Limitations of OD
• Change throughout organization	• Major time requirements
• Greater motivation	• Substantial expense
• Increased productivity	• Delayed payoff period
• Better quality of work	• Possible failure
• Higher job satisfaction	• Possible invasion of privacy
• Improved teamwork	• Possible psychological harm
• Better resolution of conflict	• Potential conformity
• Commitment to objectives	• Emphasis on group processes rather than performance
• Increased willingness to change	• Possible conceptual ambiguity
• Reduced absences	• Difficulty in evaluation
• Lower turnover	• Cultural incompatibility
• Creation of learning individuals and groups	

FIGURE 14–8

Benefits and limitations of organization development

1. Make only necessary and useful changes that have compelling support, or employees will get overwhelmed. Where possible, make evolutionary, not revolutionary, changes.

2. Alert your employees to expect an increasing pace of change and the consequent need to develop new skills throughout their careers.

3. Get a few highly visible role players on your side to lead (champion) and model the change for others.

4. Recognize the possibility of resistance to change, and develop appropriate strategies for confronting each source.

5. Involve and empower employees throughout the change process to diminish or prevent resistance.

6. Make sure that employees see, and obtain, some of the benefits from change.

7. View organizational change as an extended process with likely setbacks, and pay particular attention to the unfreezing and refreezing stages.

8. Use a systematic approach to change such as the OD model, and be willing to embrace the efforts of others (change agents) to assist you.

After an OD program in one organization, there were statistically significant improvements in trust, supportive environment, commitment to objectives, and other conditions of organizational climate. With regard to supervisory behavior, there was improvement in listening, handling of conflict, relations with others, willingness to change, and other activities. With regard to performance, there were changes in quality level and profit that were attributed to the OD program. Clearly, the effect of the program was widespread in the organization.[25]

As with any complex program, OD has problems and limitations. It is time-consuming and expensive. Some benefits have a delayed payoff period, and an organization may not be able to wait that long for potential benefits. Even when a professionally capable consultant is used, an OD program may fall flat. There are charges that participants are sometimes coerced toward group attitudes and conformity. There are other charges that excessive emphasis is given to behavioral processes rather than to job performance. Group processes seem to be given priority over needs of the organization.

A notable limitation of OD is that it may be more compatible with the humanistic values in the United States and Scandinavian countries than with the dominant values in Japan, Latin America, and Africa.[26] Therefore, to be universally successful, it must develop an arsenal of tools that are suited to a variety of cultures. The OD field would also benefit from broadening its perspective to encompass methods for helping organizations not only fine-tune themselves and adapt to changing environments but also prepare to make major transformations in their structure, strategy, and process.[27] Finally, all managers should accept their roles as being responsible for OD, since organizational improvement is almost universally needed.

SUMMARY

Change is everywhere, and its pace is increasing. The work environment is filled with change that often upsets the social system and requires employees to adjust. When they do, employees respond with their emotions as well as rational reasoning. Change has costs as well as benefits, and both must be considered to determine net effects. Employees tend to resist change because of its costs, including its psychic costs. Resistance to change can stem from the change process itself, the way it was introduced, or the perception of inequitable impact. Further, it can be logical, psychological, or sociological.

Transformational leadership can be instrumental in bringing about effective changes.

Leaders need to create and share a vision, inspire followers through their charisma, and encourage them to become double-loop learners so that future changes will be even more successful. Managers are encouraged to apply a systematic change procedure spanning unfreezing, change, and refreezing activities. Managers can reduce resistance and achieve a new equilibrium by influencing the supporting and restraining forces for change. Time is always required for the potential benefits of change to occur.

A wide range of activities to support change can be used, such as participation, shared rewards, and adequate communication. In addition, organization development (OD)—the systematic application of behavioral science knowledge at various levels to bring about planned change in the whole organization—is effective. The OD process covers the steps of diagnosis, data collection, feedback and confrontation, action planning and problem solving, use of interventions, and evaluation and follow-up. Although OD has limitations, it is an excellent practice for introducing change, making improvements, and stimulating organizational learning.

Action research	Humanistic values	**Terms and Concepts for Review**
Backsliding	Interventions	
Baseline information	Organization development (OD)	
Chain-reaction effect	Performance gaps	
Change	Proactive	
Change agents	Psychic costs	
Changing	Reactive	
Charisma	Refreezing	
Double-loop learning	Resistance to change	
Equilibrium	Single-loop learning	
Experiential learning	Transformational leaders	
Hawthorne effect	Unfreezing	
Homeostasis	Vision	

Discussion Questions

1. Think of an organizational change that you have experienced. Was there resistance to the change? Discuss. What could have been done to prevent or diminish resistance?
2. Consider again the change mentioned in question 1; list both the costs and benefits under the three headings of "logical," "psychological," and "sociological." Were the benefits greater than the costs for the employees? For the employer? Discuss.
3. Continue the analysis of this change. How did management alter the restraining and supporting forces for it? Was there an organizational learning curve for it? Discuss its length and shape, and any problems that developed.
4. There is a classic debate about the relationship between attitudes and behaviors. Some people argue that attitude changes must precede behavioral responses, but other people believe that it is easier to change an employee's behavior first and then let attitude change follow. Discuss the merits and probabilities of both approaches to change.
5. Resistance to change is often viewed negatively. Discuss some possible *benefits* of resistance to change in an organization.
6. The chapter implies that a proactive role is preferable to a reactive one. Is that always true? Explain.
7. Discuss the pros and cons of the statement: "Change is basically positive."

8. Argue *against* the necessity of having vision, charisma, and an emphasis on double-loop learning for a transformational leader to bring about change in an organization. Are these elements really needed?

9. Numerous methods for building support for change are introduced. What is one risk associated with each method that could make it backfire?

10. Review Figure 14–8, and identify the three most significant benefits and the three most important limitations of OD. Do you think the benefits outweigh the costs? Report your choices, giving reasons for your selections.

Assess Your Own Skills

How well do you exhibit good change management skills?

Read the following statements carefully. Circle the number on the response scale that most closely reflects the degree to which each statement accurately describes you when you have tried to implement a change. Add up your total points and prepare a brief action plan for self-improvement. Be ready to report your score for tabulation across the entire group.

	Good description								Poor description	
1. I prefer to be proactive rather than reactive regarding change.	10	9	8	7	6	5	4	3	2	1
2. I am acutely sensitive to the importance of employee attitudes when introducing change.	10	9	8	7	6	5	4	3	2	1
3. I am alert to the possibility of employee backsliding after a change is introduced.	10	9	8	7	6	5	4	3	2	1
4. I am aware that not only financial costs but psychic costs of change must be considered.	10	9	8	7	6	5	4	3	2	1
5. I make every effort to predict not only who might resist change but how strong their resistance might be and its source.	10	9	8	7	6	5	4	3	2	1
6. I can present a coherent set of reasons as to why employees might resist, and might not resist, a change I introduce.	10	9	8	7	6	5	4	3	2	1
7. I have the capacity to be a transformational leader by creating and communicating a vision and demonstrating charisma.	10	9	8	7	6	5	4	3	2	1
8. I pay as much attention to the unfreezing and refreezing stages as I do to the actual change stage itself.	10	9	8	7	6	5	4	3	2	1
9. I am strongly committed to involving employees in the entire change process so as to increase their commitment to the change.	10	9	8	7	6	5	4	3	2	1
10. I understand the OD process and the major characteristics that it is comprised of.	10	9	8	7	6	5	4	3	2	1

Scoring and Interpretation   Add up your total points for the ten questions. Record that number here, and report it when it is requested. _____

• If you scored between 81–100 points, you appear to have a solid capability for demonstrating good change management skills.

- If you scored between 61–80 points, you should take a close look at the items with lower self-assessment scores and explore ways to improve those items.
- If you scored less than 60 points, you should be aware that a weaker skill level regarding several items could be detrimental to your future success as a change manager. We encourage you to review relevant sections of the chapter and watch for related material in subsequent chapters and other sources.

Now identify your three lowest scores, and write the question numbers here: _____ ,

and _____ , _____ .

Write a brief paragraph, detailing to yourself an action plan for how you might sharpen each of these skills.

The New Sales Procedures

Incident

The Marin Company has more than 100 field sales representatives who sell a line of complex industrial products. Sales of these products require close work with buyers to determine their product needs, so nearly all sales representatives are college graduates in engineering and science. Other product lines of Marin Company, such as consumer products, are sold by a separate sales group.

Recently, the firm established a new companywide control and report system using a larger computer. The system doubles the amount of time the industrial sales representatives spend filling out forms and supplying information that can be fed into the computer. They estimate that they now spend as much as two hours daily processing records, and they complain that they now have inadequate time for sales effort. A field sales manager commented, "Morale has declined as a result of these new controls and reports. Sales is a rewarding, gratifying profession that is based on individual effort. Sales representatives are happy when they are making sales, since this directly affects their income and self-recognition. The more time they spend with reports, the less time they have to make sales. As a result, they can see their income and recognition declining, and thus they find themselves resisting changes."

Questions
1. Comment on the sales manager's analysis.
2. What alternative approaches to this situation do you recommend? Give reasons.

The Industrial Engineering Change

Experiential Exercise

An industrial engineer was assigned to an electronics assembly department to make some methods improvements. In one assembly operation he soon recognized that a new fixture might reduce labor costs by about 30 percent. He discussed the situation with the group leader and then with the supervisor. The group leader was indifferent, but the supervisor was interested and offered additional suggestions.

Feeling that he had the supervisor's approval, the industrial engineer had the fixture made. With the permission of the supervisor, he assigned an assembler to try the fixture. She was cooperative and enthusiastic and on the first day exceeded the expected improvement of 30 percent. When the group leader was shown the results at the end of the day, he claimed that this was one of the fastest workers in the department and that her results could not be generalized for the whole department.

The next day the industrial engineer asked the supervisor for another operator to help prove the fixture. At this point the supervisor noted that the fixture did not include her ideas fully. The industrial engineer explained that he had misunderstood but that he would include the other suggestions in the next fixture built. The supervisor, however, continued to be negative about the fixture.

When the industrial engineer attempted to instruct the second woman the way he had instructed the first one, her reaction was negative. In fact, when he stopped instructing her, it seemed that the woman deliberately stalled as she used the fixture. She also made some negative comments about the fixture and asked the industrial engineer if he felt he deserved his paycheck for this kind of effort. At the end of the day this woman's production was 10 percent below normal production by the old method.

1. Form small discussion groups, and analyze the causes of the problem.
2. Review the management activities for supporting change that are presented in this chapter (using groups, providing a rationale, participation, shared rewards, protecting employee security, communication and education, stimulating readiness, and working with the total system). Rank these from 1 (greatest) to 7 (least) in terms of their potential usefulness to the industrial engineer. Compare your rankings with those of the other discussion groups, and discuss any differences.
3. Select two people, and have them role-play a meeting of the industrial engineer and the supervisor.

Experiential Exercise

Applying Force-Field Analysis

Assume that the class is extremely unhappy with the professor's grading system and has banded together to demand a dramatic change in it.

A. Meeting in small groups, identify the *major behavioral reasons* your professor might both be inclined to accept and reject your recommendation (forces for change and reasons for resistance to it).

Forces for Change	Reasons for Resistance
1. _____	1. _____
2. _____	2. _____
3. _____	3. _____
4. _____	4. _____
5. _____	5. _____
6. _____	6. _____
7. _____	7. _____
8. _____	8. _____
9. _____	9. _____
10. _____	10. _____

B. Now attempt to predict the *strength* of each factor (high, medium, or low).

C. On the basis of this analysis, what do you *predict* your professor's overall response to the recommended change might be?

Chapter 15

Stress and Counseling

Burnout is a serious problem in today's workplace: Companies everywhere are downsizing, outsourcing, and restructuring, leaving workers at all levels feeling stressed, insecure, misunderstood, undervalued, and alienated.
–Christina Maslach and Michael P. Leiter[1]

Statistics indicate that violence has become a fundamental organizational problem.
–Anne M. O'Leary-Kelly, Ricky W. Griffin, and David J. Glew[2]

CHAPTER OBJECTIVES

TO UNDERSTAND

- The Role of Stress in Employee Health

- Extreme Forms of Stress Reactions

- Causes and Symptoms of Stress

- Organizational Effects of Stress

- Actions That May Prevent or Reduce Stress

- Different Counseling Functions

- Three Types of Counseling and Their Usefulness

Studies of stress among American workers reveal the following:

- The annual cost of stress-related absenteeism, lower productivity, rising health insurance costs, and other medical expenses is close to $300 billion and rising.
- 30 percent of executives believe their work has adversely affected their health.
- 40 percent of workers wonder whether they are going to have a job next year.
- The number of stress-related workers' compensation claims tripled in one decade, jumping from 5 percent to 15 percent of all claims.
- 46 percent of workers assess their jobs as being extremely stressful.
- 34 percent of workers have thought seriously about quitting their jobs in the past year as a result of stress.
- 69 percent of workers reported that health problems related to stress made them less productive.
- 34 percent of American workers expected to burn out on the job soon.[3]

Many people, like the employees mentioned above, develop emotional or physical problems as a result of stress. The difficulties may be temporary or enduring, and they may be caused by factors at work or out of the workplace. *No one is immune to stress,* for it can affect employees at all levels of the organization. When it is too severe or long-lasting, it can negatively affect both the individual and the employer. Fortunately, many programs exist for preventing or managing stress.

In this chapter we discuss what stress is, how it comes about, and how it affects various elements of job performance. As seen in the opening quotes for this chapter, there are often substantial costs and consequences associated with employee responses to stress. When work-related conflicts arise or when interpersonal relations become strained, a prime way to treat the resulting stress is to counsel the parties involved. We conclude the chapter by discussing three types of counseling and the ways they can be used to help employees with their problems.

EMPLOYEE STRESS

What Stress Is

Stress is the general term applied to the pressures people feel in life. The presence of stress at work is almost inevitable in many jobs. However, individual differences account for a wide range of reactions to stress; a task viewed as challenging by one person may produce high levels of anxiety in another. When pressure begins to build up, it can cause adverse strain on a person's emotions, thought processes, and physical condition. When stress becomes excessive, employees develop various symptoms of stress that can harm their job performance and health, and even threaten their ability to cope with the environment. As shown in Figure 15–1, people who are stressed may become nervous and chronically worried. They are easily provoked to anger and are unable to relax. They may be uncooperative or use alcohol or other drugs excessively. Although these conditions also occur from other causes, they are common symptoms of underlying stress.

Symptoms of stress

Stress also leads to physical disorders, because the internal body system changes to try to cope with stress. Some physical disorders are short-range, such as an upset stomach. Others are longer-range, such as a stomach ulcer. Stress over a prolonged time also leads to degenerative diseases of the heart, kidneys, blood vessels, and other

FIGURE 15–1

366

Typical negative symptoms of unmanaged stress

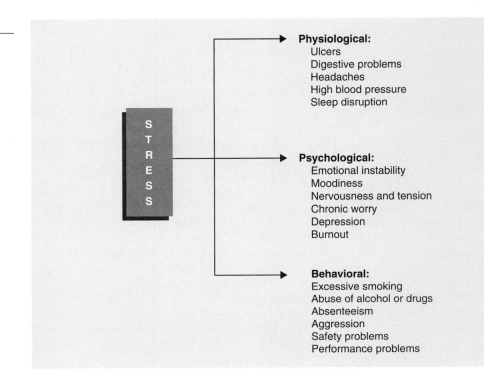

parts of the body. It can result in angina and tension headaches. Therefore it is important that stress, both on and off the job, be kept at a level low enough for most people to tolerate without developing either emotional or physical disorders.

> Peter Randall was transferred from a small city to a very large city where his commuting time to work was nearly one hour. He disliked city noises, heavy traffic, and crowds, and he felt he was wasting his time while commuting. His new job also had more responsibilities.
>
> Within a few months he developed intestinal problems. When a physical examination showed no medical cause of his difficulties, he was sent to a counselor. There was only slight improvement, and finally, his counselor in cooperation with his physician recommended that he transfer to a smaller city. His firm arranged his transfer, and within a short time his problems disappeared.

There is emerging evidence that in some situations an organization can be held legally liable for the emotional and physical impact of job stress on employees like Peter. Poor working conditions, sustained conflicts with supervisors, traumatic events, or intentional harassment of employees sometimes results in anguish, neuroses, or even suicide. If liability is established, employees could claim benefits under workers' compensation laws, as well as sue for financial damages.[4]

Extreme Products of Stress

Stress can be either temporary or long-term, either mild or severe. The effects on an employee depend mostly on how long its causes continue, how powerful they are, and how strong the employee's recovery powers are. If stress is temporary and mild, most people can handle it or at least recover from its effects rather quickly.

> Meyer Jamison, a sales representative, was transferred to a new territory after nine years in his old territory. Suddenly he found himself in a new and unknown situation with different people and job requirements. He felt frustrated, uneasy, and overloaded with work. There

was a lot to learn in a very short time. He developed conflicts with two or three customers and became less cooperative at home. He was in a condition of mild stress.

After a few weeks in his new territory, his stress gradually disappeared, and eventually he became as comfortable as he had been in his old territory.

Jamison probably rebounded from his temporary stress because of his internal **resilience,** or capacity to handle short-term tensions. Resilient individuals often have achieved a balanced life away from work, have learned to set realistic goals, and keep each irritation in perspective. They still face the same amount of stress that others face, but they handle it better.

Employees need resilience.

Burnout   In contrast to Jamison's temporary stress are some major pressures that result in stress that is sustained for long periods. Problems predictably arise when high-intensity stress continues for an extended duration. According to the theory developed by Hans Selye, the human body cannot instantly rebuild its ability to cope with stress once it is depleted.[5] As a result, people become physically and psychologically weakened from trying to combat it. This condition is called **burnout**—a situation in which employees are emotionally exhausted, become detached from their clients and their work, and feel unable to accomplish their goals. Some jobs, such as those in the helping professions (counselors, health care professionals, and social workers) and those with continuous high stress (air-traffic controllers, customer service representatives, waitstaff, and stockbrokers), are more likely than others to cause burnout.[6]

When workers become burned out, they are more likely to complain, to attribute their errors to others, and to be highly irritable. The alienation they feel drives many of them to think about leaving their jobs, to seek out opportunities to become trained for new careers, and actually to quit.[7] In addition to higher turnover, burnout also leads to increased absenteeism and decreased quality and quantity of job performance.

Symptoms of burnout

A tragic product of burnout by workers in Japan is called *karoshi,* or sudden death at work.[8] This is believed to be triggered by overwork, culminating in a fatal heart attack or stroke. Although *karoshi* was once a source of samurai-like pride, estimates of 10,000 deaths per year have prompted preventive actions. Japanese corporations are increasingly urging employees to take earned vacation days, moderate their diets, obtain exercise, and manage their stress levels.

Organizations need to identify both the jobs that lead to early burnout and the employees who exhibit some of the burnout symptoms. Sometimes it may be possible to change the parts of a job that contribute to burnout, such as reducing the frequency or intensity of interpersonal contacts. In other cases the firm can help employees learn how to cope better with their stressful work situations.

Trauma   Another severe product of stress, called **trauma,** occurs following a major threat to one's security. The event could be a natural disaster, an organizational crisis, dramatic employee abuse by the employer, or personal job loss. Employees on ocean-based oil rigs who suffer through a devastating hurricane, overseas workers who are kidnapped by terrorists and held hostage, and members of an antenna installation crew who see a coworker accidentally electrocuted are likely to experience trauma. Three types of trauma that have achieved notoriety in recent years—workplace trauma, layoff survivor's sickness, and post-traumatic stress disorder arising from workplace violence—are discussed here.

One problematic disorder is called **workplace trauma,** which is the disintegration of employees' self-concepts and beliefs in their capabilities. It can arise from harassment at work, wrongful termination, discrimination, or an employee's perceived

Causes of workplace trauma

incapacity to meet evolving performance expectations. In each case, the employee may inappropriately assume responsibility for the event, feel like a victim of circumstances, and fall into an emotional tailspin. Attitudinal clues to workplace trauma include severe moodiness, concentration difficulties, and alienation, in addition to the more distinctive behaviors of tardiness, absenteeism, and accident-proneness.

A common source of workplace trauma is *sudden job loss,* with its *potentially crushing effect on one's self-esteem.* This phenomenon became widespread in the 1990s as a consequence of the wave of corporate downsizings. Thousands of employees within individual companies—and over 9 million workers nationwide—experienced job displacement through sudden and substantial corporate layoffs. Many of these workers suffered at least short-term shock to their self-esteem. The individual impact was often magnified by two factors—the lack of warning (sometimes after hearing earlier strong assurances of no more layoffs) and the lack of insularity felt by even high-performing employees (job security has rapidly lost its meaning for *many* employees, not just marginal ones).

Even those individuals remaining employed after mass downsizings suffer stress. Some experience **layoff survivor's sickness,** with feelings of uncertainty, anger, guilt, and distrust.[9] They are simultaneously glad to have a job and guilty that their workmates were displaced. In the meantime the job pressures on them often increase dramatically as they try to shoulder the tasks of former colleagues. They also wonder, "Will I be the next to be cut?"

Another source of trauma—and product of stress—is to witness **workplace violence.** Sometimes a troubled employee takes dramatic and harmful physical action against coworkers, managers, or company property. These violent, anger-based acts can include unprovoked fights, destruction of property, or use of weapons to harm (or even murder) others. Workplace violence has catapulted homicide into the third-highest work-related cause of death in the United States.

> One highly visible organization that has been the brunt of numerous acts of workplace violence is the U.S. Postal Service. Studies show at least 100 incidents of employees beaten up by supervisors, 300 incidents of supervisors attacked by employees, and several dozen people killed in shootings at various postal stations. Many of these cases followed closely on the heels of unfair probation or dismissal, or receipt of a layoff notice. The violent acts were often perpetrated by people with low self-control—impulsive risk takers with volatile tempers.[10]

Workplace violence such as that at the Postal Service is unique in that it is often both a product of stress and the source of enormous stress on others. Any person who witnesses violence, receives injury from it, or lives under the fear of repeated future violence may suffer from **post-traumatic stress disorder.** The shock of sudden and dramatic violent incidents often produces immediate stress-related symptoms. More significantly, the effects of these traumatic crises may last for years and require lengthy treatment.

Even more important than detecting stress, burnout, and trauma is its *prevention.*

> For example, the U.S. Postal Service has established a crisis management plan that focuses on five areas: careful selection of new employees, a zero tolerance policy to deal with aberrant behavior, improvement of the work culture, mandatory training for managers to help them spot potential problems, and a threat assessment process that is automatically implemented after an employee is dismissed. As a result, actual assaults have dropped sharply, and employee fears about violence have been cut in half.[11]

Causes of Stress

An important first step in prevention is to examine and understand the causes of stress. Conditions that tend to cause stress are called **stressors.** Although even a single stressor may cause major stress, usually stressors combine to pressure an employee in a variety of ways until stress develops.

> The experience of Walter Mathis, an automobile mechanic, illustrates how various conditions combine to cause stress. Mathis felt that he was doing well, but then he failed to get a wage increase he had expected. At about the same time, his wife divorced him. A short time later, partly because of problems leading to the divorce, he underwent a detailed audit by the U.S. Internal Revenue Service. So many different problems were hitting Mathis that he began to show signs of stress.

This example illustrates a common phenomenon—the major sources of employee stress are evenly divided between organizational factors and the nonwork environment. These dual causes are noted in Figure 15–2, which shows that individual differences among employees may cause some to respond to these stressors with positive stress (which stimulates them), while others experience negative stress (which detracts from their efforts). As a result, there may be either constructive or destructive consequences for both the organization and the employee. These effects may be short-term and diminish quickly, or they may last a long time. To control stress, then, organizations usually begin by exploring its job-related causes.

Job-Related Causes of Stress

Almost any job condition can cause stress, depending on an employee's reaction to it. For example, one employee will accept a new work procedure and feel little or no stress, while another experiences overwhelming pressure from the same task. Part of the difference lies in each employee's experiences, general outlooks, and expectations, which are all internal factors. There are, however, a number of job conditions that frequently cause stress for employees. Major ones are shown in Figure 15–3.

Work overload and time deadlines put employees under pressure and lead to stress. Often these pressures arise from management, and a poor quality of management can cause stress. Examples of stress-producing factors related to management are an autocratic supervisor, an insecure job climate, lack of control over one's own job, and inadequate authority to match one's responsibilities.

Examples of job stressors

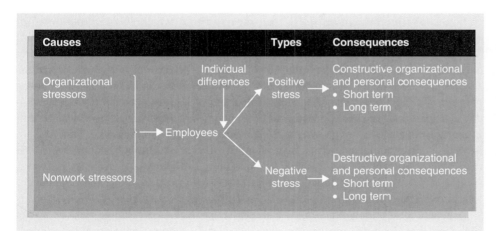

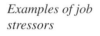

FIGURE 15–2

A model of causes, types, and consequences of stress

Source: Parts of the model are adapted from Randall S. Schuler, "An Integrative Transactional Process Model of Stress in Organizations," *Journal of Occupational Behavior,* January 1982, pp. 5–19.

FIGURE 15–3

Typical causes of stress on the job

- Work overload
- Time pressures
- Poor quality of supervision
- Insecure job climate
- Lack of personal control
- Inadequate authority to match responsibilities
- Role conflict and ambiguity
- Differences between company and employee values
- Change of any type, especially when it is major or unusual
- Frustration
- Technology with training or support

Sources vary.

Marsha Oldburg worked as a production expediter in an electronics plant. She experienced frequent emergencies, conflict, tight schedules, and pressures. She seldom had enough authority to match her responsibility. Occasionally she commented, "This job is getting me down." After three years on her job she discovered during a routine physical checkup that she had high blood pressure. After discussions with a physician, she consulted a human resources counselor, who helped her transfer to a job with less pressure and a better match of authority with responsibility. Within six months her blood pressure was under control.

Role conflict and ambiguity are also related to stress. In situations of this type, people have different expectations of an employee's activities on a job, so the employee does not know what to do and cannot meet all expectations. In addition, since the job often is poorly defined, the employee has no official model on which to depend.

A further cause of stress lies in *differences between company values and ethical practices,* as often reflected in the organization's culture, *and employee ethics and values.* Substantial differences can lead to significant mental stress as an effort is made to balance the requirements of both sets of values.

Some jobs produce more stress than others. Those which involve rotating shift work, machine-paced tasks, routine and repetitive work, or hazardous environments are associated with greater stress. Workers who spend many hours daily in front of computer screens also report high stress levels. Evidence also indicates that the sources of stress differ by organizational level. Executive stress may arise from the pressure for short-term financial results or the fear of a hostile takeover attempt. Middle managers may experience stress when their job security is threatened by news of impending corporate downsizings. Supervisory stressors include the pressures to increase quality and customer service, required attendance at numerous meetings, and responsibility for the work of others. Workers are more likely to experience the stressors of low status, lack of perceived control, resource shortages, and the demand for a large volume of error-free work.

A general and widely recognized cause of stress is change of any type (see "What Managers Are Reading" on the next page), because it requires adaptation by employees. It tends to be especially stressful when it is major or unusual, such as a tempo-

The dramatic rise in the use of technology at work in the latter decades of the twentieth century has been a mixed blessing. On the positive side, it has sped up information flows, provided people with access to vast stores of knowledge, and connected people across the globe. On the negative side, it has caused three major problems among employees:

1. Feelings that they have little control over what technology they use
2. Feelings that they received inadequate or insufficient training on how to use it

3. Feelings that there is seldom a break from the daily bombardment of information received

The combination of these feelings produces widespread "technostress," which is further compounded by a loss of privacy, inundation with messages, the demand to learn new skills, and the dramatic erosion of important face-to-face contacts. Organizations are urged to adopt a people-based model of training that reduces employee discomfort with technology by involving the entire staff in future technological choices.

Source: Michelle M. Weil and Larry D. Rosen, *Technostress: Coping with Technology @Work@Home@Play,* New York: John Wiley & Sons, 1997.

rary layoff or transfer. A related source of stress that affects many employees is worry over their financial well-being. This situation can arise when cost-saving technology is introduced, contract negotiations begin, or the firm's financial performance suffers. Clearly, there are numerous and powerful forces at work that can contribute to the feeling of stress.

Frustration

Another cause of stress is **frustration.** It is a result of a motivation (drive) being blocked to prevent one from reaching a desired goal. Imagine that you are trying to finish a report by quitting time, but one interference after another requires your attention—and your time. By the middle of the afternoon, when you see that your goal for the day may not be reached, you are likely to become frustrated. You may become irritable, develop an uneasy feeling in your stomach, or have some other reaction. These reactions to frustration are known as **defense mechanisms,** because you are trying to defend yourself from the psychological effects of the blocked goal.

What are defense mechanisms?

The example given is merely a one-day frustration that probably will be overcome tomorrow, but the situation is more serious when there is a long-run frustration, such as blocked opportunity for promotion. Then you have to live with the frustration day after day. It begins to build emotional disorders that interfere with your ability to function effectively.

Types of Reactions   One of the most common reactions to frustration is *aggression.* Whenever people are aggressive, it is likely that they are reflecting frustrations that are upsetting them. Additional reactions to frustration include apathy, withdrawal, regression, fixation, physical disorders, and substitute goals. We can illustrate them by continuing the story of the blocked promotion. Suppose that you think your supervisor is blocking your promotion. The blockage may be real or only a result of your imagination, but in any case it is real to you. As a result of your frustration, you may become aggressive by demanding better treatment and threatening to appeal to higher management. Or you may do almost the reverse and become *apathetic,* not responding to your job or associates. Another reaction is *withdrawal,* such as asking for a transfer or quitting your job. *Regression* to less mature behavior, such as self-pity and pouting, also is possible.

If there is a *fixation,* perhaps you constantly blame your supervisor for both your problems and the problems of others, regardless of the facts. You also may develop a *physical disorder,* such as an upset stomach, or choose a substitute goal, such as becoming the leader of a powerful informal group in office politics. All of these are possible reactions to frustration. It is evident that they are not usually favorable, either to the individual or to the organization, so it is desirable in organizational behavior to reduce frustrating conditions.

Sources of Frustration   Although management can be the source of frustration, it is only one of several sources. Another major source is coworkers who may place barriers in the way of goal attainment. Perhaps they withhold work inputs to you, thereby delaying your work. Or their poorly done inputs prevent you from doing quality work. You also can be frustrated by the work itself, such as a part that does not fit or a machine that breaks down. Even the environment, such as a rainy day, may prevent you from doing the work you intended.

Frequency and severity of hassles

Some research suggests that it is the little things, called **hassles,** rather than major life crises, that produce frustration. Hassles are conditions of daily living that are perceived to threaten one's well-being. They have been found to be related to both symptoms of ill health and levels of absenteeism.[12] The most frequent hassles include having too many things to do, losing items, being interrupted, and having to do unchallenging work. Some of the hassles with the greatest average severity are related to either the job or the employee's environment, such as dealing with problems of aging parents, facing prejudice and discrimination, and having insufficient personal energy. It is possible that none of these hassles alone will cause the average person to become frustrated. However, the cumulative effects of *multiple* hassles may well result in a feeling of unwelcome stress.

Managers are sometimes hardened to the effects of hassles on employee feelings and urge employees to ignore them. This has two clear consequences, however. First, such brush-aside behavior can result in **marginalized employees**—employees made to feel insignificant by the callous dismissal of their legitimate feelings. Second, it ignores the very real possibility that the employees who haven't adequately addressed the little hassles in their lives may be even less able to respond constructively to more powerful sources of frustration. Employees commonly become angry over issues such as favoritism, unfair appraisals, insufficient resources, lack of training, harassment, insensitivity, poor communication, and lack of trust. These real problems can even instigate an **incivility spiral,** wherein one frustrated employee vents unfairly on another, who then compounds the problem by making a bigger fuss on another, and so on.[13] Consequently, it is desirable for managers to be alert to, and confront, the smaller problems before they become magnified.

Frustration and Management Practice   The stronger one's motivation or drive toward a blocked goal, the stronger one's frustration will be, other things being equal. If motivation is lacking, then very little frustration is likely to develop. One implication is that when management attempts to motivate employees strongly, it also should be prepared to remove barriers and help prepare the way for employees to reach their goals. The required managerial role is a supportive one. For example, if precision machine work is demanded, the machinist needs proper training, equipment, tools, and materials for precision work. Similarly, if an employee is assigned a special project and is motivated to do it, then a suitable budget and other support are required in order to prevent frustration. The idea is not to remove all difficulties so that the assignment loses its challenge but, rather, to provide enough support to make the project reasonably possible.

Supportive management is needed.

Counseling (discussed later in this chapter) can help reduce frustrations by helping employees choose mature courses of action to overcome blockages preventing goal accomplishment. The counselor also can advise management regarding blockages so that it can try to reduce or remove them.

373

Stress and Job Performance

Stress can be either helpful or harmful to job performance, depending on its level. Figure 15–4 presents a **stress-performance model** that shows the relationship between stress and job performance. When there is no stress, job challenges are absent and performance tends to be low. As stress increases, performance tends to increase, because stress helps a person call up resources to meet job requirements. Constructive stress is a healthy stimulus that encourages employees to respond to challenges. Eventually, stress reaches a plateau that corresponds approximately with a person's top day-to-day performance capability. At this point additional stress tends to produce no more improvement.

Effects of stress on performance

Finally, if stress becomes too great, it turns into a destructive force. *Performance begins to decline at some point because excess stress interferes with performance.* An employee loses the ability to cope; she or he becomes unable to make decisions and exhibits erratic behavior. If stress increases to a breaking point, performance becomes zero; the employee has a breakdown, becomes too ill to work, is fired, quits, or refuses to come to work to face the stress.

> The significance of individual differences in the stress-performance relationship is highlighted by the results of a survey of employee perceptions of stress.[14] Sixty-two percent of the respondents reported that stress impeded their performance, while 23 percent asserted that it actually made them do their jobs better. The other 15 percent either didn't know, or reported no impact. Apparently, what works well for one person can be dysfunctional for another.

The stress-performance relationship may be compared to strings on a violin. When there is either too little or too much tension on the strings, they will not produce suitable music. Further, the violin strings may need to be readjusted to accommodate changing conditions, such as increased humidity. As with violin strings, when tension on an employee is either too high or low, the employee's performance will tend to deteriorate. The managerial challenge is to monitor tension levels and make periodic adjustments.

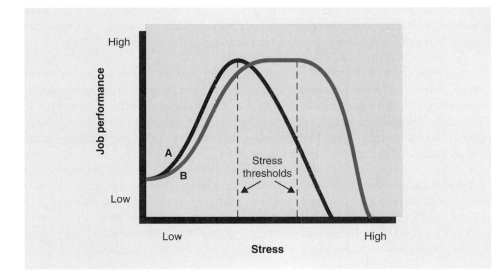

FIGURE 15–4

A stress-performance model depicting two stress thresholds

374

Athletes try to find the right balance of stress and performance. In tennis, upsets occur every year at Wimbledon when an unseeded player who is "not supposed to win" rises to the occasion and later admits to having felt only moderate stress. The vanquished opponent, who took the match too lightly, may not have experienced enough stress to stimulate early performance. Then, once the match appears to be slipping away, the favored player begins feeling too much stress to allow optimum play.

Stress Vulnerability

Stress Threshold   Two major factors help determine how stress will affect employee performance differently across similar jobs. Worker vulnerability to stress is a function of both internal (organizational) and external (nonwork) stressors, as shown earlier in Figure 15–2. One internal factor is an employee's **stress threshold**— the level of stressors (frequency and magnitude) that the person can tolerate before negative feelings of stress occur and adversely affect performance. Some people have a *low threshold,* and the stress of even relatively small changes or disruptions in their work routines causes a reduction in performance. This response is shown by line A in Figure 15–4. Others (see line *B* in the figure) have a *higher threshold,* staying cool, calm, and productive longer under the same conditions. This response may stem partly from their experience and confidence in their ability to cope. A higher stress threshold helps prevent lowered performance unless a stressor is major or prolonged.

> Marie Johnson was a cashier at a local supermarket. Every day she faced long lines, time pressures, complaints from customers, and pricing errors, but these events did not seem to trouble her. Antonio Valenzuela, a cashier at an adjoining counter, had difficulty with the complaints and pressures he received. He began to make errors and get into arguments with customers and other clerks. Finally, he asked to transfer to another job in the store. The two employees clearly had different stress thresholds.

Perceived Control   The second internal factor affecting employee stress is the amount of **perceived control** they have over their work and working conditions. Employees who have a substantial degree of independence, autonomy, and freedom to make decisions seem to handle work pressures better. Since two employees may have the same actual control and flexibility, it is clearly their relative *perception* of that freedom that counts. Managers can respond to this need for control through a variety of measures discussed earlier in this book, such as allowing flexible work schedules, enriching jobs, placing individuals on self-managing teams, or empowering employees by using participative leadership styles.

Type A behaviors

Type A and Type B People   Stress vulnerability is often related to type A and B characteristics.[15] **Type A people** are aggressive and competitive, set high standards, are impatient with themselves and others, and thrive under constant time pressures. They make excessive demands on themselves even in recreation and leisure. They often fail to realize that many of the pressures they feel are of their own making rather than products of their environment. Because of the constant stress that they feel, some type A's are more prone to physical ailments related to stress, such as heart attacks.

Type B behaviors

    Type B people appear more relaxed and easygoing. They accept situations and work within them rather than fight them competitively. Type B people are especially relaxed regarding time pressures, so they are less prone to have problems associated with stress. Still, type B individuals can be highly productive workers who meet schedule expectations; they simply obtain results in a different manner.

The research on type A and type B people is still accumulating.[16] For example, some of the type A behavior patterns, such as competitiveness and a drive for career success, appear to be consistent with society's values. At the same time, the hostility and aggression these people exhibit may make it difficult for many employees to work with them. Some studies also suggest that there may be different forms of type A personalities. As a result, the type A's who are more expressive and less hostile may be less prone to heart disease. Other type A's apparently enjoy their success so much that they disregard the surrounding stress and do not suffer from heart attacks or other physical consequences.

The distinction between type A and type B people raises several challenging questions for managers. Should an organization consider the type A or type B nature of employees when making job assignments? Should it develop training programs to help change type A employees into type B employees? Does it have a responsibility to provide training that will help both A's and B's cope with the work habits and expectations of supervisors who are different from themselves? Although stress reduction at work is a desirable goal, finding the answers to these questions will require consideration of ethical, financial, and practical issues.

Approaches to Stress Management

Both organizations and individuals are highly concerned about stress and its effects. In attempting to manage stress, they have three broad options—prevent or control it, escape from it, or learn to adapt to it (handle its symptoms). Organizations can seek to improve managerial communication skills, empower employees through participation, redesign jobs to be more fulfilling, or implement organization development programs. These steps are aimed at *reducing or eliminating stressors* for employees. Some employees can *escape* stress by requesting job transfers, finding alternative employment, taking early retirement, or acquiring assertiveness skills that allow them to confront the stressor. Several approaches also exist for *coping* with stress (see, for example, the personal prescriptions in Figure 15–5).[17] These often involve cooperative efforts among employees and management and may include social support, relaxation efforts, biofeedback, and personal wellness programs.

Three approaches: prevent, escape, or cope

Social Support   Some people experience stress because they are detached from the world around them; they lack warm interpersonal relationships. Individuals with a driving ambition and a strong need for independence may fail to develop close

Types of support

---

1. Resist working long hours or accepting overtime.
2. Volunteer for flextime or other alternative work schedules.
3. Identify the people who cause stress and avoid them.
4. Maintain a healthy diet.
5. Obtain regular exercise.
6. Avoid procrastination.
7. Set reasonable goals for yourself.
8. Develop a simple method of organizing things, and adhere to it.
9. Step back from stress and decide whether you need to fight every battle.
10. Consult with a trusted friend before becoming involved in new activities.

FIGURE 15–5

Common personal strategies for managing stress

attachments to friends and colleagues. To achieve their success, they often sacrifice fulfillment of their social needs. Their lack of social attachments may result in anger, anxiety, and loneliness—all producing stress in their lives.

A powerful antidote to this problem lies in the presence of social support at work. **Social support** is the network of helpful activities, interactions, and relationships that provides an employee with the satisfaction of important needs. There are four types of support in a total network: instrumental (task assistance), informational, evaluative, and emotional. Each is demonstrated in this example of responses to a personal stressor:

> Diane's father passed away suddenly one day. She missed a week of work while attending the funeral and getting her mother's future affairs in order. During this time (1) Aggie, a coworker, worked extra hours to keep Diane's work from falling behind (task support); (2) Marilyn, Diane's supervisor, provided helpful resources (information) to guide her mother's financial decisions; (3) Karen, her sister, kept a watchful eye on Diane and helped her recover from her grief by giving her daily feedback (evaluation) on how she was handling the situation; and (4) Diane's husband exhibited empathy and caring (emotional support) toward her by taking her on long walks and engaging her in quiet chats.

This illustration shows that social support may come from supervisors, coworkers, friends, or family. Its focus may be on either work tasks or social exchanges and may even take the form of games, jokes, or teasing. Research suggests that when employees have at least one person from whom they can receive social support (especially emotional support), they will experience lower stress.[18] Females, in particular, not only place more value on social support but seem to feel more comfortable, and capable, in providing it to others. Supervisors—male or female—need to develop the capacity to play this role for their employees when support is needed. An alternative action is to simply provide opportunities for social support and encourage it to develop among a group of workers. Managers may need to allow time for employees to develop and nurture their social support networks at work.

Relaxation   Some employees have turned to various means of mental relaxation to adjust to the stresses in their lives. Patterned after the practice of meditation, the **relaxation response** involves quiet, concentrated inner thought in order to rest the body physically and emotionally. It helps remove people temporarily from the stressful world and reduce their symptoms of stress. The ideal ingredients of this relaxation effort involve

- A comfortable position in a relatively quiet location
- Closed eyes and deep, comfortable breaths
- Repetition of a peaceful word, or focus on a pleasant mental image
- Avoidance of distracting thoughts and negative events
- Soothing background music

Practicing a simple relaxation response is like taking a time-out at work. It requires only a few minutes and can be especially fruitful just before or after a tense encounter. It is so highly regarded that a few organizations have established special lounges for employee use, and many employees who use them for momentary relaxation report favorable results regarding their capacity to deal with stress.

Biofeedback   A different approach for working with stress is **biofeedback,** by which people under medical guidance learn from instrument feedback to influence symptoms of stress, such as increased heart rate or severe headaches. Earlier, it was thought that people could not control their involuntary nervous system which, in turn, controls internal processes such as heartbeat, oxygen consumption, stomach acid flow, and brain waves. There now is evidence that people *can* exercise some control over these internal processes; thus biofeedback may be helpful in reducing undesirable effects of stress.

Sabbaticals   Whereas relaxation and biofeedback are methods for coping with stress, sometimes it is wisest to at least temporarily remove yourself from it. Some employers, recognizing this need for employees to escape, have created programs allowing **sabbatical leaves** to encourage stress relief and personal education. Some sabbaticals provide unpaid time off, others give partially paid leaves, and a few continue full pay while employees are away. Although most firms allow only four to eight weeks, some, such as Xerox, authorize up to a full year away. Most employees return emotionally refreshed, feel rewarded and valued by their employers, and often bring back new perspectives gained from readings and workshops. A side benefit sometimes reported is the cross-training that takes place among colleagues while one employee is on sabbatical. This side effect adds to organizational flexibility and raises employee competency and self-esteem.

Personal Wellness   In general, there is a trend toward in-house programs of preventive maintenance for **personal wellness** that are based on research in behavioral medicine. Corporate wellness centers may include disease screening, health education, and fitness centers. Health care specialists can recommend practices to encourage changes in lifestyle, such as breathing regulation, muscle relaxation, positive imagery, nutrition management, and exercise, enabling employees to use more of their full potential. Clearly, a preventive approach is preferable for reducing the causes of stress, although coping methods can help employees adapt to stressors that are beyond direct control. The key is to create a better fit between people and their work environment, and alternative approaches may be useful for different employees.

Preventive approaches

> Travelers Corporation created its Taking Care Program, which includes a fitness center, educational health tips, and other services. Later evaluation of the program showed that productivity gains and lower medical and absenteeism costs produced $3.40 of savings for every $1.00 spent. Total net savings in just one year added up to $9.8 million.[19]

EMPLOYEE COUNSELING

What Counseling Is

Counseling is discussion with an employee of a problem that usually has emotional content in order to help the employee cope with it better. Counseling seeks to improve employee mental health and well-being. As shown in Figure 15–6, *good mental health* means that people feel comfortable about themselves, right about other people, and able to meet the demands of life.

The goal of counseling

The definition of counseling implies a number of characteristics. It is an exchange of ideas and feelings between two people, nominally a counselor and a counselee, so it is an act of communication. Since it helps employees cope with problems, it should improve organizational performance, because the employee becomes more cooperative, worries less about personal problems, or improves in other ways. Emphasis on counseling also helps the organization become more human and considerate of people's problems.

FIGURE 15–6

Characteristics of people with good mental health

Source: Mental Health Is 1, 2, 3, Arlington, VA: Mental Health Association, n.d.

378

People with good mental health

1. **Feel comfortable about themselves**

   - Are not bowled over by their own emotions—by their fears, anger, love, jealousy, guilt, or worries
   - Can take life's disappointments in their stride
   - Have a tolerant, easygoing attitude toward themselves as well as others; can laugh at themselves
   - Neither underestimate nor overestimate their abilities
   - Can accept their own shortcomings
   - Have self-respect
   - Feel able to deal with most situations that come their way
   - Get satisfaction from simple, everyday pleasures

2. **Feel right about other people**

   - Are able to give love and to consider the interests of others
   - Have personal relationships that are satisfying and lasting
   - Expect to like and trust others, and take it for granted that others will like and trust them
   - Respect the many differences they find in people
   - Do not push people around, and do not allow themselves to be pushed around
   - Can feel they are part of a group
   - Feel a sense of responsibility to their neighbors and others

3. **Are able to meet the demands of life**

   - Do something about their problems as they arise
   - Accept their responsibilities
   - Shape their environment whenever possible; adjust to it whenever necessary
   - Plan ahead but do not fear the future
   - Welcome new experiences and new ideas
   - Make use of their natural capacities
   - Set realistic goals for themselves
   - Are able to think for themselves and make their own decisions
   - Put their best effort into what they do and get satisfaction out of it

Counseling may be performed by both professionals and nonprofessionals. For example, both a human resource specialist in counseling and a supervisor who is not trained in counseling may counsel employees. Therapists and personal physicians also counsel employees, and even an employee's friends may provide counseling.

Counseling usually is confidential so that employees will feel free to talk openly about their problems. It also involves both job and personal problems, since both types of problems may affect an employee's performance on the job. For example, one employee may be experiencing the stress of new job expectations, while another may be distraught with grief following the death of a family member. Both employees are potential candidates for receiving the benefits of counseling at work.

> Polaroid Corporation recognized that domestic violence among their employees had a powerful negative effect on workplace productivity and morale. (Four million women in the United States are abused by their husbands or partners annually; workers miss 175,000 days of paid work each year due to domestic violence.) Polaroid extended its employee assistance program to include treatment for domestic violence and developed training programs so that its managers could better recognize and deal with incidents of domestic violence.[20]

Need for Counseling

The need for counseling arises from a variety of employee problems, including stress. When these problems exist, employees benefit from the understanding and guidance that counseling can provide. For example, one employee feels insecure about retirement. Another employee is hesitant to take the risk required by a promotion and thus ceases growing on the job. A third employee may become unstable in the job. In all cases, counseling is a necessity.

> Ross Callander was an interviewer in a state employment office. Over the span of a few weeks he became unstable in his job, becoming angry easily and being rude to interviewees. His manager noticed the change and discussed it with him. When his behavior continued, he was referred to a counselor. The counselor learned that Callander's son had been arrested and in anger had accused Callander of being a failure as a parent. Callander felt resentful, frustrated, and defeated, and he was transferring these feelings to his interviewees. With the help of a community agency, Callander's family problem was solved, and he quickly returned to normal job performance.

Most problems that require counseling have some emotional content. *Emotions are a normal part of life*. Nature gave people their emotions, and these feelings make people human. On the other hand, emotions can get out of control and cause workers to do things that are harmful to their own best interests and those of the firm. They may leave their jobs because of trifling conflicts that seem large to them, or they may undermine morale in their departments. Managers want their employees to maintain good mental health and to channel their emotions along constructive lines so that they will work together effectively.

Emotions can cause problems.

What Counseling Can Do

The general objectives of counseling are to help employees grow in self-confidence, understanding, self-control, and ability to work effectively. These objectives are consistent with the supportive, collegial, and system models of organizational behavior, which encourage employee growth and self-direction. They are also consistent with Maslow's higher-order needs and Alderfer's growth needs, such as self-esteem and self-actualization.

Six functions of counseling

FIGURE 15–7

Functions of counseling

Advice	Telling a person what you think should be done; coaching
Reassurance	Giving a person courage and confidence to face a problem
Communication	Providing information and understanding
Release of emotional tension	Helping a person feel more free of frustrations and stress
Clarified thinking	Encouraging more coherent, rational, and mature thought
Reorientation	Encouraging an internal change in goals, values, and mental models

The counseling objective is achieved through one or more of the following **counseling functions.** The six activities performed by counseling are shown in Figure 15–7. As is noted later, some types of counseling perform one function better than another.

1. *Advice*   Many people view counseling as primarily an advice-giving activity, but in reality this is only one of several functions that counseling can perform. The giving of advice requires a counselor to make judgments about a counselee's problems and to lay out a course of action. Herein lies the difficulty, because it is almost impossible to understand another person's complicated problems, much less tell that person what to do about them. Advice giving may breed a relationship in which the counselee feels inferior and dependent on the counselor. In spite of all its ills, advice occurs in routine counseling because workers expect it and managers tend to provide it.

2. *Reassurance*   Counseling can provide employees with reassurance, which is a way of giving them courage to face a problem or a feeling of confidence that they are pursuing a suitable course of action. Reassurance is represented by such counselor remarks as "You are making good progress, Linda," and "Don't worry; this will come out all right."

One trouble with reassurance is that the counselees do not always accept it. They are smart enough to know that the counselor cannot know that the problem will come out all right. Even if counselees initially accept reassurance, their new self-confidence may fade away as soon as they face their problems again, which means that little real improvement has been made. Their false sense of self-confidence may even lead them to make poor personal decisions.

Though reassurance has its weaknesses, it is useful in some situations and is impossible to prohibit. Reassurance cannot be prohibited just because it is dangerous, any more than automobiles can be prohibited because they cause accidents; but, like automobiles, reassurance should be handled carefully.

3. *Communication*   Counseling can improve both upward and downward communication. In an upward direction, it is a key way for employees to express their feelings to management. As many people have said, often the top managers in an organization do not know how those at the bottom feel. The act of counseling initiates an upward signal, and if the channels are open, some of these signals will travel higher. Individual names must be kept confidential, but statements of feeling can be grouped and interpreted to management. An important part of any counselor's job is to discover emotional problems related to company policies and to interpret those types of problems to top management. Counseling also achieves downward communication because counselors help interpret company activities to employees as they discuss problems related to them.

4. *Release of Emotional Tension*   An important function of nearly all counseling is release of emotional tension; this release is sometimes called **emotional catharsis.** People tend to get an emotional release from their frustrations and other problems whenever they have an opportunity to tell someone about them. Counseling history consistently shows that as people begin to explain their problems to a sympathetic listener, their tensions begin to subside. They are more relaxed, and their speech is more coherent and rational. This release of tension does not necessarily solve people's problems, but it does remove mental blocks in the way of solution, enabling them to face their problems again and think constructively about them. In some cases emotional release accomplishes the whole job, dispelling an employee's problems as if they were mental ghosts, which they largely were.

Emotional catharsis reduces tensions.

> In a warehouse an electric-truck driver, Bill Irwin, began to develop conflicts with his supervisor. Irwin was convinced that his supervisor gave him the hardest jobs and otherwise took advantage of him. He was convinced that his supervisor did not like him and would never give him a raise. One day the company's timekeeper was in the warehouse checking time records, and Irwin, being particularly upset at the moment, cornered him and began to tell about his troubles. It all started when Irwin commented, "You don't need to worry about my time. I'll never get a rate increase, and I'll never have any overtime." The timekeeper asked, "Why?" and the conversation went on from there.
>
> The timekeeper was a staff employee working for the warehouse superintendent and was not in the chain of command from superintendent to supervisor to Irwin, so Irwin felt free to talk. Perhaps Irwin also saw the timekeeper as a means of communication around his supervisor to the superintendent. At any rate, Irwin talked. And the timekeeper listened.
>
> Since the timekeeper spent much of his time on the warehouse floor, he was closely acquainted with work assignments and the supervisor. Irwin knew this; and as he stated his grievances, he began to revise and soften them because he realized some of them did not agree with details of the situation about which the timekeeper had firsthand knowledge. As Irwin continued to bring his feelings out into the open, he felt easier and could discuss his problem more calmly. He realized that what he had said in the beginning was mostly a buildup of his own imagination and did not make sense in terms of the actual situation. He closed the conversation with the comment, "I guess I really don't have much of a problem, but I'm glad I told you anyway."

5. *Clarified Thinking*   The case of Irwin also illustrates another function of counseling, that of **clarified thinking.** Irwin began to realize that his emotional comments did not match the facts of the situation. He found that he was magnifying minor incidents and jumping to drastic conclusions. As his emotional blocks to straight thinking were eliminated, he began to think more rationally. In this case realistic thinking was encouraged because Irwin recognized that he was talking to someone who knew the facts and was not emotionally involved.

Clarified thinking tends to be a normal result of emotional release, but a skilled counselor can aid this process. In order to clarify the counselee's thinking, the counselor serves as an aid only and refrains from telling the counselee what is right. Further, the clarified thinking may not even take place while the counselor and counselee are talking. Part, or all, of it may take place later as a result of developments during the counseling relationship. The result of any clarified thinking is that a person is encouraged to accept responsibility for emotional problems and to be more realistic in solving them.

Reorientation requires a major change.

6. *Reorientation*   Another function of counseling is reorientation of the counselee. This is more than mere emotional release or clear thinking about a problem. **Reorientation** involves a change in the employee's psychic self through a change in basic goals and values. For example, it can help people recognize and accept their own limitations. Reorientation is the kind of function needed to help alcoholics return to normalcy or to treat a person with severe mental depression. It is largely a job for professional counselors who know its uses and limitations and who have the necessary training. The manager's job is to recognize those in need of reorientation before their need becomes severe, so that they can be referred to professional help in time for successful treatment.

The Manager's Counseling Role

Excluding reorientation, the counseling functions usually can be performed successfully by managers. They will at times perform all five counseling functions. On other occasions, if professional counseling services are available and a problem is significant, they will, and should, refer employees to the professional counselors. The point is that when counseling services are established, *managers must not conclude that all their counseling responsibilities have been transferred to the counseling staff.*

Training is needed for managers.

Managers are important counselors because they are the ones in day-to-day interaction with employees. If managers close their eyes to the emotional problems of employees and refuse to discuss them, it appears that managers are saying to employees, "I don't care about *you,* just your work." Managers cannot, when an emotional upset arises, say, "This is not part of my job. Go see a counselor." Emotions are part of the whole employee and must be considered a part of the total employment situation for which a manager is responsible. For this reason *all managers,* from the lowest to the highest levels, *need training to help them understand problems of employees and counsel them effectively.*

An Ethics Question

Supervisors often find themselves caught between the proverbial rock and a hard place. As part of the management team, they may be aware of impending corporate decisions that have not yet been announced to employees. They have an obligation not to disclose key information prematurely, yet they are tempted to do so. This ethical dilemma often arises during corporate downsizings, during the period when decisions are still being made regarding which employees to retain and which to release. Assume that a marginal employee—one highly likely to be on your own list of layoff recommendations—comes to you in your role as a supervisory counselor and discloses an array of deep personal problems. Then the individual changes the topic abruptly and asks, "You don't really think that this company would lay off someone with all of my stresses, do you?" How would you answer this individual?

Since almost all problems brought to a manager have a combination of factual and emotional content, a manager should not spend all day looking for emotional content when a rational answer will solve the problem.

> During a reorganization of office space, if an employee asks, "Is my desk going to be moved?" it may be that she is really wondering why anyone would want to move her desk or whether doing so would reduce her status; but it is also possible—just possible—that she only wants to know, "Is my desk going to be moved?" If you answer, "Yes, over by the window," you have solved the problem she brought you, and there is no need to try to be an amateur psychiatrist.

It is said that the father of psychiatry, Sigmund Freud, warned about the dangers of seeing emotional meaning in everything a person says or does. When a friend asked him what was the emotional meaning of the pipe he smoked, he replied, "Sometimes, sir, a pipe is just a pipe," meaning that it had no particular emotional interpretation.

TYPES OF COUNSELING

In terms of the amount of direction that a counselor gives a counselee, counseling can be viewed as a continuum from full direction (directive counseling) to no direction (nondirective counseling), as shown in Figure 15–8. Between the two extremes is participative counseling. These three counseling types are discussed in order to show how counselors may vary their direction in a counseling situation.

A continuum of counseling types

Directive Counseling

Directive counseling is the process of listening to an employee's problem, deciding with the employee what should be done, and then telling and motivating the employee to do it. Directive counseling mostly accomplishes the counseling function of *advice,* but it also may reassure, communicate, give emotional release, and—to a minor extent—clarify thinking. Reorientation is seldom achieved in directive counseling.

Almost everyone likes to give advice, counselors included, and it is easy to do. But is it effective? Does the counselor really understand the employee's problem? Does the counselor have the knowledge and judgment to make a right decision? Even if the decision is right, *will the employee follow it?* The answer to these questions is usually no; hence advice may not be helpful in counseling.

Though advice is of questionable value, some of the other functions are worthwhile. If the directive counselor is a good listener, then the employee should feel some emotional release. As the result of emotional release coupled with ideas that the counselor imparts, the employee also may clarify thinking. Furthermore, useful

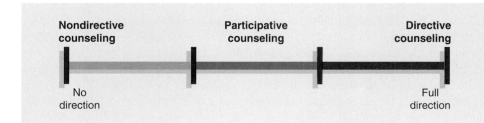

FIGURE 15–8

Types of counseling according to amount of direction that counselors provide communication probably takes place. Both advice and reassurance can be worthwhile if they give the employee more courage to take a helpful course of action that the employee supports.

Nondirective Counseling

Skillful listening is required.

Nondirective, or *client-centered,* **counseling** is at the opposite end of the continuum. It is the process of skillfully listening to and encouraging a counselee to explain troublesome problems, understand them, and determine appropriate solutions. It focuses on the counselee rather than on the counselor as judge and adviser; thus it is client-centered. Managers can use the nondirective approach; however, care should be taken to make sure that managers are not so oversold on it that they neglect their normal directive leadership responsibilities.

Nondirective counseling was developed concurrently by two groups: Elton Mayo, Fritz Roethlisberger, and others at Western Electric Company and Carl R. Rogers and his colleagues.[21] Here is the way nondirective counseling can work:

> Harold Pace went to a counselor, Janis Peterson, for assistance. Peterson attempted to build a relationship that encouraged Pace to talk freely. At this point Peterson defined the counseling relationship by explaining that she would not tell Pace how to solve his problem but that she would try to help him understand it and deal satisfactorily with it.
>
> Pace then explained his feelings, and the counselor encouraged their expression, showed interest in them, and accepted them without blame or praise. Eventually the negative feelings were drained away, giving Pace a chance to express tentatively a positive feeling or two, a fact that marked the beginning of Pace's emotional growth. The counselor encouraged these positive feelings and accepted them without blame or praise, just as she did the negative feelings.
>
> Over time, Pace began to get some insight into his problem and to develop alternative solutions to it. As he continued to grow, he was able to choose a course of positive action and see his way clear to try it. He then felt a decreasing need for help and recognized that the counseling relationship should come to an end.

Feelings need to be accepted.

Throughout the counseling relationship, it is important for the counselor to *accept* feelings—rather than *judge* them, offering blame or praise—because judgment and evaluation may discourage an employee from stating true feelings. The basic idea is to get the employee to discuss feelings, to explore solutions, and to make wise decisions. Major differences between nondirective and directive counseling are summarized in Figure 15–9. They reveal that in nondirective counseling the counselee is the key person, while the counselor is the key in a directive approach.

Use by Professionals   Professional counselors usually practice some form of nondirective counseling and often accomplish four of the six counseling functions. Communication occurs both upward and downward through the counselor. Emotional release takes place even more effectively than with directive counseling, and clarified thinking tends to follow. The unique advantage of nondirective counseling is its ability to cause the employee's reorientation. It emphasizes *changing the person* instead of *dealing only with the immediate problem,* in the usual manner of directive counseling.

Professional counselors treat each counselee as a social and organizational equal. They primarily listen in a caring and supportive fashion and try to help the counselee discover and follow improved courses of action. They especially listen between the lines to learn the full meaning of an employee's feelings. They look for the assumptions underlying the employee's statements and for the events and feelings that are so painful that the employee tends to avoid talking about them. As shown in Figure 15–10, nondirective

	Nondirective Counseling	Directive Counseling
Counseling method	The employee primarily controls the direction of the conversation and does most of the talking.	The counselor primarily controls the direction of the conversation and does most of the talking.
Responsibility for solution	Employee	Counselor
Status of participants	The employee and the counselor are on an equal level.	The counselor is at least implicitly superior to the employee.
Role of participants	The employee is psychologically independent as a person, choosing a solution and growing in ability to make choices in the future.	The employee is psychologically dependent on the counselor, whose role as a problem-solver tends to limit the employee's personal growth.
Emphasis placed	Psychological adjustment is paramount, with deep feelings and emotional problems accented.	Solution of current problems is emphasized, with feelings and emotions often ignored.

counselors follow an **iceberg model of counseling,** in which they recognize that sometimes more feelings are hidden under the surface of a counselee's communication than are revealed. For this reason they constantly encourage the counselee to open up and reveal deeper feelings that may help solve the employee's problem.

Limitations   With all its advantages, nondirective counseling has several limitations that restrict its use at work. First of all, it is more time-consuming and costly than directive counseling. Since just one employee with one problem may require many hours of

Costliness of nondirective counseling

FIGURE 15–10

Iceberg model of counseling

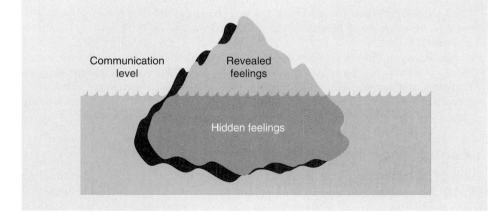

a counselor's time, the number of employees that a counselor can assist is limited. Professional counselors require professional education and consequently are expensive. Nondirective counseling also depends on a capable, willing employee. It assumes that the employee possesses a drive for well-being, has enough social intelligence to perceive what problems need solution, and has sufficient emotional stability to deal with them. The nondirective counselor needs to be careful not to become a crutch for emotionally dependent employees to lean on while they avoid their work responsibilities.

In some cases counseling itself is a weak solution because it necessarily returns the employee to the same environment that caused the problem. What is really needed is a better environment for providing employee psychological support. In this situation the counselor may step beyond the usual counseling role and give advice to management to take corrective action.

Participative Counseling

How does participative counseling work?

Nondirective counseling of employees is limited because it requires professional counselors and is costly. Directive counseling often is not accepted by modern, independent employees. The type of counseling typically used in organizations is between the two extremes of directive and nondirective counseling. This middle ground is called participative counseling.

Participative counseling (also called *cooperative counseling*) is a mutual counselor-counselee relationship that establishes a cooperative exchange of ideas to help solve a counselee's problems. It is neither wholly counselor-centered nor wholly counselee-centered. Rather, the counselor and counselee mutually apply their different knowledge, perspectives, and values to problems. Participative counseling integrates the ideas of both participants in a counseling relationship. It is, therefore, a balanced compromise that combines many advantages of both directive and nondirective counseling while avoiding most of their disadvantages.

Participative counseling starts by using the listening techniques of nondirective counseling; but as the interview progresses, participative counselors may play a more active role than nondirective counselors would. They offer bits of knowledge and insight; they may discuss the situation from their broader knowledge of the organization, thus giving an employee a different view of the problem. In general, participative counselors apply the four counseling functions of reassurance, communication, emotional release, and clarified thinking.

> Mary Carlisle was emotionally upset because she was not getting the promotions that she wanted. Although she discussed her problem with her supervisor, she was not wholly satisfied and asked to see a counselor. She and the counselor established open communication early in their discussion because at this point Carlisle was ready to open up about her problems.
>
> The counselor did not tell Carlisle what to do (directive approach) and did not merely listen (nondirective approach). Rather, the counselor explored various alternatives with Carlisle, communicated some ideas about training, and provided reassurance that Carlisle could become fully qualified for promotion. The result was that Carlisle saw her problem more clearly (clarified thinking) and chose an appropriate course of action.

A Contingency View

A manager's decision to use either directive, participative, or nondirective counseling with an employee should be based on an analysis of several contingency factors. It should not be made solely on the manager's personal preference or past experience.

Advice to Future Managers

1. Be alert for signs of stress in each of your employees; explore the factors contributing to it and the potential consequences of it.

2. Study the key behavioral phenomena underlying employee reactions to stress, such as threats to self-esteem, frustration tolerance level, loss of control, defense mechanisms, and values conflicts.

3. Pay attention to the existence of hassles, frustrations, and stressors, as well as crises. Intervene early so as to preclude a spiral of incivility.

4. Seek to identify each employee's proper stress threshold and create the conditions that best lead to employee performance under moderate stress.

5. Help employees reduce the negative stress in their lives by encouraging a variety of personal stress management practices, as well as by your provision of appropriate social support.

6. Recognize the vital importance of sensitivity to feelings and emotions in maintaining a positive work climate.

7. Remember that almost all employees will need some counseling at some time; determine whether a directive, participative, or nondirective approach is needed, and assess whether you have the training, time, and skills to proceed accordingly or whether the employee should be referred to a professional counselor.

However, the manager's knowledge and capacity to use a variety of methods are clearly critical factors in choosing how to proceed.

One of the key contingency elements to consider is the degree to which the employee's problem appears to be focusing on *facts* and the need for a timely, logical *solution* (implying the use of a more directive approach) versus focusing on personal *feelings and emotions* (implying a more nondirective approach). Another consideration is the degree to which the manager is willing to devote time and effort to the growth and development of a more independent employee. Counselees may also have different expectations for the behaviors and characteristics of their counselors, so their preferences may need to be considered. For example, some counselees prefer the nurturing role provided through participative or nondirective methods. Others seek someone with job-related expertise or problem-solving skills, which are more easily shared through the directive approach. Overall, an effective manager requires awareness of the alternatives available, the skills to be comfortable with each method, and the analytical ability to make a choice that fits the situation.

SUMMARY

Counseling occasionally is necessary for employees because of job and personal problems that subject them to excessive stress. Stress affects both physical and mental health and results in burnout when it occurs chronically. The conditions that cause stress are called stressors and include work overload, time pressures, role ambiguity, financial problems, and family problems. The stress-performance model indicates that excessive stress reduces job performance, but a moderate amount may help employees respond to job challenges. Type A people tend to show more stress than type B people.

Counseling is discussion with an employee of a problem that usually has emotional content in order to help the employee cope with it better. Its goal is improved mental health, and it is performed by both managers and professional counselors. Major counseling functions are advice, reassurance, communication, release of emotional tension, clarified thinking, and reorientation. The most appropriate type of counseling for nonprofessionals is participative counseling. Counseling programs need to be able to deal with both job and personal problems, depending on the source of the underlying stress.

Terms and Concepts for Review

Biofeedback

Burnout

Clarified thinking

Counseling

Counseling functions

Defense mechanisms

Directive counseling

Emotional catharsis

Frustration

Hassles

Iceberg model of counseling

Incivility spiral

Layoff survivor's sickness

Marginalized employees

Nondirective counseling

Participative counseling

Perceived control

Personal wellness

Post-traumatic stress disorder

Reorientation

Relaxation response

Resilience

Sabbatical leaves

Social support

Stress

Stressors

Stress-performance model

Stress threshold

Trauma

Type A people

Type B people

Workplace trauma

Workplace violence

Discussion Questions

1. List and discuss the five major sources of stress in your life during the last five years.
2. Think of someone you know who suffers from burnout. What are the symptoms? What may have caused it?
3. Discuss how stress and job performance are related. Is stress helping or interfering with your performance in college? Discuss.
4. Do you see yourself as primarily a type A or type B person? Discuss the reasons for your choice. Make a list of your five main type A characteristics and five main type B characteristics.
5. Discuss four management practices covered in earlier chapters of this book that should help reduce employee stress.
6. Discuss the six main counseling functions. Which are best performed by directive, nondirective, and participative counseling?
7. Identify someone who has lost his or her job because of corporate downsizing. Interview the person to determine how stressful the situation was and how he or she successfully managed the stress.
8. Should professional company counselors be provided in the following organizations? Discuss why or why not.
   a. A large west coast aircraft plant during rapid expansion
   b. A government office in Valdosta, Georgia, employing 700 people
   c. A job-order foundry in Chicago having unstable employment needs varying from thirty to sixty workers
9. What should be the main type of counseling used in the following situations?
   a. A traveling sales representative with fifteen years of seniority has become an alcoholic.
   b. A newly hired engineer engages in petty theft of office supplies.

c. A receptionist receives two job offers and must make a decision over the weekend.

d. A maintenance worker's spouse files for divorce.

10. Outline a preventive program for personal wellness that you could implement for yourself over the next five years. What are its elements?

Assess Your Own Skills

How well do you exhibit good stress management and counseling skills?

Read the following statements carefully. Circle the number on the response scale that most closely reflects the degree to which each statement accurately describes you when you have tried to manage stress in yourself and others. Add up your total points and prepare a brief action plan for self-improvement. Be ready to report your score for tabulation across the entire group.

	Good description									Poor description
1. I can list a comprehensive set of physiological, psychological, and behavioral symptoms of stress in employees.	10	9	8	7	6	5	4	3	2	1
2. I am aware of the ways in which I may be a direct cause of stress in employees.	10	9	8	7	6	5	4	3	2	1
3. I could spot burnout, layoff survivor's sickness, or post-traumatic stress disorder in an employee.	10	9	8	7	6	5	4	3	2	1
4. I am aware of the intimate connection between nonwork stressors and work behavior.	10	9	8	7	6	5	4	3	2	1
5. I am aware of the progressively more severe employee reactions to a frustrating situation.	10	9	8	7	6	5	4	3	2	1
6. I am aware of the nature of the relationship between stress and performance and would seek to identify each employee's stress threshold.	10	9	8	7	6	5	4	3	2	1
7. I could comfortably work for, and have working for me, both type A and type B persons.	10	9	8	7	6	5	4	3	2	1
8. I can list at least three ways in which I could provide social support to my employees.	10	9	8	7	6	5	4	3	2	1
9. I understand the contingency factors that might steer me toward using either directive, participative, or nondirective counseling.	10	9	8	7	6	5	4	3	2	1
10. I can detect whether an employee needs primarily advice, reassurance, an opportunity for communication, emotional catharsis, clarified thinking, or reorientation.	10	9	8	7	6	5	4	3	2	1

Scoring and Interpretation   Add up your total points for the ten questions. Record that number here, and report it when it is requested. _____

- If you scored between 81–100 points, you appear to have a solid capability for demonstrating good stress management and counseling skills.
- If you scored between 61–80 points, you should take a close look at the items with lower self-assessment scores and explore ways to improve those items.
- If you scored less than 60 points, you should be aware that a weaker skill level regarding several items could be detrimental to your future success as a stress manager. We encourage you to review relevant sections of the chapter and watch for related material in subsequent chapters and other sources.

Now identify your three lowest scores, and write the question numbers here _____, _____, _____. Write a brief paragraph, detailing to yourself an action plan for how you might sharpen each of these skills.

Incident

Unit Electronics Company

Unit Electronics Company produces electronic process controls for industry. The high reliability required for these controls, each designed for a specific customer, requires the production department to work closely with the test section of the quality-control department, which determines whether the product meets customer specifications. For one important order it was necessary for a production representative to work in the quality-control department with the chief test engineer. Charles Able, the manager of production, assigned William Parcel, one of his capable assistants, to this job. Parcel had worked with Able for years and was well acquainted with this equipment order, since he had coordinated its production for Able. The test engineer was named Dale Short.

A week after Parcel began working with Short, he reported to Able that he was having difficulty with Short and that Short seemed to resent his presence in the test section. Able agreed that a problem situation might be developing and said that he would visit the test section and attempt to talk with Short.

When Able visited the test section, Short immediately started complaining about Parcel. He said that Parcel undermined Short's authority by giving testers instructions that were at variance with Short's. He claimed that Parcel even contradicted him in front of the testers. After a number of other complaints he asked Able to remove Parcel from the test section and send a substitute. Short even threatened that if Able did not remove Parcel, Short would go over his head to have Parcel removed. Able listened and asked questions, but made no judgments or promises.

Parcel apparently saw Able talking to Short, so before Able left the test section, Parcel approached him with the comment, "Well, I guess Short has been telling you a tale of woe about me."

Able acknowledged that Short had complained, but he omitted mentioning Short's threat to have Parcel transferred.

"That's Short, all right," said Parcel. "He can't stand to have anyone try to correct him, but things were so fouled up I felt I had to do something."

Able admitted that the situation was sensitive, but he pointed out that Short was in charge of the test section. He ended the discussion with the comment, "Let's play it cool and not push."

Able, however, was upset by the situation, and during the next few days he gave much thought to it. Since Short felt the way he did, Able finally decided to remove

Parcel from the test section and send another employee. As he was reaching for the telephone to call Parcel in the test section, Short walked into the office smiling.

"I want to thank you, Charlie," he said. "I don't know what you said to Parcel the other day, but it sure changed his attitude. We are getting along just fine now. Funny thing, when I spoke to you the other day, I had the impression that you weren't going to do anything for me, but I guess I had you figured wrong."

Able gulped a few times and made a few vague remarks. Then Short left in high spirits.

Able was quite curious about the whole situation; so later in the day when he happened to meet Parcel alone, he commented casually, "Well, Bill, how are things with Short?"

"I have been meaning to tell you, Charlie," Parcel said. "Short has been much easier to work with the past few days. He actually takes some of my advice—even asks for it. I guess that talk you had with him really did some good."

Questions

Analyze the events in this case in terms of counseling and communication. Did counseling occur? What type of counseling? When and by whom?

Assessment of Stress-Related Behaviors

1. Evaluate yourself with regard to each of the criteria listed on the assessment form below. Circle the number that indicates your assessment of the degree to which you typically experience each source of student-related stress. Total the scores from the items, and report your total to the instructor for tabulation.
2. Examine the range of class scores and compute the average. Note that a higher score suggests the possibility of greater current stress in life.
   a. What interpretation for your own and others' scores can you provide?
   b. Which items seemed to produce the greatest stress among class members?
   c. What actions would you suggest for the reduction of student stress?

	Low Degree				High Degree
1. Inadequate privacy	1	2	3	4	5
2. Living on a tight budget	1	2	3	4	5
3. Low quality of food	1	2	3	4	5
4. Concern about personal safety	1	2	3	4	5
5. Worry about career prospects	1	2	3	4	5
6. Parental pressure for grades	1	2	3	4	5
7. Transportation problems	1	2	3	4	5
8. Ethical conflicts (e.g., alcohol, drugs)	1	2	3	4	5
9. Self-consciousness about appearance	1	2	3	4	5
10. Lack of intellectual challenge	1	2	3	4	5

Total score: _____

Part Seven

Emerging Aspects of
Organizational Behavior

Chapter 16

Organizational Behavior across Cultures

One of the biggest mistakes American expats to [other countries] make is going over with big dreams of transforming the workplace.
—Brenda Paik Sunoo[1]

Considering the fact that failure rates for overseas assignments average 45 percent, employers should understand how to best support expatriates.
—Barbara Fitzgerald-Turner[2]

CHAPTER OBJECTIVES

TO UNDERSTAND

- How Social, Legal and Ethical, Political, and Economic Conditions Vary in Different Cultures

- The Operation of Ethnocentrism and Cultural Shock

- Ways to Overcome Barriers to Cultural Adaptation

- Cultural Contingencies in Establishing High Productivity

- Theory Z as an Example of Adapting Management Practices to Fit a Host Culture

⬤ A global economy is now a reality. The shape of international trade has changed dramatically in recent years, with the emergence of the European Community, revolutionary changes in the former Soviet Union and eastern Europe, and strong markets developing in China, Japan, Korea, and many emerging nations. As a result, many organizations now do business in more than one country, and these **multinational organizations** add powerful new dimensions to organizational behavior. Expansion beyond national boundaries is much more than a step across a geographical line, however. It is also a gigantic and sometimes frightening step into different social, legal, political, and economic environments. Communication lines are lengthened, and control often becomes more difficult. Today's managers must acquire both language and intercultural skills in dealing with people—customers, suppliers, competitors, and colleagues—from other countries.

Multinational organizations

It is hard enough to operate an organization in one language and one culture. When two, three, four, five—or a dozen—languages and cultures are involved (as in Canada, Scandinavia, or Europe) communication difficulties are compounded many times over. Complex multinational organizations push a manager's behavioral skills to their limits. It often proves easier to manage the technical factors of building a sophisticated new plant than to handle the social factors of operating it thereafter. The following case illustrates the complexities that arise as different cultures are mixed in multinational operations:

> In a South American nation, a consultant from the United States was called upon to study why the West German machinery in a cellophane plant owned by South Americans was not operating properly. (This single preliminary sentence reveals that already three different cultures were involved in the incident.) When the consultant arrived, he studied the situation for several weeks. His conclusion was that there was nothing at all wrong with the machinery. It was of excellent quality and in perfect adjustment. The raw materials and other supporting factors were entirely satisfactory.
>
> The real problem, in the consultant's opinion, was the supervisors, who had a father image of the patriarchal mill manager and were unable, or unwilling, to make operating decisions without his approval. They deferred to him as their elder and superior. When something in the mill went wrong, they waited indefinitely for his decision before correcting the problem. Since he had other business interests and was frequently out of the mill for part of the day, or even for two or three days, they permitted the continuous-production machinery to produce scrap cellophane for hours or even days because of some minor maladjustment which they could have corrected. The mill manager tried to delegate decision making on these control matters to his supervisors, but neither he nor they were able to overcome this powerful custom of deference to authority which existed in their culture. The consultant finally summarized the situation this way: "The problem is the people, not the machines."
>
> The cellophane machinery was built to operate in an advanced industrial culture, but in this instance it was required to operate in a less developed culture. Neither the machinery nor the supervisors could be changed quickly to meet this new situation. Reengineering of machinery would be costly and time-consuming and, in this case, might reduce the machinery's productivity. Training of supervisors to change their cultural beliefs, even if this were possible, would likewise be time-consuming. The solution offered by the consultant was an effective compromise. He advised the manager to appoint one person as acting director during his absence, give the acting director an imposing office, and work to build the acting director's image of authority with the supervisors. Then there would always be someone at the plant to make decisions quickly.

This situation presents extreme contrasts, but it illustrates the cultural predicaments that often arise in modern times because much of the world is still less developed than the United States and other industrialized nations. In the more advanced countries (where cultural contrasts among them may be smaller), the issues raised in this chapter will often be less extreme in degree, but they continue to exist. Discussion here is limited to issues affecting work behavior, leaving other aspects of multinational operations to other books. In this chapter we examine the nature of multinational operations, ways for an organization to integrate social systems, and ways to improve motivation, productivity, and communications when operating in less developed cultures.

CONDITIONS AFFECTING MULTINATIONAL OPERATIONS

The people of the world are organized into communities and nations, each in its own way, according to its resources and cultural heritage. There are similarities among nations, but there are also significant differences. Some nations are economically developed; others are just now developing their natural and human resources. Some are still political dictatorships; others are more democratic. Some are educationally and socially advanced; others have minimal literacy and social development. In each case the conditions of work are different because of different attitudes, values, and expectations from participants. Understanding these differences and how they influence international organizational behavior is aided by examination of key social, legal and ethical, political, and economic conditions.

Social Conditions

In many countries the overriding social condition is poorly developed human resources. There are major shortages of managerial personnel, scientists, and technicians; and these deficiencies limit the ability to employ local labor productively. Needed skills must be imported temporarily from other countries, while vast training programs begin to prepare local workers.

> A Central American nation welcomed an electronic assembly plant to its capital city. The plant was labor-intensive, so the many jobs it provided reduced the nation's high unemployment rate. Wages were above community standards, working conditions were good, and the plant was environmentally clean. In addition, the valuable and tiny product that was assembled provided needed foreign exchange because it was shipped by air to assembly plants in other parts of the world.
>
> Perhaps most important of all, the company's agreement with the host nation stated that the company would supply a cadre of managers and technicians to train local employees in all phases of operating the plant. Locals would gradually become supervisors, superintendents, technicians, accountants, purchasing specialists, and so on. At the end of five years the company could have no more than eight nonlocals in the plant, including the general manager, engineers, and auditing personnel. In this manner the labor force of the nation would be upgraded.

Training multiplier effect

As this example shows, the lending of skilled people to a nation for training their local replacements may provide a more lasting benefit to its development than the lending of capital. The **training multiplier effect** is in action, by which the loaned skilled people develop others, and those trained locals become the nucleus for developing still more people. *There is a ripple effect of self-development,* much as a pebble thrown into a pond creates an impact far beyond the spot where it landed (see Figure 16–1). Just as the size and placement of the pebble dictates how far the rip-

FIGURE 16–1

The training multiplier
effect in action

397

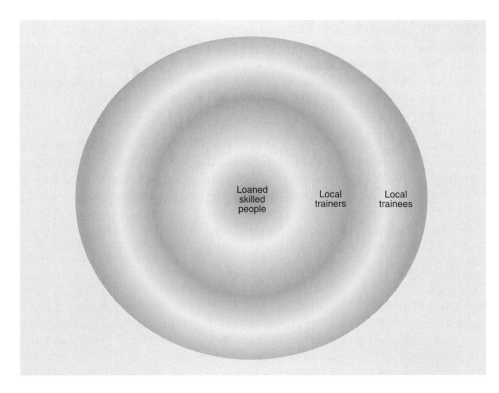

ples will radiate, the amount and focus of the initial training dictates its long-run impact. The occupational areas in which development will provide the greatest return are scientific, professional, and managerial personnel.

A significant social condition in many countries is that the local culture is not familiar with advanced technology or complex organizations. Western nations over a period of two centuries have adapted their culture to an industrial and organizational way of life, but this is not so in many other nations. The background of their employees is still largely agrarian, suggesting that they are not familiar with high-technology products and the close margin of error that they tolerate.

Another social factor on which countries are often compared is the work ethic of their employees (you may wish to review the earlier discussion in Chapter 4). When Japanese and American work hours are compared, for example, a simple conclusion emerges. Japanese employees often work several hundred more hours per year than do their U.S. counterparts. This greater number of work hours, unfortunately, is usually attributed to the higher work ethic of Japanese workers, or to the laziness of the Americans.

A recent study analyzed the reasons Japanese employees are willing to work longer hours.[3] It found that the high cost of living in Japan produced a rational response among workers— the desire to maximize wages rather than bargain for reduced working hours. Workers were also unwilling to take more than, on average, about one-half of the vacation days allotted to them. However, their decisions were driven not by preference but by a feeling of obligation, by their workload, by a sense of responsibility to the other workers who would have to do their work, and by a feeling of tacit pressure from management (who would label them selfish and disloyal if they asked for their full vacation time). Finally, many Japanese workers admitted that their willingness to remain late at work stemmed from their desire to socialize with their managers and colleagues in a more relaxed late-evening setting. Only by exploring the factors behind the statistics were the researchers able to understand the apparent differences in work ethics.

Legal and Ethical Conditions

Countries around the world vary substantially in their legal systems, and especially in their relevant employment laws and business practices. In the judicial system, some countries practice rapid disposition of cases; in other countries cases may drag on for years. In addition, the penalties for seemingly minor offenses may vary dramatically from culture to culture. A major issue affecting multinational corporations has been how to deal with contrasting local mores, customs, and ethical behaviors. Some countries condone the practice of bribery as a way of obtaining and retaining business; others strictly prohibit it. Such differences create a severe dilemma for multinational companies: Should they maintain consistent standards for all employees regardless of which country they are in, or should they pragmatically adapt their operations to fit host-country ethical standards?

Managers need to be aware of the possible differences in both laws and ethical values that define acceptable and unacceptable behaviors in foreign countries. U.S. employees operating internationally must first be guided by the Foreign Corrupt Practices Act of 1977 (as amended). This law governs the actions of American organizations abroad, particularly with regard to bribery of officials in attempts to win business. Then managers in foreign countries need to become familiar with local customs and practices. Applying their own personal and organizational value systems, they must then decide which behaviors are compatible with both parties' expectations and which are not. Finally, they need to recognize that the resolution of ethical issues is not always clear-cut (e.g., is entertaining clients at dinner unethical?). Although ethical issues pose real dilemmas, they need to be addressed and resolved.

A major issue for many firms revolves around the treatment of women and other minorities. Although Title VII of the Civil Rights Act of 1964 prohibits workplace discrimination in employment based on gender and other factors, it was not until 1991 that additional federal legislation extended those rights to U.S. citizens employed in a foreign country by an American-owned company. Because global experience is increasingly becoming a prerequisite to promotion to senior management positions, many women are interested in overseas positions offering visibility, challenge, and the opportunity for personal growth. Although the path is not easy, employers can still resolve such issues by establishing clear local policies, clarifying the legal status of local standard practices, using local consultants to identify potential problems, and carefully providing "reality training" to alert potential transferees to the cultural problems they may encounter.[4]

> The workplace in many cultures remains a male-dominated domain, with local women systematically excluded from higher managerial roles. Despite that situation success in overcoming past problems is possible. One study of fifty-two female expatriate managers from North America revealed that the vast majority (97 percent) were successful despite having no female predecessor for a role model in that position. The women attributed their success to their high visibility, cultural sensitivity, and interpersonal skills.[5] The success of these female expatriates should stimulate other firms to focus their selection of expatriate candidates on the identification of similar characteristics in both females and males.

Political Conditions

Instability and nationalism

Political conditions that have a significant effect on organizational behavior include instability of the government, nationalistic drives, and subordination of employers and labor to an authoritarian state. Instability spills over onto organizations that wish to establish or expand operations in the host country, making them cautious about further investments. This organizational instability leaves workers insecure and causes them to be passive and low in initiative. They may bring to the job an attitude of "What will be, will be; so why try to do anything about it?"

On the other hand, a strong nationalistic drive may impel locals to desire to run their country and their organizations by themselves, without interference by foreign nationals. A foreign manager simply may not be welcome.

> In a former British colony a visiting professor presented a group of trainees with a case study featuring a problem between a British shipmaster and a native crew. Expecting the group to discuss authority, interpersonal conflict, and other behavioral issues, the professor was surprised when the class focused instead on how to train the native sailors to take control from the British master. Their reasoning—that then the crew would not have to deal with the shipmaster any longer—was a clear reflection of their nationalistic values.

Organized labor in many nations is not an independent force but is mostly an arm of the authoritarian state. In other nations labor is somewhat independent, but it is socialistic, class-conscious, and oriented toward political action more than direct negotiation with organizations. Employers find that the state tends to be involved in collective bargaining and other practices affecting workers. In some nations, for example, employee layoffs are restricted by law and made costly by requiring dismissal pay. Even employee transfers may be restricted. The following is an incident that illustrates how different employment practices among nations can cause employee-employer frictions for multinational companies. In this instance, both nations were economically developed.

> Air France, a major international airline, provides service to Japan. It employs a number of Japanese flight attendants who are stationed in Tokyo and serve flights to and from that city. In order to provide further international training and integration of its flight crews, the airline transferred thirty Japanese attendants to Paris. They refused to go, so the company threatened dismissal for refusal to transfer. The attendants sought relief through the courts, and the Tokyo High Court upheld a lower-court injunction preventing Air France from dismissing the attendants. They could retain the Air France jobs in Tokyo, because transfer to Paris would "(1) restrict their civil rights as Japanese citizens, (2) cause them the anxiety of living in a place where the language and customs are different, and (3) affect their marital situation."[6]

Economic Conditions

The most significant economic conditions in less developed nations are low per capita income, rapid inflation, and unequal distribution of wealth. In terms of income, many nations of the world exist in genuine poverty compared with the United States or Canada. For example, an average family in some nations may have to survive on less than $3,000 annually. Rapid population increases coupled with a lack of national economic growth make it unlikely that family incomes will progress significantly. As a consequence, natives of those countries may not believe that additional effort on their part will earn associated rewards.

A common economic condition in many less developed countries is inflation. Despite periodic concerns in the United States over rising food, fuel, and housing prices, this country has enjoyed rather moderate inflation rates over the past few decades. By contrast, Mexico and some countries in South America, Europe, and the Middle East have suffered periods of dramatic inflation. Even residents of the former Soviet Union were painfully introduced to the ravages of inflation as they made a transition from a controlled to a market economy.

Inflation makes the economic life of workers insecure. It encourages them to spend quickly before their money loses its value, and this spending pattern adds to the country's inflationary problem. Because savings lose value rapidly, workers often do not plan for their own retirement security. They develop a dependence on the government, which is often incapable of responding. Social unrest is compounded by tremendous disparity in the distribution of wealth in these nations. The consequences are often varied; some workers passively accept their situation, while others aggressively protest. All these factors make it difficult to motivate employees.

Despite the challenges abroad and the political and economic backlash from home-country workers and consumers, some firms have moved substantial parts of their production operations into other countries. Some U.S. businesses, for example, have set up assembly plants in places such as Mexico, Malaysia, or South Korea to capitalize on the relatively lower labor costs there. These firms argue that the local economy gains by the creation of new jobs, and the U.S. economy is helped by lower production costs (assuming the cost of savings are passed on to the consumer). In essence, depressed economic conditions in another country can represent an opportunity for a firm.

Looking at social, legal and ethical, political, and economic conditions as a whole, we see that these conditions can impede the introduction of advanced technology and sophisticated organizational systems. They constrain the stability, security, and trained human resources that developing countries require to be more productive. The unfortunate fact is that these limiting conditions usually cannot be changed rapidly, because they are too well established and woven into the whole social fabric of a nation. Instead, they represent critical environmental conditions to which the managers of international operations must adapt.

Individual Differences

Are people in one country different from those in another? There are many striking differences across countries, just as there are some surprising similarities. Clearly, residents of each country have their own preferences for clothes, food, recreation, and housing. In terms of organizational behavior, there are also important contrasts across cultures regarding employee attitudes, values, and beliefs that influence how employees will act on the job. Research on national cultures in sixty countries identified five major dimensions that accounted for the sharpest differences among employees.[7] These individual-difference factors include individualism/collectivism, power distance, uncertainty avoidance, masculinity/femininity, and time orientation.

Cultures differ on five key factors.

Individualism/Collectivism   Cultures that emphasize **individualism** tend to accent individual rights and freedoms ("Look out for number 1!"), have very loosely knit social networks, and place considerable attention on self-respect. Strong emphasis is placed on the person's own career and personal rewards. **Collectivism** heavily accents the group and values harmony among members. Individual feelings are subordinated to the group's overall good, and employees are more likely to ask, "What is best for the organization?" *Face-saving* (maintaining one's self-image in front of others) is highly important in collectivistic cultures. When face-saving is accomplished, then one's status in the group can be maintained. The United States has an individualistic culture ("Every person for him- or herself"); Japan is collectivistic, with a culture that can be characterized by the proverb "The nail that sticks up gets pounded down."

Power Distance   How important are organizational status, prestige, and level in the organizational hierarchy? What rights to make decisions are given to managers as a function of their positions? To what degree should employees automatically defer to the wishes and decisions of their managers? **Power distance** refers to the belief that there are strong and legitimate decision-making rights separating managers and employees; this custom is frequently observed in Asian and South American countries. By contrast, employees in the United States and Scandinavian countries subscribe to beliefs of lower power distance and are less likely to believe that their managers are automatically correct. Therefore, many employees in the United States and Scandinavia do not blindly defer to their manager's wishes.

> Managers from various countries were asked if they thought it was important for them to have precise answers to most of the questions that their subordinates had about their work.[8] About three-fourths of Indonesian and Japanese managers agreed that it was (indicating high power distance). In sharp contrast, only about one-fourth of British, Danish, and U.S. managers agreed with that conclusion. Instead of accepting the role of an expert, the latter group believed that they should be a resource, a problem solver, and a source of personal support (indicating low power distance).

Uncertainty Avoidance   Employees in some cultures value clarity and feel very comfortable receiving specific directions from their supervisors. These employees have a high level of **uncertainty avoidance** and prefer to avoid ambiguity at work. Employees elsewhere react in an opposite manner, since ambiguity does not threaten their lower need for stability and security. These employees may even thrive on the uncertainty associated with their jobs. Employees in countries such as Greece, Portugal, and Belgium have high uncertainty avoidance characteristics and often prefer structure, stability, rules, and clarity. Countries lower in uncertainty avoidance include China, Ireland, and the United States.

Masculinity/Femininity   **Masculine societies** define gender roles in more traditional and stereotypical ways, whereas **feminine societies** have broader viewpoints on the great variety of roles that both males and females can play in the workplace and at home. In addition, masculine societies value assertive behavior and the acquisition of wealth; feminine cultures treasure relationships among people, caring for others, and a greater balance between family and work life. The Scandinavian countries have the most feminine cultures; Japan has a markedly masculine one; and the United States has a moderately masculine culture.

Time Orientation   Some cultures accent values such as the necessity of preparing for the future, the value of thrift and savings, and the merits of persistence. Members of these cultures, exemplified by Hong Kong, China, and Japan, have a **long-term orientation.** Other cultures value the past and accent the present, with a rich respect for tradition and the need to fulfill historical social obligations. These societies, including France, Russia, and West Africa, generally have a **short-term orientation.**

An Intercultural Comparison   Figure 16–2 highlights the differences between two countries—Japan and the United States—on these five dimensions. It should be noted that neither country has a better culture than the other; they are simply quite different. Managers in all countries, however, need to become more aware of their

FIGURE 16–2

Comparison of typical cultural differences between Japan and the United States

Cultural Dimension	Japan	United States
Individualism/collectivism	Collectivistic	Individualistic
Power distance	High	Low
Uncertainty avoidance	Strong	Weak
Masculinity/femininity	High masculinity	Moderate masculinity
Time orientation	Long-term	Short-term

own cultural characteristics, to search for the uniqueness in the cultures of other countries, and to learn how to use the local culture to their advantage. However, they must avoid the tendency to stereotype people whom they do not know. Avoiding problems of cultural adaptation is particularly important in foreign work assignments, which are discussed next.

MANAGING AN INTERNATIONAL WORKFORCE

Roles of expatriates

Whenever an organization expands its operations so that its geographic boundaries span two or more countries, it tends to become multicultural and will then face the challenge of blending various cultures. **Multiculturalism** occurs when the employees in two or more cultures interact with each other on a regular basis. Managers and technical employees entering another nation to install an advanced organizational system need to adjust their leadership styles, communication patterns, and other practices to fit the culture of their host country. In some instances these new employees are *parent-country nationals* from the nation in which the home office is located, or they may be *third-country nationals* from some other nation. In either case they are called **expatriates,** since they come from another nation. Their role is to provide a fusion of cultures in which both parties adjust to the new situation of seeking greater productivity for the benefit of both the organization and the citizens of the country in which the organization operates.

Barriers to Cultural Adaptation

Problems expatriates may experience

An expatriate manager may find several obstacles to a smooth adaptation to a new culture. An early requirement for overcoming such obstacles is to *acquire cultural awareness* of the multiple ways in which cultures differ (language, religion, food, personal space, and social behaviors). For example, some cultures can be classified as high context, meaning that people from those countries use situational cues to develop a complete portrait of a visitor. **High-context cultures,** such as China, Korea, and Japan, tend to emphasize personal relations, place high value on trust, focus on nonverbal cues, and accent the need to attend to social needs before business matters. Other cultures are classified as low context, meaning that people from those countries tend to interpret cues more literally. **Low-context cultures,** such as Germany, the United States, and Scandinavian countries, tend to rely on written rules and legal documents, conduct business first, and value expertise and performance. Lack of attention to these factors results in costly failures for expatriates; the rate varies from a low of 18 percent of those sent to London, to 36 percent in Tokyo, to 68 percent in Saudi Arabia.[9]

In addition to the major areas of individual differences already discussed, parochialism, ethnocentrism, cultural distance, and cultural shock can also have an impact (see Figure 16–3). These barriers to cultural adaptation must be understood and addressed.

Parochialism *The dominant feature of all international operations is that they are conducted in a social system different from the one in which the organization is based.* This new social system affects the responses of all persons involved. Managers and other employees who come into a host country in order to get a new operation established naturally tend to exhibit a variety of behaviors that are often true of citizens in their homeland. For example, many people are predisposed to **parochialism,** meaning that they see the situation around them from their own perspective. They may fail to recognize key differences between their own and others' cultures. Even if they do, they tend to conclude that the impact of those differences is insignificant. In effect, they are assuming that the two cultures are more similar than they actually are.

Ethnocentrism Another potential barrier to easy adaptation to another culture occurs when people are predisposed to believe that their homeland conditions are the best. This predisposition is known as the *self-reference criterion,* or **ethnocentrism.** Though this way of perceiving conditions is very natural, it interferes with understanding human behavior in other cultures and obtaining productivity from local employees. In order to integrate the imported and local social systems, expatriate employees minimally need to develop **cultural empathy.** This is the awareness of differences across cultures, an understanding of the ways in which those differences can affect business relationships, and an appreciation of the contributions each culture makes to overall success. Cultural empathy is similar, on an international scale, to the idea of valuing diversity discussed in Chapter 4. Cultural empathy, when demonstrated consistently, will result in geocentric organizations which largely ignore a person's nationality while accenting employee ability in selection, assignment, and promotional decisions.[10] **Geocentric organizations** seek to integrate the interests of the various cultures involved. The attempt to build a sense of community is consistent with a supportive approach to human behavior in its productive use of all employees.

Cultural empathy

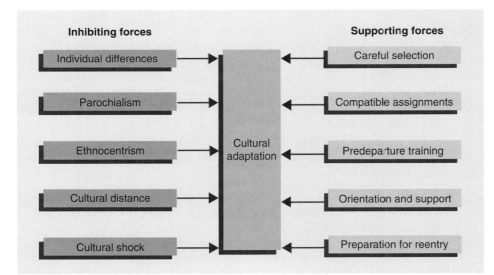

FIGURE 16–3

Forces inhibiting and supporting cultural adaptation

Inhibiting forces | Supporting forces

Individual differences → Cultural adaptation ← Careful selection

Parochialism → ← Compatible assignments

Ethnocentrism → ← Predeparture training

Cultural distance → ← Orientation and support

Cultural shock → ← Preparation for reentry

Cultural Distance   Predicting the amount of adaptation that may be required when an expatriate manager moves to another country requires an understanding of the **cultural distance** between the two countries. Cultural distance is the amount of difference between any two social systems and may range from minimal to substantial. As a citizen of one country accurately expressed the contrast, "We are only one day (geographically) but many years distant (technologically and socially) from Washington, D.C." Research has shown that some measures of cultural distance from the United States are greater for countries in the Mediterranean area and Asia and smaller for Scandinavian and English-speaking countries.[11]

Whatever the amount of cultural distance, it does affect the responses of all people to business-related issues. Expatriate managers naturally tend to be somewhat ethnocentric and to judge conditions in a new country according to the standards of their homeland. These problems will be magnified if the cultural distance is great. Nevertheless, expatriates must be adaptable enough to integrate the interests of the two or more cultures involved. Such cultural adaptation is not easy, as this U.S.–Asian example demonstrates:

> Executives of a U.S. firm in an Asian nation were unable to adapt to the philosophy of the local partner regarding the employment of relatives (nepotism). The home office in the United States had strong rules against this practice, so the expatriate managers tried to apply the same policy in their Asian branch. The Asian partner and manager, on the other hand, saw the business as a source of jobs for family members, so he employed many of them, even when they were poorly qualified. His actions were consistent with the cultural belief that as the senior male member of his family, he should help provide for the economic needs of his entire extended family. The Asian–United States differences on this issue were so great, largely because of cultural distance, that the partners finally separated.[12]

Cultural Shock   Companies often assign employees to new job assignments in different areas to provide them with invaluable breadth of experience. The employees who move to new job locations often experience various degrees of **cultural shock,** which is a feeling of confusion, insecurity, and anxiety caused by a strange new environment.[13] They are rightfully concerned about not knowing how to act and about losing their self-confidence when the wrong responses are made.

A cultural change does not have to be dramatic to cause some degree of shock. For example, when an employee moves from a small town to the Chicago home office, both the employee and his or her family are likely to suffer cultural shock. A similar shock may occur when a Boston native is transferred to a small town in rural Kansas. The whole family may not know what to do with their time or how to act or dress. For unprepared employees, the new environment can appear to be chaotic and somewhat overwhelming. However, the new culture has a unique systematic structure of behavioral patterns; indeed, it is probably as systematic as the culture the employee left behind. Although it is different, it can be understood if employees have receptive attitudes, dedicate themselves to learn about the new culture, and adapt to it.

> Maria was born and raised in Houston, Texas. After completing college there, she found a job in northern Wisconsin. However, she discovered many differences in her new community and found it difficult to adapt to them. "I can't locate any decent [spicy] chili in the restaurants here," she complained. "Also, people up here talk differently, and that makes them hard to understand." She soon learned that the pace of work was different from the one she was used to, and worst of all, she proclaimed, "There's nothing here to do all win-

ter except go ice fishing and snowmobiling!" Maria was experiencing cultural shock from her new social environment.

Cultural shock is even greater when an employee moves from one nation to another. Increasingly, employees in multinational companies receive job assignments in new countries, or at least need to collaborate with people from different national backgrounds. This exposure to a new culture may result in initial shock. When employees enter another nation, they may experience several reactions in a series of four phases, as follows.

Transferred employees may experience stimulation, disillusionment, shock, and adaptation.

- In the first phase, they are often *excited and stimulated* by the challenge of a new job, home, and culture. Each day is filled with new discoveries.

- This positive attitude is soon followed by a second phase, that of *disillusionment,* as they discover various problems they had not anticipated regarding travel, shopping, or language skills.

- In the third and most critical stage, they tend to suffer cultural shock, which is the *insecurity and disorientation* caused by encountering all parts of a different culture. They may not know how to act, may fear losing face and self-confidence, or may become emotionally upset. In severe cases their surroundings appear to be social chaos, and this perception diminishes their ability to perform effectively. Some individuals isolate themselves, and a few even decide to return home on the next airplane. But a different culture is not behavioral chaos; it is a systematic structure of behavior patterns, probably as systematic as the culture in the employee's home country. Nevertheless, it *is* different, and these differences place a strain on newcomers regardless of their flexibility.

- Usually, if they can emotionally survive the first few weeks, they will reach the fourth phase, that of *adaptation.* At this point they accept the new culture, regain a sense of self-esteem, and respond constructively to their new surroundings at work and at home.

Cultural shock is virtually universal. It occurs in response to dramatic differences in language, forms of courtesy, customs, housing conditions, and cultural orientations in the use of space (relative emphasis on privacy), time (focus on the past, present, or future), and activity (accent on life achievements versus life experiences). It happens even on a move from one advanced nation to another. For example, many Japanese firms have established assembly plants, made substantial investments in real estate, or distributed their electronic and photographic products in the United States in recent years. When they send their managers to oversee foreign operations, these individuals suffer cultural shock; and when U.S. employees move to Japan or other countries, they also suffer cultural shock.[14]

Social customs vary widely among countries. Consider the following examples:

- In the United States, people tend to greet each other with a simple handshake; in other cultures, greetings may occur through a warm embrace, a bow, or an exchange of kisses.

- In the United States, people tend to demand responses, fill voids of silence with conversation, and use direct eye contact; in other cultures, people may show respect through averting their eyes, and they appreciate silence as a time to think and evaluate a topic.

- In the United States, Americans are often driven by time, deadlines, promptness, and schedules; people in other cultures often arrive late for appointments and devote hours to developing social rapport before turning to business issues.

Some of the factors that are most likely to contribute to cultural shock are shown in Figure 16–4. Many expatriates report difficulty adjusting to different human resource management philosophies, the strange language, the unfamiliar currency, and the differing work attitudes in another culture.

Overcoming Barriers to Cultural Adaptation

In spite of the strong evident need for expatriate employees to understand local culture and to be adaptable, they often arrive unprepared. Their selection is typically based upon their job performance in the home country or their need to better understand the company's international operations as a prerequisite to obtaining top-management positions. Because of their parochial, individualistic, or ethnocentric beliefs, they might not be concerned about the fact that they will be doing business with people whose traditional beliefs are different from their own. They may not know the local language and might have little interest in becoming a part of the community. They also may have been selected largely on the basis of their technical qualifications, with the employer overlooking the need for a good fit between the expatriate and the local culture. Companies seem to be stating, "Our main concern is that they can do the technical job we send them to do." However, cultural understanding is essential to avoid errors and misunderstandings that can be costly to an organization. There are, fortunately, several actions that firms can take to prevent cultural shock and reduce the impact of the other barriers discussed previously. Some of the most useful actions are the following (refer to the supporting forces in Figure 16–3).

Careful Selection Employees who are low in ethnocentrism and other possibly troublesome characteristics can be chosen. The *desire* to experience another culture and live in another nation may also be an important prerequisite attitude worth assessing. Potential expatriates might be screened to determine which employees are already capable of speaking the language of the nation where they will be assigned, or which ones have traveled to that region previously. Learning the attitudes of the employee's spouse and family toward the assignment also can be important to ensure that there is strong support for becoming expatriates.[15]

FIGURE 16–4

Factors that contribute to cultural shock and reverse cultural shock

Cultural Shock May Result from Encountering	Reverse Cultural Shock May Result from Encountering
• Different management philosophies	• A loss of decision-making authority
• An unfamiliar language	• A loss of responsibility
• New foods, styles of dress, driving patterns, and the like	• Changes in one's level of status in the organization
• An unfamiliar currency system	• Changes in personal lifestyle
• Reduced availability of goods	• Technological and organizational changes
• Different attitudes toward work and productivity	
• Separation from friends and work colleagues	

Compatible Assignments   Adjustment to new surroundings is easier if employees, especially on their first international assignment, are sent to nations that are similar to their own. This practice is more likely to be possible in giant firms like Exxon and IBM that have widespread foreign operations than in smaller organizations that have only a few international offices.

Analysis of industrialized nations in the free world shows that most of these can be grouped into six sociocultural clusters (see Figure 16–5). The *Anglo-American* cluster includes the United States, the United Kingdom, Canada, and Australia; the *Nordic* group includes Norway, Finland, Denmark, and Sweden; the *Latin European* group has Portugal, Spain, Italy, France, and Belgium; the *Latin American* cluster includes Peru, Mexico, Argentina, Chile, and Venezuela; the *Pacific Rim* cluster includes Japan, China, Hong Kong, Taiwan, and Korea; and the *Central European* group contains Germany, Austria, and Switzerland. Some nations—such as Israel, India, and Brazil—do not fit cleanly into any of the clusters.

Some cultures are relatively similar; they can be grouped into clusters.

Using this information about clusters, a firm can attempt to assign expatriate employees within their own cluster of nations, with the result being easier adjustment and less cultural shock. For example, a Canadian employee assigned to Australia is likely to adjust more quickly than a Spanish employee would in the same assignment.

Analysis of sociocultural clusters can also provide an explanation for the complexity involved in blending of practices within the European Community. Although there are similarities among some of the members (e.g., within the Nordic group), the cultural differences are substantial within the Community when it is viewed in its entirety. These differences in power distance, masculinity/femininity, individualism/collectivism, uncertainty avoidance, and time orientation suggest that organizational behavior practices will need to be somewhat varied and flexible to succeed.[16]

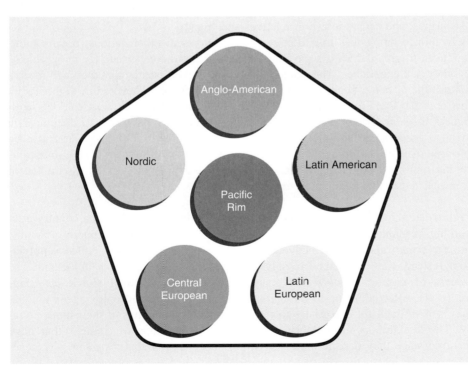

FIGURE 16–5

Primary sociocultural clusters of industrialized nations

Source: Adapted from Simcha Ronen and Allen I. Kraut, "Similarities among Countries Based on Employee Work Values and Attitudes," *Columbia Journal of World Business,* Summer 1977, p. 94.

Predeparture Training   As a minimum, many organizations try to hasten adjustment to a host nation by encouraging employees to learn the local language. They offer language training prior to the assignment, and some even give pay differentials to expatriate employees who learn the local language (a form of knowledge-based pay). The added language capacity seems to be well worth its personal and organizational costs, because those who possess it can speak with local employees in their native language. Fluency in the host language contributes to cultural adaptation in two ways. First, it helps avoid the misunderstandings that can arise when communications have to be translated by someone else. Second, it creates a better impression of the expatriate as someone who is willing to invest personal time and effort in adapting to the local environment. Predeparture training now often includes orientation to the geography, customs, culture, and political environment in which the employee will be living.[17]

Orientation and Support in the New Country   Adjustment is further encouraged after arrival in the new country if a special effort is made to help the employee and family get settled. This task may include assistance with housing, transportation, and shopping. It is especially helpful if a mentor can be assigned to ease the transition. Sometimes this role can be filled by the previous jobholder, who stays for a short period to share useful experiences before moving to a new assignment. Another valuable mentor would be a local national working for the same organization who is available to answer questions and provide advice regarding culturally acceptable behavior.

Another problem that can arise when employees transfer to another culture is that of intensified need deficiencies. This situation arises because expatriates' need satisfactions may not be as great as those of comparable employees who remain at home. Although a move to another nation may be an exciting opportunity that provides new challenges, responsibilities, authority, and recognition, the lack of basic goods and services can severely interfere with the enjoyment of those other factors. Specifically, an international job assignment may bring about financial difficulties, inconveniences, insecurities, and separation from relatives and friends.

Incentives and guarantees

To induce employees to accept such assignments in other nations, organizations may need to give them extra pay and fringe benefits to compensate for the problems that they will experience. The employees also need to be assured that they will receive comparable or better positions within the organization upon their return to the homeland and that their foreign experiences will be appreciated. The organization's willingness to value the expatriate's experience is especially important to document in advance, since some at-home managers suffer from **xenophobia**—a fear and even rejection of ideas and things foreign to them. The effect of this fear can be disastrous for the returning expatriate, whose international experiences may be discounted or even rejected by the xenophobic manager.[18]

Xenophobia

Preparation for Reentry   Employees typically return to their home country after working in another nation for one to three years and need to be smoothly blended into the organization and effectively utilized there. This process is called **repatriation.** Instead, they often tend to suffer cultural shock in their own homeland. The process of *cross-cultural reentry* may cause **reverse cultural shock** (see Figure 16–4). After adjusting to the culture of another nation and enjoying its uniqueness, it is difficult for expatriates to readjust to the surroundings of their home country. The situation is made more difficult by the multitude of changes that have occurred since they departed. Just as philosophers suggest that a person may never

Reverse cultural shock

step into the same river twice, it is also unlikely that one's home environment will remain the same. Not only does the actual homeland change, but expatriates are likely to idealize the positive aspects of it while they are away, only to be surprised at the reality they later find.

Furthermore, in their host country expatriates may have enjoyed higher status, better pay, and special privileges (such as servants), but back home they are merely one of several employees with similar rank in the home office. Colleagues who remained at home might have been promoted, leaving returning employees with a feeling that they were bypassed and therefore have lost valuable advancement opportunities. As noted in Figure 16–4, overseas executives often report difficulty with insufficient decision-making authority and diminished responsibility after reentry. For example, 46 percent of American repatriates reported reduced autonomy and authority upon their return home, and 60 to 70 percent faced the uncertainty of not even knowing what their new assignments would be.[19] As a result, companies need repatriation policies and programs to help returning employees obtain suitable assignments and adjust to the "new" environment.

PRODUCTIVITY AND CULTURAL CONTINGENCIES

The Challenge of Achieving Productivity

Productivity—achieving quantity and quality of results while controlling inputs—is the central idea that the people of a country need to absorb and embrace in order to develop the capacity to progress. Without a devotion to productivity, the conditions of poverty, inefficiency, and wastefulness of natural resources continue, while new capital inputs are dissipated. Without a belief in productivity, more education merely increases one's desire for gaining additional personal status. Unless productivity increases, whatever one person gains is usually achieved at the expense of others.

Expatriates often find, however, that some local managers do not understand the idea of productivity. Even those who do may still have difficulty communicating it to their supervisors and workers. Despite the simple notions of a results-orientation and productivity (introduced in Chapter 1), local managers and employees may view productivity in terms of production (a net increase in output regardless of inputs). In contrast, the extensive publicity and educational efforts devoted to productivity in Europe, the United States, and Japan have resulted in a resurgence of understanding and active pursuit of quality products that will satisfy or exceed customer expectations.

The gap in understanding productivity in other nations is widened by the fact that local managers often ignore rational methods of solving problems and making decisions. They tend to treat management as a personal art, solving problems subjectively without adequate attention to whether their decisions will produce the desired result. Since decision patterns like these are firmly ingrained, it is difficult to change them, regardless of the quality of communication efforts and the number of training programs provided by the home organization. Problems are further compounded when these subjective decisions are not followed with objective measures to determine whether productivity and customer satisfaction were in fact increased.

Cultural Contingencies

Even when nations want to reduce waste of their resources and have more goods and services for their citizens, results are not obtained easily. Since each nation is different, effective business practices from one country cannot be transferred directly to

Match practice to the culture.

another country. The idea of **cultural contingency** means that the most productive practices for a particular nation will depend heavily on its culture. The ideas that work in one nation's culture must be blended with the social system, level of economic development, and employees' values in a host country. The difficult lesson for both expatriate and local managers to accept is that neither the home nation's productivity approaches nor the host nation's traditional practices are used exclusively. Instead, a third set of practices must be developed that integrates the most workable ideas from both nations. In this way both the new firm and the host nation gain benefits from the company's operations.

Theory Z Cultural contingencies are illustrated by **Theory Z,** an integrative model of organizational behavior proposed by William Ouchi.[20] Theory Z provides a useful example of the way in which *behavioral prescriptions for management must be adapted to fit the organization's cultural environment.* Its blending of American and Japanese concepts has been used by many American companies. Whereas a pure Japanese model of management practices includes many features that would be inappropriate in the United States (company unions, women as temporary workers, seniority-based evaluation and promotions), *Theory Z selectively adapts some Japanese practices to the American culture.*[21]

The distinguishing features of Theory Z companies are listed in Figure 16–6. Use of the Theory Z model is believed to foster close, cooperative, trusting relationships among workers, managers, and other groups. The central notion is the creation of an industrial team within a stable work environment where employee needs for affiliation, independence, and control are met while the organization's needs for high-quality work are satisfied. The first step in this direction is to create and publicize a humanistic statement of corporate philosophy, which will guide the firm's policies. Many corporate giants, such as Eli Lilly, Rockwell International, and Target, claim to hold Theory Z values. Some of the most visible illustrations of Japanese management practices in action have occurred in the automotive assembly plants operated in the United States by Toyota, Honda, and Nissan.

> By accenting quality, teamwork, just-in-time production, and nonadversarial labor relations, Japanese managers at the Toyota–General Motors joint venture in Fremont, California, attained results dramatically different from the previous GM operation. Production levels of new autos were attained with one-half the previous workforce, outstanding grievances dropped from 5,000 to 2, and absenteeism rates plummeted from 20 percent to under 2 percent. "The Japanese philosophy is to make people an important item," concludes the general manager of human resources,[22] and the evidence seems to support that contention.

Pros and cons of Theory Z

Evaluations of Theory Z approaches suggest that there are both positive and negative features. On the positive side, Theory Z organizations have made a commendable attempt to adapt, not transplant, Japanese ideas into their firms. Theory Z is based on a shared concern for multiple employee needs, and it clearly typifies the trend

FIGURE 16–6

Typical features of Theory Z organizations

- Long-term employment
- Nonspecialized careers
- Individual responsibility
- Concern for the total person
- Less formal control systems
- Consensus decision making
- Slower rates of promotion

toward supportive systems and collegial approaches by its use of consensus-oriented decisions. Further, there is some evidence that Theory Z firms have been, and can be, productive (as seen in the above example at the Fremont plant).

Ouchi's Theory Z has not been immune to criticism.[23] It has been suggested that Theory Z is not new but merely an extension of earlier theories that received less popular acclaim. In particular, Theory Z appears to reflect the assumptions underlying McGregor's Theory Y and provides a set of behavioral practices that are consistent with it. Other critics have concluded that the research supporting its effectiveness is limited. Perhaps the most damaging criticism is the idea that Theory Z fails to provide useful contingency criteria for helping managers decide *when* to use it and when *not* to use it. Some firms in volatile industries such as electronics have difficulty balancing their desire to provide lifetime employment with the need to adjust their workforces to meet market demands. Finally, U.S. employees, accustomed to frequent promotions in rapid-growth industries, may become frustrated with the much slower rates of promotions in Theory Z firms—but even Japanese employees are beginning to show impatience with their system. Despite these initial problems, Ouchi's Theory Z model has served a very important function by stimulating many managers to examine the nature and probable effectiveness of their current model of organizational behavior.

Managerial Implications   The idea of cultural contingency suggests that expatriate managers must learn to operate effectively in a new environment. Although they must operate within the limits of most home-office policies, managers also must be flexible enough to respond to local conditions. Labor policy, personnel practices, and production methods need to be adapted to a different labor force. Organization structures and communication patterns need to be suitable for local operation as well as coordinated with the home office and other branches. There is a much greater probability of achieving productivity improvements when a business and its expatriates adapt to host-country conditions.

Management's Integrating Role   Once managers are on location in a host country, their attention needs to be directed toward integrating the technological approaches with the local cultures involved. Where local practices that interfere with productivity cannot be changed, they can perhaps be bypassed or integrated into a modified production plan. If, for example, a one-hour siesta must be accepted, perhaps siesta hours can be staggered so that equipment can be kept operating and service maintained for customers.

Blend technology and culture.

The job of international managers is to try to retain in their management practices the essential elements of both familiar and new cultures so that their employees may work with the security of some familiar practices but also with greater productivity than the old culture normally has accomplished. As both experience and research demonstrate, technological change is also accompanied by social change. The technological part of change usually can be aided by the tools and logical approaches of science, but the social part is dependent on effective leadership.

Managers as well as technicians need to restrain their tendency to set up complex administrative and production systems in the host country to match those in their own country. These systems may be beyond the skills or educational backgrounds of local people and may be misunderstood and inefficiently operated. A simpler system may operate better, as the following situation shows:

> A human resource management specialist on assignment in another country set up a complicated performance appraisal system having ten items, just like the one used in the Chicago home office. Local supervisors nodded their heads as instructions were given, so

the specialist thought that everything was fine and that they understood completely. When the completed appraisal forms were returned, however, he found that all seven supervisors had rated each employee exactly alike on all ten items.

Investigation disclosed that the supervisors nodded yes because they wished not to offend the specialist, who was to them a guest and a superior, but they did not understand the appraisal system concept. Furthermore, they could not culturally accept the idea of judging their employees (who were also their neighbors) in writing because neither party in that kind of situation could save face.

The Community Role of Expatriate Managers   Expatriate managers need to consider what their role will be in a local community. Although they generally are respected figures with considerable economic power, they are in a country as guests and may not be readily absorbed into the social and power structures of a local community. Even if they speak the local language and live in a community for years, they still may not be fully accepted into its social structure. Because of their marginal role and subsequent insulation from important insights, they risk misinterpreting much of the community's value structure. As a result, they must be cautious not to violate local customs by getting too familiar. The Spanish language and some other languages, for example, have certain familiar pronouns and verb conjugations that are used only among close personal friends and relatives. One manager related the following experience on this subject:

> I was assigned to a country whose people spoke the Spanish language. I had been there two years, and since I speak the language fluently, I felt that I was working very well with the community. On one occasion I was particularly pleased when our top local manager asked me to his home to meet his grandmother, who was the family matriarch and revered by all of the family. When I was introduced to her in rather formal circumstances, without thinking I spoke to her using the familiar form of the verb. Immediately the atmosphere in the room turned to ice, and my visit was hastily terminated. I still didn't know what had happened, but on my way home I asked our local manager, and he emotionally told me that this kind of familiarity is not accepted in his culture. It took me weeks to make the proper apologies through necessary intermediaries, and I felt I never did recover socially from this setback.

Though these kinds of cultural errors may seem minor to an outsider, they can be highly important to a local citizen. Expatriate managers must not establish the image that they are callous to local culture or desire to change it. They are more likely to succeed by maintaining a balance of respect for the local culture and its compatibility with the parent company's culture. If local culture is ignored, the resulting imbalance in the social system interferes with productivity. Likewise, if the organization submits wholly to the culture of the host country, the lack of fit with the technological system will cause loss of efficiency. Both local culture and advanced technology must be integrated.

CROSS-CULTURAL COMMUNICATION

In addition to the desirability of learning to speak and understand the language of the host country, expatriates also need to gain an appreciation for important differences in nonverbal communication. If they do not, they risk making serious errors that might damage their relationships with their employees, partners, customers, and suppliers. Areas in which orientations to **cross-cultural communication** may differ include contrasts in the relative value placed on time efficiency, thought patterns, values placed

Virtual teams in the global realm—individuals who work together by electronic communication across national borders—are becoming increasingly commonplace in firms such as Shell Oil, Verifone, and Nortel Networks. Authors Duarte and Snyder recommend several strategies to avoid the potential pitfalls in virtual teams:

- Make sure the virtual team has key connections to the power brokers in the firm for support—team sponsors, stakeholders, and champions for its cause.

- Create a clear team charter endorsed by the team members, management, and key stakeholders that clarifies the team's mission and goals.

- Recruit strong team members, and brief them on their

type of role expectation—core members, support members, and others whose sole job is to review and approve results.

- Facilitate introductions of team members, and orient them to the task and each other—preferably in a face-to-face context.

- Decide on a team process for exchanging information, managing the work, and sharing information.

Source: Deborah Duarte and Nancy Tennant Snyder, *Mastering Virtual Teams: Strategies, Tools, and Techniques That Succeed,* San Francisco: Jossey-Bass, 1999.

---

on seeing the future, the need for personal space, eye contact, physical appearance, posture, gestures, the meaning of silence, and the legitimacy of touch. These factors make it immensely challenging to communicate effectively with another person in an international setting. As a consequence, they are important contingency factors that must be considered carefully by managers.

Despite the desirability for American managers to learn the language of a host country when dealing there, a countertrend has been established—the increasing acceptance of English as the dominant language of business in Europe. Sixty-nine percent of western European managers now speak English, and over 90 percent of European students study English. What stimulated this widespread usage? Explanations vary, but they include both its rich vocabulary and capacity for change, as well as a powerful technological force—the impact of e-mail and the Internet, where English is a common denominator in the business realm.[24]

Transcultural Managers

It is evident that careful attention should be given to cultural preparation of expatriate employees. Eventually a cadre of employees with cross-cultural adaptability can be developed in organizations with large international operations. These employees are **transcultural employees** because they operate effectively in several cultures. They are low in ethnocentrism and adapt readily to different cultures without major cultural shock. They usually can communicate fluently in more than one language.

Transcultural employees are needed.

Transcultural employees are especially needed in large, multinational firms that operate in a variety of national cultures. For a firm to be truly multinational in character, it should have ownership, operations, markets, and managers truly diversified without primary dominance of any one of these four items by any one nation. Its leaders look to the world as an economic and social unit; but they recognize each local culture, respect its integrity, acknowledge its benefits, and use its differences effectively in their organization.

SUMMARY

The world of business has been transformed into a global economy. Many U.S. businesses have become multinational, extending their operations into other countries. Similarly, corporations in other countries have begun extensive operations in the

1. Learn as much as you can about a variety of cultures, both locally and internationally.
2. Develop regular collaborative (joint learning) relationships with foreign colleagues.
3. Participate in cross-cultural and diversity training.
4. Interview previous expatriates, as well as foreign nationals working in this country, to learn from their valuable experiences.
5. Start now to acquire fluency in at least one additional language.
6. Identify a mentor who is willing and able to advise you on cross-cultural issues.
7. Examine the cultural characteristics (e.g., individualism/collectivism) of the country to which you are most likely to be assigned.
8. Consciously strive to avoid the behavioral problems of xenophobia, ethnocentrism, and so forth.

United States and elsewhere. Managers of these firms encounter a wide variety of social, legal, ethical, political, and economic environments as well as individual differences. Among many other factors, the difficulty in understanding local views of productivity can be a major barrier to improvement. However, when expatriate managers are effective, they help create a training multiplier effect, providing skills which become multiplied many times in the host country.

Employees entering another nation may have difficulty adapting to it because of their parochialism or ethnocentrism, or because of the differences in cultural distance among nations. Cultural shock is a potential barrier to success, but it can be prevented or minimized through careful selection, compatible assignments, predeparture training, and orientation and support. Returning employees also need attention so that their reentry will be smooth and productive.

Expatriate managers must recognize that their organizational behavior practices cannot be transferred directly from one country to another, especially if the host country is less developed. Models for understanding and managing people need to be adapted to the particular social culture. The best results occur when neither the home country's nor the host nation's traditional practices are used. Theory Z provides an example of organizational approaches that integrate the most workable ideas from both sets of existing practices. Transcultural managers—those who can adapt successfully to a number of other cultures and still achieve their goals of improved productivity—will be increasingly needed.

Terms and Concepts for Review

Collectivism

Cross-cultural communication

Cultural contingency

Cultural distance

Cultural empathy

Cultural shock

Ethnocentrism

Expatriates

Feminine societies

Geocentric organizations

High-context cultures

Individualism

Long-term orientation

Low-context cultures

Masculine societies

Multiculturalism

Multinational organizations

Parochialism

Power distance

Repatriation

Reverse cultural shock

Short-term orientation

Theory Z

Training multiplier effect

Transcultural employees

Uncertainty avoidance

Xenophobia

1. Select a foreign country that has recently been in the news. Seek information about key social, legal, ethical, political, and economic factors that would help a manager who is about to move there to understand that country's culture.
2. Identify firms in your region that are multinational. In what parts of the world do they operate? How recently have they become multinational? If possible, invite a representative of one of the firms to speak to the class about policies, experiences, and problems the firm has encountered in its multinational operations.
3. Examine the five factors that represent major individual differences across cultures (e.g., power distance). To what degree do you fit the image of a person from your country on those particular dimensions? Could you work with someone with the opposite characteristics?
4. Discuss the effects of parochialism and ethnocentrism. How would employees behave if they had those characteristics? How would you respond to workers from another country if they demonstrated those traits?
5. Think of a time when you may have experienced cultural shock. How did you react? How could you have better anticipated and prevented it? Is it possible to experience cultural shock by just traveling across the United States? Explain.
6. Evaluate the various recommendations for minimizing or overcoming barriers to cultural adaptation. Which do you think have the greatest likelihood of succeeding?
7. Which person do you predict will experience the greatest amount of cultural shock upon moving to a new country, the expatriate or that person's spouse? Why?
8. Offer several suggestions for preventing or at least minimizing the problem of cross-cultural reentry (reverse cultural shock).
9. Why is the concept of a results orientation (emphasis on productivity) difficult to grasp for some host-country employees? Would it be easier to explain its necessity in an oil-rich country or in one with very limited natural resources? Explain.
10. Theory Z adapts selected Japanese management practices to the U.S. environment. Speculate on the reasons some U.S. employees working for a Theory Z firm might still resist those practices. Now try to create a Theory ZZ approach, in which American practices would be adapted to the Japanese environment and culture. What might Theory ZZ be like, and how would it be received?

How well do you exhibit good intercultural management skills?

Read the following statements carefully. Circle the number on the response scale that most closely reflects the degree to which each statement accurately describes you when you have tried to manage behavior across cultures. Add up your total points and prepare a brief action plan for self-improvement. Be ready to report your score for tabulation across the entire group.

**Assess Your
Own Skills**

	Good description					Poor description			
1. I am able to adapt to different levels of the work ethic that I might find across cultures.	10	9	8	7	6	5	4	3	2	1
2. I believe that female expatriates can be equally effective as male expatriates.	10	9	8	7	6	5	4	3	2	1
3. I am sensitive to the need for people of all cultures, but especially collectivist cultures, to engage in face-saving.	10	9	8	7	6	5	4	3	2	1

416

4. I am capable of assessing differences across national cultures on the basis of five key factors (e.g., power distance, uncertainty avoidance).	10	9	8	7	6	5	4	3	2	1
5. I could be equally comfortable operating in a high-context or low-context culture.	10	9	8	7	6	5	4	3	2	1
6. I speak at least two languages fluently.	10	9	8	7	6	5	4	3	2	1
7. I can demonstrate a substantial degree of cultural empathy for any country I might visit or work in.	10	9	8	7	6	5	4	3	2	1
8. I am aware of the typical stages of cultural shock and believe that I could move to the adaptation stage fairly rapidly in a new culture.	10	9	8	7	6	5	4	3	2	1
9. I know which countries tend to cluster into similar sociocultural groupings.	10	9	8	7	6	5	4	3	2	1
10. I can list the characteristics of, and advantages to, a Theory Z approach to management.	10	9	8	7	6	5	4	3	2	1

Scoring and Interpretation   Add up your total points for the ten questions. Record that number here, and report it when it is requested. _____

- If you scored between 81–100 points, you appear to have a solid capability for demonstrating good intercultural management skills.
- If you scored between 61–80 points, you should take a close look at the items with lower self-assessment scores and explore ways to improve those items.
- If you scored less than 60 points, you should be aware that a weaker skill level regarding several items could be detrimental to your future success as an intercultural manager. We encourage you to review relevant sections of the chapter and watch for related material in subsequent chapters and other sources.

Now identify your three lowest scores, and write the question numbers here: _____ , _____, _____. Write a brief paragraph, detailing to yourself an action plan for how you might sharpen each of these skills.

Incident

The Piedmont Company

The Piedmont Company is a major multinational manufacturer with branch operations in several nations around the world. Its home office is in the United States, but it has sent expatriate managers to work in its various branches. The company recently conducted a survey of its middle managers to determine their relative levels of need satisfaction in their jobs. The results of the survey are reported in the following table:

Approximate Need Satisfaction Levels of Middle-Level American Managers in U.S. Operations versus Overseas Branches

Survey Items	Managers in United States	Expatriate (U.S.) Managers in Branches
Satisfaction with		
Job security	High	Moderate
Opportunity for friendships	High	Low
Feelings of self-esteem	High	Moderate
In-company prestige	Moderate	Moderate
Community prestige	Moderate	High
Opportunity for autonomy	Moderate	High
Level of authority	Low	High
Feeling of accomplishment	Moderate	Moderate
Feeling of self-fulfillment	Low	Moderate

Questions

1. Analyze the results shown, and give your interpretation of the kinds of problems that exist. Offer possible explanations for them.
2. Prepare a set of recommendations for resolving or diminishing the problems that you have identified.
3. Speculate about what the results might look like if the nonsupervisory employees in each country had been surveyed. What is the basis for your conclusions?

Adaptability to a Multicultural Assignment

Experiential Exercise

Assume that you have been hired by a firm with extensive operations in many different countries around the world. Your first job assignment will take you out of the United States for approximately three years, and you will depart about thirty days from now.

1. Review the text discussion of parochialism, ethnocentrism, and cultural shock. Think about the degree to which you would be likely to exhibit each of these barriers to cultural adaptation, and record your responses on the top portion of the following chart. Then on the bottom portion of the chart indicate the degree to which you would honestly expect to experience difficulty adapting to the culture in each of the six sociocultural clusters.

Low Degree						**High Degree**
Barrier						
Parochialism	1	2	3	4	5	6	7
Ethnocentrism	1	2	3	4	5	6	7
Cultural shock	1	2	3	4	5	6	7

Sociocultural cluster

Anglo-American	1	2	3	4	5	6	7
Latin American	1	2	3	4	5	6	7
Latin European	1	2	3	4	5	6	7
Nordic	1	2	3	4	5	6	7
Central European	1	2	3	4	5	6	7
Pacific Rim	1	2	3	4	5	6	7

2. Share your personal assessments with the rest of the class. (Create a frequency distribution of the responses.) Explore why differences exist among students and what the overall pattern implies regarding the capacity of class members to become transcultural employees. What could you, or your employer, do to improve the likelihood of your success in view of your assessments?

Part Eight

Case Problems

INTRODUCTION

Case problems provide a useful medium for testing and applying some of the ideas in this textbook. They bring reality to abstract ideas about organizational behavior. All the case problems that follow are true situations recorded by case research. Certain case details are disguised, but none of the cases is a fictional creation. All names are disguised, and any similarity to actual persons is purely coincidental.

These cases have a decision-making emphasis; that is, they end at a point that leaves managers or employees with certain decisions to make. Most of the cases emphasize decisional problems of managers. One decision often is based on the question, Do I have a further problem? If the answer is yes, then further analysis must be made: What problems exist? Why are they problems? What can be done about them within the resource limits available (i.e., what alternatives are available)? Finally, what *should* be done to solve this particular problem in this specific organization? Making decisions based on the answers to such questions is the reality that every manager faces in operating situations. There is no escaping it.

Even a person who does not plan to be a manager can gain much from analyzing these cases, because all employees need to develop their own analytical skills about human behavior in order to work successfully with their associates and *with management* in organizations. Placing yourself in the employee role in a case, you can ask: Why do my associates act the way they do in this situation? Why is management acting the way it is in this instance? Was there something in my behavior that caused these actions? How can I change my behavior in order to work more effectively with the organization and my associates and thereby reach my goals more easily?

Since these case problems describe real situations, they include both good and bad practices. These cases are not presented as examples of good management, effective organizational behavior, bad management, or ineffective organizational behavior. Readers may make these judgments for themselves. The primary value in studying these cases lies in the development of analytical skills and the application of organizational behavior knowledge to solve challenging problems.

Case 1

The Virtual Environment Work Team

T.A. Stearns was a national tax accounting firm whose main business was its popular tax preparation service for individuals. Stearns's superior reputation was based on the high quality of its advice and the excellence of its service. Key to the achievement of its reputation were the superior computer databases and analysis tools that its agents used when counseling clients. These programs were developed by highly trained individuals, usually lawyers and tax accountants who had picked up programming skills on the side.

The programs that these individuals produced were highly technical both in terms of the tax laws they covered and the code in which they were written. Perfecting them required high levels of programming skill as well as the ability to understand the law. New laws and interpretations of existing laws had to be integrated quickly and flawlessly into the existing regulations and analysis tools.

The work was carried out in a virtual environment by four programmers in the greater Boston area. Four work sites were connected to each other and to the company by e-mail, telephone, and conferencing software. Formal meetings among all of the programmers took place only a few times a year, although the workers sometimes met informally outside of these scheduled occasions.

The following paragraphs describe the members of the virtual work team.

Tom Andrews was a tax lawyer, a graduate of State University and a former hockey player there. At thirty-five years old, Tom had worked on the programs for six years and was the longest-standing member of the group. Along with his design responsibilities, Tom was the primary liaison with Stearns. He was also responsible for training new group members. Single, he worked out of his farm in southern New Hampshire where in his spare time he enjoyed hunting and fishing.

Cy Crane, a tax accountant and computer science graduate of State University, was thirty-two years old, married with two children ages four and six. His wife worked full-time in a law firm in downtown Boston, whereas he commuted from his kitchen to his computer in their home in the Boston suburbs. In his spare time he enjoyed biking and fishing.

Marge Dector, tax lawyer, graduate of Outstate Unversity, thirty-eight years old, was married with two children ages eight and ten. Her husband worked full-time as an electrical engineer at a local defense contractor. She lived and worked in her suburban Boston home, and she enjoyed golf and skiing.

Megan Harris, tax accountant and graduate of Big Time University, was twenty-six years old and single. She had recently relocated to Boston to take advantage of the wide range of opportunities in her field and to enjoy the beauty of New England. She worked out of her Back Bay apartment.

In the course of their work, these four people exchanged e-mail messages many times every day, and it was not unusual for one of them to step away from guests or children to log on and check in with the others. Often their e-mails were amusing as well as work-related. Sometimes they helped each other with the work, as, for example, when a parent with a sick child was facing a deadline. Tom occasionally invited the others to visit with him on his farm, and once in a while Marge and Cy got their families together for dinner. About once a month the whole group got together for lunch.

All of these workers were on salary, which, according to company custom, each had negotiated separately and secretly with management. A major factor in their commitment to the job was its flexibility. Although they were required to check in regularly during every workday, they could do the work whenever they wanted to. When they got together, they often joked about the managers and workers who had to be in the office during specific hours, referring to them as "face timers" and to themselves as "free agents."

When the programmers were asked to make a major program change, they often developed programming tools called macros that would help them to do their work more efficiently. These macros greatly enhanced the speed at which a change could be written into the programs. Cy in particular really enjoyed hacking around with macros. For example, on one recent project, he became obsessed by the prospect of creating a shortcut that could save him a huge amount of time. One week after he had turned in his code and his release notes to the company, Cy bragged to Tom that he had created a new macro that had saved him eight hours of work that week. "The stripers are running," he had said, "And I want to be on the beach." Tom was skeptical about the shortcut, but after trying it out in his own work, he found that it actually did save him many hours.

T.A. Stearns had an employee suggestion program that rewarded employees for innovations that saved the company money. The program gave an employee 5 percent of the savings generated by their innovation over a period of three months. The company also had a profit-sharing plan. Tom and Cy felt that the small amount of money that would be generated by a company reward would not offset the free time that they gained using their new macro. They wanted the time either for leisure or for other consulting, and furthermore, they agreed that because the money came out of profits, the money was really coming out of the employees' pockets anyhow. There seemed to be little incentive to share their innovation macro with management.

They also believed that their group could suffer if management learned about the innovation. They could now do the work so quickly that only three programmers might be needed. If management were to learn about the macro, one of them would probably lose their job, and the remaining workers would have more work thrown at them.

Cy and Tom decided that there was not enough incentive to tell the company about the macro. However, they were just entering their busy season and they knew that everyone in the group would be stressed by the heavy workload. They decided to distribute the macro to the other members of the group and swore them to secrecy.

Over lunch one day, the group set for itself a level of production that it felt would not arouse management's suspicion. Several months passed, and they used some of their extra time to push the quality of their work even higher. The rest of the time gained they used for their own personal interests.

Dave Regan, the manager of the work group, picked up on the innovation several weeks after it was first implemented. He had wondered why production time had gone down a bit, while quality had shot up, and he got his first inkling of an answer when he saw an e-mail from Marge to Cy thanking him for saving her so much time with his "brilliant mind." Not wanting to embarass his group of employees, the manager hinted to Tom that he wanted to know what was happening, but he got nowhere. He did not tell his own manager about his suspicions, reasoning that since both quality and productivity were up he did not really need to pursue the matter further.

Then one day Dave heard that Cy had boasted about his trick to a member of another virtual work group in the company. Suddenly the situation seemed to have gotten out of hand. Dave took Cy to lunch and asked him to explain what was happening. Cy told him about the innovation, but he insisted that the group's action had been justified to protect itself.

Dave knew that his own boss would soon hear of the situation, and that he would be looking for answers—from him.

Study Guides

1. Why is this group a team?
2. What characteristics of the team predispose it to making ineffective decisions?
3. What are the characteristics of groupthink that are manifested in the work team?
4. Has Dave been an effective group leader? What should Dave do now?

Case 2

The Teaching Hospital

Dr. Robert Uric was the head of the Renal Medicine Unit at a large university medical school and teaching hospital. The teaching hospital, a regional medical center, had over 1,000 beds and was considered a reasonably prestigious medical facility.

There was a steady undercurrent of hostility and competition between the hospital and the medical school. The two institutions, a state school and a state-supported hospital, had only one top official in common—the provost. From the provost down, the organization split in half, with the medical school, its physician faculty, and its nursing faculty on one side, and the hospital administrator, nonmedical hospital employees, and ancillary service staff on the other (see Figure 1).

The physical plant, designed in the shape of an H, paralleled and accentuated the organizational structure. The medical school ran east-west, ten floors high on the north side, and the hospital ran east-west, eight stories high on the south. They were connected only by the bar of the H, an officeless corridor connecting the medical school and the hospital on each of the first six floors.

A large part of the problem was the unusual nature of the financial arrangements. The physicians, as faculty members, received salaries but no money for patient services. Patients *were* billed for professional services, but the revenues went into departmental funds that were disbursed at the discretion of the department chairs. The hospital, on the other hand, turned in every patient-revenue dollar to the state and then had to turn around and beg for, and account for, every penny of operating revenue it got.

Grant monies further complicated the situation, especially in the area of salaries. Hospital employees were civil service workers, strictly regulated by job classifications and wage scales; no exceptions were made. The medical school faculty, however, could frequently use grant money to supplement state salary scale, to hire peo-

This case was prepared by Roberta P. Marquette and Michael H. Smith under the supervision of Theodore T. Herbert. The case is not intended to reflect either effective or ineffective administrative or technical practices; it was prepared for class discussion. Copyright Theodore T. Herbert, Crummer Graduate School of Business, Rollins College, Winter Park, FL 32789.

ple outright at higher salaries, or to provide nonsalary perquisites. Because of the financial flexibility, working conditions were also frequently better on the medical school side, and medical school staff had money for more equipment, more travel, and even more parties.

The inconsistencies between the operations of the hospital and those of the medical school were highlighted by the integration of medical school faculty into hospital functions. The situation was aggravated by the reports of technicians, patient-floor employees, and clinical clerks. These hospital personnel worked directly under the physicians and nurses from the medical school faculty, who were also administrative heads of clinical hospital departments and were in rather good positions to observe and hear of differences between the hospital and medical school sides. (Qualified physicians were felt to be necessary in heading clinical hospital departments because of the technical natures of the departments' functions and from medical necessity.)

Assistant hospital directors were in charge of most administrative matters, including administration of wage and benefit programs; department heads (physicians), however, were responsible for supervising departmental activities, evaluating employees,

FIGURE 1

Teaching hospital–medical school organization chart

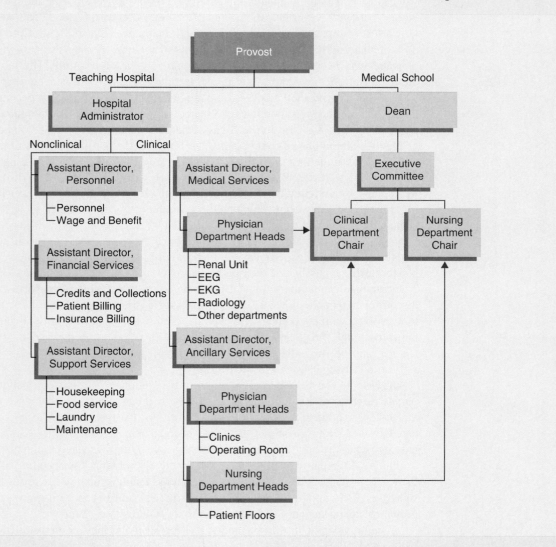

and recommending raises and promotions. The dual reporting relationship left the employees in a situation of very divided responsibilities. Further, the general disdain that the physicians felt for hospital administrators left the assistant directors in the position of mere figureheads in the area of clinical services. The hospital personnel, seemingly from the administrators down to the clinic clerks, complained that the physicians were prima donnas, who considered themselves the next best thing to being divine. The medical personnel, on the other hand, complained that hospital personnel were civil service, time-serving incompetents.

One exception was Dr. Robert Uric, head of the renal unit. Despite the difficulty of his job and his membership in the faculty group, Dr. Uric was roundly liked by the hospital employees with whom he worked. One reason was that, whenever possible, he shared his grant monies with the hospital employees in his unit. Financially and emotionally, the hospital renal unit, not the medical school department of medicine, was Dr. Uric's home and favorite child.

The Renal Medicine Unit at the teaching hospital, like many other renal units, received what might be termed "stepchild" treatment, banished to a subbasement where most of the other faculty and staff could avoid the painful realities of chronic kidney patients. Nevertheless, the renal unit *was* a cheerful place. The staff, under Uric's leadership, maintained high morale, remarkably high in view of the hopelessness of many cases and the frequent deaths of patients who spent years visiting the unit and who became, in time, almost members of a large family. The job done by the renal staffers—residents, interns, and technicians alike—was sincerely appreciated by the patients and their families, and was a source of wonder to those outside faculty and staff who were familiar with the conditions of the dungeonlike renal unit. As a matter of fact, Dr. Uric himself was something of a wonder.

On nice afternoons he could be seen strolling the grounds, pop bottle and hero sandwich in hand, trailed by a half-dozen students, teaching Socratic-style among the birch trees and the squirrels. Brown-bagging his lunch was not the least of Uric's peculiarities; many stories circulated, including the tale of his being given a ticket for speeding down one of the steep campus hills on his bicycle. Also, through those who knew someone in the renal unit, other stories began to leak out—tales of Friday afternoon parties fueled with grain alcohol and fruit punch, and worse yet, rumors of a monthly rabbit roast in which experimental animals whose transplants were not successful were put to death painlessly and then barbecued over a pair of Bunsen burners.

Other faculty members found Uric to be a constant source of embarrassment and discomfort. His actions were "undignified"; for a research physician, he was entirely too involved with his patients. He actually cried openly when his patients died—most unprofessional! Still, he was a fine director of renal medicine and a remarkable teacher, and he was, after all, an inside joke.

That all changed with Flower Life.

Dr. Uric had several federal grants from the National Institutes of Health (NIH) to pursue research on kidney transplantation. He had begun doing active research within the first year after taking over the renal unit. Not the type of man to become fascinated by academic questions, Uric had become almost obsessed with the need for answers when he saw his patients suffering and dying because treatments were not available. He began by solving small, individual problems for specific patients and then generalizing and publishing the solutions. Gaining confidence from his initial successes, Uric applied for, and got, grant money and began working on the larger problems facing patients with chronic kidney failure.

A major problem in transplantation is keeping the kidney properly diffused (alive and full of fluid) between donor and recipient, and Uric was involved in this problem. In the course of his work he discovered a fluid that was absorbed much faster than water at the cellular level. Testing showed it to be ineffective as a solution for diffusion, but it occurred to Uric that if plants absorbed it as well as human cells did, it might make a good fluid for cut flowers, extending their life. After finding the right combination of fluid and an acid substance to keep the cut stem end from closing, Dr. Uric decided he did have a substance superior to anything then on the market.

As required by the grant agreement, Uric reported his discovery to the NIH. NIH officials said they did not want the fluid. Ownership belonged to the university. But when Uric offered it to them, the university officials smiled indulgently and said he could keep it. Not a man to be easily discouraged, Uric next offered his discovery to a large nursery-supply manufacturer. The firm bought it, named it Flower Life, and began making millions. All of a sudden NIH had a change of heart and filed suit. The story broke in the newspapers, first locally, then regionally, then nationally; needless to say, Dr. Uric made fun copy.

Uric and his peculiarities were no longer a private joke, and the faculty became concerned about the reputation of the school. At the next executive committee meeting, the heads of the clinical departments discussed the situation with the dean and suggested that perhaps Uric should be put in a less visible position until things quieted down. The dean agreed. The executive committee felt it should move carefully; Uric was, after all, tenured and very popular with the students and house staff. It would not do to let this move look like persecution. The committee finally settled on approaching the provost with a plan to establish a new research chair in medicine. Backed by the dean, and financed by money donated from the chairs' department funds, the plan was approved and Uric was hastily offered the position. At first he refused, but it was subtly made clear that if he expected the university to back him in the impending litigation, he would have to help out by surrounding himself with an air of respectability. Uric accepted and was given a big raise and transferred to a beautifully equipped new lab on the tenth floor of the main building; the chief resident of renal medicine, Dr. George Conrad, was placed in charge of the dialysis unit.

The chief resident had a reputation for being hard-nosed. He had gone to medical school at a smaller university and had been very happy to get an internship and residency at a large teaching hospital. An excellent student, Conrad had also applied to Bellevue, the hospital arm of New York University, and to several other major teaching hospitals. His only acceptance came from his current employer, and the evaluation committee had looked long and hard at his application before accepting him. While his grades and aptitude tests showed him to be an extremely bright and an extraordinarily dedicated young man, his reference letters revealed him to be inflexible and rather ruthless. Born and raised in very poor surroundings, George Conrad was determined to become a doctor and to surround himself with that safe and apparently impenetrable aura of the physician—financially, socially, and professionally secure. He had an image of the physician as being wise, aloof, self-controlled, and as close to infallible as a person can get. Somewhat insecure about his origins, Conrad had long ago assumed a facade of what he thought a physician should look like; now it was hard, even for him, to tell whether the facade had become reality.

With Uric's removal, the members of the executive committee felt that Conrad was the ideal person to assume the responsibility for the renal unit. They felt Conrad would apply a strong hand. The assignment was turned over to him by the chair of the anesthesiology department, a powerful and respected member of the committee. The chair told Conrad that the committee was certain he could handle the renal unit, and that they did not expect to hear of any problems from the unit under his capable guidance. The chair also suggested that Conrad be firm in asking Uric to stay away from the unit and thereby allow the transition of authority to proceed quickly.

The executive committee expected a period of adjustment, but disruptions of routine exceeded anything the members imagined. Serious personnel problems arose in the dialysis unit, with increased absences and constant grievances about impossible working conditions. While these complaints were pouring into the hospital personnel office through grievance procedures, few or no messages were coming through to the executive committee or the dean. The hospital administration, unable to alter matters without the concurrence of the department head, in this case Dr. Conrad, waited for appropriate authorization to investigate the matter and attempt to improve conditions.

By the end of the first month the turnovers had started; after three months ninety of the old employees were gone. Dr. Conrad did not believe in becoming involved with patients on a personal basis, and he appeared to feel the same way about subordinates. Interns on rotation through renal medicine complained bitterly about Conrad's attitude toward and treatment of them; the roster of residents applying to the service dropped dramatically.

Meanwhile upstairs, Uric's research work was stale, as was his disposition. He failed to turn in a grant progress report on time, and the granting agency flexed its muscle and canceled the remainder of his funding.

The dean was not happy and the executive committee was far from delighted, but everyone still believed the situation would straighten itself out. Nobody, however, believed the problem to be serious enough to investigate the effects on the kidney patients down in the subbasement. The dean and the committee might have even forgotten that the dialysis unit was down there. When news did come out, it revealed that the effects were far more damaging than any tales of Dr. Uric's weird habits could possibly have been.

A patient who had been on dialysis three times a week for several years had given up her place and gone home to die. Because she had a rare blood and tissue type, the woman had been waiting a long time for a transplant. She had seen many other patients die waiting and even more patients get transplants while her odds appeared ever slimmer. Sometime after Uric left the unit, she had made her decision; the story leaked out after she died.

Shocked by the realization of how bad the situation had become, the dean and the executive committee immediately placed Uric back as head of the renal unit; they then began to analyze what had happened, and what could be done to put the renal unit—and the hospital's reputation—back together again.

Study Guides

1. Identify the barriers to communication in this case, and describe their impact on the hospital's effectiveness.
2. Compare and contrast the two doctors' styles of management and the apparent reflections of Theory X and Theory Y assumptions of each of the doctors.
3. Relate various motivational theories, such as McClelland's drives, Herzberg's two-factor theory, and the expectancy model, to this case.

Case 3

Creative Toys Company

The Creative Toys Company, a small firm that specializes in producing small wooden toys, was started by John Wilson. A carpenter by hobby, Mr. Wilson had made numerous toys for his children. He found these toys to be quite marketable in an age of plastic, battery-operated, easily broken toys. The company is proud of its history and stability and growth in the industry. Low turnover rates are the result of good wages and fringe benefits.

One department in particular had been highly productive. The transportation department at one time surpassed all other departments in production for twelve months. The only reason for this success is the low turnover rate within the department. All eight people in the department have held their current jobs for at least two years.

This department is responsible for producing all the toy cars and trucks in the firm's product line. Each department member has all the tools and equipment at his or her workstation to produce a complete toy. Four workers make cars in the morning while the other four produce trucks. The system is reversed in the afternoon to decrease monotony.

In the past, upper management allowed each department to determine its own procedure and methods, as long as production orders were filled on time. This departmental autonomy allowed the transportation department to rearrange its eight work areas in a circular fashion (see Figure 1). This circular arrangement let the department members converse with each other and keep informed of each other's work habits and productivity. They not only were high producers but also got along well outside of work.

The plant manager recently decided to bring in consultants to determine if production could be increased without physical expansion; demand for company products had outstripped production capacity. One recommendation dealt with the transportation department. The physical layout of the department did not facilitate efficient traffic flow to and from the other departments. The transportation department was located between the painting department and the wooden block department. Supplies and completed products were placed in a storage area in the shipping and receiving department, creating considerable traffic through the departments. One employee on a forklift would bring supplies to all the departments and simultaneously remove the completed products.

The consultants recommended rearranging the work areas in the transportation department into eight individual areas to facilitate traffic flow (see Figure 2). In their report the consultants viewed the department's productivity as having the potential for substantial improvements. The plant manager agreed with the assessment and had the workstations rearranged during the next weekend.

After two months it was obvious that the transportation department's productivity was declining. The plant manager spoke to all members of the department, hoping to find some answers; however, department members could not articulate the problem. They knew only that something had changed besides the physical arrangement of the work areas.

Mr. Wilson asked the plant manager for an explanation of the department's declining productivity.

PLANT MANAGER: I see no obvious reason for this decline. The department is composed of the same people, doing the same work. The only difference is the work area layout, and the workers seem to have adapted well. Perhaps a raise is the answer. In the past this department put out more than the other departments. Monetary recognition could be the answer.

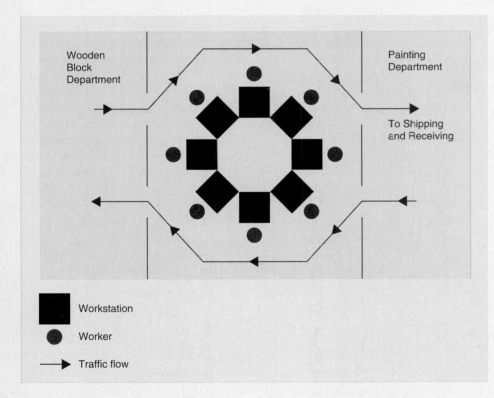

FIGURE 1

Initial transportation department work layout

■ Workstation

● Worker

→ Traffic flow

434

MR. WILSON: We have done some rearranging in other, more unstable departments. These other departments have increased productivity; that suggests to me that the rearrangement is not the problem. I think the department must have built in slack time on purpose. The workers want a raise, and this is their way of getting our attention. I won't be blackmailed this way! They'll not get raises until they have met their prior production performance.

The plant manager left the meeting feeling that they had not solved the real problem but only bypassed it, although he was unsure of what the real problem was.

Study Guides

Discuss the role of social systems and their impact on productivity in this case. Be sure to include comments on change, informal organization, communication, and motivation.

FIGURE 2

Rearranged transportation department work layout

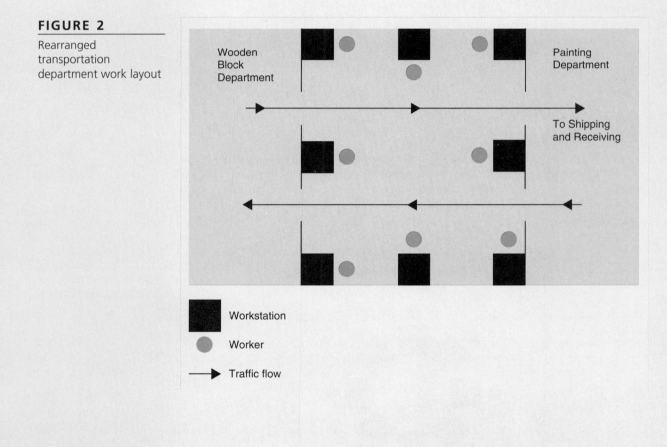

Case 4

Eastern International Food Service Corporation

Stanley Strayhorn, general manager of Eastern International Food Service Corporation's Ocean Point Division, has a problem. For the past week, labor turnover has been increasing, employee morale has been dropping, and food cost percentage is climbing, while profit margins on sales are declining. Mr. Strayhorn is deeply concerned, for there are still two weeks left in the summer season. Not only is it too late to train new workers, but it is difficult even to find replacements. A shortage of labor will drastically affect potential sales for the next two weeks, a period noted for heavy sales.

BACKGROUND INFORMATION

Eastern International Food Service Corporation (EI) was a food service corporation in the eastern area of the United States. Its services were offered in many amusement parks. Ocean Point Amusement Park was one of its biggest branches, in sales as well as in number of employees—300. Eastern International had a contract with Ocean Point to operate all its food service concessions on the park's premises. Fifteen EI concession stands were distributed throughout the 500-acre park. Food sales included hotdogs, hamburgers, french fries, popcorn, ice cream, beverages, and so on. Each concession stand had a manager and an assistant manager, as well as between five and twenty workers, depending on the size of the stand. Jobs ranged from cleaning grills and fryers to waiting on the customers over the counter.

In addition to the concession stands, the company also operated six different restaurants on the premises, including fast-food services, cafeterias, and a sit-down dining room. Each had its own manager and two or three assistant managers, as well as a full complement of line servers, dishwashers, kitchen helpers, cooks, waiters, and waitresses.

This case was adapted from materials prepared by David Hau under the supervision of Theodore T. Herbert. The case is not intended to reflect either effective or ineffective administrative or technical practices, but was prepared as a basis for class discussion. Copyright Theodore T. Herbert, Crummer Graduate School of Business, Rollins College, Winter Park, FL 32789.

Since the park was open only in the summer, student employees fit perfectly into the schedule. With room and board provided, and a work season which coincided with summer vacation, high school and college students found employment with EI both convenient and well-paying. Besides, there were hundreds of other students of the same age with whom to associate, both on and off the job. Almost all the positions—managers and workers—were held by student employees.

All stand and restaurant managers reported to one of several supervisors, each of whom was a full-time, nonstudent Eastern International employee. The functions of the supervisors were to check on all stands and restaurants to make sure everything was running properly, no employee was loafing, and food cost and profit margin targets were met. Above the supervisors was the general manager of this division—Mr. Strayhorn himself—and the assistant manager, Mr. Edwards.

Summer employment was regarded as part-time employment, so there was no union established. In other words, there was nothing to guarantee full-term employment. Nevertheless, EI tried to keep its employees as long as possible. Most employees hired were inexperienced, fresh out of high school. They often needed a few days to be trained; several weeks on the job were needed to become a fast worker. The secret behind working in a concession stand was that the faster a person worked, the more sales he or she could make, an important consideration for being reemployed by EI the next season. Usually a returning employee would get a 20 to 25 percent increase in pay or perhaps a promotion, if initiative and managerial abilities were demonstrated. In essence, the company tried to maintain regular and well-experienced employees, a difficult task considering the long work hours and the nature of its student labor force.

PROBLEM SITUATION

Everyone who worked at Ocean Point knew that Eastern International Food Service was a lessee. The contract was to terminate on Labor Day. Only two weeks remained in the contract period and the season, but the question of whether Ocean Point would choose to renew the contract for next year remained unanswered.

Complicating the issue was the fact that, starting three years ago, Ocean Point had established specialty-food concession stands of its own. Such was its contractual right, to set up and administer food concessions not directly competitive with the foods offered by EI. Ocean Point now had four stands in operation serving pizza, tacos, and frozen bananas. Ocean Point used its own employees, currently employed in the park, to run the stands. The amusement park manager had found that he could relieve sweepers in the morning hours (before litter had a chance to accumulate) and put them on the early shift in the concession stands. Sweepers would be relieved, in turn, by ticket sellers in the afternoon hours when few tickets were sold and when litter cleaning was a full-time proposition. Such a clever arrangement allowed the addition of selling functions with no increase in labor costs.

Rumors flew, fueled by the concession operations of the park. Some said that the stands were set up to allow the park to develop the skills needed to administer concessions. Once the skills were developed, the contract with EI would be allowed to lapse, and park employees would run the former EI stands next season. An elaborate seniority and promotion system used by the park would effectively preclude EI employees from transferring to park employment.

If the contract was renewed, then everything would remain unchanged; nobody would be disturbed. If, however, the contract was not renewed, Eastern International would have no operation in Ocean Point next year and between 200 and 300 college students would not be returning to summer jobs.

Rumors spread among the EI employees. Some said EI would be back next year, and others said it would not. Neither rumor was verified by EI management. Even when confronted with the question point-blank, all that the supervisors could, or would, say was that EI *might* not be back. (Several Ocean Point stand managers were spotted wandering around in front of EI stands. They were believed to be spying.) The season was approaching its end, and the management had maintained silence. By now, the accepted rumors were that Eastern International would *not* return next summer and that Ocean Point did not wish to hire any person who had worked for EI.

The attitude of the EI employees had gotten steadily worse. Morale had declined. Managers of stands had become irresponsible and were losing control of their subordinates. Food costs were rising as a result of the amount of theft and waste. Workers slowed their pace and thereby failed to serve numerous customers, who were quite vocal in their displeasure. Some students had quit, "knowing" that they would not be rehired anyhow. While the *potential* sales of the season were reaching their peak, *actual* sales and profits had declined. Never was there, in the history of the company, such a tremendous decline in sales and profit during this time of the season.

Study Guides

1. Assess Strayhorn's communication effectiveness. What impact has his approach had on morale and productivity?
2. Comment on the impact of anxiety, stress, and crises on employee use of informal communications (the grapevine) in this case.

Case 5

Goodman Company

THE COMPANY

The Goodman Company manufactures small rubber automotive parts. Its products include boots for floor-mounted automobile and truck transmissions, boots for brakes, and clutch and accelerator pedals. These products are sold exclusively to assembly plants for new cars and trucks.

The company operates a single plant. Joe Smith is the production manager. He reports directly to the president of the company, Robert Goodman. Joe has three supervisors under him, each responsible for one of the three production shifts.

Goodman Company has been doing quite well lately. Employees have been added until all machines in the plant are fully staffed on each shift. In fact, for the past quarter the plant has operated six days a week in an effort to keep up with its increased orders.

Robert Goodman, in viewing the outlook for the company, foresees greater opportunities in the years ahead if output can be expanded to meet future demands. Any increase in production must occur within the present physical plant, because money is not available for the proposed multimillion-dollar expansion that was thought possible last year.

Because the purchase of new equipment is out of the question, Mr. Goodman decided to hire a production analyst to see if greater efficiency could be achieved with current equipment. Ann Bennet was hired for the job of generating recommendations for wringing greater productivity from the plant.

This case was prepared by Paul Seifert, Dave Thirion, Roger Young, Gene Sitarz, and Debra Mooney under the supervision of Theodore T. Herbert. The case is not intended to reflect either effective or ineffective administrative or technical practices, but was prepared as a basis for class discussion. Copyright Theodore T. Herbert, Crummer Graduate School of Business, Rollins College, Winter Park, FL 32789.

ANN BENNET

Ann Bennet earned a bachelor's degree in finance in 1988. In 1990 she earned an M.B.A. with a concentration in production management. She did her graduate work at a well-known university, from which she graduated magna cum laude.

Before accepting her new position, Ms. Bennet worked for a management consulting firm. After two years she was promoted to project leader. She held that position for three years before going with Goodman Company.

Her reasons for leaving the consulting firm are numerous. She has received a handsome salary increase from Goodman. Whereas her previous job demanded that she travel about 40 percent of the time, no traveling is required by her new job. Finally, she feels that her new job is more challenging and that better opportunities for advancement exist with Goodman.

The Goodman Company was very impressed with Ms. Bennet's interview, her credentials, and her references. They feel that she will be an asset to the firm and that the position will be an asset to her professionally.

PRODUCTION: BEFORE

Presently, the entire production process is handled by each individual worker. Sheets of rubber, in slabs 3 feet by 3 feet, are purchased from a major rubber company; these sheets are the only raw material for the manufactured products. The sheets of rubber are located in the center of the work area. Each worker procures his or her own material and then, in the storage area, cuts it to size for a particular product. The worker then transports the cut material back to a steam-fed curing press. Each press has twelve molds in which the cut material is placed; the press is then activated for the five-minute curing cycle. During the five-minute interval, the worker trims the excess rubber from parts previously extracted from the press. After ten to twelve boxes have been filled, the worker transports the boxes to the shipping area. All production workers are paid an hourly rate.

PRODUCTION: AFTER

Ms. Bennet's proposal involves using the same equipment but in a mass-production format. Each worker will no longer perform the entire process. One will be assigned to raw material preparation and will be responsible for cutting the raw material to the appropriate size for curing. Another worker will be responsible for material handling—moving raw material to the curing presses and transporting bins of finished products from the work area to shipping.

The final finish operation, which involves trimming the excess rubber from the cured parts and placing them in bins for shipment, will be handled by still another worker. Finally, a worker will be assigned to the curing process: to place parts into the press, activate the press, and eject the parts and place them on a conveyor that leads to the final finish operation. The curing worker will operate a total of five presses.

All production workers under the proposed process will be compensated under a piecework system. This approach is used in an effort to increase motivation, which thereby will increase production.

THE PRODUCTION SHIFTS

Ms. Bennet's plan was eagerly accepted by Goodman and the members of the board of directors. The plan was made final and sent to the production supervisors for implementation. Mr. Goodman and the board anxiously awaited the results. Mr. Brown, a board member, observed each shift before and after the production plan was in full operation.

First Shift

Before   Cleverson Anthony is the supervisor on the first shift. "Clev," as he is fondly referred to by the workers under him, looks and thinks just the same as he did when he was first hired by Goodman back in 1965. When asked a question about plant operations, Clev sits back, drags on his cigar, and talks extemporaneously about plant performance. Top management has a lot of respect for old Clev; he is considered one of the loyal employees who helped make the company what it is today.

Clev really has no need to work. His brother-in-law died several years back, leaving Clev and his wife a considerable amount of money. Since then, Clev has been traveling around the country looking for the perfect place to retire. He does his searching during his six weeks of vacation; sometimes he stretches a holiday by taking off a day before and after. The department runs itself and he can do this unnoticed. Clev still has eight years to go before retirement, but he still spends a lot of work time talking about the as yet unfound place to which he is going to retire.

Nancy Pearson, the timekeeper, is in her late twenties; she handles the paperwork of the department. She schedules production, orders materials, inventories finished goods, and then types the shipping labels.

Joe Bob Haymaker, the first press operator, is proud of the fact that he and Clev were hired on the same day. The two of them have an agreement to retire to the same place. Clev comes over about once a shift and helps Joe Bob run his press while they talk about the different places Clev has been to visit recently.

John (Fireball) Malone is the second press operator. Although Fireball is in his late fifties, he attends school in the evenings in the hope of becoming a computer programmer. He likes to make a show of bringing his books to the lunchroom and discussing the latest things he has learned. Computer programming is one of the many different courses he has started. Last year, he was taking a home-study course in accounting.

Fireball is the shift's self-elected spokesman. He walks around the department during the day and takes notes of complaints and of improvements that could be made in the operations. The workers tolerate Fireball but make derogatory remarks about him; whenever he sees Joe Smith or Robert Goodman, he runs up to them and reads his suggestions from the notebook he carries in his pocket.

The others on the first shift are in the same age bracket as Clev, Joe Bob, and Fireball, yet they do not socialize with each other. They get along fine at work, but after working hours they go their separate ways. For the most part, the workers on the first shift feel they have made the company what it is. They feel that the company has not been entirely fair to them through the years by not sharing the high profits they have earned for the company. Consequently, whenever they have the chance, they take off work early or show up late.

The first shift never loses any production. The workers see to that by helping Nancy plan the intended work schedule every Monday. Clev sees nothing wrong with that tactic; after all, these workers have the most knowledge anyone could possess about equipment capabilities.

The quality level of the first shift is top-rate. Whenever a bad product is returned by a customer, Fireball and Clev go down to the front office to inspect it. The part is almost always thought to be from one of the "goof-off" shifts. The workers of the first shift just have too much experience to make costly mistakes!

After   The production and the quality of the work of the first shift dropped off considerably after the change. After two weeks of working under Ms. Bennet's plan, Clev asked if he could take early retirement. Upper management hated to lose such a good man, so it created a job for him in the front office. Because Fireball is always such a progressive thinker when it comes to work, management thinks he will make a fine foreman.

No one on the first shift likes the changes. There is constant complaining over the new process. Products are not being readied properly for the next step of the production process.

Joe Bob, who complained that the company has put the screws to them by implementing piecework rates, is trying to organize a union. The rest of the workers appear willing to go along with the idea. They feel the company must not think much of their abilities or else the job would not have been simplified, and there would be no need to degrade them with the piecework requirement.

Second Shift

Before   The second shift supervisor is Norm Leonard. He is fifty-four years old and has been with the company for only three years. Norm was hired directly into the company as a supervisor by his good friend and lodge brother Bob Goodman.

Before he came to Goodman, Norm had been an assistant floor supervisor in production control at another company. He had taken his thirty-years-and-out retirement option when he was fifty years old. After a year of retirement he learned that his pension was not sufficient to live on, and if he wanted full Social Security benefits when he was sixty-five, he would have to continue paying into the program for ten or eleven more years.

Bob Goodman told Norm that there was a place for him at Goodman Company. The firm could use Norm's experience, and Norm could use the extra money to ease his transition from full employment to full retirement. Norm figured it would be an easy job.

In September, Norm took over supervision of the second shift at Goodman. This shift consists of twelve men who are in their mid-thirties. Most have been with the company for seven or eight years; overall, they seem to be a productive group. When Norm took the job, the men did not exactly accept him with open arms, but no one particularly disliked him either.

So far Norm's job has been relatively easy. Whenever the men have problems with material or machines, they go to Jim Fask. Jim is one of the senior men on the shift; it appears that he knows exactly how every machine and product should be run on the second shift. Jim has no formal authority over the men, but they all seem to like and trust him.

Other than Jim, Norm has noticed no other stars on his shift. Norm socializes very little with his men; he feels that the men should do their jobs and he should do his. He follows the rules and regulations set down by the company and keeps the shift running at a satisfactory rate. In other words, Norm does not want to rock the boat.

After   Reflecting on what has happened since Ms. Bennet's program was implemented, Norm feels that he has cooperated in every way possible. He is convinced that the dramatic decrease in the production on this shift is a result of Ms. Bennet's new program.

First of all, she took Jim Fask out of the regular production crew and reassigned him as the shift set-up man and mechanic because of his experience. Norm speculates that this move alone accounts for a large decrease in production, since Jim outproduced all the others on the shift and used to make up any slack that the guys acquired by goofing off.

After the new plan was in operation, Norm had stayed right on the production floor all the time. He wanted to watch to make sure that the men were following Ms. Bennet's plan to a T.

Norm does not see anything basically wrong with Ms. Bennet's plan. In fact, he wishes he had thought of it. It would have shown Bob Goodman that he appreciated the job and the company. He felt sure that if a man had thought up and implemented the plan, the workers would have been more willing to adopt it. Now that he thought about it, he was sure the men were rebelling against the plan because a woman had thought of it.

Third Shift

Before The third shift was added in late May to meet rising demand caused by the auto industry's model changeover. Twelve workers were placed on this shift; only five of them were full-time employees, each having less than five years' service. Seven college students, hired for the summer, made up the remainder of the crew.

Strong ties of friendship had quickly developed between the regular employees, nicknamed the "Jackson Five" by the students in honor of shift supervisor Bob Jackson, and the "Magnificent Seven," a tongue-in-cheek title bestowed on the students during their first week of training. Socializing among members of the shift was not uncommon after work. Cooperation on the job was extremely high, with fellow workers helping each other with mechanical or material difficulties.

Heading the shift was twenty-nine-year old, ex-Marine sergeant Bob Jackson. Bob had been working for Goodman for the last four and one-half years. His military experience qualified him for a supervisory training program upon joining the company. After being assigned various smaller crews, Bob was placed in charge of the new shift, after three weeks of extensive training relating to all aspects of the operation.

Being the only person of supervisory status on the shift, Bob did not believe that he constantly had to push his workers to reach the company's production quotas; some other supervisors pushed hard to impress any supervisors who might be observing. He had been known to work side by side with those members of his shift who were experiencing difficulties with their machines or with the materials.

The remaining four full-time employees were machine operators relatively new to the system previously described. Together with the seven college students, they spent their first two weeks in the department familiarizing themselves with the operations. All part changeovers during this period were handled by the prior shifts. Production improved over the next three weeks as the workers became used to the procedures.

When the order came down that the production process would be changed, Bob notified his shift and finalized the plans that soon followed. Bob found out that six machine operators would be kept on production, one of his workers would be trained as the shift's mechanic, and the remaining four would function as stockers, trimmers, and curers.

After   Because the machines were automated, the only real skills required were in the maintenance of the machines and the knowledge necessary to make part changeovers. John Baluck, a three-year employee, was the former operator chosen to be trained as a mechanic. The remaining three veterans were to remain on the machines; Jackson felt that they, along with the Magnificent Seven, should be rotated as operators.

To break up the boredom of running the molds, the operators often broke up into two groups to challenge each other to production races; the losers bought the beer during one of the afterwork outings. Often the quota was reached five hours into the shift. Those who were not operating the molds went along with the game, for they knew that the coming week would see them on the machines.

Concerned that this practice could decrease the product quality, Jackson set up an elaborate scoring system penalizing any group for its defects. The entire process worked so well that Jackson was not bothered by the one and one-half hour "lunch" breaks his workers took in the middle of the night. His shift was consistently over its production quotas and had outproduced the other two shifts through the month of August.

Product changeovers and mechanical adjustments, a problem in other shifts, were nonexistent. John Baluck was able to make all the adjustments during the workers' lunches. Should some work be required at any other time, the workers shortened the time spent on lunch to make up any downtime.

Jackson encouraged ideas. He wanted to make the new system work. The workers responded by suggesting ways that production could be made easier. Neither Bob nor his workers wanted to set new production goals. They were satisfied to be performing slightly better than the norm. The crew realized that the more efficient the process was made, the more free time they would have to shoot the breeze. As long as everything remained normal, Jackson was not going to upset anyone by pushing for greater output, especially because his shift was outstripping the others.

Other crews and supervisors were amazed at the third shift's performance. Ann Bennet attributed its record to her ideas, but she had never been able to discover why the one shift had met with success and the others failed. Even observing Jackson's crew a couple of nights did not produce any insight. The Jackson Five and the Magnificent Seven knew that they had a good thing going; they were not about to ruin it for themselves by letting anyone else know about their special arrangements and methods.

OVERALL EFFECTS

Implementation of the change in the manufacturing process met with disturbing results. Output decreased on the first and second shifts. Output on the newly created third shift remained relatively unchanged but continued to meet the standardized production quota. Mr. Goodman was quite displeased with the overall results and wondered if hiring Ann Bennet as a production analyst had been a mistake.

Study Guides

1. What changes took place at Goodman, and what contributed to the difficulty in implementing them?
2. What problems in communication, motivation, and leadership can you identify?
3. Discuss the role of informal groups in the Goodman Company.

Case 6

Falcon Computer

A small group of managers at Falcon Computer met regularly on Wednesday mornings to develop a statement capturing what they considered to be the "Falcon culture." Their discussions were wide-ranging, covering what they thought their firm's culture was, what it should be, and how to create it. They were probably influenced by other firms in their environment, since they were located in the Silicon Valley area of California.

Falcon Computer was a new firm, having been created just eight months earlier. Since the corporation was still in the start-up phase, managers decided that it would be timely to create and instill the type of culture they thought would be most appropriate for their organization. After several weeks of brainstorming, writing, debating, and rewriting, the management group eventually produced a document called "Falcon Values," which described the culture of the company as they saw it. The organizational culture statement covered such topics as treatment of customers, relations among work colleagues, preferred style of social communication, the decision-making process, and the nature of the working environment.

Peter Richards read over the Falcon Values statement shortly after he was hired as a software trainer. After observing managerial and employee behaviors at Falcon for a few weeks, he was struck by the wide discrepancy between the values expressed in the document and what he observed as actual practice within the organization. For example, the Falcon values document contained statements such as this: "Quality: Attention to detail is our trademark; our goal is to do it right the first time. We intend to deliver defect-free products and services to our customers on the date promised." However, Richards had already seen shipping reports showing that a number of defective computers were being shipped to customers. And his personal experience supported his worst fears. When he borrowed four brand-new Falcon computers from the shipping room for use in a training class, he found that only two of them started up correctly without additional technical work on his part.

This case was prepared by Mel Schnake, who adapted it from the article by Peter C. Reynolds, "Imposing a Corporate Culture," *Psychology Today,* March 1987, pp. 33–38.

Another example of the difference between the Falcon values document and actual practice concerned this statement on communication: "Managing by personal communication is part of the Falcon way. We value and encourage open, direct, person-to-person communication as part of our daily routine." Executives bragged about how they arranged their chairs in a circle to show equality and to facilitate open communications whenever they met to discuss the Falcon values document. Richards had heard the "open communication" buzzword a lot since coming to Falcon, but he hadn't seen much evidence of such communication. As a matter of fact, all other meetings used a more traditional layout, with top executives at the front of the room. Richards believed that the real organizational culture that was developing at Falcon was characterized by secrecy and communications that followed the formal chain of command. Even the Falcon values document, Richards was told, had been created in secret.

Richards soon became disillusioned. He confided in a coworker one afternoon that "the Falcon values document was so at variance with what people saw every day that very few of them took it seriously." Employees quickly learned what was truly emphasized in the organization—hierarchy, secrecy, and expediency—and focused on those realities instead, ignoring many of the concepts incorporated in the values document. Despite his frustration, Richards stayed with Falcon until it filed for bankruptcy two years later. "Next time," he thought to himself as he cleaned out his desk, "I'll pay more attention to what is actually going on, and less to what top management says is true. Furthermore," he thought to himself, "I guess you just can't create values."

Study Guides

1. What is more important, the statements in a corporate culture document or actual managerial behavior?
2. Why did the Falcon executives act as they did?
3. Why didn't employees like Richards blow the whistle on Falcon, challenging the inconsistency between values and behavior?
4. How can executives go about changing the old values that govern an organization?

Case 7

Consolidated Life

PART 1

It all started so positively. Three days after graduating with his degree in business administration, Mike Wilson started his first day at a prestigious insurance company—Consolidated Life. He worked in the policy issue department. The work of the department was mostly clerical and did not require a high degree of technical knowledge. Given the repetitive and mundane nature of the work, the successful worker had to be consistent and willing to grind out paperwork.

Rick Belkner was the division's vice president, "the man in charge" at the time. Rick was an actuary by training, a technical professional whose leadership style was laissez-faire. He was described in the division as "the mirror of whoever was the strongest personality around him." It was also common knowledge that Rick made $60,000 a year while he spent his time doing crossword puzzles.

Mike was hired as a management trainee and promised a supervisory assignment within a year. However, because of a management reorganization, it was only six weeks before he was placed in charge of an eight-person unit.

The reorganization was intended to streamline work flow, upgrade and combine the clerical jobs, and make greater use of the computer system. It was a drastic departure from the old way of doing things and created a great deal of animosity and anxiety among the clerical staff.

Management realized that a flexible supervisory style was necessary to pull off the reorganization without immense turnover, so the managers gave their supervisors a free hand to run their units as they saw fit. Mike used this latitude to implement group meetings and training classes in his unit. In addition, he assured all members raises if they worked hard to attain them. By working long hours, participating in the mundane task with his unit, and being flexible in his management style, he was able to increase productivity, reduce errors, and reduce lost time. Things improved so dra-

This case was prepared by Joseph Weiss, Mark Wahlstrom, and Edward Marshall, and is used with permission of the authors and the publisher, Elsevier Science Publishing Co., Inc.

matically that he was noticed by upper management and earned a reputation as a superstar despite being viewed as free-spirited and unorthodox. The feeling was that his loose, people-oriented management style could be tolerated because his results were excellent.

A Chance for Advancement

After a year Mike received an offer from a different Consolidated Life division located across town. Mike was asked to manage an office in the marketing area. The pay was excellent, and the position offered an opportunity to turn around an office in disarray. The reorganization in his present division at Consolidated was almost complete and most of his mentors and friends in management had moved on to other jobs. Mike decided to accept the offer.

In his exit interview he was assured that if he ever wanted to return, a position would be made for him. It was clear that he was held in high regard by management and staff alike. A huge party was thrown to send him off.

The new job was satisfying for a short time, but it became apparent to Mike that it did not have the long-term potential he had been promised. After bringing on a new staff, computerizing the office, and auditing the books, he began looking for a position that would both challenge him and give him the autonomy he needed to be successful.

Eventually word got back to his former vice president, Rick Belkner, at Consolidated Life that Mike was looking for another job. Rick offered Mike a position with the same pay he was now receiving and control over a fourteen-person unit in his old division. After considering other options, Mike decided to return to his old division, feeling that he would be able to progress steadily over the next several years.

Enter Jack Greely; Return Mike Wilson

Upon his return to Consolidated Life, Mike became aware of several changes that had taken place in the six months since his departure. The most important change was the hiring of a new divisional senior vice president, Jack Greely. Jack had been given total authority to run the division. Rick Belkner now reported to Jack.

Jack's reputation was that he was tough but fair. It was necessary for people in Jack's division to do things his way and get the work out.

Mike also found himself reporting to one of his former peers, Kathy Miller, who had been promoted to manager during the reorganization. Mike had always hit it off with Kathy and foresaw no problems in working with her.

After a week Mike realized the extent of the changes that had occurred. Gone was the loose, casual atmosphere that had marked his first tour in the division. Now, a stricter, task-oriented management doctrine was practiced. Morale of the supervisory staff had decreased to an alarming level. Jack Greely was the major topic of conversation in and around the division. People joked that MBO now meant "management by oppression."

Mike was greeted back with comments like "Welcome to prison" and "Why would you come back here? You must be desperate!" It seemed as if everyone was looking for new jobs or transfers. The negative attitudes were reflected in the poor quality of work being done.

Mike's Idea: Supervisors' Forum

Mike felt that a change in the management style of his boss (Jack) was necessary in order to improve a frustrating situation. Realizing that it would be difficult to affect Jack's style directly, Mike requested permission from Rick Belkner to form a

Supervisors' Forum for all the managers on Mike's level in the division. Mike explained that the purpose would be to enhance the existing management-training program. The forum would include weekly meetings, guest speakers, and discussions of topics relevant to the division and the industry. Mike thought the forum would show Greely that he was serious not only about doing his job but also about improving morale in the division. Rick gave the okay for an initial meeting.

The meeting took place and ten supervisors who were Mike's peers in the company eagerly took the opportunity to engage in the discussion. There was a euphoric attitude in the group as the members drafted their statement of intent. It read as follows:

To:	Rick Belkner
From:	New Issue Services Supervisors
Subject:	Supervisors' Forum

On Thursday, June 11, the Supervisors' Forum held its first meeting. The objective of the meeting was to identify common areas of concern among the managers and to determine topics that we might be interested in pursuing.

The first area addressed was the void that we perceive exists in the management-training program. As a result of conditions beyond anyone's control, many of us over the past year have held supervisory duties without the benefit of formal training or proper experience. Therefore, we propose that we use the Supervisors' Forum as a means to enhance the existing management-training program. The areas that we hope to affect with this supplemental training are as follows: (a) morale/job satisfaction, (b) quality of work and services, (c) productivity, and (d) management expertise as it relates to the life insurance industry. With this objective in mind, we have outlined below a list of activities that we would like to pursue:

1. Further use of the existing in-house training programs provided for manager trainees and supervisors, i.e., Introduction to Supervision, EEO, and Coaching and Counseling.

2. A series of speakers from various sections in the company, which would help expose us to the technical aspects of their departments and their managerial styles.

3. Invitations to outside speakers to address the forum on topics such as managerial development, organizational structure and behavior, business policy, and the insurance industry. Speakers could be area college professors, consultants, and state insurance officials.

4. Outside training and visits to the field. This activity could include attendance at seminars on managerial theory and development relative to the insurance industry. Attached is a representative sample of a program we would like to have considered in the future.

In conclusion, we hope that this memo clearly illustrates what we are attempting to accomplish with this program. It is our hope that the above outline will give the forum credibility and establish it as an effective tool for all levels of management within New Issue Services. By supplementing our on-the-job training with a series of speakers and classes, we aim to develop prospective managerial personnel with a broad perspective of both the life insurance industry and management's role in it. Also, we would like to extend an invitation to the underwriters to attend any programs that might be of interest to them.

cc: J. Greely
Managers

The group felt that the memo accurately and diplomatically stated its dissatisfaction with the current situation. However, the members pondered what the results of their actions would be and what else they could have done.

PART 2

An emergency management meeting was called by Rick Belkner at Jack Greely's request to address the union being formed by the supervisors. Four general managers, Rick Belkner, and Jack Greely were at that meeting. During the meeting it was suggested that the forum be disbanded to "put them in their place." However, Rick Belkner felt that if guided in the proper direction, the forum could die from lack of interest. His stance was adopted, but it was common knowledge that Jack Greely was strongly opposed to the group and wanted its founders dealt with. His comment was, "It's not a democracy and they're not a union. If they don't like it here, then they can leave." An investigation was begun by the managers to determine who the main authors of the memo were so that they could be dealt with.

At about this time, Mike's unit had made a mistake on a case, which Jack Greely was embarrassed to admit to his boss. This embarrassment was more than Jack Greely cared to take from Mike Wilson. At the managers' staff meeting that day Jack stormed in and declared that the next supervisor to "screw up" was out the door. He would permit no more embarrassments of his division and repeated his earlier statement about "people leaving if they didn't like it here." It was clear to Mike and everyone else present that Mike Wilson was a marked man.

Mike had always been a loose, amiable supervisor. The major reason his units had been successful was the attention he paid to each person and how he or she interacted with the group. He had a reputation for fairness, was seen as an excellent judge of personnel for new positions, and was noted for his ability to turn around people who had been in trouble. He motivated people through a dynamic, personable style and was noted for his general lack of regard for rules. He treated rules as obstacles to management and usually used his own discretion as to what was important. His office had a sign saying "Any fool can manage by rules. It takes an uncommon person to manage without any." It was an approach that flew in the face of company policy, but it had been overlooked in the past because of his results. However, because of Mike's actions with the Supervisors' Forum, he was now regarded as a troublemaker, not a superstar, and his oddball style only made matters worse.

Faced with the fact that he was rumored to be out the door, Mike sat down to appraise the situation.

PART 3

Mike decided on the following course of action:

1. Keep the forum alive but moderate its tone so that it didn't step on Jack Greely's toes.
2. Don't panic. Simply outwork and outsmart the rest of the division. This plan included a massive retraining and remotivation of his personnel. He implemented weekly meetings, cross-training with other divisions, and a lot of interpersonal stroking to motivate the group.
3. Evoke praise from vendors and customers through excellent service, and direct that praise to Jack Greely.

The results after eight months were impressive. Mike's unit improved the speed of processing 60 percent and lowered errors 75 percent. His staff became the most highly trained in the division. Mike had a file of several letters to Jack Greely that praised the unit's excellent service. In addition, the Supervisors' Forum had grudgingly attained credibility, although the scope of activity was restricted. Mike had even improved to the point of submitting reports on time as a concession to management.

Mike was confident that the results would speak for themselves. However, one month before his scheduled promotion and one month after an excellent merit raise in recognition of his exceptional work record, he was called into the office of his supervisor, Kathy Miller. She informed him that after long and careful consideration the decision had been made to deny his promotion because of his lack of attention to detail. Denial of the promotion did not mean he was not a good supervisor, just that he needed to follow more instead of taking the lead. Mike was stunned and said so. But before he said anything else, he asked to meet with Rick Belkner and Jack Greely the next day.

The Showdown

Sitting face-to-face with Rick and Jack, Mike asked if they agreed with the appraisal Kathy had discussed with him. They both said they did. When asked if any other supervisor surpassed his ability and results, each stated that Mike was one of the best, if not *the* best they had. Then why, Mike asked, would they deny him a promotion when others of less ability were approved? The answer came from Jack: "It's nothing personal; we just don't like your management style. You're an oddball. We can't run a division with ten supervisors all doing different things. What kind of a business do you think we're running here? We need people who conform to our style and methods so we can measure their results objectively. There is no room for subjective interpretation. It's our feeling that if you really put your mind to it, you can be an excellent manager. It's just that you now create trouble and rock the boat. We don't need that. It doesn't matter if you're the best now. Sooner or later as you go up the ladder, you will be forced to pay more attention to administrative duties and you won't handle them well. If we correct your bad habits now, we think you can go far."

Mike was shocked. He turned to face Rick and blurted out, "You mean it doesn't matter what my results are? All that matters is how I do things?" Rick leaned back in his chair and said in a casual tone, "In a word, yes."

Mike left the office knowing that his career at Consolidated was over and immediately started looking for a new job. What had gone wrong?

Study Guides

1. This case can be treated as a three-part predictive exercise.
   a. Read only Part 1 and stop. How do you think the supervisors' statement of intent will be received by top management at Consolidated Life?
   b. Read Part 2. What do you think Mike will do now? What do you recommend that he do?
   c. Read Part 3. Should Mike try to continue his career with Consolidated Life or find a job elsewhere? How does the self-fulfilling prophecy affect this situation? If he leaves, do you think he can be successful in another organization?
2. Was Mike wise to attempt to change the behavior of his boss? Was such an attempt ethical? What methods have you read about that he could have used? What would you have done differently?
3. How do you think that Mike would describe the organizational culture at Consolidated Life? What is an employee's responsibility for reading a firm's culture and for adjusting to it?
4. Evaluate the memo that Mike wrote. Now assess the fairness and motivational impact of the feedback that Mike received. Will such feedback be useful in changing his behavior? What advice could you have given Rick and Jack prior to the meeting with Mike?

Case 8

Video Electronics Company

Frank Simpson, president and controlling stockholder of the Video Electronics Company, now in its tenth year, was faced with the problem of gearing his plant to meet both increased production demands brought on by the expanding electronics industry and increased competition from other producers of his line of products. The plant tripled its number of employees during the past year, but production per worker decreased nearly 20 percent and costs rose nearly to the break-even point. For the preceding quarter, profit on sales was less than 1 percent and profit on invested capital was under 3 percent. These profit rates were one-fourth of what Simpson considered normal.

The company employed mostly unskilled labor, who were trained by the company. Employees were not represented by a labor union. All employees were paid hourly wages rather than incentive wages.

The company was founded by Simpson and a few investor friends for production of a narrow line of specialized small electronics parts that were sold to other manufacturers. It grew slowly and had a labor force of only 105 workers at the beginning of last year. Its reputation for quality was excellent. This reputation for quality was the primary reason for a flood of orders from new clients in the spring of last year, requiring the firm to triple its labor force by July. Simpson remarked, "I didn't seek those orders. *They* came to us. I didn't want to expand that fast, but what could I do? If you want to stay in business, you can't tell your customers you are too busy to sell them anything."

The company was located in a manufacturing town of 15,000 people in rural New York, about 60 miles from any large town. Enough untrained people were available locally for hiring for the expansion, which required the operation of two shifts instead of one. Management's forecasts indicated that the expansion would be permanent, with the additional possibility of moderate growth during the next five years or longer.

Simpson, in consultation with the board of directors, concluded that he needed to establish the new position of general manager of the plant so that he (Simpson) could spend more of his time on high-level work and less of it ironing out production difficulties. He also concluded that under present conditions he needed to build an industrial engineering staff that could both cope with present production problems and give his company the developmental work that was needed to stay ahead of the competitors.

Almost all his present supervisory personnel had been with the company since the year it was founded. They were all skilled people in their particular phases of the operations, but Simpson felt that none of them had the training or overall insight into company problems to take charge as general manager.

After much thought, Simpson decided to employ a general manager from outside the company. This person would report directly to him and would have full responsibility for production of the product and development of a top-notch industrial engineering department. Simpson called a meeting of all his supervisory personnel and explained his decision to them in detail. He described the need for this plan of action and stressed the necessity for the utmost in cooperation. The older supervisors did not seem to be pleased with this turn of events but promised that they would cooperate fully with the new manager.

About four months after his meeting with his supervisors, Simpson found a suitable general manager, John Rider. Rider, age thirty-six, was a mechanical engineer who had been a general supervisor in a large Philadelphia electronics plant. One of his first jobs as general manager was to find a qualified person to develop the industrial engineering function. Paul Green, an industrial engineer thirty-one years of age, was hired from the industrial engineering department of a large steel company in Pittsburgh. Green had an M.B.A., a good academic record, an honorable discharge from the military, and two years of relevant experience.

Green and Rider both felt that the company was in bad condition in relation to machine utilization, employee utilization, waste, and reject rates. On the basis of their first impressions of the production facilities they estimated that production management and industrial engineering changes might be able to increase productivity at least 25 percent and reduce unit costs 35 percent.

Green wanted time to get acquainted with the processes and the supervisory personnel before recommending major improvements. Rider granted this wish, and Green spent two months getting acquainted with the supervisors. During this period he recommended to Rider only minor changes, which the supervisors seemed to accept, with only minor disagreement. However, after this period Simpson, Rider, and Green felt that major steps had to be taken to improve both production and quality. They decided that the first industrial engineering project should be a study of production processes, department by department. The study was to cover every operation done on the products. All processes were to be put in writing, since many of the processes had developed without anyone's ever writing down just how they were to be performed. Several of the supervisors were the only ones who understood how certain operations were to be set up and performed, and any supervisor who left the company often took valuable knowledge that was difficult to replace.

At the next supervisory meeting (of all managerial personnel), Simpson announced the plan for the production study. No estimated completion date for the study was given. No comments were made by the production supervisors, but it was plain to Rider and Green that several of the older supervisors were not happy about the idea. Simpson tried to get across the idea that full cooperation was required and that the company had "to meet its competition or go out of business."

Green started the survey the following week. There was outward rebellion in some cases, but he smoothed this over by discussing with the supervisor the reasons for the survey and then leaving that department alone for a few days. Green thought he was convincing the people who objected, so he proceeded with the study without comment to either Rider or Simpson about the resistance.

About five weeks after Green started the study, he and Rider left town together on a business trip that kept them away from the plant for two days. On the night of the second day one of the second-shift supervisors telephoned Simpson, who happened to be working late at the office. The supervisor said that a group of them would like to talk to Simpson. Since many of these supervisors had known Simpson for a long time and called him by his first name, he did not object and told them to "come on up."

The group that arrived consisted of all supervisors with more than one year's company seniority. First-shift supervisors were there, even though they had been off duty for three hours. As soon as the group arrived, it was apparent to Simpson that they were troubled about something and that this was no social call. All the supervisors entered his office, and Charles Warren, an older man who had been supervisor for nine years, acted as speaker for the group.

"Frank," he said, "all of us here have been in this game for a good many years. We know more about this business than anyone else around here, and we don't like people standing around in our departments watching what we are doing. We also don't like the idea of some young guy telling us that we should do this and that to improve our production and quality. This industry is different, and those new ideas about industrial engineering just won't work for us. We want you to tell that new guy, Green, that his ideas won't work for a company like this." Warren then paused to give Simpson a chance to answer. The other supervisors stood there quietly.

Study Guides

1. If you were Simpson, what would you do now? What would you do later, if anything? What behavioral models and ideas are involved in your decisions?
2. Should Simpson have permitted the supervisors to see him, since they now report directly to Rider?
3. What kinds of changes are taking place in this case? What are the effects of these changes? What ideas about change would be helpful in dealing with this situation?
4. Do the three stages in change (unfreezing, changing, refreezing) apply in this case? Discuss.

Role-Playing Situations

1. You are Simpson. Reply to Warren and the other supervisors gathered in your office.
2. Have people play the roles of Simpson, Rider, and Green in a meeting in Simpson's office to discuss the situation on the day Rider and Green return from their trip.
3. Role-play the supervisory meeting in which Simpson announces to his supervisors the production process study. Include people in the roles of Rider and Green.

Case 9

Elite Electric Company

Elite Electric Company is a moderately small manufacturing subsidiary of a large European conglomerate. The company manufactures electric components supplied to its parent company for sale to consumer retail outlets as well as for commercial distribution. Sales five years ago were approximately $10 million and grew to $35 million last year. Elite Electric Company has two plants, one in Pennsylvania and the other in Massachusetts. The plant in Pennsylvania is relatively new and can manufacture three times the number of units manufactured by the Massachusetts plant. The Massachusetts plant was established in the early 1920s and is on a large, beautifully manicured estate. The buildings are quite old, and the machinery is antiquated. However, the company headquarters is at the Massachusetts plant, and the company's president is insistent upon keeping both plants active. (See the table for the five-year production history of the plants.)

In order to cope with the growth of the company administratively, additional staff were hired. However, there was no organized plan to establish systems and procedures for training, mechanization, and so on, in anticipation of the increased workload and the specialization of activities and functions that would eventually arise. People who had been with the company for a long period of time knew their assignments and, by and large, carried the company through its day-to-day activities. When many of these people left suddenly during a personnel reduction, an information void was created because there was little in the way of written procedures to guide those who remained and the replacement staff who were hired.

Another significant factor in the company's history was employee turnover. An administrative employee organization chart shows that 40 percent of the people employed as of just two years ago are no longer associated with the company. Of those remaining, 90 percent have different assignments today. Many of the losses in staff were in important positions, and all levels were affected. (Figures 1 and 2 show the organization charts for the company and for the Massachusetts plant, respectively.)

This case was prepared by Barry R. Armandi, and is used with permission of the author and the publisher, Elsevier Science Publishing Co., Inc.

THE MASSACHUSETTS PLANT

The president of the company, Mr. William White, originally came from LTV, which is located in Dallas, Texas. From there he was recruited to be plant operations manager in Massachusetts. When the original owners sold out to the European concern, White was made president. The next year, he opened the Pennsylvania plant.

As president, White developed a six-item operational philosophy. The components of this philosophy are as follows:

1. Make product quality and customer service top priorities.
2. Foster a human-oriented working atmosphere.
3. Maximize communication, interaction, and involvement.
4. Minimize the layers of organizational structure, and control the growth of bureaucracy.
5. Value and respect our form of company organization.
6. Strive for excellence in our business performance.

Upon being appointed president, White promoted Peter Johnson to the position of plant operations manager from his previous position of production manager. White told Johnson that he (Johnson) had a lot to learn about running a plant and to go easy with changes until he got his feet wet. He also indicated that with the projected operation of the new plant the following year, Johnson should expect some reduction in production demand. But White felt this reduction would be temporary. Further, White emphatically reminded Johnson of the company's operational philosophy.

While White was plant operations manager, he initiated daily operations meetings with the following people: the purchasing manager (Paul Barbato), the production manager (Brian Campbell), the quality-control manager (Elizabeth Schultz), the engineering manager (David Arato), the safety manager (Martin Massell), the personnel manager (Jane Wieder), the customer service manager (Michael St. John), and one of the assistant controllers (Harvey Jones).

Five-Year Production History for Elite Electric Company
(in units)

	Year 1	Year 2	Year 3*		Year 4		Year 5	
			Mass.	Penn.	Mass.	Penn.	Mass.	Penn.
Transistors (thousands)	800	600	500	400	475	535	452	629
Large integrated circuit boards (thousands)	475	479	325	201	300	227	248	325
Small integrated circuit boards (thousands)	600	585	480	175	250	212	321	438
Large-capacity chips (millions)	1.2	1.1	0.7	0.5	0.6	0.7	0.6	0.9
Small-capacity chips (millions)	1.8	2.0	0.5	1.3	0.2	2.0	0.3	2.7
Cathode-ray tubes (thousands)	325	250	210	22	126	46	147	63
Percent with defects	0.1	0.15	0.9	4.2	1.6	2.5	2.5	1.2

*New plant begins operations.

When Johnson took over, he decided to continue the daily meetings. One day, after discussing problems of the company at an open meeting, it was decided that individuals from various other line and staff areas should attend the daily meetings. The transcript of a typical meeting is given below.

PETER JOHNSON: Okay, everybody, it's 9:00, so let's get started. You all know what the agenda is, so let's start with safety first.

MARTIN MASSELL (Safety Manager): Well Peter, I have a number of things to go over. First, we should look into feedback from maintenance. The other day we had an incident where the maintenance crew was washing down the walls and water leaked into the electrical wiring. Nobody was told about this, and subsequently, seepage began Friday and smoke developed.

PETER JOHNSON: Okay, we will have maintenance look into it and they will get back to you. What else, Marty?

MARTIN MASSELL: We found out that the operators of the forklifts are operating them too fast in the plant. We are sending out a memo telling them to slow down.

DAVID ARATO (Engineering Manager): Why don't we just put some bumps in the floor so they can't speed over them?

MARTIN MASSELL: Well, we are looking at that. We may decide to do it, but we have to get some cost estimates and maintenance will have to fill us in.

PETER JOHNSON: By the way, where is the representative from maintenance? Well, I will have to contact Irving (Maintenance Manager). Anything else, Marty?

MARTIN MASSELL: Oh yeah, I forgot to tell you yesterday the entire loading dock has been cleaned. We shouldn't be having any more problems. By the way, Brian, make sure you contact Irv about the spill in the area.

FIGURE 1

Elite Electric Company organization chart

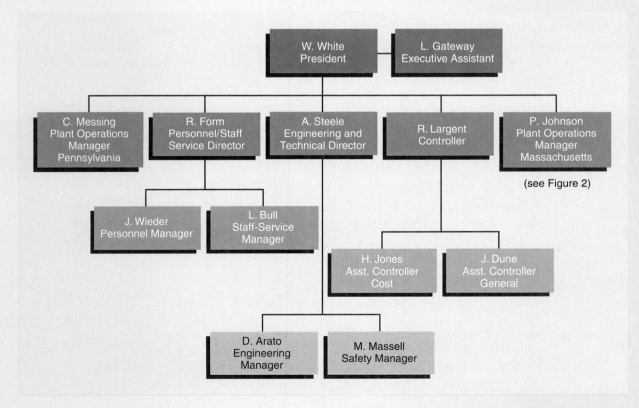

(see Figure 2)

BRIAN CAMPBELL (Production Manager): Oh, I forgot to tell you, Peter, but Irv said that we would have to close down machines 1 and 6 to get at the leak that is causing the oil spill. I have already gone ahead with that.

PETER JOHNSON: Gee, Brian, I wish you would clear these things with me first. How badly will this affect our production?

BRIAN CAMPBELL: Not badly, we should be able to get away with a minimum of overtime this weekend.

PETER JOHNSON: Customer service is next. Mike, how are we doing with our parent company?

MICHAEL ST. JOHN (Customer Service Manager): Nothing much new to report. We are starting to get flack for not taking that Japanese order, but the guys at the parent company understand. They may not like it, but they can deal with it. Oh, Paul, are you going to have enough transistors on hand to complete the order by next Tuesday?

PAUL BARBATO (Purchasing Manager): Sure, Mike, I sent you a memo on that yesterday.

MICHAEL ST. JOHN: Sorry, but I haven't had a chance to get to my morning mail yet. I was too busy with some visitors from Europe.

PETER JOHNSON: Are these people being taken care of, Mike? Is there anything we can do to make their stay here more comfortable?

MICHAEL ST. JOHN: No, everything is fine.

PETER JOHNSON: Okay. Let's move on to employee relations. Jane?

FIGURE 2

Massachusetts plant organization chart

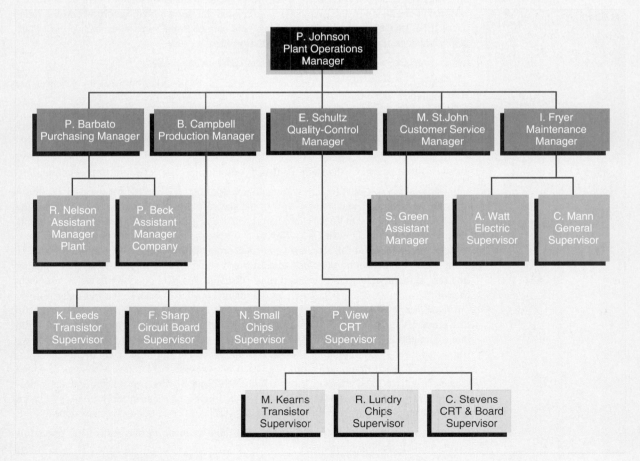

JANE WIEDER (Personnel Manager): I would like to introduce two guests from Training Programs, Inc. As you know, we will be embarking upon our final training program shortly. The grievance with Al Janow has been resolved. At the management/employee meeting last week, an agreement was reached that a representative from each department would attend. As you are aware, this meeting is once a month. It's funny, the biggest complaint at the meeting was an extra chair for the conference room. [*Laughter.*] The Interview Workshop memo is done, Peter, and here it is. Also, Peter, we have to work on a posting of dates for the Annual Family Get-Together. I don't know if July will work out.

MICHAEL ST. JOHN: July does not look that good. We have a great deal of overtime since that Australian order is due the beginning of August. Can we push it up to June?

HARVEY JONES (Assistant Controller): Don't forget that in June, revised budgets are due. [*The meeting continues to discuss the best date for the Annual Family Get-Together for another 15 minutes.*]

JANE WIEDER: One more thing, please notify us of any changes in marital status, address, etc. We have to keep our records up to date. Also, please be advised that the company cars can be purchased by employees. Sales will take place through a lottery system.

DAVID ARATO: Will we get a memo on this?

JANE WIEDER: Yes, I will have one out by the end of the week.

PETER JOHNSON: Let's move on to quality control. Elizabeth?

ELIZABETH SCHULTZ (Quality-Control Manager): Our number 1 and 8 machines have been throwing out bent transistor leads. Over the weekend, these two machines will be down. Irv and Brian are aware of this. We have to straighten out this problem before we do the order from IBM. I have also noticed that the last gold shipment had some other metals in it. Paul, can you check this out to see what was the problem?

PAUL BARBATO: What amount of extraneous metals was present?

ELIZABETH SCHULTZ: We didn't do complete tests of the material, but it seems 5 ounces per 100 pounds.

PAUL BARBATO: That doesn't seem to be a significant amount.

ELIZABETH SCHULTZ: Well, it is according to our estimates, and I would like it to be checked out.

PETER JOHNSON: Okay. Elizabeth, Paul will look into it. Now let's turn to production.

BRIAN CAMPBELL: Last Monday we manufactured 3,000 transistors. Machines 1, 2, and 8 did 300, machines 2 and 4 were down, and the rest of the production was done by the remaining machines. On Tuesday we had to change to produce the larger integrated circuits that were needed by Control Data. We had two hours of downtime to change the machines. Machines 6 and 7 did 20 percent of the total production run of 5,000 boards. Machine 1 continued to manufacture the small transistorized chips, with machines 2 and 5 completing the rest of the integrated circuit board runs. [*At about this time, two people get up and walk out of the room as Brian is talking.*] Wednesday we switched back to the transistor runs on all machines. Unfortunately, machine 2 was down for the entire day, and machine 7 was up for preventive maintenance. We manufactured 2,700 transistors. Machines 3, 5, and 8 did approximately 60 percent of the work. [*A number of people start yawning.*] Thursday we produced only 1,000 transistors and had to ship part of our run to the cathode-ray tube production for Digital Equipment Corp. We produced 500 units for Digital. Machines 3, 4, and 5 were used for the DEC run, and machines 1, 2, and 8 were kept on the transistor production. Machine 7 was down. On Friday we had half a day and in the morning we had a blackout and were only about to get 100 transistors and 22 cathode-ray tubes done.

PETER JOHNSON: Brian, do you think you will able to make up the rest of the order this week without much overtime?

BRIAN CAMPBELL: I don't know. I think we should talk to Harry. [*Harry Brown is the union representative.*]

PETER JOHNSON: That may be difficult since Harry is on vacation, but I will try to get in touch with him. If I can't, let's go ahead with it anyway and we will take the consequences. All right, let's go around the room and see what anybody has to say.

PAUL BARBATO: Nothing.

BRIAN CAMPBELL: Dave, I want to talk to you about the machine changeover and also if we can design a better ramp.

ELIZABETH SCHULTZ: Peter, can I see you after the meeting to discuss a personal matter?

DAVID ARATO: Nothing.

MARTIN MASSELL: I just wanted to let everyone know that we had a problem in one of the machine wells. It appears that while they were pouring some concrete around the well, some slipped in and it took us a couple of days to get it cleaned up.

JANE WIEDER: Paul, see me on Mary Bernstein's problem.

MICHAEL ST. JOHN: Just wanted to let you know we may be getting a very big order from Grumman.

HARVEY JONES: The following people have not reported their exempt status to payroll. [*He lists about twelve names.*] Remember this was from Jane's memo about three weeks ago.

PETER JOHNSON: Brian, I want to take a tour with a couple of people from the university next week. I will call you and set something up. Okay? Good meeting. See you tomorrow, same time, same place.

Study Guides

1. Comment on White's operational philosophy, from the standpoint of
   a. The motivational impact of the six goals.
   b. The overall type of organizational culture that probably exists at Elite Electric
2. Assess the nature and quality of the communications that took place in the meeting conducted by Johnson, indicating the strengths and weaknesses that were illustrated there. Does anyone exhibit assertive communication? What interpersonal relations patterns are apparent?
3. Examine some of the group dynamics present in Johnson's meeting. What task and social leadership roles were used by participants? How could the meeting have been improved?
4. Why do you think that Johnson concluded that it was a "good meeting"? Do you agree? Explain.

Case 10

The Patterson Operation

BACKGROUND

Carrington, Inc., is an international company engaged in the production and distribution of pharmaceuticals, proprietary drugs, and cosmetics and toiletries. In its worldwide operations, Carrington employs over 15,000 people and has sales of over $500 million annually.

At the midsouth plant of Carrington, Inc., management was faced with problems of low productivity, low employee morale, and high unit costs in the section responsible for the assembly of various kinds of packages containing assortments of different products made by the company. These "prepaks," or "deals," as they are referred to within the organization, are specially prepared to the specifications of the individual customer. Each package may contain from 24 to 480 items, and the total number of packages for a customer may range from 10 to 1,500 units. Most of these packages are prepared in such a way that the retailer can set them up as freestanding, point-of-sale promotional displays. From Carrington's standpoint, the objective of using these product displays is to create additional shelf space for Carrington's products. In the stores these displays could be placed in aisles or used as shelf extenders. Assembling the deals is essentially a job-shop-type process, and prior to last year the assembly room was located in a part of the main plant known as Section 10.

The employees in Carrington's manufacturing and assembly operations are unionized, and the firm uses a Halsey 50-50 Incentive Plan, a time-saved bonus plan. Under the Halsey Plan, a worker who can do her or his job in less than the standard time receives a bonus of 50 percent of the hourly wage rate multiplied by the time saved. For example, an employee who completed 10 standard hours of work in 8 hours would be paid 8 hours plus 1 of the 2 hours saved. Thus, if the hourly pay rate is $8.50, the worker would earn $76.50 for the day.

This case was prepared by James M. Todd and Thomas R. Miller, and is used with permission of the authors and the publisher, *Journal of Case Studies*.

PROBLEMS WITH SECTION 10

The assembly of prepaks in Section 10 used roller-type conveyor belts which supplied each worker with the products to be included in a particular package. The working conditions were outstanding; the work area was very clean, well lighted, and air-conditioned. An attractive cafeteria for employee use was available in the same large building.

In spite of good working conditions and the chance to earn extra pay through the company's incentive system, the operation in Section 10 had encountered a marked trend of increases in unit costs and decreases in output per labor hour. In fact, during the last three years cost figures revealed that the section was below the break-even point. Contributing to this deteriorating situation was low productivity and failure of employees to meet the work standard. This latter problem was made particularly evident by the fact that no employees were able to earn a bonus under the incentive plan.

Discipline in Section 10 was poor and supervisors were constantly having problems. A number of grievances had been generated. Morale was not helped by the fact that any employee quite often was moved from one assembly line to another. This action tended to increase production costs because the employees had little chance of moving down a particular learning curve before being moved to another operation. Another factor indicative of low morale was the employees' attitudes. There was no spirit of mutual cooperation and the attitude of "that's not my job" was prevalent.

All in all, working in Section 10 was considered an unpopular work assignment. The work required manual labor and was perceived as relatively hard work compared with work on the automated lines in the other work areas. Also, word had spread that no one could "make bonus" working there. Eventually, through the bidding system used by the organization, the workforce in Section 10 came to consist, in large part, of young inexperienced employees, problem workers, and malcontents. As one manager described the situation, "Section 10 had the pits of the workforce."

A NEW OPERATION

Early last year management at Carrington was confronted with a severe space problem for its expanding manufacturing and assembly operations. Several alternatives were considered, but none seemed to offer an economically feasible solution to the space problem. In near desperation, managers held a brainstorming session that led to a decision to move a large part of the assembly of the deals to a facility already leased by the company and presently used as a warehouse. This facility was located on Patterson Street; thus the new deal room became known in the company as the "Patterson operation."

The new facility fell far short of providing work space and conditions comparable to those in Section 10. The building was located in an entirely separate area approximately 3 miles from the main plant in a neighborhood of run-down, low-income housing and other warehouse operations.

The building housing the Patterson operation had been thought to be acceptable only for warehouse use. It was an old brick structure with a number of large open bays for shipping and receiving. The building was dark, poorly ventilated, not air-conditioned, and inadequately heated. It was poorly suited for use by workers involved in assembly operations. Temperatures averaged approximately 50 degrees during the winter months and well over 90 degrees in the summer. There was no cafeteria or food service, and employees either brought their own lunch or went to a small neighborhood grocery in the vicinity and bought food. Other worker facilities, such as restrooms and break areas, were poor. In summary, working conditions contrasted sharply with those of Section 10, with its clean, air-conditioned, well-heated facilities in a good neighborhood and with a first-class company cafeteria available.

Despite these tremendous obstacles and seemingly against its best judgment, management, pressed for manufacturing space, decided to move the assembly of prepaks to the Patterson warehouse. Little money was spent on modifications of the Patterson facility.

RESULTS OF THE MOVE

Moving to Patterson involved the transfer of approximately 40 employees from the main plant, most of whom were African Americans with low seniority. Under the new structure, all these workers were managed by Fred Hammond, an African-American first-line supervisor.

As foreman, Fred made some drastic changes in the assembly operation. He set up the assembly line so that individual workers could work on the same job until that particular order was completed. The situation was entirely different from the one in Section 10 where an employee could work on as many as three different assemblies during a day's time. Under the new plan, the repetition of working on only one line enabled workers to develop speed, which facilitated their earning bonuses.

The new foreman introduced some other innovations. He allowed employees the opportunity to influence decisions concerning their work hours and the times of their rest breaks. While at the main plant the playing of radios in a production area was not permitted, at Patterson it gradually became acceptable to have radios tuned to popular music, usually played at a high volume level. Other nonstandard conditions existed at Patterson. Employees did not have to observe dress codes, wear bonnets, or refrain from wearing jewelry on the job. Because of the rather remote location of Patterson off the main plant site, managers or supervisors from the plant visited the new facility rather infrequently. Where violations of certain company policies existed, a somewhat liberal attitude was taken by management.

In order to have some place to eat or to take a break, the employees got together and furnished a small room with enough tables and chairs to modestly equip a rather austere dining room and break area. Eventually this room was air-conditioned. In addition, the employees were attempting to get the company to furnish some paint so that they could repaint the room.

With these and other changes, a shift in worker attitudes began to evolve. Employees came to view Patterson as their own "company." A feeling of mutual cooperation prevailed, as evidenced by the willingness of individual workers to assist others when possible. An esprit de corps developed among the Patterson workers. Productivity increased to such an extent that employees were receiving bonuses, which had very seldom been the case in the old location. The jobs at Patterson became more popular and the composition of the workforce there gradually changed from one of inexperienced and dissatisfied workers to one in which older and better-qualified people began to bid actively for the jobs. Since the Patterson operation opened, there has been only one grievance filed, and during the first year of operation there was a 32.8 percent increase in productivity over that of Section 10.

Since the inception of the Patterson operation, Fred Hammond, the first-line supervisor initially in charge, was promoted. He was replaced by May Allison who has continued to run the operation in the same manner as Hammond. To an outside observer, it is rather amusing to watch May, who is less than 5 feet tall and weighs approximately 100 pounds, in her supervisory relationship with the workforce, particularly the burly male employees and the older female workers. It is apparent that she has been able to earn the respect and admiration of the employees and has developed effective work relationships with them. Recent data indicate higher productivity and more bonuses at Patterson than in comparable work in the main plant. May is well liked personally as evidenced by employee contributions of about $75 for her birthday gift.

May has continued to get the employees to participate in decision making, for example, in the decision to change work hours at Patterson during the summer months from 5:30 A.M. to 2:00 P.M. rather than 7:30 A.M. to 4:00 P.M. as in the other plant areas. This change was initiated because of the nearly unbearable heat of the late afternoon in the warehouse. This change in work schedule was not in accordance with company policy, but it has been tolerated by management. The workers at Patterson really preferred an even earlier workday, but that choice was not feasible because of coordination problems in receiving goods from the main plant.

Another interesting development at Patterson is the formation of the workers' own softball team, called the Patterson Warriors. Normally, the company fields a team composed of players from all units instead of from only one particular section. Again, Patterson employees made a decision and acted independently, without reference to overall company personnel policy.

Work records at the Patterson operation concerning absenteeism, tardiness, and turnover are not better than those in the main plant. In a few cases they are slightly worse although this difference is not considered to be significant by management. However, the very low grievance rate, the high level of worker morale, and the better productivity at Patterson are pleasant surprises to management.

The activities of the Patterson operation are fairly well known among the managers at the mid-south plant of Carrington. Management reactions range from positive to negative, with some managers ambivalent about Patterson. All, however, seem to agree that the Patterson operation is, at least, interesting.

Study Guides

1. Has the Patterson operation been successful? To the degree that it can be judged a success, what factors have contributed to it?
2. Identify the leadership styles of Fred Hammond and May Allison. Apply several of the leadership models to the case, such as Fiedler's contingency model and the Hersey-Blanchard situational model.
3. Comment on the informal organization at Patterson. In what ways did the employees create their own "company"?
4. Review Herzberg's two-factor model. Why didn't the change in physical working conditions (a deterioration of a hygiene factor) have a negative effect on productivity? What *did* cause the workers to be productive?

Case 11

TRW—Oilwell Cable Division

It was July 5, and Bill Russell had been expecting the phone call he had just received from the corporate office of TRW in Cleveland naming him general manager. Bill had been the acting general manager of the Oilwell Cable Division in Lawrence, Kansas, since January when Gino Strippoli left the division for another assignment. He had expected to be named general manager, but the second part of the call informing him that he must lay off twenty people or achieve an equivalent reduction in labor costs was greatly disturbing to him. It was now 8:00 A.M., and Bill had called a meeting of all plant personnel at 8:15 A.M. to announce his appointment and, now, to also announce the impending layoffs. He was wondering how to handle the tough decisions that lay before him.

TRW

TRW is a diversified, multinational manufacturing firm that has sales approaching $5.5 billion. Its roots can be found in the Cleveland Cap Screw Company, which was founded in 1901 with a total investment of $2,500 and with twenty-nine employees. Today, through a growth strategy of acquisition and diversification, the company employs 88,000 employees at over 300 locations in seventeen countries. The original shareholders' investment has grown to over $1.6 billion. As quoted from a company publication, "This growth reflects the company's ability to anticipate promising new fields and to pioneer in their development—automotive, industrial, aircraft, aerospace, systems, electronics, and energy. We grew with these markets and helped create them."

OILWELL CABLE DIVISION, LAWRENCE, KANSAS

The Oilwell Cable Division is part of the Industrial and Energy Segment of TRW. This segment of TRW's business represents 24 percent of its sales and 23 percent of its operating profits. The pumps, valves, and energy-services group, of which the Oil-

This case was prepared by Michael G. Kolchin, Thomas J. Hyclak, and Sheree Deming, and is used with permission of the authors and the publisher, Elsevier Science Publishing Co., Inc.

well Cable Division is a part, accounts for 30 percent of the Industrial and Energy Segment's net sales.

The Oilwell Cable Division had its beginning as the Crescent Wire and Cable Company of Trenton, New Jersey. When TRW acquired Crescent, the company was losing money, occupied an outmoded plant, and had significant labor problems. In order to improve the profitability of the recent division, TRW decided to move its operations out of Trenton. The first decision was to move oilwell cable production to Lawrence, Kansas, about ten years ago. The line was moved into a new building and all new equipment was purchased. Only Gino Strippoli, the plant manager, and three other employees made the move from Trenton to Lawrence.

The reason for choosing Lawrence as the new site for the Crescent division was fourfold. Most important, Lawrence was considerably closer to the customer base of the division, which was in northeast Oklahoma. Second, Kansas was a right-to-work state, and given the labor problems of the Trenton plant, TRW was looking for a more supportive labor environment for its new operations. Third, the wage rates for the Lawrence area were very reasonable compared with those in Trenton. Finally, there was an already existing building that could house the oilwell cable production line in an industrial park in North Lawrence. In addition, considerable acreage next to the building would allow for future expansion.

By just moving the oilwell cable line to Lawrence, TRW hoped to be able to focus in on this product and make it more profitable before moving the other products from the Crescent plant in Trenton. Soon thereafter, when the oilwell cable plant had reached division status, no further consideration was given to moving the rest of the Trenton plant. The remaining operations in Trenton were sold.

Team Management at Lawrence

When Gino Strippoli was given the task of starting up operations in Lawrence, he saw a great opportunity to establish a new management system. With a new plant, new equipment, and almost all new employees, the time seemed perfect to test the value of team management. Gino had long been a supporter of team management, and now a golden opportunity was being presented to him to set up an experiment to test his ideas.

Team Structure

Team	Number of Teams	Composition
Management	1	Members of management
Resource	1	Management information systems, design engineering, process engineering, employment, accounting, etc.
Technical	1	Nonexempt laboratory personnel
Administration	1	
Maintenance	1	Boiler, electrical, and mechanical maintenance personnel
Shipping and receiving	1	
Production	5	Extruding, armoring, braiding

469

In the case of the TRW-Lawrence plant, eleven teams exist, ranging in size from four to seventeen members. The titles of the teams and brief descriptions of their makeup are shown in the table. Figure 1 depicts the current organization of the Oilwell Cable Division.

The five production teams are formed around the production process in use at TRW-Lawrence. Each team meets on a weekly basis or as needed, with the exception of the resource team, which meets every two weeks. The typical meeting lasts an hour and a half to two hours. There is no formal structure for team meetings, but most meetings adhere to an agenda similar to this one:

1. Scheduling labor hours and overtime
2. Round-robin discussion and reporting from various plant committees (e.g., safety, gain sharing)
3. Area managers' comments regarding scrap, labor efficiency, and any new information since the last meeting

Other decisions made by the team are listed in Figure 2, which illustrates the roles of the various levels of management at the Oilwell Cable Division. Figure 2 also shows the relationships between levels. For instance, top management has the responsibility for setting overall divisional goals and objectives and for providing the resources necessary for the teams to attain those targets.

The role of the area managers is that of intermediaries. They are present at most team meetings to act as facilitators and to provide the teams with information necessary to carry out their scheduling functions. In addition, the area managers fill a coordination function by meeting twice a week to discuss mutual problems and to discuss other items that should be presented at the weekly team meetings.

As can be seen in Figure 2, the teams are filling managerial roles, and the decisions they make are more typical of those made by supervisory levels in more traditional plants. In essence, they, the team members, are given control over their work areas.

For decisions that affect the entire plant, a task force or a divisionwide committee is established that includes representatives from all the teams. Examples of some of these divisionwide committees include safety, gain sharing, and benefits.

FIGURE 1

Organizational structure at the Oilwell Cable Division

Note: An organizational chart for the Oilwell Cable Division does not exist. This figure represents the casewriters' depiction of the structure existing at TRW-Lawrence based on discussions with division personnel.

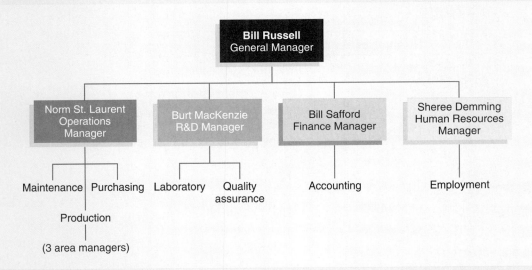

Results from Team Management

After some initial start-up problems with the team management concept, the experiment started by Gino Strippoli seems to be a success. In an article in *Fortune* (Burck, 1981) titled "What Happens When Workers Manage Themselves," Gino is quoted as saying: "In the beginning we considered it [team management] an experiment, but somewhere along the way we said, 'This is no longer an experiment; this is how we operate.' "

The success of the experiment not only was written up in *Fortune* but also was the subject of several case studies. But this success was not achieved easily. In the beginning, there was a good deal of mistrust among employees regarding management's motives. Also, when the Lawrence facility was first started up, there was only one union employee brought from Trenton. The rest of the people hired had little experience with the production process involved in making wire cable. As a result, there was a lot of frustration with a high level of turnover. The turnover rate was 12 percent in the first two years of operations, compared with a national average of 3.8 percent at that time (U.S. Department of Labor, p. 180).

But Gino was not to be deterred from seeing his experiment succeed. He realized that he was concentrating too heavily on team involvement concepts and not paying enough attention to technical concerns. A compensation scheme was developed that encouraged employees to master the various pieces of equipment in the plant. This action seemed to have the desired effect, for the division became profitable for the first time two years after his arrival.

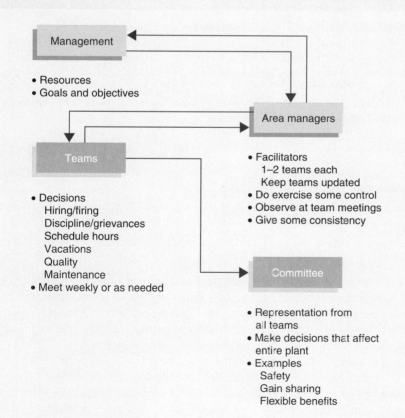

FIGURE 2

Relationships between the various levels in the team management concept

By that time, employment had dropped from a high of 132 to what seemed to be a more optimal level of 125. Turnover dropped from in excess of 12 percent to a range of 2 to 4 percent, which was more in line with the national average for manufacturing firms. More impressive was the absentee rate, which hovered in the range of 2.5 to 3 percent for several years. The national average during that period was closer to 6.5 percent (U.S. Department of Labor, p. 136). Productivity was improving steadily as well. The Oilwell Cable Division now enjoyed the highest productivity of any plant in the oilwell cable industry.

It was not only the objective data that indicated that team management was succeeding; comments from employees at the Oilwell Cable Division seemed to confirm this success as well. By and large, all employees rated TRW-Lawrence a good company and preferred the team management concept to more traditional methods of management.

Some sample comments from the various levels of management verify this conclusion.

Team Members

". . . an excellent place to work."

"Team management gives employees a good deal of responsibility."

"Now at least we have some control over scheduling."

"The company gains as much as the employee because of the flexibility. Now there is little idle time."

"Team management gives the employee a feeling of equality."

"System allows for the maximum contribution of each member of the team."

Area Managers

"The plant is not a Utopia, but I do feel better at the end of the day."

"Decision making is more difficult, but team management results in easier implementation and better understanding by team members."

Management

"System allows for crossing over lines of responsibility. There is not the turf issue that exists in traditionally structured plants."

"Team management concept has resulted in an excellent labor climate. TRW-Lawrence is a good place to work and the workers here are receptive to change."

"The major benefit of the team management concept is flexibility while maintaining goal orientation."

This last statement is one of the real keys to team management—flexibility. Under such a management system, idle time is greatly reduced, as is the involvement of the plant manager in day-to-day operating problems. As noted by Strippoli, "I really feel for the first time that I am managing rather than putting out fires. The teams are putting out the fires way down in the organization. (Burck, p. 69)"

From the workers' point of view, the major benefit of team management is their ability to control their jobs. This control has resulted in a high level of commitment by the employees, as evidenced by the numerous suggestions made by the teams that have resulted in significant improvements in quality and productivity.

Of course, the team management concept is not without its difficulties. As noted earlier, there are numerous problems with start-up. It takes a while for participants to become comfortable with the system and to accept the responsibility of managing themselves. In this case, it took nearly two years. However, after the first year's settling-in period, productivity improved dramatically and has been maintained at that level. This achievement is illustrated in Figure 3.

In addition to dealing with start-up problems, the people who filled middle-management positions had great difficulty in adjusting to their new roles as facilitators as opposed to being bosses in the traditional sense. This role conflict is an area that is often overlooked in implementing participation schemes in factories. In the case of the Oilwell Cable Division, the inability to adapt to a new position resulted in four area managers' leaving their positions. Plant management tried to deal with this problem by providing facilitator training for area managers. Although the current area managers still express some frustration at not being able to simply *tell* workers what to do, they do feel the team management concept is a much more effective system than traditional supervisory systems, and they would not want to go back to a traditional system.

All in all, Gino was very pleased with the experiment. After five years, he left the Lawrence facility for another assignment, and Bill Russell, who had been Gino's operations manager replaced him as the acting general manager.

THE OILWELL CABLE DIVISION'S MARKET

The basic product produced by the Oilwell Cable Division is wire that provides power to submersible pumps used in oil drilling. As a result, the demand for its product is directly dependent on the demand for submersible pumps, a demand that is a function of the price of crude oil. As the price of oil increases, the demand for pumps increases as it becomes economically feasible to drill deeper wells.

Drilling deeper wells also produces a need for cables that are able to withstand the harsher environments found in such wells. For example, these wells often

FIGURE 3

Productivity at
TRW-Lawrence

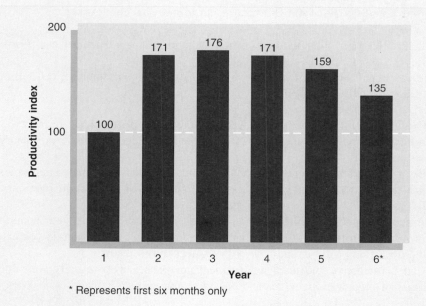

* Represents first six months only

474

require the use of lead jackets to protect the cables from the corrosive effects of hydrogen sulfide.

With the Iranian oil crisis and the resulting increase in oil prices, cable producers were able to sell almost all they were able to produce. Prices were determined on the basis of quality and delivery. However, with the advent of an oil glut, demand for submersible pumps had dropped and the competitive factors in the market were determined more on the basis of price.

In all, TRW had ten competitors in the cable market. TRW was the market leader with a significant share of the market, but it was facing strong competition from both domestic and foreign producers.

Location was also a competitive factor that foreign competitors enjoyed, especially with regard to oil and gas drilling in Southeast Asia and the Middle East. As the production of cable was basically a semicontinuous process, economies of scale were important. With this in mind, it was not feasible to build smaller plants nearer to a customer base that was widely dispersed. As noted earlier, one of the reasons for moving to Lawrence was so that TRW could be closer to its primary customers in Oklahoma.

By the end of June the market for cable had declined dramatically. As Bill Russell reviewed the quarterly financial data and observed the idle equipment and employees in the plant, he knew he had to do something soon if his division was to maintain market share and profitability.

THE LAYOFF DECISION

As Bill Russell prepared to meet with all personnel at the Lawrence facility, he wondered how he would handle the process of laying off 16 percent of the current workforce of 125. Two things particularly troubled him. First, his predecessor, Gino Strippoli, had implied to the employees that there would never be a layoff at the Oilwell Cable Division. Second, and perhaps more important, he had to determine whether the decision regarding how to reduce labor costs was a decision he should make alone or one that the teams should undertake as their responsibility.

It was now 8:15 A.M., and Bill headed out to meet his employees.

References

Burck, Charles G., "What Happens when Workers Manage Themselves," *Fortune,* July 27, 1981, pp. 62–69.

U.S. Department of Labor, *Handbook of Labor Statistics,* Washington, D.C.: Bureau of Labor Statistics, 1983.

Study Guides

1. Evaluate team management at TRW's Lawrence plant. What organizational behavior system is it most similar to? Does it reflect Theory X or Theory Y assumptions?
2. Examine the results from team management at Lawrence. Do they support a satisfaction causes productivity or a productivity causes satisfaction relationship? Explain.
3. Assume the role of Bill Russell at the end of the case. Prepare your announcement regarding the layoffs to the cable division's employees. What do you expect their reactions will be, and how will you respond to them?
4. Can participative and team management approaches work equally well during times of organizational crisis and during normal times? Explain.

Absences   Employees who fail to show up for work as scheduled.

Achievement motivation   Drive to overcome challenges and obstacles in the pursuit of goals.

Acquired immune deficiency syndrome (AIDS)   Contagious viral disease of the human immune system.

Action research   Cyclical process of identifying system problems, gathering data, taking corrective action, assessing progress, making ongoing adjustments, and learning from the experience.

Active listening   Using a variety of principles and behaviors to receive both the factual and the emotional message being sent by another person.

Affiliation motivation   Drive to relate to people on a social basis.

Affirmative action   Effort by employers to increase employment opportunities for qualified members of protected groups that appear to be inadequately represented in a firm's labor force.

Appraisal interview   Session in which supervisors provide feedback to their employees on past performance, discuss problems, and invite a response.

Area of job freedom   Area of discretion after all restraints have been applied.

Assertiveness   Process of expressing feelings, asking for legitimate changes, and giving and receiving honest feedback.

At-risk pay   Amount of employee pay that will not be received if employee does not achieve certain individual performance targets.

Attitudes   Feelings and beliefs that largely determine how employees will perceive their environment, commit themselves to intended actions, and ultimately behave.

Attribution   Process by which people interpret the causes of their own and others' behavior.

Autocratic leaders   People who centralize power and decision-making authority in themselves.

Autocratic model   Managerial view that power and formal authority are necessary to control employee behavior.

Autonomy   Policy of giving employees some discretion and control over job-related decisions.

Backsliding   The tendency of an individual or group to return to its perceived best way of life after any change occurs.

Baseline information   An organization's current level of operations, which can be used for later comparison to the effects of a change program.

Bases of power   Sources by which leaders gain and extend their influence over others; these bases include personal, legitimate, expert, reward, and coercive power.

Behavioral bias   Narrow viewpoint of some people that emphasizes satisfying employee experiences while overlooking the broader system of the organization in relation to all its publics.

Behavioral intentions   Employee plans and predispositions to act in a certain way (e.g., arrive late, skip work, slow down, be creative, or resign).

Biofeedback   Approach by which people under medical guidance learn from instrument feedback to influence symptoms of stress, such as increased heart rate.

Body language   Way in which people communicate meaning to others with their bodies in interpersonal interaction.

Boundary roles   Positions that require an ability to interact with different groups in order to keep a project successful.

Boundary spanners   Employees with strong communication links within their department, with people in other units, and often with the external community.

Brainstorming   Group structure that encourages creative thinking by deferring judgment on ideas generated.

Burnout   Condition in which employees are emotionally exhausted, become detached from their work, and feel helpless in accomplishing their goals.

Chain-reaction effect   Situation in which a change, or other condition, that directly affects only one or a few persons may lead to a reaction from many people, even hundreds or thousands, because of their mutual interest in it.

Change   Any alteration occurring in the work environment that affects the way in which employees must act.

Change agents   People whose roles are to stimulate, facilitate, and coordinate change within a system while remaining independent of it.

Changing   Learning new ideas and practices of thinking, reasoning, and performing.

Charisma   Leadership characteristic that inspires and influences employees to take early and sustained action to carry out a vision.

Clarified thinking   Removal of emotional blocks to rational and realistic thinking.

Closed-end questions   Those questions presented in an interview or survey format which direct the respondent to simply select and mark the answers that best represent his or her own feelings.

Closed questions   Questions that focus on a narrow topic and direct the receiver to provide a specific response.

Cluster chain   Grapevine chain in which one person tells several others, and a few of those tell more than one person.

Coach   Leadership role in which a leader prepares, guides, facilitates, cheers, and directs the team but does not play the game.

Codetermination   Government-mandated worker representation on the board of directors of a firm.

Coercive power   Capacity to punish other people (or to create the perceived threat to do so) so as to influence them.

Cognitive dissonance   Internal conflict and anxiety that occurs when people receive information incompatible with their value systems, prior decisions, or other information they may have.

Cohesiveness   Degree to which employees stick together, rely on one another, and desire to remain members of a group.

Collectivism   Process of placing heavy emphasis on the group and valuing harmony among its members.

Collegial model   Managerial view that teamwork is the way to build employee responsibility.

Committee   Specific type of group meeting in which members in their group role have been delegated authority with regard to the problem at hand.

Communication   Transfer of information and understanding from one person to another person.

Communication overload   Condition in which employees receive more communication inputs than they can process or more than they need.

Communication process   Steps by which a sender reaches a receiver with a message and receives feedback on it. See *Two-way communication process.*

Comparable worth   Attempt to give employees in comparable jobs—those of equal value to the employer—similar levels of pay.

Complete pay program   Comprehensive reward system that uses different bases of pay to accomplish various objectives (e.g., retention, production, teamwork).

Conceptual skill   Ability to think in terms of models, frameworks, and broad relationships.

Conditional strokes   Strokes offered to employees if they perform correctly or avoid problems.

Conflict   Disagreement over the goals to attain or the methods to be used to accomplish them.

Conformity   Dependence on the norms of others without independent thinking.

Confronting   Facing a conflict directly and working through it to a mutually satisfactory resolution. Also known as *problem solving* or *integrating.*

Consensus   Agreement of most of the members of a group.

Consideration   Leader's employee orientation, which reflects concern about employees' human needs.

Consultative leaders   Managers who approach one or more employees and ask for inputs prior to making a decision.

Contingency approach to OB   Philosophy that different environments require different behavioral practices for effectiveness.

Contingency model of leadership   Model which states that the most appropriate leadership style depends on the favorableness of the situation, especially in relation to leader-member relations, task structure, and position power.

Core dimensions   Five factors of jobs—skill variety, task identity, task significance, autonomy, and feedback—identified in a job characteristics approach to job enrichment.

Corrective discipline   Action taken to discourage further infractions so that future acts will be in compliance with standards.

Cost-benefit analysis   Determination of net effects of an action that has both positive and negative impacts (financial and other).

Cost-reward comparison   Process in which employees identify and compare personal costs and rewards to determine the point at which they are approximately equal.

Counseling   Discussion of a problem that usually has emotional content with an employee in order to help the employee cope with it better.

Counseling functions   Six activities that may be performed by counseling, including advice, reassurance, communication, release of emotional tension, clarified thinking, and reorientation.

Credibility gap   Difference between what someone says and what she or he does.

Cross-cultural communication   Capacity of an expatriate to speak and understand the language of a host country, as well as its nonverbal cues.

Cross-functional teams   Teams that draw their members from more than one specialty area.

Cultural contingency   Recognition that the most productive OB practices for a particular nation will depend heavily on its culture.

Cultural distance   Amount of difference between any two social systems.

Cultural diversity   Recognition, acknowledgment, appreciation, and positive use of the rich variety of differences among people at work.

Cultural empathy   Awareness and appreciation of differences across cultures and the way those differences affect business relationships.

Cultural shock   Feeling of confusion, insecurity, and anxiety caused by a strange new environment.

Custodial model   Managerial view that security needs are dominant among employees.

Decision-making model of leadership   Structured approach to selecting a leadership style, developed by Vroom and others, that encourages assessment of a variety of problem attributes and matches the results of that analysis with one of five leadership options.

Defense mechanisms   Reactions to frustration that attempt to defend a person from the psychological effects of a blocked goal.

Defensive reasoning   Communication behaviors used by people about to lose an argument, in which they inappropriately blame others, selectively gather and use data, seek to remain in control, and suppress negative feelings.

Deferred judgment   Advantage of brainstorming, by which all ideas are encouraged and criticism is delayed until after the session.

Delegation   Assignment of duties, authority, and responsibility to others.

Delphi decision group   Group structure in which a series of questionnaires are distributed to the respondents for their response, but group members do not need to meet face-to-face.

Development level   Task-specific combination of employee competence and motivation to perform that helps determine which leadership style to use.

Devil's advocate   Person who challenges the ideas of others, probes for supporting facts, provides constructive criticism, and challenges logic so as to improve the quality of a group decision.

Dialectic decision method (DDM)   Creation of two or more competing proposals, identification of underlying assumptions, examination by advocacy subgroups, and whole-group decision making.

Directive counseling   Process of listening to an employee's problem, deciding with the employee what should be done, and then telling and motivating the employee to do it.

Discharge   Separation of an employee from the company for cause.

Discipline   Management action to enforce organizational standards.

Discrimination   Biased treatment of other individuals or groups.

Division of work   Creation of levels of authority and functional units.

Double-loop learning   Process of using current information about a change to prepare participants to manage future changes even more effectively.

Downward communication   Flows of information from higher to lower levels of an organization.

Drives   Employee motivation for achievement, affiliation, or power.

Dysfunctional effect   Unfavorable impact of an action or a change on a system.

Ecological control   Alteration of the surroundings so as to influence another's feelings and behavior.

Economic incentive system   System that varies an employee's pay in proportion to some criterion of individual, group, or organizational performance.

Elaborating   Adding one's own strong feelings and reasoning to a communication.

Electronic brainstorming   Use of personal computers to facilitate idea generation and recording during brainstorming sessions.

Electronic grapevine   Transmission of informal messages by the use of computers.

Electronic mail (e-mail)   Computer-based communication system that allows messages to be sent to multiple parties simultaneously.

Electronic monitoring   Surveillance of employee behavior through a wide array of technological methods.

Emotional catharsis   Release of emotional tension and frustrations, often through telling someone else about it.

Employee ownership   Program in which employees provide the capital to purchase control of an existing operation.

Employee territories   Spaces that employees can call their own, where they can design their work layout, decorate to their satisfaction, and generally control what happens.

Empowerment   Process that provides greater autonomy to employees through the sharing of relevant information and the provision of control over factors affecting job performance.

Enhancers for leadership   Elements that amplify a leader's impact on the employees.

Equal employment opportunity (EEO)   Provision of equal opportunities to secure jobs and earn rewards in them, regardless of conditions unrelated to job performance.

Equal Pay Act of 1963   Federal legislation demanding that reward systems be designed and administered so that persons doing the same or equal work receive equal pay regardless of their sex.

Equilibrium   The state existing when there is a dynamic balance between forces supporting and restraining any existing practice.

Equity sensitivity   Recognition that employees have different preferences for over-reward, equity, or underreward.

Equity theory   Employee tendency to judge fairness by comparing their relevant inputs to the outcomes they receive, and also comparing this ratio to those of other people.

E-R-G model   Motivational model, developed by Clayton Alderfer, suggesting that there are three need levels—existence, relatedness, and growth.

Escalating commitment   Act of persevering to advocate a course of action, and possibly allocating additional resources to a project, despite rational evidence that it will result in failure.

Ethical imperative   Belief that participation ought to be used by managers for moral reasons.

Ethical leadership   Leadership based on high ethical and moral integrity, which follows such principles as social responsibility, open communication, and cost benefit analysis.

Ethical treatment   Belief that organizations and their managers should treat employees and customers in an ethical fashion.

Ethnocentrism   Predisposition to use oneself and one's own culture as the criteria for judging others.

Existence needs   Physiological and security factors.

Expatriates   Employees who work in a nation (and culture) different from their own.

Expectancy   Strength of belief that work-related effort will result in successful completion of a task (performance).

Expectancy model   Theory that motivation is a product of three factors: valence, expectancy, and instrumentality.

Experiential learning   Process in which participants learn by experiencing in the training environment the kinds of human relations problems they face on the job.

Expert power   Power that arises from a person's knowledge of and information about a complex situation.

Extinction   Withholding of significant positive consequences that were previously provided for a desirable behavior.

Extrinsic motivators   External rewards that occur apart from work.

Face-saving   Drive to maintain a desired self-image.

Facilitators   People who act as process consultants, getting employees to examine their roles within a team.

Fact premises   Descriptive views of how the world behaves, based on research and personal experience.

Feedback   Information from the job itself, management, or other employees that tells workers how well they are performing.

Feedback-seeking behavior   Act of monitoring one's performance and inquiring about progress toward goals.

Feminine societies   Societies characterized by a broader viewpoint of the great variety of roles that both males and females can play in the workplace and at home and by the value placed on interpersonal relationships.

Filtering   Reducing a communication to a few basic details that can be remembered and passed on to others.

Fixed interval schedule   Provision of a reinforcement after a certain period of time.

Followership   Behaviors that help a person to be an effective subordinate to a leader.

Formal groups   Groups established by the organization that have a public identity and goal to achieve.

Frustration   Result of a motivation (drive) being blocked to prevent one from reaching a desired goal.

Functional effect   Favorable impact of an action or a change on a system.

Fundamental attribution bias   Tendency to attribute others' achievements to good luck or easy tasks and their failures to not trying hard enough or not having the necessary personal characteristics.

Gain sharing   Policy of giving employees a substantial portion of the cost savings produced when their jobs are improved.

Gain-sharing plan   Program that establishes a historical base period of organizational performance, measures improvements, and shares the gains with employees on some formula basis. Also known as *production sharing*.

Genetic monitoring   Identifying harmful substances in the workplace, examining their effects on the genetic makeup of employees, and using the information for corrective action.

Genetic testing   Process of predicting whether an employee may be genetically susceptible to one or more types of illness or harmful substances.

Geocentric organizations   Organizations that largely ignore nationality while integrating the community of interest of the various cultures involved.

Goal setting   Establishment of targets and objectives for successful performance, both long-run and short-run.

Goals   Concrete formulations of achievements that the organization aims for within set periods of time.

Goals of organizational behavior   To describe, understand, predict, and control (favorably affect) human behavior at work.

Gossip chain   Grapevine in which a person contacts many others.

Grapevine   Informal communication system within an informal organization.

Group decision support system   Use of computers, decision models, and technological advances to remove communication barriers, structure the decision process, and generally direct the group's discussion.

Group dynamics   Social process by which people interact face-to-face in small groups.

Groupthink   Tendency of a group to bring individual thinking in line with the average quality of the group's thinking.

Growth needs   Needs related to the desire for self-esteem and self-actualization.

Hassles   Little conditions of daily living that are perceived to threaten one's sense of well-being.

Hawthorne effect   Concept that the mere observation of a group tends to change the way the group operates.

Hidden agendas   Private emotions and motives of group members.

Hierarchy of needs   Philosophy, developed by Abraham Maslow, that different groups of needs have a specific order of priority among most people, so that one group of needs precedes another in importance.

High-context cultures   Cultures in which people tend to use situational cues to develop a complete portrait of a visitor.

Higher-order needs   Need levels 3 to 5 (social, esteem, and self-actualization) on the Maslow hierarchy of needs.

Holistic OB   Philosophy that interprets people–organization relationships in terms of the whole person, whole group, whole organization, and whole social system.

Homeostasis   Self-correcting mechanism in a group by which energies are called up to restore balance whenever change threatens.

Honesty tests   Methods for assessing employee integrity and propensity to engage in unethical behaviors. Also known as *integrity tests.*

Human resources approach to OB   Belief that organizations should be concerned with the growth and development of people toward higher levels of competency, creativity, and fulfillment. Also known as the *supportive approach.*

Human skill   Ability to work effectively with people and to build teamwork.

Humanistic values   Positive beliefs about the potential and desire for growth among employees.

Hygiene factors   Conditions that tend to satisfy workers when they exist and to dissatisfy workers when they do not exist, but their existence tends not to be strongly motivating. Also known as *maintenance factors.*

Iceberg model of counseling   Viewpoint that recognizes that more feelings are hidden under the surface of a counselee's communication than are revealed.

Impairment testing   Determination of employee capacity to perform without the influence of illegal drugs by subjecting the individual to a brief motor-skills test performed on a computer.

Imposter phenomenon   Belief that one's personal capabilities are not as great as other people believe them to be.

Impression management   Ability to protect one's self-image while intentionally affecting another's assessment of oneself.

Incentives   Environmental factors that are established for the purpose of motivating a person.

Incivility spiral   The result of one frustrated employee venting unfairly on another, who then compounds the problem by making a bigger fuss on another.

Individual differences   Idea that each person is different from all others and that these differences usually are substantial rather than meaningless.

Individualism   Cultural emphasis on placing greatest importance on individual rights and freedoms, loosely knit social networks, and self-respect.

Individualization   Process through which employees successfully exert influence on the social system around them.

Industrial democracy   Government-mandated worker participation at various levels of the organization with regard to decisions that affect workers.

Inference   Interpretation of symbols that is based on assumptions, not facts.

Informal groups   Groups formed on the basis of common interests, proximity, and friendships.

Informal leader   Person who has the largest amount of status in the informal organization and emerges to exhibit influence on informal group members.

Informal organization   Network of personal and social relations not established or required by the formal organization but arising spontaneously as people associate with one another.

Inputs   All the rich and diverse elements that employees believe they bring, or contribute, to their job.

Instrumentality   Belief that a reward will be received once a task is accomplished.

Interpersonal orientation   The dominant way of treating people that a person believes in and displays.

Interventions   Structured activities designed to help individuals or groups improve their work effectiveness.

Intrinsic motivators   Internal rewards that a person feels when performing a job, so that there is a direct and immediate connection between work and reward.

Job breadth   Number of different tasks for which an individual is directly responsible.

Job content   Conditions that relate directly to the job itself and the employee's performance of it, rather than conditions in the environment external to the job.

Job context   Job conditions in the environment surrounding the job, rather than those directly related to job performance.

Job depth   Amount of control, responsibility, and discretion employees have over how their job is performed.

Job Diagnostic Survey   Instrument used to determine the relative presence of the five core dimensions in jobs.

Job enlargement   Policy of giving workers a wider variety of duties in order to reduce monotony.

Job enrichment   Policy of adding motivators to a job to make it more rewarding.

Job involvement   Degree to which employees immerse themselves in their jobs, invest time and energy in them, and view work as a central part of their overall lives.

Job rotation   Periodic assignment of an employee to completely different sets of job activities.

Job satisfaction   Set of favorable or unfavorable feelings with which employees view their work.

Job satisfaction survey Procedure by which employees report their feelings toward their jobs and work environment.

Job scope Assessment of a job on two dimensions—job breadth and job depth—to determine its potential for enlargement or enrichment.

Just-in-time training Provision to employees of key information in convenient small modules that they can access when they need to.

Lateral communication Communication across chains of command. Also known as *cross-communication.*

Law of diminishing returns Principle that a declining amount of extra output is received when more of a desirable input is added to an operating system.

Law of effect Tendency of a person to repeat behavior that is accompanied by favorable consequences and not to repeat behavior accompanied by unfavorable consequences.

Law of individual differences Belief that each person is different from all others.

Layoff survivor's sickness Feelings of uncertainty, anger, guilt, and distrust that follow the termination of workmates.

Leader–member exchange model Idea that leaders and their followers exchange information, resources, and role expectations that determine the quality of their interpersonal relationships.

Leader–member relations Degree to which the leader is accepted by the group (a variable in Fiedler's contingency model of leadership).

Leader-position power Organizational power that goes with the position the leader occupies (a variable in Fiedler's contingency model of leadership).

Leadership Process of encouraging and helping others to work enthusiastically toward achieving objectives.

Leadership style Total pattern of a leader's philosophy, skills, traits, and attitudes that is exhibited in the leader's behavior.

Legitimacy of organizational influence Interaction of two variables—conduct on or off the job and conduct that is or is not job-related—to produce varying degrees of acceptability of an act.

Legitimate power Power that is delegated legitimately from higher-established authorities to others.

Liaison individuals People who are active communicators on the grapevine.

Linking pin Managerial role of connecting the group with the remainder of the organization.

Locus of control Beliefs about whether an employee's achievements are the product of the employee's efforts (internal) or of outside forces (external).

Long-term orientation Cultural value that emphasizes preparing for the future, valuing thrift and savings, and the merits of persistence.

Loose rates Payment at rates that allow employees to reach standard output with less than normal effort.

Low-context cultures Cultures in which people tend to interpret cues literally, rely on written rules and legal documents, conduct business first, and value expertise and performance.

Lower-order needs Need levels 1 and 2 (physiological and safety/security) on the Maslow hierarchy of needs.

Management by objectives (MBO) Process of jointly setting objectives, creating action plans, conducting periodic reviews, and engaging in annual performance evaluations to facilitate desired performance.

Management by walking around (MBWA) Communication and learning that occurs when managers take the initiative to systematically make contact with a large number of employees.

Managerial grid Framework of management styles based on the dimensions of concern for people and concern for production.

Manipulation of people The use of organizational behavior knowledge and techniques to make people act in unethical ways or for one's personal gain.

Marginalized employees People who are made to feel that they, or their jobs, are insignificant.

Masculine societies Societies defining gender roles in traditional and stereotypical ways, valuing assertive behavior, and encouraging the acquisition of wealth.

Matrix organization Overlay of one type of organization on another so that there are two chains of command directing individual employees.

Mechanistic organizations Organizations characterized by the use of hierarchy, centralized direction, certainty of task assignments, and strict definition of roles.

Mentor Person who serves as a role model to help other employees gain valuable advice on roles to play and behaviors to avoid.

Mission Statement that identifies what business an organization is operating in, the market niches it is trying to serve, its customers, and the reasons for its existence.

Mixed stroke A message in which an individual sends or (receives) a combination of both positive and negative messages; it is thus often unclear what the overall intent was meant to be.

Models of OB Underlying theories or frameworks that act as conscious or unconscious but powerful guides to managerial thought and behavior. Also known as *paradigms*.

Morale Level of job satisfaction within a group.

Motivating potential score (MPS) Index that indicates the degree to which a job is perceived to be meaningful, foster responsibility, and provide knowledge of results.

Motivation Strength of the drive toward an action.

Motivational factors Conditions that tend to motivate workers when they exist, but their absence rarely is strongly dissatisfying.

Multi-skilling Learning of a wide range of relevant skills by team members so they can flexibly float between areas and perform multiple tasks.

Multiculturalism Successful blending of two or more cultures when employees from each interact on a regular basis.

Multinational organizations Those organizations that do business in more than one country.

Mutuality of interest Idea that people need organizations and organizations need people, which gives them a superordinate goal of joint interest to bring them together.

Mutual trust Mutual faith in the responsibility and actions of all parties involved in a relationship.

Negative affectivity A personal characteristic of employees that inclines them to be predisposed to be dissatisfied at work.

Negative reinforcement Removal of an unfavorable consequence that accompanies behavior.

Negative strokes   Recognition provided that hurts physically or emotionally when received and detracts from another's sense of well-being.

Neighborhoods of offices   Centers of related individual offices arranged to encourage the formation of social groups.

Network   Group of people who develop and maintain contact to exchange information informally, usually about a shared interest.

Network charts   Informal organization charts that document patterns of feelings expressed or behaviors exhibited.

Networking   Being active in a networked group of people.

Neutralizers   Attributes of subordinates, tasks, and organizations that interfere with or diminish a leader's attempts to influence employees.

Noise   Physical or emotional barriers to communication that limit a receiver's understanding.

Nominal group   Group structure that combines individual input, group discussion, and independent decision making.

Nondirective counseling   Process of skillfully listening to and encouraging a counselee to explain troublesome problems, understand the problems, and determine appropriate solutions. Also known as *client-centered counseling.*

Nonverbal communication   Actions, or inactions, that people take that serve as a means of communication.

Norm of reciprocity   Principle that two people in a continuing relationship feel a strong obligation to repay their social debts to one another.

Norms   Informal group requirements for the behavior of group members.

Ombudsperson   Person who receives and responds to inquiries, complaints, requests for policy clarifications, or allegations of wrongdoing from employees.

Open-book management   Providing employees with the company's financial statements and other operating data that enable them to independently track and understand the organization's performance.

Open-door policy   Statement encouraging employees to come to their supervisor or higher managers with any matter that concerns them.

Open-end questions   Those questions presented in an interview or survey format in which employees respond in their own words to express their feelings, thoughts, and intentions.

Open questions   Those questions which introduce a broad topic during counseling or conversation and give the receiver an opportunity to respond in many ways.

Open systems   Systems that engage in exchanges with their environments through their boundaries, receiving inputs and providing outputs.

Organic organizations   Organizations characterized by flexible tasks and roles, open communications, and decentralized decision making.

Organization development (OD)   Systematic application of behavioral science knowledge at various levels (group, intergroup, and total organization) to bring about planned change.

Organizational behavior (OB)   Study and application of knowledge about how people—as individuals and groups—act within organizations.

Organizational behavior modification (OB Mod)   Behavior modification used in organizations to shape individual behavior through the use of positive and negative consequences.

Organizational behavior system   Integrated framework of elements that portrays how behavior is guided toward achievement of organizational goals.

Organizational citizens   Employees who engage in discretionary positive social acts that promote the organization's success, such as volunteering their efforts, sharing their resources, or cooperating with others.

Organizational citizenship behaviors   Discretionary actions that promote the organization's success.

Organizational commitment   Degree to which an employee identifies with the organization and wants to continue actively participating in it.

Organizational culture   The values, beliefs, and norms that are shared by an organization's members.

Organizational politics   Use of behaviors that enhance or protect a person's influence and self-interest.

Organizational socialization   Continuous process of transmitting key elements of an organization's culture to its employees.

Outcomes   Rewards employees perceive they get from their job and employer.

Output restriction   Situation in which workers choose to produce less than they could produce with normal effort.

Overparticipation   Condition in which employees have more participation than they want.

Paradigms   Frameworks of possible explanations of how things work.

Parochialism   Seeing the situation around oneself from one's own perspective only.

Participation   Mental and emotional involvement of people in group situations that encourages them to contribute to group goals and share responsibility for them.

Participative counseling   Mutual counselor-counselee relationship that establishes a cooperative exchange of ideas to help solve a counselee's problems. Also known as *cooperative counseling.*

Participative leaders   Leaders who decentralize authority by consulting with followers.

Participative management   Use of programs that develop a substantial sense of empowerment among employees.

Path-goal leadership   Model that states that the leader's job is to create a work environment through structure, support, and rewards that helps employees reach the organization's goals.

Perceived control   Amount of control that employees believe they have over their work and working conditions.

Perception   Individual's own view of the world.

Perceptual set   People's tendency to perceive what they expect to perceive.

Performance appraisal   Process of evaluating the performance of employees.

Performance feedback   Timely provision of data or judgment regarding task-related results.

Performance gaps   Deficiencies in the way an organization operates.

Performance monitoring   Observing behavior, inspecting output, or studying documents of performance indicators.

Performance-satisfaction-effort loop   Flow model that shows the directional relationship between performance, satisfaction, and effort.

Personal barriers   Communication interferences that arise from human emotions, values, and poor listening habits.

Personal power   Ability of leaders to develop followers from the strength of their own personalities.

Personal wellness Programs of preventive maintenance that help individuals reduce the causes of stress or cope with stressors that are beyond their direct control.

Philosophy of OB Integrated set of explicit or implicit assumptions and beliefs about the way things are and the way they should be.

Physical barriers Communication interferences that occur in the environment in which the communication takes place.

Physical withdrawal Unauthorized absences, early departures, extended breaks, work slowdowns, or acts of aggression and retaliation.

Piece rate Reward system that pays employees according to the number of acceptable pieces produced.

Polarization Rigid and extreme position in one's attitudes.

Polarized The situation that results when two parties take extreme positions or viewpoints on a subject.

Political power Ability to work with people and social systems to gain their allegiance and support.

Politics Ways that leaders gain and use power.

Polygraph Instrument (lie detector) that attempts to measure the physiological changes when a person tells a significant lie.

Positive affectivity A personal characteristic of employees that inclines them to be predisposed to be satisfied at work.

Positive reinforcement Favorable consequence that accompanies behavior and encourages repetition of the behavior.

Positive strokes Recognition provided that feels good when received and contributes to another's sense of well-being.

Post-traumatic stress disorder Residual stress-related consequences for an employee who has experienced sudden and dramatic negative incidents (e.g., violence or injury).

Power Ability to influence other people and events.

Power distance Belief that there are strong and legitimate decision-making rights separating managers and employees.

Power motivation Drive to influence people and change situations.

Practice Conscious application of conceptual models and research results with the goal of improving individual and organizational performance.

Prejudice Negative attitudes toward other individuals or groups.

Preventive discipline Action taken to encourage employees to follow standards and rules so that infractions do not occur.

Primary needs Basic physiological and security needs.

Primary outcomes Rewards that employees receive directly as a result of their actions.

Proactive Anticipating events, initiating change, and taking control of one's destiny.

Process consultation Set of activities that help others perceive, understand, and react constructively to current behavioral events around them.

Productivity Ratio that compares units of output with units of input.

Profit sharing System that distributes to employees some portion of the profits of business.

Progressive discipline Policy that provides stronger penalties for repeated offenses.

Protégé Person who receives and accepts advice and examples from a trusted mentor.

Proxemics Exploration of different practices and feelings about interpersonal space within and across cultures.

Psychic costs Costs that affect a person's inner self or psyche.

Psychological contract Unwritten agreement that defines the conditions of each employee's psychological involvement with the system—what they intend to give to it and receive from it.

Psychological distance Feeling of being emotionally separated from another that acts as a personal barrier to effective communication.

Psychological stress evaluator Instrument that analyzes changes in voice patterns in an attempt to determine whether a lie is being told.

Psychological support Condition in which leaders stimulate people to want to do a particular job.

Psychological withdrawal Emotional detachment from one's job, such as engaging in daydreaming.

Punishment Unfavorable consequence that accompanies behavior and discourages repetition of the behavior.

Quality circles Voluntary groups that receive training in statistical techniques and problem-solving skills and then meet to produce ideas for improving productivity and working conditions.

Quality of work life (QWL) Favorableness or unfavorableness of a total job environment for people.

Quick fix Managerial use of a fad that addresses symptoms while ignoring underlying problems.

Rate setting Process of determining the standard output for each job.

Reactive Responding to events, adapting to change, and tempering its consequences.

Readability Degree to which writing and speech are understandable to receivers.

Realistic job previews Employment process in which job candidates are given a small sample of organizational reality.

Reference group Group whose norms a person accepts.

Refreezing Term applying to situations involving change and referring to the action of integrating what has been learned into actual practice.

Reinforcement Behavior modification consequence that influences future behavior.

Reinforcement, continuous Reinforcement accompanying each correct behavior.

Reinforcement, fixed-interval Reinforcement after a certain period of time.

Reinforcement, fixed ratio Reinforcement after a certain number of correct responses.

Reinforcement, partial The act of encouraging learning by reinforcing some correct behaviors on one of four possible schedules.

Reinforcement, variable-interval Reinforcement after a variety of time periods.

Reinforcement, variable-ratio Reinforcement after a variable number of correct responses.

Reinforcement schedules Frequency with which reinforcement accompanies a desired behavior.

Relatedness needs Needs that involve the desire of an employee to be understood and accepted.

Relaxation response Use of quiet, concentrated inner thought in order to rest the body physically and emotionally, thus reducing symptoms of stress.

Reliability   Capacity of a survey instrument to produce consistent results.

Reorientation   Change in an employee's psychic self through a change in basic goals and values.

Repatriation   Return of an employee to the home country, smooth blending into the original culture, and effective utilization in the organization after working in another nation for several years.

Research   Process of gathering and interpreting relevant evidence that will either support a behavioral theory or help change it.

Resilience   A person's capacity to handle short-term tensions.

Resistance to change   Desire not to accept a change or to accept it only partially, often resulting in actions designed to discredit, delay, or prevent the implementation of a work change.

Results-oriented approach to OB   Emphasis on relevant organizational outcomes, often expressed in terms of productivity.

Reverse cultural shock   Difficulty experienced by expatriates in readjusting to the surroundings of their home country upon their reentry.

Reward power   Capacity to control and administer items that are valued by other people so as to influence them.

Rights of privacy   Freedom from organizational invasion of a person's private life and unauthorized release of confidential information about a person.

Risky shift   Act of a group becoming more willing to take chances when its members are dealing with the resources of others and cannot be held individually accountable.

Role   Pattern of actions expected of a person in activities involving others.

Role ambiguity   Feeling that arises when roles are inadequately defined or are substantially unknown.

Role conflict   Feeling that arises when others have different perceptions or expectations of a person's role.

Role models   Leaders who serve as examples for their followers.

Role perceptions   How people think that they are supposed to act in their own roles and others should act in their roles.

Rumor   Grapevine information that is communicated without secure standards of evidence being present.

Sabbatical leaves   Provision to employees of paid or unpaid time off from work to encourage stress relief and personal education.

Sanctions   Rewards and penalties that a group uses to persuade members to conform to its norms.

Secondary needs   Social and psychological needs.

Secondary outcomes   Rewards that employees receive indirectly, following their primary outcomes.

Selective perception   Act of paying attention to those features of the work environment that are consistent with or reinforce one's own expectations.

Self-actualization   Need to become all that one is capable of becoming.

Self-appraisal   Process of asking individuals to identify and assess their accomplishments, strengths, and weaknesses.

Self-concept   An employee's "face," or level of self-esteem.

Self-efficacy   Internal belief that one has the necessary capabilities and competencies to perform a task, fulfill role expectations, or meet a challenging situation successfully.

Self-fulfilling prophecy   Condition that exists when a manager's expectations for an employee will cause the manager to treat the employee differently, and the employee will respond in a way that confirms the initial expectations. Also known as the *Pygmalion effect.*

Self-leadership   Act of leading oneself to perform naturally motivating tasks and of managing oneself to do work that is required but not naturally rewarding.

Self-managing teams   Natural work groups that are given a large degree of decision-making autonomy and expected to control their own behavior and results. Also known as *self-directing teams, self-reliant teams, sociotechnical teams,* or *semi-autonomous work groups.*

Self-perceived task ability   Degree of employee confidence in his or her potential to perform a task successfully.

Self-serving bias   Tendency to claim undue credit for one's own success and minimize personal responsibility for problems.

Semantic barriers   Communication limitations caused by the variety of meanings in the symbols used.

Semantics   Science of meaning.

Sexual harassment   Process of making employment or promotion decisions contingent on sexual favors; also, any verbal or physical conduct that creates an offensive working environment.

Shaping   Systematic and progressive application of positive reinforcement as behavior comes closer to the desired behavior.

Short-circuiting   Situation in which people skip one or more steps in the communication hierarchy.

Short-term orientation   Cultural value that emphasizes valuing the past and accenting the present while respecting tradition and the need to fulfill historical social obligations.

Single-loop learning   Process of solving immediate problems and adapting to changes which are imposed upon employees.

Situational leadership model   Theory of leadership that suggests that a leader's style should be determined by matching it with the task-related development (maturity) level of each subordinate.

Skill-based pay   System that rewards individual employees for what they know how to do. Also known as *knowledge-based pay* or *multiskill pay.*

Skill variety   Policy of allowing employees to perform different operations that often require different skills.

Social cues   Positive or negative bits of information that employees receive from their social surroundings and that act to influence how they react to a communication.

Social culture   Social environment of human-created beliefs, customs, knowledge, and practices that defines conventional behavior in a society.

Social desirability bias   Modifying one's responses to a survey or an interviewer based on what the respondent thinks that society values.

Social equilibrium   Dynamic working balance among the interdependent parts of a system.

Social facilitation   Process by which individuals often try harder to contribute to a task just because other people are present.

Social information processing   Recognition that social cues provided by peers and others affect employee perceptions of their jobs.

Socialization   See *Organizational socialization.*

Social leader   Person who helps restore and maintain group relationships.

Social loafing   Employee lessening of output when employees think their contributions to a group cannot be measured.

Social responsibility   Recognition that organizations have significant influence on the social system, which must be considered and balanced in all organizational actions.

Social support   Network of activities and relationships that satisfies an employee's perceived need to be cared for, esteemed, and valued.

Social system   Complex set of human relationships interacting in many ways.

Spillover effect   Impact of job satisfaction on life satisfaction, and vice versa.

Stages of team development   Movement of a group through the evolutionary phases of forming, storming, norming, performing, and (possibly) adjourning.

Status   Social rank of a person in a group.

Status anxiety   Employees' feelings of being upset because of differences between their actual and desired status levels.

Status deprivation   Loss of status, or a level of insufficient status, for a person. Also known as *losing face*.

Status symbols   Visible, external things that attach to a person or workplace and serve as evidence of social rank.

Status systems   Hierarchies of status that define employee rank relative to others in the group.

Storytelling   The process of using memorable stories to help forge a culture and communicate key values to employees.

Stress   General term applied to the pressures people feel in life.

Stressors   Conditions that tend to cause stress.

Stress-performance model   Visual portrait of the relationship between stress and job performance, illustrating different thresholds for different people.

Stress threshold   Level of stressors that one can tolerate before feelings of stress occur and adversely affect performance.

Stroking   Performing any act of recognition for another person.

Structure   Leader's task orientation that, at the extreme, ignores personal issues and emotions of employees.

Substitutes for leadership   Characteristics of the task, employees, or organization that may reduce the need for leadership behaviors.

Sucker effect   Lessening of output by a team member under the belief that others are doing so and that it would be foolish not to do the same thing.

Suggestion programs   Formal plans to encourage individual employees to recommend work improvements. A monetary award frequently is offered for acceptable suggestions.

Superleadership   Actively working to unleash the abilities of subordinates and encouraging them to become capable of self-leadership.

Superordinate goal   Goal that integrates the efforts of individuals or groups.

Supportive approach to OB   Philosophy of working with people in ways that seek to satisfy their needs and develop their potential.

Supportive model   Managerial view that leaders should support employees in their attempts to grow in their jobs and to perform them well.

Surface agenda   Official task of a group.

Surveillance devices   Equipment and procedures for observing employee actions (often done secretly).

System model   Managerial view that employees are concerned about finding meaning at work; having a work context infused with integrity, trust, and a sense of community; and receiving care and compassion from managers.

Systems approach to OB   Belief that there are many variables in organizations and that each of them affects all the others in a complex relationship.

Tardiness   Arriving late for work.

Task identity   Practice of allowing employees to perform a complete piece of work.

Task leader   Person who helps the group accomplish its objectives and stay on target.

Task significance   Amount of impact, as perceived by the worker, that the work has on other people.

Task structure   Degree to which one specific method is required to do the job (a variable in Fiedler's contingency model of leadership).

Task support   Condition in which leaders provide the resources, budgets, power, and other elements that are essential in getting the job done.

Task team   Cooperative small group in regular contact that is engaged in coordinated action.

Team building   Process of making teams more effective by encouraging members to examine how they work together, identify their weaknesses, and develop more effective ways of cooperating.

Teamwork   State that occurs when members know their objectives, contribute responsibly and enthusiastically to the task, and support one another.

Technical skill   Knowledge of and ability in any type of process or technique.

Telecommuting   Process of accomplishing all or a part of an employee's work at home through computer links to the office. Also known as an *electronic cottage*.

Theft   Unauthorized removal of company resources by an employee.

Theories   Explanations of how and why people think, feel, and act as they do.

Theory X   Autocratic and traditional set of assumptions about people.

Theory Y   Humanistic and supportive set of assumptions about people.

Theory Z   Model that adapts the elements of Japanese management systems to the U.S. culture and emphasizes cooperation and consensus decision processes.

360-degree feedback   Process of systematically gathering data on a person's skills, abilities, and behaviors from a variety of sources, such as their manager, peers, subordinates, and customers, so as to see where problems exist and improvements can be made.

Total quality management (TQM)   Process of getting every employee involved in the task of searching for continuous improvements in their operations.

Training multiplier effect   Process by which skilled people develop others, who then become the nucleus for developing still others.

Traits   Physical, intellectual, or personality characteristics that differentiate between leaders and nonleaders or between successful and unsuccessful leaders.

Transcultural employees   Employees who have learned to operate effectively in several cultures.

Transformational leaders   Managers who initiate bold strategic changes to position the organization for its future.

Trauma   Stress resulting from a severe threat to one's security.

Triple reward system   Term applied to practices that jointly benefit the needs and objectives of three groups: people, organizations, and the whole social system.

Trust   Capacity to depend on another's word and actions.

Tunnel vision   Holding narrow viewpoints, while missing the broader perspective.

Turnover   Rate at which employees leave an organization.

Two-factor model of motivation   Motivational model developed by Frederick Herzberg, which concludes that one set of job conditions (motivators) primarily motivates an employee and produces satisfaction if they are adequate, while a different set (hygiene factors) primarily dissatisfies the employee if they are inadequate.

Two-way communication process   Eight-step process in which a sender develops, encodes, and transmits an idea, with the recipient receiving, decoding, accepting, and using it, followed by sending feedback to the sender.

Type A people   People who are aggressive and competitive, set high standards, and put themselves under constant time pressures.

Type B people   People who are relaxed and easygoing and accept situations readily.

Uncertainty avoidance   Lack of comfort with ambiguity that drives some employees to avoid it and seek clarity.

Unconditional strokes   Strokes presented without any connection to behavior.

Underparticipation   Condition in which employees want more participation than they have.

Unfreezing   Term applying to situations that involve change and referring to the act of casting aside old ideas and practices so that new ones can be learned.

Upward communication   Flows of information from lower to higher levels in an organization.

Valence   Strength of a person's preference for receiving a reward.

Validity   Capacity of a survey instrument to measure what it claims to measure.

Value premises   Personal views of the desirability of certain goals and activities.

Valuing diversity   Philosophy and programs asserting that differences among people need to be recognized, acknowledged, appreciated, and used to collective advantage.

Variable interval schedule   Provision of a reinforcement after a variety of time periods.

Violence   Various forms of verbal or physical aggression at work.

Virtual offices   Layouts in which physical office space and individual desks are replaced with an array of portable communication tools, allowing employees to work almost anywhere.

Virtual teams   Working groups that meet without all their members being in the same location; such teams often rely heavily on technology to achieve their communication and coordination needs.

Vision   Challenging and crystallized long-range portrait of what the organization and its members can and should be—a possible, and desirable, image of the future.

Wage incentives   Reward systems that provide more pay for more production.

Whistle-blowing   Disclosing alleged misconduct to an internal or external source.

Willingness to accept the influence of others   Contingency factor in the path-goal model of leadership that suggests a leader's choice of style is partially dependent on an employee's readiness to accept direction from others.

Win-win outcome of conflict   Outcome in which both parties perceive that they are in a better position than they were before a conflict began.

Work ethic   Employee attitude of viewing work as a central life interest and desirable goal in life.

Work moods   Employee feelings about their jobs that can change within a day, hour, or minute.

Workplace trauma   Disintegration of employee self-concepts and beliefs in their capabilities arising from dramatic negative factors or experiences at work.

Workplace violence   Dramatic action harming employees, their coworkers, managers, or company property.

Xenophobia   Fear and rejection of ideas and things foreign to a person.

REFERENCES

Chapter 1

1. Daniel Goleman, "What Makes a Leader?" *Harvard Business Review,* November–December 1998, p. 102.
2. Karlene H. Roberts et al., "Reflections on the Field of Organizational Behavior," *Journal of Management Systems,* vol. 2, no. 1, 1990, p. 33.
3. Larry Hirschhorn and Thomas Gilmore, "The New Boundaries of the 'Boundaryless' Company," *Harvard Business Review,* May–June 1992, pp. 104–15.
4. See, for example, Ramon J. Aldag and Timothy M. Stearns, "Issues in Research Methodology," *Journal of Management,* June 1988, pp. 252–76.
5. One author suggests that a dozen different organizational behavior models all assume that it is possible to achieve both employee satisfaction and organizational performance at the same time through this mutuality of interest. See Barry M. Staw, "Organizational Psychology and the Pursuit of the Happy/Productive Worker," *California Management Review,* Summer 1986, pp. 40–53.
6. Early emphasis on the human resources approach to organizational behavior is provided in Raymond E. Miles, "Human Relations or Human Resources?" *Harvard Business Review,* July–August 1965, pp. 148–63.
7. The opportunity to perform work is discussed in Melvin Blumberg and Charles D. Pringle, "The Missing Opportunity in Organizational Research: Some Implications for a Theory of Work Performance," *Academy of Management Review,* October 1982, pp. 560–69.
8. This discussion is adapted from Keith Davis, "A Law of Diminishing Returns in Organizational Behavior?" *Personnel Journal,* December 1975, pp. 616–19.
9. Jack Stack, *The Great Game of Business,* New York: Currency Doubleday, 1992, p. 203.
10. Adapted from Keith Davis, "Five Propositions for Social Responsibility," *Business Horizons,* June 1975, pp. 5–18.
11. See, for example, John Micklethwait and Adrian Wooldridge, *The Witch Doctors: Making Sense of the Management Gurus,* New York: Times Business, 1996.
12. Roberts et al., pp. 25–38.

Chapter 2

1. Geoffrey Colvin, "Managing in the Info Era," *Fortune,* March 6, 2000, p. F9.
2. Pamela Leigh, "The New Spirit at Work," *Training and Development,* March 1997, p. 26.
3. Edmund J. Metz, "Managing Change toward a Leading-Edge Information Culture," *Organizational Dynamics,* August 1986, pp. 28–40. Another example of an organization that manages by explicitly examining its values and philosophy is in Diane Filipowski, "The Tao of Tandem," *Personnel Journal,* October 1991, pp. 72–78.
4. Judith Simpson, "Visioning: More than Meets the Eye," *Training and Development Journal,* September 1990, pp. 70–72. For a cautionary note on visioning,

see Jay A. Conger, "The Dark Side of Leadership," *Organizational Dynamics,* Autumn 1990, pp. 44–45.

5. Theory X and Theory Y were first published in Douglas McGregor, "The Human Side of Enterprise," in *Proceedings of the Fifth Anniversary Convocation of the School of Industrial Management,* Cambridge, MA: Massachusetts Institute of Technology, April 9, 1957.

6. Joel Arthur Barker, *Paradigms: The Business of Discovering the Future,* New York: Harper Business, 1992.

7. The distinctions between the first four models of organizational behavior were originally published in Keith Davis, *Human Relations at Work: The Dynamics of Organizational Behavior,* 3rd ed., New York: McGraw-Hill, 1967, p. 480.

8. "The Law of the Hog: A Parable about Improving Employee Effectiveness," *Training,* March 1987, p. 67.

9. See, for example, programs at 3M Corporation and IBM, in "3M Offers Buyouts to 1,300 Employees," *Duluth News Tribune,* December 10, 1995, p. 5B; and Aaron Bernstein, Scott Ticer, and Jonathan B. Levine, "IBM's Fancy Footwork to Sidestep Layoffs," *Business Week,* July 7, 1986, pp. 54–55.

10. Dawn Anfuso, "Creating a Culture of Caring Pays Off," *Personnel Journal,* August 1995, pp. 70–77.

11. An example of this early research is a study of the Prudential Insurance Company in Daniel Katz, Nathan Maccoby, and Nancy C. Morse, *Productivity, Supervision, and Morale in an Office Situation,* Part 1, Ann Arbor, MI: Institute for Social Research, University of Michigan, 1950. The conclusion about job satisfaction and productivity is reported on p. 63.

12. Rensis Likert, *New Patterns of Management,* New York: McGraw-Hill, 1961, pp. 102–3. Italics in original.

13. Elton Mayo, *The Human Problems of an Industrial Civilization,* Cambridge, MA: Harvard University Press, 1933; F. J. Roethlisberger and W. J. Dickson, *Management and the Worker,* Cambridge, MA: Harvard University Press, 1939; and F. J. Roethlisberger, *The Elusive Phenomena: An Autobiographical Account of My Work in the Field of Organizational Behavior at the Harvard Business School,* Cambridge, MA: Harvard University Press, 1977. The symposium on the fiftieth anniversary of the Western Electric Company, Hawthorne Studies, is reported in Eugene Louis Cass and Frederick G. Zimmer (eds.), *Man and Work in Society,* New York: Van Nostrand Reinhold Company, 1975. Recollections of the participants are reported in Ronald G. Greenwood, Alfred A. Bolton, and Regina A. Greenwood, "Hawthorne a Half Century Later: Relay Assembly Participants Remember," *Journal of Management,* Fall–Winter 1983, pp. 217–31. The earliest general textbook on human relations was Burleigh B. Gardner and David G. Moore, *Human Relations in Industry,* Chicago: Irwin, 1945.

14. For example, see Alex Carey, "The Hawthorne Studies: A Radical Criticism," *American Sociological Review,* June 1967, pp. 403–16; and Richard Herbert Franke and James D. Kaul, "The Hawthorne Experiments: First Statistical Interpretations," *American Sociological Review,* October 1978, pp. 623–43.

15. Frank Harrison, "The Management of Scientists: Determinants of Perceived Role Performance," *Academy of Management Journal,* June 1974, pp. 234–41.

16. Naomi Weiss, "How Starbucks Impassions Workers to Drive Growth," *Workforce,* August 1998, pp. 59–64.

17. Interested readers may wish to consult the history of organizational behavior, as traced by Keith Davis in "Human Relations, Industrial Humanism, and Organi-

zational Behavior," in a presentation to the Southern Division of the Academy of Management, November 13, 1986.

18. Sandra L. Robinson, Matthew S. Kraatz, and Denise M. Rousseau, "Changing Obligations and the Psychological Contract: A Longitudinal Study," *Academy of Management Journal,* February 1994, pp. 137–52.

Chapter 3

1. Jennifer J. Salopek, "Is Anyone Listening?" *Training and Development,* September 1999, p. 59.

2. Edward M. Hallowell, "The Human Moment at Work," *Harvard Business Review,* January–February 1999, p. 58.

3. Interested readers may wish to consult a fascinating collection and interpretation of a wide array of colloquialisms in Keith Davis, *Popular American Colloquialisms: Their Meaning and Origin,* Tempe, AZ: Keith Davis, 1991.

4. J. David Pincus, "Communication Satisfaction, Job Satisfaction, and Job Performance," *Human Communication Research,* Spring 1986, pp. 395–419.

5. Chris Argyris, "Good Communication That Blocks Learning," *Harvard Business Review,* July–August 1994, pp. 77–85.

6. Rudolph Flesch, *The Art of Readable Writing,* rev. ed., New York: Harper & Row, 1974. (The earlier edition was published in 1949.)

7. James M. Kouzes and Barry Z. Posner, "The Credibility Factor: What Followers Expect from Their Leaders," *Management Review,* January 1990, pp. 29–33; and Alan Farnham, "The Trust Gap," *Fortune,* December 4, 1989, pp. 57–78.

8. For a retrospective analysis of a classic study in misperception of employee needs by supervisors, see Stephen A. Rubenfeld, John W. Newstrom, and Thomas Duff, "Caveat Emptor: Avoiding Pitfalls in Data-Based Decision Making," *Review of Business,* Winter 1994, pp. 20–23.

9. James R. Larson, Jr., "The Dynamic Interplay between Employees' Feedback-Seeking Strategies and Supervisors' Delivery of Performance Feedback," *Academy of Management Review,* July 1989, pp. 408–22.

10. "Communications: Key to Product Redesign at McDonnell Douglas," *Quality Digest,* July 1994, pp. 62–65.

11. Sandra L. Kirmeyer and Thung-Rung Lin, "Social Support: Its Relationship to Observed Communication with Peers and Superiors," *Academy of Management Journal,* March 1987, pp. 138–51.

12. Jennifer J. Laabs, "Interactive Sessions Further TQM Effort," *Personnel Journal,* March 1994, pp. 22–28.

13. See, for example, M. M. Extejt, "Teaching Students to Correspond Effectively Electronically: Tips for Using Electronic Mail Properly," *Business Communication Quarterly,* June 1998, pp. 57–67; and Charlene Marmer Solomon, "Building Teams across Borders," *Global Workforce,* November 1998, pp. 12–17.

14. Jonathan N. Goodrich, "Telecommuting in America," *Business Horizons,* July–August 1990, pp. 31–37.

15. Robert C. Ford and Frank McLaughlin, "Questions and Answers about Telecommuting Programs," *Business Horizons,* May–June 1995, pp. 66–71; and Edward C. Baig, "Welcome to the Wireless Office," *Business Week,* June 26, 1995, pp. 104, 106.

16. Thomas H. Davenport and Keri Pearlson, "Two Cheers for the Virtual Office," *Sloan Management Review,* Summer 1998, pp. 51–65; Michael Adams, "Remote

Control," *Performance,* March 1995, pp. 44–48; and David Stamps, "The Virtual Office," *Training,* February 1994, pp. 17–18.

17. Keith Davis, "Management Communication and the Grapevine," *Harvard Business Review,* September–October 1953, p. 44.

18. Our own research discloses an accuracy of 80 to 99 percent for noncontroversial company information. Accuracy probably is lower for personal or highly emotional information.

19. John W. Newstrom, Robert M. Monczka, and William E. Reif, "Perceptions of the Grapevine: Its Value and Influence," *Journal of Business Communication,* Spring 1974, pp. 12–20.

Chapter 4

1. Chip R. Bell, "The Bluebirds' Secret: Mentoring with Bravery and Balance," *Training and Development,* February 1997, p. 33.

2. Dawn Anfuso, "Core Values Shape W. L. Gore's Innovative Culture," *Workforce,* March 1999, p. 50.

3. Kenneth Labich, "Hot Company, Warm Culture," *Fortune,* February 27, 1989, pp. 74–78.

4. Alex Taylor III, "The Odd Eclipse of a Star CEO," *Fortune,* February 11, 1991, pp. 87–96.

5. Elizabeth Wolfe Morrison and Sandra L. Robinson, "When Employees Feel Betrayed: A Model of How Psychological Contract Violation Develops," *Academy of Management Review,* January 1997, pp. 226–56.

6. Meena Wilson, "The Intercultural Values Questionnaire," *Issues and Observations,* Center for Creative Leadership, vol. 15, no. 1, 1995, pp. 10–11.

7. Charlene Solomon, "Affirmative Action: What You Need to Know," *Personnel Journal,* August 1995, pp. 56–67.

8. Karen Stinson, "Managing a Diverse Workforce," *Corporate Report Ventures,* August 1995, pp. 40–41.

9. Frances J. Milliken and Luis L. Martens, "Searching for Common Threads: Understanding the Multiple Effects of Diversity in Organizational Groups," *Academy of Management Review,* April 1996, pp. 402–33.

10. "For Bottom-Line Benefits, Develop a Diverse Workforce," *ASTD National Report,* July–August 1995, pp. 1, 3.

11. Ahmad Diba and Lisa Muñoz, "America's Most Admired Corporations," *Fortune,* February 19, 2001, pp. 64–66.

12. Susan M. Schor, "Separate and Unequal: The Nature of Women's and Men's Career-Building Relationships," *Business Horizons,* September–October 1997, pp. 51–58; and Belle Rose Ragins, "Diversified Mentoring Relationships in Organizations: A Power Perspective," *Academy of Management Review,* April 1997, pp. 482–521. For a discussion of mentoring programs for high school students, see Rebecca Ganzel, "Reaching Tomorrow's Workers," *Training,* June 2000, pp. 70–75.

13. Terri A. Scandura, "Dysfunctional Mentoring Relationships and Outcomes," *Journal of Management,* vol. 24, no. 3, 1998, pp. 449–67.

14. Robert L. Kahn et al., *Organizational Stress: Studies in Role Conflict and Ambiguity,* New York: John Wiley & Sons, 1964, pp. 56, 99–124.

15. Chester I. Barnard, "Functions and Pathology of Status Systems in Formal Organizations," in William F. Whyte (ed.), *Industry and Society,* New York: McGraw-Hill, 1946, p. 69.

16. For definitions of corporate culture, see Edgar H. Schein, *The Corporate Culture Survival Guide: Sense and Nonsense about Culture Change,* San Francisco: Jossey-Bass, 1999; and Daniel Denison, "What *Is* the Difference between Organizational Culture and Organizational Climate? A Native's Point of View on a Decade of Paradigm Wars," *Academy of Management Review,* July 1996, pp. 619–54.

17. Stephenie Overman, "A Company of Champions," *HRMagazine,* October 1990, pp. 58–60.

18. J. Robert Carleton, "Cultural Due Diligence," *Training,* November 1997, pp. 67–75.

19. John Sheridan, "Organizational Culture and Employee Retention," *Academy of Management Journal,* December 1992, pp. 1036–56.

20. Elizabeth R. Moore, "Prudential Reinforces Its Business Values," *Personnel Journal,* January 1993, pp. 84–89.

21. "Storytelling," *ASTD Info-Line,* no. 0006, June 2000, pp. 1–16; and Beverly Kaye and Betsy Jacobson, "True Tales and Tall Tales: The Power of Organizational Storytelling," *Training and Development,* March 1999, pp. 45–50.

22. "Organizational Culture," *ASTD Info-Line,* no. 9304, April 1993, pp. 1–16.

Chapter 5

1. Brenda Paik Sunoo, "Praise and Thanks—You Can't Give Enough," *Workforce,* April 1999, p. 56.

2. Thomas L. Quick, "Expectancy Theory in Five Simple Steps," *Training and Development Journal,* July 1988, p. 30.

3. James E. Ellis, "Feeling Stuck at Hyatt? Create a New Business," *Business Week,* December 10, 1990, p. 195.

4. The original work on achievement motivation is David C. McClelland, *The Achieving Society,* New York: Van Nostrand, 1961.

5. A. H. Maslow, "A Theory of Motivation," *Psychological Review,* vol. 50, 1943, pp. 370–96; and A. H. Maslow, *Motivation and Personality,* New York: Harper & Row, 1954. The need for students of organizational behavior to read the originally published work of classics like these is stressed in W. Dennis Patzig and Barry L. Wisdom, "Some Words of Caution about Having Students Read the Classics," in Dennis Ray (ed.), Southern Management Association Proceedings, Mississippi State, MS: Southern Management Association, 1986.

6. For a fuller discussion, see Richard M. Steers and Lyman W. Porter, *Motivation and Work Behavior,* 5th ed., New York: McGraw-Hill, 1991.

7. Frederick Herzberg, Bernard Mausner, and Barbara Snyderman, *The Motivation to Work,* New York: John Wiley & Sons, 1959; Frederick Herzberg, *Work and the Nature of Man,* Cleveland: World Publishing Company, 1966; and Frederick Herzberg, *The Managerial Choice: To Be Efficient or to Be Human,* rev. ed., Salt Lake City: Olympus, 1982.

8. Early criticisms were in Martin G. Evans, "Herzberg's Two-Factor Theory of Motivation: Some Problems and a Suggested Test," *Personnel Journal,* January 1970, pp. 32–35; and Valerie M. Bockman, "The Herzberg Controversy," *Personnel Psychology,* Summer 1971, pp. 155–89. The latter article reports the first ten years of research on the model.

9. Clayton P. Alderfer, "An Empirical Test of a New Theory of Human Needs," *Organizational Behavior and Human Performance,* vol. 4, 1969, pp. 142–75.

10. B. F. Skinner, *Science and Human Behavior,* New York: Macmillan (Free Press), 1953; and B. F. Skinner, *Contingencies of Reinforcement,* New York: Appleton-Century-Crofts, 1969. OB Mod is discussed in Fred Luthans and Robert Kreitner, *Organizational Behavior Modification and Beyond: An Operant and Social Learning Approach,* Glenview, IL: Scott, Foresman, 1985.

11. Tawn Nhan, "A Little Thoughtfulness Can Mean More than Lots of Pay," *Duluth News-Tribune,* December 11, 1995, pp. B1, B3.

12. "Productivity Gains from a Pat on the Back," *Business Week,* January 23, 1978, pp. 56–62.

13. See, for example, Alexander D. Stajkovic and Fred Luthans, "Going beyond Traditional Motivational and Behavioral Approaches," *Organizational Dynamics,* Spring 1998, pp. 62–74.

14. Helen Rheem, "Performance Management," *Harvard Business Review,* May–June 1995, pp. 11–12.

15. Victor H. Vroom, *Work and Motivation,* New York: John Wiley & Sons, 1964; and Lyman W. Porter and Edward E. Lawler III, *Managerial Attitudes and Performance,* Homewood, IL: Dorsey Press and Richard D. Irwin, 1968.

16. The original meaning of instrumentality, as offered by Victor Vroom, reflected the level of association between performance and reward and thus was a correlation that could range between -1 and $+1$. However, later interpretations and modifications to the expectancy model by other writers have generally limited the effective range of instrumentality to include only positive associations from 0 to $+1$. For a more thorough discussion, see Craig C. Pinder, "Valence-Instrumentality-Expectancy Theory," in Richard M. Steers and Lyman W. Porter (eds.), *Motivation and Work Behavior,* 4th ed., New York: McGraw-Hill Book Company, 1987, pp. 69–89.

17. J. S. Adams, "Inequity in Social Exchange," in L. Berkowitz (ed.), *Advances in Experimental Social Psychology,* vol. 2, New York: Academic Press, 1965, pp. 267–99. For a discussion of the impact of different cultural backgrounds, see Lynda M. Kilbourne and Anne M. O'Leary-Kelly, "A Reevaluation of Equity Theory: The Influence of Culture," *Journal of Management Inquiry,* June 1994, pp. 177–88.

18. Jerald Greenberg, "Employee Theft as a Reaction to Underpayment Inequity: The Hidden Cost of Pay Cuts," *Journal of Applied Psychology,* October 1990, pp. 561–68.

19. Richard C. Huseman, John D. Hatfield, and Edward W. Miles, "A New Perspective on Equity Theory: The Equity Sensitivity Construct," *Academy of Management Review,* April 1987, pp. 222–34; also see Richard J. Huseman and John D. Hatfield, "Equity Theory and the Managerial Matrix," *Training and Development Journal,* April 1990, pp. 98–102.

20. Developed from an article by Liz Roman Gallese, "Stephen Jellen Builds Pianos Not for Money but for Satisfaction," *The Wall Street Journal* (Pacific Coast edition), September 6, 1973, pp. 1, 12.

Chapter 6

1. Jean-Francois Manzoni and Jean-Louis Barsoux, "The Set-Up-to-Fail Syndrome," *Harvard Business Review,* March–April 1998, p. 101.

2. Larry Cipolla, "Make Performance Appraisals Count," *Corporate Report Ventures,* August 1995, p. 20.

3. A five-level reward strategy is described in Elizabeth J. Hawk, "Culture and Rewards," *Personnel Journal,* April 1995, pp. 30–37.

4. Carolyn Wiley, "Incentive Plan Pushes Production," *Personnel Journal,* August 1993, pp. 86–91.

5. Three field tests of the underpaid/overpaid equity hypotheses support a curvilinear relationship with pay satisfaction in Paul D. Sweeney, "Distributive Justice and Pay Satisfaction: A Field Test of an Equity Theory Predication," *Journal of Business and Psychology,* Spring 1990, pp. 329–41.

6. This trade-off between extrinsic rewards and intrinsic satisfaction was originally proposed by Edward L. Deci, "Effects of Externally Mediated Rewards on Intrinsic Motivation," *Journal of Personality and Social Psychology,* vol. 18, 1971, pp. 105–15. Recent field-research support for his proposal appears in Paul C. Jordan, "Effects of an Extrinsic Reward on Intrinsic Motivation: A Field Experiment," *Academy of Management Journal,* June 1986, pp. 405–12.

7. Jackee McNitt, "In Good Company: An Employee Recognition Plan with Staying Power," *Compensation and Benefits Management,* Spring 1990, pp. 242–46.

8. See, for example, Linda Davidson, "The Power of Personal Recognition," *Workforce,* July 1999, pp. 44–49; and Shari Caudron, "Flattery Will Get You Everywhere," *Workforce,* July 1999, pp. 25–26.

9. One unique problem is the possibility that some employees will engage in negative impression management for a variety of reasons. See Thomas E. Becker and Scott L. Martin, "Trying to Look Bad at Work: Methods and Motives for Managing Poor Impressions in Organizations," *Academy of Management Journal,* February 1995, pp. 174–99.

10. Mary N. Vinson, "The Pros and Cons of 360-Degree Feedback: Making It Work," *Training and Development,* April 1996, pp. 11–12.

11. Robert Carey, "Coming around to 360-Degree Feedback," *Performance,* March 1995, pp. 56–60.

12. The four problems are drawn from Robert E. Lefton, "Performance Appraisals: Why They Go Wrong and How to Do Them Right," *National Productivity Review,* Winter 1985–1986, pp. 54–63.

13. The attribution process was first presented in Fritz Heider, *The Psychology of Interpersonal Relations,* New York: John Wiley & Sons, Inc., 1958. It was elaborated upon in H. H. Kelley, "The Processes of Causal Attribution," *American Psychologist,* February 1973, pp. 107–28.

14. The self-fulfilling prophecy was initially presented in Robert K. Merton, "The Self-Fulfilling Prophecy," *Antioch Review,* vol. 8, 1948, pp. 193–210. Recent studies are reported in R. H. G. Field, "The Self-Fulfilling Prophecy Leader: Achieving the Metharme Effect," *Journal of Management Studies,* March 1989, pp. 151–75; and Dov Eden, "Pygmalion without Interpersonal Contrast Effects: Whole Groups Gain from Raising Manager Expectations," *Journal of Applied Psychology,* August 1990, pp. 394–98.

15. The Nucor system is described in "Nucor's Ken Iverson on Productivity and Pay," *Personnel Administrator,* October 1986, pp. 46 ff.

16. Arvid Wellman, "1987 Profit Sharing Rate Announced," *The Frame Maker* (Andersen Corporation newsletter), January 16, 1988, p. 1.

17. Useful overviews of gain sharing are in Susan C. Hanlon, David C. Meyer, and Robert R. Taylor, "Consequences of Gainsharing: A Field Experiment Revisited," *Group and Organizational Management,* vol. 19, no. 1, 1994, pp. 87–111; and Denis Collins, Larry Hatcher, and Timothy L. Ross, "The Decision to Implement

Gainsharing: The Role of Work Climate, Expected Outcomes, and Union Status," *Personnel Psychology,* Spring 1993, pp. 77–104.

18. Garry M. Ritzky, "Incentive Pay Programs That Help the Bottom Line," *HRMagazine,* April 1995, pp. 68–74.

19. Timothy L. Ross, Larry Hatcher, and Ruth Ann Ross, "From Piecework to Companywide Gainsharing," *Management Review,* May 1989, pp. 22–26.

20. Elements of the at-risk program at Du Pont are described in Robert P. McNutt, "Sharing Across the Board: Du Pont's Achievement Sharing Program," *Compensation and Benefits Review,* July–August 1990, pp. 17–24; and Edward J. Ost, "Team-Based Pay: New Wave Strategic Incentives," *Sloan Management Review,* Spring 1990, pp. 19–27.

21. Edward E. Lawler III, Gerald E. Ledford, Jr., and Lei Chang, "Who Uses Skill-Based Pay, and Why," *Compensation and Benefits Review,* March–April 1993, pp. 22–26; also see, for example, the entire issue devoted to skill-based pay at General Mills, Honeywell's Ammunition Assembly Plant, and Northern Telecom in *Compensation and Benefits Review,* March–April 1991.

Chapter 7

1. Gregory G. Dess and Joseph C. Picken, "Changing Roles: Leadership in the 21st Century," *Organizational Dynamics,* Winter 2000, p. 19.

2. Brent B. Allred, Charles C. Snow, and Raymond E. Miles, "Characteristics of Managers in the 21st Century," *Academy of Management Executive,* November 1996, p. 25.

3. John A. Byrne, "The Shredder," *Business Week,* January 15, 1996, pp. 56–61.

4. Eli Cohen and Noel Tichy, "How Leaders Develop Leaders," *Training and Development,* May 1997, pp. 58–73.

5. Shelley A. Kirkpatrick and Edwin A. Locke, "Leadership: Do Traits Matter?" *Academy of Management Executive,* May 1991, pp. 48–60.

6. For another perspective on leadership continuums—from micro to team to macro leadership—see Ed Kur, "Developing Leadership in Organizations: A Continuum of Choices," *Journal of Management Inquiry,* June 1995, pp. 198–206.

7. Gregory H. Dobbins and Stephen J. Zaccaro, "The Effects of Group Cohesion and Leader Behavior on Subordinate Satisfaction," *Group and Organization Studies,* September 1986, pp. 203–19; and Chester A. Schriesheim, "The Great High Consideration–High Initiating Structure Leadership Myth: Evidence on Its Generalizability," *Journal of Social Psychology,* April 1982, pp. 221–28.

8. Examples of early reports from each university are Daniel Katz et al., *Productivity, Supervision and Morale in an Office Situation,* Ann Arbor: University of Michigan Press, 1950; and E. A. Fleishman, *Leadership Climate and Supervisory Behavior,* Columbus, OH: Personnel Research Board, Ohio State University Press, 1951.

9. Robert R. Blake and Jane S. Mouton, *The Managerial Grid,* Houston: Gulf Publishing Company, 1964.

10. Fred E. Fiedler, *A Theory of Leadership Effectiveness,* New York: McGraw-Hill, 1967; and Fred E. Fiedler and Martin M. Chemers, *Leadership and Effective Management,* Glenview, IL: Scott, Foresman, 1974. For a critique, see Arthur G. Jago and James W. Ragan, "The Trouble with Leader Match Is That It Doesn't Match Fiedler's Contingency Model," *Journal of Applied Psychology,* November 1986, pp. 555–59.

11. Paul Hersey and Kenneth H. Blanchard, *Management of Organizational Behavior,* 5th ed., Englewood Cliffs, NJ: Prentice Hall, 1988. A slightly modified approach featuring directing, coaching, supporting, and delegating styles is in Kenneth H. Blanchard et al., *Leadership and the One Minute Manager,* New York: William Morrow, 1985. The authors provide a retrospective look at their model in Paul Hersey and Ken Blanchard, "Great Ideas Revisited," *Training and Development,* January 1996, pp. 42–51.

12. Critical perspectives on the Hersey-Blanchard situational leadership model appear in Barry-Craig P. Johansen, "Situational Leadership: A Review of the Research," *Human Resource Development Quarterly,* Spring 1990, pp. 73–85; and Warren Blank, John R. Weitzel, and Stephen G. Green, "A Test of the Situational Leadership Theory," *Personnel Psychology,* Autumn 1990, pp. 579–97. However, the model continues to be used widely in industry, as reported by Marshall Whitmire and Philip R. Nienstedt, "Lead Leaders into the '90s," *Personnel Journal,* May 1991, pp. 80–85.

13. Robert J. House, "A Path Goal Theory of Leadership Effectiveness," *Administrative Science Quarterly,* September 1971, pp. 321–28. For the original explanation, see M. G. Evans, *The Effects of Supervisory Behavior upon Worker Perceptions of Their Path-Goal Relationships,* unpublished doctoral dissertation, New Haven, CT: Yale University, 1968. For a broad review of the path-goal literature, see J. C. Wofford and Laurie Z. Liska, "Path-Goal Theories of Leadership: A Meta-Analysis," *Journal of Management,* Winter 1993, pp. 857–76.

14. "Mgr. Forum," *Mgr.* (American Telephone and Telegraph Company, Long Lines Division), no. 4, 1976, p. 2.

15. V. H. Vroom and P. W. Yetton, *Leadership and Decision Making,* Pittsburgh: University of Pittsburgh Press, 1973, contains both an individual (consultative) model and a similar one for group decision making. Subsequent research and modifications to the original model are reported in Victor H. Vroom and Arthur G. Jago, *The New Leadership: Managing Participation in Organizations,* Englewood Cliffs, NJ: Prentice Hall, 1988. Research supporting the importance of the problem attributes is reported in Richard H. G. Field, Peter C. Read, and Jordan J. Louviere, "The Effect of Situation Attributes on Decision Method Choice in the Vroom-Jago Model of Participation in Decision Making," *Leadership Quarterly,* Fall 1990, pp. 165–76. For an update, see Victor H. Vroom, "Leadership and the Decision-Making Process," *Organizational Dynamics,* vol. 28, no. 4, 2000, pp. 82–94.

16. Steven Kerr and J. M. Jermier, "Substitutes for Leadership: Their Meaning and Measurement," *Organizational Behavior and Human Performance,* December 1978, pp. 375–403.

17. Jon P. Howell et al., "Substitutes for Leadership: Effective Alternatives to Ineffective Leadership," *Organizational Dynamics,* Summer 1990, pp. 20–38.

18. Charles C. Manz and Henry P. Sims, Jr., "Leading Workers to Lead Themselves: The External Leadership of Self-Managing Work Teams," *Administrative Science Quarterly,* vol. 32, 1987, pp. 106–27; and Charles C. Manz, *Mastering Self-Leadership: Empowering Yourself for Personal Excellence,* Englewood Cliffs, NJ: Prentice Hall, 1991.

19. Charles C. Manz and Henry P. Sims, Jr., "SuperLeadership: Beyond the Myth of Heroic Leadership," *Organizational Dynamics,* Summer 1991, pp. 18–35.

20. Christopher A. Bartlett and Sumantra Ghoshal, "Changing the Role of Top Management: Beyond Systems to People," *Harvard Business Review,* May–June 1995,

pp. 132–42; and Walter Kiechel III, "The Boss as Coach," *Fortune,* November 4, 1991, pp. 201–2.

21. See, for example, John O. Burdett, "Forty Things Every Manager Should Know about Coaching," *Journal of Management Development,* vol. 17, no. 2, 1998, pp. 142–52; and William Q. Judge and Jeffrey Cowell, "The Brave New World of Executive Coaching," *Business Horizons,* July–August 1997, pp. 71–76.

Chapter 8

1. Chris Argyris, as reported in Suzy Wetlaufer, "Organizing for Empowerment: An Interview with AES's Roger Sant and Dennis Bakke," *Harvard Business Review,* January–February 1999, p. 111.

2. Jay Klagge, "The Empowerment Squeeze—Views from the Middle Management Position," *Journal of Management Development,* vol. 17, no. 8, 1998, p. 557.

3. Robert C. Ford and Myron D. Fottler, "Empowerment: A Matter of Degree," *Academy of Management Executive,* vol. 9, no. 3, 1995, pp. 21–31; a case and multiple perspectives on it appear in Lawrence R. Rothstein, "The Empowerment Effort That Came Undone," *Harvard Business Review,* January–February 1995, pp. 20–31.

4. David E. Bowen and Edward E. Lawler III, "Empowering Service Employees," *Sloan Management Review,* Summer 1995, pp. 73–83.

5. Gretchen M. Spreitzer, Mark A. Kizilos, and Stephen W. Nason, "A Dimensional Analysis of the Relationship between Psychological Empowerment and Effectiveness, Satisfaction, and Strain," *Journal of Management,* vol. 23, no. 5, 1997, pp. 679–704.

6. Peter Lazes, "Employee Involvement Activities: Saving Jobs and Money Too," *New Management,* Winter 1986, pp. 58–60.

7. F. J. Roethlisberger and W. J. Dickson, *Management and the Worker,* Cambridge, MA: Harvard University Press, 1939; and Lester Coch and John R. P. French, Jr., "Overcoming Resistance to Change," *Human Relations,* vol. 1, no. 4, 1948, pp. 512–32. The presence of conflicting views on the value of participation is illustrated in these two articles: Carrie R. Leana, Edwin A. Locke, and David M. Schweiger, "Fact and Fiction in Analyzing Research on Participative Decision Making: A Critique of Cotton, Vollrath, Froggatt, Lengnick-Hall, and Jennings," *Academy of Management Review,* January 1990, pp. 137–46; and John L. Cotton et al., "Fact: The Form of Participation Does Matter—A Rebuttal to Leana, Locke, and Schweiger," *Academy of Management Review,* January 1990, pp. 147–53.

8. John A. Wagner III, "Participation's Effects on Performance and Satisfaction: A Reconsideration of Research Evidence," *Academy of Management Review,* vol. 19, no. 2, 1994, pp. 312–30. Also see David J. Glew, Ricky W. Griffin, and David D. Van Fleet, "Participation in Organizations: A Preview of the Issues and Proposed Framework for Future Analysis," *Journal of Management,* vol. 21, no. 3, 1995, pp. 395–421.

9. This interest is demonstrated by the wide popularity of books on management; see Jon L. Pierce and John W. Newstrom, *The Manager's Bookshelf: A Mosaic of Contemporary Views,* 6th ed., Englewood Cliffs, NJ: Prentice Hall, 2002.

10. See, for example, "Companies Hit the Road Less Traveled," *Business Week,* June 5, 1995, pp. 82–83; and Donald W. McCormick, "Spirituality and Management," *Spirit at Work,* Winter 1995, pp. 1–3.

11. A summary of strengths and weaknesses of participative approaches by level of analysis is in Robert E. Cole, Paul Bacdayan, and M. Joseph White, "Quality,

Participation, and Competitiveness," *California Management Review,* Spring 1993, pp. 68–81.

12. Support for the participative process is in Carla S. Smith and Michael T. Brannick, "A Role and Expectancy Model of Participative Decision-Making: A Replication and Theoretical Extension," *Journal of Organizational Behavior,* March 1990, pp. 91–104. For results in another culture, see James P. Guthrie, "High Involvement Work Practices, Turnover, and Productivity: Evidence from New Zealand," *Academy of Management Journal,* vol. 44, no. 1, 2001, pp. 180–90.

13. This model was originally presented in F. Dansereau, Jr., G. Graen, and W. J. Haga, "A Vertical Dyad Linkage Approach to Leadership within Formal Organizations: A Longitudinal Investigation of the Role Making Process," *Organizational Behavior and Human Performance,* vol. 13, 1975, pp. 46–68. Recent additions include Raymond T. Sparrowe and Robert C. Liden, "Process and Structure in Leader-Member Exchange," *Academy of Management Review,* vol. 22, no. 2, 1997, pp. 522–52; and Elaine M. Engle and Robert G. Lord, "Implicit Theories, Self-Schemas, and Leader-Member Exchange," *Academy of Management Journal,* vol. 40, no. 4, 1997, pp. 988–1010.

14. A readable portrait of how empowerment increases power for both parties is in William C. Byham (with Jeff Cox), *Zapp! The Lightning of Empowerment,* Pittsburgh: DDI Press, 1989; the overall dynamics of managing with power are explored in Jeffrey Pfeffer, "Understanding Power in Organizations," *California Management Review,* Winter 1992, pp. 29–50.

15. A unique team approach to submitting suggestions at Black and Decker is described in Steve Paloncy, "Team Approach Cuts Costs," *HRMagazine,* November 1990, pp. 61–62; a case report showing an 82 percent participation rate is in Rosalie A. Steele, "Awards Energize a Suggestion Program," *Personnel Journal,* October 1992, pp. 96–100.

16. Mitchell Lee Marks et al., "Employee Participation in a Quality Circle Program: Impact on Quality of Work Life, Productivity, and Absenteeism," *Journal of Applied Psychology,* February 1986, pp. 61–69. A discussion of options for various levels of participation is in C. Philip Alexander, "Voluntary Participation," *Quality Digest,* October 1994, pp. 50–52.

17. An example is the H. J. Heinz company, a global food-processing organization. See "O'Reilly Supports Total Quality Management at Heinz," *Beta Gamma Sigma Newsletter,* Summer 1991, p. 1.

18. Katherine J. Klein, "Employee Ownership," *New Management,* Spring 1986, pp. 55–61.

19. Some have argued that it is necessary for employees to psychologically experience ownership before results can be expected from them. See Jon L. Pierce, Stephen A. Rubenfeld, and Susan Morgan, "Employee Ownership: A Conceptual Model of Process and Effects," *Academy of Management Review,* January 1991, pp. 121–44; and Jon L. Pierce and Candace A. Furo, "Employee Ownership: Implications for Management," *Organizational Dynamics,* Winter 1990, pp. 32–43.

20. Randall Hanson, Rebecca I. Porterfield, and Kathleen Ames, "Employee Empowerment at Risk: Effects of Recent NLRB Rulings," *Academy of Management Executive,* vol. 9, no. 2, 1995, pp. 45–56.

21. Robert E. Quinn and Gretchen M. Spreitzer, "The Road to Empowerment: Seven Questions Every Leader Should Consider," *Organizational Dynamics,* Autumn 1977, p. 46.

22. Chris Lee and Ron Zemke, "The Search for Spirit in the Workplace," *Training,* June 1993, pp. 21–28; and Peter Block, "From Paternalism to Stewardship," *Training,* July 1993, pp. 45–50.

Chapter 9

1. George M. C. Fisher, "A New Relationship with Employees," *CEO Series* (Washington University in St. Louis), no. 14, March 1997, p. 1.
2. Diane E. Lewis, "Employee Perks Keep Workers from Leaving," *Minneapolis Star Tribune,* November 8, 1999, p. D9.
3. Hugh Aaron, "Recession-Proofing a Company's Employees," *The Wall Street Journal,* March 4, 1991, p. A10.
4. Jack C. Davis and Denny Organ, "The Happy Curve," *Business Horizons,* May–June 1995, pp. 1–3.
5. See, for example, Donald L. Kanter and Philip H. Mirvis, "Managing Jaundiced Workers," *New Management,* Spring 1986, pp. 50–54. Interested readers may also refer to Jeffrey S. Rain, Irving M. Lane, and Dirk D. Steiner, "A Current Look at the Job Satisfaction/Life Satisfaction Relationship: Review and Future Considerations," *Human Relations,* vol. 44, no. 3, 1991, pp. 287–307.
6. Relevant discussions and research are reported in Charlene Marmer Solomon, "The Loyalty Factor," *Personnel Journal,* September 1992, pp. 52–62; R. D. Iverson and P. Roy, "A Causal Model of Behavioral Commitment: Evidence from a Study of Australian Blue-Collar Employees," *Journal of Management,* Spring 1994, pp. 15–42; and Thomas E. Slocombe and Thomas W. Dougherty, "Dissecting Organizational Commitment and Its Relationship with Employee Behavior," *Journal of Business and Psychology,* Summer 1998, pp. 469–91. For a discussion of practices leading to the more common synonym for commitment, see Caroline Louise Cole, "Building Loyalty," *Workforce,* August 2000, pp. 43–52.
7. See, for example, J. M. George and A. P. Brief, "Feeling Good—Doing Good: A Conceptual Analysis of the Mood at Work-Organizational Spontaneity Relationship," *Psychological Bulletin,* 1992, vol. 112, pp. 310–29.
8. A systematic classification of active/passive and constructive/destructive employee responses is in C. Rusbult et al., "Impact of Exchange Variables on Exit, Voice, Loyalty, and Neglect: An Integrative Model of Responses to Declining Job Satisfaction," *Academy of Management Journal,* vol. 31, no. 3, 1988, pp. 599–627.
9. For a classic description of this relationship, see Edward E. Lawler III and Lyman W. Porter, "The Effect of Performance on Job Satisfaction," *Industrial Relations,* October 1967, pp. 20–28. For an update on the antecedents and consequences of absenteeism, see David A. Harrison and Joseph J. Martocchio, "Time for Absenteeism: A 20-Year Review of Origins, Offshoots, and Outcomes," *Journal of Management,* vol. 24, no. 3, 1998, pp. 305–50.
10. W. H. Mobley, "Intermediate Linkages in the Relationship between Job Satisfaction and Employee Turnover," *Journal of Applied Psychology,* vol. 6, 1977, pp. 237–40.
11. "New Behavioral Study Defines Typical 'Turnover Personality,'" *Human Resource Measurements,* Supplement to *Personnel Journal,* April 1992, p. 4; the "turnover personality" is supported by Timothy A. Judge and Shinichiro Watanabe, "Is the Past Prologue? A Test of Ghiselli's Hobo Syndrome," *Journal of Management,* vol. 21, no. 2, 1995, pp. 211–29.

12. See, for example, Nicholas Stein, "Winning the War to Keep Top Talent," *Fortune,* May 29, 2000, pp. 132–38; and "Twelve Ways to Keep Good People," *Training,* April 1999, p. 19.

13. John Putzier and Frank T. Nowak, "Attendance Management and Control," *Personnel Administrator,* August 1989, pp. 58–60.

14. Theft is discussed in Samuel Greegard, "Theft Control Starts with HR Strategies," *Personnel Journal,* April 1993, pp. 81–91; and Alan Weiss, "Seven Reasons to Examine Workplace Ethics," *HRMagazine,* March 1991, pp. 69–74.

15. Kevin Dobbs, "The Lucrative Menace of Workplace Violence," *Training,* March 2000, pp. 55–62.

16. Dennis W. Organ, "Personality and Organizational Citizenship Behavior," *Journal of Management,* Summer 1994, pp. 465–78; and John R Deckop, Robert Mangel, and Carol C. Cirka, "Getting More than You Pay for: Organizational Citizenship Behavior and Pay-for-Performance Plans," *Academy of Management Journal,* August 1999, pp. 420–28.

17. Mark C. Bolino, "Citizenship and Impression Management: Good Soldiers or Good Actors?" *Academy of Management Review,* January 1999, pp. 82–98.

18. The Index of Organizational Reactions is described in F. J. Smith and L. W. Porter, "What Do Executives Really Think about Their Organizations?" *Organizational Dynamics,* Autumn 1977, pp. 68–80. The Job Descriptive Index is reported in P. C. Smith, L. M. Kendall, and C. L. Hulin, *The Measurement of Satisfaction in Work and Retirement,* Chicago: Rand McNally & Company, 1969. The example of a numerical scale used to indicate degree of agreement or disagreement with a statement is adapted from Lyman W. Porter, "A Study of Perceived Need Satisfactions in Bottom and Middle Management," *Journal of Applied Psychology,* January 1961, pp. 1–10. The Minnesota Satisfaction Questionnaire is presented in D. J. Weiss et al., *Manual for the Minnesota Satisfaction Questionnaire,* Minnesota Studies in Vocational Rehabilitation: XXII, University of Minnesota Industrial Relations Center, Work Adjustment Project, 1967.

19. Brad Fishel, "A New Perspective: How to Get the Real Story from Attitude Surveys," *Training,* February 1998, pp. 91–94.

20. "Bringing Sears into the New World," *Fortune,* October 13, 1997, pp. 183–84.

21. Karen B. Paul and David W. Bracken, "Everything You Always Wanted to Know about Employee Surveys," *Training and Development,* January 1995, pp. 45–49; Terrence R. Gray, "A Hospital Takes Action on Employee Survey," *Personnel Journal,* March 1995, pp. 74–77; and Claire Krulikowski, "Measuring Employee Satisfaction," *Quality Digest,* September 1994, pp. 58–63.

Chapter 10

1. Samuel Greengard, "Privacy: Entitlement or Illusion?" *Personnel Journal,* May 1996, p. 242.

2. Janet P. Near and Marcia P. Miceli, "Effective Whistle-Blowing," *Academy of Management Review,* July 1995, p. 680.

3. Edgar H. Schein and J. Steven Ott, "The Legitimacy of Organizational Influence," *American Journal of Sociology,* May 1962, pp. 682–89; and Keith Davis, "Attitudes toward the Legitimacy of Management Efforts to Influence Employees," *Academy of Management Journal,* June 1968, pp. 153–62.

4. Paul Tolchinsky et al., "Employee Perceptions of Invasion of Privacy: A Field Simulation Experiment," *Journal of Applied Psychology,* June 1982, pp. 308–13.

5. Adapted from Virginia E. Schein, "Privacy and Personnel: A Time for Action," *Personnel Journal,* December 1976, pp. 604–7.

6. Gene Bylinski, "How Companies Spy on Employees," *Fortune,* November 4, 1991, pp. 131–40; see also Peter Coy, "Big Brother, Pinned to Your Chest," *Business Week,* August 17, 1992, p. 38; Jennifer J. Laabs, "Surveillance: Tool or Trap?" *Personnel Journal,* June 1992, pp. 96–104; and Wayne E. Barlow, "Do Employees' Electronic Messages Spell Trouble for You?" *Personnel Journal,* October 1995, pp. 135 ff.

7. Ron Zemke, "Do Honesty Tests Tell the Truth?" *Training,* October 1990, pp. 75–81.

8. David E. Nagle, "The Polygraph Shield," *Personnel Administrator,* February 1989, pp. 18–23; and Lawrence S. Kleiman, Robert H. Faley, and David W. Denton, "Legal Issues Concerning Polygraph Testing in the Public Sector," *Public Personnel Management,* Winter 1990, pp. 365–79.

9. H. John Bernardin and Donna K. Cooke, "Validity of an Honesty Test in Predicting Theft among Convenience Store Employees," *Academy of Management Journal,* October 1993, pp. 1097–1108; see also Paul R. Sackett, Laura R. Burris, and Christine Callahan, "Integrity Testing for Personnel Selection: An Update," *Personnel Psychology,* Autumn 1989, pp. 491–529.

10. Robert J. Nobile, "The Drug-Free Workplace: Action on It!" *Personnel,* February 1990, pp. 21–23; and Minda Zetlin, "Combating Drugs in the Workplace," *Management Review,* August 1991, pp. 17–19.

11. Timothy L. Baker, "Preventing Drug Abuse at Work," *Personnel Administrator,* July 1989, pp. 56–59.

12. Cory R. Fine, "Video Tests Are the New Frontier in Drug Detection," *Personnel Journal,* July 1992, pp. 146–61.

13. The data cited are from Gary N. Powell, "Sexual Harassment: Confronting the Issue of Definition," *Business Horizons,* July–August 1983, pp. 24–28; and Diane Feldman, "Sexual Harassment: Policies and Prevention," *Personnel,* September 1987, pp. 12–17.

14. S. Trowers Crowley, *ADA Primer: A Concise Guide to the Americans with Disabilities Act of 1990,* Englewood Cliffs, NJ: Maxwell Macmillan, 1990.

15. Michael A. Campion, Lisa Cheraskin, and Michael J. Stevens, "Career-Related Antecedents and Outcomes of Job Rotation," *Academy of Management Journal,* December 1994, pp. 1518–42.

16. Edward E. Lawler III, "For a More Effective Organization—Match the Job to the Man," *Organizational Dynamics,* Summer 1974, pp. 19–29.

17. J. Richard Hackman et al., "A New Strategy for Job Enrichment," *California Management Review,* Summer 1975, pp. 57–71.

18. "The Signature of Quality," *Management in Practice,* American Management Associations, March–April 1977, pp. 2–3.

19. J. Richard Hackman and Greg R. Oldham, "Development of the Job Diagnostic Survey," *Journal of Applied Psychology,* April 1975, pp. 159–70.

20. Fred Luthans et al., "The Impact of a Job Redesign Intervention on Salespersons' Observed Performance Behaviors: A Field Experiment," *Group and Organization Studies,* March 1987, pp. 55–72.

21. Ricky W. Griffin et al., "Objective and Social Factors as Determinants of Task Perceptions and Responses: An Integrated Perspective and Empirical Investigation," *Academy of Management Journal,* September 1987, pp. 501–23.

22. The idea of ethical leadership is in Richard P. Nielson, "Changing Unethical Organizational Behavior," *Academy of Management Executive,* May 1989, pp.

123–30; survey results on policies are in Timothy R. Barnett and Daniel S. Cochran, "Making Room for the Whistleblower," *HRMagazine,* January 1991, pp. 58–61; and tips for whistle-blowers appear in Amy Dunkin, "Blowing the Whistle without Paying the Piper," *Business Week,* June 3, 1991, pp. 138–39.

509

23. Janet P. Near and Marcia Miceli, "Effective Whistle-Blowing," *Academy of Management Review,* July 1995, pp. 679–708; and Marcia P. Miceli and Janet P. Near, "Relationships among Value Congruence, Perceived Victimization, and Retaliation against Whistle-Blowers," *Journal of Management,* Winter 1994, pp. 773–94.

24. Richard W. Stevenson, "A Whistle Blower to Get $7.5 Million in Big Fraud Case," *New York Times,* July 15, 1992.

Chapter 11

1. Jennifer Laabs, "Managing-up Secrets: I Did It the Boss's Way," *Workforce,* August 2000, p. 22.

2. Len Schlesinger, "It Doesn't Take a Wizard to Build a Better Boss," *Fast Company's* "Handbook of the Business Revolution," n.d., p. 20.

3. Kenneth W. Thomas and Warren H. Schmidt, "A Survey of Managerial Interests with Respect to Conflict," *Academy of Management Journal,* June 1976, pp. 315–18.

4. Ellen Van Velsor and Jean Brittain Leslie, "Why Executives Derail: Perspectives Across Time and Cultures," *Academy of Management Executive,* vol. 9, no. 4, 1995, pp. 62–72.

5. M. K. Mount and M. R. Barrick, "The Big Five Personality Dimensions: Implications for Research and Practice in Human Resources Management," *Research in Personnel and Human Resources Management,* 1995, pp. 153–200.

6. W. L. Gardner and M. J. Martinko, "Using the Myers-Briggs Type Indicator to Study Managers: A Literature Review and Research Agenda," *Journal of Management,* vol. 22, 1996, pp. 45–83.

7. Robert R. Blake and Jane S. Mouton, *Managing Intergroup Conflict in Industry,* Houston: Gulf Publishing Co., 1964. Note that these authors and others often include an intermediate strategy called compromising. Also see Evert Van de Viert and Boris Kabanoff, "Toward Theory-Based Measures of Conflict Management," *Academy of Management Journal,* March 1990, pp. 199–209.

8. A useful approach to negotiating is the use of internal dispute resolution. See, for example, Bryan Downie, Mary Lou Coates, and Gary Furlong, "Meet Me Inside," *Ivey Business Quarterly,* Summer 1998, pp. 56–61.

9. Eric Berne, *Transactional Analysis in Psychotherapy,* New York: Grove Press, 1961; Eric Berne, *Games People Play,* New York: Grove Press, 1964; and Thomas A. Harris, *I'm OK—You're OK: A Practical Guide to Transactional Analysis,* New York: Harper & Row, 1969.

10. The importance of management support and other actions to encourage behavioral change is discussed in John W. Newstrom, "Leveraging Management Development through Transfer of Training Strategies," *Journal of Management Development,* vol. 5, no. 5, 1986, pp. 33–45.

11. J. R. P. French and B. H. Raven, "The Bases of Social Power," in D. Cartwright (ed.), *Studies in Social Power,* Ann Arbor: University of Michigan Press, 1959.

12. See, for example, Daniel Sandowsky, "The Charismatic Leader as Narcissist: Understanding the Abuse of Power," *Organizational Dynamics,* Spring 1995, pp. 57–71.

13. Christopher P. Parker, Robert L. Dipboye, and Stacey L. Jackson, "Perceptions of Organizational Politics: An Investigation of Antecedents and Consequences,"

Journal of Management, vol. 21, no. 5, 1995, pp. 891–912; and Amos Drory and Tsilia Romm, "The Definition of Organizational Politics: A Review," *Human Relations,* November 1990, pp. 1133–54.

14. Jeffrey K. Pinto and Om P. Kharbanda, "Lessons for an Accidental Profession," *Business Horizons,* March–April 1995, pp. 41–50.

15. Jeffrey Gandz and Victor Murray, "The Experience of Workplace Politics," *Academy of Management Journal,* June 1980, p. 244.

16. Allen R. Cohen and David L. Bradford, *Influence without Authority,* New York: John Wiley & Sons, 1990.

17. Martin Kilduff and David V. Day, "Do Chameleons Get Ahead? The Effects of Self-Monitoring on Managerial Careers," *Academy of Management Journal,* vol. 37, no. 4, 1994, pp. 1047–60.

18. Sandy J. Wayne and Robert C. Liden, "Effects of Impression Management on Performance Ratings: A Longitudinal Study," *Academy of Management Journal,* vol. 38, no. 1, 1995, pp. 232–60.

Chapter 12

1. Eric Matson, "The Seven Sins of Deadly Meetings," *Handbook of the Business Revolution,* Fast Company n.d., p. 27.

2. Bob Filipczak, "Critical Mass: Putting Whole-Systems Thinking into Practice," *Training,* September 1995, p. 33.

3. The idea that the informal organization's activities, interactions, and sentiments emerge from the formal organization is drawn from George C. Homans, *The Human Group,* New York: Harcourt Brace Jovanovich, 1950.

4. Beatrice Shultz, "Communicative Correlates of Perceived Leaders in the Small Group," *Small Group Behavior,* February 1986, pp. 51–65.

5. Stuart Drescher, Gary Burlingame, and Addie Fuhriman, "Cohesion: An Odyssey in Empirical Understanding," *Small Group Behavior,* February 1985, pp. 3–30. For discussion of a reliable instrument to measure cohesion, see Nancy J. Evans and Paul A. Jarvis, "The Group Attitude Scale: A Measure of Attraction to Group," *Small Group Behavior,* May 1986, pp. 203–16.

6. Four types of work group reactions (acceptance, avoidance, confrontation, and nurturance) are discussed by James W. Fairfield-Sonn, "Work Group Reactions to New Members: Tool or Trap in Making Selection Decisions?" *Public Personnel Management,* Winter 1984, pp. 485–93.

7. Daniel Feldman, "The Development and Enforcement of Group Norms," *Academy of Management Review,* January 1984, pp. 47–53.

8. Monika Henderson and Michael Argyle, "The Informal Rules of Working Relationships," *Journal of Occupational Behaviour,* vol. 7, 1986, pp. 259–75.

9. The saying "sent to Coventry" is derived from the following situation: The citizens of Coventry, England, so disliked soldiers that people seen talking to one were isolated from their social community, so those few citizens who felt like talking to soldiers did not dare do so. Hence a soldier sent to Coventry was isolated from community interaction.

10. David Krackhardt and Jeffrey R. Hanson, "Informal Networks: The Company Behind the Chart," *Harvard Business Review,* July–August 1993, pp. 104–11.

11. Bernard Johann, "The Meeting as a Lever for Organizational Improvement," *National Productivity Review,* Summer 1994, pp. 369–77.

12. Mary Lippitt Nichols, "An Exploratory Study of Committee Composition as an Administrative Problem-Solving Tool," *Decision Sciences,* April 1981, pp. 338–51.

13. The importance of a planned agenda is presented in Gary English, "How about a Good Word for Meetings?" *Management Review,* June 1990, pp. 58–60. Other useful suggestions appear in Wayne Hensley, "Guidelines for Success and Failure in Groups," *Supervision,* September 2000, pp. 9–10.

14. Task and social roles were originally presented by R. F. Bales, *Interaction Process Analysis,* Cambridge, MA: Addison-Wesley, 1950.

15. Bob Rosener, "What Are Your Secrets for Running a Successful Meeting?" *Workforce,* January 1999, pp. 22–23.

16. Brainstorming was developed by Alex F. Osborn and is described in his book *Applied Imagination,* New York: Charles Scribner's Sons, 1953. A review of brainstorming and other structured approaches is in Ron Zemke, "In Search of Good Ideas," *Training,* January 1993, pp. 46–52. For current applications at IDEO, see Michael Schrage, "Playing Around with Brainstorming," *Harvard Business Review,* March 2001, pp. 149–154.

17. Greg Bachman, "Brainstorming Deluxe," *Training and Development,* January 2000, pp. 15–17.

18. R. Brent Gallupe, Lana M. Bastianutti, and William H. Cooper, "Unblocking Brainstorms," *Journal of Applied Psychology,* January 1991, pp. 137–42; for comparative results, see Alan R. Dennis and Joseph S. Valacich, "Group, Sub-Group, and Nominal Group Idea Generation: New Rules for a New Media?" *Journal of Management,* vol. 20, no. 4, 1994, pp. 723–36. Applied discussion of groupware appears in David Kirkpatrick, "Groupware Goes Boom," *Fortune,* December 27, 1993, pp. 99–106; and Michael Finley, "Groupware Gives Whole New Meaning to Meeting," *St. Paul Pioneer Press,* April 23, 1995.

19. Gene E. Burton, "The 'Clustering Effect': An Idea-Generation Phenomenon during Nominal Grouping," *Small Group Behavior,* May 1987, pp. 224–38.

20. Recommendations ranging from two to five iterations of the Delphi process have been made. One study found that results stabilized after four rounds; see Robert C. Erffmeyer et al., "The Delphi Technique: An Empirical Evaluation of the Optimal Number of Rounds," *Group and Organization Studies,* March–June 1986, pp. 120–28.

21. Richard A. Cosier and Charles R. Schwenk, "Agreement and Thinking Alike: Ingredients for Poor Decisions," *The Executive,* February 1990, pp. 69–74; and David M. Schweiger, William R. Sandberg, and Paula L. Rechner, "Experiential Effects of Dialectical Inquiry, Devil's Advocacy, and Consensus Approaches to Strategic Decision Making," *Academy of Management Journal,* December 1989, pp. 745–72.

22. A surprising finding—that structured techniques raise consensus—is reported in Richard L. Priem, David A. Harrison, and Nan Kanoff Muir, "Structured Conflict and Consensus Outcomes in Group Decision Making," *Journal of Management,* vol. 21, no. 4, 1995, pp. 691–710.

23. Steven Saint and James R. Lawson, *Rules for Reaching Consensus,* San Diego: Pfeiffer & Company, 1994.

24. Irving L. Janis, *Victims of Groupthink,* Boston: Houghton-Mifflin, 1972; see also Glen Whyte, "Groupthink Reconsidered," *Academy of Management Review,* January 1989, pp. 40–56. A related problem—the Nut Island Effect—is discussed in Paul F. Levy, "When Good Teams Go Wrong," *Harvard Business Review,* March 2001, pp. 51–59.

25. Zemke, "In Search of Good Ideas."

26. See, for example, Gail Kay, "Effective Meetings through Electronic Brainstorming," *Journal of Management Development,* vol. 14, no. 6, 1995, pp. 4–25; and *Basics of Electronic Meeting Support,* Alexandria, VA: ASTD, 1995.

Chapter 13

1. Thomas R. Keen and Cherie N. Keen, "Conducting a Team Audit," *Training and Development,* February 1998, p. 13.
2. David X. Swenson, "Teams: Good, Bad, and Often Just Plain Hard," *Business North,* August 2000, p. 6B.
3. Carrie R. Leana, "Predictors and Consequences of Delegation," *Academy of Management Journal,* December 1986, pp. 754–74; see also Stephen C. Bushardt, David L. Huhon, and Aubrey R. Fowler, Jr., "Management Delegation Myths and the Paradox of Task Assignment," *Business Horizons,* March–April 1991, pp. 38–43.
4. T. Burns and G. M. Stalker, *The Management of Innovation,* London: Tavistock Publications, 1961.
5. William F. Joyce, "Matrix Organization: A Social Experiment," *Academy of Management Journal,* September 1986, pp. 536–61.
6. The five stages noted here were originally identified by B. W. Tuckman, "Developmental Sequence in Small Groups," *Psychological Bulletin,* vol. 63, 1965, pp. 384–99; an extension of the model is in Anthony R. Montebello and Victor R. Buzzotta, "Work Teams That Work," *Training and Development,* March 1993, pp. 59–64.
7. Russ Forester and Allan B. Drexler, "A Model for Team-Based Organization Performance," *Academy of Management Executive,* August 1999, pp. 36–49.
8. Beverly Geber, "The Bugaloo of Team Pay," *Training,* August 1995, pp. 25–34; and Sam T. Johnson, "Work Teams: What's Ahead in Work Design and Rewards Management," *Compensation and Benefits Review,* March–April 1993, pp. 35–41.
9. Melville Cottrill, "Give Your Work Teams Time and Training," *Academy of Management Executive,* August 1997, pp. 87–89.
10. Miriam Erez and Anit Somech, "Is Group Productivity Loss the Rule or the Exception? Effects of Culture and Group-Based Motivation," *Academy of Management Journal,* December 1996, pp. 1513–37.
11. An example of team building in the public sector is in Robin N. Amadei and Lyn Wade, "Government Employees Learn to Work in Sync," *Personnel Journal,* September 1996, pp. 91–94.
12. The effects of team building on satisfaction and productivity, respectively, are in George A. Neuman, Jack E. Edwards, and Nambury S. Raju, "Organizational Development Interventions: A Meta-Analysis of Their Effects on Satisfaction and Other Attitudes," *Personnel Psychology,* Autumn 1989, pp. 461–89; and Paul Buller and Cecil H. Bell, Jr., "Effects of Team Building and Goal Setting on Productivity: A Field Experiment," *Academy of Management Journal,* June 1986, pp. 305–28.
13. "Team Building at Its Best," *ASTD Info-Line,* no. 701, January 1987, p. 4.
14. An example is in Heidi Campbell, "Adventures in Teamland," *Personnel Journal,* May 1996, pp. 56–62. A critique of wilderness programs is in John W. Newstrom, "'Mod' Management Development: Does It Deliver What It Promises?" *Journal of Management Development,* vol. 4, no. 1, 1985, pp. 3–11.
15. Edgar H. Schein, *Process Consultation Revisited: Building the Helping Relationship,* Reading, MA: Addison-Wesley Longman, 1998.
16. Lawrence Holpp, "Applied Empowerment," *Training,* February 1994, pp. 39–44. Also see the survey results reporting what self-managing teams manage (most often—work schedules; least often—firing) in "1994 Industry Report," *Training,* October 1994, p. 62.

17. James Kochanski, "Hiring in Self-Regulating Work Teams," *National Productivity Review,* Spring 1987, pp. 153–59. Other examples appear in Richard W. Wellins, "Building a Self-Directed Work Team," *Training and Development,* December 1992, pp. 24–28.

18. Dale E. Yeatts, Martha Hipskind, and Debra Barnes, "Lessons Learned from Self-Managed Work Teams," *Business Horizons,* July–August 1994, pp. 11–18.

Chapter 14

1. "On the Paradox of Competence," *Fast Company,* January–February 2000, p. 232.

2. Thomas S. Bateman and J. Michael Crant, "Proactive Behavior: Meaning, Impact, Recommendations," *Business Horizons,* May–June 1999, p. 63.

3. Tom Duening, "Our Turbulent Times: The Case for Evolutionary Organizational Change," *Business Horizons,* January–February 1997, pp. 2–8.

4. F. J. Roethlisberger, *Management and Morale,* Cambridge, MA: Harvard University Press, 1941, p. 10. See also F. J. Roethlisberger and William J. Dickson, *Management and the Worker,* Cambridge, MA: Harvard University Press, 1939. An update is Ronald G. Greenwood et al., "Hawthorne a Half Century Later: Relay Assembly Participants Remember," *Journal of Management,* Fall–Winter 1983, pp. 217–31.

5. John Donne (1572–1631), *The Complete Poetry and Selected Prose of John Donne and the Complete Poetry of William Blake,* New York: Random House, 1941, p. 332. Emphasis in original.

6. An extensive discussion of costs and benefits is in Wayne F. Cascio, *Costing Human Resources: The Financial Impact of Behavior in Organizations,* 3rd ed., Boston: PWS-Kent, 1991.

7. Jennifer J. Laabs, "Expert Advice on How to Move Forward with Change," *Personnel Journal,* July 1996, pp. 54–63.

8. W. Warner Burke et al., "Managers Get a 'C' in Managing Change," *Training and Development,* May 1991, pp. 87–92.

9. Bernard M. Bass, "From Transactional to Transformational Leadership: Learning to Share the Vision," *Organizational Dynamics,* Winter 1990, pp. 19–31. Research supporting the dimensionality and positive effects (extra effort and satisfaction) of transformational leadership is in Philip M. Podsakoff et al., "Transformational Leader Behaviors and Their Effects on Followers' Trust in Leader, Satisfaction, and Organizational Citizenship Behaviors," *Leadership Quarterly,* Summer 1990, pp. 107–42; and Francis J. Yammarino and Bernard M. Bass, "Transformational Leadership and Multiple Levels of Analysis," *Human Relations,* October 1990, pp. 975–95.

10. The role of vision in GE's Crotonville plant's success is described in Noel M. Tichy, "GE's Crotonville: A Staging Ground for Corporate Revolution," *Academy of Management Executive,* May 1989, pp. 99–106; a countering view of the limitations of the role of vision is provided by Jay A. Conger, "The Dark Side of Leadership," *Organizational Dynamics,* Autumn 1990, pp. 44–55.

11. Discussions of charisma are in David A. Nadler and Michael L. Tushman, "Beyond the Charismatic Leader: Leadership and Organizational Change," *California Management Review,* Winter 1990, pp. 77–97; see also Jay A. Conger, "Inspiring Others: The Language of Leadership," *Academy of Management Executive,* February 1991, pp. 31–45. Charismatic leadership was originally proposed in Robert J. House, "A 1976 Theory of Charismatic Leadership," in J. G. Hunt

and L. L. Larson (eds.), *Leadership: The Cutting Edge,* Carbondale: Southern Illinois University Press, 1977.

12. Chris Argyris, "Teaching Smart People How to Learn," *Harvard Business Review,* May–June 1991, pp. 99–109. These ideas were originally presented in Chris Argyris, "The Executive Mind and Double-Loop Learning," *Organizational Dynamics,* Autumn 1982, pp. 4–22. A parallel set of ideas are first-order change (single-loop learning) and second-order change (double-loop learning); see Andrew H. Van De Ven and Marshall Scott Poole, "Explaining Development and Change in Organizations," *Academy of Management Review,* July 1995, pp. 510–40.

13. Linda Honold, "The Power of Learning at Johnsonville Foods," *Training,* April 1991, pp. 54–58.

14. A study using the three steps is reported in Paul E. O'Neill, "Transforming Managers for Organizational Change," *Training and Development Journal,* July 1990, pp. 87–90.

15. Paul Strebel, "Choosing the Right Change Path," *California Management Review,* Winter 1994, pp. 29–51.

16. Albert S. King, "Expectation Effects in Organizational Change," *Administrative Science Quarterly,* June 1974, pp. 221–30; and Dov Eden and Gad Ravid, "Pygmalion versus Self-Expectancy: Effects of Infrastructure and Self-Expectancy on Trainee Performance," *Organizational Behavior and Human Performance,* December 1982, pp. 351–64.

17. David Dorsey, "Change Factory," *Fast Company,* June 2000, pp. 211–24.

18. A systematic model for the change process is in Paul Dainty and Andrew Kakabadse, "Organizational Change: A Strategy for Successful Implementation," *Journal of Business and Psychology,* Summer 1990, pp. 463–81.

19. Jim Grieves, "Introduction: The Origins of Organizational Development," *Journal of Management Development,* vol. 19, no. 5, 2000, pp. 345–51.

20. W. Harvey Hegarty, "Organizational Survival Means Embracing Change," *Business Horizons,* November–December 1993, pp. 1–4.

21. A pioneering effort to identify causal variables in organizational systems was in Rensis Likert, *The Human Organization: Its Management and Value,* New York: McGraw-Hill, 1967; and Rensis Likert, *New Patterns of Management,* New York: McGraw-Hill, 1961.

22. Debra D. Burrington, "Organization Development in the Utah Department of Public Safety," *Public Personnel Management,* Summer 1987, pp. 115–25.

23. A. M. Barrat, "Organizational Improvement in Mobil Oil," *Journal of Management Development,* vol. 1, no. 2, 1982, pp. 3–9.

24. A study of the results of OD through the perceptions of OD practitioners is in Jerry I. Porras and Susan J. Hoffer, "Common Behavior Changes in Successful Organization Development Efforts," *Journal of Applied Behavioral Science,* vol. 22, no. 4, 1986, pp. 477–94.

25. John R. Kimberly and Warren R. Nielsen, "Organizational Development and Change in Organizational Performance," *Administrative Science Quarterly,* June 1975, pp. 191–206.

26. Richard W. Woodman, "Organizational Change and Development: New Arenas for Inquiry and Action," *Journal of Management,* June 1989, pp. 205–28.

27. See, for example, Daniel J. McCarthy, "View from the Top: Henry Mintzberg on Strategy and Management," *Academy of Management Executive,* August 2000, pp. 31–42.

Chapter 15

1. Christina Maslach and Michael P. Leiter, "Take This Job and Love It!" *Psychology Today,* September–October 1999, p. 50.

2. Anne M. O'Leary-Kelly, Ricky W. Griffin, and David J. Glew, "Organization-Motivated Aggression: A Research Framework," *Academy of Management Review,* vol. 21, no. 1, 1996, p. 225.

3. Leslie Brooks Suzukamo, "Fed Up, Fired Up or (Gulp) Fired," *Duluth News-Tribune,* February 26, 1996, pp. 1B, 4B; and Jennifer J. Laabs, "Job Stress," *Personnel Journal,* April 1992, p. 43.

4. Resa W. King and Irene Pave, "Stress Claims Are Making Business Jumpy," *Business Week,* October 14, 1985, pp. 152, 154.

5. Hans Selye, *The Stress of Life,* rev. ed., New York: McGraw-Hill, 1976.

6. Cynthia L. Cordes and Thomas W. Dougherty, "A Review and an Integration of Research on Job Burnout," *Academy of Management Review,* October 1993, pp. 621–56.

7. Susan E. Jackson, Richard L. Schwab, and Randall S. Schuler, "Toward an Understanding of the Burnout Phenomenon," *Journal of Applied Psychology,* November 1986, pp. 630–40; and Joseph Seltzer and Rita E. Numeroff, "Supervisory Leadership and Subordinate Burnout," *Academy of Management Journal,* June 1988, pp. 439–46.

8. Karen Lowry Miller, "Now Japan Is Admitting It: Work Kills Executives," *Business Week,* August 3, 1992, p. 35.

9. David M. Noer, "Leadership in an Age of Layoffs," *Journal of Management Development,* vol. 14, no. 5, 1995, pp. 27–38.

10. Comprehensive discussions of contributing factors are in Michael G. Harvey and Richard A. Cosier, "Homicides in the Workplace: Crisis or False Alarm?" *Business Horizons,* March–April 1995, pp. 11–20; and Romauld A. Stone, "Workplace Homicide: A Time for Action," *Business Horizons,* March–April 1995, pp. 3–10.

11. Samuel Greengard, "Zero Tolerance: Making It Work," *Workforce,* May 1999, pp. 28–34. See also Helen Frank Bensimon, "What to Do about Anger in the Workplace," *Training and Development,* September 1997, pp. 28–32.

12. John M. Ivancevich, "Life Events and Hassles as Predictors of Health Symptoms, Job Performance, and Absenteeism," *Journal of Occupational Behaviour,* January 1986, pp. 39–51.

13. Lynne M. Andersson and Christine M. Pearson, "Tit for Tat? The Spiraling Effect of Incivility in the Workplace," *Academy of Management Review,* July 1999, pp. 452–71.

14. "Employees Value Workplace Relationships," *Personnel Journal,* June 1996, p. 25.

15. Meyer Friedman and Ray H. Rosenman, *Type A Behavior and Your Heart,* New York: Alfred Knopf, 1974; see also Meyer Friedman and Diane Ulmer, *Treating Type A Behavior and Your Heart,* New York: Alfred A. Knopf, 1984.

16. A metaanalysis, or quantitative review and synthesis of previous research results, is provided by Stephanie Booth-Kewley and Howard S. Friedman, "Psychological Predictors of Heart Disease: A Quantitative Review," *Psychological Bulletin,* May 1987, pp. 343–62; a readable update is Joshua Fischman, "Type A on Trial," *Psychology Today,* February 1987, pp. 42–50, 64.

17. Sacha Cohen, "De-Stress for Success," *Training and Development,* November 1997, pp. 77–80; and "Tips for Reducing Work-Related Stress," *Workforce,* July 1999, p. 24.

18. Monika Henderson and Michael Argyle, "Social Support by Four Categories of Work Colleagues: Relationships between Activities, Stress, and Satisfaction," *Journal of Occupational Behaviour,* July 1985, pp. 229–39.
19. Mike McNamee, Chris Roush, and Sandra D. Atchison, "A Health-Care Winner that May Get Zapped," *Business Week,* August 9, 1993, p. 33.
20. Charlene Marmer Solomon, "Picture This: A Safer Workplace," *Workforce,* February 1998, pp. 82–86.
21. F. J. Roethlisberger and William J. Dickson, *Management and the Worker,* Cambridge, MA: Harvard University Press, 1939, pp. 189–205, 593–604; and William J. Dickson and F. J. Roethlisberger, *Counseling in an Organization: A Sequel to the Hawthorne Researches,* Boston: Harvard Business School, Division of Research, 1966.

Chapter 16

1. Brenda Paik Sunoo, "Adapting to the Land Down Under," *Global Workforce,* January 1998, p. 24.
2. Barbara Fitzgerald-Turner, "Myths of Expatriate Life," *HRMagazine,* June 1997, p. 70.
3. Robert E. Cole, "Work and Leisure in Japan," *California Management Review,* Spring 1992, pp. 52–63. Another contributing factor to the workplace environment in some Japanese organizations is known as *ijime*—the building of employees to work hard by their supervisors, even to the point of dying on the job, a phenomenon called *karoshi.* See Christopher B. Meek, "Ganbatte: Understanding the Japanese Employee," *Business Horizons,* January–February 1999, pp. 27–36.
4. Patricia Feltes, Robert K. Robinson, and Ross L. Fink, "American Female Expatriates and the Civil Rights Act of 1991: Balancing Legal and Business Interests," *Business Horizons,* March–April 1993, pp. 82–85. A variety of suggestions for helping cultivate female candidates for expatriate assignments are in Charlene Marmer Solomon, "Women Expats: Shattering the Myths," *Global Workforce,* May 1998, pp. 11–14.
5. Mariann Jelinek and Nancy J. Adler, "Women: World-Class Managers for Global Competition," *Academy of Management Executive,* February 1988, pp. 11–19.
6. "Court Invalidates Airline's Policy for Transfers to Foreign Cities," *Japan Labor Bulletin,* November 1, 1974, p. 7.
7. Geert Hofstede, "Cultural Constraints in Management Theories," *Academy of Management Executive,* February 1993, pp. 81–94.
8. Andre Laurent, "The Cultural Diversity of Western Conceptions of Management," *International Studies of Management and Organization,* Spring–Summer 1983, pp. 75–96.
9. Gary Bonvillian and William A. Nowlin, "Cultural Awareness: An Essential Element of Doing Business Abroad," *Business Horizons,* November–December 1994, pp. 44–50; and Mary Munter, "Cross-Cultural Communication for Managers," *Business Horizons,* May–June 1993, pp. 69–78.
10. Geocentric attitudes are discussed in Lennie Copeland and Lewis Griggs, "The Internationable Employee," *Management Review,* April 1988, pp. 52–53.
11. Geert Hofstede, "Motivation, Leadership, and Organization: Do American Theories Apply Abroad?" *Organizational Dynamics,* Summer 1980, pp. 42–63.

517

12. John I. Reynolds, "Developing Policy Responses to Cultural Differences," *Business Horizons,* August 1978, pp. 28–35.

13. Jean McEnery and Gaston DesHarnais, "Culture Shock," *Training and Development Journal,* April 1990, pp. 43–47.

14. Richard G. Linowes, "The Japanese Manager's Traumatic Entry into the United States: Understanding the American-Japanese Cultural Divide," *Academy of Management Executive,* vol. 7, no. 4, 1993, pp. 21–40.

15. "As Costs of Overseas Assignments Climb, Firms Select Expatriates More Carefully," *The Wall Street Journal,* January 9, 1992, pp. B1, B8.

16. Richard M. Hodgetts and Fred Luthans, "U.S. Multinationals' Compensation Strategies for Local Management: Cross-Cultural Implications," *Compensation and Benefits Review,* March–April 1993, pp. 42–48.

17. Discussions of predeparture training appear in Gary W. Hogan and Jane R. Goodson, "The Key to Expatriate Success," *Training and Development Journal,* January 1990, pp. 50–52; and "Why Aren't American Firms Training for Global Participation?" *Management Development Report* (ASTD), Summer 1990, pp. 1–2.

18. Hoon Park and J. Kline Harrison, "Enhancing Managerial Cross-Cultural Awareness and Sensitivity: Transactional Analysis Revisited," *Journal of Management Development,* vol. 12, no. 3, 1993, pp. 20–29.

19. Charlene Marmer Solomon, "Repatriation: Up, Down or Out?" *Personnel Journal,* January 1995, pp. 28–37; see also Marvina Shilling, "How to Win at Repatriation," *Personnel Journal,* September 1993, pp. 40–46.

20. William Ouchi, *Theory Z: How American Business Can Meet the Japanese Challenge,* Reading, MA: Addison-Wesley, 1981.

21. J. B. Keys et al., "The Japanese Management Theory Jungle—Revisited," *Journal of Management,* Summer 1994, pp. 373–402.

22. Aaron Bernstein, Dan Cook, Pete Engardio, and Gregory L. Miles, "The Difference Japanese Management Makes," *Business Week,* July 14, 1986, pp. 47–50.

23. See, for example, Jeremiah J. Sullivan, "A Critique of Theory Z," *Academy of Management Review,* January 1983, pp. 132–42; and Edgar H. Schein, "Does Japanese Management Style Have a Message for American Managers?" *Sloan Management Review,* Fall 1982, pp. 55–68.

24. Justin Fox, "The Triumph of English," *Fortune,* September 18, 2000, pp. 209–12.

SUBJECT INDEX

528